the Adobe® photoshop *book* for digital photographers

for Versions CS6 and CC

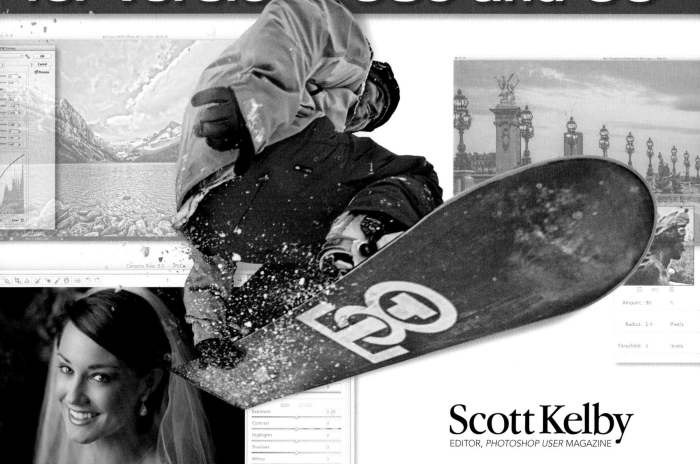

Scott Kelby
EDITOR, *PHOTOSHOP USER* MAGAZINE

D0730835

THE ADOBE PHOTOSHOP BOOK FOR DIGITAL PHOTOGRAPHERS
(for Versions CS6 and CC)

The Adobe Photoshop Book for Digital Photographers Team

CREATIVE DIRECTOR
Felix Nelson

TECHNICAL EDITORS
Kim Doty
Cindy Snyder

TRAFFIC DIRECTOR
Kim Gabriel

PRODUCTION MANAGER
Dave Damstra

ART DIRECTOR
Jessica Maldonado

COVER PHOTOS BY
Scott Kelby

Published by
New Riders

Composed in Avenir, Myriad Pro, and Helvetica by Kelby Media Group, Inc.

Trademarks
All terms mentioned in this book that are known to be trademarks or service marks have been appropriately capitalized. New Riders cannot attest to the accuracy of this information. Use of a term in this book should not be regarded as affecting the validity of any trademark or service mark.

Photoshop is a registered trademark of Adobe Systems, Inc.
Macintosh is a registered trademark of Apple, Inc.
Windows is a registered trademark of Microsoft Corp.

Warning and Disclaimer
This book is designed to provide information about Photoshop for digital photographers. Every effort has been made to make this book as complete and as accurate as possible, but no warranty of fitness is implied.

The information is provided on an as-is basis. The author and New Riders shall have neither the liability nor responsibility to any person or entity with respect to any loss or damages arising from the information contained in this book or from the use of the discs, electronic files, or programs that may accompany it.

THIS PRODUCT IS NOT ENDORSED OR SPONSORED BY ADOBE SYSTEMS INCORPORATED, PUBLISHER OF ADOBE PHOTOSHOP.

ISBN 13: 978-0-321-93384-3
ISBN 10:   0-321-93384-2

9 8 7 6 5 4 3 2 1

http://kelbytraining.com
www.newriders.com

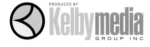

This book is dedicated to the coolest six-year-old ever:
my amazing, hilarious, smart, adorable, loving daughter Kira.
You are a clone of your mom and that's the best thing
I could ever wish for you. Daddy loves you very much!!!

ACKNOWLEDGMENTS

I've been writing books for 14 years now, and I still find that the thing that's the hardest for me to write in any book is writing the acknowledgments. It also, hands down, takes me longer than any other pages in the book. For me, I think the reason I take these acknowledgments so seriously is because it's when I get to put down on paper how truly grateful I am to be surrounded by such great friends, an incredible book team, and a family that truly makes my life a joy. That's why it's so hard. I also know why it takes so long—you type a lot slower with tears in your eyes.

To my remarkable wife, Kalebra: We've been married nearly 23 years now, and you still continue to amaze me, and everyone around you. I've never met anyone more compassionate, more loving, more hilarious, and more genuinely beautiful, and I'm so blessed to be going through life with you, to have you as the mother of my children, my business partner, my private pilot, Chinese translator, and best friend. You truly are the type of woman love songs are written for, and as anyone who knows me will tell you, I am, without a doubt, the luckiest man alive to have you for my wife.

To my son, Jordan: It's every dad's dream to have a relationship with his son like I have with you, and I'm so proud of the bright, caring, creative young man you've become. I can't wait to see the amazing things life has in store for you, and I just want you to know that watching you grow into the person you are is one of my life's greatest joys.

To my precious little girl, Kira: You have been blessed in a very special way, because you are a little clone of your mom, which is the most wonderful thing I could have possibly wished for you. I see all her gifts reflected in your eyes, and though you're still too young to have any idea how blessed you are to have Kalebra as your mom, one day—just like Jordan—you will.

To my big brother Jeff, who has always been, and will always be, a hero to me. So much of who I am, and where I am, is because of your influence, guidance, caring, and love as I was growing up. Thank you for teaching me to always take the high road, for always knowing the right thing to say at the right time, and for having so much of our dad in you.

I'm incredibly fortunate to have part of the production of my books handled in-house by my own book team at Kelby Media Group, which is led by my friend and longtime Creative Director, Felix Nelson, who is hands down the most creative person I've ever met. He's surrounded by some of the most talented, amazing, ambitious, gifted, and downright brilliant people I've ever had the honor of working with, and thank God he had the foresight to hire Kim Doty, my Editor, and the only reason why I haven't totally fallen onto the floor in the fetal position after writing both a Lightroom 4 book and a CS6 book, back to back. Kim is just an incredibly organized, upbeat, focused person who keeps me calm and on track, and no matter how tough the task ahead is, she always says the same thing, "Ah, piece of cake," and she convinces you that you can do it, and then you do it. I cannot begin to tell you how grateful I am to her for being my Editor, and to Felix for finding her. I guess great people just attract other great people.

Working with Kim is Cindy Snyder, who relentlessly tests all the stuff I write to make sure I didn't leave anything out, so you'll all be able to do the things I'm teaching (which with a Photoshop book is an absolute necessity). She's like a steel trap that nothing can get through if it doesn't work just like I said it would.

http://kelbytraining.com

The look of the book comes from an amazing designer, a creative powerhouse, and someone whom I feel very, very lucky to have designing my books—Jessica Maldonado. She always adds that little something that just takes it up a notch, and I've built up such a trust for her ideas and intuition, which I why I just let her do her thing. Thanks Jess!

I owe a huge debt of gratitude to my Executive Assistant and Chief Wonder Woman, Kathy Siler. She runs a whole side of my business life, and a big chunk of our conferences, and she does it so I have time to write books, spend time with my family, and have a life outside of work. She's such an important part of what I do that I don't know how I did anything without her. Thank you, thank you, thank you. It means more than you know.

To my best buddy and book-publishing powerhouse, Dave Moser (also known as "the guiding light, force of nature, miracle birth, etc."), for always insisting that we raise the bar and make everything we do better than anything we've done before.

Thanks to everyone at New Riders and Peachpit, and in particular to my way cool Editor, Ted Waitt (who is one heck of a photographer and a vitally important part of everything I do in "Bookland"), my wonderful Publisher Nancy Aldrich-Ruenzel, marketing maven Scott Cowlin, marketing diva Sara Jane Todd, and the entire team at Pearson Education who go out of their way to make sure that we're always working in the best interest of my readers, that we're always trying to take things up a notch, and who work hard to make sure my work gets in as many people's hands as possible.

Thanks to my friends at Adobe: Bryan O'Neil Hughes, John Nack, Mala Sharma, Terry White, Cari Gushiken, Julieanne Kost, Tom Hogarty, Scott Morris, Russell Preston Brown, and the amazing engineering team at Adobe (I don't know how you all do it). Gone but not forgotten: Barbara Rice, Jill Nakashima, Rye Livingston, Addy Roff, Bryan Lamkin, Jennifer Stern, Deb Whitman, Kevin Connor, John Loiacono, and Karen Gauthier.

Thanks to Matt Kloskowski for all his input and ideas for this edition of the book. I'm very grateful to have his advice, and his friendship. I want to thank all the talented and gifted photographers who've taught me so much over the years, including: Moose Peterson, Joe McNally, Anne Cahill, Vincent Versace, Cliff Mautner, Dave Black, Bill Fortney, David Ziser, Helene Glassman, Kevin Ames, and Jim DiVitale.

Thanks to my mentors, whose wisdom and whip-cracking have helped me immeasurably, including John Graden, Jack Lee, Dave Gales, Judy Farmer, and Douglas Poole.

Most importantly, I want to thank God, and His Son Jesus Christ, for leading me to the woman of my dreams, for blessing us with two amazing children, for allowing me to make a living doing something I truly love, for always being there when I need Him, for blessing me with a wonderful, fulfilling, and happy life, and such a warm, loving family to share it with.

OTHER BOOKS BY **SCOTT KELBY**

Professional Portrait Retouching Techniques for Photographers Using Photoshop

The Digital Photography Book, parts 1, 2, 3, and 4

*Light It, Shoot It, Retouch It: Learn Step by Step How to Go from
Empty Studio to Finished Image*

Scott Kelby's 7-Point System for Adobe Photoshop CS3

The iPhone Book

The Adobe Photoshop Lightroom 4 Book for Digital Photographers

Photoshop Down & Dirty Tricks

The Photoshop Elements Book for Digital Photographers

*Photo Recipes Live: Behind the Scenes: Your Guide to Today's
Most Popular Lighting Techniques*, parts 1 & 2

ABOUT THE AUTHOR

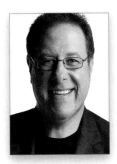

Scott Kelby

Scott is Editor, Publisher, and co-founder of *Photoshop User* magazine, Executive Editor and Publisher of *Light It* (the how-to magazine for studio lighting and off-camera flash), and is host of *The Grid*, the weekly live videocast talk show for photographers, as well as co-host of the top-rated weekly videocast series, *Photoshop User TV.*

He is President of the National Association of Photoshop Professionals (NAPP), the trade association for Adobe® Photoshop® users, and he's President of the training, education, and publishing firm, Kelby Media Group, Inc.

Scott is a photographer, designer, and award-winning author of more than 50 books, including *The Adobe Photoshop Lightroom 4 Book for Digital Photographers, Professional Portrait Retouching Techniques for Photographers Using Photoshop, Light It, Shoot It, Retouch It: Learn Step by Step How to Go from Empty Studio to Finished Image, The iPhone Book, The iPod Book,* and *The Digital Photography Book,* parts 1, 2, 3 & 4.

For the past three years, Scott has been honored with the distinction of being the world's #1 best-selling author of photography books. His book, *The Digital Photography Book,* vol. 1, is now the best-selling book on digital photography in history.

His books have been translated into dozens of different languages, including Chinese, Russian, Spanish, Korean, Polish, Taiwanese, French, German, Italian, Japanese, Dutch, Swedish, Turkish, and Portuguese, among others, and he is a recipient of the prestigious ASP International Award, presented annually by the American Society of Photographers for "…contributions in a special or significant way to the ideals of Professional Photography as an art and a science."

Scott is Training Director for the Adobe Photoshop Seminar Tour and Conference Technical Chair for the Photoshop World Conference & Expo. He's featured in a series of Adobe Photoshop training DVDs and online courses at KelbyTraining.com and has been training Adobe Photoshop users since 1993.

For more information on Scott, visit him at:

His daily blog: **http://scottkelby.com**
Google+: **Scottgplus.com**
Twitter: **http://twitter.com@scottkelby**
Facebook: **www.facebook.com/skelby**

www.kelbytraining.com

CONTENTS

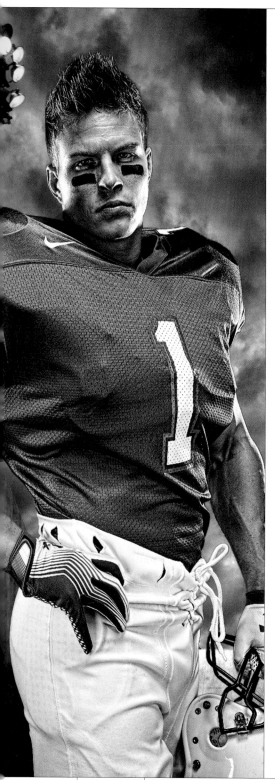

CONTENTS

Attitude Adjustment
Camera Raw's Adjustment Tools

Scream of the Crop
How to Resize and Crop Photos

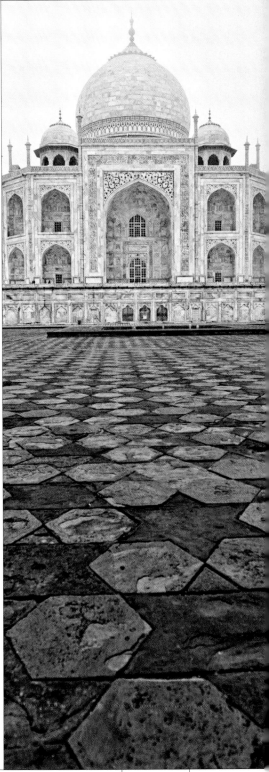

CONTENTS

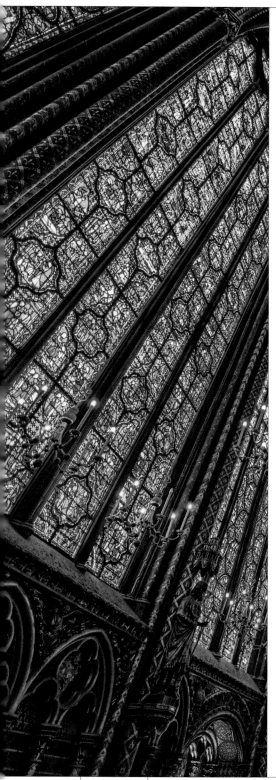

CONTENTS

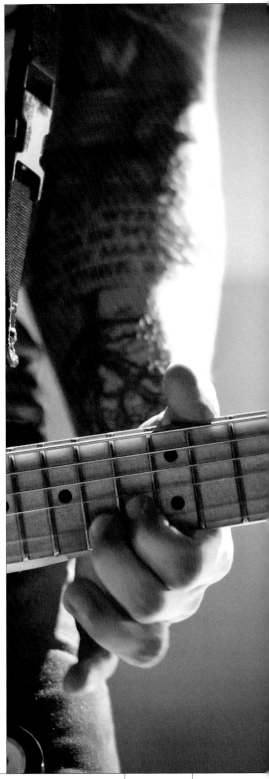

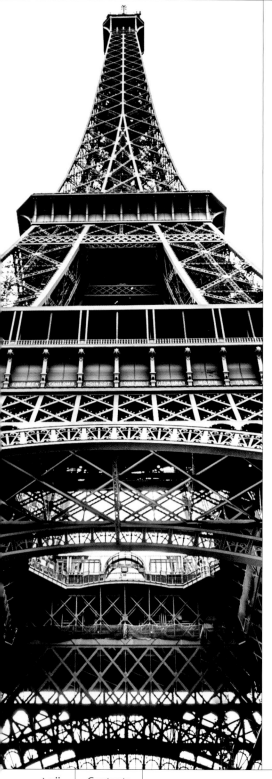

CONTENTS

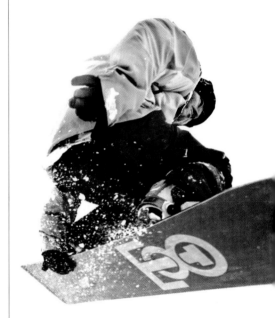

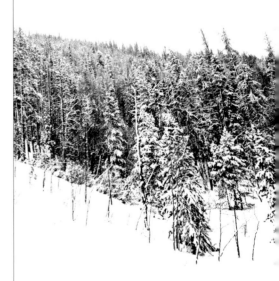

Seven Things You'll Wish You Had Known Before Reading This Book

It's really important to me that you get a lot out of reading this book, and one way I can help is to get you to read these seven quick things about the book that you'll wish later you knew now. For example, it's here that I tell you about where to download something important, and if you skip over this, eventually you'll send me an email asking where it is, but by then you'll be really aggravated, and well… it's gonna get ugly. We can skip all that (and more), if you take two minutes now and read these seven quick things. I promise to make it worth your while.

(1) You don't have to read this book in order.

I designed this book so you can turn right to the technique you want to learn, and start there. I explain everything as I go, step-by-step, so if you want to learn how to remove dust spots from a RAW image, just turn to page 84, and in a couple of minutes, you'll know. I did write the book in a logical order for learning CS6, but don't let that tie your hands—jump right to whatever technique you want to learn— you can always go back, review, and try other stuff. And if you are a Creative Cloud member, those new features are covered in their own chapter at the end of the book.

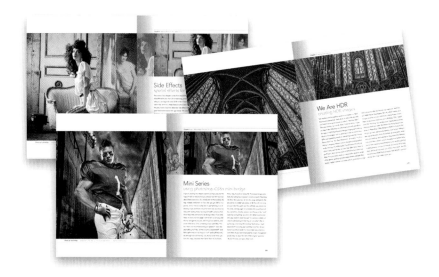

(2) Practice along with the same photos I used here in the book.

As you're going through the book, and you come to a technique like "Working with HDR Pro in Photoshop CS6," you might not have an HDR-bracketed set of shots hanging around, so in those cases I usually made the images available for you to download, so you can follow along with the book. You can find them at **http://kelbytraining.com/books/cs6** (see, this is one of those things I was talking about that you'd miss if you skipped this and went right to Chapter 1).

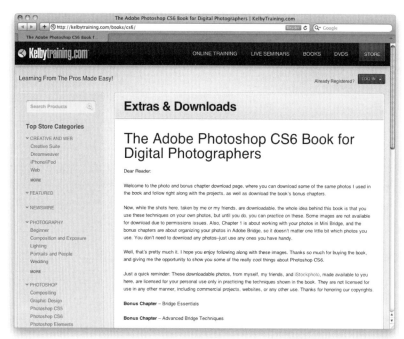

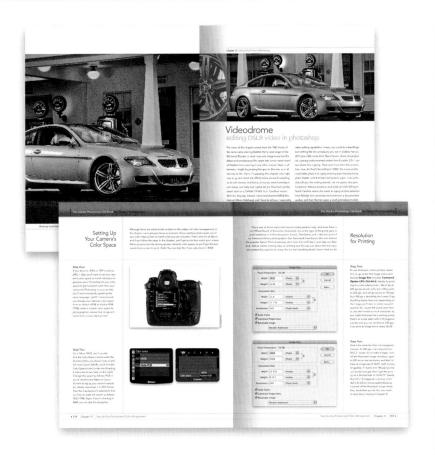

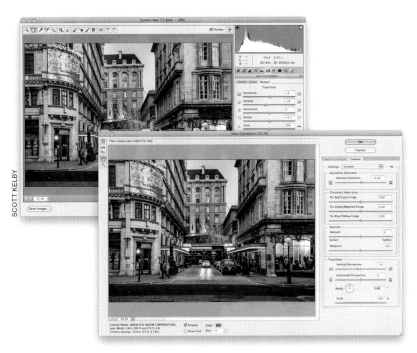

SCOTT KELBY

(3) The intro pages at the beginning of each chapter are not what they seem.

The chapter introductions are designed to give you a quick mental break between chapters, and honestly, they have little to do with what's in the chapter. In fact, they have little to do with anything, but writing these quirky chapter intros has become kind of a tradition of mine (I do this in all my books), so if you're one of those really "serious" types, I'm begging you—skip them and just go right into the chapter because they'll just get on your nerves. However, the short intros at the beginning of each individual project, up at the top of the page, are usually pretty important. If you skip over them, you might wind up missing stuff that isn't mentioned in the project itself. So, if you find yourself working on a project, and you're thinking to yourself, "Why are we doing this?" it's probably because you skipped over that intro. So, just make sure you read it first, and then go to Step One. It'll make a difference—I promise.

(4) There are things in Photoshop CS6 and in Camera Raw that do the exact same thing.

For example, there's a Lens Corrections panel in Camera Raw, and there's a Lens Correction filter in Photoshop, and they are almost identical. What this means to you is that some things are covered twice in the book. As you go through the book, and you start to think, "This sounds familiar…," now you know why. By the way, in my own workflow, if I can do the exact same task in Camera Raw or Photoshop, I always choose to do it in Camera Raw, because it's faster (there are no progress bars in Camera Raw) and it's non-destructive (so I can always change my mind later).

(Continued)

(5) I included a chapter on my CS6 workflow, but don't read it yet.

At the end of this book I included a special chapter detailing my own CS6 workflow, but please don't read it until you've read the rest of the book, because it assumes that you've read the book already, and understand the basic concepts, so it doesn't spell everything out (or it would be one really, really long drawn-out chapter).

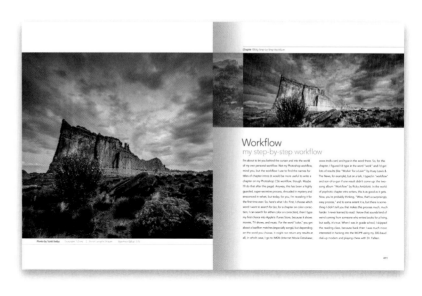

(6) Where's the Bridge stuff?

A version of Bridge is built right into Photoshop itself. It's called "Mini Bridge" (I am not making this up), and it does about 85% of what "Big Bridge" does (Adobe doesn't call it Big Bridge, they call it Adobe Bridge). This is great because now you don't have to leave Photoshop and jump to a separate application for finding and working with your images. So, since Mini Bridge is part of CS6, I start the book with a chapter on Mini Bridge. So, what did Adobe add to Big Bridge in CS6? Well, barely anything (which gives you some hint as to the future of Bridge, eh?). Anyway, they did greatly improve and streamline Mini Bridge, but since some of you may still be using Big Bridge for at least a little while longer (at least until you fall in love with Mini Bridge), I did update two Big Bridge chapters, and put them on the web for you to download free. You'll find these at **http://kelbytraining.com/books/cs6**.

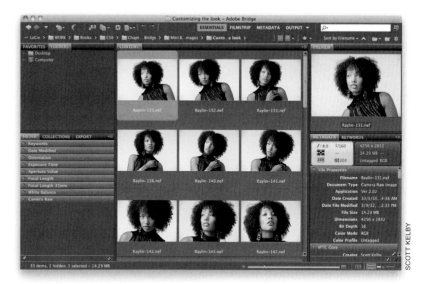

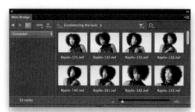

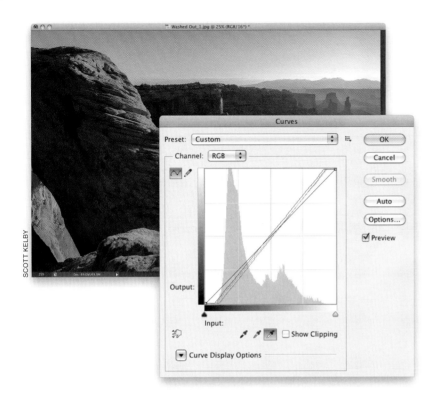

SCOTT KELBY

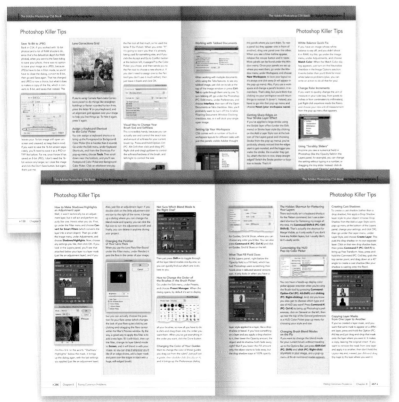

(7) Photography is evolving, Photoshop is evolving, and this book has to, too.

This is the first edition of this book that doesn't include a chapter on using Curves, and that's because today we use a different tool—Camera Raw (even if we don't shoot in RAW, because it works for JPEGs and TIFFs, too!). I spent years teaching Curves in books and in podcasts and here in this book, but honestly, today I really don't use Curves (and if I do, I use the Tone Curve in Camera Raw, which I do cover here in the book). In fact, I had a hard time finding any photographers I know still using Curves, which just shows how Photoshop has evolved over time. Although Curves isn't covered here in the book, I did provide a color correction chapter using Curves on the book's downloads page (ya know, just in case you want to go "old school"). You can find it at the web address just mentioned in #6.

(8) Each chapter includes my "Photoshop Killer Tips"!

Hey, I thought you said it was "Seven Things"? Well, consider this eighth a "bonus thing," because it's about another bonus I included in this CS6 edition of the book. At the end of every chapter is a special section I call "Photoshop Killer Tips" (named after the book of the same name I did a few years ago with Felix Nelson). These are those time-saving, job-saving, "man, I wish I had known that sooner" type tips. The ones that make you smile, nod, and then want to call all your friends and "tune them up" with your new status as Photoshop guru. These are in addition to all the other tips, which already appear throughout the chapters (you can never have enough tips, right? Remember: He who dies with the most tips, wins!). So, there you have it, seven (or so) things that you're now probably glad you took a couple minutes to read. Okay, the easy part is over—turn the page and let's get to work.

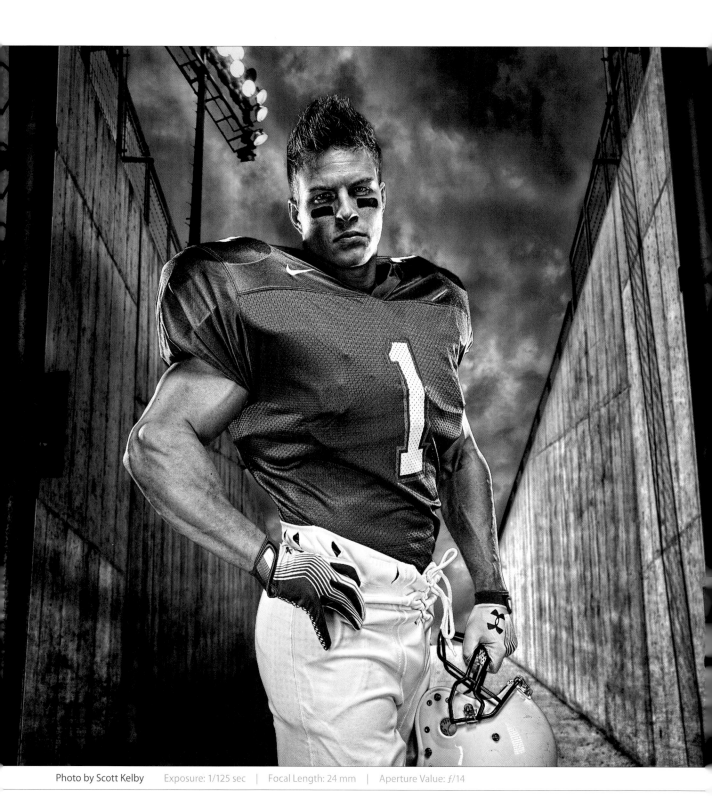

Photo by Scott Kelby | Exposure: 1/125 sec | Focal Length: 24 mm | Aperture Value: ƒ/14

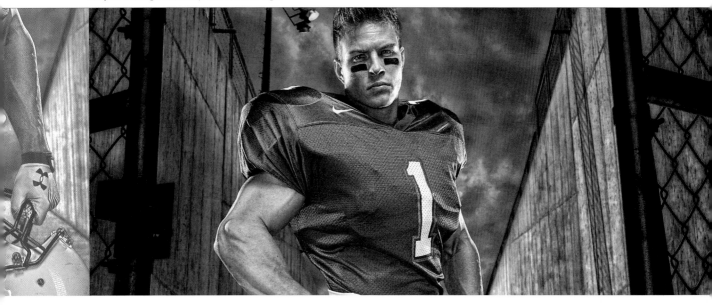

Mini Series
using photoshop CS6's mini bridge

If you're reading this chapter opener (and you are, by the way), it's safe to assume that you already read the warning about these openers in the introduction to the book (by the way, nobody reads that, so if you did, you get 500 bonus points, and a chance to play later in our lightning round). Anyway, if you read that and you're here now, you must be okay with reading these, knowing full well in advance that these have little instructional (or literary) value of any kind. Now, once you turn the page, I turn all serious on you, and the fun and games are over, and it's just you and me, and most of the time I'll be screaming at you (stuff like, "No, no—that's too much sharpening you goober!" and "Are you kidding me? You call that a Curves adjustment?" and "Who spilled my mocha Frappuccino?" and stuff like that), so although we're all friendly now, that all ends when you turn the page, because then we're down to business.

That's why, if you're a meany Mr. Frumpypants type who feels that joking has no place in a serious book of learning like this, then you can: (a) turn the page and get to the discipline and order you crave, or (b) if you're not sure, you can take this quick quiz that will help you determine the early warning signs of someone who should skip all the rest of the chapter openers and focus on the "real" learning (and yelling). Question #1: When was the last time you used the word "poopy" in a sentence when not directly addressing or referring to a toddler? Was it: (a) During a morning HR meeting? (b) During a legal deposition? (c) During your wedding vows? Or, (d) you haven't said that word in a meaningful way since you were three. If you even attempted to answer this question, you're clear to read the rest of the chapter openers. Oh, by the way: pee pee. (Hee hee!)

Getting to Your Photos Using Mini Bridge

Way back in Photoshop 7, we had a feature I loved called the File Browser, which let you access your images from right within Photoshop. Well, when Photoshop CS came along, they took the File Browser away and gave us the more powerful Adobe Bridge. I loved that it was more powerful, but I hated that it was a totally separate program, and now I had to leave Photoshop to get to my images. Thankfully, in Photoshop CS5, they added Mini Bridge, and in CS6, it's faster, easier to use, and so convenient that in most cases we don't have to leave Photoshop (wild cheers ensue!).

Step One:

By default, Mini Bridge lives at the bottom of Photoshop's workspace, and to make it visible, you just click directly on its tab and it pops right up (as seen here). When it appears, click on the Launch Bridge button, and it launches "Big Bridge" (what I call the full-sized Adobe Bridge) in the background (you won't see it, but Mini Bridge actually needs Big Bridge open to do its thing, but again, this happens in the background, so you won't actually see it at all). By the way, if you already have Big Bridge open, of course you won't see a button asking you to launch it.

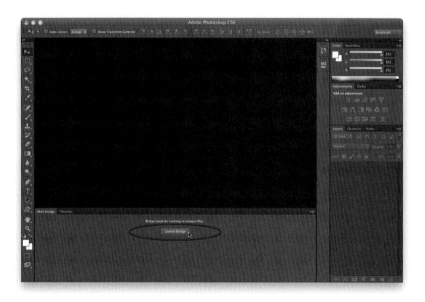

Step Two:

Once Big Bridge launches in the background, Mini Bridge comes alive, displaying your images in a horizontal filmstrip layout (as seen here). On the left side of the panel is the Navigation pod, which is where you navigate to the photos you want to appear in Mini Bridge. There's a pop-up menu at the top to help you make your way to the photos on your computer (or even ones on your memory card, if it's connected to your computer). Here, I chose my Pictures folder, and below the pop-up menu, it lists the folders I have inside that folder. To see what's inside any of the folders, you just double-click on one.

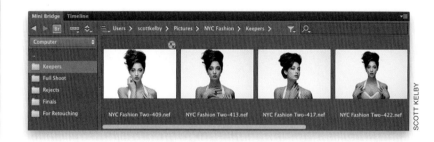

SCOTT KELBY

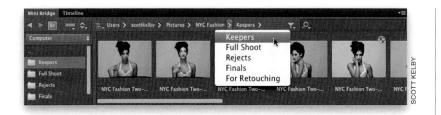

SCOTT KELBY

Step Three:

My favorite way to navigate is to use the new pop-up menus that appear right above the filmstrip itself—these make getting right to the folder you want really quick and easy. That area above the thumbnail filmstrip gives you a "breadcrumb trail" showing the path to the folder that is currently displayed in Mini Bridge (Adobe calls this the "Path Bar"). If you click on the little right-facing arrow to the right of each folder in the Path Bar, a pop-up menu appears with a list of the subfolders inside that folder. To display what's in one of those folders, just choose it from the pop-up menu (as shown here). Once you try this a few times, you'll love how quickly you can drill down to find the photos you want to work on. By the way (and this may seem insanely obvious, but…), to open any of these images in Photoshop, just double-click on one.

Step Four:

To change the size of the thumbnails when Mini Bridge is docked to the bottom of the screen, you just change the size of the Mini Bridge panel itself. Click-and-drag the top of the panel upward and, as you do, the thumbnails grow to fill in the space (as seen here).

TIP: Learning More About Big Bridge

If you want to learn more about Big Bridge, make sure you download the two free bonus chapters I posted on the book's download website, mentioned in the introduction of this book.

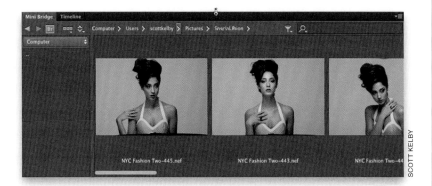

SCOTT KELBY

Viewing Your Photos in Mini Bridge

Okay, now that you've found Mini Bridge, let's put it to work and find out which style of Mini Bridge works best for your workflow (luckily, you get to set it up the way you like it), and how to use it quickly to find and view your images.

Step One:

By default, Mini Bridge is set up in a wide filmstrip layout, and is docked to the bottom of your screen, like the one you see here. However, you can undock it and have it work like any other floating panel in Photoshop.

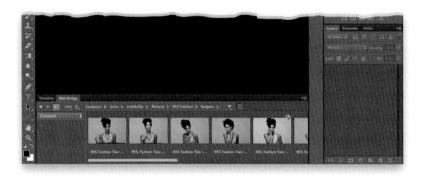

Step Two:

To undock Mini Bridge, click-and-drag its tab up toward the center of Photoshop's image area, and it becomes a floating panel with multiple columns and rows (as seen here). Doing this also reveals a thumbnail size slider in the bottom-right corner of the Mini Bridge panel (shown circled here in red). Also, once you've found the images you want to work with, you can hide the Navigation pod along the left side (so you can see more of the thumbnails) by clicking on the panel's flyout menu in its upper-right corner and choosing **Hide Navigation Pod**.

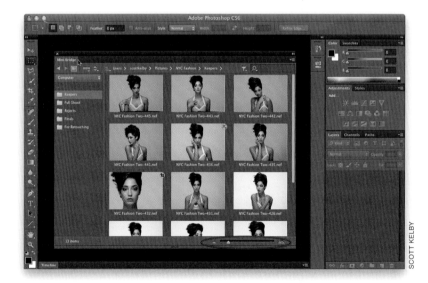

SCOTT KELBY

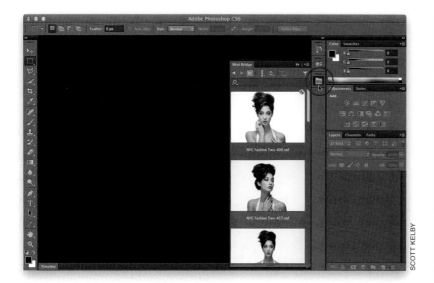

SCOTT KELBY

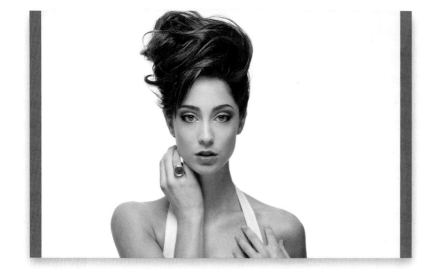

Step Three:

If you don't want Mini Bridge docked to the bottom of your screen, or floating around untethered, then you can dock it to your right side panels, which gives you a vertical filmstrip layout, and now you can show/hide it by clicking on its icon (as shown here). Again, if you want your thumbnails bigger, you have to drag the left side of Mini Bridge out to the left, and as it gets wider, the thumbnails grow to fill in the space. Technically, you could "nest" it with your other panels, like the Layers panel or the Color panel, but then its size would be really constricted by those other panels (drag its tab over next to the Layers tab and you'll see what I mean), so it's really better off positioned like you see here, so it kind of pops-out to the left.

Step Four:

To view any of these thumbnails much larger, you don't have to resize Mini Bridge. Instead, you can get an instant full-screen preview by clicking on a thumbnail, and then pressing the **Spacebar** on your keyboard. That image goes full screen (as shown here), so you can get a good look at it. To see the next image in the filmstrip, just press the Right Arrow key on your keyboard (and, of course, to go to a previous image, use the Left Arrow key). When you're done seeing this full-screen preview, you can either press the Spacebar again, or press the Esc key on your keyboard.

Use Full-Screen Review Mode to Find Your Best Shots Fast

One of my favorite features of Mini Bridge is Review mode, because this is where Mini Bridge really feels big! By making your images much larger onscreen, it makes it much easier to find your best shots, and Review mode really makes whittling things down to just the best shots from your shoot so much easier.

Step One:

To see the images in Mini Bridge in Review mode, make sure either no images are selected or all the images you want to see are selected (by Command-clicking [PC: Ctrl-clicking] on them), then choose **Review Mode** from the View icon's pop-up menu at the top left of the panel (as shown here). By the way, if you have less than four images, it doesn't go into the full carousel slide show version of Review mode like you see in the next step—it just puts the four in Full Screen Preview mode (yawn).

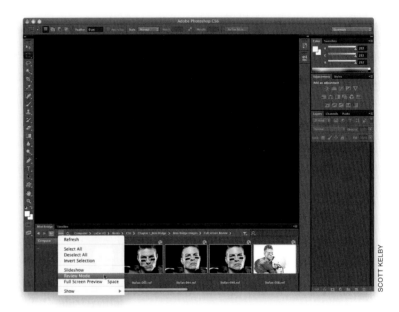

Step Two:

When you choose Review Mode, it enters a full-screen view with your images in a cool carousel-like rotation (as seen here). This mode is great for two big reasons: The first being it makes a really nice on-screen slide show presentation. You can use the **Left** and **Right Arrow keys** on your keyboard to move through the photos or the arrow buttons in the lower-left corner of the screen (as a photo comes to the front, it becomes larger and brighter). If you want to open the image in front in Photoshop, press the letter **O**. To open the front photo in Adobe Camera Raw, press **R**. To open all your images in Camera Raw, press **Option-R (PC: Alt-R)**. To leave Review mode, press the **Esc key**. If you forget any of these shortcuts, just press **H**.

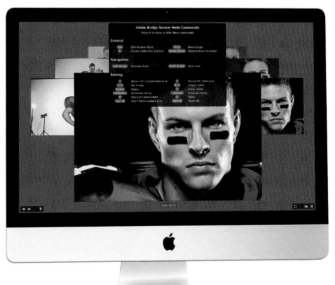

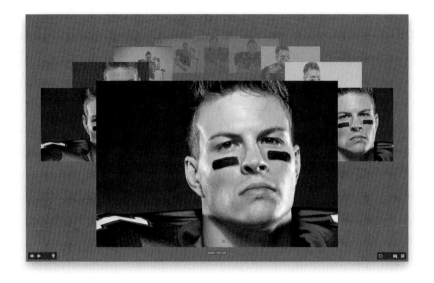

Step Three:

The second reason to use Review mode is to help you narrow things down to just your best photos from a shoot. Here's how: Let's say you have five or six similar photos, or photos of a similar subject (in this case, a football player), and you want to find the single best one out of those. Start by Command-clicking (PC: Ctrl-clicking) on just those photos (in the filmstrip) to select them, and enter Review mode. As you move through the photos (using the Left and Right Arrow keys on your keyboard), and you see one come to the front that's not going to make the cut, just press the **Down Arrow key** on your keyboard (or click the Down Arrow button onscreen) and that photo is removed from the screen. Keep doing this until you've narrowed things down to just the final image.

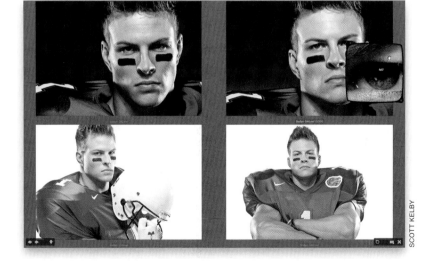

Step Four:

Like I mentioned, once you fall below five images, you no longer get the carousel view. Instead, it looks more like regular Full Screen Preview mode—it's just full screen (as seen here). In Review mode, you can zoom in tight on a particular area using the built-in Loupe. Just move your cursor over the part of the photo you want a closer look at, and click to bring up the Loupe for that photo (as shown here, in the image in the top right). To move it, click-and-hold inside the Loupe and drag it where you want it. To make it go away, just click once inside it. Once you've whittled things down to just your keepers, you can give each a star rating (like a 5-star rating by pressing **Command-5 [PC: Ctrl-5]**)—more on this on the next page.

SCOTT KELBY

Sorting and Arranging Your Photos

Ah, finally we get to the fun part—sorting your photos. We generally always have the same goal here: quickly finding out which are the best shots from your shoot (the keepers), marking them as your best shots, and then separating those from the rest, so they're just one click away when you need them. That way, you can view them as slide shows, post them on the web, send them to a client for proofing, or prepare them for printing.

Step One:

When you view your images in Mini Bridge, by default, they're sorted manually by filename, so it's pretty likely that the first photo you shot will appear in the left end of the filmstrip. I say it's "pretty likely" because there are exceptions (if you did multiple shoots on different cameras, or shot on different memory cards, etc.), but most likely they'll appear first one shot first. If you want to change how they are sorted, click on the Sort icon (it looks like up and down arrows) near the left end of the Toolbar, and a pop-up menu of options will appear (as seen here).

Step Two:

Let's start by quickly rating our photos to separate the keepers from the rest of the bunch. First, I switch to a view mode that's better for decision making, like Full Screen Preview mode (select any photo and then press the **Spacebar**) or Review mode (we just went through this). Now, use the **Left** and **Right Arrow keys** on your keyboard to move through the full-screen images.

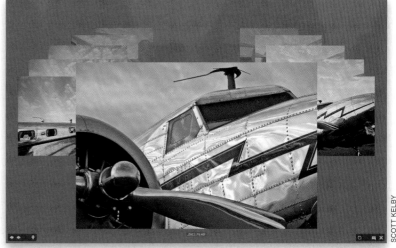

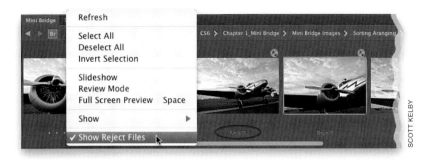

SCOTT KELBY

Step Three:

Probably the most popular method for sorting your images is to rate them using Mini Bridge's 1- to 5-star rating system (with 5 being your best images). That being said, I'm going to try to convince you to try a rating system that is faster and more efficient. Let's start by finding the bad ones. When you see a photo that is really bad (way out of focus, the flash didn't fire, the subject's eyes are closed, etc.), press **Option-Delete (PC: Alt-Delete)** to mark that photo as a Reject. The word Reject appears in red in the bottom-left after you do this in Full Screen Preview mode, below the photo in Review mode, and below the thumbnail, as well (shown circled here in red), if you choose **Labels and Ratings**, under Show in the View icon's pop-up menu. It doesn't delete them; it just marks 'em as Rejects. *Note:* Mini Bridge displays your Rejects right alongside your other photos, but if you don't want to see your Rejects, you can hide them by going under the View icon's pop-up menu and choosing **Show Reject Files** (as shown here).

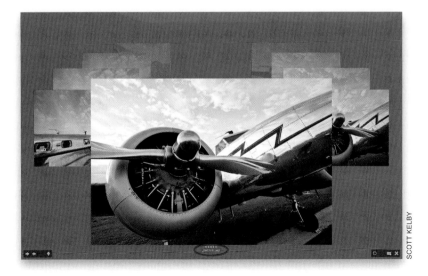

SCOTT KELBY

Step Four:

When you see a "keeper" (a shot you may want to print, or show to the client, etc.), then you'll press **Command-5 (PC: Ctrl-5)** to mark that photo as a 5-star image, and this star rating will appear below the selected photo (shown circled here in red). So that's the drill—move through your photos and when you see a real keeper, press Command-5, and when you see a totally messed up photo, press Option-Delete to mark it as a Reject. For all the rest of the photos, you do absolutely nothing. So, why not use the entire star rating system? Because it takes way, way too long (I'll explain why on the next page).

(Continued)

Step Five:

Here's why I don't recommend using the entire star rating system: What are you going to do with your 2-star images? They're not bad enough to delete, so we keep 'em, right? What about your 3-star ones? The client won't see these either, but we keep 'em. What about your 4-star photos (the ones that weren't quite good enough to be five stars)? We keep them, too. See where I'm going? Why waste your valuable time deciding if a photo is a 2- or a 3- or a 4-star, if all you're go-ing to do is keep 'em anyway? The only shots we really care about are the ones we want off our computer (they're mess-ed up and just wasting disk space) and our best shots from that shoot. So, once you've gone through and ranked them, let's get rid of the dogs. Click-and-hold on the Filter Items by Rating icon at the right end of the Toolbar (it looks like a funnel) and choose **Show Rejected Items Only** (as shown here) to see just the Rejects.

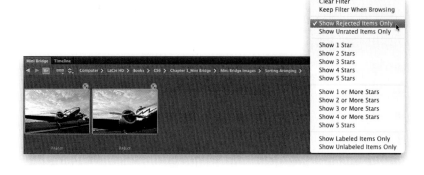

Step Six:

Now, Command-click (PC: Ctrl-click) on all the Rejects, then press the Spacebar to open them in Full Screen Preview mode, and press **Command-Delete (PC: Ctrl-Delete)** on each one to move them to your Trash (PC: Recycle Bin). Next, go under the Filter Items by Rat-ing icon's pop-up menu again, but this time choose **Show 5 Stars** (as shown here) to filter things down so just your keepers—your 5-star images—are visible in Mini Bridge.

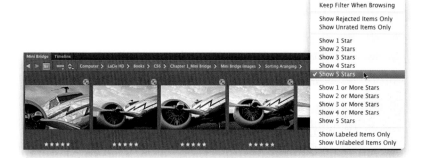

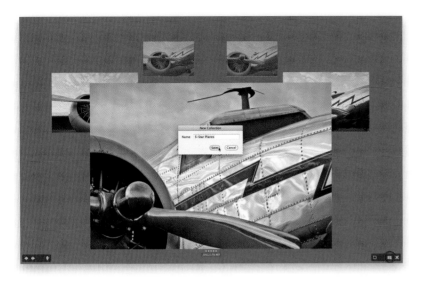

Step Seven:

At this point, we want to set things up so that, in the future, these 5-star photos are just one click away at any time, and we do that using collections (which are stored in Big Bridge). Here's how it works: Select all your 5-star photos, then enter Review mode. You'll see a button in the bottom-right corner (to the left of the X [Close] button, and shown circled here in red). Click it, and it brings up a dialog where you can name and save your images to a collection. Type in a name (I used "5-Star Planes") and click the Save button.

TIP: Removing Ratings and Reject Labels

To remove a photo's star rating, just click on the photo, then press **Command-0** (zero; **PC: Ctrl-0**). You can use the same shortcut to remove the Reject label.

Step Eight:

When you click that Save button, a collection of just these photos is saved. Now these best-of-that-shoot photos will always be just one click away. From the panel's flyout menu, choose **Show Navigation Pod** to make the Navigation pod visible again. Then, from the pop-up menu at the top of the pod, choose **Collections**, then click on the 5-Star Planes collection (as shown here), and just that shoot's 5-star photos appear.

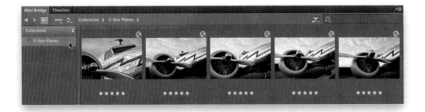

Finding Your Photos by Searching

Mini Bridge has a search function that lets you either use your computer's built-in search (like the Mac's Spotlight search or Windows Desktop Search), or you can use Mini Bridge's Advanced Search, which has searching power more like the one in Big Bridge. Here's how it works:

Step One:

At the top-right corner of the Mini Bridge panel is a search field. If you click on the little down-facing arrow in the field, you'll see that you have three different choices in the pop-up menu for how to search: (1) You can use your computer's built-in search to search your entire computer (which is surprisingly handy), or (2) just the current folder. Or, (3) you can use a standard Bridge search (which searches just the filename and any embedded keywords) to narrow things down in just your current folder.

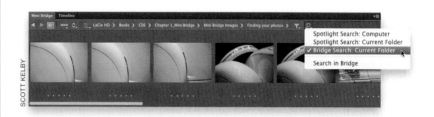

Step Two:

Here, I typed in the keyword "Tires" and chose the basic Bridge search of the current folder, and Mini Bridge displayed the results of this keyword search, which in this case was just three images with a clear view of a tire (as seen here). To leave the search results and return to your previous folder of images, just click the Back button (the left arrow) at the top-left corner of the Mini Bridge panel.

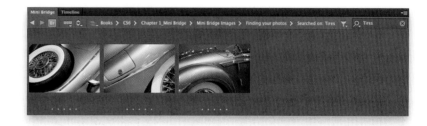

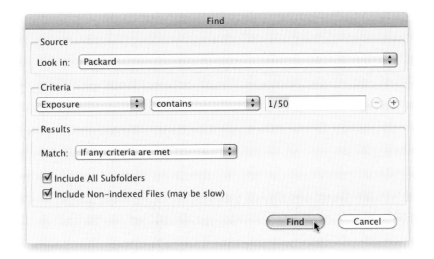

Step Three:
If you want more search control, then choose **Search in Bridge** from the search field's pop-up menu, and it brings up the Find dialog you see here in Big Bridge. You choose where it's going to search from the Source Look In pop-up menu up top (by default, it includes your Pictures folder, any favorite locations you've saved in Big Bridge, and your desktop). You choose what to search for using the Criteria pop-up menus, and the best way to see what you can search for is simply to click-and-hold on the first pop-up menu (it's a pretty darn amazing list, including searching through all the EXIF data embedded into your photo at the moment you took the shot).

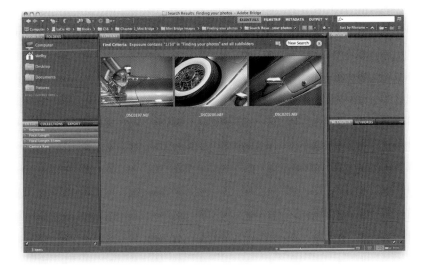

Step Four:
When you click Find, the results of your search are displayed in the Content panel of Big Bridge itself (as seen here) and you can open any of the images directly into Photoshop (just double-click on them) or Camera Raw (if they're RAW images, they'll automatically open in Camera Raw first. If not, you can open JPEG or TIFF images in Camera Raw by clicking on them, then pressing **Command-R [PC: Ctrl-R]**. Easy to remember—just think "R" for "RAW").

TIP: Deleting Photos in Mini Bridge
You can delete photos in Mini Bridge by going into Full Screen Preview mode and pressing Delete (Mac or PC). You'll get a dialog asking if you want to reject the file or delete it. If you press **Command-Delete (PC: Ctrl-Delete)**, it automatically puts it in the Trash (PC: Recycle Bin) and moves on to the next image.

Photoshop Killer Tips

Syncing Mini Bridge with Big Bridge

If you want to sync Adobe Bridge (I call it "Big Bridge") and Mini Bridge (so they both display the same images at the same time), start in Mini Bridge and click the Reveal in Bridge icon at the top left of the panel. This sends you over to Big Bridge, where you'll need to click the Return to Adobe Photoshop icon (it's a little boomerang) near the top left of the window, and it boomerangs you back to Photoshop. Now, Mini Bridge and Big Bridge will both display the same folder of images. To turn off the syncing, press **Command-Option-O (PC: Ctrl-Alt-O)** to switch applications and choose a new folder, or just change applications using the Dock (on a Mac) or the taskbar (on a PC).

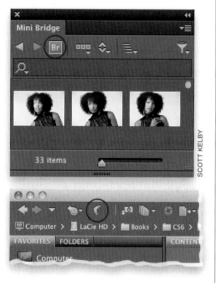

Hiding the Path Bar & Tools

If you don't wind up using the Path Bar a lot in your workflow, you can actually hide it from view altogether (which makes your thumbnails a little bit larger without resizing Mini Bridge) by clicking on the down-facing arrow in the top-right corner of the

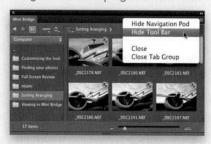

panel and choosing **Hide Toolbar**. This hides the Path Bar and the icons for the View, Sort, and Filter menus.

Seeing Just the Thumbnails Alone

When I'm searching for just the right image, I want my distractions at a minimum, and if that sounds like you, try choosing **Thumbnail Only**, under Show, from the View icon's pop-up menu near the left end of the Tool-

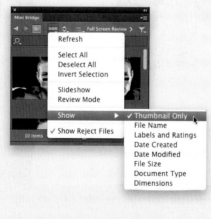

bar. That hides the file's name, any star ratings, color labels, or any other distracting stuff, so you can focus on the images.

Review Mode Time Saver

I mentioned earlier in the chapter that if you're in Mini Bridge's Review mode (see page 6) and you find an image you want to work on, you can press **R** to open the image in Camera Raw (it doesn't matter whether it's a RAW image, a JPEG, or a TIFF), and if you want to open a JPEG, TIFF, or even a PSD from Review mode directly into Photoshop, you can press **O**, but you can also Right-click on the image and choose **Open** from the pop-up menu,

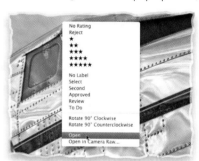

and it opens right up. You can also do other things from this pop-up menu, like add a color label to your image, or add a star rating, or rotate the file.

Dragging-and-Dropping Right from Mini Bridge

If you already have a document open in Photoshop, you can drag-and-drop an image directly from Mini Bridge right into that document and it appears as a smart object (not too shabby!). If the

Photoshop Killer Tips

photo is in RAW format, it opens in Camera Raw first (for any last minute tweaking), but then opens when you click OK. But my favorite drag-and-drop tip is this: You don't have to have a document already open. Just drag-and-drop your image from Mini Bridge right into the center area where your document would normally be, and it opens your photo in a new image window. You gotta try this! (If you're using a Mac, though, you need to have Application Frame turned on [under the Window menu] for this to work. If you don't, your image will just copy to your desktop.)

Hidden Slide Show Shortcuts

If you select a bunch of images in Mini Bridge, and choose **Slideshow** from the View icon's pop-up menu (at the top left of the panel), you get a full-screen, auto-advancing slide show complete with transitions. But there are

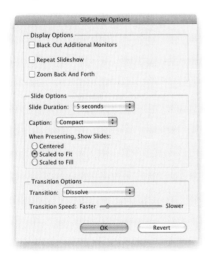

some hidden shortcuts you can use while it's running that are pretty handy. For example: Press the **R key** to pause the slide show and open the current photo in Camera Raw (just press the **Spacebar** to resume the slide show once you're done in Camera Raw); press the **Period key** to add a 1-star rating, press it twice to add a 2-star rating, and so on; press the **Left Bracket key** to rotate counterclockwise, and the **Right Bracket key** to rotate clockwise; press the **L key** to bring up the Slideshow Options dialog (shown here); and press the **+ (plus sign) key** to zoom in, and the **– (minus sign) key** to zoom out. The numbers **1–5** also add star ratings, and **6–9** add color labels. Lastly, just press the **H key** to get a list of the slide show shortcuts.

The Path Bar Is Live

The Path Bar that shows the path to the current folder you're viewing isn't just for looks—it's live—meaning you can click on any of the folder names in the path and jump to that folder.

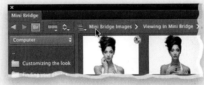

Changing a File's Name

If you want to change a file's name, just Right-click on its thumbnail in Mini Bridge and choose **Rename**. This highlights the name field and you can just type in the new name you want. Technically, you can

also click directly on the name of the file itself and it will highlight, but the Right-click method works better, because it's too easy to accidentally open the image when you're trying to get that name field to highlight. One thing to know: this only works with one image at a time. If you want to batch rename a bunch of files, then you'll need to jump over to Big Bridge.

Adding Favorites to Mini Bridge

So, how do you get your favorite, most-used folders added to Mini Bridge's Navigation pod, so they're just one click away? Click the Reveal in Bridge icon at the top left of the panel to jump to Big Bridge, then in the Folders panel (at the top left of the window), find the folder you want to make a favorite. Once you find it, Right-click on it and choose **Add to Favorites** from the pop-up menu, then click the Return to Adobe Photoshop icon (the boomerang icon in the top left of the window) to jump back to Photoshop. Now, you'll see that folder added to your Favorites list in Mini Bridge.

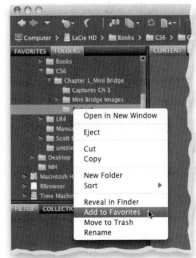

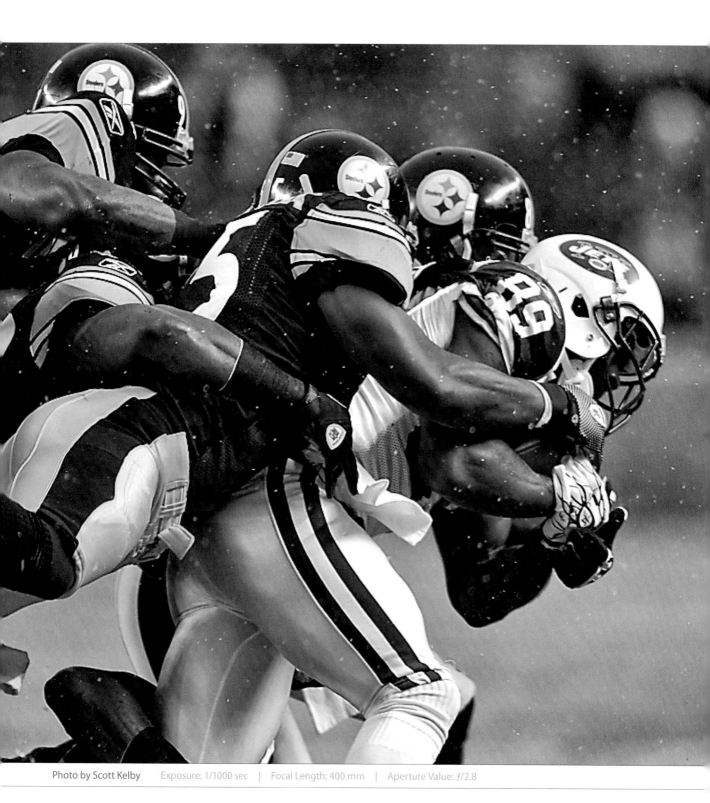

Photo by Scott Kelby   Exposure: 1/1000 sec | Focal Length: 400 mm | Aperture Value: f/2.8

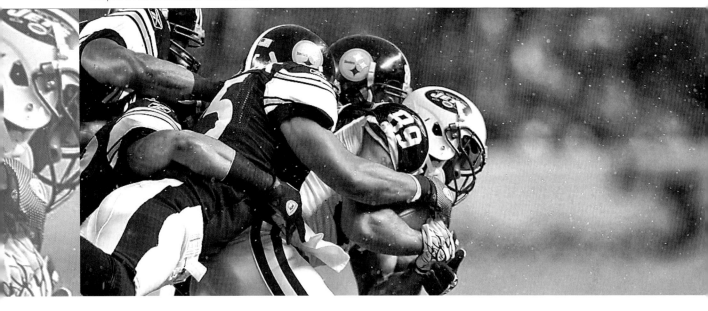

WWF Raw
the essentials of camera raw

Now, if you're reading the English-language version of this book, you probably instantly recognized the chapter title "WWF Raw" from the wildly popular American TV series *Wasabi with Fries Raw* (though in Germany, it's called *Weinerschnitzel Mit Fischrogen Raw*, and in Spain, it's called simply *Lucha Falsa*, which translated literally means "Lunch Feet"). Anyway, it's been a tradition of mine, going back about 50 books or so, to name the chapters after a movie title, song title, or TV show, and while "WWF Raw" may not be the ideal name for a chapter on Camera Raw essentials, it's certainly better than my second choice, "Raw Meat" (named after the 1972 movie starring Donald Pleasence. The sequel, *Steak Tartare*, was released straight to DVD in 1976, nearly 20 years before DVDs were even invented, which is quite remarkable for a movie whose French version wound up being called *Boeuf Gâté Dans la Toilette*, with French

actor Jean-Pierre Pommes Frites playing the lead role of Marcel, the dog-faced boy). Anyway, finding movies, TV shows, and song titles with the word "raw" in them isn't as easy as it looks, and since this book has not one, not two, not three, but...well, yes, actually it has three chapters on Camera Raw, I'm going to have to do some serious research to come up with something that tops "WWF Raw," but isn't "Raw Meat," and doesn't use the same name I used back in the CS4 edition of this book, which was "Raw Deal" (from the 1986 movie starring California Governor Arnold from *Happy Days*. See, that was a vague reference to the guy who played the diner owner in the '70s sitcom *Happy Days*, starring Harrison Ford and Marlon Brando). But what I really can't wait for is to see how the people who do the foreign translations of my books translate this intro. C'est magnifique, amigos!

Working with Camera Raw

Although Adobe Camera Raw was originally created to process photos taken in your camera's RAW format, you can also use it to process your JPEG and TIFF photos. A big advantage of using Camera Raw that many people don't realize is that it's just plain easier and faster to make your images look good using Camera Raw than with any other method. Camera Raw's controls are simple, they're instantaneous, and they're totally undoable, which makes it hard to beat. But first, you've got to open your images in Camera Raw for processing.

Opening RAW Images:

Since Camera Raw was designed to open RAW images, if you double-click on a RAW image (whether in Mini Bridge or just in a folder on your computer), it will launch Photoshop and open that RAW image in Camera Raw (its full official name is Adobe Camera Raw, but here in the book, I'll just be calling it "Camera Raw" for short, because…well…that's what I call it). *Note:* If you double-click on what you know is a RAW image and it doesn't open in Camera Raw, make sure you have the latest version of Camera Raw—images from newly released cameras need the latest versions of Camera Raw to recognize their RAW files.

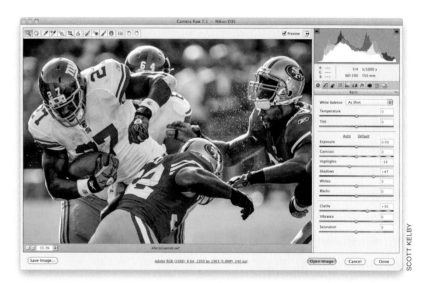

Opening JPEG & TIFF Images from Mini Bridge:

If you want to open a JPEG or TIFF image from Mini Bridge, it's easy: Right-click on it and, from the pop-up menu, under Open With, choose **Camera Raw**.

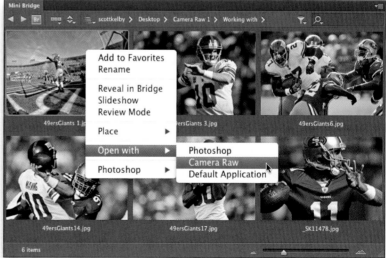

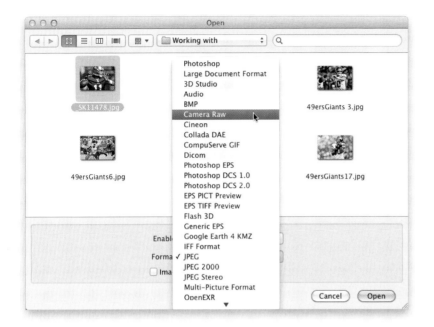

Opening JPEG & TIFF Images from Your Computer:

If you want to open a JPEG or TIFF image from your computer, then here's what you do: On a Mac, go under Photoshop's File menu and choose **Open**. When the Open dialog appears, click on your JPEG (or TIFF, but we'll use a JPEG as our example) image, and in the Format pop-up menu, it will say JPEG. You need to click-and-hold on that Format pop-up menu, and from that menu choose **Camera Raw**, as shown here. Then click the Open button, and your JPEG image will open in Camera Raw. In Windows, just go under Photoshop's File menu and choose **Open As**, then navigate your way to that JPEG or TIFF image, change the Open As pop-up menu to **Camera Raw**, and click Open.

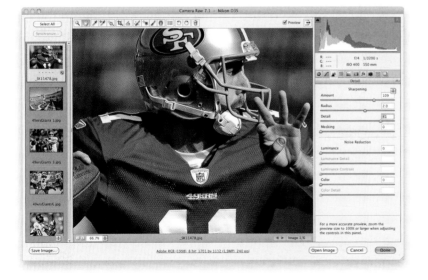

Opening Multiple Images:

You can open multiple RAW photos in Camera Raw by selecting them first (either in Mini Bridge or in a folder on your computer), then just double-clicking on any one of them, and they'll all open in Camera Raw and appear in a filmstrip along the left side of the Camera Raw window (as seen here). If the photos are JPEGs or TIFFs, in Mini Bridge, select 'em first, then switch to Review mode, and press **Option-R (PC: Alt-R)**. If they're in a folder on your computer, then you'll need to use Mini Bridge to open them, as well (just use the Path Bar in Mini Bridge to navigate to where those images are located).

(Continued)

Editing JPEG & TIFF Images in Camera Raw:

One thing about editing JPEGs and TIFFs in Camera Raw: When you make adjustments to a JPEG or TIFF and you click the Open Image button, it opens your image in Photoshop (as you'd expect). However, if you just want to save the changes you made in Camera Raw without opening the photo in Photoshop, then click the Done button instead (as shown here), and your changes will be saved. But there is a big distinction between editing JPEG or TIFF images and editing a RAW image. If you click the Done button, you're actually affecting the real pixels of the original JPEG or TIFF, whereas, if this were a RAW image, you wouldn't be (which is another big advantage of shooting in RAW). If you click the Open Image button, and open your JPEG or TIFF in Photoshop, you're opening and editing the real image, as well. Just so you know.

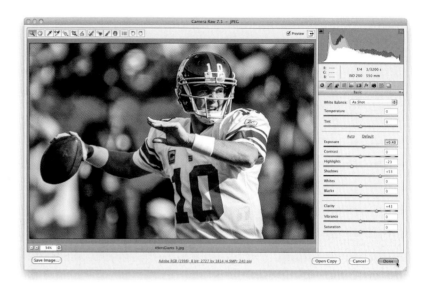

The Two Camera Raws:

Here's another thing you'll need to know: there are actually two Camera Raws—one in Photoshop, and a separate one in Bridge. The advantage of having two Camera Raws comes into play when you're processing (or saving) a lot of RAW photos—you can have them processing in Bridge's version of Camera Raw, while you're working on something else in Photoshop. If you find yourself using Bridge's Camera Raw most often, then you'll probably want to press **Command-K (PC: Ctrl-K)** to bring up Bridge's Preferences, click on General on the left, and then turn on the checkbox for Double-Click Edits Camera Raw Settings in Bridge (as shown here). Now, double-clicking on a photo opens RAW photos in Bridge's Camera Raw, rather than Photoshop's.

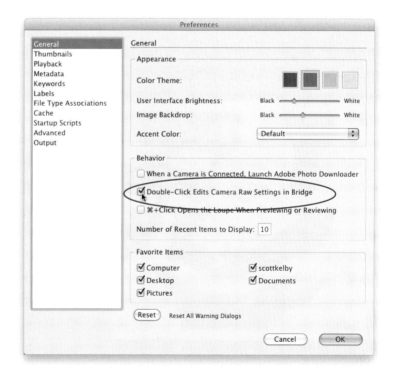

Not only are there new sliders in Photoshop CS6's version of Camera Raw, but some of the old sliders now do different things, and understanding that now (before we just dive right in) will help it all make more sense. I'm going to borrow the way the histogram works in the current version of Adobe Photoshop Lightroom, which has the latest Camera Raw built into it, because it will help you visually understand the changes of these new sliders.

For CS4/CS5 Users Only: Understanding CS6's New Camera Raw Sliders

CS4/CS5 CAMERA RAW HISTOGRAM

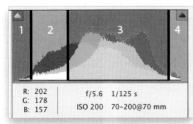

1. Affected by the Blacks slider
2. Affected by the Fill Light slider
3. Affected by the Exposure slider
4. Affected by the Recovery slider

NEW CS6 CAMERA RAW HISTOGRAM

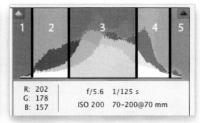

1. Affected by the Blacks slider
2. Affected by the Shadows slider
3. Affected by the Exposure slider
4. Affected by the Highlights slider
5. Affected by the Whites slider

CS4/CS5 CAMERA RAW BASIC PANEL

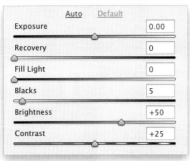

CS4/CS5: Recovery slider

CS4/CS5: Fill Light slider

CS4/CS5: Brightness slider

NEW CS6 CAMERA RAW BASIC PANEL

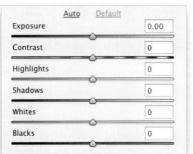

CS6: Now use Highlights & Exposure sliders

CS6: Now use Shadows slider

CS6: Now use Exposure slider

Old CS4/CS5 Camera Raw:
Four sliders controlled the entire tonal range, which limited your editing. One problem was that the Exposure slider covered too much of that range—from the midtones all the way through the highlights (see #3 in the histogram on the left here). Plus, you could only *increase* the amounts of Recovery, Fill Light, and Blacks—you couldn't decrease them.

New CS6 Camera Raw:
Now, five sliders control the overall tonal range (so you have more control), and they're consistent now—all starting in the center, so that dragging a slider to the left darkens the adjustment and dragging to the right brightens it. Also, the Exposure slider now controls a smaller range (mostly the midtones, as seen in the histogram on the right above), and it has a Recovery algorithm built in now, so you can increase it much more than you could in CS4/CS5 without clipping the highlights. If you do clip the highlights (perhaps in-camera), you now use the Highlights slider first to fix the clipping, and tweak the Exposure slider, if necessary. The Highlights and Shadows sliders are somewhat like the Levels adjustment's white and black points. Shadows is a more subtle, but far better looking, Fill Light control (think Fill Light without the halos and HDR-effect look).

Updating to the Latest Camera Raw Editing Features (Not for New Users)

Okay, this is only for those who have been using Camera Raw in previous versions of Photoshop (like CS5, CS4, etc.), because if this is the first time you'll be using it, this won't affect you at all, so you can skip this. Here's why: in Photoshop CS6, Adobe dramatically improved the math and controls for the Basic panel, so if you have RAW images you edited in earlier versions of Camera Raw, when you open them in CS6's updated version of Camera Raw, you'll have the choice of keeping the old look (and old controls) or updating to the new, vastly improved Basic panel controls (called the 2012 process version).

Step One:

Even before you bought this book, you probably heard that Camera Raw now has a different set of sliders that offer more powerful, and overall just better, control over your images, but when you open a RAW image in CS6's Camera Raw that you previously edited in an earlier version of Camera Raw, you might be surprised to see that all the sliders look exactly the same as they did before. That's because Adobe didn't want to change the way your already-processed photo looks without your permission, so at this point, your image looks the same (and so do Camera Raw's sliders—the Fill Light and Recovery sliders are still there).

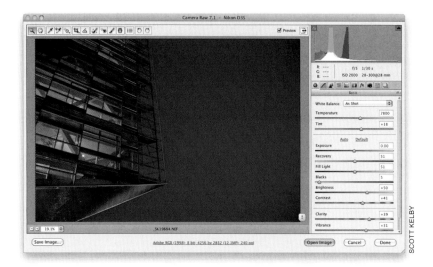

Step Two:

However, the processing technology being used on your photo at this point is actually out-of-date. If fact, it's either old technology from 2010, or if you're moving up from CS4, it's actually processing technology from back in 2003. Adobe calls these "process versions"—if you go to the Camera Calibration panel and click on the Process pop-up menu (as shown here), you can choose from the three different versions (the 2010 version improved the sharpening and noise reduction quality pretty dramatically).

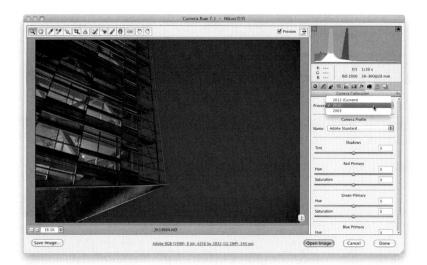

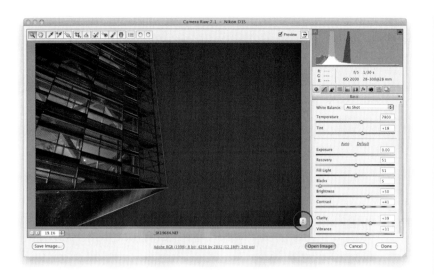

Step Three:

Of course, you could choose the 2012 (current) process version from that pop-up menu and your image will be updated to the current processing power, and all the new, improved sliders will appear in the Basic panel. But, I'd only do that if I were charging by the hour, because there's a much quicker way to do it. When you open an image edited in a previous version of Camera Raw, you'll see a warning icon in the bottom-right corner of the Preview area (actually, it's an exclamation point, shown circled here in red). To instantly update to the latest version, just click directly on that exclamation point and it's updated.

TIP: Getting Fill Light & Recovery Back

If you ever decide that you just can't live without the old Fill Light and/or Recovery sliders, just go to the Camera Calibration panel and from the Process pop-up menu up top, choose **2010**, and they instantly reappear (but you'll be using the old processing technology now, as well).

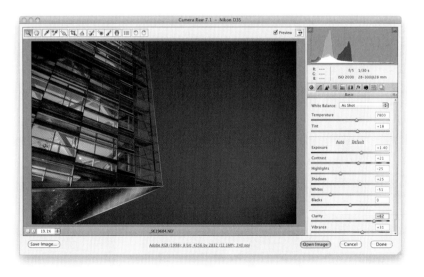

Step Four:

Now your image is updated to the latest processing technology, and it's been my experience that just by converting to the new process version, my photos look instantly better (well, in the vast majority of cases—in some cases, they look the same, but I've never had one I thought looked worse). However, if you didn't apply any Basic panel adjustments to your image previously, there's nothing for it really to update, so you're not going to notice a change when you update. In this image, once I updated to the 2012 process version, I was able to increase the Clarity more (without creating halos), and I bumped up the Exposure a bit, too.

Miss the JPEG Look? Try Applying a Camera Profile

If you've ever wondered why RAW images look good on your camera's LCD, but look flat when you open them in Camera Raw, it's because what you see on your LCD is a JPEG preview (even though you're shooting in RAW), and your camera automatically adds color correction, sharpening, etc., to them. When you shoot in RAW, you're telling the camera, "Turn all that color enhancement and sharpening off—just leave it untouched, and I'll process it myself." But, if you'd like that JPEG-processed look as a starting place for your RAW photo editing, camera profiles can get you close.

Step One:

Click on the Camera Calibration icon (the third icon from the right) near the top of the Panel area, and in the Camera Profile section, click-and-hold on the Name pop-up menu, and you'll see a list of camera profiles available for your particular camera (it reads the embedded EXIF data, so it knows which brand of camera you use). For example, if you shoot Nikon, you'll see a list of the in-camera picture styles (shown here) you could have applied to your image if you had taken the shot in JPEG mode (if you shoot in RAW, Camera Raw ignores those in-camera profiles, as explained above). If you shoot Canon, you'll see a slightly different list, but it does the same type of thing.

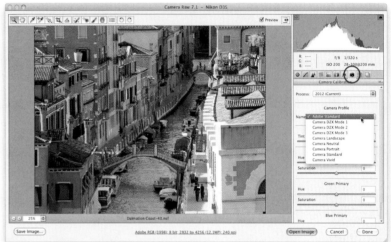

Step Two:

The default profile will be Adobe Standard. Now, ask yourself this: "Does the word 'Standard' ever mean 'Kick Butt?'" Not usually, which is why I suggest you try out the different profiles in this list and see which ones you like. At the very least, I would change it to **Camera Standard**, which I think usually gives you a better starting place (as seen here).

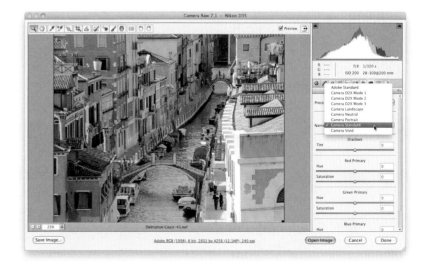

SCOTT KELBY

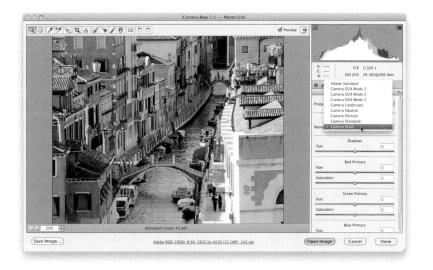

Step Three:

Depending on the individual photo you're editing, Camera Standard might not be the right choice, but as the photographer, this is a call you have to make (in other words, it's up to you to choose which one looks best to you). I usually wind up using either Camera Standard, Camera Landscape, or Camera Vivid for images taken with a Nikon camera, because I think Landscape and Vivid look the most like the JPEGs I see on the back of my camera. But again, if you're not shooting Nikon, Landscape or Vivid won't be one of the available choices (Nikons have eight picture styles and Canons have six). If you don't shoot Canon or Nikon, or one of a handful of other cameras, then you'll only have Adobe Standard, and possibly Camera Standard, to choose from, but you can create your own custom profiles using Adobe's free DNG Profile Editor utility, available from Adobe at http://labs.adobe.com.

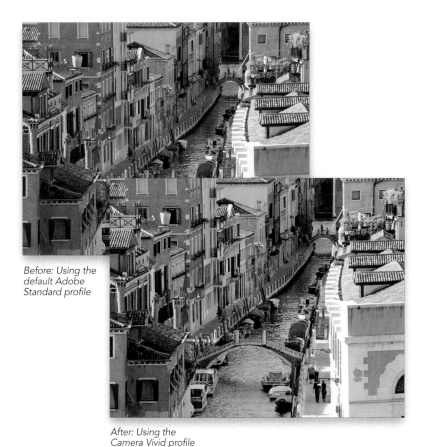

Before: Using the default Adobe Standard profile

After: Using the Camera Vivid profile

Step Four:

Here's a before/after with only one thing done to this photo: I chose Camera Vivid (as shown in the pop-up menu in Step Three). Again, this is designed to replicate the color looks you could have chosen in the camera, so if you want to have Camera Raw give you a similar look as a starting point, give this a try. Also, since Camera Raw allows you to open more than one image at a time (in fact, you can open hundreds at a time), you could open a few hundred images, then click the Select All button that will appear at the top-left corner of the window, change the camera profile for the first-selected image, and then all the other images will have that same profile automatically applied. Now, you can just click the Done button.

The Essential Adjustments: White Balance

If you've ever taken a photo indoors, chances are it came out with kind of a yellowish tint. Unless you took the shot in an office, and then it probably had a green tint. If you just took a shot of somebody in the shade, the photo probably had a blue tint. Those are white balance problems, and if we properly set our white balance in the camera, we won't see these color problems (the photos will just look normal), but since most of us shoot with our cameras set to Auto White Balance, we're going to run into them. Luckily, we can fix them pretty easily.

Step One:

The white balance is usually the very first thing I adjust in my own Camera Raw workflow, because getting the white balance right will eliminate 99% of your color problems right off the bat. At the top of the Basic panel (on the right side of the Camera Raw window), are the White Balance controls. If you look to the right of the words "White Balance," you'll see a pop-up menu (shown circled here in red), and by default it shows you the "As Shot" white balance (you're seeing the white balance you had set in your camera when you took the shot). I had been shooting indoors under regular indoor lighting, so my white balance had been set to Tungsten, but then I went into the studio and didn't change my white balance, so the first few shots came out with a heavy bluish tint (as seen here—yeech!) and that's why the white balance is way, way off.

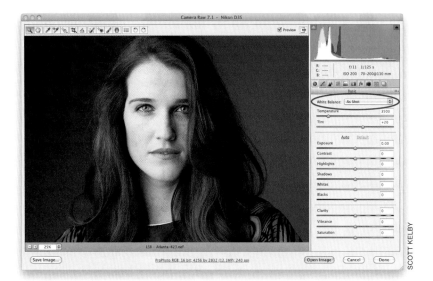

SCOTT KELBY

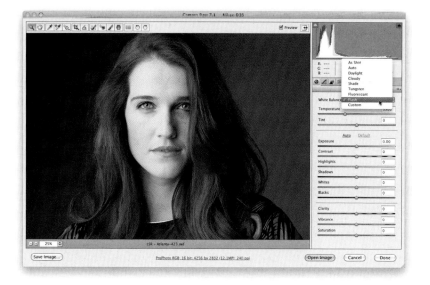

Step Two:

There are three ways to change the white balance in your photo, and the first is to simply choose one of the built-in White Balance presets. Fairly often, that's all you need to do to color correct your image. Just click on the White Balance pop-up menu, and you'll see a list of white balance settings you could have chosen in the camera. Just choose the preset that most closely matches what the lighting situation was when you originally took the photo (for example, if you took the shot in the shade of a tree, you'd choose the Shade preset). Here I tried each preset and Flash seemed to look best— it removed the bluish tint and made the background gray again. (*Note:* This is the one main area where the processing of RAW and JPEG or TIFF images differs. You'll only get this full list of white balance presets with RAW images. With JPEGs or TIFFs, your only choice is As Shot or Auto white balance.)

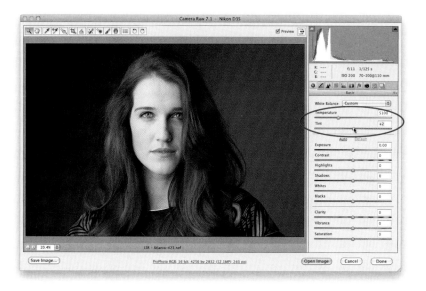

Step Three:

The second method is to use the Temperature and Tint sliders (found right below the White Balance preset menu). The bars behind the sliders are color coded so you can see which way to drag to get which kind of color tint. What I like to do is use the built-in presets to get close (as a starting point), and then if my color is just a little too blue or too yellow, I drag in the opposite direction. So, in this example, the Flash preset was close, but made it a little too yellow, so I dragged the Temperature slider a little bit toward blue and the Tint slider a tiny bit toward magenta.

(Continued)

The Essentials of Camera Raw | Chapter 2 |

Step Four:

Just a couple of other quick things about manually setting your white balance using the Temperature and Tint sliders: If you move a slider and decide you didn't want to move it after all, just double-click directly on the little slider "nub" itself, and it will reset to its previous location. By the way, I generally just adjust the Temperature slider, and rarely have to touch the Tint slider. Also, to reset the white balance to where it was when you opened the image, just choose **As Shot** from the White Balance pop-up menu (as seen here).

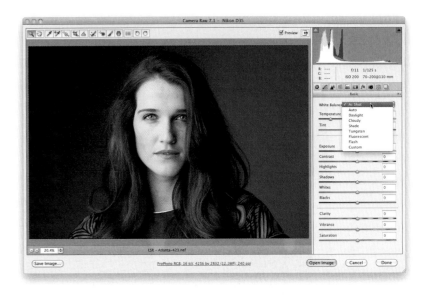

Step Five:

The third method is my personal favorite, and the method I use the most often, and that is setting the white balance using the White Balance tool **(I)**. This is perhaps the most accurate because it takes a white balance reading from the photo itself. You just click on the White Balance tool in the toolbar at the top left (it's circled in red here), and then click it on something in your photo that's supposed to be a light gray (that's right—you properly set the white balance by clicking on something that's light gray). So, take the tool and click it once on the background near her hair (as shown here) and it sets the white balance for you. If you don't like how it looks, then just click on a different light gray area. (It was a little dark, so I bumped up the Exposure a little, too.)

TIP: Quick White Balance Reset

To quickly reset your white balance to the As Shot setting, just double-click on the White Balance tool up in the toolbar.

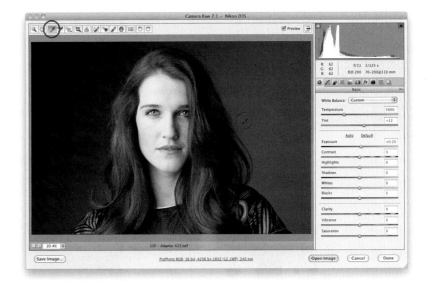

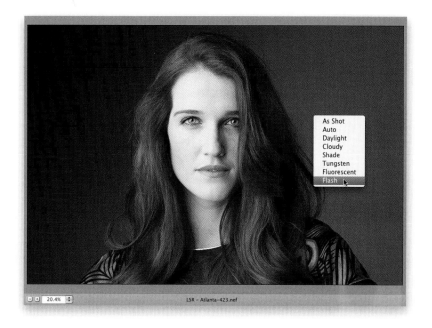

As Shot
Auto
Daylight
Cloudy
Shade
Tungsten
Fluorescent
Flash

LSR - Atlanta-423.nef

Step Six:

Now, here's the thing: although this can give you a perfectly accurate white balance, it doesn't mean that it will look good. White balance is a creative decision, and the most important thing is that your photo looks good to you. So don't get caught up in that "I don't like the way the white balance looks, but I know it's accurate" thing that sucks some people in—set your white balance so it looks right to you. You are the bottom line. You're the photographer. It's your photo, so make it look its best. Accurate is not another word for good. By the way, you can just Right-click on your image to access the White Balance pop-up menu (as shown here).

Step Seven:

Here's a before/after so you can see what a difference setting a proper white balance makes (by the way, you can see a quick before/after of your white balance edit by pressing the letter **P** on your keyboard to toggle the Preview on/off).

TIP: Using the Gray Card

To help you find that neutral light gray color in your images, I've included an 18% gray card in the back of this book (it's perforated, so you can tear it out). Once your lighting is set, just have your subject hold it while you take one shot. Then, open that image in Camera Raw, and click the White Balance tool on the card in your image to instantly set your white balance. Now, apply that same white balance to all the other shots taken under that same light (more on how to do that coming up in the next chapter).

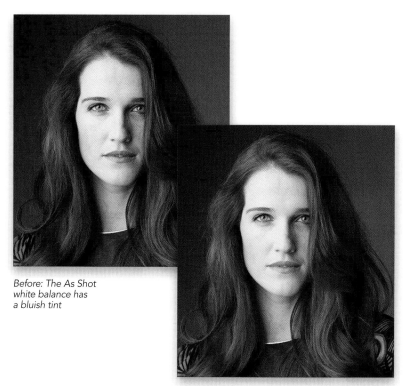

Before: The As Shot white balance has a bluish tint

After: With one click of the White Balance tool, everything comes together

The Essential Adjustments #2: Exposure

The next thing I fix (after adjusting the white balance) is the photo's exposure. Now, some might argue that this is the most essential adjustment of them all, but if your photo looks way too blue, nobody will notice if the photo's underexposed by a third of a stop, so I fix the white balance first, then I worry about exposure. However, exposure in Camera Raw isn't just the Exposure slider. It's actually five sliders: Exposure (midtones), Blacks (deep shadows), Shadows (regular shadows), Highlights (well-named), and Whites (extreme highlights).

Step One:

I recommend (and so does Adobe) starting with the top tonal slider in the Basic panel (Exposure) and working your way down through the other sliders in order, which is a different workflow than in previous versions of Camera Raw, where it didn't matter too much which slider you moved when. However, in CS6, it works best if you start by getting the Exposure (midtones) set first, and then if things look kind of washed out, adding some Contrast (the contrast slider in CS6 is way, way better than the one in CS5 and earlier, which I generally avoided). This photo, well, it's a mess. Taken in harsh, unflattering light, it needs some serious Camera Raw help.

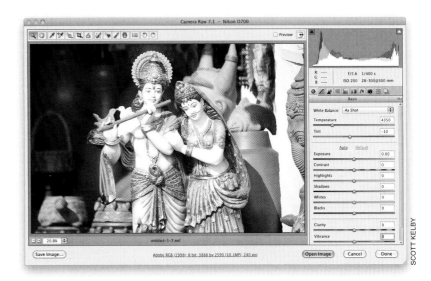

Step Two:

Start by adjusting the Exposure slider. This photo is way overexposed, so drag it to the left to darken the midtones and the overall exposure. Here, I dragged it over to –1.25 (it looks a lot better already), but the image is still kind of flat looking, and that's why your next step should be to adjust the contrast (by the way, although you can drag the Contrast slider to the left to make things less contrasty, I can't remember an occasion where I wanted my image to look more flat, so I don't drag to the left. Ever. But, hey, that's just me).

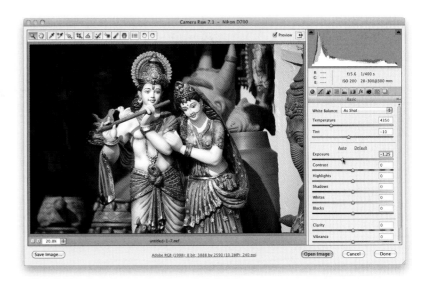

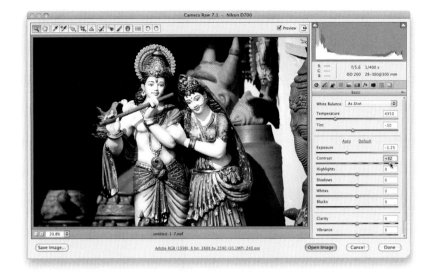

Step Three:

In previous versions of Camera Raw, when I saw an image looking flat like this one did back in Step Two, I would reach for the Blacks slider, but in CS6, now you increase the contrast using the Contrast slider, which makes the bright areas brighter and the dark areas darker (here, I dragged it to the right to +82, which helped deal with the flat, low-contrast look). These two steps—adjusting the Exposure and then the Contrast slider (if necessary)—should be your starting points every time. This top-down approach helps, because the other sliders build off this exposure foundation, and it will keep you from having to constantly keep tweaking slider after slider. So, think of these two as the foundation of your exposure, and the rest are kind of optional based on the image you're working on.

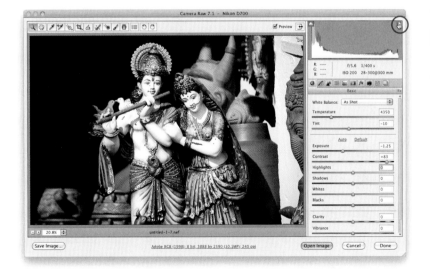

Step Four:

Before we go any further, increasing our contrast to where we wanted it created a clipping problem, meaning we are clipping off our highlights (part of our photo got so bright that it won't have any detail in that area at all. It's blown out. If all that sounds bad, well, that's 'cause it is). Luckily, Camera Raw will give you a warning if you're clipping, in the upper-right corner of the histogram. See that triangle? That's the highlight clipping warning (although I just call it "the white triangle of death"). Now, if you do see a white triangle, don't freak out. First, go up and click directly on that white triangle and the areas that are clipping will appear in red (look on her arm). We do this to find out if what's clipping is an area of important detail, or if it's like a tiny highlight on a chrome bumper or something meaningless in the background of your image.

(Continued)

Step Five:

If that red highlight shows over an area you feel has important detail (her arm and other areas here certainly seem important to me), go to the Highlights slider and drag it to the left until the red areas disappear (here, I dragged the Highlights slider to the left to –18). For those of you upgrading from an earlier version of Camera Raw, I kind of hesitate to say this replaces the Recovery slider, because there's more going on than just that, due to the way Adobe reworked the Exposure slider. Now when you adjust the Exposure slider, there's less chance of clipping than ever before, so it's kind of like the Exposure slider has some built-in Recovery power, too! That being said, I still look to the Highlights slider to re-cover clipped highlights first, and then if that doesn't do the trick, I try lowering the Exposure amount, but I rarely have to do that.

TIP: The Color Warning Triangles

If you see a red, yellow, magenta, etc., color warning triangle (rather than white), it's not great, but it's not nearly as bad as white. It means you're clipping just that one color channel (and there's still detail in the other channels).

Step Six:

The next slider down, Shadows, is another one you only use if there's a problem (just like the Highlights slider), and in this case, the problem is we can't see any detail in the upper-left corner of the photo. We can see that something's there, but we can't see exactly what. That's when you reach for the Shadows slider—drag it to the right to brighten the shadows (like I did here, where I dragged it over to +87) and look how you can now see the pottery in the background.

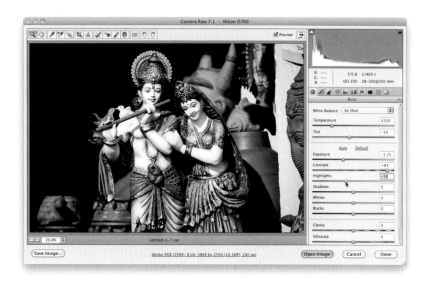

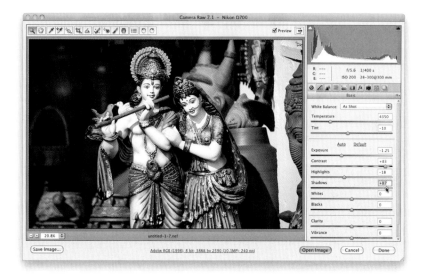

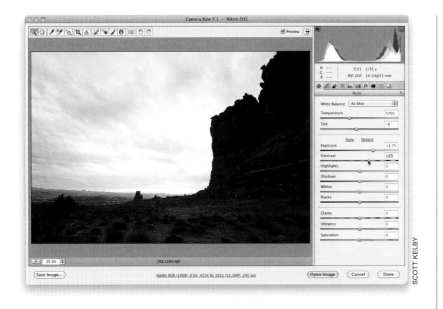

SCOTT KELBY

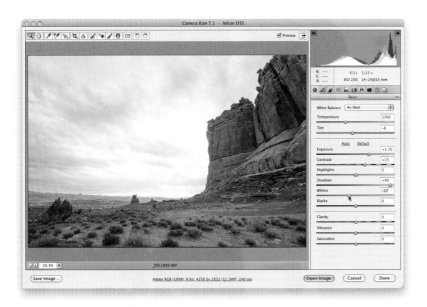

Step Seven:

Before we leave the Shadows slider, we need to switch to another image for just a moment (we'll come back to the other image shortly), because I want to point out that one of the most common times you'll use the Shadows slider is when your subject is backlit like this one, where the sky is pretty well exposed, but the fore-ground is really dark. When I was standing there, of course my eye compensated perfectly for the two vastly different ex-posures, but our cameras still aren't as sophisticated as the human eye, so we get shots that look like this. In previous versions of Camera Raw, I'd reach for the Fill Light slider to fix this problem, but of course, it created its own problems (if you bumped it way up, your image started to look a bit HDR-like, but not in a good way). Now, in CS6, the Shadows slider works with the Exposure slider to give you better results than the old Fill Light slider alone could give. Start by bumping up the Exposure, and then the Contrast (the Shadows slider will work much better when you tweak these first).

Step Eight:

Now, drag the Shadows slider way over to the right to open up those rocks and the foreground, so the whole image looks more balanced (here, I dragged over to +90). That overprocessed Fill Light look from previous versions of Cam-era Raw is gone. Instead, we have a much more natural-looking edit. Believe it or not, bumping the Shadows up this much created some highlight clipping in the Red channel (I saw the red highlight warning triangle appear in the upper-right corner), but that's an easy fix—I just dragged the Whites slider a little bit to the left (to –17, as shown here) to re-duce the brightest highlights. Now we can jump back to our original image.

(Continued)

Step Nine:

The last two essential exposure sliders are the Whites and Blacks. If you're used to working with Levels in Photoshop, you'll totally get these, because they're like setting your highlight and shadow points (or your white and black points). Most of the time, if I use the Whites slider (which controls the brightest highlights), I find myself dragging it to the right to make sure the whites are nice and bright white (and not light gray), but in this instance, I was using the Whites slider to pull the whites back a bit (to help hide the fact that it was shot in harsh, direct daylight), so I dragged it to the left (to darken the whites) to around –28. I also increased the deepest shadows by dragging the Blacks slider to the left just a little bit (here, I dragged over to –10). I still use this slider if, near the end of the editing process, I think the color needs more oomph, as this helps the colors look saturated and less washed out. Here's a before/after, but I did add two last finishing touches, which were to increase the Clarity a little (more on this coming up on page 36) and I increased the Vibrance amount a bit. Again, I recommend doing all of this in a top-to-bottom order, but just understand that not every image will need an adjustment to the Highlights and Shadows—only mess with those if you have a problem in those areas. Otherwise, skip 'em.

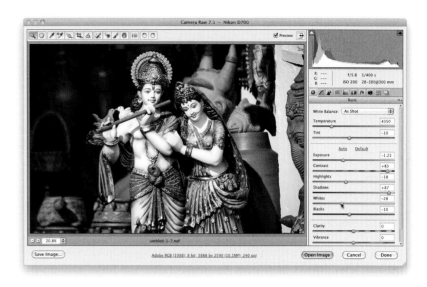

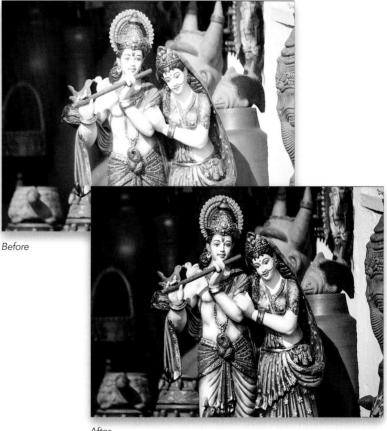

Before

After

If you're not quite comfortable with manually adjusting each image, Camera Raw does come with a one-click Auto function, which takes a stab at correcting the overall exposure of your image (including contrast, highlights, shadows, etc.), and at this point in Camera Raw's evolution, it's really not that bad. If you like the results, you can set up Camera Raw's preferences so every photo, upon opening in Camera Raw, will be auto-adjusted using that same feature.

Letting Camera Raw Auto-Correct Your Photos

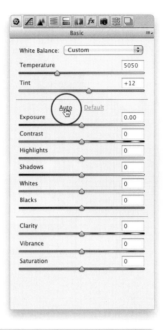

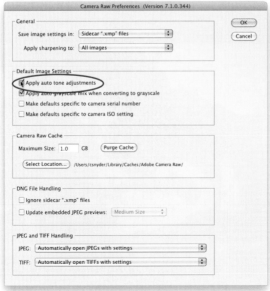

Step One:
Once you have an image open in Camera Raw, you can have Camera Raw take a stab at setting the overall exposure (using the controls in the Basic panel) for you by clicking on the Auto button (shown circled in red here). In older versions of Camera Raw, this Auto correction feature was…well…let's just say it was less than stellar, but it's gotten much better since then, and now it does a somewhat decent job (especially if you're stuck and not sure what to do), so click on it and see how it looks. If it doesn't look good, no sweat—just press **Command-Z (PC: Ctrl-Z)** to Undo.

Step Two:
You can set up Camera Raw so it automatically performs an Auto Tone adjustment each time you open a photo—just click on the Preferences icon up in Camera Raw's toolbar (it's the third icon from the right), and when the dialog appears, turn on the checkbox for Apply Auto Tone Adjustments (shown circled here), then click OK. Now, Camera Raw will evaluate each image and try to correct it. If you don't like its tonal corrections, then you can just click on the Default button, which appears to the right of the Auto button (the Auto button will be grayed out because it's already been applied).

Adding Punch to Your Images with Clarity

This is one of my favorite features in Camera Raw, and whenever I show it in a class, it never fails to get "Oooohs" and "Ahhhhs." I think it's because it's just one simple slider, yet it does so much to add "snap" to your image. The Clarity slider (which is well-named) basically increases the midtone contrast in a way that gives your photo more punch and impact, without actually sharpening the image. I add lots of Clarity anytime I want to enhance the texture in an image, and it works great on everything from landscapes to cityscapes, from travel photos to portraits of men—anything where emphasizing texture would look good.

Step One:

The Clarity slider is found in the bottom section of the Basic panel in Camera Raw, right above the Vibrance and Saturation sliders. (Although its official name is Clarity, I heard that at one point Adobe engineers considered naming it "Punch" instead, as they felt using it added punch to the image.) To clearly see the effects of Clarity, first zoom in to a 100% view by double-clicking on the Zoom tool up in the toolbar (it looks like a magnifying glass). In the example shown here, I only zoomed to 25% so you could see more of the image.

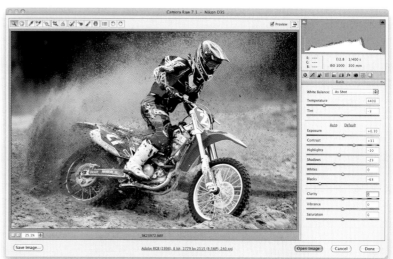

Step Two:

Using the Clarity control couldn't be easier—drag the slider to the right to increase the amount of punch (midtone contrast) in your image (compare the top and bottom images shown here). Here, I dragged it over to +100, which is something you really couldn't get away with in earlier versions of Camera Raw (you'd get horrible halos around everything), but in CS6, you can crank that puppy up and it looks awesome! Any image I edit where I want to emphasize the texture (landscapes, cityscapes, sports photos, etc.) gets between +25 and +50 Clarity, but now you can crank it up even higher in most cases (as seen here).

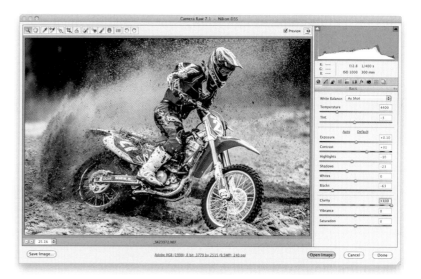

SCOTT KELBY

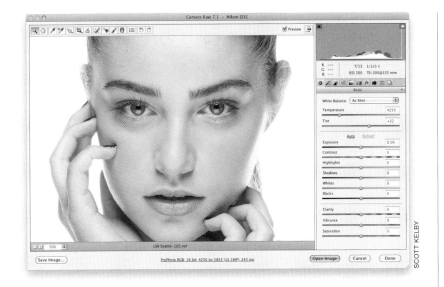

SCOTT KELBY

Step Three:

Of course, there are subjects where you don't want to emphasize texture (like women and children), and in those cases, I don't apply any positive Clarity. However, you can also use the Clarity control in reverse—to soften skin. This is called adding negative Clarity, meaning you can apply less than 0 (zero) to reduce the midtone contrast, which gives you a softening effect, but you don't want to apply it to the entire image, so you'd use the Adjustment Brush to apply it (more on the Adjustment Brush in Chapter 4). Here's an original image without any negative Clarity applied.

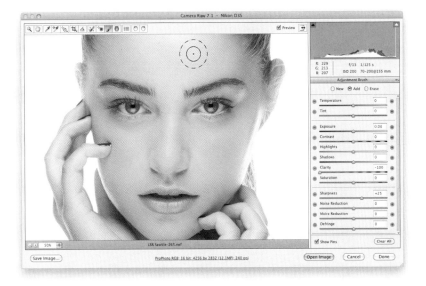

Step Four:

Here, I've taken the Adjustment Brush (again, lots on how to use this in Chapter 4), and I set the Clarity all the way to the left, to –100, for super-soft skin softening. To balance all that softness, I also increased the Sharpness amount to +25 (more on this soon, too), and then I painted over just her skin, being careful to avoid any areas that should stay nice and sharp, like her eyes, eyebrows, nostrils, lips, hair, and the edges of her face. Take a look at how much softer our subject's skin looks now. Now, if you need to soften up some skin really quickly, and you're not super-fussy about how it looks, negative Clarity can do the trick.

Adjusting Contrast Using Curves

The much-improved Contrast slider in CS6's Camera Raw will still only take you so far, but luckily there's Curves, which is a powerful ally in your fight against flat-looking photos. While I've got you here, there's something else new in this new version, another feature from regular Photoshop made its way into Camera Raw: the ability to edit individual R, G, and B channels with Curves. Okay, I don't use this feature, but somebody could really have some fun with it (for cross-processing effects, if nothing else).

Step One:

After you've done all your exposure adjustments in the Basic panel, and you feel you need more contrast (hey, it's possible), it's time to head for the Tone Curve panel (click on the second icon from the left, near the top of the Panel area, shown circled here in red). There are two different types of curves available here: the Point curve, and the Parametric curve. We'll start with the Point curve, so click on the Point tab at the top of the panel. Here's what the photo shown here looks like with no added contrast in the Point curve (notice that the Curve pop-up menu above the curve is set to Linear, which is a flat, unadjusted curve). *Note:* In previous versions of Camera Raw, RAW images had the default curve set to Medium Contrast (since your camera didn't add any contrast), but now in CS6, just like when you shoot in JPEG, no additional contrast will be added by default.

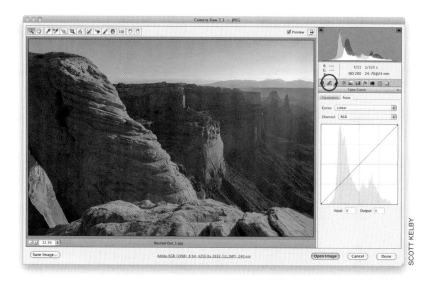

Step Two:

If you want more contrast, choose **Strong Contrast** from the Curve pop-up menu (as shown here), and you can see how much more contrast this photo now has, compared with Step One. The difference is the Strong Contrast settings create a steeper curve, and the steeper the curve, the more contrast it creates.

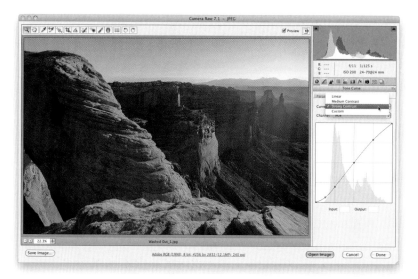

SCOTT KELBY

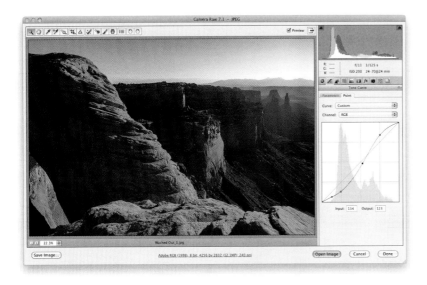

Step Three:

If you're familiar with Photoshop's Curves and want to create your own custom curve, start by choosing any one of the preset curves, then either click-and-drag the adjustment points on the curve or use the **Arrow keys** to move them (I think it's easier to click on a point, then use the Up and Down Arrow keys on your keyboard to move that part of the curve up or down). If you'd prefer to start from scratch, choose **Linear** from the Curve pop-up menu, which gives you a flat curve. To add adjustment points, just click along the curve. To remove a point, just click-and-drag it right off the curve (drag it off quickly, like you're pulling off a Band-Aid).

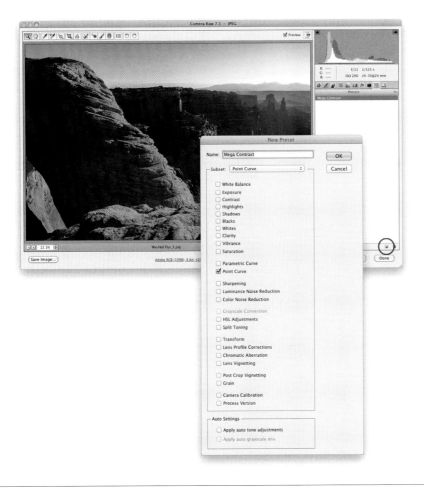

Step Four:

If you create a curve that you'd like to be able to apply again to other photos, you can save this curve as a preset. To do that, click on the Presets icon (the second icon from the right) near the top of the Panel area to bring up the Presets panel. Next, click on the New Preset icon (which looks just like Photoshop's Create a New Layer icon) at the bottom of the panel. This brings up the New Preset dialog (shown here). If you just want to save this curve setting, from the Subset pop-up menu near the top, choose **Point Curve**, and it turns off the checkboxes for all the other settings available as presets, and leaves only the Point Curve checkbox turned on (as shown here). Give your preset a name (I named mine "Mega Contrast") and click OK.

(Continued)

Step Five:

If you're not comfortable with adjusting the Point curve, try the Parametric curve, which lets you craft your curve using sliders that adjust the curve for you. Click on the Parametric tab, and you'll see four sliders, which control the four different areas of the curve, but before you start "sliding," know that the adjustments you make here are added to anything you did in the Point tab (if you did anything there first—I reset the Point tab's Curve pop-up menu to Linear here).

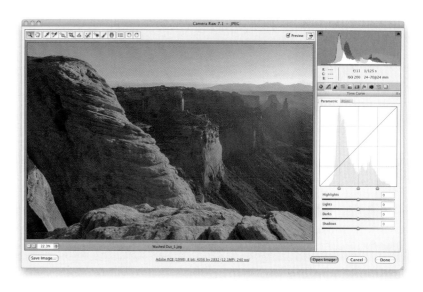

Step Six:

The Highlights slider controls the highlights area of the curve (the top of the curve), and dragging it to the right arcs the curve upward, making the highlights brighter. Right below that is the Lights slider, which covers the next lower range of tones (the area between the midtones and the highlights). Dragging this slider to the right makes this part of the curve steeper, and increases the upper midtones. The Darks and Shadows sliders do pretty much the same thing for the lower midtones and deep shadow areas. But remember, dragging to the right opens up those areas, so to create contrast, you'd drag both of those to the left instead. Here, to create some really punchy contrast, I dragged both the Highlights and Lights sliders to the right, and the Darks and Shadows sliders to the left.

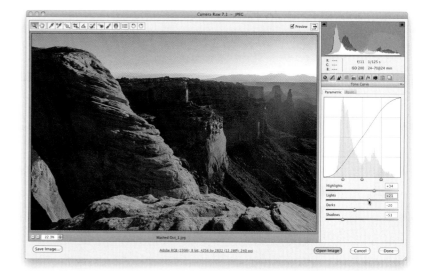

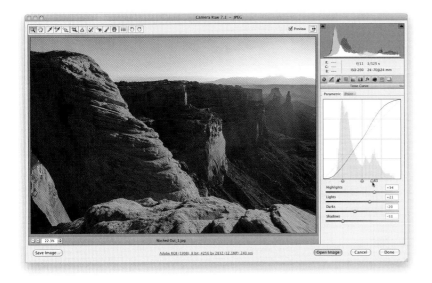

Step Seven:

Another advantage of the Parametric curve is that you can use the region divider controls (under the curve) to choose how wide a range each of the four sliders covers. So, if you move the far-right region divider to the right, it expands the area controlled by the Lights slider. Now the Highlights slider has less impact, flattening the upper part of the curve, so the contrast is decreased. If I drag that same region divider control back to the left instead (shown here), it expands the Highlights slider's area, which steepens the curve and increases contrast.

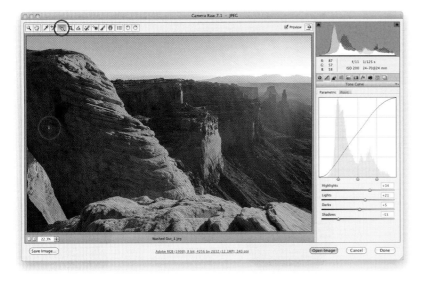

Step Eight:

If all of this makes you a bit squeamish, have I got a tool for you: it's called the Targeted Adjustment tool (or TAT for short) and you'll find it up in the toolbar at the top of the window (it's the fifth tool from the left, shown circled here). Just move the tool over the part of the image you want to adjust, then drag upward to lighten that area, or downward to darken it (this just moves the part of the curve that represents that part of the image). A lot of photographers love the TAT, so make sure you give it a try, because it makes getting that one area you want brighter (or darker) easier. Now, there is one caveat (I've been waiting to use that word for a while), and that is: it doesn't just adjust that one area of your photo—it adjusts the curve itself. So, depending on the image, other areas may get lighter/darker, too, so just keep an eye on that while you're adjusting. In the example shown here, I clicked and dragged upward to brighten up that shadowy area on the left, and the curve adjusted to make that happen automatically.

(Continued)

Step Nine:

Before we finish up with curves, there's another new feature in the CS6 version of Camera Raw, and that's the ability to tweak the individual RGB curves in the Point curve. Although this works great for creating cross-processing effects (which we'll cover in a moment), you'll probably wind up using it most for fixing tough white balance problems (like a color cast that just won't go away). You choose which channel you want to adjust by going to the Point tab, and then choosing the individual channel from the Channel pop-up menu (as shown here, where I'm choosing Blue to help me remove a color cast from the background and her skin—the background is supposed to be solid gray, and her skin isn't supposed to be bluish).

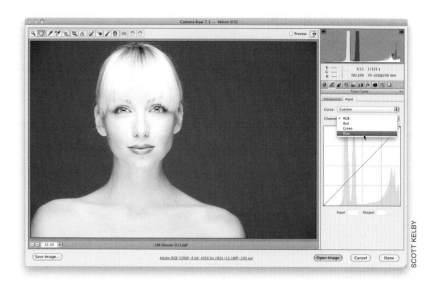

Step 10:

So, now that you have just the Blue channel selected (notice that the Curve readout is now tinted blue, as well, as a visual cue to you that you're adjusting just this one channel), how do you know which part of the curve to adjust? You can get Camera Raw to tell you exactly which part to adjust. Move your cursor over the background area you want to affect, press-and-hold the **Command (PC: Ctrl) key**, and your cursor temporarily changes into the Eyedropper tool. Click once on your image and it adds a point to the curve that corresponds to the area you want to adjust. Now, click on that curve point and drag at a 45° angle down toward the bottom-right corner, and it removes the blue from the background (as seen here).

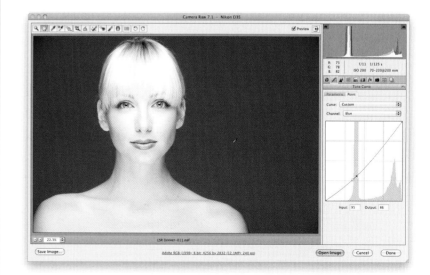

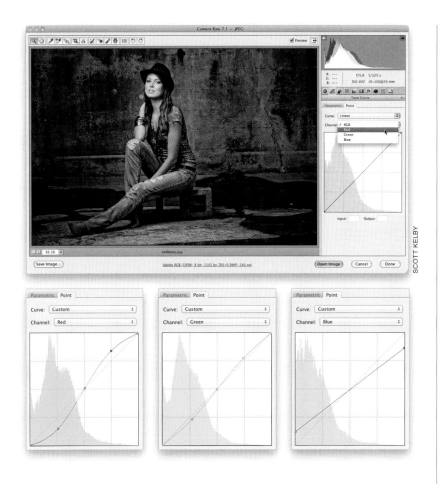

SCOTT KELBY

Step 11:

If you want to use these RGB curves to create a cross-processing effect (a classic darkroom technique from the film days, but still popular today, especially in fashion photography), it's actually fairly easy. There are dozens of different combinations, but here's one I like: Start by choosing **Red** in the Point tab's Channel pop-up menu, and create kind of a steep S-curve shape by clicking three times along the diagonal curve (once in the center, once at the next grid line above, and once below), so they're evenly spaced along the line. Now, leave the center point where it is, drag the top point straight upward, and drag the bottom point straight down to create the curve you see here at the far left. Then, switch to the Green channel and make another three-point S-curve, but one that's not as steep (as seen here, in the center). Lastly, go to the Blue channel, don't add any points, and just drag the bottom-left point straight upward along the left edge (as shown here at right) and drag the top-right point down along the right edge.

Step 12:

Of course, based on the particular image you use, you might have to tweak these settings a bit (usually, it's the amount you drag in the Blue channel, but again, it depends on the photo you're applying it to). If you come up with a setting you like, don't forget to save it as a preset in the Preset panel (just like you did with your Mega Contrast curve earlier).

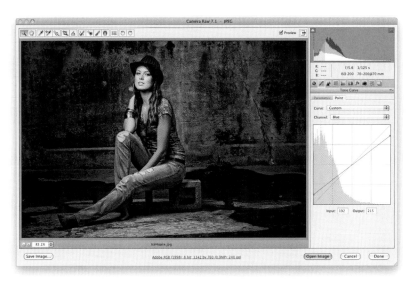

Cropping and Straightening

There's a distinct advantage to cropping your photo here in Camera Raw, rather than in Photoshop CS6 itself, and that is you can return to Camera Raw later and bring back the uncropped version of the image. This even holds true for JPEG and TIFF photos, as long as you haven't overwritten the original JPEG or TIFF file. To avoid overwriting, when you save the JPEG or TIFF in Photoshop, just change the filename (that way the original stays intact). With RAW images, you don't have to worry about that, because it doesn't let you overwrite the original.

Step One:

The Crop tool **(C)** is the sixth tool from the left in the toolbar. By default, you click-and-drag it out around the area you want to keep, and like in Photoshop, you have access to a list of preset cropping ratios. To get them, click-and-hold on the Crop tool and a pop-up menu will appear (as shown here). The Normal setting gives you the standard drag-it-where-you-want-it cropping. However, if you choose one of the cropping presets, then your cropping is constrained to a specific ratio. For example, choose the 2 to 3 ratio, click-and-drag it out, and you'll see that it keeps the same aspect ratio as your original uncropped photo.

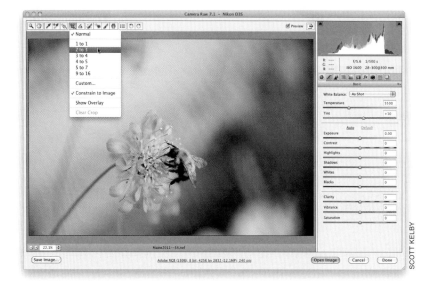

Step Two:

Here's the 2-to-3-ratio cropping border dragged out over my image. The area to be cropped away appears dimmed, and the clear area inside the border is how your final cropped photo will appear. If you want to see the cropped version before you leave Camera Raw, just switch to another tool in the toolbar. (Note: If you draw a set size cropping border and want to switch orientation, click on the bottom-right corner and drag down and to the left to switch from wide to tall, or up and to the right to switch from tall to wide.)

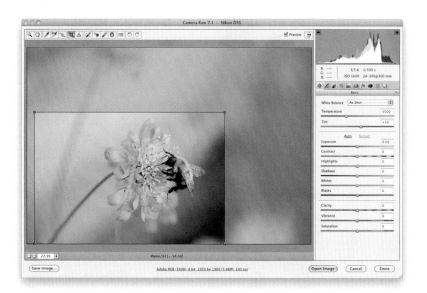

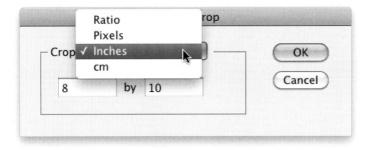

Step Three:

If you re-open your cropped photo again in Camera Raw, you'll see the cropped version. To bring back the cropping border, just click on the Crop tool. To remove the cropping altogether, press the **Esc** or **Delete (PC: Backspace) key** on your keyboard (or choose **Clear Crop** from the Crop tool's pop-up menu). If you want your photo cropped to an exact size (like 8x10", 13x19", etc.), choose **Custom** from the Crop tool's pop-up menu to bring up the dialog you see here. You can choose to crop by inches, pixels, or centimeters.

Step Four:

Here, we're going to create a custom crop so our photo winds up being exactly 8x10", so choose **Inches** from the Crop pop-up menu, then type in your custom size. Click OK, click-and-drag out the cropping border, and the area inside it will be exactly 8x10". Click on any other tool in the toolbar or press **Return (PC: Enter)**, and you'll see the final cropped 8x10" image. If you click the Open Image button, the image is cropped to your specs and opened in Photoshop. If, instead, you click the Done button, Camera Raw closes and your photo is untouched, but it keeps your cropping border in place for the future.

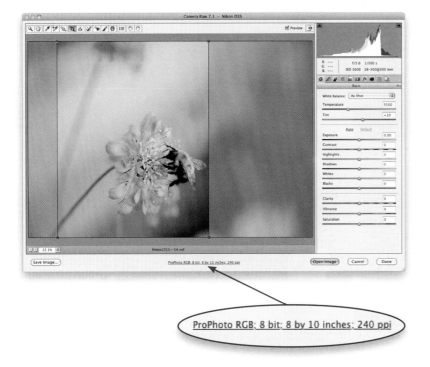

ProPhoto RGB; 8 bit; 8 by 10 inches; 240 ppi

TIP: Seeing Image Size

The size of your photo (and other information) is displayed below the Preview area of Camera Raw (in blue underlined text that looks like a web link). When you drag out a cropping border, the size info for the photo automatically updates to display the dimensions of the currently selected crop area.

(Continued)

Step Five:

If you save a cropped JPEG or TIFF photo out of Camera Raw (by clicking the Done button), the only way to bring back those cropped areas is to reopen the photo in Camera Raw. However, if you click the Save Image button and you choose **Photoshop** from the Format pop-up menu (as shown), a new option will appear called Preserve Cropped Pixels. If you turn on that checkbox before you click Save, when you open this cropped photo in Photoshop, it will appear to be cropped, but the photo will be on a separate layer (not flattened on the Background layer). So the cropped area is still there—it just extends off the visible image area. You can bring that cropped area back by clicking-and-dragging your photo within the image area (try it—use the Move tool **[V]** to click-and-drag your photo to the right or left and you'll see what I mean).

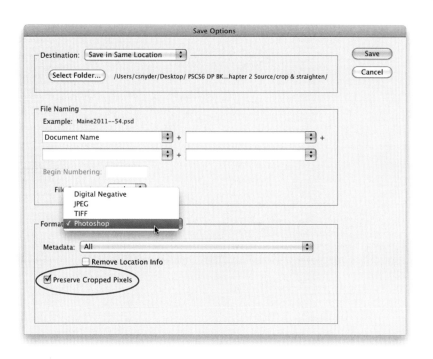

Step Six:

If you have a number of similar photos you need to crop the same way, you're going to love this: First, select all the photos you want to crop in Camera Raw (either in Mini Bridge or on your computer), then open them all in Camera Raw. When you open multiple photos, they appear in a vertical filmstrip along the left side of Camera Raw (as shown here). Click on the Select All button (it's above the filmstrip) and then crop the currently selected photo as you'd like. As you apply your cropping, look at the filmstrip and you'll see all the thumbnails update with their new cropping instructions. A tiny Crop icon will also appear in the bottom-left corner of each thumbnail, letting you know that these photos have been cropped in Camera Raw.

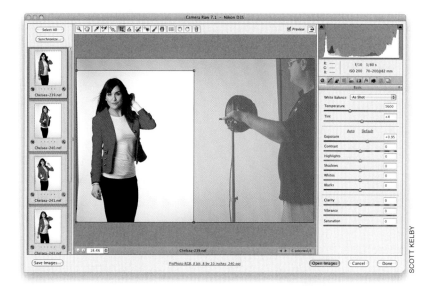

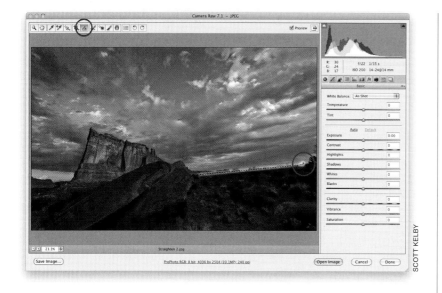

SCOTT KELBY

Step Seven:

Another form of cropping is actually straightening your photos using the Straighten tool. It's a close cousin of the Crop tool because what it does is essentially rotates your cropping border, so when you open the photo, it's straight. In the Camera Raw toolbar, choose the Straighten tool (it's immediately to the right of the Crop tool and shown circled here in red). Now, click-and-drag it along the horizon line in your photo (as shown here). When you release the mouse button, a cropping border appears and that border is automatically rotated to the exact amount needed to straighten the photo (as shown in Step Eight).

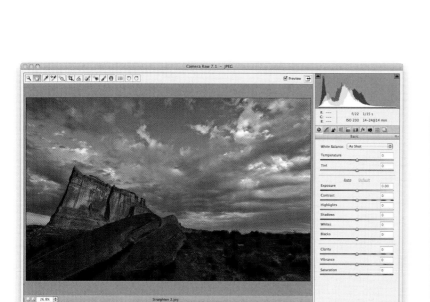

Step Eight:

You won't actually see the straightened photo until you switch tools, press **Return (PC: Enter)**, or open the photo in Photoshop (which means, if you click Save Image or Done, Camera Raw closes, and the straightening information is saved along with the file. So if you open this file again in Camera Raw, you'll see the straightened version, and you won't really know it was ever crooked). If you click Open Image instead, the straightened photo opens in Photoshop. Again, if this is a RAW photo (or if it's a JPEG or TIFF and you clicked the Done button), you can always return to Camera Raw and remove this cropping border to get the original uncropped photo back.

TIP: Canceling Your Straightening

If you want to cancel your straightening, just press the **Esc key** on your keyboard, and the straightening border will go away.

Photoshop Killer Tips

Skipping the Camera Raw Window Altogether

If you've already applied a set of tweaks to a RAW photo, you probably don't need the Camera Raw editing window opening every time you open the file. So, just press-and-hold the Shift key when you double-click on the RAW file in Mini Bridge, and the image will open in Photoshop, with the last set of edits already applied, skipping the Camera Raw window altogether. If you didn't apply any tweaks in Camera Raw, it just opens with the Camera Raw defaults applied. Either way, it's a big time saver.

Handy Shortcuts for Blend Modes

Most people wind up using the same handful of layer blend modes—Multiply, Screen, Overlay, Hard Light, and Soft Light. If those sound like your favorites, you can save yourself some time by jumping directly to the one you want using a simple keyboard shortcut. For example, to jump directly to Screen mode, you'd press **Option-Shift-S (PC: Alt-Shift-S)**, for Multiply mode, you'd press **Option-Shift-M (PC: Alt-Shift-M)**, and so on. To run through the different shortcuts, just try different letters on your keyboard.

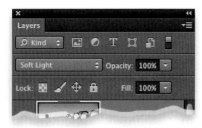

Seeing a True Before/After

The weird thing about the way Camera Raw handles previews is it does them on a panel-by-panel basis, so if you make a bunch of changes in the Basic panel, then switch to the Detail panel and make changes there, when you turn off the Preview checkbox (on the top right of the Preview area), it doesn't give you a real before/after. It just gives you a before/after of the panel you're in right now, which doesn't give you a true before/after of your image editing. To get a real before/after of all your edits in Camera Raw, click on the Presets icon (the second icon from the right near the top of the Panel area) or

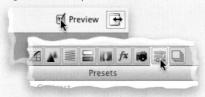

the Snapshots icon (the far right icon), and now when you toggle on/off the Preview checkbox, it shows you the real before/after.

Don't Get Fooled by the Default Button

If you've edited your image in Camera Raw, and then you decide you want to start over, clicking the Default button in

the Basic panel (it's to the left of the Auto button) won't return your image to how it looked when you opened it. Instead, to get back to the original way your image looked when you first opened it in Camera Raw, go to the Camera Raw flyout menu and choose **Camera Raw Defaults**. You can also press-and-hold the Option (PC: Alt) key, and the Cancel button will change to a Reset button.

Deleting Multiple Images While Editing in Camera Raw

If you have more than one image open in Camera Raw, you can mark any of them you want to be deleted by selecting them (in the filmstrip on the left side of Camera Raw), then pressing the Delete key on your keyboard. A red "X" will appear on those images. When you're done in Camera Raw, click on the Done button, and those images marked to be deleted will be moved to the Trash (PC: Recycle Bin) automatically. To remove the mark for deletion, just select them and press the Delete key again.

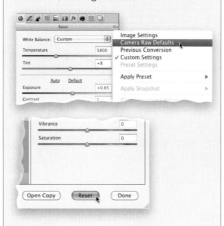

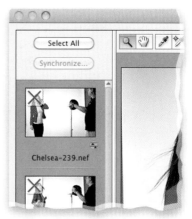

Photoshop Killer Tips

Cool Raw Retouching Trick

There's a pretty common retouching technique in Photoshop for reducing hot spots (shiny areas on a subject's face), which uses the Healing Brush to completely remove the hot spot, then under the Edit menu, you choose Fade Healing Brush, and lower the Opacity there. A little hint of the hot spot comes back, so it looks more like a highlight than a shine (it actually works really well). You can do something similar in Camera Raw when using the Spot Removal tool (set to Heal) by removing the hot spot (or freckle, or wrinkle) and then using the Opacity slider in the Spot Removal options panel.

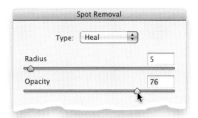

Get a Larger Preview Area

If you have multiple images open in Camera Raw, and need more room to see the preview of the image you're currently working on, just double-click right on that little divider that separates the filmstrip from the Preview area, and

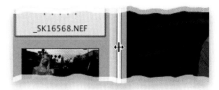

the filmstrip tucks in over to the left, out of the way, giving you a larger preview. To bring it back, just double-click on that divider again (it's now over on the far-left side of the Camera Raw window) and it pops back out.

Rate Your Images in Camera Raw

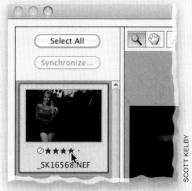

SCOTT KELBY

You don't have to be in Mini Bridge to add or change star ratings. If you've got multiple images open, you can do it right in Camera Raw. Just press **Command-1, -2, -3 (PC: Ctrl-1, -2, -3)**, and so on, to add star ratings (up to five stars). You can also just click directly on the five little dots that appear below the thumbnails in the filmstrip on the left.

Rule-of-Thirds Cropping

This one Adobe borrowed from Camera Raw's sister program Photoshop Lightroom, because (like in Lightroom) you can have the "Rule-of-Thirds" grid appear over your cropping border anytime by just clicking-and-holding on the Crop tool in the toolbar, then choosing **Show Overlay**.

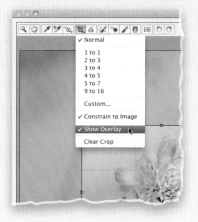

Jump to Full Screen Mode in Camera Raw

If you want to see your image in Camera Raw as large as possible, just press the **F key**, and Camera Raw expands to Full Screen mode, with the window filling your monitor, giving you a larger look at your image.

Shortcut for Viewing Sharpening

The best zoom magnification to view your

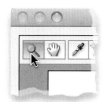

sharpening in Camera Raw is a 100% view, and the quickest way to get there is to just double-click the Zoom tool.

Don't Know Where to Start When Editing an Image? Try Auto Levels or Curves (They're Better in CS6)

In Photoshop CS6, Adobe greatly improved the results of the Auto button found in the Levels and Curves adjustment layer settings in the Properties panel, as well as in the Levels and Curves adjustment dialogs. It often actually makes a pretty decent starting point for editing your image, especially if you have a tricky image and you're not sure where to start.

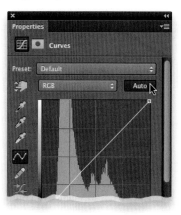

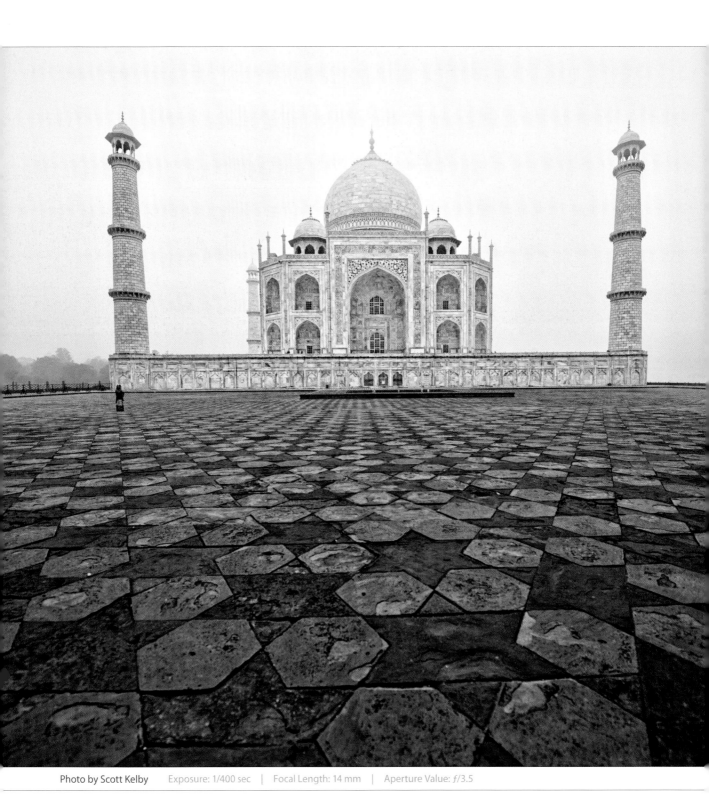

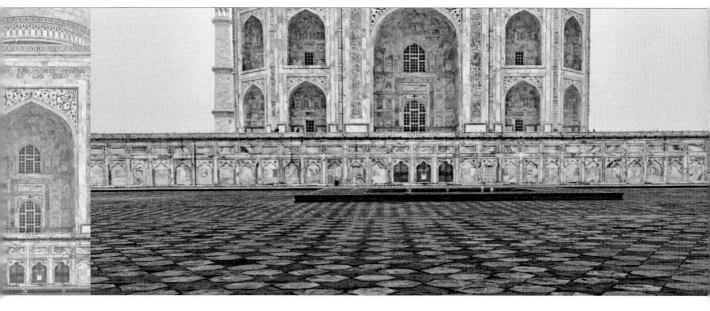

Raw Justice
camera raw—beyond the basics

When I searched The Internet Movie Database (IMDb) for movies or TV shows containing the word "Raw," I was pleasantly surprised to find out just how many choices I actually had. However, I went with the 1994 movie *Raw Justice*, but I don't want you to think for one minute that I was influenced in any way by the fact that the star of the movie was Pamela Anderson. That would be incredibly shallow of me. Like any serious movie buff, I was drawn to this movie by what drew most of the audience to this movie: actor Robert Hays (who could forget his role in 2007's *Nicky's Birthday Camera* or the Michael Tuchner–directed film *Trenchcoat*). Of course, the fact that Stacey Keach was in the movie was just the icing on the cake, but everybody knows the real draw of this flick clearly was Hays. However, what I found most puzzling was this: in the movie poster, Pamela Anderson totally dominates the poster with a large,

full-color, ¾-length pose of her wearing a skimpy black dress, thigh-high boots, and holding a pistol at her side, yet the other actors appear only as tiny black-and-white, backscreened headshots. I have to admit, this really puzzles me, because while Pamela Anderson is a fine actress— one of the best, in fact—I feel, on some level, they were trying to fool you into watching a movie thinking it was about Pamela Anderson's acting, when in fact it was really about the acting eye candy that is Hays. This is called "bait and switch" (though you probably are more familiar with the terms "tuck and roll" or perhaps "Bartles & Jaymes"). Anyway, I think, while "Raw Justice" makes a great title for a chapter on going beyond the basics of Camera Raw, there is no real justice in that this finely crafted classic of modern cinematography wound up going straight to DVD.

Double-Processing to Create the Uncapturable

As good as digital cameras have become these days, when it comes to exposure, the human eye totally kicks their butt. That's why we shoot so many photos where our subject is backlit, because with our naked eye we can see the subject just fine (our eye adjusts). But when we open the photo, the subject is basically in silhouette. Or how about sunsets, where we have to choose which part of the scene to expose for—the ground or the sky—because our camera can't expose for both? Well, here's how to use Camera Raw to overcome this exposure limitation:

Step One:

Open the photo you want to double-process. In this example, the camera properly exposed for the sky in the background, so the rock formation in the foreground is a silhouette. Of course, our goal is to create something more like what our eye sees, but our camera can't—a photo where both the foreground rocks and the sky are each exposed properly. Plus, by double-processing (editing the same RAW photo twice), we can choose one set of edits for the sky and another for the rocks, to create just what we want.

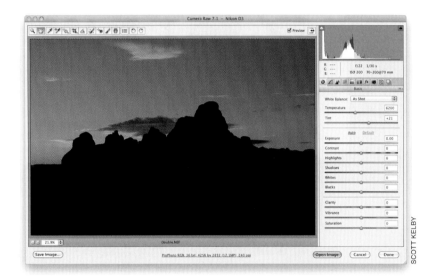

Step Two:

Let's start by making the rocks visible. Drag the Shadows slider all the way to the right, and now at least you can see them, but it's still not enough, so you'll have to bump up the Exposure slider, as well (here, I've dragged it over to +1.00). The rocks look kind of "flat" contrast-wise, so bump up the Contrast a bit, too (let's go to +28). Lastly, since these are rocks, and we want to accentuate their texture, let's crank the Clarity up to around +40, and then make the little bit of color that's there more vibrant by increasing the Vibrance to around +37. Now, press-and-hold the Shift key, and the Open button changes to Open Object (as seen here). Click it.

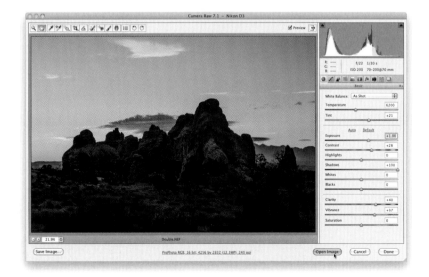

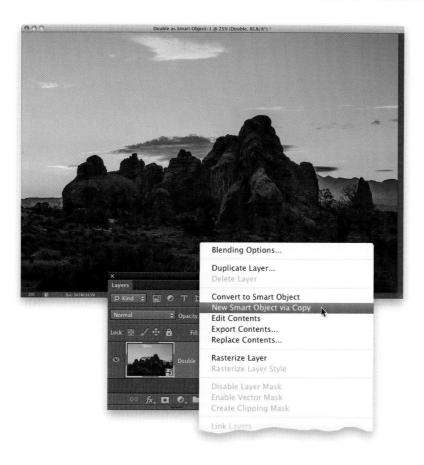

Step Three:

Clicking Open Object makes your image open in Photoshop as a smart object (you'll see the layer thumbnail has a little page icon in the bottom-right corner). Now we need a second version of this image, because the sky looks way too light in this version. In our second version of this RAW file, we'll focus on just the sky. If you were to duplicate the layer by dragging it onto the Create a New Layer icon, the double-processing wouldn't work. That's because the duplicate layer would be tied to the original layer, so any changes you made to the duplicate would also automatically be applied to the original layer. We need to be able to edit these two layers separately from each other. Basically, we need to break the link between the two layers. To do that, go to the Layers panel, Right-click on the layer, and from the pop-up menu that appears, choose **New Smart Object via Copy**. This gives you a duplicate layer, but breaks the link to the original layer.

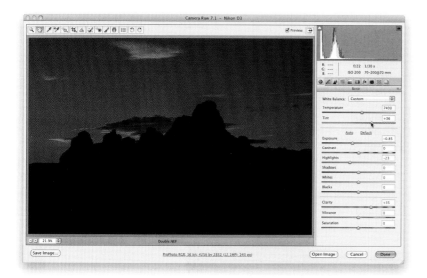

Step Four:

Now, double-click directly on this duplicate layer's thumbnail and it opens this duplicate in Camera Raw. Here, you're going to expose for the sky, without any regard for how the foreground looks (it will turn really dark, but who cares—you've already got a version with it properly exposed on its own separate layer, right?). So, drag the Exposure slider way over to the left (I went to –0.85), and drag the Highlights slider to –23 to help darken the sky. I also dragged the Temperature and Tint sliders a little to the right to warm the color of the sky, and lastly, I increased the Clarity to +35 (it made the clouds look a little more interesting). Once the sky looks good, click OK.

(Continued)

Step Five:

You now have two versions of your photo, each on a different layer—the brighter one exposed for the rocks in the foreground on the bottom layer, and the darker sky version on the layer directly on top of it—and they are perfectly aligned, one on top of the other. This is why we call it "double-processing," because you have two versions of the same image, each processed differently. Now what we need to do is combine these two different layers (with different exposures) into one single image that combines the best of both. It'll be easier if we have the image with the properly exposed rocks as our top layer, so click on that layer and drag it above the darker sky layer (as seen here). We'll combine the images with a layer mask, but rather than painstakingly painting it, we can cheat and use the Quick Selection tool **(W)**. So, get it from the Toolbox and paint over the rocks and foreground, and it selects them for you in just a few seconds (as shown here).

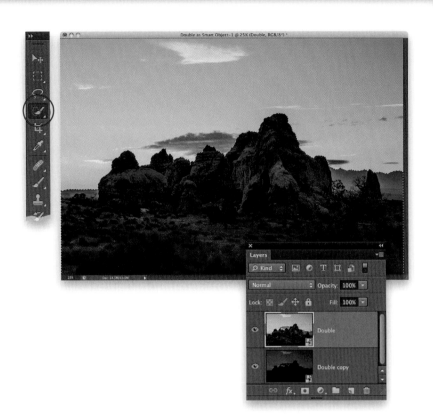

Step Six:

Go to the Layers panel and click on the Add Layer Mask icon at the bottom of the panel (shown circled here in red). This converts your selection into a layer mask, which hides the light sky and reveals the new darker sky layer in its place (as seen here). It still needs some tweaking (for sure), but at least now you can see what we're aiming for—the brighter foreground rocks from one layer blended with the darker sky from the other layer.

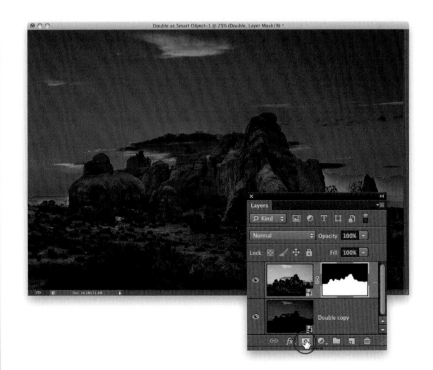

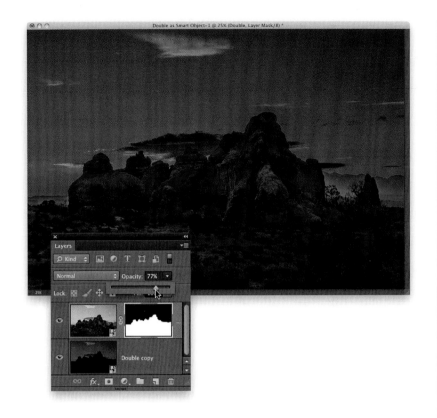

Step Seven:

Now, you're going to lower the Opacity of this top layer (the brighter rocks layer), so it blends in a little better with the darker sky layer. Here, I've lowered it to 77%, and the colors match much better. Well, except for those blue mountain areas on either side of the base of the rocks, which look kind of funky. They're too bright, and a bit "glowy." We're going to have to fix that. Uggh!

TIP: Always Opening Your Images as Smart Objects

If you always want your RAW-processed images to open as smart objects, click on the workflow options link at the bottom of the Camera Raw dialog (the blue text below the Preview area), and when the dialog appears, turn on the Open in Photoshop as Smart Objects checkbox.

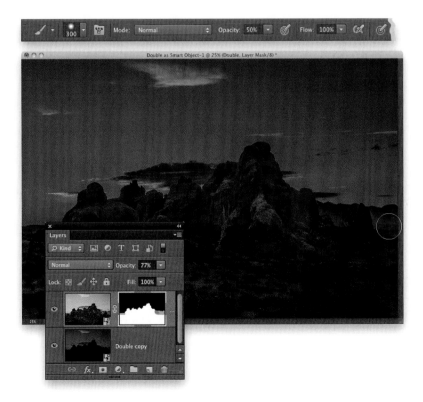

Step Eight:

Press the letter **B** to get the Brush tool, then click on the Brush icon in the Options Bar and choose a medium-sized, soft-edged brush from the Brush Picker. Also, to help blend this a little better, lower the Opacity of the brush (up in the Options Bar) to just 50%. Now, press **D**, then **X** to set your Foreground color to black, start painting over those blue mountain areas on the sides of the photo, and it paints back in 50% of the darker image, so it helps to hide those areas without making them solid black. If you make a mistake, switch your Foreground color to white and paint over your mistake to erase the spillover.

(Continued)

Step Nine:

Now, we have a pretty common problem to deal with here: along the edge, where the brighter rocks meet the darker sky, there's a little bit of a white fringe happening (I zoomed in here to 100%, so you can see it better). Luckily, that's fairly easy to fix, without having to take a tiny brush and paint all along that edge (which is how we used to do it, and we still sometimes do that for a little touch-up, but this isn't a little touch-up).

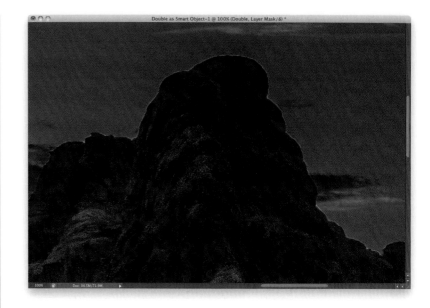

Step 10:

We're going to shift the edge of our mask a few pixels, so you don't see that white edge fringe any longer, and we'll let Photoshop do all the heavy lifting. Go under the Select menu and choose **Refine Mask**. This brings up the Refine Mask dialog you see here. First, to make seeing this white edge easier, from the View pop-up menu up top, choose **On Black** and now it really stands out, so you can see it clearly for what you're going to do next. In the Edge Detection section, turn on the Smart Radius checkbox and drag the Radius slider to the right until the white edge is almost gone (I dragged to 8.2). Then, under Adjust Edge, drag the Shift Edge slider to the left (as shown here) until the white edge disappears (as you see here, where I dragged to –25), then click OK. See, that was fairly easy. Again, if after doing this, you still notice a white pixel or two here or there, just take a very small brush (you're still at 50% Opacity with this brush) and simply paint over it to hide it.

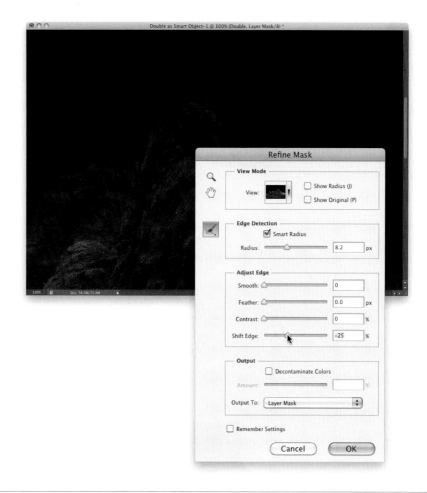

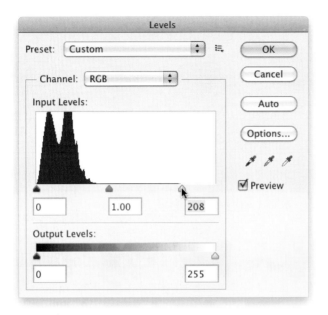

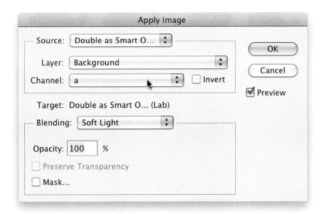

Step 11:

Now, let's finish this baby off. Go to the Layers panel and, from the flyout menu at the top right, choose **Flatten Image** to flatten the image down to one layer. The image looks a little dark overall, so press **Command-L (PC: Ctrl-L)** to bring up the Levels dialog, and bring back some of the overall highlights by dragging the white Input Levels highlights slider (right below the far-right side of the histogram) to the left to brighten things up.

Step 12:

Lastly, I would do something to make the image a little more vibrant (and applying an effect to the combined image helps unify the look). You could reopen the image in Camera Raw (it's not a smart object any longer, so you'd have to do it the old-fashioned way—see page 18). Instead, let's do a quick Lab Color move. Go under the Image menu, under Mode, and choose **Lab Color**. Now, go under the Image menu again and choose **Apply Image**. When the dialog appears, in the Source section, choose the "**a**" channel, then change your Blending mode to **Soft Light**. This adds color and contrast. Click OK, and then go back under the Image menu, under Mode, and switch back to **RGB Color**.

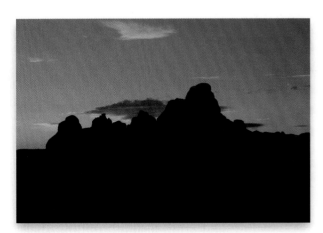

Before

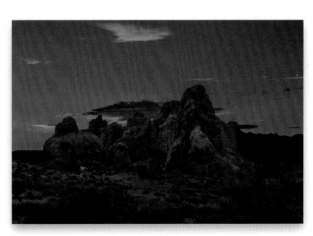

After

Editing Multiple Photos at Once

One of the biggest advantages of using Camera Raw is that it enables you to apply changes to one photo, and then easily apply those exact same changes to a bunch of other similar photos taken in the same approximate setting. It's a form of built-in automation, and it can save you an incredible amount of time when editing your shoots.

Step One:

The key to making this work is that the photos you edit all are shot in similar lighting conditions, or all have some similar problem. In this case, our photos are of a vintage airplane at the Sun 'n Fun International Fly-In & Expo, and they're a little underexposed. In Mini Bridge, start by selecting the images you want to edit (click on one, press-and-hold the Command [PC: Ctrl] key, then click on all the others). If they're RAW images, just double-click on any one of them and they open in Camera Raw, but if they're JPEG or TIFF images, you'll need to select them, switch to Review mode, and then press **Option-R (PC: Alt-R)**.

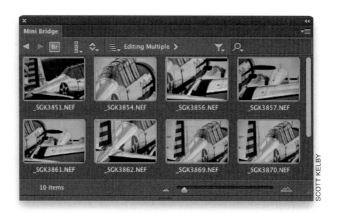

Step Two:

When the images open in Camera Raw, you'll see a filmstrip along the left side of the window with all the images you selected. Now, there are two ways to do this and, while neither one is wrong, I think the second method is faster (which you'll see in a moment). We'll start with the first: Click on an image in the film-strip, then make any adjustments you want to make this one image look good (I tweaked the Temperature, Exposure, Contrast, Blacks, and Clarity to brighten it and make it more contrasty).

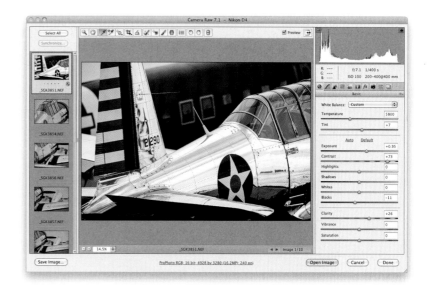

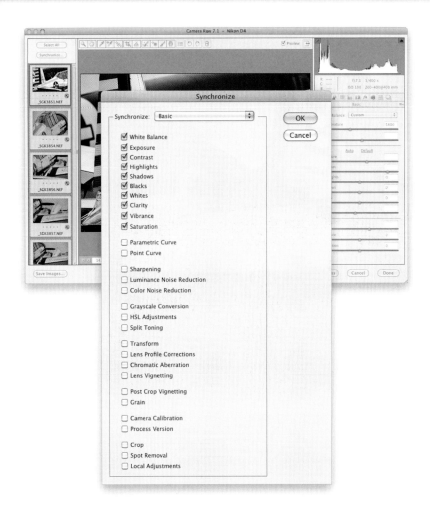

Step Three:

Once you've got one of the photos looking good, click the Select All button up at the top of the filmstrip to select all the photos (even though it selects the rest of the photos, you'll notice that the image you edited is actually the "most selected" image, with a highlight border around it). Now click the Synchronize button (it's right below the Select All button) to bring up the Synchronize dialog (seen here). It shows you a list of all the things you could copy from this "most selected" photo and apply to the rest of the selected photos. Choose **Basic** from the pop-up menu at the top, and it unchecks all the other stuff, and leaves just the Basic panel checkboxes turned on.

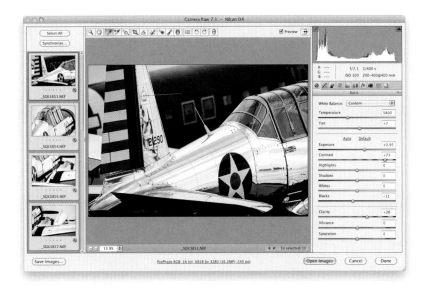

Step Four:

When you click the OK button, it applies the Basic panel settings from the "most selected" photo to all the rest of the selected photos (if you look in the filmstrip, you'll see that all the photos have had those settings adjusted). Okay, so why don't I like this method? Although it does work, it takes too many clicks, and decisions, and checkboxes, which is why I prefer the second method.

TIP: Editing Only Select Photos

If you only want certain photos to be affected, and not all the ones open in Camera Raw, then in the filmstrip, Command-click (PC: Ctrl-click) on only the photos you want affected and click the Synchronize button.

(Continued)

Step Five:

In the second method, as soon as Camera Raw opens, click the Select All button to select all your images, then go ahead and make your changes. As you make the changes to your "most selected" photo, all the others are updated with your new settings almost instantly, so you don't have to remember which settings you applied—when you move one slider, all the images get the same treatment, so you don't need the Synchronize dialog at all. Try out both methods and see which one you like, but if you feel the need for speed, you'll probably like the second one much better.

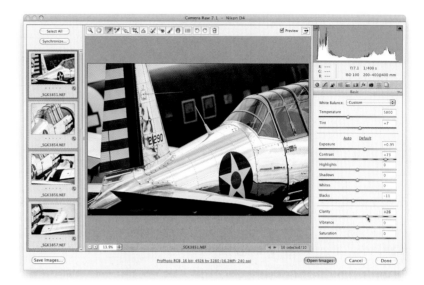

If you shoot in JPEG, your digital camera applies sharpening to your photo right in the camera itself, so no sharpening is automatically applied by Camera Raw. But if you shoot in RAW, you're telling your camera to ignore that sharpening, and that's why, when you bring a RAW image into Camera Raw, by default, it applies some sharpening, called "capture sharpening." In my workflow, I sharpen twice: once here in Camera Raw, and once more right before I output my final image from Photoshop (called "output sharpening"). Here's how to apply capture sharpening in Camera Raw:

Sharpening in Camera Raw

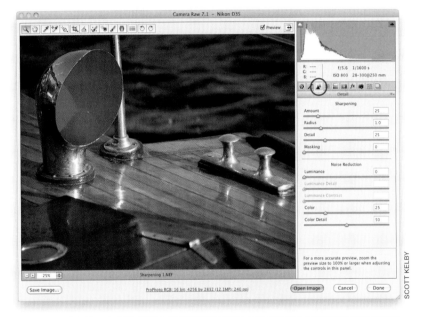

SCOTT KELBY

Step One:

When you open a RAW image in Camera Raw, by default, it applies a small amount of sharpening to your photo (not the JPEGs or TIFFs, only RAW images). You can adjust this amount (or turn it off altogether, if you like) by clicking on the Detail icon (it's the third icon from the left) at the top of the Panel area, or using the keyboard shortcut **Command-Option-3 (PC: Ctrl-Alt-3)**. At the top of this panel is the Sharpening section, where by a quick glance you can see that sharpening has already been applied to your photo. If you don't want any sharpening applied at this stage (it's a personal preference), then simply click-and-drag the Amount slider all the way to the left to lower the amount of sharpening to 0 (zero), and the sharpening is removed.

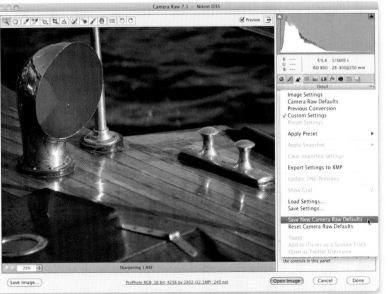

Step Two:

If you want to turn off this automatic, by default sharpening (so capture sharpening is only applied if you go and manually add it yourself), first set the Sharpening Amount slider to 0 (zero), then go to the Camera Raw flyout menu and choose **Save New Camera Raw Defaults** (as shown here). Now, RAW images taken with that camera will not be automatically sharpened.

(Continued)

Step Three:

Before we charge into sharpening, there's one more thing you'll want to know: if you don't actually want sharpening applied, but you'd still like to see what the sharpened image would look like, you can sharpen just the preview, and not the actual file. Just press **Command-K (PC: Ctrl-K)** while Camera Raw is open, and in the Camera Raw Preferences dialog, choose **Preview Images Only** from the Apply Sharpening To pop-up menu (as shown here), and then click OK to save this as your default. Now the sharpening only affects the preview you see here in Camera Raw, but when you choose to open the file in Photoshop, the sharpening is not applied.

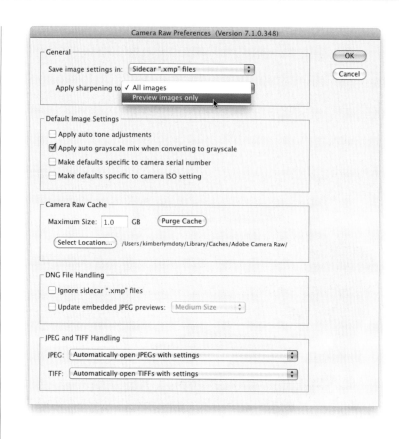

Step Four:

If you've been using Camera Raw for a while now, you probably remember back to older versions of Photoshop where you had to view your image at 100% to really see any effects of the sharpening. They pretty much fixed that back in CS5, so it's not as necessary to be at a 100% size view, but it still seems to me to render the most accurate view of the sharpening. The quickest way to jump to that 100% view is to double-click directly on the Zoom tool in the toolbar (shown circled here). (*Note:* You'll see a message about zooming to 100% at the bottom of the Detail panel, but it'll disappear after you zoom in to 100%.)

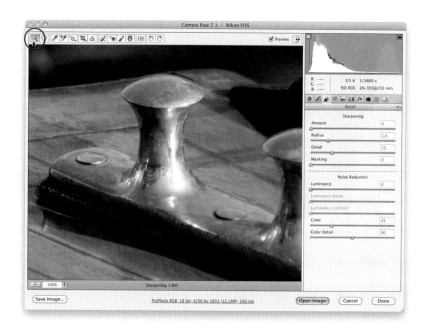

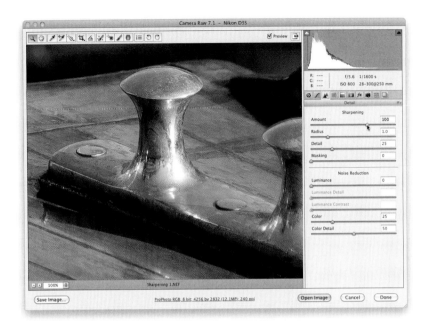

Step Five:

Dipping into the realm of the painfully obvious, dragging the Amount slider to the right increases the amount of sharpening. Compare the image shown here, with the one in Step Four (where the Sharpening Amount was set to 0), and you can see how much sharper the image now appears, where I dragged it to 100.

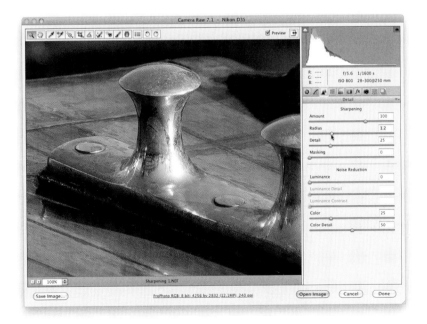

Step Six:

The next slider down is the Radius slider, which determines how far out the sharpening is applied from the edges being sharpened in your photo. This pretty much works like the Radius slider in Photoshop's Unsharp Mask filter, which is probably why the default is 1 (because that's probably where we'll leave it most of the time). I use less than a Radius of 1 if the photo I'm processing is only going to be used on a website, in video editing, or somewhere where it's going to be at a very small size or resolution. I only use a Radius of more than 1 when: (1) the image is visibly blurry, (2) it has lots of detail (like this photo, where I pushed the Radius to 1.2), so it can take some serious sharpening, or (3) the image needs some "emergency" sharpening. If you decide to increase the Radius amount above 1 (unlike the Unsharp Mask filter, you can only go as high as 3 here), just be careful, because if you go too much above 1, your photo can start to look fake, oversharpened, or even noisy, so be careful out there (in the next step, I set it back to 1).

(Continued)

Step Seven:

The next slider down is the Detail slider, which determines how much of the edge areas are affected by sharpening. You'll apply lower amounts of Detail if your photo is slightly blurred, and higher amounts if you really want to bring out texture and detail (which is why this slider is aptly named). So, how much Detail you apply depends on the subject you're sharpening. With an image like this one, with lots of metal and texture in the deck, it's an ideal candidate for a high amount of Detail (so are most landscapes, city-scapes, motorcycle shots—stuff with lots of edges), so I dragged the slider to the right (all the way to 78), until the detail really came out.

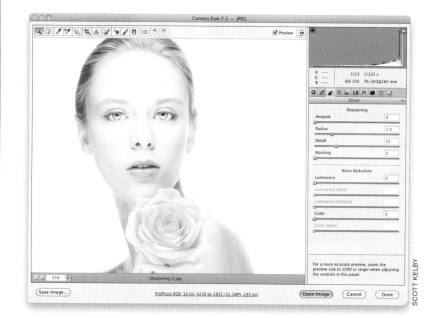

Step Eight:

I'm going to change photos to show you the Masking slider. This one's easier to understand, and for many people, I think it will become invaluable. Here's why: When you apply sharpening, it gets applied to the entire image evenly. But what if you have an image where there are areas you'd like sharpened, but other softer areas that you'd like left alone (like the photo here, where you want to keep her skin soft, but have her eyes, lips, etc., sharpened)? If we weren't in Camera Raw, you could apply the Unsharp Mask filter to a duplicate layer, add a layer mask, and paint away (cover) those softer areas, right? Well, that's kind of what the Masking slider here in Camera Raw does—as you drag it to the right, it re-duces the amount of sharpening on non-edge areas. The default Masking setting of 0 (zero) applies sharpening to the en-tire image. As you drag to the right, the non-edge areas are masked (protected) from being sharpened.

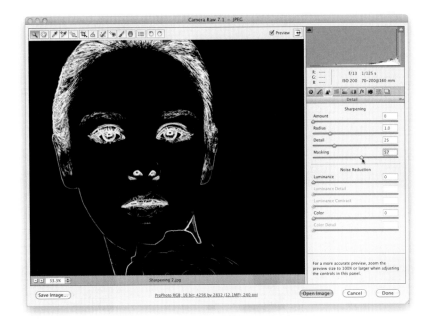

Step Nine:

All four sliders in the Sharpening section of the Detail panel let you have a live preview of what the sharpening is affecting—just press-and-hold the Option (PC: Alt) key as you drag; your screen will turn grayscale, and the areas that the slider you're dragging will affect appear as edge areas in the Preview area. This is particularly helpful in understanding the Masking slider, so press-and-hold the Option key and drag the Masking slider to the right. When Masking is set to 0, the screen turns solid white (because sharpening is being evenly applied to everything). As you drag to the right, in the preview (shown here), the parts that are no longer being sharpened turn black (those areas are masked). Any areas you see in white are the only parts of the photo receiving sharpening (perfect for sharpening women, because it avoids sharpening their skin, but sharpens the things you want sharp, like the eyes, hair, eyebrows, lips, edges of her face, and so on). Below is a before/after of our boat deck shot, with these settings—Amount: 100, Radius: 1, Detail: 78, Masking: 0.

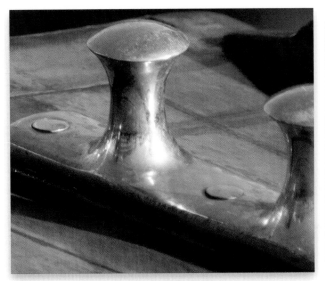

Before

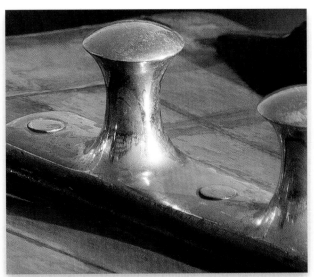

After

Automatically Fixing Lens Problems

Earlier versions of Camera Raw have had lens correction features, but Camera Raw can now automatically apply corrections for common lens problems (like barrel or/and pin-cushion distortion, or edge vignetting). It does this by reading the embedded camera data (so it knows which camera and lens you used), and it applies a profile to fix the problem. It's amazingly fast, and it takes just one check-box, but what if there is no profile for your camera/lens, or there's no EXIF data for your image (maybe you scanned it), or if you don't like the profile (it was too little or too much)? You're about to learn all of that.

Step One:
Open the image with a lens problem in Camera Raw. Now, if you've been using Photoshop for a while, you already know there's a Lens Correction filter found under Photoshop's Filter menu, and they've updated that with pretty much the same features as the Camera Raw version, but it's better to do the correction here because: (1) it's non-destructive, and (2) it's faster. So I always fix lens problems here, rather than using the Photoshop filter.

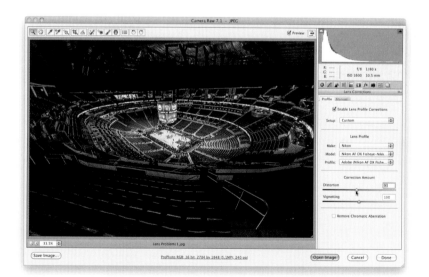

Step Two:
Click on the Lens Corrections icon (the fifth icon from the right at the top of the Panel area) and on the Profile tab, turn on the Enable Lens Profile Corrections checkbox. Now, chances are that you're done. Boom. It's fixed. That's because, as I said above, it looks at the camera data embedded in the shot to find out which camera and lens you used, then it searches its internal database for a profile of that lens, and it immediately fixes the photo (as seen here). If it can't find a profile, it lets you know at the bottom of the panel (as seen in the next step). Also, I usually have to back down the amount of correction just a bit with fisheye lenses by dragging the Distortion slider a little bit to the left (as seen here).

SCOTT KELBY

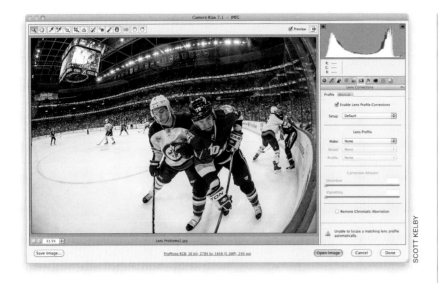

SCOTT KELBY

Step Three:

So, what happens in a case like this, where you open a photo and it can't find a profile automatically, or the image doesn't have any embedded EXIF data (for example, if you're trying to fix a scanned image, or an image you copied-and-pasted from another document)? Take a look at the photo here. Camera Raw couldn't find a profile for it, so in the Lens Profile section, the Make is set to None and the Model and Profile pop-up menus are grayed out. What this really means is that you have to help it out by telling it what equipment you used to take the photo (if you know), or you'll have to make your best guess (if you don't).

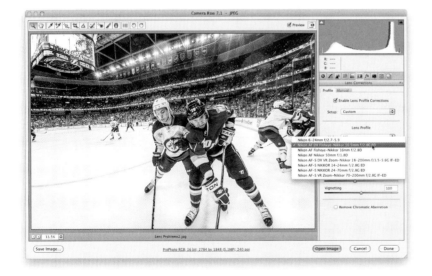

Step Four:

I shoot Nikon cameras, so I pretty much knew this was taken with a Nikon, so from the Make field I chose Nikon, and as soon as I did, it did the rest—it found a lens match and fixed the photo. Now, it's not always 100% sure it has the right lens match, so it gives you a list of lenses it thinks might be right. You can click on the Model pop-up menu, and you'll see a list of lenses it thinks it could be (as seen here). You can try out any of the other lenses listed there and see if it gives you a better result than the one that it chose for you (it does a surprisingly good job, so I usually wind up using the one it chose, but every once in a while I find a lens in that list I like better, even though sometimes I know it's not the actual lens I used). Here, I actually used the 10.5mm fisheye lens, so I chose that from the pop-up menu.

(Continued)

Step Five:

Our last two images were taken with a 10.5mm fisheye lens, but now let's look at a situation where the lens problem is so large, a built-in profile alone isn't going to get the job done. Take at look at the image shown here, where the building and tower look like they're leaning in toward the center (look at how the tower on the left side is leaning to the right). This is a pretty common problem for photos taken with a wide-angle lens on a full-frame camera (this was taken with a 28–300mm lens, at 28mm). Besides the lens distortion problems (look at the foundation—how it bends up on the left side), this image has lens vignetting (darkening) in all four corners, it's way underexposed, and it's lacking contrast in a big way. I kind of like the mystery of the fog, but it is just kind of a mess overall.

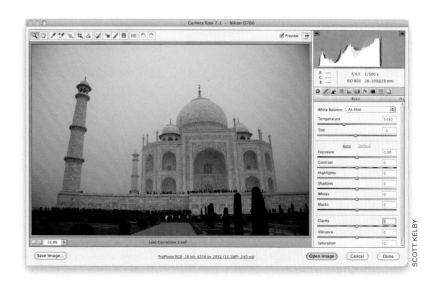

Step Six:

Let's start by quickly fixing the exposure and contrast, because it's really distracting. We can fix this in just a few clicks. When something is this underexposed and flat-looking (lacking contrast), it's a perfect candidate for a click on the Auto button, so start there. It actually looks okay, but let's just use that as a starting point. Now, add more contrast by dragging the Contrast slider over to +20, then drag the Blacks slider down to –50 to keep the shadows from looking washed out, and lastly, crank up that Clarity a bunch (here, I dragged it over to +71 to really bring out the detail). We still have some nasty edge vignetting, but we'll fix that next.

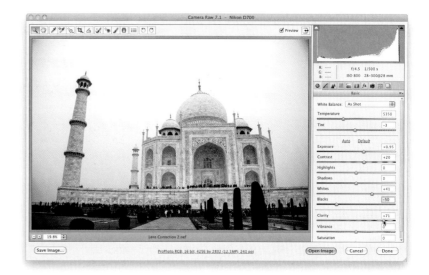

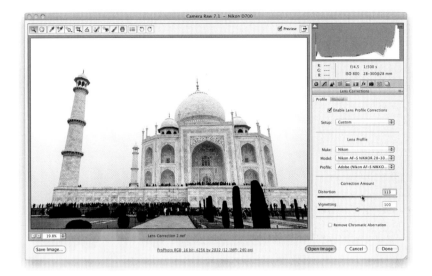

Step Seven:
Click on the Lens Corrections icon and turn on the Enable Lens Profile Corrections checkbox (at the top of the Profile tab). It looks at the camera data embedded into your photo and, if it finds a match in its database, it applies the fix automatically, as it did here by flattening out the foundation of the building, removing the bloated look from the front of the palace, and removing the edge vignetting from all the corners. Ahhhhhh, that's starting to look a bit better. After it applied its profile correction, the foundation beneath the building still didn't look perfectly straight, but luckily you can tweak the amount of Distortion correction applied by the profile by using the Correction Amount sliders at the bottom (here, I had to drag the Distortion slider over to 113 to get the foundation perfectly straight).

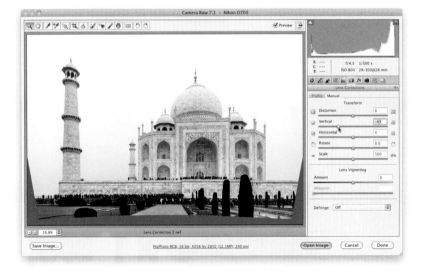

Step Eight:
If you need more than a little tweak to the profile (which we definitely do—look at how the building and tower are leaning back, back in Step Seven), then you need to click on the Manual tab and basically do it yourself. (*Note:* The changes you make in the Manual tab are added on top of what you already did in the Profile tab.) In this case, we need to fix the vertical geometric distortion, so drag the Vertical slider to the left, and as you do, keep an eye on the tower on the left. Your goal is to make it straight, so simply drag to the left until it is (in this case, I dragged over to –43, as shown here). Now, pinching the perspective of the image like this will leave a dark gray gap at the bottom and sides of the image (as seen here), but we'll deal with that in just a moment. For now, at least we've fixed the "leaning tower of Agra" problem.

(Continued)

Step Nine:

Go ahead and click the Open Image button to open the corrected photo (complete with the dark gray gaps) in Photoshop. You'll notice that to fix the leaning problems, it had to kind of squash the image a bit, so now the building looks a little squatty. To fix the squattiness (not a word, I know) and cover that dark gray gap at the bottom, get the Rectangular Marquee tool **(M)**, and click-and-drag it around the image, going across the bottom edge, right above the dark gray gap. Now, press **Command-T (PC: Ctrl-T)** to bring up Free Transform. Grab the bottom-center transform handle and drag the image straight down—stretching it to fill the dark gray gap at the bottom (as shown here). Press **Return (PC: Enter)** to lock in your change, then press **Command-D (PC: Ctrl-D)** to deselect. The bonus here is that the building doesn't look squatty anymore. Two birds. One stone.

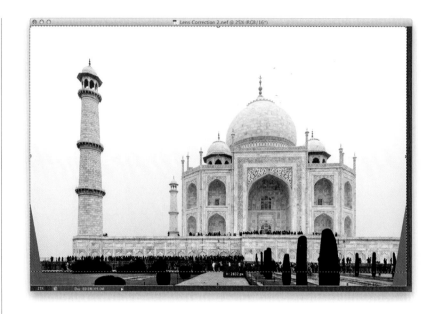

Step 10:

Now, when it comes to those two gray triangles in the corners, you have two choices here: (1) The most common choice is simply to crop away those gray empty areas, so get the Crop tool **(C)**, drag it out over as much of the photo as you can without extending into the gaps, and then press Return. (2) However, we could pull a fast one, and instead try a little Content-Aware Fill (it's definitely worth a try, because fairly often it works like magic). Get the Magic Wand tool (press **Shift-W** until you have it), and click it once in a gray area to select it, then Shift-click in the other one. Go under the Select menu, under Modify and choose **Expand**, and enter 4 pixels (Content-Aware Fill seems to work better if you expand out your selection by 4 pixels. I learned that from Adobe themselves).

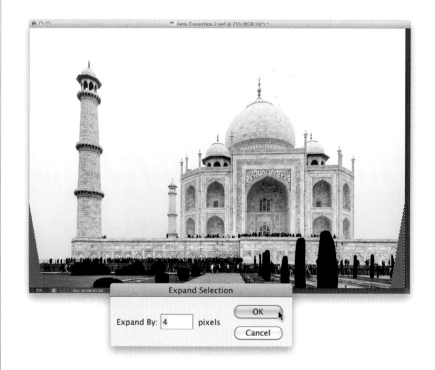

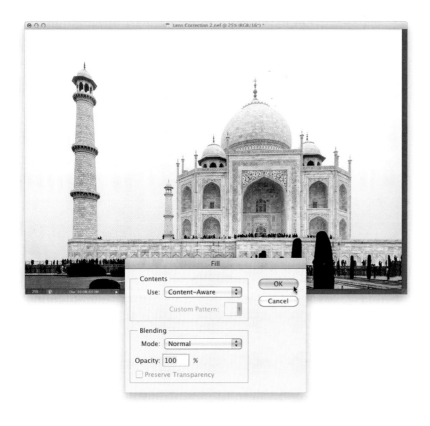

Step 11:

Next, press the **Delete (PC: Backspace) key** to bring up the Content-Aware Fill dialog (that Delete key trick only works if your image is flattened. If this image was on a layer, you'd need to go under the Edit menu and choose **Fill**), and then choose **Content-Aware** from the Use pop-up menu. Click OK, and let's see how it worked (like how I create fake anticipation here, since you know and I know that it worked?). Hey, look at that— it worked. Well, it could probably use a tiny bit of cloning here and there, but all-in-all it did about 98% of the job. Nice! Press Command-D to deselect the triangular areas.

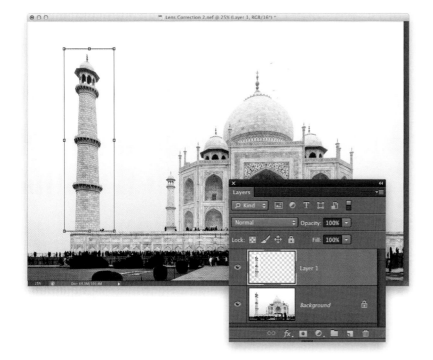

Step 12:

That tower isn't leaning anymore, but it is kind of skewed to the right a bit. We're going to pull another fast one and fix this while nobody's looking (nobody is looking, are they?). Get the Rectangular Marquee tool again, and click-and-drag out a rectangular selection around the tower—just make sure you select some of the sky around it (that way, it can cover the old tower that's about to be behind it). Now press **Command-J (PC: Ctrl-J)** to put this selected area up on its own layer. Then, press Command-T to bring up Free Transform (as seen here).

(Continued)

Step 13:

Press-and-hold the Command (PC: Ctrl) key, grab the top-right Free Transform handle, and drag upward to straighten out the tower (as shown here). Stretching out the tower like this might make it a little too tall, so once it's fairly straight, release the Command key, grab the top-center handle, and drag straight down a little to shrink the tower back down to size. By the way, while Free Transform is in place, you can go to the Layers panel and lower the Opacity of this top layer so you can see the original tower below it. That way, you can match up the height correctly. Just don't forget to raise your Opacity back up to 100% when you're done. Now, press the Return (PC: Enter) key to lock in your transformation. So, is all this "moving the tower thing" cheating? You betcha! I love it!!!! (Just make sure you're not doing stuff like this if you're a photojournalist reporting the news. However, if you're like me, someone trying to create beautiful images, then my friend, have at it!)

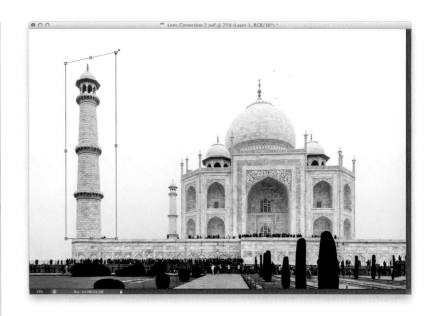

Step 14:

The final step would be to sharpen this puppy to death! (I mean, add a significant amount of sharpening.) Go under the Filter menu, under Sharpen, and choose **Unsharp Mask**. For Amount, enter between 90% and 100%, increase the Radius to 1.5 pixels, and set the Threshold at 3 levels. This is some major sharpening, but when you have a photo with something this detailed, it can take a lot of sharpening (meaning, it *loves* to be sharpened). Now, click OK to finish your lens correction problem (and then some!). A before and after is shown on the next page.

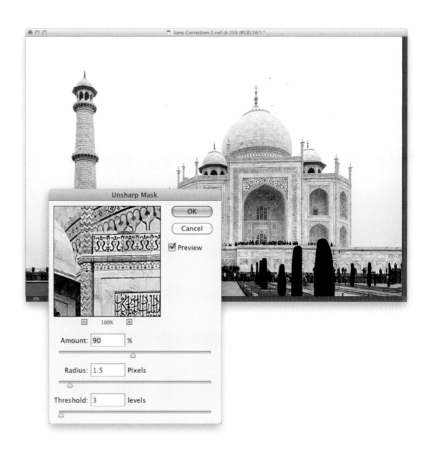

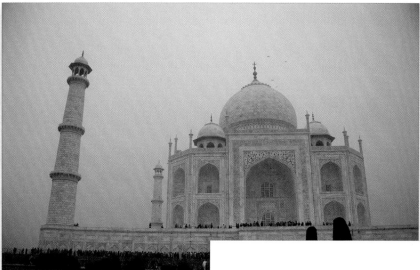

Before

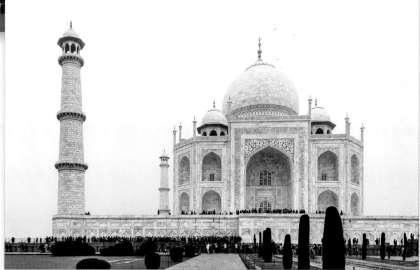

After

Fixing Chromatic Aberrations (That Colored-Edge Fringe)

Chromatic aberration is a fancy name for that thin line of colored fringe that sometimes appears around the edges of objects in photos. Sometimes the fringe is red, sometimes green, sometimes purple, blue, etc., but all the time it's bad, so we might as well get rid of it. Luckily, Camera Raw has a built-in fix that does a pretty good job.

Step One:

Open a photo that has signs of chromatic aberrations. If they're going to appear, they're usually right along an edge in the image that has lots of contrast (like along the edges of these stone stairs).

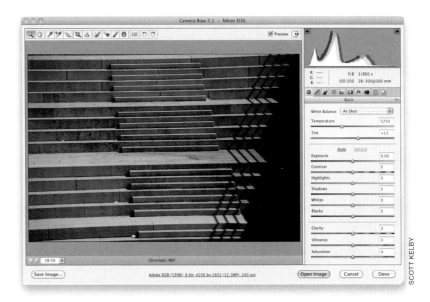

Step Two:

Press **Z** to get the Zoom tool and zoom in on an area where you think (or see) the fringe might be fairly obvious (here, I've zoomed in on the steps on the top left, and you can see thin purple and green lines at the top and bottom of the steps). To remove this, start by clicking on the Lens Corrections icon (the sixth icon from the left) at the top of the Panel area, then click on the Color tab (in the center) to make the Chromatic Aberration controls visible.

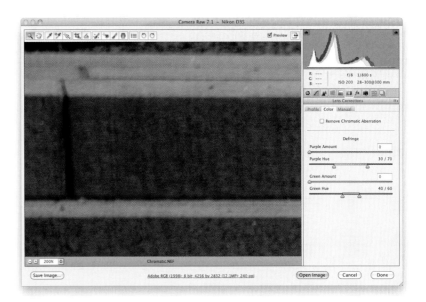

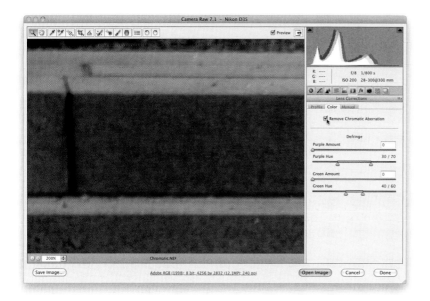

Step Three:

In most cases, all you'll have to do is turn on the Remove Chromatic Aberration checkbox (as shown here) and you're done—Photoshop removes the color fringe based on your lens' make and model, which it learns from the meta-data embedded into the image at the moment you took the shot. However, if for some reason the image still needs more correction (the checkbox alone didn't do the trick), then you can try getting rid of the fringe manually using the sliders in the Defringe section below the checkbox (just so you can see how this works, go ahead and turn off the Remove Chromatic Aberration checkbox).

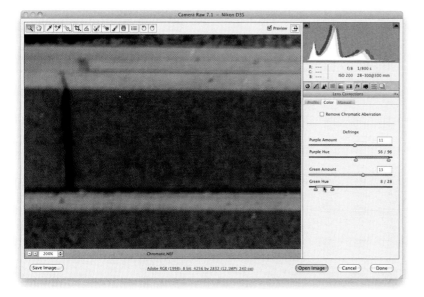

Step Four:

We'll start by trying to remove the purple (or often magenta) line by dragging the Purple Amount slider to the right until you see it's gone. In this case, it removed most of it, but left a little bit (especially on the left). That's because the hue in the aberration is a little different (it happens), and that's when you use the Purple Hue slider to dial in just the right color. Click right between the two knobs and drag the slider way over to the right, and the residual color is now gone (sometimes you might have to drag to the left—it just depends on the image. So, try dragging it in both directions first to quickly see which direction is the right one). You can do the same thing for the green aberration—drag the Green Amount slider to the right first, and if anything is left over, drag the Green Hue slider to dial in just the right hue, until it's completely gone (like you see here). Again, I rarely have to go beyond turning on the Remove Chromatic Aberration checkbox, but at least now if it doesn't do the job for you, you'll know what to do instead.

Edge Vignetting: How to Fix It and How to Add It for Effect

If you're looking at a photo and the corners of the photo appear darker, that's lens vignetting. Generally, I look at it this way: If it's just the corners, and they're just a little bit dark, that's a problem and I fix it. However, sometimes I want to focus the viewer's attention on a particular area, so I create a vignette, but I expand it significantly beyond the corners, so it looks like an intentional soft spotlight effect. Here's how to fix (or create) vignettes:

Step One:

Here, you can see the dark areas in the corners (that's the bad vignetting). This is normally caused by the camera's lens, so don't blame yourself (unless you bought a really cheap lens—then feel free to give yourself as much grief as you can bear). To remove this vignetting from the corners, start by clicking on the Lens Corrections icon (the sixth icon from the left) at the top of the Panel area. In the Profile tab, turn on the Enable Lens Profile Corrections checkbox and Photoshop tries to remove the edge vignetting based on your lens' make and model (it learns this from your image's EXIF data. See page 66 for more on this). If the image still needs correcting, try the Vignetting slider under Correction Amount.

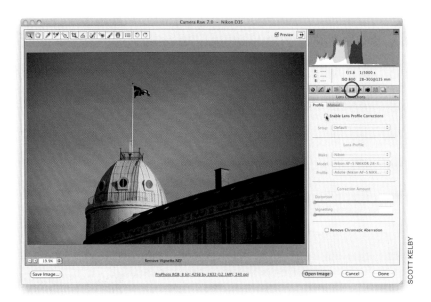

Step Two:

If the automatic way just isn't working, do it manually by clicking on the Manual tab. In the Lens Vignetting section, click on the Amount slider and drag it to the right until the vignetting in the corners disappears. Once you move the Amount slider, the Midpoint slider beneath it becomes available. It determines how wide the vignetting repair extends into your photo, so drag it to the left to expand the lightening farther toward the center of your photo.

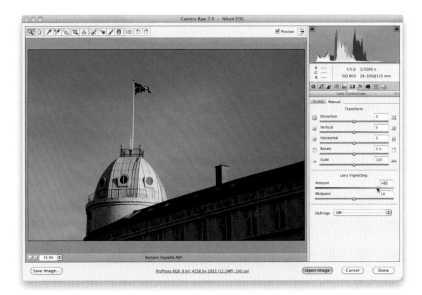

SCOTT KELBY

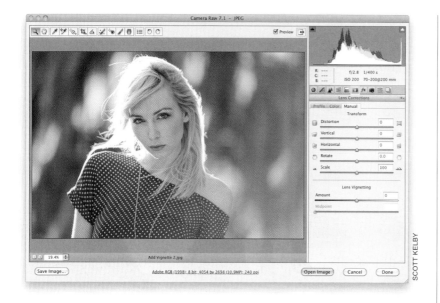

SCOTT KELBY

Step Three:

Now for the opposite: adding vignetting to focus attention (by the way, in the "Special Effects for Photographers" chapter, I also show you how to get the same effect outside of Camera Raw). For this, we'll switch to a different photo.

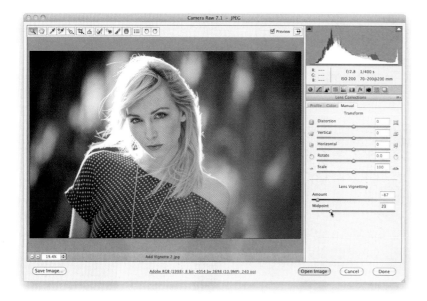

Step Four:

This time, in the Lens Vignetting section, you're going to drag the Amount slider to the left, and as you drag left, you'll start to see vignetting appear in the corners of your photo. But since it's just in the corners, it looks like the bad kind of vignetting, not the good kind, so you'll need to make the vignetting look more like a soft spotlight falling on your subject. Drag the Midpoint slider quite a bit to the left, which increases the size of the vignetting and creates a soft, pleasing effect that is very popular in portraiture, or anywhere you want to draw attention to your subject. That's it—how to get rid of 'em and how to add 'em. Two for the price of one!

(Continued)

Step Five:

So far, adding the vignette has been pretty easy—you just drag a couple of sliders, right? But where you'll run into a problem is when you crop a photo, because you're also cropping the vignetting effect away, as well (after all, it's an edge effect, and now the edges are in a different place, and Camera Raw doesn't automatically redraw your vignette at the newly cropped size). So, start by applying a regular edge vignette (as shown here).

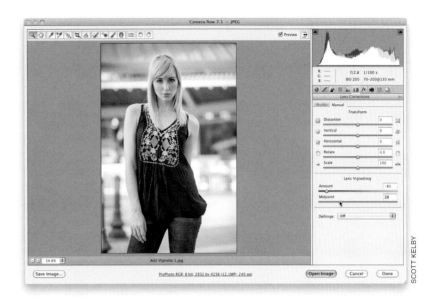

Step Six:

Now, let's get the Crop tool **(C)** from the toolbar, crop that photo in pretty tight, and you can see what the problem is—the vignette effect we just added is pretty much gone (the dark edges were cropped away).

Note: Adobe originally added the ability to add a vignette after you've cropped an image (called Post Crop Vignetting) back in Photoshop CS4, but the problem was when you added it, it didn't look nearly as good as the regular non-cropped vignetting (even though it offered more control, as seen at the bottom of the Effects panel shown in Step Seven). It kind of looked just like adding muddy dark gray to the edges. Yeech!

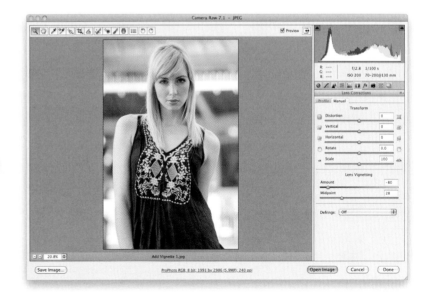

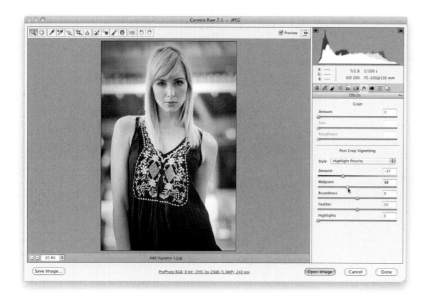

Step Seven:

Let's go add a post-crop vignette by clicking on the Effects icon (the fourth icon from the right) at the top of the Panel area and, under Post Crop Vignetting, dragging the Amount slider to the left to darken the edges, then using the Midpoint slider to choose how far into your image this vignetting will extend (as seen here). Now, here's what they added in CS5 (it makes all the difference in the world): At the top of the Post Crop Vignetting section is a pop-up menu with three different types of vignetting: Highlight Priority (which I think far and away looks the best, and the most like the original vignetting we applied back in Step Five), which tries to maintain the highlight details as the edges are darkened; Color Priority tries to maintain the color while the edges are darkened (it's okay, but not great); and Paint Overlay is the old method from CS4 that almost everybody hated (apparently somebody liked it, because it's still there). I would stay away from this one altogether.

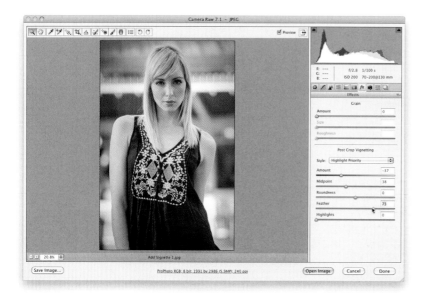

Step Eight:

Below the Midpoint slider is the Roundness slider that gives you control over the roundness of the vignetting (lower the Feather amount to 0, so you can get a better idea of what the Roundness slider does). The farther to the right you drag, the rounder the shape gets, and when you drag to the left, it actually becomes more like a large, rounded-corner rectangle. The Feather slider determines how soft that oval you created with the Roundness slider becomes. I like it really soft, so it looks more like a spotlight, so I usually drag this slider quite a bit over to the right (here I dragged it over to 73, but I wouldn't hesitate to go higher, depending on how it looks on the photo).

The Advantages of Adobe's DNG Format for RAW Photos

Adobe created DNG (an open archival format for RAW photos) because, at this point in time, each camera manufacturer has its own proprietary RAW file format. If, one day, one or more manufacturers abandon their proprietary format for something new (like Kodak did with their Photo CD format), will we still be able to open our RAW photos? With DNG, it's not proprietary—Adobe made it an open archival format, ensuring that your negatives can be opened in the future, but besides that, DNG brings another couple of advantages, as well.

Step One:

There are three advantages to converting your RAW files to Adobe DNG: (1) DNG files are generally about 20% smaller. (2) DNG files don't need an XMP sidecar file to store Camera Raw edits, metadata, and keywords—the info's embedded into the DNG file, so you only have one file to keep track of. And, (3) DNG is an open format, so you'll be able to open them in the future (as I mentioned in the intro above). If you have a RAW image open in Camera Raw, you can save it as an Adobe DNG by clicking the Save Image button (as shown here) to bring up the Save Options dialog (seen in the next step). *Note:* There's really no advantage to saving TIFF or JPEG files as DNGs, so I only convert RAW photos.

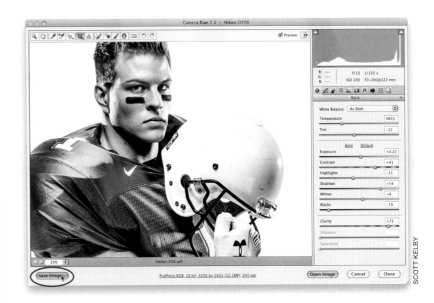

SCOTT KELBY

Step Two:

When the Save Options dialog appears, at the bottom of the dialog, from the Format pop-up menu, choose **Digital Negative** (shown here). Once you choose Digital Negative, a new set of options appears at the bottom of the dialog (seen in Step Three).

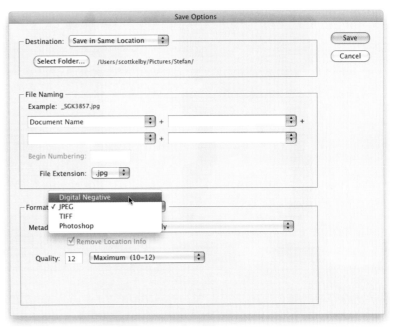

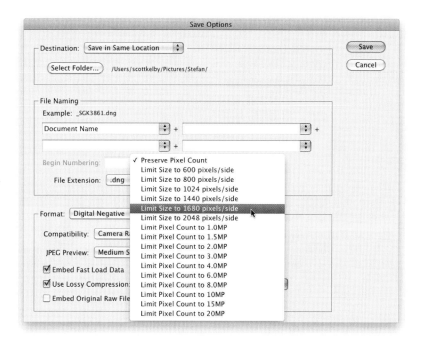

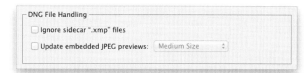

Step Three:

New in CS6 is the Embed Fast Load Data checkbox, which uses a smaller embedded RAW preview that makes switching between images faster (I turn this feature on). Below that is a somewhat controversial option, but if used in the right way, I think it's okay. It uses a JPEG-like lossy compression (meaning there is a loss in quality), but the trade-off (just like in JPEG) is that your file sizes are dramatically smaller (about 25% of the size of a full, uncompressed RAW file). So, if there's a loss of quality, why would you use this? Well, I wouldn't use it for my Picks (the best images from a shoot—ones I might print, or a client might see), but what about the hundreds the client rejected or you don't like? Those might (it's your call) be candidates to be compressed to save drive space. It's something to consider. If you do want to do it, turn on that checkbox, then choose (from its pop-up menu) which option is most important to you: saving the same physical dimensions (pixel size) or file size (megapixels). Once you've made your choices, click OK, and you've got a DNG.

TIP: Setting Your DNG Preferences

With Camera Raw open, press **Command-K (PC: Ctrl-K)** to bring up Camera Raw's Preferences dialog. There are two preferences in the DNG File Handling section: Choose Ignore Sidecar ".xmp" Files only if you use a different RAW processing application (other than Camera Raw or Lightroom), and you want Camera Raw to ignore any XMP files created by that application. If you turn on the Update Embedded JPEG Previews checkbox (and choose your preferred preview size from the pop-up menu), then any changes you make to the DNG will be applied to the preview, as well.

Adjusting or Changing Ranges of Color

In the next chapter, you're going to learn how to paint an adjustment over any part of your image, but sometimes you need to affect an entire area (like you need the entire sky bluer, or the sand warmer, or a piece of clothing to be an entirely different color). In those cases, where you're adjusting large areas, it's usually quicker to use the HSL adjustments, which not only let you change color, but also let you change the saturation and the lightness of the color. It's more powerful, and handier than you might think.

Step One:
Here's the original image of the washed-out top of a tugboat's mast against a bland blue sky. What I'd like to do is tweak the color of that sky so it's a richer blue, and then make the red crow's nest on the boat more vivid so it really stands out. You tweak individual colors, or ranges of color, in the HSL/Grayscale panel, so click on its icon at the top of the Panel area (it's the fourth one from the left—circled here in red). Now, click on the Saturation tab (as shown here) to bring up the Saturation sliders (which control the intensity of the colors).

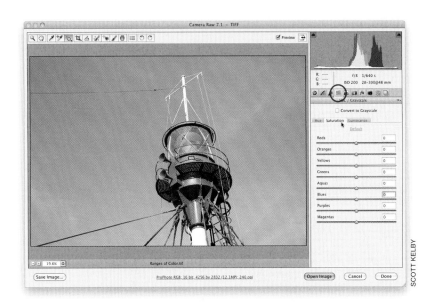

Step Two:
We'll start by bringing some richness and depth back into that bland blue sky. You can just drag the Blues slider to the right, and it will get bluer (the color will get more intense), but most of the time, the color your eye sees (blue, in this case) is made up of more than just that color. So, rather than guessing, and messing with the individual sliders, I recommend grabbing the Targeted Adjustment tool (or TAT, for short) from the toolbar up top (it's the fifth tool from the left), then clicking it somewhere in the sky, and dragging straight upward. As you do this, it knows which sliders control that area, and it moves them for you (in this case, it moved the Blues slider a lot, but it also moved the Purples slider a little, too).

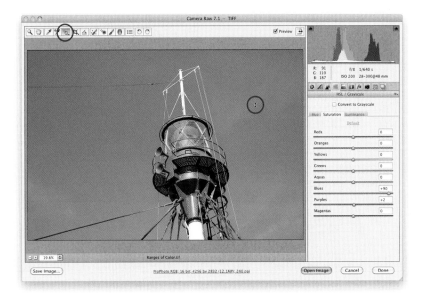

SCOTT KELBY

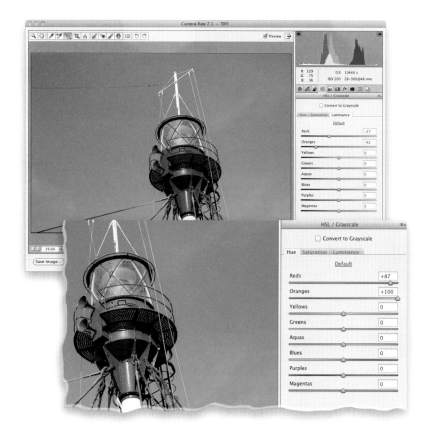

Step Three:

By the way, dragging upward with the TAT increases the saturation amounts, and dragging downward decreases them. Just so you know. Okay, now that the sky looks pretty decent, let's work on that red crow's nest (or mini-lighthouse). So, take the TAT, click it on the side of it (I clicked between the walkway and the horn), and drag straight upward to increase the color saturation (intensity) of those reds. Go look at the sliders, and you'll see it moved the Reds and Oranges sliders (so that color was made up of red and orange), but beyond that, the TAT knows the right percentage of each, which is why using it gives you such an advantage (in fact, I don't use these HSL sliders without using the TAT).

Step Four:

If you think the red color looks too bright now, then all you have to do is click on the Luminance tab (it controls how bright the colors appear), click on a bright area of red, and drag downward (as shown here, where I clicked below the walkway), and now the red tower isn't nearly as bright (compare it with what you see in Step Three). It kind of helps make the harsh light not as harsh, in this case. So, that's how it works for tweaking Saturation and Luminance. However, if you want to actually change a color (and not just tweak the existing color), then click on the Hue tab. The controls are the same: click your TAT on the tower and drag upward to change the color (as I did here in the inset). Again, you could always drag the sliders around, and eventually you'd find out which slider controls which part of the image, but I think you can see why Adobe invented the TAT—to make our lives in this panel easier.

Removing Spots, Specks, Blemishes, Etc.

If you need to remove something pretty minor from your photo, like a spot from some dust on your camera's sensor, or a blemish on your subject's face, or something relatively simple like that, you can use the Spot Removal tool right within Camera Raw. If it's more complicated than just a simple spot or two, you'll have to head over to Photoshop and use its much more powerful and precise retouching tools (like the Healing Brush tool, Patch tool, and Clone Stamp tool).

Step One:

This photo has some simple problems that can be fixed using Camera Raw's Spot Removal tool. You start by clicking on the Spot Removal tool (the seventh tool from the right in the toolbar) or by pressing **B** to get it, and a set of options appears in the Spot Removal panel on the right (seen here). Using the tool is pretty simple—just move your cursor over the center of a spot that needs to be removed (in this case, it's those spots in the sky where my camera's sensor got dirty), then click, hold, and drag outward, and a red-and-white circle will appear, growing larger as you drag outward. Keep dragging until that circle is a little larger than the spot you're trying to remove (as shown here below). Don't forget, you can use the Zoom tool **(Z)** to zoom in and get a better look at your spots before you drag out your circle.

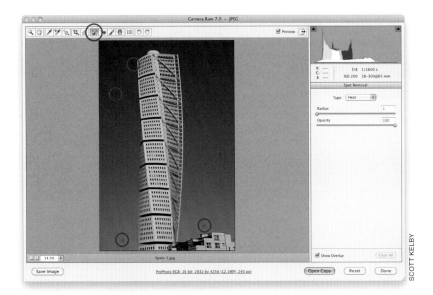

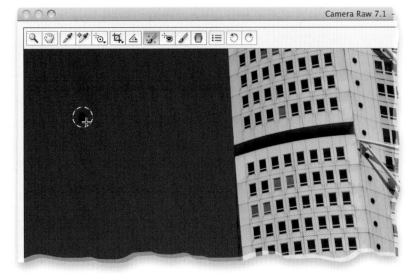

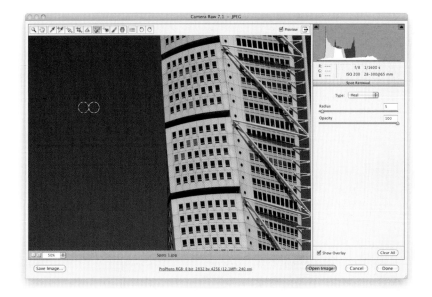

Step Two:

When you release the mouse button, a second circle (this one is green and white) appears to show you the area where Camera Raw chose to sample your repair texture from (it's usually very close by), and your spot or blemish is gone (as seen here).

TIP: When to Fix Blemishes in Camera Raw

So, what determines if you can fix a blemish here in Camera Raw? Basically, it's how close the blemish, spot, or other object you need to remove is to the edge of anything. This tool doesn't like edges (the edge of a door, a wall, a person's face, etc.), so as long as the blemish (spot, etc.) is all by itself, you're usually okay.

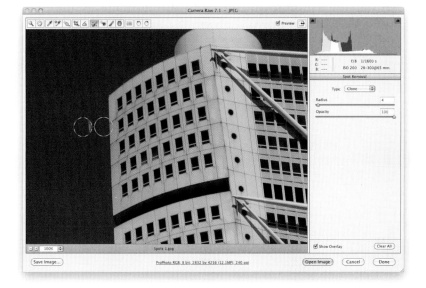

Step Three:

To remove a different spot (like the one near the top of the building here), you use the same method: move over that spot, click, hold, and drag out a circle that's slightly larger than the spot, then release the mouse button. In this case, Camera Raw did sample a nearby area, but unfortunately it also sampled a bit of the building, and it copied it to the sky area where we were retouching, making the retouch look very obvious with that piece of building hanging out there.

(Continued)

Step Four:

If this happens, here's what to do: move your cursor inside the green-and-white circle, and drag that circle to a different nearby area (here, I dragged it to a clean area to the left of the spot I'm removing), and when you release the mouse button, it resamples texture from that area. Another thing you can try, if the area is at all near an edge, is to go to the top of the Spot Removal panel and choose Clone rather than Heal from the Type pop-up menu (although I use Heal about 99% of the time, because it generally works much better).

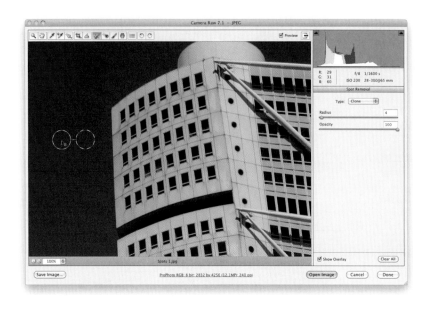

Step Five:

When you're done retouching, just change tools and your retouches are applied (and the circles go away). Here's the final retouch after removing all the spots in the sky from my dirty sensor. Use this tool the next time you have a spot on your lens or on your sensor (where the same spot is in the same place in all the photos from your shoot)—fix the spot on one photo, then open multiple photos, and paste the repair onto the other selected RAW photos using Synchronize (see "Editing Multiple Photos at Once," earlier in this chapter, and just turn on the Spot Removal checkbox in the Synchronize dialog).

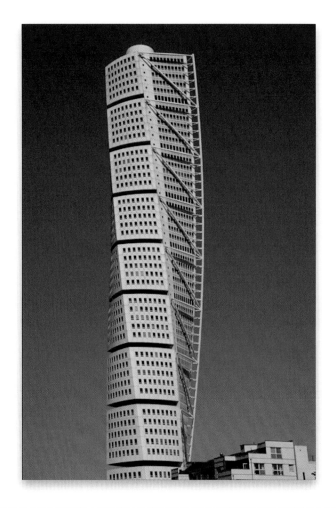

Some cameras seem to have their own "color signature," and by that I mean that every photo seems to be a little too red, or every photo is a little too green, etc. You just know, when you open a photo from that camera, that you're going to have to deal with the slight color cast it adds. Well, if that's the case, you can compensate for that in Camera Raw, and then set that color adjustment as the default for that particular camera. That way, any time you open a photo from that camera, it will automatically compensate for that color.

Calibrating for Your Particular Camera

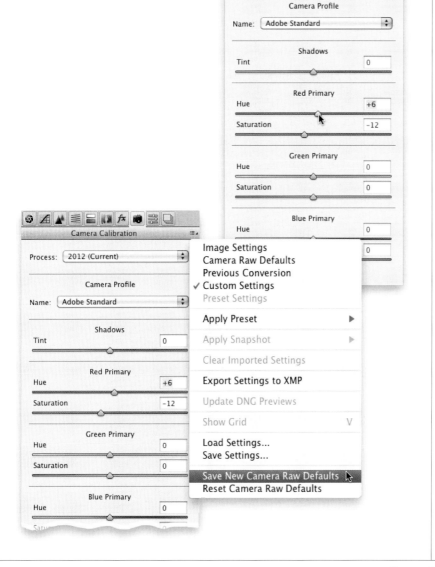

Step One:
To calibrate Camera Raw so it fixes a persistent color cast added by your camera, open a typical photo taken with that camera in Camera Raw, and then click on the Camera Calibration icon (it looks like a camera and is the third icon from the right at the top of the Panel area). So, let's say that the shadow areas in every photo from your camera appear slightly too red. In the Camera Calibration panel, drag the Red Primary Saturation slider to the left, lowering the amount of red in the entire photo. If the red simply isn't the right shade of red (maybe it's too hot and you just want to tone it down a bit), drag the Red Primary Hue slider until the red color looks better to you (dragging to the right makes the reds more orange).

Step Two:
To have Camera Raw automatically apply this calibration each time a photo from that particular camera is opened in Camera Raw, go to Camera Raw's fly-out menu (in the top right of the panel), and choose **Save New Camera Raw Defaults** (as shown here). Now, when you open a photo from that camera (Camera Raw reads the EXIF data so it knows which camera each shot comes from), it will apply that calibration. *Note:* You can adjust your blues and greens in the same way.

Reducing Noise in Noisy Photos

This is, hands down, not only one of the most-requested features by photographers, but one of the best since the upgrade in CS5. Now, if you're thinking, "But Scott, didn't Photoshop and Camera Raw both have built-in noise reduction before CS5?" Yes, yes they did. And did it stink? Yes, yes it did. But, does the current noise reduction rock? Oh yeah! What makes it so amazing is that it removes the noise without greatly reducing the sharpness, detail, and color saturation. Plus, it applies the noise reduction to the RAW image itself (unlike most noise plug-ins).

Step One:

Open your noisy image in Camera Raw (the Noise Reduction feature works best on RAW images, but you can also use it on JPEGs and TIFFs, as well). The image shown here was shot at a high ISO using a Nikon D3S, which didn't do a very good job in this low-light situation, so you can see a lot of color noise (those red, green, and blue spots) and luminance noise (the grainy looking gray spots).

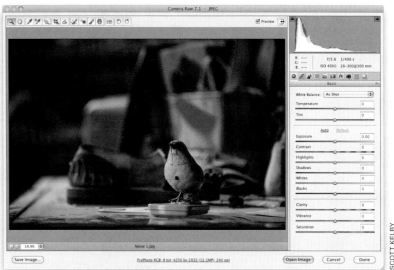

Step Two:

Sometimes it's hard to see the noise until you really zoom in tight, so zoom into at least 100% (here, I zoomed into 200%), and there it is, lurking in the shadows (that's where noise hangs out the most). Click on the Detail icon (it's the third icon from the left at the top of the Panel area) to access the Noise Reduction controls. I usually get rid of the color noise first, because that makes it easier to see the luminance noise (which comes next). Here's a good rule of thumb to go by when removing color noise: start with the Color slider over at 0 (as shown here) and then slowly drag it to the right until the moment the color noise is gone. *Note:* A bit of color noise reduction is automatically applied to RAW images—the Color slider is set to 25. But, for JPEGs or TIFFs, the Color slider is set to 0.

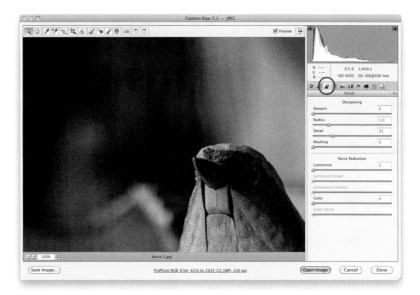

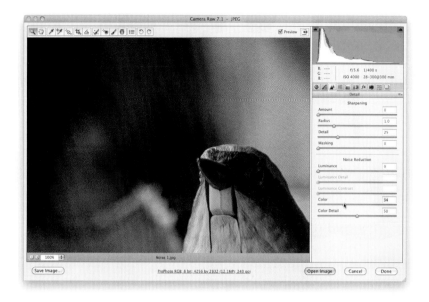

Step Three:

So, click-and-drag the Color slider to the right, but remember, you'll still see some noise (that's the luminance noise, which we'll deal with next), so what you're looking for here is just for the red, green, and blue color spots to go away. Chances are that you won't have to drag very far at all—just until that color noise all turns gray. If you have to push the Color slider pretty far to the right, you might start to lose some detail, and in that case, you can drag the Color Detail slider to the right a bit, though honestly, I rarely have to do this for color noise.

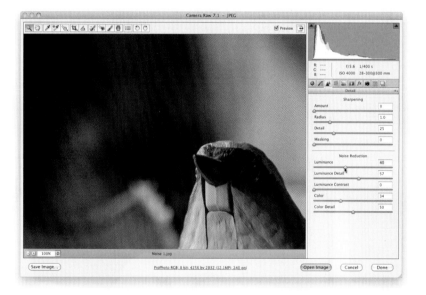

Step Four:

Now that the color noise is gone, all that's left is the luminance noise, and you'll want to use a similar process: just drag the Luminance slider to the right, and keep dragging until the visible noise disappears (as seen here). You'll generally have to drag this one farther to the right than you did with the Color slider, but that's normal. There are two things that tend to happen when you have to push this slider really far to the right: you lose sharpness (detail) and contrast. Just increase the Luminance Detail slider if things start to get too soft (but I tend not to drag this one too far), and if things start looking flat, add the missing contrast back in using the Luminance Contrast slider (I don't mind cranking this one up a bit, except when I'm working on a portrait, because the flesh tones start to look icky). You probably won't have to touch either one all that often, but it's nice to know they're there if you need them.

(Continued)

Step Five:

Rather than increasing the Luminance Detail a bunch, I generally bump up the Sharpening Amount at the top of the Detail panel (as shown here), which really helps to bring some of the original sharpness and detail back. Here's the final image, zoomed back out, and you can see the noise has been pretty much eliminated, but even with the default settings (if you're fixing a RAW image), you're usually able to keep a lot of the original sharpness and detail. A zoomed-in before/after of the noise reduction we applied here is shown below.

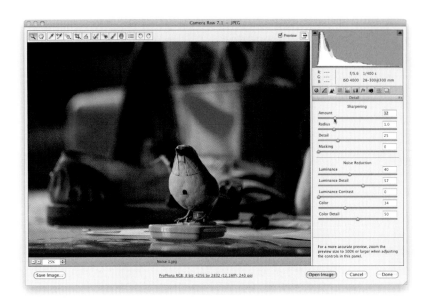

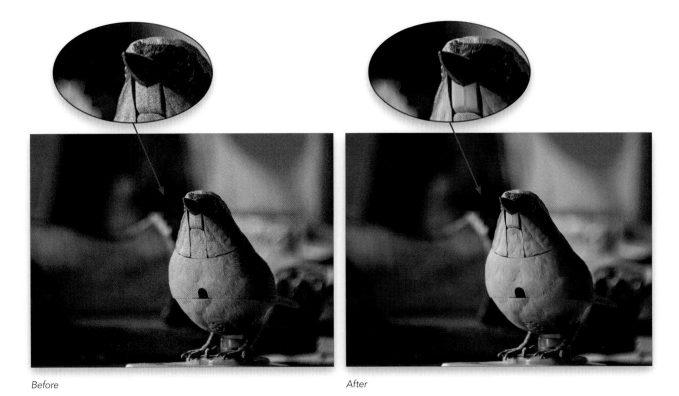

Before

After

Setting Your Resolution, Image Size, Color Space, and Bit Depth

Since you're processing your own images, it only makes sense that you get to choose what resolution, what size, which color space, and how many bits per channel your photo will be, right? These are workflow decisions, which is why you make them in the Workflow Options dialog. Here are my recommendations on what to choose, and why:

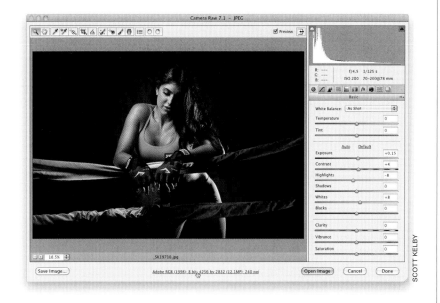

SCOTT KELBY

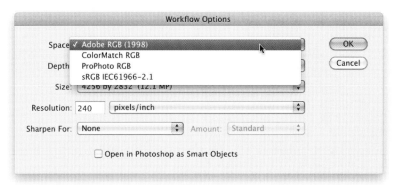

Step One:
Once you've made all your edits, and the photo is generally looking the way you want it to, it's time to choose your resolution, size, etc. Directly below the Camera Raw Preview area (where you see your photo), you'll see your current workflow settings—they are underlined in blue like a website link. Click on that link to bring up the Workflow Options dialog (which is seen in the next step).

Step Two:
We'll start at the top by choosing your photo's color space. By default, it shows the color space specified in your digital camera, but you can ignore that and choose the color space you want the photo processed with. I recommend choosing the same color space that you have chosen as Photoshop's color space. For photographers shooting in RAW or using Lightroom, I recommend that you choose ProPhoto RGB, but if you're shooting in JPEG or TIFF format, then I still recommend that you choose Adobe RGB (1998) for Photoshop's color space, and then you would choose the same color space here, from the Space pop-up menu. See my color management and printing chapter (Chapter 11) for more on why you should use ProPhoto RGB or Adobe RGB (1998).

(Continued)

Step Three:

When it comes to choosing your photo's bit depth, I have a simple rule I go by: I always work in 8 Bits/Channel (Photoshop's default), unless I have a photo that is so messed up that after Camera Raw, I know I'm still going to have to do some major Curves adjustments in Photoshop just to make it look right. The advantage of 16-bit is those major Curves adjustments (you'd get less banding or posterization because of the greater depth of 16-bit). The reasons I don't use 16-bit more often are: (1) many of Photoshop's tools and features aren't available in 16-bit, (2) your file size is approximately double, which makes Photoshop run a lot slower, and (3) 16-bit photos take up twice as much room on your computer. Still, some photographers insist on only working in 16-bit and that doesn't bother me one bit. (Get it? One bit? Aw, come on, that wasn't that bad.)

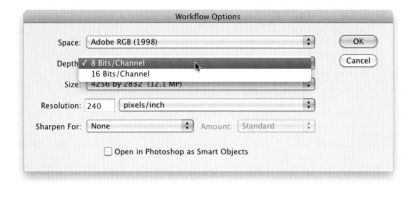

Step Four:

The next option down is Size. By default, the size displayed in the Size pop-up menu is the original size dictated by your digital camera's megapixel capacity (in this case, it's 4256 by 2832 pixels—the size generated by a 12.1-megapixel camera). If you click-and-hold on the Size pop-up menu, you'll see a list of image sizes Camera Raw can generate from your RAW original (the number in parentheses shows the equivalent megapixels that size represents). The sizes with a + (plus sign) by them indicate that you're scaling the image up in size from the original. The – (minus sign) means you're shrinking the size from the original, which quality-wise isn't a problem. Usually, it's fairly safe to increase the size to the next largest choice, but anything above that and you risk having the photo look soft and/or pixelated.

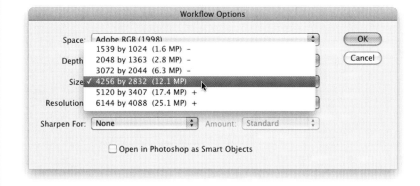

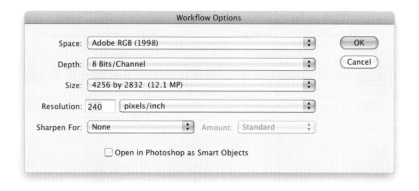

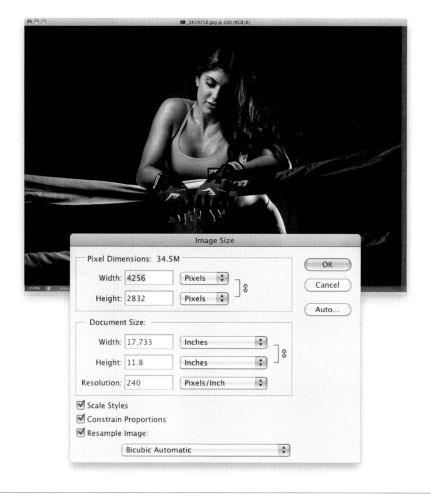

Step Five:

The last Workflow Options choice is what you want the resolution of your processed file to be. The topic of resolution is something entire training DVDs are dedicated to, so we won't go in-depth about it here, but I'll give you some quick guidelines. If your photo will wind up on a printing press, use 300 ppi (you don't really need that much, but many print shops still think you do, so just play it safe at 300 ppi). When printing to an inkjet printer at larger than 8x10" size, I use 240 ppi (although some argue that the sweet spot for Epson printers is 360 ppi, so you might try printing the same image at both resolutions and compare). For prints smaller than 8x10" (which are viewed at a very close distance), try 300 ppi. If your photos are only going to be viewed on the web, you can use 72 ppi. (By the way, the proper resolution is debated daily in Photoshop discussion forums around the world, and everybody has their own reason why their number is right. So, if ever you're bored one night....)

Step Six:

When you click OK and then click Open Image in the Camera Raw dialog, your photo is processed using those settings and opened in Photoshop (here's the processed photo in Photoshop with the Image Size dialog open, so you can see the settings). These workflow settings now become your defaults, so you don't have to mess with them again, unless: (a) you want to choose a different size, (b) you need to work in 16-bit, or (c) you need to change the resolution. Personally, I work at the original size taken by my camera, in 8-bit mode, and at a resolution of 240 ppi, so I don't have to change these workflow options very often.

Getting the Old CS5-Style Fill Light Slider Back

As much as I love the new improved Shadows slider in Camera Raw—it does a better-quality job of opening up shadows—it's not as powerful (meaning, the old Fill Light slider would let you go a little "over-the-top"). I particularly liked the Fill Light slider's look for certain things like opening up shadow areas in hair, or creating faux-HDR effects. Here's a little workaround I came up with that lets you blend the new sliders with the old Fill Light slider, thanks to a little smart object trick.

Step One:

Start by opening your image in Camera Raw and doing your standard edits (in this case, I tweaked the white balance a little by dragging the Temperature slider a little bit to the right to make it warmer. I also increased the Exposure a little—to +0.25—to make it a bit brighter, and I opened up the Shadows a little bit, too, by dragging it over to +13, as seen here). Nothing drastic, but I did do a few little tweaks here. Now, press-and-hold the Shift key and you'll see that the Open Image button changes to the Open Object button (it's shown circled here in red). Go ahead and click it to open this image in Photoshop as a smart object.

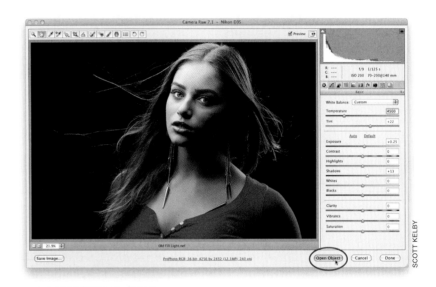

Step Two:

Once the image appears in Photoshop as a smart object (you can tell it's a smart object by looking in the Layers panel—in the bottom-right corner of the layer's thumbnail, you should see a little page icon), go ahead and Right-click just to the right of the layer's name and, when the pop-up menu appears, choose **New Smart Object Via Copy** (as shown here). This makes a duplicate of your smart object layer, but it is no longer tied to the original layer, so we can edit these as two totally independent RAW images.

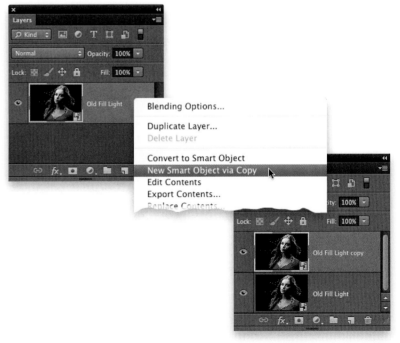

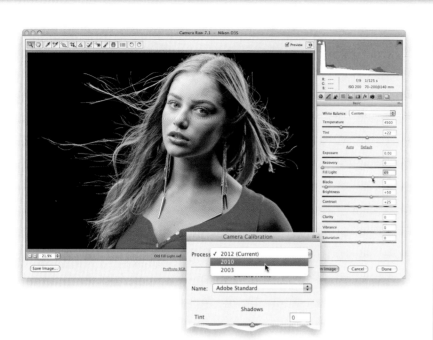

Step Three:

Double-click on the thumbnail for this duplicated smart object layer, and it reopens in Camera Raw. Now, click on the Camera Calibration icon (it's the third one from the right and looks like a camera) at the top of the Panel area and, at the top of that panel, click on the Process menu and choose **2010** (as shown here at the bottom). This changes just this duplicate layer back to the old process version, so it has the controls from Photoshop CS5. Now, go to the Basic panel and, lo and behold, there is the old Fill Light slider. Go ahead and crank that Fill Light slider up (here, I dragged it over to 69). This really opens up the shadows in her hair (much more so than the Shadows slider set to +100 in the current process version). However, you can see the weird look it gives the rest of the image, which is why Adobe thought this control needed some improvements. When it looks good to you, click OK.

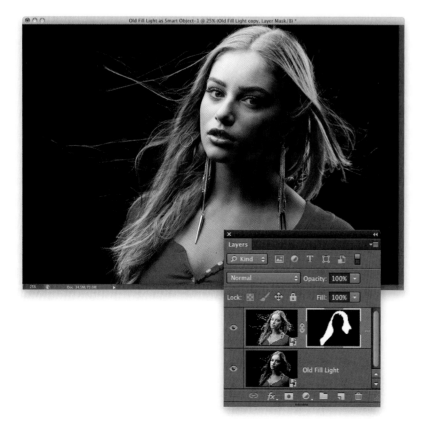

Step Four:

With the top layer active in the Layers panel, Option-click (PC: Alt-click) on the Add Layer Mask icon at the bottom of the panel to hide this newly processed layer behind a black mask. Now, get the Brush tool **(B)**, make sure your Foreground color is set to white, then paint over the areas you want to have the old Fill Light look (for example, here I painted over her hair and earrings, which is primarily what I wanted). Here's the final image, using a combination of the old Camera Raw Fill Light slider and the new, improved Camera Raw processing power. Sweet!

Photoshop Killer Tips

Don't Use the Reduce Noise Filter in Photoshop

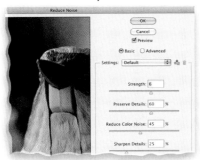

There are two different places you can reduce noise in Photoshop: The Noise Reduction controls in Camera Raw rock, however the Reduce Noise filter in Photoshop (under the Filter menu, under Noise) does not. We used to joke that the sliders weren't connected to anything, and if they were, it was a blur filter. My advice—only use the Noise Reduction in the Detail panel of Camera Raw, and avoid the other altogether.

Rotating Your Images

Finally, a shortcut that makes perfect sense: To rotate your image to the left, press **L**; to rotate to the right, press **R**. The nice thing is, once you learn one, you'll never forget the other.

Making Camera Raw Full Screen

To have Camera Raw expand to fill your entire screen, click the Full Screen mode icon to the right of the Preview checkbox, at the top of the window or just press the **F key**.

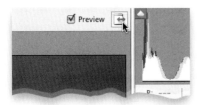

Avoiding Noise Problems

If there's noise in your photo, chances are it's in the shadow areas, so keep this in mind when you're editing your images. If you open up the shadows a lot (using the Shadows slider, Blacks, or in some cases, even the Exposure slider), any noise that was already in the image is going to become magnified. If you can't avoid opening up those shadows, just make sure you use Camera Raw's Noise Reduction to reduce the visible amount.

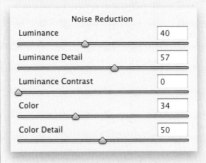

Tip for Wacom Tablet Users Who Use Their Tablet in Their Lap

Back in CS4, Adobe introduced Fluid Canvas Rotation, which lets tablet users who work with their tablet in their lap rotate the screen to match the current angle of their tablet (you turn this on

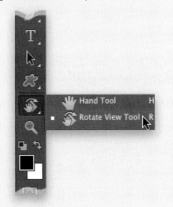

by clicking on the Hand tool, choosing the Rotate View tool, and then clicking-and-dragging that within your image to rotate the canvas). There was only one problem, though: when you rotated the canvas, it rotated your brushes, too (which wouldn't happen in real life). Luckily, now when your canvas rotates, your brushes stay intact.

Get Automatic Auto Corrections

The Auto correction one-click fix feature got dramatically better in previous versions of Photoshop. So, now it's to the point where the Auto button is pretty decent. Not great, not amazing, but decent. Anyway, if you want to have Camera Raw automatically apply an Auto correction to every photo you open (to get a better starting point for your editing), then click on the Preferences icon in Camera Raw's toolbar (it's the third icon from the right), and in the Default Image Settings section, turn on the Apply Auto Tone Adjustments checkbox. Now, every image will get an automatic correction as soon as it's opened.

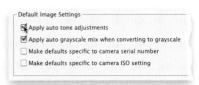

Photoshop Killer Tips

Assigning a Color Profile to Your RAW Image

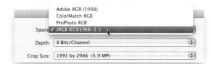

If you shoot in RAW, your camera doesn't embed a color profile in the image (like it does with JPEG and TIFF images). You assign a color profile in Camera Raw, and if you're using Camera Raw for all your editing, and then you're just saving your file as a JPEG for emailing or posting to the web, you're going to want to assign a color profile that keeps the colors looking like you saw in Photoshop. You do this by clicking on the blue link beneath the Preview area in Camera Raw. This brings up the Workflow Options dialog, where you choose which color profile gets embedded into your image (you choose it from the Space pop-up menu). If you're emailing the image, or posting it on the web, choose **sRGB** as your color space—that way it pretty much maintains the colors that you saw while you were in Camera Raw (if you left it at ProPhoto RGB, or even Adobe RGB [1998], the colors on the web, or in the email, will probably look drab and washed out).

Get a Histogram for the Most Important Part of Your Photo

If you're editing a portrait in Camera Raw, the most important part is, of course, your subject, but the histogram in Camera Raw shows you a readout for the entire image (so if you shot your subject on a white background, the histogram isn't going to be much help in determining if the skin

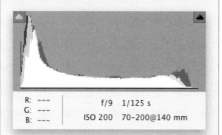

tone is correct). To get around this, grab the Crop tool **(C)**, and drag out a cropping border tight right around your subject's face (but don't actually crop the image). With the cropping border in place, if you look at the histogram (in the top right of the window), it shows you a readout for just what's inside the cropping border— your subject's face. Very handy!

The Hidden Trash Can

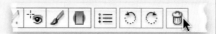

If you're wondering why you've never seen the Trash icon in Camera Raw (where you can click to delete files), it's because it only appears when you have multiple images open there (it appears at the end of the toolbar). Click on it, and it marks your selected image(s) for deletion. Click the Done button, and it deletes that image (well, it moves it to the Trash on a Mac, or Recycle Bin on a PC).

Finding Your Best Images Fast

I mentioned in the last chapter that if you have multiple images open in Camera Raw, you can assign star ratings and labels to photos just as if you were in Mini Bridge (you even use the same shortcuts). But, a little-known tip is that if you press-and-hold the Option (PC: Alt) key, the Select

All button at the top of the filmstrip on the left changes into the Select Rated button. Click it, and any images that have either a star rating or a label will be instantly selected for you, letting you get to your best images fast.

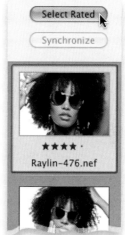

Right-Click to Choose Your Zoom

If you Right-click directly on your image in Camera Raw's Preview area, a pop-up menu with different zoom percentages appears.

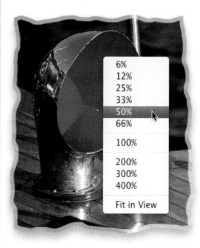

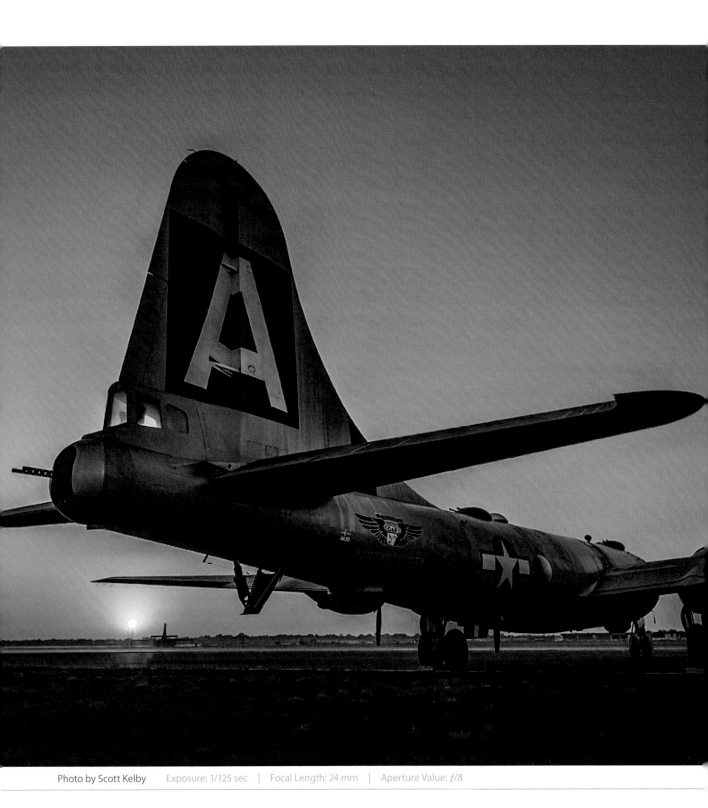

Photo by Scott Kelby   Exposure: 1/125 sec | Focal Length: 24 mm | Aperture Value: *f*/8

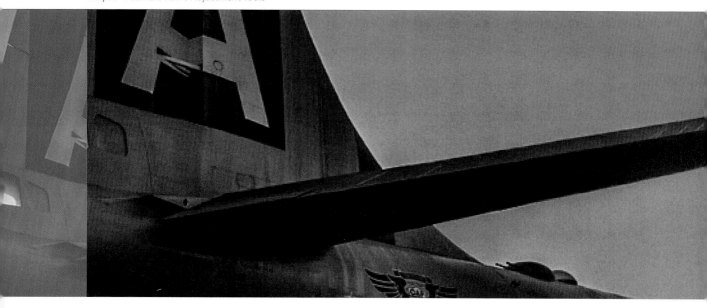

Attitude Adjustment
camera raw's adjustment tools

When I went searching for songs with the word "adjustment" in them, I quickly found Aerosmith's "Attitude Adjustment," which would make this an easy choice for me as an Aerosmith fan, but there's no real way for you to know if the title I'm referencing up there is actually the one by Aerosmith, or if I secretly went with another song with the exact same title by hip hop artists Trick Trick and Jazze Pha. In iTunes, this song was marked with the Explicit label, so I thought I'd better listen to the free 90-second preview first, because I wanted to make sure I didn't pick a song whose free preview was too explicit, but while listening to that preview, something very unexpected happened to me that I haven't gotten over to this very day. The sad truth is that I couldn't understand a word they were saying. I even played it back a couple of times, and I was waiting for naughty words to jump out at me, but I could barely make out anything they said. It just sounded like a bunch of noise. This can only mean one thing—I'm old. I remember playing songs for my parents when I was younger, and I remember my mom saying, "I can't understand a word they're saying" and she had that irritated look that only old people who can't understand a word they're hearing can get. But this time it was me. Me—that young, cool guy (stop giggling) experiencing my first "old people" moment. I was sad. I just sat there for a moment in stunned silence, and then I said "F&*$ S#!& A@# M*%$#%" and in no time flat, my wife stuck her head in the room and said, "Are you writing rap lyrics again?" At that moment, I felt young again. I jumped up out of my chair, but then I grabbed my back and yelled "F*%$#% R%^$!" My wife then said, "I can't understand a word you're saying." Peace out!

Dodging, Burning, and Adjusting Individual Areas of Your Photo

One of my favorite features in Camera Raw is the ability to make non-destructive adjustments to individual areas of your photos (Adobe calls this "localized corrections"). The way they've added this feature is pretty darn clever, and while it's different than using a brush in Photoshop, there are some aspects of it that I bet you'll like better. We'll start with dodging and burning, but we'll add more options in as we go.

Step One:

This photo has two areas that need completely different adjustments: (1) the sky needs to be darker with more vibrant colors, and (2) the plane needs to be brighter and punchier. So, get the Adjustment Brush from up in the toolbar (it's shown circled here in red) or just press the letter **K** on your keyboard. However, I recommend that you do all the regular edits to your photo in the Basic panel first (exposure, contrast, etc.), just like normal, before you grab the brush.

Step Two:

Once you click on the brush, an Adjustment Brush panel appears on the right side of the window, with most of the same sliders you have in the Basic panel (except for Vibrance), along with some extra ones (like Sharpness, Noise Reduction, and Moire Reduction). Let's start by darkening the sky. With the Adjustment Brush, you (1) choose what kind of adjustment you want first, then (2) you start painting, and then (3) you tweak the amount of your adjustment after the fact. So, start by clicking on the – (minus sign) button to the left of the Exposure slider, which resets all the sliders to 0 and lowers the Exposure (the midtones control) to –0.50, which is a decent starting place.

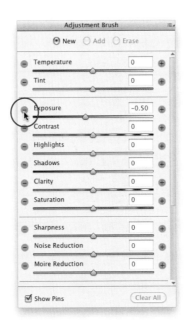

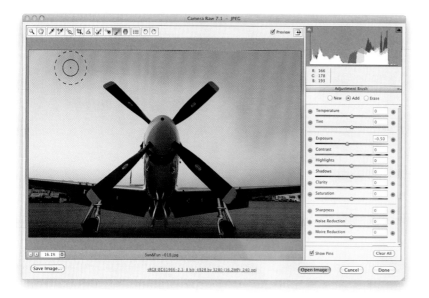

Step Three:

At the bottom of the Adjustment Brush panel, there is a really amazing Adjustment Brush feature called "Auto Mask," which helps to keep you from accidentally painting on things you don't want to paint on (so it's great around the edges of things). But, when you're painting over something like a big sky, it actually slows things down because it keeps trying to find an edge. So, I leave the Auto Mask checkbox turned off for stuff like this, and here, I'll just avoid getting close to the edges of the plane (for now, anyway). Go ahead and paint over the sky (with Auto Mask turned off), but of course, avoid getting too close to the propeller blades or the wings of the plane—just stick to open areas of sky (as seen here). Notice how the sky gets darker as you paint?

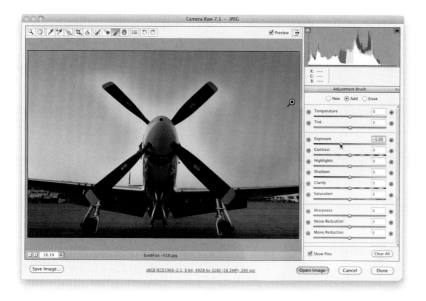

Step Four:

Once you've painted in most of the sky (but avoided the prop and wings of the plane), now you can tweak how dark it is. Try lowering the Exposure to –1.00 (as shown here) and the area you painted over gets a lot darker. This is what I meant by "you tweak it after the fact." Also, you see that green pin on the right side of the image? That represents this one adjustment (you can have more than one, which is why you need a way to keep track of them. More on this coming up).

TIP: Deleting Adjustments

If you want to delete any adjustment you've made, click on the adjustment's pin to select that adjustment (the center of the pin turns black), then press the Delete (PC: Backspace) key on your keyboard.

(Continued)

Step Five:

Okay, now that "glow" around the prop and wings where we haven't painted is starting to get on my nerves, so let's deal with that before we tweak our settings any more. When we're getting near the edges of the prop and wings is when you want to turn Auto Mask back on (shown here). That way, you can paint right up against them, filling in all those areas, without accidentally painting over the blades and wings. The key to using Auto Mask is simple—don't let that little + (plus sign) inside the inner circle of your brush stray over onto the blades or wings, because that's what determines what gets affected (if that + crosses over onto a wing, it starts painting over the wing). It's okay if the outer circle crosses right over the wings and blades—just not that + (see how the brush here is extending over onto the cone in front of the prop, but it's not getting darker? That's Auto Mask at work).

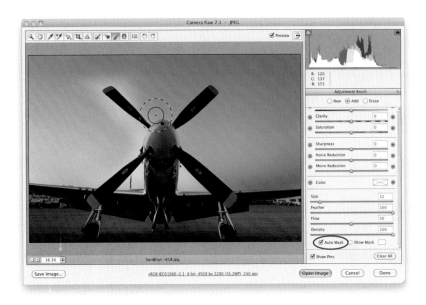

Step Six:

So, how do you know if you've really painted over the entire area you wanted to adjust? How do you know whether you've missed a spot? Well, if you turn on the Show Mask checkbox near the bottom of the panel, it puts a tint over the area you painted (as seen here, where I changed my tint color to red by clicking on the color swatch to the right of the checkbox), so you can see if you missed anything. If you don't want this on all the time, you can just hover your cursor over any pin (which is what I'm doing here) and it will temporarily show the masked area for that pin. Now that you know where you painted, you can go back and paint over any areas you missed. If you want to keep the mask turned on while you paint, just press the letter **Y** on your keyboard.

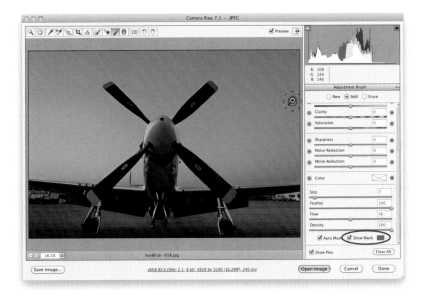

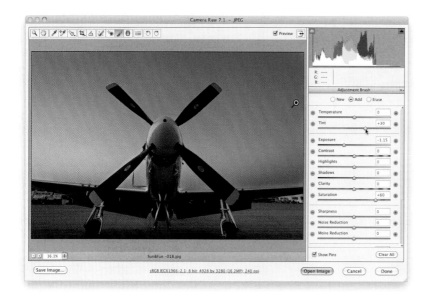

Step Seven:

Now, let's unlock a little more of the Adjustment Brush's power by adjusting more sliders. That's right, once you've painted over (masked) an area, you can adjust any of the other sliders and they affect just the area you painted over (here, they'll just affect the sky). Starting at the top, let's drag the Tint slider to the right, toward magenta, to make the sky color more interesting (I dragged it over to +30), then let's make it even darker by lowering the Exposure amount to –1.15. Now, head down to Saturation and crank that up a bit (I took it up to +60), and that flat dawn sky gets much more vibrant (as seen here). Yeah, that's just like I remember it (wink). The ability to paint over one area, and stack up a number of adjustments on just that area, is what gives this tool so much power.

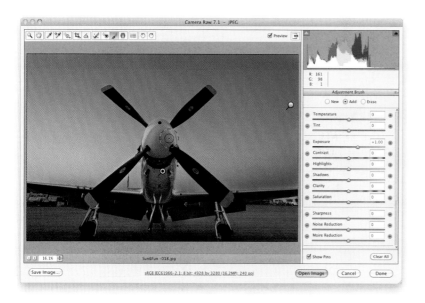

Step Eight:

Next, let's work on the plane (a P-51 Mustang). First, click the New radio button at the top of the panel, so we can paint over a new area (otherwise, the plane would get the same settings we used on the sky). Then, click the + button to the right of Exposure twice to reset all the other sliders to 0 and bump up the Exposure amount to +1.00 (twice the one-click amount). Now, with Auto Mask turned on, paint over the underside of the plane and the propeller blades (as shown here), which lightens those areas because you increased the Exposure amount by quite a bit. Also, notice there are now two pins, and the sky's pin is now white, letting you know it's no longer active. If you wanted to adjust the sky again, you'd click on its pin, and all the sky settings would come back.

(Continued)

Step Nine:

Finish painting over the rest of the plane (wings, propeller blades), and then let's add some more "juice" to it by increasing the Exposure amount a bit more (here, I dragged it over to +1.50), then open the shadow areas by dragging the Shadows slider a little to the right (here, I went to +10), and then let's add some punch by adding Clarity (drag it over to around +17). Now the plane is really starting to pop, but you can see that I let the little + in the middle of the brush extend off the bottom of the wings a bit, and it started to brighten the tarmac (concrete runway) below them, which looks bad. So, we'll have to deal with that next.

TIP: Choosing What to Edit

If you have multiple pins and you drag a slider, Camera Raw will adjust whichever pin is currently active (the green-and-black one). To choose which adjustment you want to edit, click on the pin to select it, then make your changes.

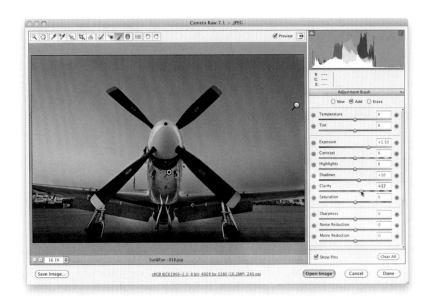

Step 10:

If you make a mistake, or need to erase something that spilled over, just press-and-hold the **Option (PC: Alt) key** and the brush switches to Erase mode. Now, just paint the area where you spilled over and it erases the spillover (as shown here). You can also switch to Erase mode by clicking on the Erase radio button at the top of the Adjustment Brush panel. When you switch this way, you get to choose the Size, Feather, Flow, and Density of the Erase brush (more on this in just a moment), so it's at least good to click on the radio button, choose your preferred brush size (I set the Feather and Density to 100% for this brush), then from that point on, just press-and-hold the Option key to get it when you need it.

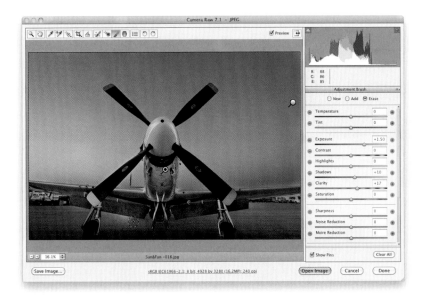

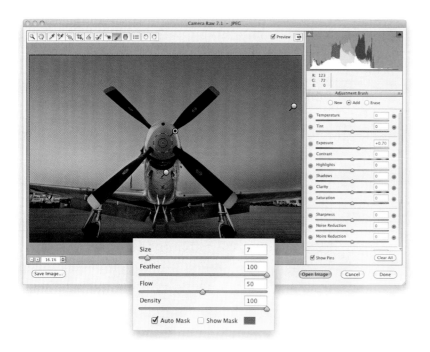

Step 11:

Here are a couple of other things about the Adjustment Brush you'll want to know: The Feather slider controls how soft the brush edges are—the higher the number, the softer the brush (I paint with a soft brush about 90% of the time). For a hard-edged brush, set the Feather slider to 0. The default brush settings are designed to have it build up as you paint, so if you paint over an area and it's not dark enough, paint another stroke over it. This build-up amount is controlled by the Flow and Density sliders at the bottom of the panel. The Density slider kind of simulates the way Photoshop's airbrush capabilities work with its Brush tools, but the effect is so subtle here that I don't ever change it from its default setting of 100. The Flow slider controls the amount of paint that comes out of the brush (I leave the Flow set at 100 most of the time these days, but if I decide I want to "build up," then I lower it to 50). Below is a before/after, which shows how useful dodging and burning with the Adjustment Brush can be.

Note: I felt I needed to make one more change to this image. If you look back at Step 10, the yellow nose cone looks too bright, so I used the Erase brush to erase over it entirely. Then, I clicked the New button, reset everything to 0, increased the Exposure amount to +70, and painted over just the cone (as shown in Step 11) to get the final image here.

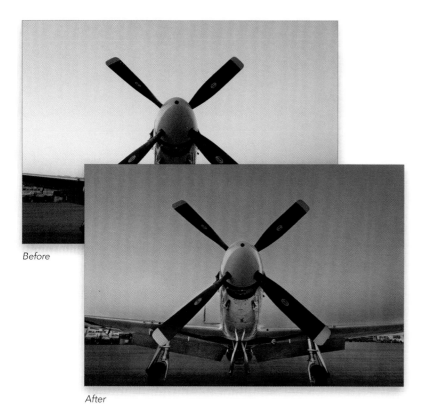

Before

After

Retouching Portraits in Camera Raw

One of the main things we've always had to go to Photoshop for was retouching portraits, but now, by using the Spot Removal tool, along with the Adjustment Brush, we can do a lot of simple retouching jobs right here in Camera Raw, where they're completely non-destructive and surprisingly flexible.

Step One:

In the portrait shown here (which I shot on stage during my *Light It, Shoot It, Retouch It* class at the Photoshop World Conference & Expo), we want to make three retouches: (1) we want to remove any blemishes and soften her skin, (2) we want to lighten the whites of her eyes, brighten her eyes in general, and add contrast, and (3) we want to sharpen her eyes, eyebrows, and eyelashes.

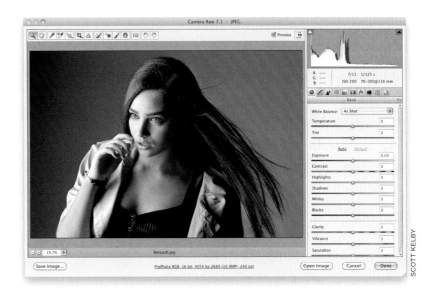

Step Two:

We'll start with removing blemishes. First, zoom in on her face, then get the Spot Removal tool **(B)** from the toolbar up top (it's shown circled here in red) and set your brush Radius (a fancy name for the brush's size) to where it's just slightly larger than the blemish you want to remove. Now, move your cursor over the blemish and just click. Don't paint a stroke or any-thing—just click once and it's gone. If the removal doesn't look quite right, it just means that Camera Raw chose a bad place to sample clean skin from to make its repair. So, click on the green sample circle and drag it to a nearby area and it redoes the retouch (as shown here). Now, remove the rest of the blemishes with just a single click each, adjusting the position of their green sample circles, if necessary.

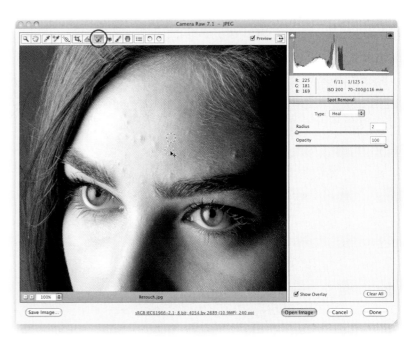

SCOTT KELBY

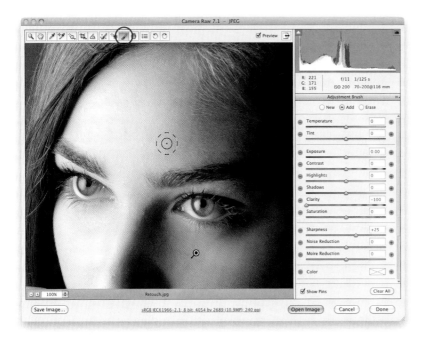

Step Three:

Next, let's do some skin softening. Click on the Adjustment Brush (shown circled here) in the toolbar, then click the – (minus sign) button to the left of Clarity four times to set the Clarity amount at –100 (this is called "negative clarity" by people who love to give everything a name). Now, increase the Sharpness slider to +25 and you're ready to go. Increase the size of your brush (by using either the Size slider or the **Right Bracket key** on your keyboard), and then paint over her skin to soften it (as shown here), but be careful to avoid any areas that should stay sharp and retain lots of detail, like her eyebrows, eyelids, lips, nostrils, hair, etc. While you're painting, you might not feel like it's really doing that much, but toggle on/off the Preview checkbox at the top, and you'll see that it's doing a lot more than you might think. Of course, once you're done painting, if you think you've applied too much softening, just raise the Clarity (try –75 or –50).

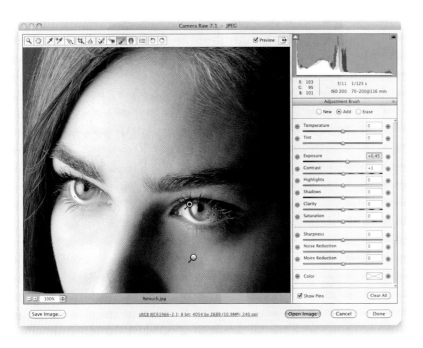

Step Four:

Let's work on the eyes next. Click the New radio button at the top of the panel (to work on a new area), then reset the Clarity and Sharpness sliders to 0 by double-clicking directly on the slider knobs. Now, drag the Exposure slider a little to the right, decrease the size of your brush, then paint over the whites of her eyes (as shown here). Once that looks good, click the New radio button again and zero out the sliders, so we can work on adding contrast and brightness to her irises.

(Continued)

Step Five:

To add more contrast, we're really going to crank up the Contrast slider (here, I dragged it over to +73), but to brighten and enhance the texture of the irises a bit at the same time, increase the Exposure to +15 and the Clarity to +18, then paint directly over the irises, and see how much better they look! Lastly, let's sharpen the eyes, eyelashes, and eyebrows. Click the New button once again, reset all the sliders to 0 (just click the + [plus sign] button to the right of Sharpness and it re-sets them all and moves Sharpness up to +25). Now, paint over her pupils and irises (but not out all the way to the edge of the iris), then paint over her eyelashes and eyebrows to help make them look sharper and crisper, completing the re-touch (a before/after is shown below).

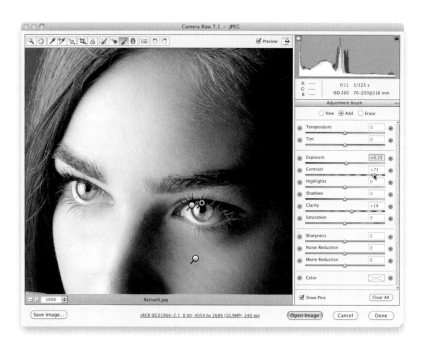

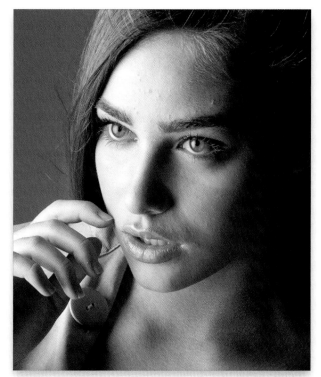

Before

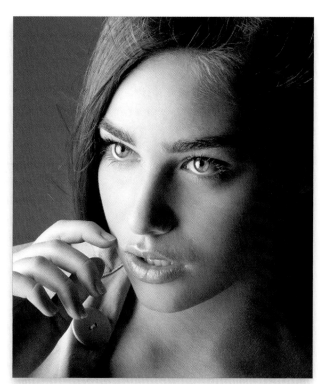

After

The Graduated Filter (which acts more like a tool) lets you recreate the look of a traditional neutral density gradient filter (these are glass or plastic filters that are dark on the top and then graduate down to fully transparent). They're popular with landscape photographers because you're either going to get a photo with a perfectly exposed foreground, or a perfectly exposed sky, but not both. However, with the way Adobe implemented this feature, you can use it for much more than just neutral density gradient effects (although that probably will still be its number one use).

Fixing Skies (and Other Stuff) with the Graduated Filter

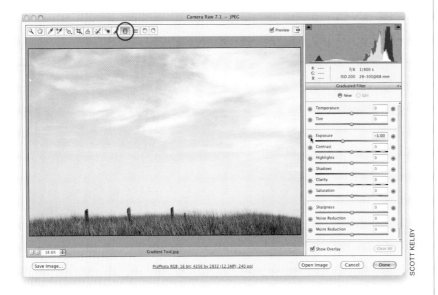

Step One:
Start by selecting the Graduated Filter tool **(G)** up in the toolbar (it's shown circled in red here). When you click on it, its options panel appears (shown here) with a set of effects you can apply that are similar to the ones you can apply using the Adjustment Brush. Here we're going to replicate the look of a traditional neutral density gradient filter and darken the sky. Start by dragging the Exposure slider to the left, or just click on the – (minus sign) button two times to get to –1.00 (as seen here).

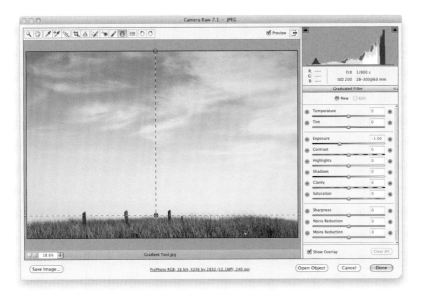

Step Two:
Press-and-hold the Shift key (to keep your gradient straight), click at the top center of your image, and drag straight down until you reach the top of the grass (as shown here). Generally, you want to stop dragging the gradient before it reaches the horizon line, or it will start to darken your properly exposed foreground. You can see the darkening effect it has on the sky and the photo already looks more balanced. *Note:* Just let go of the Shift key to drag the gradient in any direction.

(Continued)

Step Three:

The green pin shows the top of your gradient; the red pin shows the bottom. In this case, we'd like the sky a little darker still, so drag the Exposure slider to the left a bit to darken the midtones in the sky. What's nice about this tool is, like the Adjustment Brush, once we've dragged out the Graduated Filter, we can add other effects to that same area. So, if you'd like the sky to be bluer, you can click on the Color swatch, and when the Color Picker appears, click on a blue color to complete your effect.

TIP: Gradient Tips

You can reposition your gradient after the fact—just click-and-drag downward on the line connecting the green and red pins to move the whole gradient down. Click-and-drag either pin to rotate your gradient after it's in place. You can also have more than one gradient (click on the New radio button at the top of the panel) and to delete a gradient, just click on it and press the Delete (PC: Backspace) key.

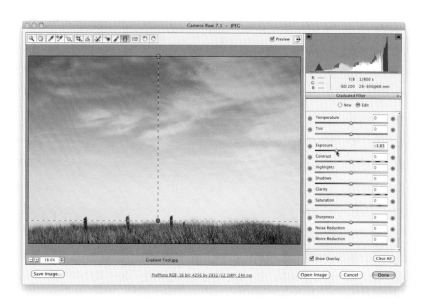

Before

After

There are some really nice special effects you can apply from right within Camera Raw itself, and some of these are easier to achieve here than they are by going into the rest of Photoshop and doing it all with layers and masks. Here are two special effects that are popular in portrait and wedding photography: (1) drawing attention by turning everything black and white, but leaving one key object in full color (very popular for wedding photography and photos of kids), and (2) creating a soft, dramatic spotlight effect by "painting with light."

Special Effects Using Camera Raw

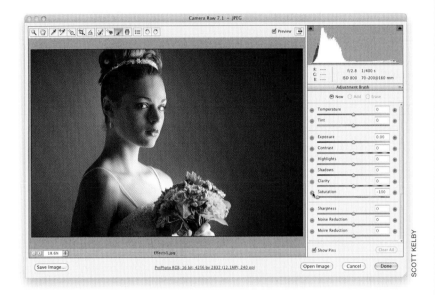

Step One:

For the first effect (where we make one part of the image stand out by leaving it in color, while the rest of the image is black and white [I know it's cheesy, you know it's cheesy, but clients love it]), we want to set up the Adjustment Brush so it paints in black and white. Start by getting the Adjustment Brush **(K)**, then in the Adjustment Brush options panel, click on the – (minus sign) button to the left of Saturation four times to reset all the other sliders to 0 and set the Saturation to –100. That way, whatever you paint over becomes black and white.

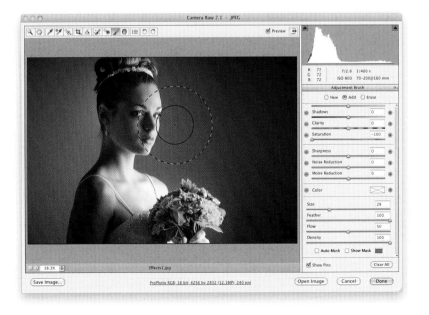

Step Two:

In just a moment, we're going to paint over most of the image, and this will go a lot faster if you turn off the Auto Mask checkbox near the bottom of the panel (so it's not trying to detect edges as you paint). Once that's off, make your brush nice and big (drag the Size slider to the right or press the **Right Bracket key**), and paint over most of the image, but make sure you don't get too close to the area right around the bouquet, as shown here, where I left about a ½" area untouched all around the bouquet.

(Continued)

Step Three:

Now you'll need to do two things:
(1) make your brush size smaller, and
(2) turn on the Auto Mask checkbox. The
Auto Mask feature is really what makes
this all work, because it will automatically
make sure you don't accidentally make
the object in your image that you want
to remain color, black and white, as long
as you follow one simple rule: don't let
that little plus-sign crosshair in the center
of the brush touch the thing you want to
stay in color (in our case, it's the bouquet
of flowers). Everything that little crosshair
touches turns black and white (because
we lowered the Saturation to –100), so
your job is to paint close to the flowers,
but don't let that crosshair actually touch
the flowers. It doesn't matter if the edges
of the brush (the round rings) extend over
onto the flowers (in fact, they'll have to,
to get in really close), but just don't let
that little crosshair touch, and you'll be
fine. This works amazingly well (you just
have to try it for yourself and you'll see).

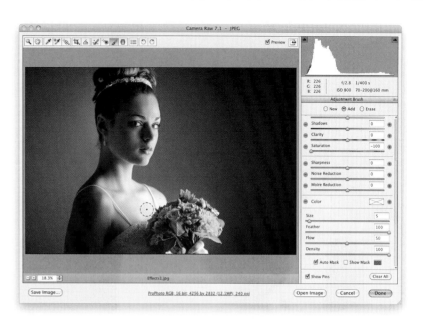

Step Four:

Here, we've painted right up close to
the bouquet and yet the flowers and
even the green leaves are still in color
because we were careful not to let that
crosshair stray over onto them. Okay,
now let's use a similar technique in a different way to create a dark, dramatic
effect using the same image. Start by
pressing the Delete (PC: Backspace) key
to get rid of this adjustment pin and
start over from scratch with the original
color image.

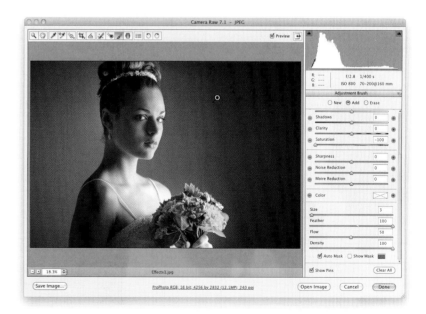

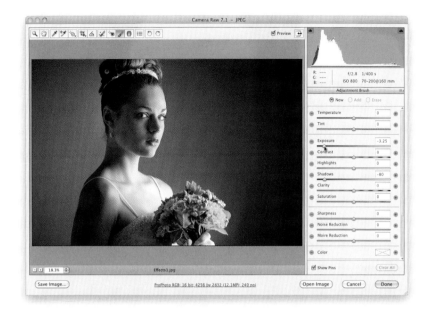

Step Five:
Here's the original full-color image again. Get the Adjustment Brush and click the – (minus sign) button beside Exposure to zero everything out. Then drag the Exposure slider almost all the way over to the left. You can also drag the Shadows slider way over to the left, too (to make sure that, when we paint, things get really dark).

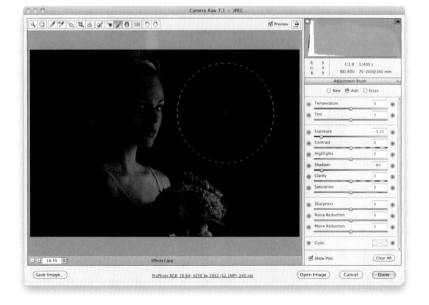

Step Six:
Turn off the Auto Mask checkbox and, using a large brush, paint over the entire image (as shown here) to greatly darken it.

(Continued)

Step Seven:

Now, click the Erase radio button at the top of the Adjustment Brush's options panel (or just press-and-hold the Option [PC: Alt] key to temporarily switch to the Erase tool), set your brush to a very large brush size (like the one shown here), set your Feather (softness) amount to around 90, then click once right over the area you want lit with a soft spotlight (like I did here, where I clicked on the bride's face). What you're doing is essentially revealing the original image in just that one spot, by erasing the darkening you added in the previous step.

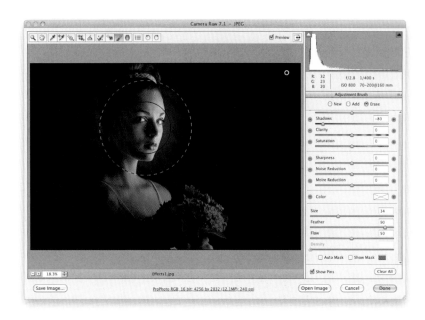

Step Eight:

Click just a few more times on the image, maybe moving ½" or so around her head and shoulders, to reveal just the areas where you want light to appear, and you'll wind up with the image you see here as the final effect. If the effect seems too intense, undo those last few steps by pressing **Command-Option-Z (PC: Ctrl-Alt-Z)** a few times, then lower the Flow amount. That way, it builds up more gradually as you click the brush.

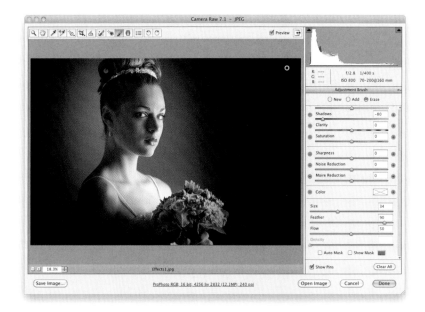

This is the first version of Camera Raw that lets us paint with white balance, and of all the new things added to Camera Raw, believe it or not, this is one you'll probably wind up using the most. It's pretty common to have a natural light photo where part of the photo is in shadows, which usually means the parts in daylight have one color, and the parts in shadows are usually bluish (especially if you use Auto White Balance, which most of us do, because it works pretty well for most situations). Here's how to paint with white balance to make all the color in your image consistent:

Fixing Color Problems (or Adding Effects) by "Painting" White Balance

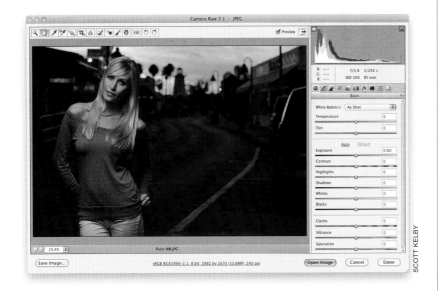

Step One:

Here's a location portrait, where our subject has a nice warm skin tone (partially because I put an orange gel over the off-camera flash), but take a look at the background behind her—the street and buildings are in the shade and that makes them look blue (like it was taken at dawn), even though it was taken at sunset. If I try to warm up the white balance, she is going to turn really yellow. Luckily, now we can adjust the white balance in just one area.

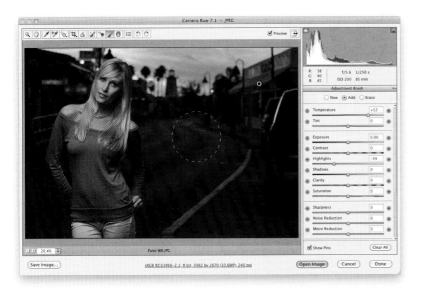

Step Two:

Get the Adjustment Brush **(K)**, click on the + (plus sign) button to the right of Temperature (this resets all the other sliders to 0 and sets the Temperature to +25), and start painting over these bluish background areas (as shown here). Once you've painted over them, you can adjust the Temperature slider (drag to the right to warm up the color and make this area less blue, as I did here, or to the left if the default setting of +25 makes things too warm). This is the beauty of using the Adjustment Brush for this—once you paint over the bluish area, you can "dial in" just the right amount of white balance correction by dragging the slider after you've painted. Now the street looks more neutral, and I also painted over the sky a bit to make it even more "sunsetty" (I know—that's not really a word). I also decreased the Highlights a bit to finish it up.

SCOTT KELBY

Reducing Noise in Just the Shadow Areas

If you shoot at a high ISO (like 800 or above), you're going to see some noise in your image (depending on your camera's make and model, of course), but the area where it's going to show up the most is in the shadow areas (that's where noise tends to be its worst, by far). Worse yet, if you have to brighten the shadow areas, then you're really going to see the noise big time. Well, as good as Camera Raw's noise reduction works, like any noise reduction, the trade-off is it makes your photo a bit softer (it kind of blurs the noise away). This technique lets you paint noise reduction just where you need it, so the rest of the image stays sharp.

Step One:

We'll start by brightening up the wall at the end of this hallway. This shot was taken at ISO 800, so when we brighten up that area, it's going to exaggerate any noise in those shadow areas big time, but at least now we can do something about it. Start by getting the Adjustment Brush **(K)**, click on the + (plus sign) button to the right of Shadows (this resets all the other sliders to 0), then drag the Shadows slider to around +88, and paint over that green-ish wall in the back. Even after that, it's still too dark, so try brightening the Highlights by dragging that slider over to +75 and increase the Exposure to +0.45. Lastly, drag the Clarity slider over to +42 (to enhance the texture). It definitely looks better now (well, to me anyway), but if you look at the inset, you now see lots of noise that was once hidden in those shadows.

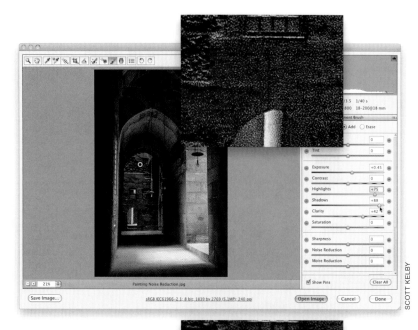

Step Two:

Now, zoom in to 100%, so you can really see the noise in these shadow areas (and drag the Noise Reduction slider to the right as you keep an eye on the amount of noise in your image. Keep dragging until you find that sweet spot, where the noise has been reduced but these shadow areas haven't gotten too blurry (remember, it's noise reduction, not noise removal). This noise reduction only affects that wall area where you painted, and the rest of the image keeps its original sharpness.

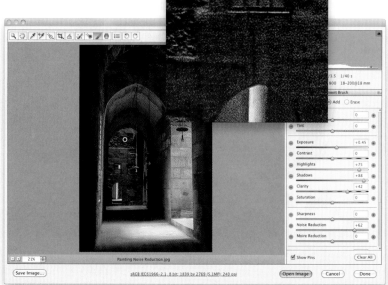

SCOTT KELBY

Let's say you feel like a particular part of your photo needs more Clarity, so you've set the Clarity slider to 100 and painted over that part of your image. You look at that area and think, "Even though I painted with the slider at 100%, I still need more!" (Basically, you need your amp to go to 11. :) Here's what to do (it's a trick I picked up from my buddy, Matt Kloskowski, which he calls "double stacking" and it really works great!):

How to Get More Than 100% Out of Any Adjustment Brush Effect

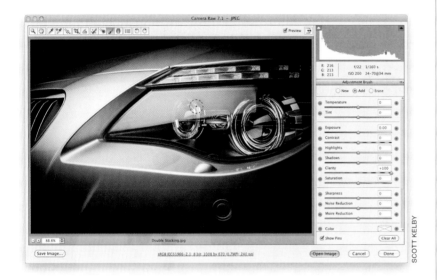

SCOTT KELBY

Step One:

Here's the image we want to work on, and our goal is to bring out extra detail in the headlamps of the car. So, go ahead and get the Adjustment Brush **(K)**, click on the + (plus sign) button to the right of the Clarity slider (to reset all the other sliders to 0), and then drag just that Clarity slider way over to +100. Next, fully paint over just the two circular headlamps. Now, if you think they still need more detail to really make them "pop," but you've already painted with your Clarity maxed out at +100, what do you do? You can't drag the slider over to +200 or anything like that, right? Well, not without a workaround anyway.

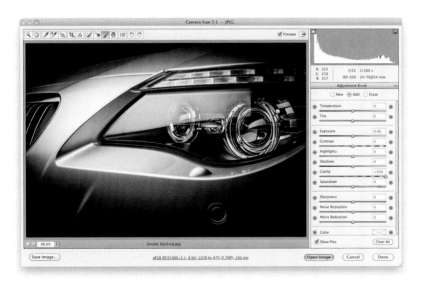

Step Two:

Click the New radio button at top of the Adjustment Brush panel, and you'll notice that your Clarity is still set to +100. Now, all you have to do is paint over that same area again—just start your brush stroke in a different place along the headlamps and now you're stacking a second pass of Clarity on that same area (so you have two pins on this area now: the original pin where you applied 100% Clarity, and now a second pin with another 100% Clarity on top of that). Basically, you've got 200% Clarity applied on those headlamps. Of course, this doesn't just work for Clarity—it works for any of the sliders here in the Adjustment Brush panel.

Photoshop Killer Tips

Painting a Gaussian Blur

Okay, technically it's not a Gaussian blur, but in Camera Raw, you can paint with a blur effect by lowering the Sharpness amount (in the Adjustment Brush panel) below 0 (actually, I'd go all the way to

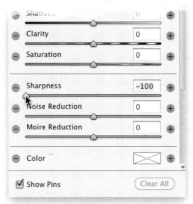

–100 to get more of a Gaussian-type blur look). This is handy if you want to add a blur to a background for the look of a more shallow depth of field, or one of the 100 other reasons you'd want to blur something in your photo.

Why There Are Two Cursors

When you use the Adjustment Brush, you'll see there are two brush cursors displayed at the same time, one inside the other. The smaller one shows the size of the brush you've selected; the larger (dotted-line circle) shows the size of the feathering (softening) you've applied to the brush.

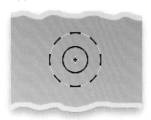

How to Set the Color to None

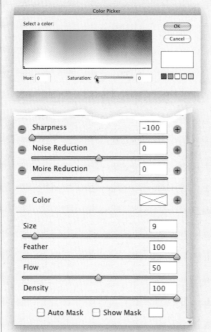

Once you pick a color using the Adjustment Brush's Color Picker, it's not really obvious how to reset the color to None (no color). The trick is to click on the Color swatch (in the middle of the Adjustment Brush options panel) to reopen the Color Picker, then drag the Saturation slider down to 0. Now, you'll see the X over the Color swatch, letting you know it's set to None.

How to See Just One of Your Layers

Just **Option-Click (PC: Alt-click)** on the Eye icon beside the layer you want to see, and all the others are hidden from view. Even though all the other layers are hidden, you can scroll through them by pressing-and-holding the **Option (PC: Alt) key**, and then using the **Left** and **Right Bracket keys** to move up/down the stack of layers. Want to bring them all back? Just Option-click on that Eye icon again.

Painting Straight Lines

If you want to paint a straight line using the Adjustment Brush, you can use the same trick we use with Photoshop's Brush tool: just click once where you want the line to start, press-and-hold the Shift key, then click once where you want the straight line to end, and the Adjustment Brush will draw a perfectly straight line between the two. Really handy when working on hard edges, like the edge of a building where it meets the sky.

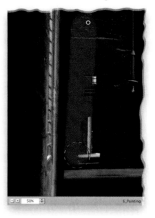

Save a "Jump Back" Spot

If you're familiar with Photoshop's History panel, and how you can make a snapshot at any stage of your editing, so you can jump back to that look with just one click, well…good news: you can do that in Camera Raw, too! You can save a snapshot while you're in any panel by pressing **Command-Shift-S (PC: Ctrl-Shift-S)**. Then you can jump back to how the image looked when you took that snapshot by clicking on it in the Snapshots panel.

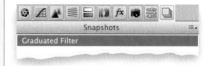

Photoshop Killer Tips

Starting Over from Scratch

If you've added a bunch of adjustments using the Adjustment Brush, and you realize you just want to start over from scratch, you don't have to click on each one of the edit pins and hit the Delete (PC: Backspace) key. Instead, click on the Clear All button in the bottom-right corner of the Adjustment Brush options panel.

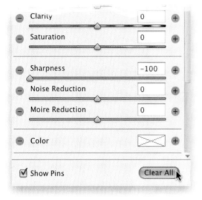

Changing Brush Size with Your Mouse

If you Right-click-and-hold with the Adjustment Brush in Camera Raw, you'll see a little two-headed arrow appear in the middle of your brush. This lets you know you can drag side-to-side to change the size of your Adjustment Brush (drag left to make it smaller and right to make it bigger).

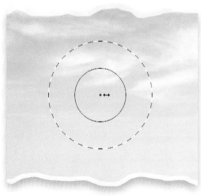

Seeing Paint as You Paint

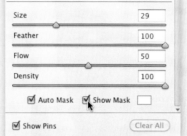

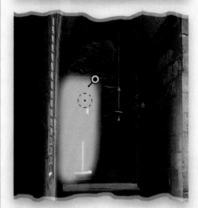

Normally, when you paint with the Adjustment Brush, you see the adjustment (so if you're darkening an area, as you paint, that area gets darker), but if you're doing a subtle adjustment, it might be kind of hard to see what you're actually painting (and if you're spilling over into an area you don't want darkened). If that's the case, try this: turn on the Show Mask checkbox (near the bottom of the Adjustment Brush panel). Now, when you paint, it paints in white (the default mask color, which you can change by clicking on the color swatch to the right of the checkbox), so you can see exactly the area you're affecting. When you're done, just press the **Y key** to turn the Show Mask checkbox off. This one's worth a try.

Add Your Own Color Swatches

When you click on the Color swatch in the Adjustment Brush panel, you see that there are five color swatches in the bottom-right corner of the Color Picker. They're there for you to save your most-used colors, so they're one click away. To add a color to the swatches, first choose the color you want from the color gradient, then press-and-hold the Option (PC: Alt) key and when you move your cursor over any of those five color swatches, it will change into a paint bucket. Click that little bucket on any one of the swatches, and it changes the swatch to your currently selected color.

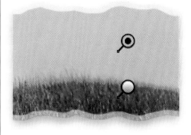

Hiding the Edit Pins

To temporarily hide the edit pins that appear when you use the Adjustment Brush, just press the **V key** on your keyboard (it toggles the pins' visibility on/off).

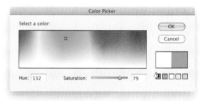

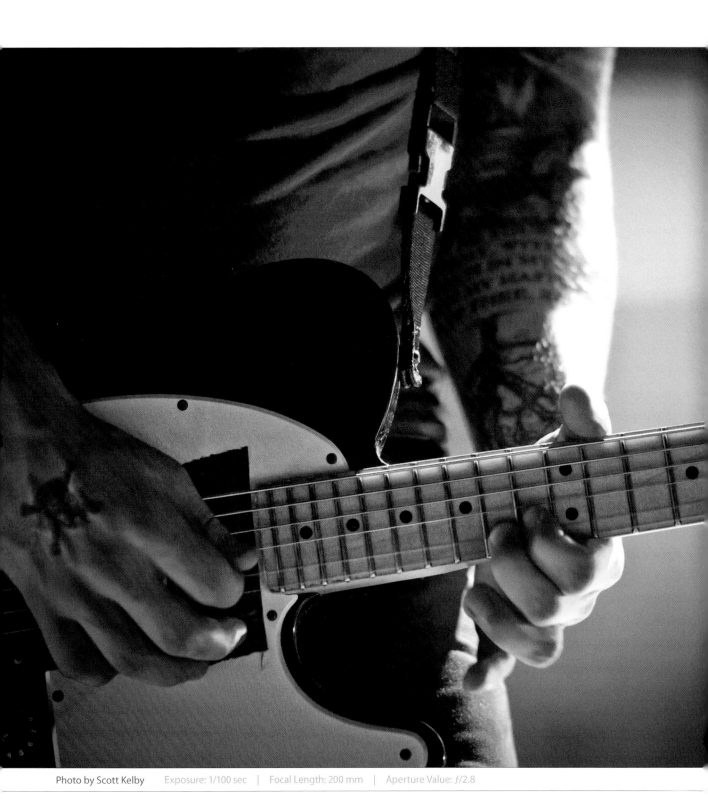

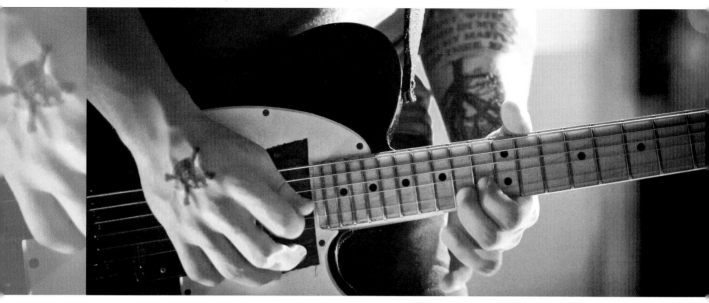

Scream of the Crop
how to resize and crop photos

I love the title of this chapter—it's the name of an album from the band Soulfarm (tell me that Soulfarm wouldn't make a great name for a horror movie!). Anyway, I also found a band named Cash Crop, which would make a great title, too, but when I looked at their album, every song was marked with the Explicit warning. I listened to a 90-second preview of the first track (which was featured in the original motion picture soundtrack for the movie *Sorority Row*), and I immediately knew what kind of music they did. Naughty, naughty music. Anyway, while I was listening, and wincing from time to time as F-bombs exploded all around me, I realized that someone at the iTunes Store must have the full-time job of listening to each song and choosing the 90-second preview. I imagine, at this point, that person has to be 100% completely numb to hearing things like the F-bomb, the S-missile, and the B-grenade (which means

they could totally do a stint as Joe Pesci's nanny). But, I digress. The "Scream of the Crop" title (which would make a great title for a movie about evil corn) is almost ideal for this chapter, except for the fact that this chapter also includes resizing. So, I thought, what the heck, and searched for "resize" and found a song called "Undo Resize" by electronic ambient artist DJ Yanatz Ft. The Designers, and it literally is an 8:31 long background music track with two European-sounding women whispering the names of menu commands from Adobe products. Stuff like "Select All," "Fill," "Distort," "Snap to Grid," and so on. I am not making this up (I listened to the free 90-second preview). It was only 99¢, which was a bargain for 8+ minutes of menu commands set to music. Normally, this many minutes of menu commands set to music would be more like, I dunno, $1.29 or so.

Basic Cropping for Photos

Adobe completely overhauled cropping in Photoshop CS6, and it's a big improvement (it was long overdue, since aside from a few minor enhancements, cropping has been essentially unchanged since Photoshop 1.0). Here, we'll cover the basic garden-variety cropping (and the new way of cropping in CS6), but since there are many different ways to crop a photo in Photoshop (and different reasons why you'd use one over another), we'll cover them all. If you're a Lightroom user, you'll be right at home with this new cropping, because it works more like Lightroom's cropping.

Step One:

Press the letter **C** to get the Crop tool and you instantly see the first improvement over previous versions of the tool: you don't have to drag the cropping border out over your photo—it's automatically added around your image for you (yay!). Now, just grab one of the corner or side handles and start dragging inward to start cropping (as seen here) and it crops in toward the center of the image (the area to be cropped away will appear dimmed). If you want to keep the image proportions the same in your crop (I usually do), just press-and-hold the Shift key while you drag any of the cropping handles. Also, you can reposition your image within the border by clicking-and-dragging on it.

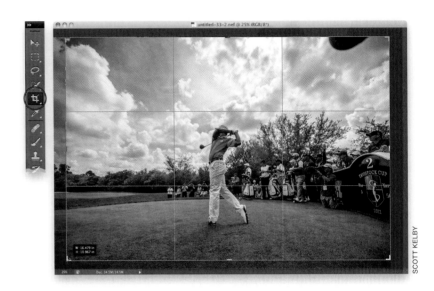

SCOTT KELBY

Step Two:

The Rule of Thirds overlay grid that you see in Step One doesn't appear over your photo until you actually drag one of the cropping handles. If you see a different overlay, just click on the View pop-up menu in the Options Bar and you'll see a list of the different overlays you can choose (if you're not sure which one you want, you can cycle through them by pressing the letter **O**). There are also three overlay options in the menu: Always Show Overlay (once you start cropping, it's visible even when you're not cropping), Never Show Overlay, and Auto Show Overlay (my favorite—it only appears when you're actually cropping).

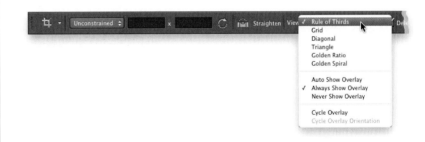

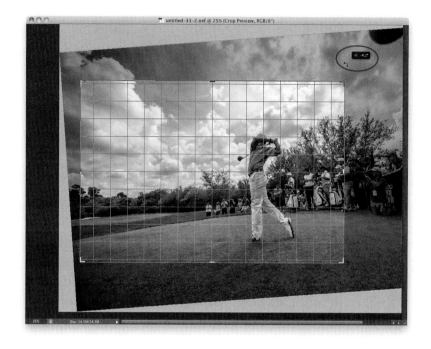

Step Three:

While you have the cropping border in place, if you need to rotate your photo, just move your cursor anywhere outside the border. When you do this, the cursor will change into a double-headed arrow. Just click, hold, and drag up (or down) and the cropping border will rotate in the direction you choose. One big thing that has changed in how this works in Photoshop CS6 is that now the image actually rotates (rather than the border), which makes the process much easier (especially when you're trying to straighten a horizon line or a building). A little pop-up now appears, too, with the angle of rotation (it's shown circled here in red).

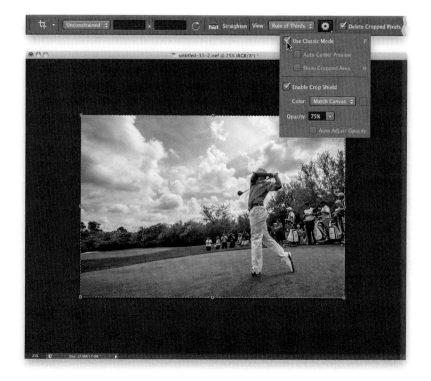

Step Four:

If you decide you want to return to the old way of rotating your crop (where the border rotates, rather than your image), click on the Set Additional Crop Options icon (it looks like a gear) in the Options Bar and turn on the Use Classic Mode checkbox (also known as "old school" or "ancient cropping" by today's hipster croppers), and then you're back to the old method. However, I really recommend giving this new way a try—it takes a little getting used to, but once you do, you'll really find it useful. While we're in this options menu, when you're not in Classic mode, you have two options available here: (1) to turn off having your crop centered automatically (it's on by default), and we'll talk about the next one on the next page (it's a little more involved).

(Continued)

Step Five:

That other option (2) is more powerful than it sounds, because it pretty much brings one of the most popular cropping features of Lightroom over here to Photoshop CS6. In Lightroom, it's called Lights Out cropping, and when you use this, it blacks out everything surrounding your crop area, so as you drag a cropping handle, you see exactly what the final image will look like without any distractions. If you click on the Set Additional Crop Options icon, you can toggle this on/off with the Show Cropped Area checkbox, but honestly it's quicker just to press the letter **H** on your keyboard (it's easy to remember—H for hide the distracting stuff; click on a cropping handle first or it'll switch to the Hand tool). Want to take it up a notch? Once you've hidden the extra stuff, hit the Tab key on your keyboard and everything else (the Toolbox, panels, Options Bar, etc.) hides temporarily, too. The other options here only kick in if you do have that dimmed cropped away area visible (called the Crop Shield), and you can make it lighter or darker by changing the Opacity amount, or you can turn it off altogether by turning off the Enable Crop Shield checkbox.

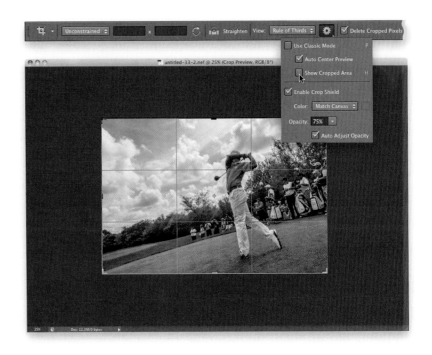

Step Six:

If you want to save some time, there's a list of preset standard cropping sizes in the pop-up menu at the left end of the Options Bar (seen here). Just choose the crop ratio you'd like (here, I chose a square 1x1 ratio), and your crop border automatically resizes to that size or ratio (as shown here).

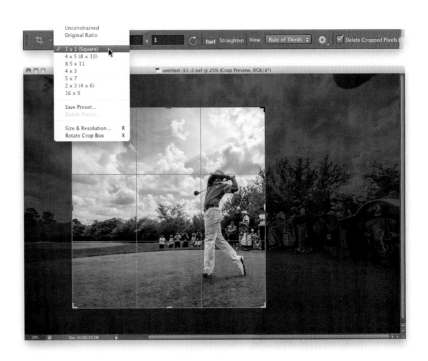

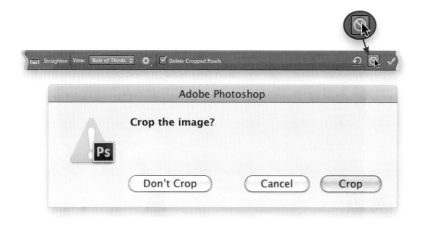

Step Seven:

If you decide at some point you don't want to crop the image at all, you can either press the **Esc key** on your keyboard, click on the "No!" symbol in the Options Bar (as shown here), or just click on a different tool in the Toolbox, which will bring up a dialog asking if you want to crop the image or not.

TIP: Flipping Your Crop Horizontal/Vertical

Want to flip the cropping border after you've clicked on it, so you can crop your wide photos with a tall crop that maintains the same aspect ratio (or vice versa)? You can click the little circular arrow button in the middle of the Options Bar, but there's an even faster way—just press the letter **X** on your keyboard.

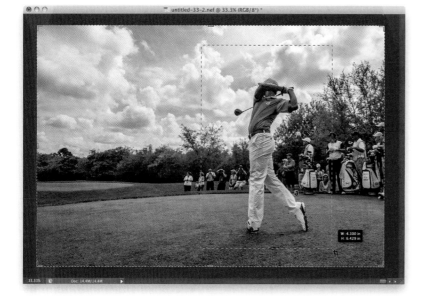

Step Eight:

So far, we've looked at the standard way of cropping in CS6—click on the tool and then drag the handles where you want them—but you can also use the freestyle way of cropping (like in previous versions of Photoshop) by taking the Crop tool itself and just clicking-and-dragging over the area you want to crop (as shown here). Don't let it freak you out that there's a cropping border already in place—just click-and-drag it out, and when you release the mouse button, it will display your new cropping border. Of course, now you can tweak the handles just like before. If you go back and look at the original image in Step One, you'll see how much we've already cropped away (it's quite a bit).

(Continued)

Step Nine:

This is something you could actually do in previous versions of Photoshop, but it's just easier and more intuitive in CS6, and that is to add canvas area around your image using the Crop tool. One quick thing to check first: if you want a white background for your canvas area (and my guess is, most times you will), then before you even click on the Crop tool, press the letter **D** on your keyboard to set your Background color to white. Then, once you click on the Crop tool, make sure **Unconstrained** is selected in the pop-up menu at the left end of the Options Bar, otherwise the cropping border will be constrained to the aspect ratio of your image (in this case, we want the bottom section to be deeper than the sides and top). Now, grab a cropping handle and drag the border outward to add canvas area. Here, I clicked on the top-left cropping handle and dragged up and to the left (at a 45° angle), and it expanded the top and left side areas around my image.

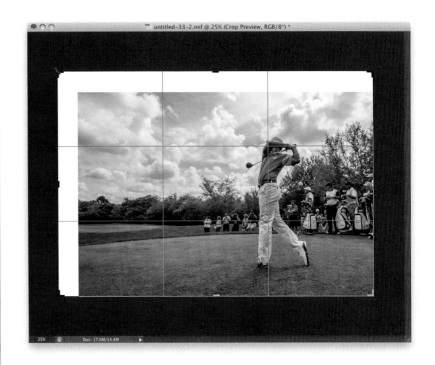

Step 10:

Here, I dragged the right side out and then dragged the bottom-center handle down quite a bit to add a fine art poster mat look around my image.

TIP: Skip Holding the Shift Key

You already know that to keep your cropping proportional, you press-and-hold the Shift key, right? Here's how to skip having to hold that key ever again, yet still keep it proportional: close any open images, grab the Crop tool, and then choose **Original Ratio** from the pop-up menu at the left end of the Options Bar. Now, it's your default setting. How cool is that?

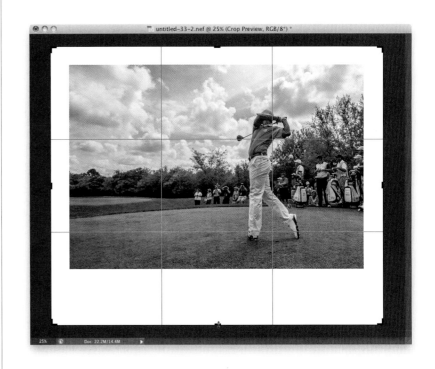

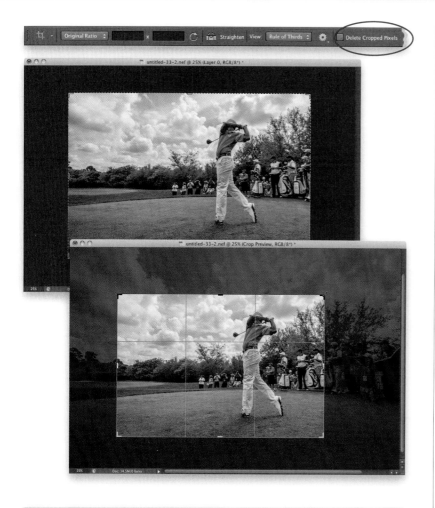

Step 11:

Before you actually commit to cropping your image, you have a decision to make. Luckily, it's probably a decision you'll make once, based on how you like to do things, so you won't have to make it every time. You get to decide if the part of your image that gets cropped away from view is: (a) gone forever, or (b) just hidden from view and, if necessary, can be brought back. You choose this by turning on/off the Delete Cropped Pixels checkbox up in the Options Bar (shown circled here in red). With it turned on, when you crop, the stuff outside the border is cropped away (and you get a smaller file size). If you turn if off, it keeps those areas in the file, even though you can't see them (well, not until you click on the Crop tool again and click-and-drag the cropping border back out). If you need the photo a specific size, but aren't happy with the way your first crop looks, you can move the image around with the Move tool (V), or click on the cropping border while the Crop tool is active, then click on the image and move it.

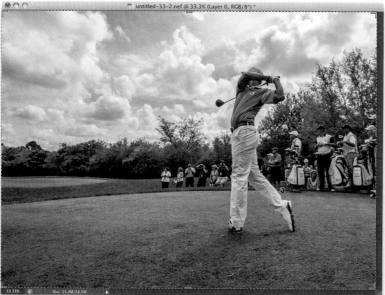

Step 12:

Once you have the cropping border right where you want it, press the **Return (PC: Enter) key** to crop your image. The final cropped image is shown here, where we cropped off some of the crowd on the right side, and the lens peeking into the frame from above my shooting position (down on one knee), and some of the excess grass on the tee box.

Cropping to a Specific Size

If you're using one of the standard size or cropping ratio presets that appear in the Crop tool's pop-up menu, then you're set. However, there are only a few common sizes in that pop-up menu, so you're going to need to know (a) how to create custom sizes, and (b) how to save that custom size to the pop-up menu, so you don't have to build it from scratch again next time. Plus, I'm going to show you another way to crop an image that, well, I'm not proud of, but I know a lot of photographers that do it this way. (Now, I'm not saying that I've done it that way, but…well…I've done it that way. More times than I care to admit.)

Step One:

Here's the image I want to print as a wide 20x16" print (a very common size today, even though it's based on the size of traditional film, not digital images, so you have to crop just to make it fit). Start by clicking on the Crop tool **(C)** in the Toolbox, then from the pop-up menu at the left end of the Options Bar, choose **Size & Resolution** (as shown here).

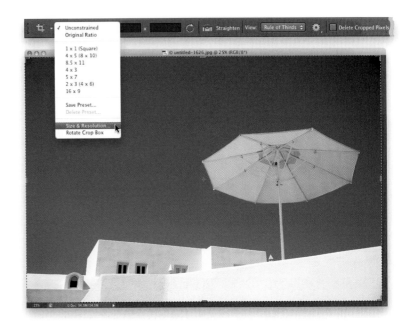

Step Two:

This brings up the Crop Image Size & Resolution dialog (shown here). Type in the custom size you want (in this case, 20x16" at a resolution of 240 ppi, which is pretty ideal for most color inkjet printing). If you think you'll be using this size again (and chances are, you will), turn on the Save as Crop Preset checkbox (as shown here), and it adds this new size to that pop-up menu, so you don't have to recreate it every time. When you click OK, it resizes the cropping border so it's 20" wide by 16" deep. You can click-and-drag the border left/right to get the part of the photo you want to appear inside the cropping border. Now press the **Return (PC: Enter) key** and it crops your image to that size.

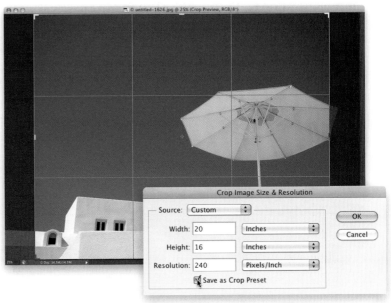

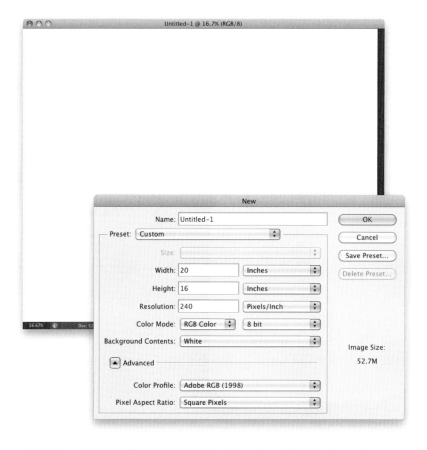

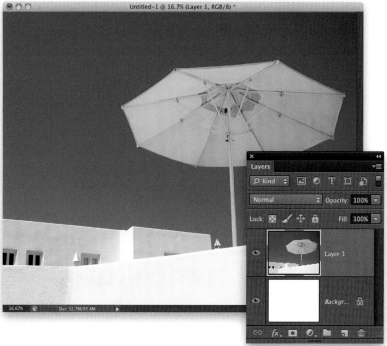

Step Three:

Okay, here's that (ahem) other method: Go under the File menu, under New, and choose **Document**. When the New dialog appears, enter 20 inches by 16 inches, and enter 240 for Resolution, then click OK to create a new blank document in the exact size and resolution you need (as seen here).

TIP: Cropping to Another Photo's Size

If you already have a photo that is the exact size and resolution that you'd like to apply to other images, you can use its settings as the crop dimensions. First, open the photo you'd like to resize, and then open your ideal-size-and-resolution photo. Get the Crop tool, and then from the pop-up menu at the left end of the Options Bar, choose **Size & Resolution**. In the dialog that appears, choose **Front Image** from the Source pop-up menu, and click OK. Photoshop will automatically input that photo's dimensions into the Crop tool's Width and Height fields. All you have to do is crop the other image, and it will share the exact same specs as your ideal-size photo.

Step Four:

Now, get the Move tool **(V)**, click on the image you want cropped to that size, and drag it onto that new blank document. While you still have the Move tool, click-and-drag the image around within the window so it's cropped the way you want it, then press **Command-E (PC: Ctrl-E)** to merge this layer with the Background layer, and you're set. As you can see, they both kind of do the exact same thing, so which one's right? The one you like best.

Creating Your Own Custom Crop Tools

Although it's more of an advanced technique, creating your own custom tools isn't complicated. In fact, once you set them up, they will save you time and money. We're going to create what are called "tool presets." These tool presets are a series of tools (in this case, Crop tools) with all our option settings already in place so, we can create a 5x7", 6x4", or whatever size Crop tool we want. Then, when we want to crop to 5x7", all we have to do is grab the 5x7" Crop tool preset. Here's how:

Step One:
Press the letter **C** to switch to the Crop tool, and then go under the Window menu and choose **Tool Presets** to bring up the Tool Presets panel. You'll find that five Crop tool presets are already there. (Make sure that the Current Tool Only checkbox is turned on at the bottom of the panel, so you'll see only the Crop tool's presets, and not the presets for every tool.)

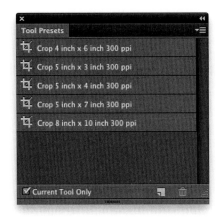

Step Two:
Go up to the Options Bar and enter the dimensions for the first tool you want to create (in this example, we'll create a Crop tool that crops to a wallet-size image). In the Width field, enter 2 in, then press the **Tab key** to jump to the Height field, enter 2.5 in, and press Return (PC: Enter). *Note:* If you want to include the resolution in your tool preset, go to the pop-up menu at the left end of the Options Bar, and choose **Size & Resolution**. Enter your Height, Width, and Resolution in the dialog that appears, and click OK.

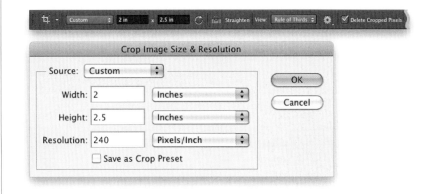

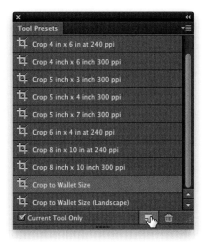

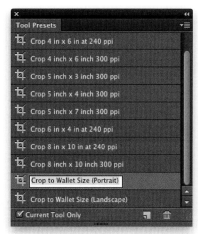

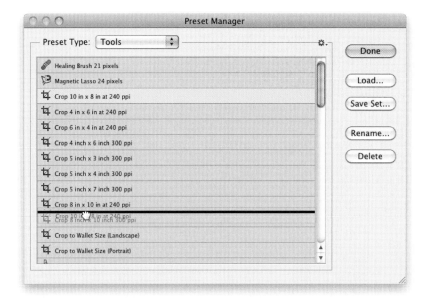

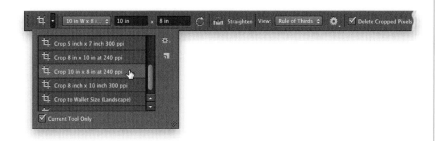

Step Three:

In the Tool Presets panel, click on the Create New Tool Preset icon at the bottom of the panel (to the left of the Trash icon). This brings up the New Tool Preset dialog, in which you can name your new preset. Name it, click OK, and the new tool is added to the Tool Presets panel. Continue this process of typing in new dimensions in the Crop tool's Options Bar and clicking on the Create New Tool Preset icon until you've created custom Crop tools for the sizes you use most. Make sure the name is descriptive (for example, add "Portrait" or "Landscape"). If you need to change the name of a preset, just double-click directly on its name in the panel, and then type in a new name.

Step Four:

Chances are your custom Crop tool presets won't be in the order you want them, so go under the Edit menu, under Preset, and choose **Preset Manager**. In the resulting dialog, choose **Tools** from the Preset Type pop-up menu, and scroll down until you see the Crop tools you created. Now just click-and-drag them to wherever you want them to appear in the list, and then click Done.

Step Five:

Now you can close the Tool Presets panel because there's an easier way to access your presets: With the Crop tool selected, just click on the Crop icon on the left end of the Options Bar. A tool preset picker will appear. Click on a preset, and your cropping border will be fixed to the exact dimensions you chose for that tool.

Custom Sizes for Photographers

Photoshop's dialog for creating new documents has a pop-up menu with a list of preset sizes. You're probably thinking, "Hey, there's a 4x6", 5x7", and 8x10"— I'm set." The problem is there's no way to switch the resolution of these presets (so the Portrait, 4x6 will always be a 300 ppi document). That's why creating your own custom new document sizes is so important. Here's how:

Step One:

Go under the File menu and choose **New**. When the New dialog appears, click on the Preset pop-up menu to reveal the list of preset types, and choose **Photo**. Then click on the Size pop-up menu to see the preset sizes, which include 2x3", 4x6", 5x7", and 8x10" in both portrait and landscape orientation. The only problem with these is that their resolution is set to 300 ppi by default. So, if you want a different size preset at less than 300 ppi, you'll need to create and save your own.

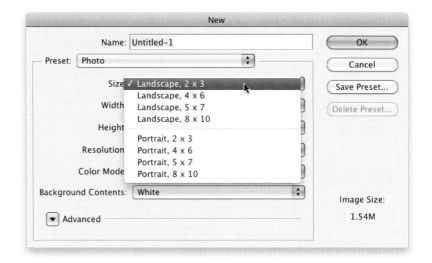

Step Two:

For example, let's say that you want a 5x7" set to landscape (that's 7" wide by 5" tall). First, choose Photo from the Preset pop-up menu, then choose Landscape, 5x7 from the Size pop-up menu. Choose your desired Color Mode (below Resolution) and Color Profile (under Advanced), and then enter a Resolution (I entered 212 ppi, which is enough for me to have my image printed on a high-end printing press). Once your settings are in place, click on the Save Preset button.

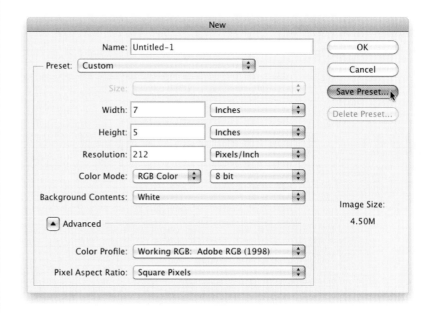

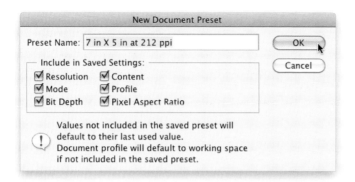

Step Three:

This brings up the New Document Preset dialog. In the Preset Name field, enter your new resolution at the end of the size. You can turn on/off the checkboxes for which parameters you want saved, but I use the default setting to include everything (better safe than sorry, I guess).

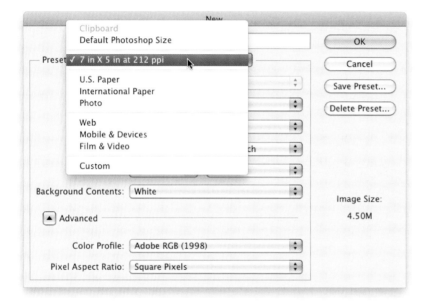

Step Four:

Click OK and your new custom preset will appear in the New dialog's Preset pop-up menu. You only have to go through this once. Photoshop will remember your custom settings, and they will appear in this Preset pop-up menu from now on.

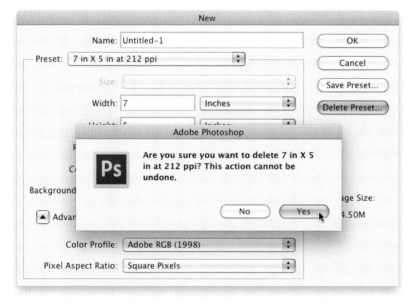

Step Five:

If you decide you want to delete a preset, it's simple—just open the New dialog, choose the preset you want to delete from the Preset pop-up menu, and then click the Delete Preset button. A warning dialog will appear asking you to confirm the delete. Click Yes, and it's gone!

Resizing Digital Camera Photos

If you're used to resizing scans, you'll find that resizing images from digital cameras is a bit different, primarily because scanners create high-res scans (usually 300 ppi or more), but the default settings for many digital cameras produce an image that is large in physical dimensions, but lower in pixels-per-inch (usually 72 ppi). The trick is to decrease the physical size of your digital camera image (and increase its resolution) without losing any of its quality. Here's the trick:

Step One:
Open the digital camera image that you want to resize. Press **Command-R (PC: Ctrl-R)** to make Photoshop's rulers visible. As you can see from the rulers, the photo is about 59" wide by 39" high.

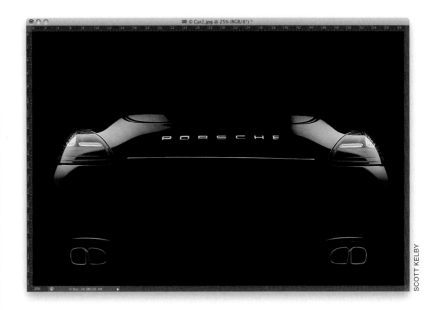

SCOTT KELBY

Step Two:
Go under the Image menu and choose **Image Size** (or press **Command-Option-I [PC: Ctrl-Alt-I]**) to bring up the Image Size dialog. Under the Document Size section, the Resolution setting is 72 ppi. A resolution of 72 ppi is considered "low resolution" and is ideal for photos that will only be viewed onscreen (such as web graphics, slide shows, and so on), but it's too low to get high-quality results from a color inkjet printer, color laser printer, or for use on a printing press.

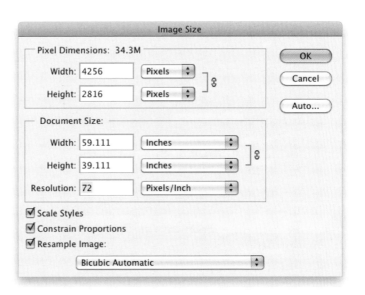

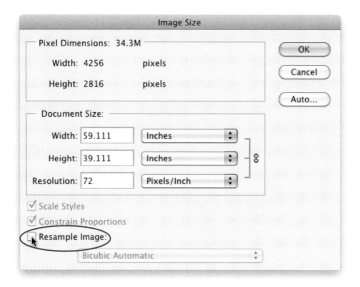

Step Three:

If we plan to output this photo to any printing device, it's pretty clear that we'll need to increase the resolution to get good results. I wish we could just type in the resolution we'd like it to be in the Resolution field (such as 200 or 240 ppi), but unfortunately this "resampling" makes our low-res photo appear soft (blurry) and pixelated. That's why we need to turn off the Resample Image checkbox (it's on by default). That way, when we type in a Resolution setting that we need, Photoshop automatically adjusts the Width and Height of the image down in the exact same proportion. As your Width and Height come down (with Resample Image turned off), your Resolution goes up. Best of all, there's absolutely no loss of quality. Pretty cool!

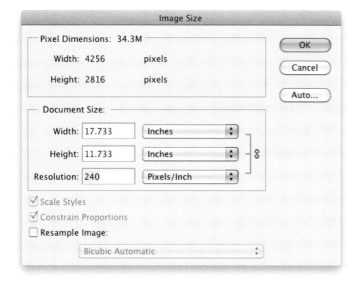

Step Four:

Here I've turned off Resample Image and I entered 240 in the Resolution field for output to a color inkjet printer. (I know, you probably think you need a lot more resolution, but you don't. In fact, I never print with a resolution higher than 240 ppi.) This resized my image to nearly 12x18" so it's just about perfect for printing to my Epson Stylus Photo R2880 printer, which makes up to 13x19"-sized prints—perfect!

(Continued)

Step Five:

Here, I've lowered the Resolution setting to 180 ppi. (Again, you don't need nearly as much resolution as you'd think, but 180 ppi is pretty much about as low as you should go when printing to a color inkjet printer.) As you can see, the Width of my image is now almost 24" and the Height is now almost 16". Best of all, we did it without damaging a single pixel, because we were able to turn off Resample Image, which normally, with things like scans, we couldn't do.

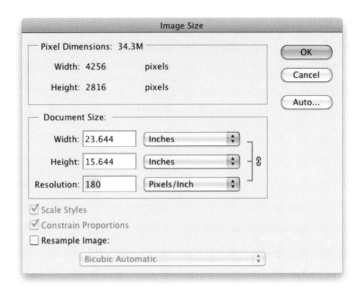

Step Six:

When you click OK, you won't see the image window change at all—it will appear at the exact same size onscreen—but look at the rulers. You can see that it's now almost 16" high by almost 24" wide. Resizing using this technique does three big things: (1) it gets your physical dimensions down to size (the photo now fits easily on a 16x24" sheet); (2) it increases the resolution enough so you can output this image on a color inkjet printer; and (3) you haven't softened, blurred, or pixelated the image in any way—the quality remains the same—all because you turned off Resample Image. *Note:* Do not turn off Resample Image for images that you scan on a scanner—they start as high-res images in the first place. Turning Resample Image off like this is only for low-res photos taken with a digital camera.

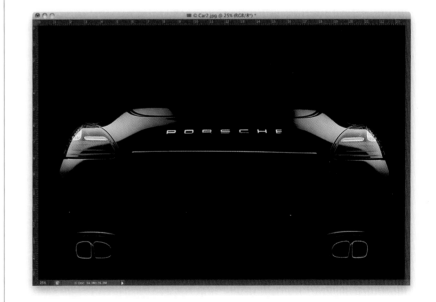

If you have a bunch of images that you need resized, or converted from TIFFs to JPEGs (or from PSDs to JPEGs, for that matter), then you will love the built-in Image Processor. It's kind of hidden in a place you might not expect it (under the Scripts menu), but don't let that throw you—this is a really handy, and really easy-to-use, totally automated tool that can save you tons of time.

Automated Saving and Resizing

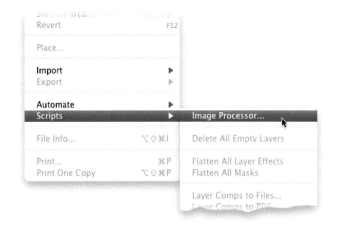

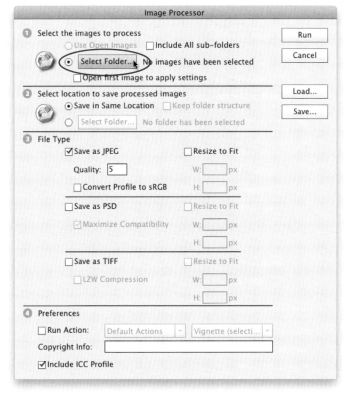

Step One:
Go under the File menu, under Scripts, and choose **Image Processor**. By the way, if you're working in Adobe Bridge (rather than Photoshop), you can Command-click (PC: Ctrl-click) on all the photos you want to apply the Image Processor to, then go under the Tools menu, under Photoshop, and choose Image Processor. That way, when the Image Processor opens, it already has those photos pegged for processing. Sweet!

Step Two:
When the Image Processor dialog opens, the first thing you have to do is choose the folder of photos you want it to "do its thing" to by clicking on the Select Folder button, then navigating to the folder you want and clicking Choose (PC: OK). If you already have some photos open in Photoshop, you can click on the Use Open Images radio button (or if you chose Image Processor from Bridge, the Select Folder button won't be there at all—instead it will list how many photos you have selected in Bridge). Then, in the second section, decide whether you want the new copies to be saved in the same folder or copied into a different folder. No big whoop (that's a technical term).

(Continued)

Step Three:

The third section is where the fun begins. This is where you decide how many copies of your original you're going to wind up with, and in what format. If you turn on the checkboxes for Save as JPEG, Save as PSD, and Save as TIFF, you're going to create three new copies of each photo. If you turn on the Resize to Fit checkboxes (and enter a size in the Width and Height fields), your copies will be resized, too (in the example shown here, I chose a small JPEG of each file, then a larger TIFF, so in my folder I'd find one small JPEG and one larger TIFF for every file in my original folder).

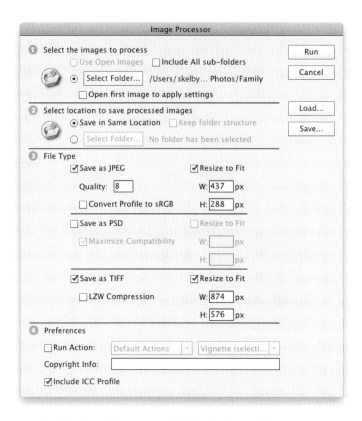

Step Four:

In the fourth section, if you've created an action that you want applied to your copies, you can also have that happen automatically. Just turn on the Run Action checkbox, then from the pop-up menus, choose which action you want to run. If you want to automatically embed your copyright info into these copies, type your info in the Copyright Info field. Lastly, there's a checkbox that lets you decide whether to include an ICC profile in each image or not (of course, I'm going to try to convince you to include the profile, because I included how to set up color management in Photoshop in Chapter 11). Click the Run button, sit back, and let it "do its thing," and before you know it, you'll have nice, clean copies aplenty.

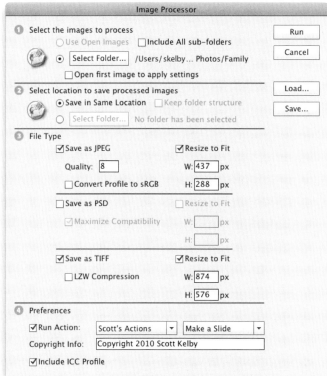

So, since you saw earlier how much resolution you need to have to create a decent-sized print, how do photographers get those huge poster-sized prints without having super-high-megapixel cameras? It's easy—they upsize the images in Photoshop, and the good news is that unless you need to resize your image by more than 300%, you can do this all right in Photoshop without having to buy a separate resizing plug-in (but if you need more than a 300% size increase, that's where those plug-ins, like OnOne Software's Perfect Resize, really pay off).

Resizing for Poster-Sized Prints

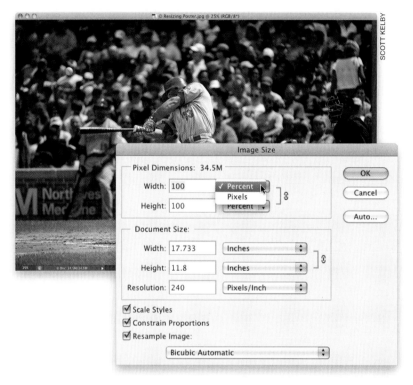

SCOTT KELBY

Step One:
Open the photo you want to resize, then go under the Image menu and choose **Image Size**. When the Image Size dialog appears, in the Pixel Dimensions section at the top, to the right of the Width field, you'll see a pop-up menu where Pixels is chosen (if this section isn't active, turn on the Resample Image checkbox at the bottom). Click on that menu and choose **Percent** (as shown here). Both the Width and Height will change to Percent, because they're linked together by default.

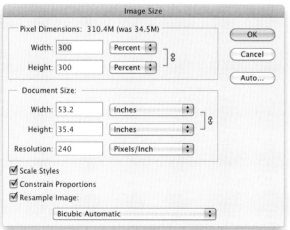

Step Two:
Now, type in either 200% or 300% (although there is some debate about this, it seems to work best if you move up/down in 100% increments) in the Width field (again, since they're linked, the Height field will automatically change to the same number).

(Continued)

Step Three:

At the bottom of the dialog is a pop-up menu that decides which algorithm is used to upsize your photo. The default is Bicubic Automatic, and I use that for most everyday resizing stuff, but when it comes to jumping in big increments, like 200% or 300%, I switch to **Bicubic Smoother** (which Adobe says is "best for enlargement"), as shown here.

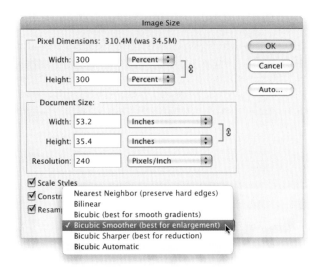

Step Four:

My buddy (and Epson printing expert) Vincent Versace breaks this rule. According to Vincent's research, the key to his resizing technique is to not use the sampling method Adobe recommends (Bicubic Smoother), but instead to choose Bicubic Sharper, which he feels provides better results. So, which one is the right one for you? Try both on the same image (that's right—just do a test print), and see if you can see a visible difference. Here's the final image resized to around 53x35" (you can see the size in the rulers by pressing **Command-R [PC: Ctrl-R]**).

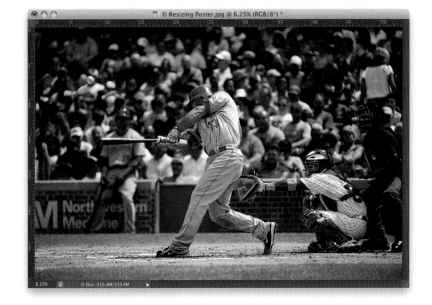

Straightening Crooked Photos

Adobe has been tweaking the way we straighten images for the past few versions of Photoshop, and in Photoshop CS6, it's now the fastest and easiest way yet, and it's built right into the Crop tool's options. (Back in CS5, you had to use the Ruler tool in the Toolbox for straightening, which wasn't exactly obvious—they needed a tool named Straighten, so people could actually find it. Thankfully, now there is just that.)

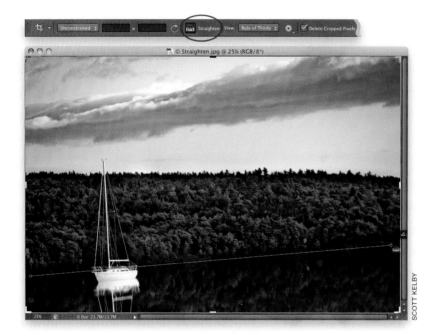

SCOTT KELBY

Step One:

Open the photo that needs straightening, click on the Crop tool **(C)** in the Toolbox, and then click on the Straighten tool up in the Options Bar. Now, find something in your photo that's supposed to be straight or relatively straight (the water's edge, in this example). Click-and-drag the Straighten tool horizontally along this straight edge in your photo, starting from the left and extending to the right (as shown here).

(Continued)

Step Two:

When you release the mouse button, your photo rotates the exact amount to perfectly straighten the photo. One nice feature here is that it automatically resizes the cropping border, so that when you lock in your crop, you don't have any gray gaps in the corners (if you ignore the cropping border, and look at the whole image now, see those triangular gray areas? Those would be white if Photoshop didn't crop in like this). Now, just press the **Return (PC: Enter) key** to lock in your straightening, and it straightens and crops the image down to just what you see inside the cropping border (the final straightened image is shown here below).

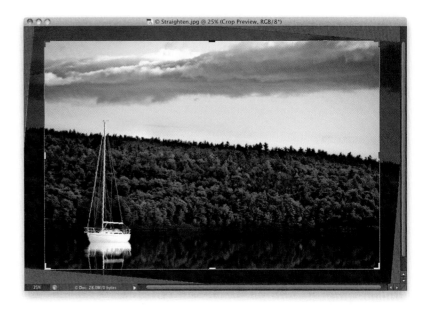

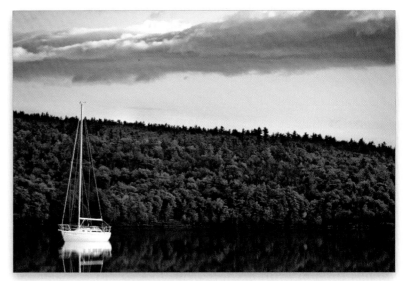

There's a different set of rules we use for maintaining as much quality as possible when making an image smaller, and there are a couple of different ways to do just that (we'll cover the two main ones here). Luckily, maintaining image quality is much easier when sizing down than when scaling up (in fact, photos often look dramatically better—and sharper—when scaled down, especially if you follow these guidelines).

Making Your Photos Smaller (Downsizing)

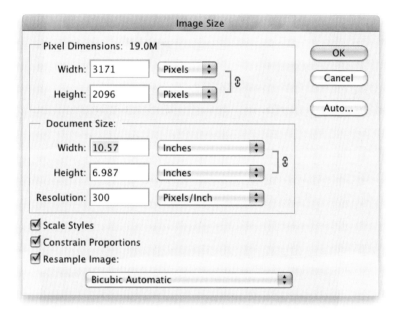

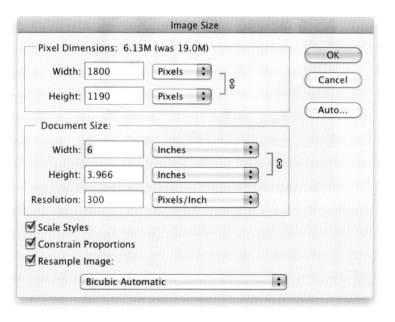

Downsizing photos where the resolution is already 300 ppi: Although earlier we discussed how to change image size if your digital camera gives you 72-ppi images with large physical dimensions (like 24x42" deep), what do you do if your camera gives you 300-ppi images at smaller physical dimensions (like a 10x6" at 300 ppi)? Basically, you turn on Resample Image (in the Image Size dialog under the Image menu), then simply type in the desired size (in this example, we want a 6x4" final image size), and click OK (don't change the Resolution setting, just click OK). The image will be scaled down to size, and the resolution will remain at 300 ppi. *IMPORTANT:* When you scale down using this method, it's likely that the image will soften a little bit, so after scaling, you'll want to apply the Unsharp Mask filter to bring back any sharpness lost in the resizing (go to Chapter 10 to see what settings to use).

(Continued)

Making one photo smaller without shrinking the whole document:

If you're working with more than one image in the same document, you'll resize a bit differently. To scale down a photo on a layer (like this photo of a Venice canal, which is on its own layer), first click on that photo's layer in the Layers panel, then press **Command-T (PC: Ctrl-T)** to bring up Free Transform (it puts little handles around your image on that layer, kind of like what the Crop tool does). Press-and-hold the Shift key (to keep the photo proportional), grab a corner handle, and drag inward (here, I've grabbed the top-right corner handle and dragged inward to shrink the image). When the size looks good, press **Return (PC: Enter)**. If the image looks softer after resizing it, apply the Unsharp Mask filter (see Chapter 10 for settings) to bring that sharpness back.

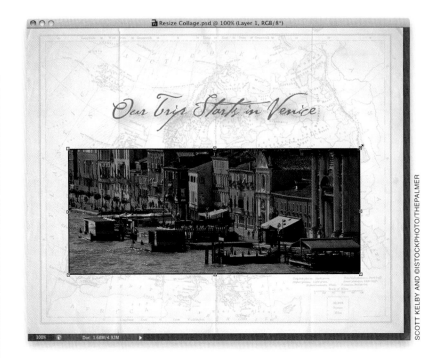

TIP: Reaching the Free Transform Handles

If you drag an image from one open document to another (like I did here, where I dragged the original Venice canal photo over onto the old world map document), there's a pretty good chance you'll have to resize the dragged image, so it fits within your other image. And, if the image is larger (as in this case), when you bring up Free Transform, you won't be able to reach the resizing handles (they'll extend right off the edges of the document). Luckily, there's a trick to reaching those handles: just press **Command-0 (PC: Ctrl-0)**, and your window will automatically resize so you can reach all the handles—no matter how far outside your image area they once were. Two things: (1) This only works once you have Free Transform active, and (2) it's Command-0—that's the number zero, not the letter O.

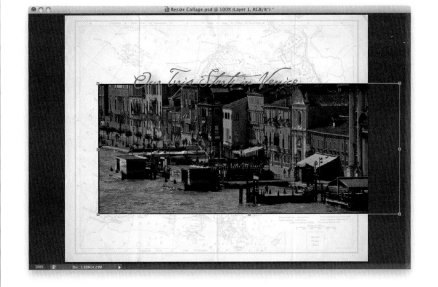

SCOTT KELBY AND ©ISTOCKPHOTO/THEPALMER

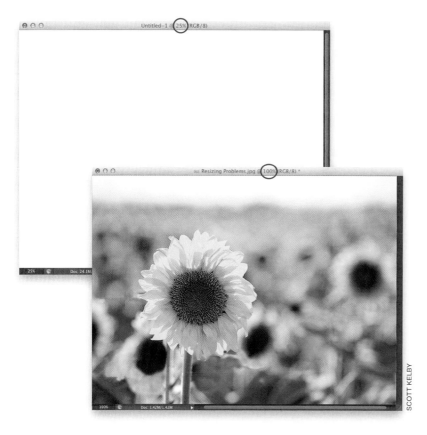

SCOTT KELBY

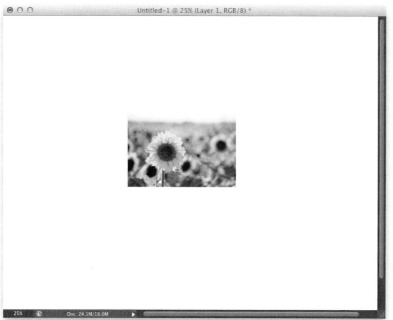

Resizing problems when dragging between documents:

This one gets a lot of people, because at first glance it just doesn't make sense. You have two documents open, and they look approximately the same size (as seen here, at top), but when you drag the sunflower photo onto the blank document, the sunflower photo appears really small (as seen below). Why? Although the documents appear to be the same size, they're not. The sunflower photo is a low-resolution, 72-ppi (pixels per inch) image, but the blank document is a high-resolution, 300-ppi image. The tip-off that you're not really seeing them at the same size is found in each photo's title bar. Here, the sunflower image is displayed at 100%, but the Untitled-2 document is displayed at only 25% (so, it's much larger than it appears). The key is that when you're dragging images between documents, they need to be the same size and resolution.

TIP: Automated Cropping & Straightening

Want to save time the next time you're scanning prints? Try gang scanning (fitting as many photos on your flatbed scanner as you can and scanning them as one big single image), and then you can have Photoshop automatically straighten each individual image and place it into its own separate document. You do this by going under the File menu, under Automate, and choosing **Crop and Straighten Photos**. No dialog will appear. Instead, Photoshop will look for straight edges in your photos, straighten the photos, and copy each into its own separate document.

Resizing Just Parts of Your Image Using "Content-Aware" Scaling

We've all run into situations where our image is a little smaller than the area where we need it to fit. For example, if you resize a digital camera image so it fits within a traditional 8x10" image area, you'll have extra space either above or below your image (or both). That's where Content-Aware Scaling comes in—it lets you resize one part of your image, while keeping the important parts intact (basically, it analyzes the image and stretches, or shrinks, parts of the image it thinks aren't as important). Here's how to use it:

Step One:

Create a new document at 8x10" and 240 ppi. Open a digital camera image, get the Move tool **(V)**, and drag-and-drop it onto the new document, then press **Command-T (PC: Ctrl-T)** to bring up Free Transform. Press-and-hold the Shift key, then grab a corner point and drag inward to scale the image down, so it fits within the 8x10" area (as shown here on top), and press **Return (PC: Enter)**. Now, in the image on top, there's white space above and below the photo. If you want it to fill the 8x10 space, you could use Free Transform to stretch the image to do so, but you'd get a short, squatty version of the jet (seen at bottom). This is where Content-Aware Scale comes in.

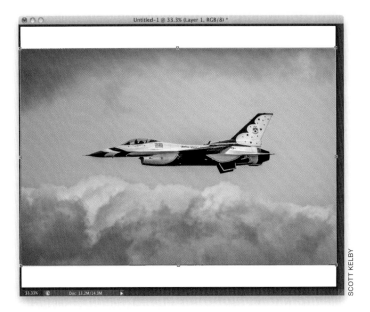

SCOTT KELBY

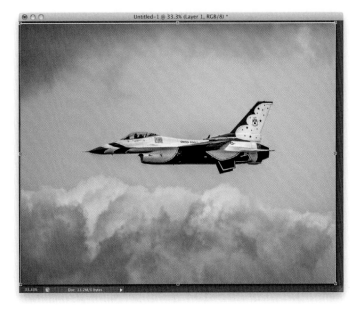

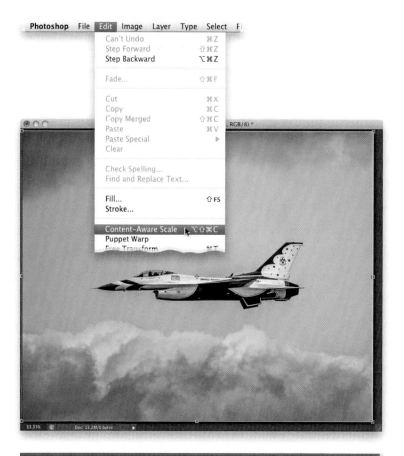

Step Two:

Go under the Edit menu and choose **Content-Aware Scale** (or press **Command-Option-Shift-C [PC: Ctrl-Alt-Shift-C]**). Grab the top handle, drag straight upward, and notice that it stretches the sky upward, but pretty much leaves the jet intact. When you've dragged far enough, press **Return (PC: Enter)** to lock in your change. (*Note:* The button that looks like a person in the Options Bar tells Content-Aware Scale that there are people in the photo, so it tries to avoid stretching anything with a skin tone.)

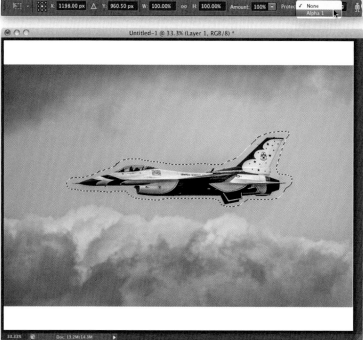

Step Three:

There are two more controls you need to know about: First, if you try Content-Aware Scale and it stretches your subject more than you want, get the Lasso tool **(L)** and draw a selection around your subject (as shown here), then go under the Select menu and choose **Save Selection**. When the Save Selection dialog appears, just click OK. Then bring up Content-Aware Scale again, but this time, go up in the Options Bar and choose your selection from the Protect pop-up menu (as shown here) to tell Photoshop where your subject is. Now you can drag up or down to fill the empty space with the least possible stretching.

(Continued)

Step Four:

There's also an Amount control up in the Options Bar, which determines how much stretching protection is provided. At its default of 100%, it's protecting as much as possible. At 50%, it's a mix of protected resizing and regular Free Transform, and for some photos that works best. The nice thing is the Amount control is live, so as long as your handles are still in place, you can lower the Amount and see live onscreen how it affects your resizing.

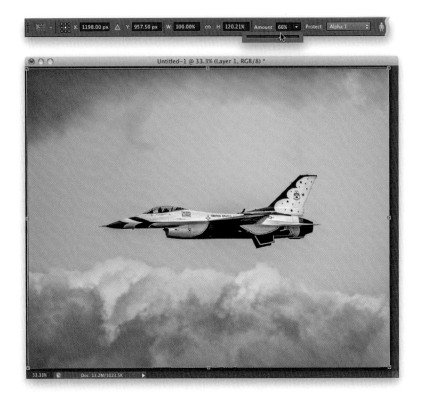

Photoshop Killer Tips

Instant Background Layer Unlocking

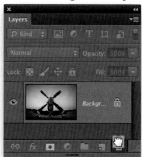

This is one of those little tips that just makes you smile. To instantly turn your Background layer into a regular layer without having a dialog pop up first, just click-and-drag the little lock icon to the right of the word "Background" straight into the trash (thanks to Adobe's Julieanne Kost for sharing this one).

Get Your Channel Shortcuts Back

Back in CS3, and all earlier versions of Photoshop, you could look at the individual color channels for a photo by pressing **Command-1**, **Command-2**, **Command-3**, and so on (on a PC, you'd use **Ctrl-1**, **Ctrl-2**, etc., instead). In CS4, they changed the shortcuts, which totally bummed out a lot of longtime users, but you have the option of bringing those glory days of channel shortcuts back to the pre-CS4 era. Go under the Edit menu, choose **Keyboard Shortcuts**, then near the top of the dialog, turn on the Use Legacy Channel Shortcuts checkbox.

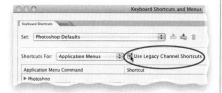

Set Defaults in Layer Styles

You can set your own custom defaults for layer styles like Drop Shadow or Glow. All you have to do is create a new layer in the Layers panel by clicking on the Create a New Layer icon, then choose the layer style you want from the Add a Layer Style icon's pop-up menu (like Outer Glow, for example). In the Layer Style dialog, enter your own settings (like changing the glow from yeech yellow to white, or black, or anything but yeech yellow), then click on the Make Default button near the bottom of the dialog. To return to the factory default (yeech) settings, click the Reset to Default button.

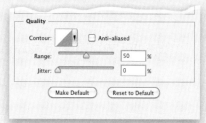

How to Know if You Used the "Blend If" Sliders on a Layer

CS6 now adds an icon on the right of any layer where you've adjusted the Blend If sliders in the Blending Options of the Layer Style dialog. The icon looks like two little over-lapping squares, but it's more than an icon—it's a button. Click on it and it brings up the Blend If sliders in the Layer Style dialog.

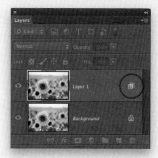

Layer Mask from Layer Transparency

Here's a nice time saver: you can make the transparent areas of any layer into a mask in just one step: go under the Layer menu, under Layer Mask, and choose **From Transparency**.

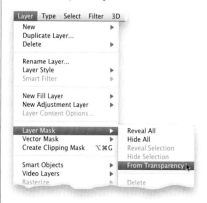

Seeing Your Final Crop in Camera Raw

When you crop a photo in Camera Raw, you can see the final cropped image without having to open the image in Photoshop. Once your cropping border is in place, just change tools and you'll see the cropped version (in some previous versions, the cropped away area was still visible; it was just dimmed).

One Click to Close All Your Tabs

If you're using the Tabs feature (all your documents open as tabs), then you'll definitely want to know this tip: to close all your open tabs at once, just Right-click on any tab and choose **Close All**.

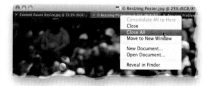

Photoshop Killer Tips

Save 16-Bit to JPEG

Back in CS4, if you worked with 16-bit photos (and a lot of RAW shooters do, since that's the default bit-depth for RAW photos), when you went to the Save dialog to save your photo, there was no option to save your image as a JPEG, because JPEGs have to be in 8-bit mode, so you'd have to close the dialog, convert to 8-bit, then go and Save again. That has changed and JPEG is now a choice, but what it does is makes a copy of the file, which it converts to 8-bit, and saves that instead. This

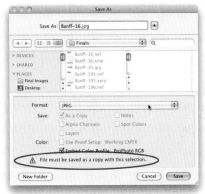

leaves your 16-bit image still open on-screen and unsaved, so keep that in mind. If you want to save the 16-bit version separately, you'll need to save it as a PSD or TIFF like before. For me, once I know it has saved an 8-bit JPEG, I don't need the 16-bit version any longer, so I close the image and click the Don't Save button, but again, that's just me.

Lens Corrections Grid

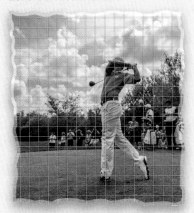

If you're using Camara Raw's Lens Corrections panel to do things like straighten buildings or flatten rounded horizon lines, press the letter **V** on your keyboard, and an alignment grid appears over your image to help you line things up. To hide it again, press V again.

Assign a Keyboard Shortcut to the Color Picker

You can assign a keyboard shortcut to bring up the Foreground (or Background) Color Picker (this is handier than it sounds). Go under the Edit menu, under Keyboard Shortcuts, and from the Shortcuts For pop-up menu, choose **Tools**. Then scroll down near the bottom, and you'll see Foreground Color Picker and Background Color Picker. Click on whichever one you want, and type in the shortcut you want. I have to tell you up front: most of the good shortcuts are already taken (in fact, almost all combinations of shortcuts are already taken), but my buddy Dave Cross came up with a good idea. He doesn't use

the Pen tool all that much, so he used the letter P (for Picker). When you enter "P," it's going to warn you that it's already being used for something else, and if you click the Accept and Go to Conflict button at the bottom left, it assigns P to the Color Picker you chose, and then sends you to the Pen tool to choose a new shortcut. If you don't need to assign one to the Pen tool (you don't use it much either), then just leave it blank and click OK.

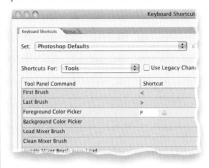

Visual Way to Change Your Brush Size and Softness

This is incredibly handy, because you can actually see and control the exact size and amount of softness for your current brush tip. Press-and-hold Option-Ctrl (PC: Alt-Ctrl) then click-and-drag (PC: Right-click-and-drag) up/down to control the softness/hardness of the brush, and left/right to control the size.

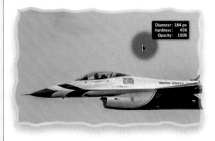

Photoshop Killer Tips

Working with Tabbed Documents

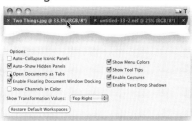

When working with multiple documents while using the Tabs features, to see any tabbed image, just click on its tab at the top of the image window or press **Ctrl-Tab** to cycle through them one by one. To turn tabbing off, go under the Photoshop (PC: Edit) menu, under Preferences, and choose **Interface**, then turn off the Open Documents as Tabs checkbox. Also, you'll probably want to turn off the Enable Floating Document Window Docking checkbox, too, or it will dock your single open image.

Setting Up Your Workspace

CS6 comes with a number of built-in workspace layouts for different tasks with just the panels visible Adobe thought

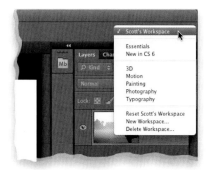

you'd need. You can find them by clicking on the pop-up menu at the right end of the Options Bar. To create your own custom workspace layout, just click-and-drag

the panels where you want them. To nest a panel (so they appear one in front of another), drag one panel over the other. When you see a blue outline appear, release the mouse button and it nests. More panels can be found under the Window menu. Once your panels are set up where you want them, go under the Window menu, under Workspace, and choose **New Workspace**, to save your layout so it's always one click away (it will appear in the pop-up menu). Also, if you use a workspace and change a panel's location, it remembers. That's okay, but you'd think that clicking on your workspace would return things to normal. It doesn't. Instead, you have to go into that pop-up menu and choose **Reset [your workspace name]**.

Getting Sharp Edges on Your Stroke Layer Effect

If you've applied a large stroke using the Stroke layer effect (under the Edit menu) or Stroke layer style (by clicking on the Add a Layer Style icon at the bottom of the Layers panel and choosing Stroke from the pop-up menu), you've probably already noticed that the edges start to get rounded, and the bigger you make the stroke, the rounder they get. So, what's the trick to nice, sharp straight edges? Switch the Stroke position or location to Inside. That's it!

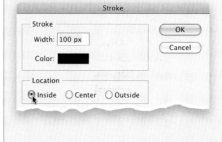

White Balance Quick Fix

If you have an image whose white balance is way off, and you didn't shoot it in RAW, try this: go under the Image menu, under Adjustments, and choose **Match Color**. When the Match Color dialog appears, just turn on the Neutralize checkbox in the Image Options ssection. It works better than you'd think for most white balance problems (plus, you can write an action to do all that for you).

Change Ruler Increments

If you want to quickly change the unit of measure in your ruler (say, from pixels to inches or from centimeters to millimeters), just Right-click anywhere inside the Rulers and choose your new unit of measurement from the pop-up menu that appears.

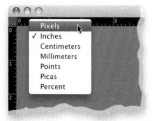

Using "Scrubby Sliders"

Anytime you see a numerical field in Photoshop (like the Opacity field in the Layers panel, for example), you can change the setting without typing in a number, or dragging the tiny slider. Instead. click directly on the word "Opacity" and drag left (to lower the opacity) or right (to increase it). This is very fast, and totally addictive, and if you're not using it yet, you've got to try it. There's no faster way to make quick changes (also, press-and-hold the Shift key while using it, and it goes even faster).

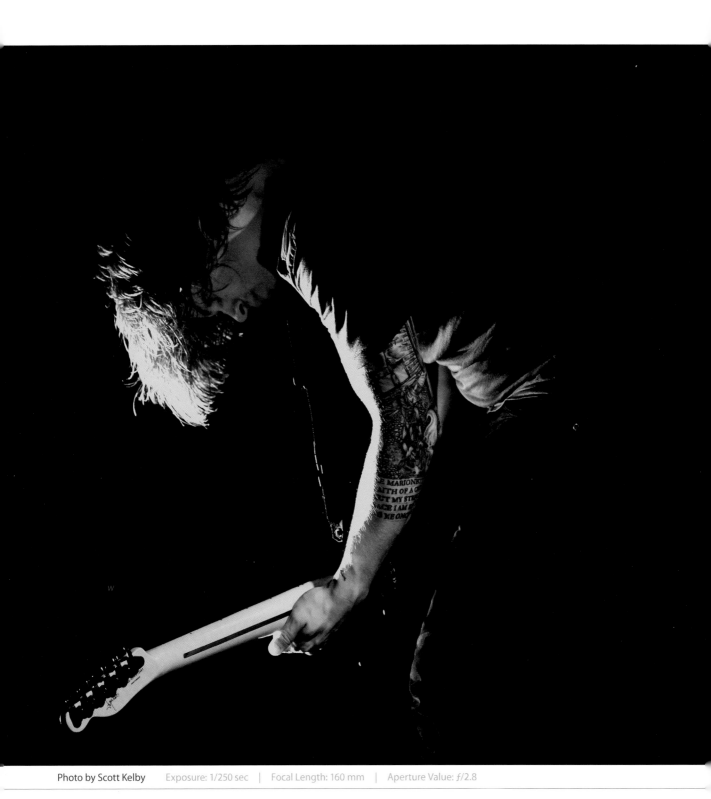

Photo by Scott Kelby   Exposure: 1/250 sec | Focal Length: 160 mm | Aperture Value: *f*/2.8

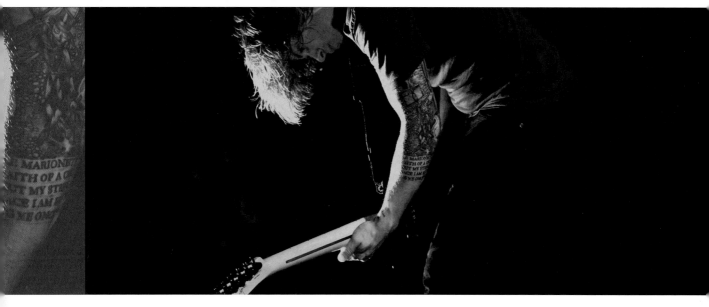

Black & White
how to create stunning b&w images

I know what you're thinking: "He's given up on the whole movie name/song title/TV show thing." But, actually, the "Black & White" you see above is from the song by the 1970s hit machine Three Dog Night. (Remember the song: "The ink is black. The page is white. Together we learn to read and write"? I can't believe with captivating lyrics like that, these guys aren't still crankin' out the hits.) Anyway, back in the CS4 intro for this chapter, I wrote that I had toyed with the idea of using the song "Black Widow" by Mötley Crüe, but I chose not to for a very legitimate (yet, secret until now) reason: I couldn't figure out how to add those two little dots above the letter "u" in Crüe, so I went with Elvis Costello's "Black and White World" instead (it was an easy choice, as it contains no crazy dots above any letters). I have to admit, I am a bit embarrassed that I didn't know what those little dots are called, so I did a Google search for this phrase: "two little dots above the letter U." It returned six search results, including a Facebook group called (and I'm not making this up): "It is a crime to write über without the Umlaut." At that moment I realized two things: (1) it's called an umlaut, and (2) people get totally psychotic about things like a missing umlaut. This is probably why, in the printed version of my CS4 book, not only did my editor Kim add the umlaut above the "u" for me, but she also added an umlaut over the "o" in Mötley. You're thinking, "Wow, she's good!" and she totally is, but I know her dirty little secret. She only knew there was a problem there to fix because she's a huge "big hair bands from the '80s" fan. If, instead, she had been a fan of Sheena Easton or Garth Brooks back then, you know and I know she would have changed it to read "Motley Crew," just like she referred to the song "Walk This Way" as being performed by Arrow Smith. (Kidding, Kim. Just a joke. really!)

Converting to Black and White Using Camera Raw

Although Photoshop has its own Black & White conversion adjustment layer, I never, ever use it, but that's only because it totally stinks (I don't know any pros who use it). I think you can create a much better black-and-white conversion using Camera Raw, and it's much faster and looks infinitely better. Well, that is as long as you don't get suckered into using the HSL/Grayscale panel in Camera Raw, which is nothing more than the Black & White adjustment layer hiding in Camera Raw, trying to sucker in some poor unsuspecting soul.

Step One:

We'll start by opening a color image in Camera Raw (as seen here). Converting from color to black and white is simple—just click on the HSL/Grayscale icon (the fourth one from the left) and then turn on the Convert to Grayscale checkbox at the top of the panel (as seen here). That's all you want to do here (trust me). By the way, I did two little fixes to the photo unrelated to the B&W conversion: (1) I straightened it using the Straighten tool (it was a little crooked), and (2) the building (the back side of the Taj Mahal) had a lens distortion problem, so I adjusted the Vertical distortion in the Lens Corrections panel (as shown here).

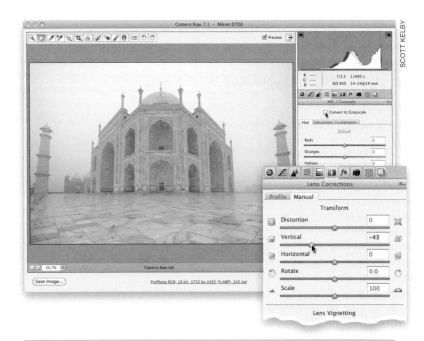

Step Two:

Once you click on that Convert to Grayscale checkbox, it gives you an incredibly flat conversion (like you see here), and you might be tempted to drag those color sliders around, until you realize that since the photo is already converted to black and white, you're kind of dragging around in the dark. So, the best advice I can give you is to get out of this panel just as fast as you can. It's the only hope for making this flat-looking grayscale image blossom into a beautiful butterfly of a B&W image (come on, I at least get five points for the butterfly metaphor).

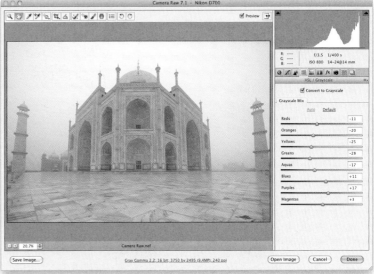

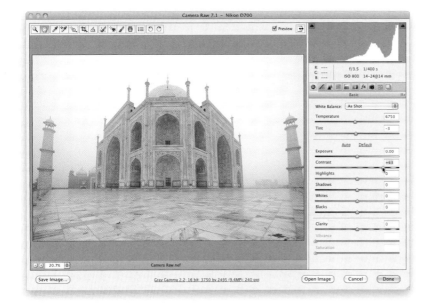

Step Three:

When you talk to photographers about great B&Ws, you'll always hear them talk about high-contrast B&Ws, so you already know what you need to do—you need to add *lots* of contrast. That basically means making the whites whiter and the blacks blacker, which has been made easier to do in Photoshop CS6 now that the Basic panel has both Whites and Blacks sliders (not to mention a Contrast slider that now actually does a good job). So, start in the Basic panel. Normally, you'd adjust the Exposure slider to start things off, but in this case, the image looks okay in the midtones (actually, the image is all mid-tones), so if you wanted, you could drag a little to the left to darken it, but I'm just leaving it set as-is. However, this flat-look-ing image needs lots of contrast, so let's drag the Contrast slider way over to the right (here, I dragged to +63). That looks a little better, but not a bunch—we've got more to do!

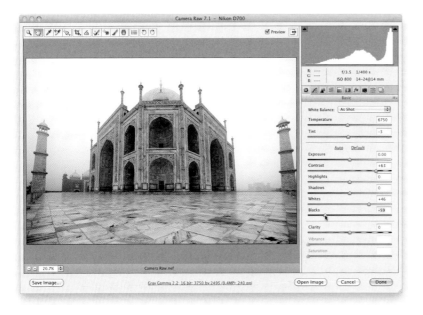

Step Four:

Now, let's set our white and black points. Start by dragging the Whites slider as far to the right as you can without clipping the highlights (in other words, drag until you see the white triangle in the top right of the histogram appear [that's the high-light clipping warning], then back it off just a tiny bit, until it turns black again). Here, I dragged it over to +46. Now, drag the Blacks slider to the left until it really starts to look nice and contrasty (as shown here, where I dragged to –59). Okay, it's start-ing to look a lot better, but we're not quite there yet.

(Continued)

Step Five:

The insides of the arches are kind of dark, so drag the Shadows slider to the right to lighten those areas a bit (I dragged to +41). Then, increase the Clarity amount quite a bit, which adds midtone contrast and makes the image more punchy and a little brighter, too (here, I pushed it over to +58). Also, the sky looks really white, so let's pull back those highlights by dragging the Highlights slider to the left (here, I dragged to –43). Now, if you feel like it could still be more contrasty (I do), then go to the Tone Curve panel and choose **Strong Contrast** from the Curve pop-up menu at the top of the Point tab (as shown here on the right). If it's too much contrast, try Medium Contrast instead.

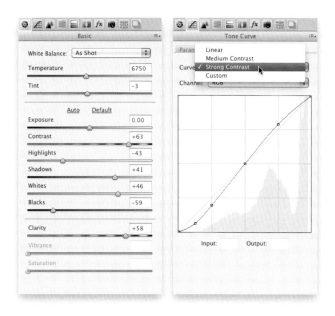

Step Six:

There is one problem that is unique to this particular photo—the towers on the left and right look washed out, so get the Adjustment Brush **(K)**, click on the + (plus sign) button to the right of Contrast (to reset the sliders to 0), and then increase the Contrast slider a bunch. Now, drag the Shadows slider to the left and then paint over the towers (as shown here). A before/after is shown on the next page. Pretty striking difference, eh?

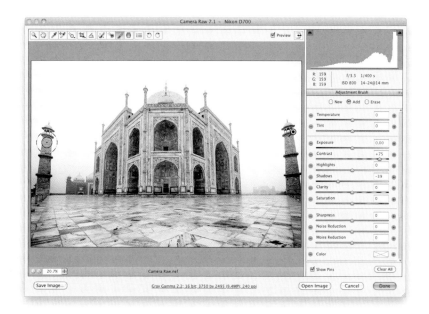

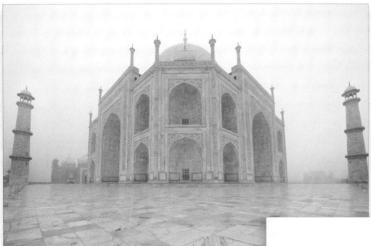

Before

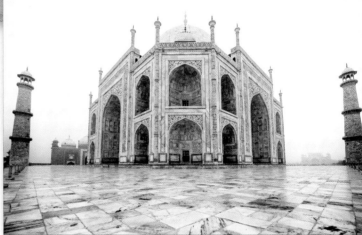

After

My Three-Click Method for Converting to B&W (Once You're Already in Photoshop)

Some of the best techniques unfold when you least expect it, and this technique is a perfect example. I was working on a completely different technique when I stumbled upon this and I fell in love, and now you're only three clicks away from a nice, crisp, high-contrast B&W image (once you're already in Photoshop. Otherwise, I would do it in Camera Raw, because you have more control). Plus, I'll show you how you can tweak your conversion, along with a variation, with just a couple more clicks. It's a B&W clicking lovefest.

Step One:
Open the color photo you want to convert into a high-contrast B&W image. You start by pressing the letter **D** to set your Foreground color to black, and then in the Adjustments panel, click on the Gradient Map icon (it looks like a horizontal gradient— it's shown circled in red here).

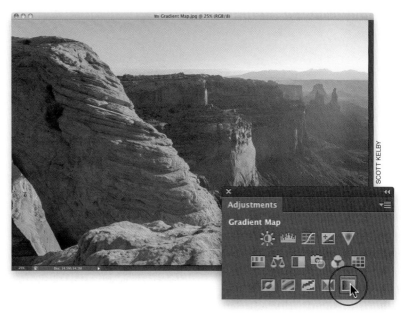

Step Two:
Once you click that icon, the Gradient Map options appear in the Properties panel, but you don't have to do anything there. Not a bad B&W conversion, eh? Believe it or not, just the simple act of applying this black-to-white gradient map will almost always give you a much better conversion than choosing Grayscale from the Image menu's Mode submenu, and I feel it's generally even better than both the default and Auto settings in the Black & White adjustment dialog. However, we can add another click or two and take this conversion up a big notch.

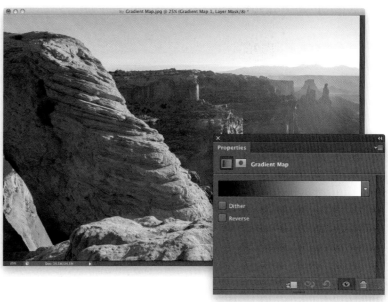

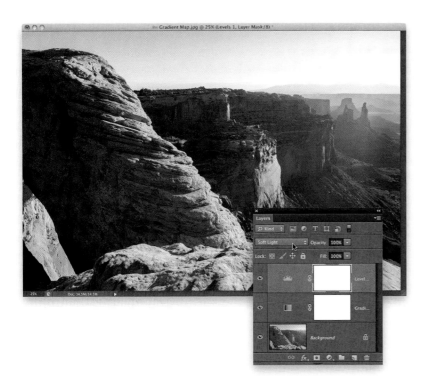

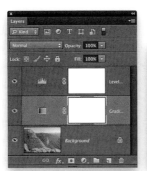

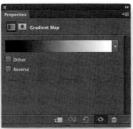

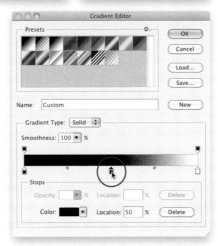

Step Three:

Now you're going to add some contrast the easy way. Click on the Levels adjustment layer icon in the Adjustments panel (it's the second icon on the top row). Here's the good news: when the Levels options appear in the Properties panel, you're not actually going to adjust the Levels. All you need to do is change the layer blend mode of this adjustment layer from Normal to **Soft Light** (at the top of the Layers panel, as shown here) and look how much more contrasty, and just generally yummy, this photo looks now. If choosing Soft Light for the particular photo you're working on doesn't add enough contrast, then try Overlay mode instead (it's more contrast). Okay, that's it—three clicks and you're done. Now, if you're feeling "clicky," there is a way to tweak your conversion if you really feel like it (not necessary usually, but in case you want to, I'll show ya).

Step Four:

In the Layers panel, click on the Gradient Map adjustment layer (the middle layer) to make it active. Now, click directly on the gradient in the Properties panel, which brings up the Gradient Editor dialog. Once it appears, click once directly in the center, right below the gradient ramp (as shown circled here) to add a color stop (it looks like a little house) right below your gradient. Don't click OK yet. At this point, your image will look really dark, but that's okay—we're not done yet.

(Continued)

Step Five:

Double-click directly on that color stop you just created and Photoshop's Color Picker appears (seen here). Click-and-drag your cursor all the way over to the left side of the Color Picker, right up against the edge (as shown here), and pick a medium gray color. As you slide up and down that left side, let go of the mouse button and look at your photo. You'll see the midtones changing as you drag, and you can stop at any point where the image looks good to you. Once you find a spot that looks good (in our case, one in the center), click OK to close the Color Picker (don't close the Gradient Editor, just the Color Picker at this point, because there's another tweak you can do. Of course, this is all optional [you could have stopped back at Step Three], but now we have some extra editing power if we want it).

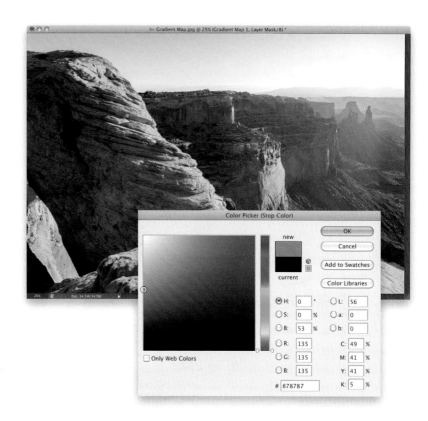

Step Six:

Once you're back at the Gradient Editor, and your color stop is now gray, you can drag that middle gray stop around to adjust the tone of your image (as shown here). What's weird is you drag the opposite way that the gradient shows. For example, to darken the photo, you drag to the right, toward the white end of the gradient, and to lighten the photo, you drag left toward the dark end. Freaky, I know. One other thing: unlike almost every other slider in all of Photoshop, as you drag that color stop, you do not get a live preview of what's happening—you have to release the mouse button and then it shows you the results of your dragging. Click OK, and you're done.

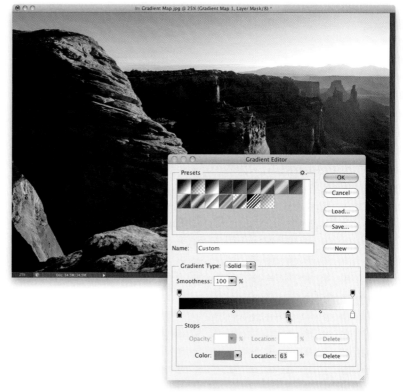

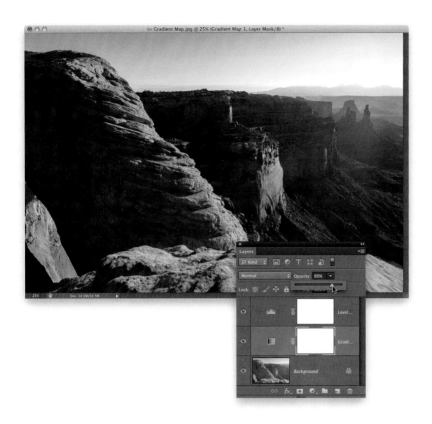

Step Seven:

Here's a quick variation you can try that's just one more click: go to the Layers panel and lower the Opacity of your Gradient Map adjustment layer to 80% (as shown here). This bleeds back in a little of the color, and gives a really nice subtle "wash" effect (compare this slightly-colored photo with the full-color photo in Step One, and you'll see what I mean. It's kinda nice, isn't it?). A before and after is shown below, but it's just the three-click version (not all the other tweaking we added after the fact).

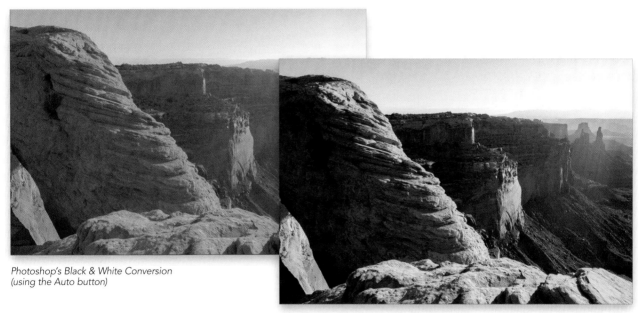

Photoshop's Black & White Conversion (using the Auto button)

Scott's "Three-Click Method" (using just the three clicks, not the extra tweaking)

Split Toning

Split toning is a traditional darkroom special effect where you apply one tint to your photo's highlights, and one tint to your photo's shadow areas, and you even can control the saturation of each tint and the balance between the two for some interesting effects. Although split-toning effects can be applied to both color and B&W photos, you probably see it most often applied to a B&W image, so here we'll start by converting the photo to black and white, then apply the split-tone effect.

Step One:

Start by converting your full-color image to black and white by clicking on the HSL/Grayscale icon (the fourth icon from the left) at the top of the Panel area and then just turning on the Convert to Grayscale checkbox at the top of the panel (see page 154 for one of my favorite methods for converting to black and white). *Note:* I made some adjustments in the Basic panel (shown here), before I turned on the checkbox.

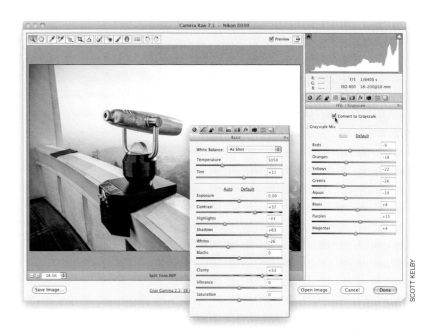

Step Two:

Now, click on the Split Toning icon (the fifth icon from the left) at the top of the Panel area. At this point, dragging either the Highlights or Shadows Hue slider does absolutely nothing because, by default, the Saturation sliders are set to 0. So, do yourself a favor and drag the Highlights Saturation slider over to around 25, so at least you can see what it looks like while you're dragging the Hue slider. As soon as you do this, you'll see the default tint color for Hue (which is kind of pinkish).

TIP: Seeing Your Colors

To temporarily see your hues at their full 100% saturation, just press-and-hold the Option (PC: Alt) key, then click-and-drag a Hue slider. It helps when picking your colors, if you don't feel like taking my advice and increasing the saturation (like I mentioned at the end of Step Two).

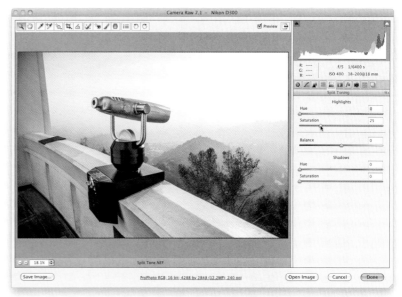

SCOTT KELBY

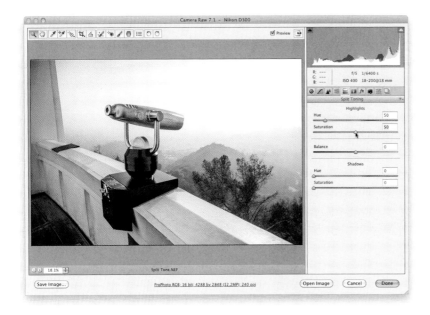

Step Three:

Now that you can see what's going on, click-and-drag the Highlights Hue slider until you find a highlight hue you like. For this image, I'm using a Hue setting of 50, and I also increased the Highlights Saturation amount to around 50 to make the tint a bit heavier.

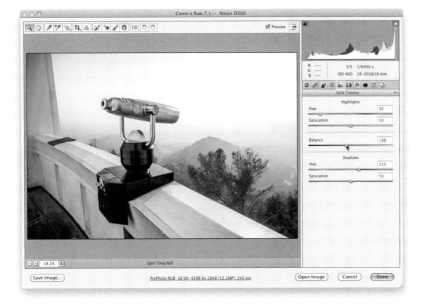

Step Four:

Let's add a teal tint to the shadows (a fairly popular spilt-tone combination) by dragging the Shadows Saturation slider to 50 (so you can see the shadows hue), then drag the Shadows Hue slider over to 215, and now you see that teal tint in the shadow areas. There is one more control—a Balance slider, which lets you control whether your split tone favors your highlight or shadow color. Just drag left, then back right, and you'll instantly see what this slider does (here, I dragged the Balance slider over to the left to –10, and you can see that the split tone now has more teal in the shadow areas). If you do find a split-toning combination you like (hey, it could happen), I'd definitely jump to page 167 to find out how to turn that into a one-click preset, so you don't have to go through all this every time you want a quick split-tone effect.

Duotones Made Crazy Easy

Don't let the fact that this technique fits neatly on one page make you think it's not a rocking technique, because this is the best and fastest duotone technique I've ever used (and it's the only one I use in my own workflow). I used to do a more complicated version, but then my buddy Terry White showed me a technique he learned from one of his buddies whose duotones he adored, and well…now I'm passing it on to you. It's very easy, but man does it work like a charm.

Step One:
Start by converting your color image to black and white by clicking on the HSL/Grayscale icon (the fourth icon from the left) at the top of the Panel area and then turning on the Convert to Grayscale checkbox at the top of the panel (see page 154 for one of my favorite methods for converting to black and white).

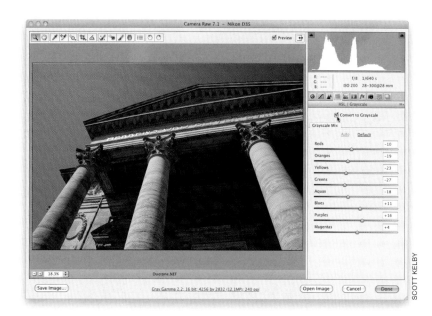

Step Two:
Now, click on the Split Toning icon at the top of the Panel area (it's the fifth icon from the left), and then, in the Shadows section, increase the Saturation amount to 25 as a starting point. Next, just drag the Shadows Hue slider until you have a nice sepia-tone hue (I generally use something around 28). If you think it's too intense, lower the Saturation and you're done. That's right—completely ignore the Highlights controls altogether, and you'll love the results you get (ignore the powerful pull of the Highlights sliders. I know you feel on some level that they will make things better, but you are already holding the magical key to great duotones. Don't blow it!). That's it—that's the whole ball of wax (I told you it was easy, but don't let that fool you. Try printing one of these and you'll see what I mean). Mmmm. Duotone.

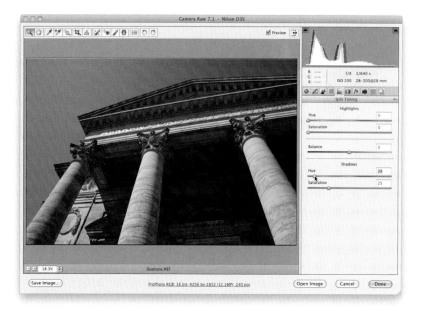

SCOTT KELBY

Quadtoning for Richer B&Ws

If you've ever wondered how the pros get those deep, rich-looking B&W photos, you might be surprised to learn that what you were looking at weren't just regular B&W photos, instead they were quadtones or tritones—B&W photos made up of three or four different grays and/or brown colors to make what appears to be a B&W photo, but with much greater depth. For years, Photoshop had a bunch of very slick presets buried somewhere on your computer, but luckily, in CS6, they're just one click away.

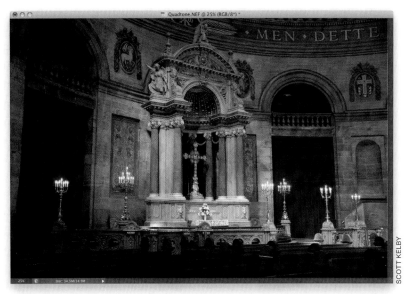

SCOTT KELBY

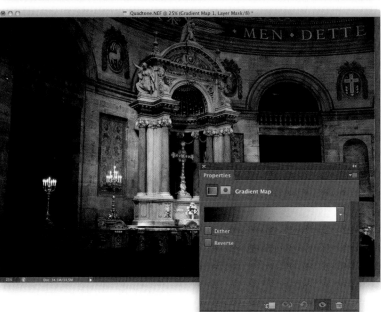

Step One:

Open the photo you want to apply your quadtoning effect to (the term quad-toning just means the final photo will use four different inks mixed together to achieve the effect. Tritones use three inks, and do I really have to mention how many duotones use?). Quadtoning effects seem to look best with (but are not limited to) two kinds of photos: (1) landscapes, and (2) people. But, here, we're going to apply it to an image of the inside of a church.

Step Two:

To create a quadtone, you'll have to convert to Grayscale mode first, but by now you know what a flat-looking B&W photo that creates, so instead try this (from a few pages ago): Press the letter **D** to set your Foreground and Background colors to their defaults of black and white, then click on the Gradient Map icon in the Adjustments panel. When the Gradient Map options appear in the Properties panel, you don't need to make any changes. Now, before you can make a quadtone, you need to convert this image to **Grayscale** mode by going under the Image menu, under Mode, and choosing Grayscale. It will ask you if you want to flatten your layers, so click the Flatten button. (It will also ask you if you want to discard the color info. Click Discard.)

(Continued)

Step Three:

Once your photo is in Grayscale mode, the Duotone menu item (which has been grayed out and unchoosable until now) is now open for business (if you're in 8-bit mode). So, go under the Image menu, under Mode, and choose **Duotone**. When the Duotone Options dialog appears (shown here), the default setting is for a one-color Monotone (a cruel joke perpetrated by Adobe engineers), but that's no big deal, because we're going to use the built-in presets from the pop-up menu at the top. Here, you'll literally find 137 presets (I counted). Now, you'd think they'd be organized by duotones first, tritones, then quadtones, right? Nope—that makes too much sense (in fact, I'm not sure they're in any order at all).

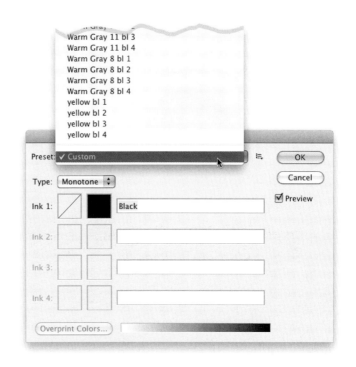

Step Four:

I thought I'd give you a few of my favorites to get you started. One I use often is named "Bl 541 513 5773" (the Bl stands for black, and the three sets of numbers are the PMS numbers of the three other Pantone colors used to make the quad-tone). How about a nice duotone? It uses black and it adds a reddish brown to the mix. It's called "478 brown (100%) bl 4," and depending on the photo, it can work really well (you'll be surprised at how different these same quadtones, tritones, and duotones will look when applied to different photos). There's a nice tritone that uses black and two grays, named "Bl WmGray 7 WmGray 2." We'll wrap things up with another nice duotone—this one's named "Warm Gray 11 bl 2," and gives you the duotone effect shown here. Well, there you have it—four of my favorites (and don't forget, when you're done, convert back to RGB mode for color inkjet printing).

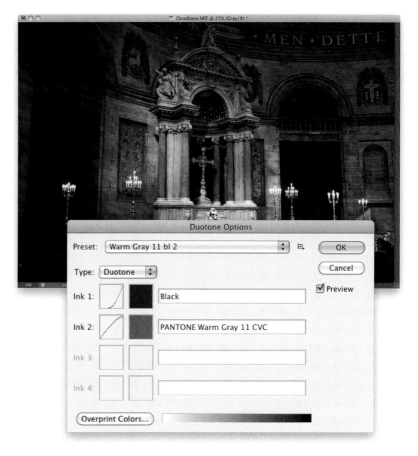

Now that we created split tones and duotones, this is the perfect time to start making your own one-click presets. That way, the next time you open a photo that you want to have that same effect, you don't have to go through all those steps (converting it to black and white, tweaking it, then applying the Split Toning settings), you can just click one button and all those settings are applied at once, giving you an instant one-click effect anytime. Of course, these presets aren't just for split tones and duotones—make one anytime you want to reuse any settings from Camera Raw.

Creating Your Own One-Click Presets in Camera Raw

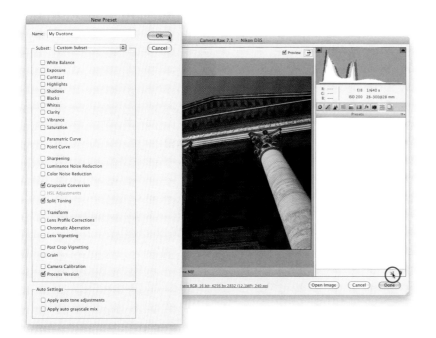

Step One:
Since we just created that duotone effect in Camera Raw, we'll go ahead and use that to create a one-click preset there. Just remember—anytime you come up with a look you like, you can save it as a preset. To create a preset, you click on the Presets icon (it's the second icon from the right at the top of the Panel area), and then click on the New Preset icon (shown circled here in red) to bring up the New Preset dialog (seen here). Now, just turn on the checkboxes for the adjustments you want copied to your preset (as I did here), give your preset a name, and then click the OK button.

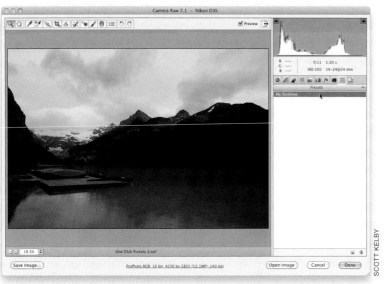

Step Two:
Once you've saved the preset, it appears in the Presets list (since there's only one preset here, I'm not sure it qualifies as a list at this point, but you get the idea, right?). To apply it is really a one-click process—just open a different photo, go to the Presets panel, and click on the preset (as shown here), and all those settings are applied. Keep in mind, though, because the exposure is different for every photo, if you save a preset where you had to tweak the exposure a lot, that same exposure will be applied anytime you apply this preset. That's why you might want to save just the split-tone/duotone settings and not all the exposure stuff, too.

If You're Really, Really Serious About B&W, Then Consider This Instead

I saved this for the last page, because I wanted to share all my favorite techniques for doing B&W using just Photoshop's tools, and although I still use those techniques from time to time, it would be pretty disingenuous of me if I didn't tell you what I do most of the time, which is: I use Nik Software's Silver Efex Pro 2 black-and-white plug-in. Almost all the pros I know use it as well, and it's absolutely brilliant (and super-easy to use). You can download the free 15-day trial copy from www.niksoftware.com and see for yourself. Here's how I use it:

Step One:

Once you install Silver Efex Pro 2, open the image you want to convert from color to B&W, then go under Photoshop's Filter menu, under Nik Software, and choose **Silver Efex Pro 2**. When the window opens, it gives you the default conversion (which isn't bad all by itself), and a host of controls on the right side (but honestly, I literally never touch those controls).

Step Two:

The magic of this plug-in is its B&W (and duotone) presets. They're listed along the left side of the window, complete with a small preview of how the effect will look, but here's where I always start: on their High Structure preset. Eight times out of 10, that's the one I choose, because it has its own high-contrast, sharpened look that is wonderful for so many images. However, if I'm converting a portrait, I'll often wind up using a different preset, because High Structure can be too intense when your subject is a person. So, I click on the top preset in the list, and then click on each preset below it until I find one that looks good to me, then I click OK in the bottom-right corner and I'm done. That's all I do. It's fast, easy, and it looks fantastic. That's just what I want.

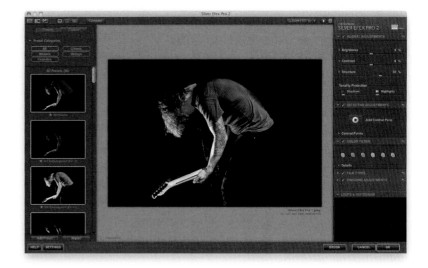

SCOTT KELBY

Photoshop Killer Tips

Why the Fill Dialog Shows Up Sometimes, but Not Others

If you have a flattened image (so, it's just a Background layer), and you make a selection and press the **Delete (PC: Backspace) key**, the Fill dialog appears (Content-Aware is selected in the Use pop-up menu, by default). But there are times when hitting Delete won't bring up the Fill dialog. Instead, if you have a multi-layered document, it will delete whatever is inside the selection on your current layer, making it transparent. (That's either, "Yikes!" or "Great!" depending on how you look at it.) Also, if you have only one single layer (that is not a Background layer), you'll again delete anything inside your selection and make it transparent. So, to bring up the Fill dialog in those instances, just use **Shift-Delete (PC: Shift-Backspace)** instead.

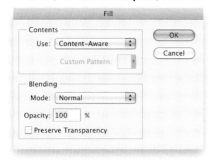

Doing a Smooth Zoom In

Another way to zoom in on your image is to click-and-hold the Zoom tool (the magnifying glass icon) on the spot where you want to zoom, and it smoothly zooms in right on that spot. The only downside is that it does it so smoothly, it's actually slow. It does look cool, but again, it's slow. That's why clicking with the tool and dragging to the right works so much better (although it's not nearly as cool to show to your friends as the "slow zoom").

Move an Object Between Documents and Have It Appear in the Exact Same Place

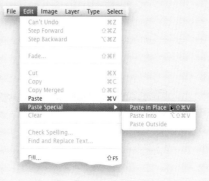

If you have something on a layer in one document, and you want the object to appear in the exact same place in another open document, here's what you do: First, press-and-hold the Command (PC: Ctrl) key, go to the Layers panel and click on the layer's thumbnail to put a selection around your object. Then, press **Command-C (PC: Ctrl-C)** to Copy that object into memory. Switch to the other document, then go under the Edit menu, under Paste Special, and choose **Paste in Place**. Now it will appear in the exact same position in the other document (provided, of course, the other document is the same size and resolution). This also works with selected areas—not just layers.

Removing Red Eye

If you have a photo that has someone with the dreaded red-eye problem, it's a 15-second fix. Use the Zoom tool **(Z)** to zoom in tight on the eye, then get the Red Eye tool from the Toolbox (it's under the Spot Healing Brush, or press **Shift-J** until you have it). Click it once on the red area of the eye, and in just a second or two, the red is gone. If your first try doesn't select all the red, increase the

Pupil Size up in the Options Bar. If the retouch doesn't look dark enough (the pupil looks gray, rather than black), just increase the Darken Amount up in the Options Bar.

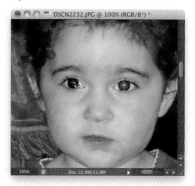

Dragged-and-Dropped Images Don't Have to Appear as Smart Objects

You learned earlier that you can drag-and-drop images from Mini Bridge right into open documents (and if there isn't a document open, it'll open as a new document), but by default it always drags in as a smart object. If you'd rather it didn't, press **Command-K (PC: Ctrl-K)** to bring up Photoshop's Preferences, click on General on the left, then turn off the checkbox for Place or Drag Raster Images as Smart Objects near the bottom of the Options section.

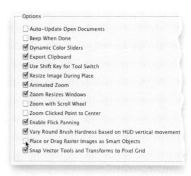

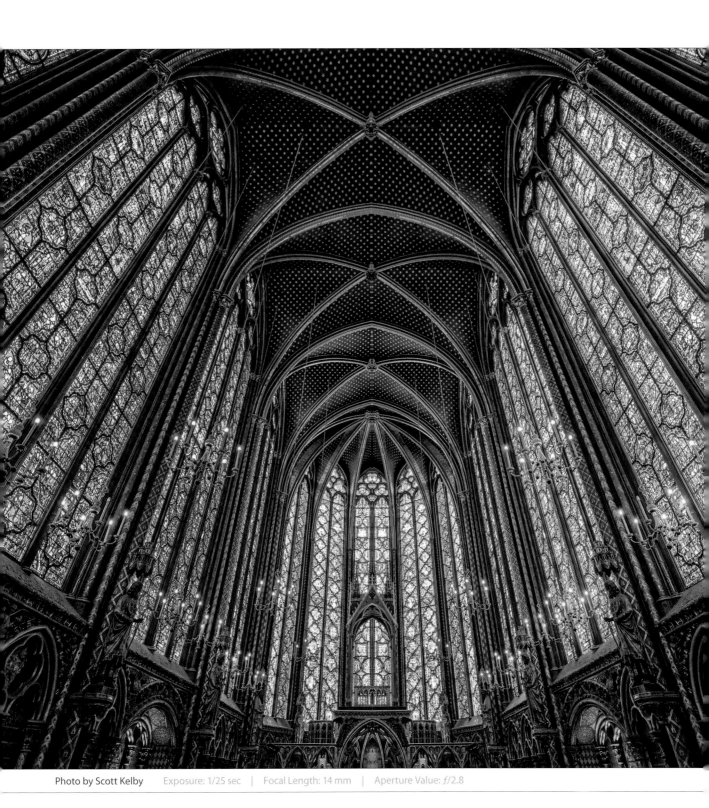

Photo by Scott Kelby   Exposure: 1/25 sec | Focal Length: 14 mm | Aperture Value: *f*/2.8

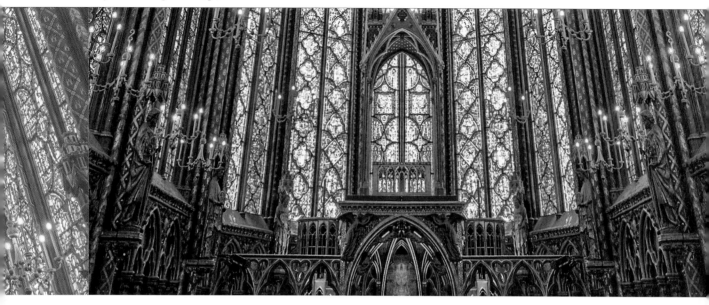

We Are HDR
creating HDR images

Tell me this isn't the perfect name for a chapter on HDR. The band is named hdr, their album is called *We Are Hdr*, and there's a song on the album called, "We Are HDR." This was destiny, my friends. Now, I have to admit, I have no idea if the HDR they are referring to actually stands for the type of HDR (High Dynamic Range) imaging we're talking about in this chapter, but on some level, I like to think it does (although it probably stands for something more like "Heavy Donut Raid" or "Her Darn Rottweiler" or maybe "Hi, Don Rickles"). Anyway, if there's a topic that gets photographers really riled up, it's HDR (Highly Decaffeinated Roast), so I don't really want to take us down that rabbit hole. Now, as you'll learn, there are two types of HDR (Hardee's Delicious Ribs): The good one, where you expand the dynamic range of the photo, getting a greater range of tone and light than today's digital cameras can create, which gives you an image that's closer to what the human eye captures. And the evil HDR (House Developers' Revolt), which makes your images look like a movie still from a Harry Potter movie. Now, I know as you read this, you're thinking, "Oh, I would want that first thing" and at this point, I totally believe that's what you think you want. But here's the thing: there's one slider in Photoshop CS6's Merge to HDR Pro feature that lets you go from real to surreal pretty much by just sliding it one way or the other. And I know that, at some point, when nobody's looking, you're going to drag toward the fantasy side, and then—bam!—you're hooked, and before long, you're tone mapping everything from your wedding photos to baby photos, and you're friends and family will sit you down and try to help wean you off the "hard stuff," but the lure of surreal HDR (Hallucinogenic Deli Relish) is just too strong. Don't say I didn't warn you.

Setting Up Your Camera to Shoot HDR

For the HDR (High Dynamic Range) technique to work, you have to "shoot for HDR" (in other words, you have to set up your camera to shoot exposure-bracketed shots that can be used by Photoshop to create an HDR image). Here, I'm going to show you how to set up both Nikon and Canon cameras (the two most popular DSLR brands) to shoot three- and five-stop brackets, so all you have to do is hold the shutter button and your camera will do the rest.

Step One:

When you're shooting for HDR, you're going to be shooting multiple shots of the exact same scene (at different exposures), and since these images need to be perfectly aligned with one another, you really need to be shooting on a tripod. Now, that being said, Photoshop does have an Auto-Align feature that does an amazingly good job, so if you don't have a tripod, or you're in a situation where you can't use one, you can try hand-holding—just make sure you're shooting in a well-lit area, so your shutter speed will be fast enough that your images won't be blurry.

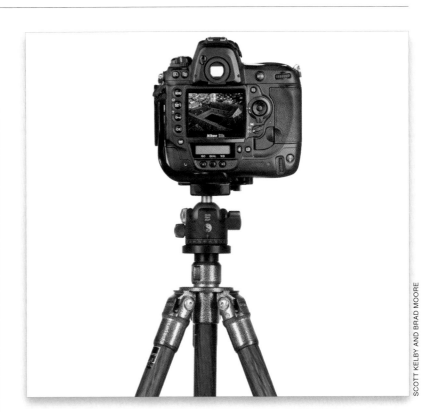

SCOTT KELBY AND BRAD MOORE

Step Two:

We'll need to vary our exposure as we take each HDR shot, but we can't vary the f-stop or our depth of field will change from shot to shot, so instead we vary our shutter speed (actually, the camera will do this for us). So, switch your camera to Aperture Priority mode (the A mode on Nikon cameras, like a D300S, D700, D3S, D3X, and D4, and the Av mode on Canon cameras like the 60D, 60Da, 7D, 5D Mark III, 1D Mark IV, etc.). In Aperture Priority mode, we choose an aperture (like f/8 or f/11 for outdoor shots), and then the camera will vary the shutter speed for us.

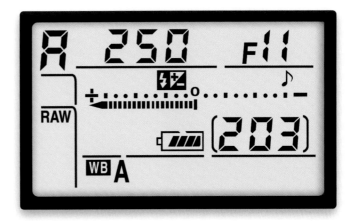

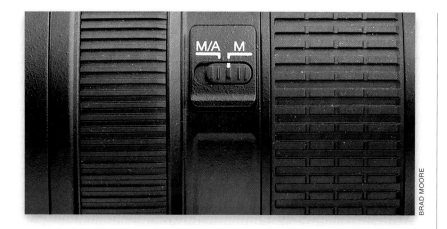

BRAD MOORE

Step Three:

Go ahead and compose your shot, and focus on the scene you want to shoot. Once it's in focus, switch your lens to Manual focus. That way, while your camera is taking multiple shots, it doesn't accidentally change focus. Now, just so we're clear, you're not going to manually focus—you're going to use Auto focus just like always, but once it's focused on your scene, just switch off Auto focus, and then don't touch the lens.

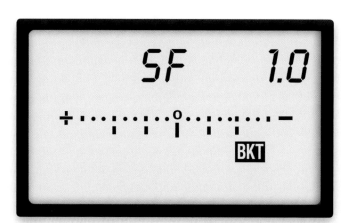

Step Four:

Now we set up the camera to shoot bracketed, which tells the camera to shoot the regular exposure, and then extra photos that are exposed both brighter and darker. The minimum number of exposures you can use for HDR is three, but I generally take five bracketed photos for my HDR images (although some folks take as many as nine). So, with five, I wind up with one shot with my normal exposure, then two darker shots (one 1 stop underexposed and one 2 stops underexposed), followed by two brighter ones (one 1 stop overexposed and one 2 stops overexposed). Here's how to set up your camera to shoot bracketed (we'll start with a Nikon D3S, for example): To turn on bracketing on a Nikon D3S, press the Fn (function) button on the front of the camera, below the lens. Then use the main command dial to choose how many exposures to bracket (the control panel on the top of the camera shows the bracketing settings; choose 5F, so you get five bracketed shots). Use the sub-command dial (in front of the shutter button) to set the bracketing amount to 1 stop (as seen here).

(Continued)

Step Five:

Now, switch your Nikon camera to Continuous High shooting mode, and just press-and-hold the shutter button until it takes all five bracketed shots for you. That's it. Okay, on to the setup for Canon cameras.

TIP: Use a Low ISO

Because HDR shots are likely to increase any noise in your image, try to shoot your HDR shots using the lowest ISO you can get away with (100 ISO on most Canon cameras, or 200 ISO on Nikon DSLRs).

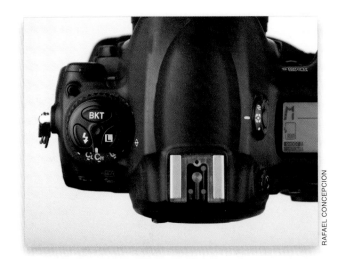

RAFAEL CONCEPCION

Step Six:

To turn on bracketing for a Canon camera (like the Canon 60D), start by going to the Camera Tab menu in the LCD on the back of the camera, then scroll down to Expo Comp/AEB (Auto Exposure Bracketing), and press the Set button. Now, use the Main Dial to choose 2 stops brighter, then press the Set button again (this automatically sets the bracketing to also shoot 2 stops darker). Now set your camera to High-Speed Continuous Shooting mode, and then press-and-hold the shutter button and your camera will automatically shoot all five bracketed photos (once all five are taken, you can release the shutter button). That's all there is to it.

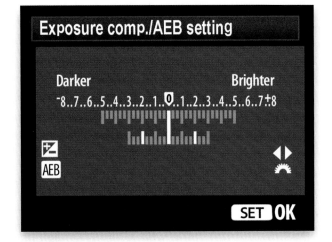

Note: Because I shoot with a Nikon camera, and most Nikon models only bracket in 1-stop increments, I have to shoot five bracketed images to have one that's 2 stops underexposed and one that's 2 stops overexposed. However, Canon DSLRs (and some Nikons, like the D4 and D7000) bracket in 2-stop increments, so you'll only need to shoot three bracketed images. They contain enough depth to make the HDR (actually, the darker image is more important than the lighter one), and by only using three photos, the processing is much faster.

In the next project, I'm going to go through what all the sliders in Photoshop's built-in HDR feature do, but for now we're going to start off with a quick, "down & dirty" HDR crash course that will have your HDR image compiled, tone mapped, sharpened, and finished off in just about six clicks (great for people with attention spans like mine, who want it done now without a lot of fuss). I use this exact HDR workflow a lot and thanks to something they included in Photoshop CS6, we can just dive right in and do it (you couldn't do this without some serious prep work back in CS5—you'll see why in a moment). Hang on—here we go!

Scott's "Down & Dirty" HDR Workflow (Six Clicks to Done!)

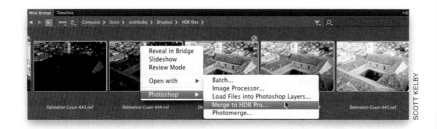

SCOTT KELBY

Step One:

If you shot for HDR (like I talked about in the previous tutorial), you can easily take those images straight from Mini Bridge to Photoshop's Merge to HDR Pro feature. Here, I've selected the five shots I bracketed with my camera (one that's 2 stops underexposed, one that's 1 stop underexposed, the normal exposure, one that's 1 stop overexposed, and one that's 2 stops overexposed). Once you've selected your bracketed shots in Mini Bridge, Right-click on any one of those thumbnails and from the pop-up menu that appears, under Photoshop, choose **Merge to HDR Pro** (as shown here).

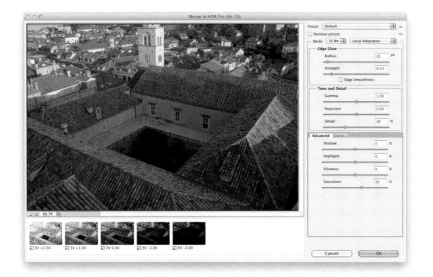

Step Two:

In a few moments, the Merge to HDR Pro dialog will appear (I'm being pretty gratuitous when I say "a few moments," because I just timed it and, on my laptop, it took 22 seconds before the dialog appeared. For everything else in life, that's a very short time, but when you're waiting for a dialog to open, it feels more like 3½ hours). Anyway, it merges these five images, with five different exposures, into one single HDR image that looks pretty bad, because it's using the default settings, which should be named simply "Bad" for the sake of clarity.

(Continued)

Step Three:

When Merge to HDR Pro came out, I made a lot of fun of the presets that came with it, because I couldn't find a single image that they didn't look awful on (none of them looked like the traditional tone-mapped HDR images you see all over the web). So, I set out to create an HDR Pro preset that worked pretty consistently for most of the images I tried it on. It took a while, but I came up with one, and I'm totally jazzed to say that Adobe liked it enough that they included it here, in Photoshop CS6. It's called "Scott5" (it was my fifth try, and it took a lot longer than it sounds). So, since Adobe included it in their Preset menu, all you have to do for this "Down & Dirty HDR" technique is choose **Scott5** from the pop-up menu (as shown here. My buddy RC Concepcion had a couple of his presets included here, as well. They're called "RC5" and "City Twilight").

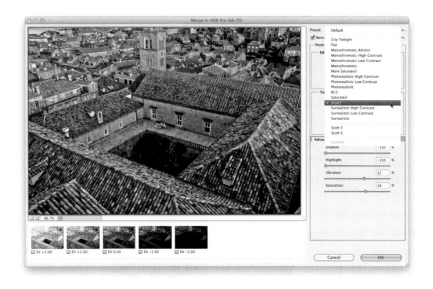

Step Four:

With this preset, there's really only one slider that I ever need to tweak and, depending on the photo, it might not even make a difference, but it's worth a try. It's the Shadow slider. If part of your HDR image looks pretty dark (like the courtyard in the center does back in Step Three), then you can open up those shadows a bit by dragging the Shadow slider way over to the right (as seen here). Now, you can see the trees in the courtyard pretty well. Click OK to process the image (it's waiting time again).

TIP: Presets Can Look Very Different

The Scott5 preset looks pretty good most of the time, but I do find some images where it doesn't look good and, in those cases, I try out the other presets to see if one gives me a better look. If they don't, then turn to page 179.

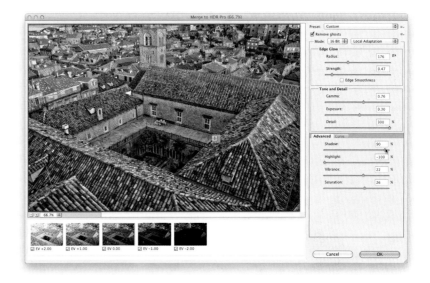

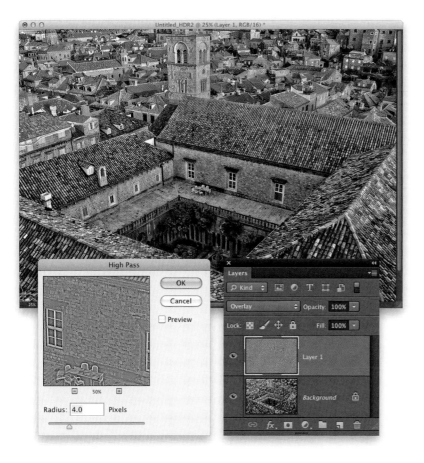

Step Five:

Once the image opens in Photoshop (as seen here), it's time to add some sharpening. High Pass sharpening is really popular on HDR images (rather than Unsharp Mask), because it's kind of a mega-sharpening and really enhances the details that are already there (and I think its look really suits HDR images). Start by duplicating the Background layer (press **Command-J [PC: Ctrl-J]**), then go under the Filter menu, under Other, and choose **High Pass**. When the High Pass filter dialog appears (shown here), I generally enter 4 pixels and click OK for a nice snappy sharpening. (*Note:* When the filter dialog appears, it will turn your duplicate layer solid gray with just an outline of the edges in your image. That's normal.) Now, to change this gray layer into sharpening, go to the Layers panel, change this layer's blend mode from Normal to **Overlay** (as I did here), and now you see the sharpening. If you think it's too much, just lower the Opacity of this layer until it looks right to you.

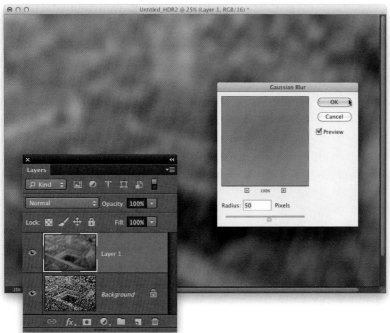

Step Six:

Another popular HDR "finishing move" is to add a soft glow over the entire image. It helps to take away some of the harshness of an HDR image and gives the image a little bit of a surreal feel to it (in a good way, not in an over-the-top, crazy surreal HDR way that drives people nuts). First, choose **Flatten Image** from the Layers panel's flyout menu to flatten your layers, duplicate your Background layer again, then go under the Filter menu, under Blur, and choose **Gaussian Blur**. Enter 50 pixels to blur the heck out of it, and click OK (as shown here). Don't worry, you're not done yet.

(Continued)

Step Seven:

Now, to finish this puppy off, lower the Opacity of this blurry layer to 70% (as shown here) and then (this is really important) change the layer blend mode from Normal to **Soft Light** (as seen here). This is what blends the glow effect in nicely and gives you the final effect you see at the bottom right.

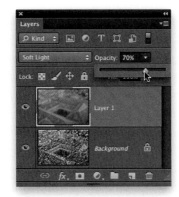

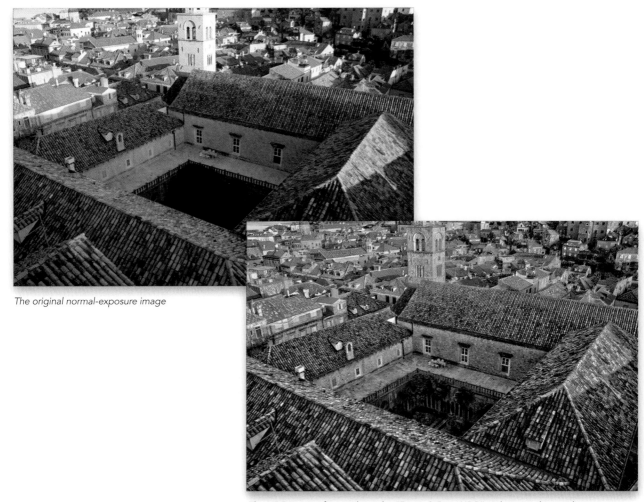

The original normal-exposure image

The HDR image after applying the "Down & Dirty HDR" technique, along with sharpening and the glow finishing move

Okay, now that you've learned my "Down & Dirty" method, you probably want to branch out a little further and get a feel for what all the sliders and controls in HDR Pro actually do. Here, I'll take you through HDR Pro from start to finish and then you can start to develop some of your own presets with the looks that you want to get.

Working with HDR Pro in Photoshop CS6

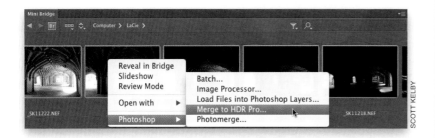

Step One:
Go to Mini Bridge (or Big Bridge), press-and-hold the Command (PC: Ctrl) key, and click on the images you want to combine into a single HDR image. Once they're selected, Right-click on any one of those thumbnails and, from the pop-up menu that appears, under Photoshop, choose **Merge to HDR Pro** (as shown here).

Step Two:
After a few moments, you'll see the Merge to HDR Pro dialog appear (seen here) with the default settings applied, but they are so subtle (and lame) you may not notice that anything's been done to your image at all. At the bottom of the dialog, you'll see thumbnails of the images it combined to create the single HDR exposure, and it shows the Exposure Value [EV] of each one (so you can see which one is the normal exposure and which are the over- or underexposed ones. These actually come into play if you turn on the Auto Ghosting feature—more on that later in the chapter). Near the top right of the dialog, you'll see a pop-up menu that says **Local Adaptation**, and that's the only option you want to use (the others are holdovers from the "bad HDR" of CS4 and earlier. Yecch!).

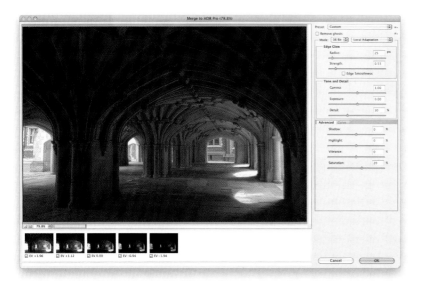

(Continued)

Step Three:

As I mentioned in the previous (Down & Dirty) HDR project, there's a Preset pop-up menu at the top right of the dialog, and you might be tempted to choose one of those presets, until you actually try a few (well, I'm kind of partial to Scott5, but outside of that one, and maybe City Twilight or RC5, my guess is that'll be the last time you try 'em. Yes, they're that bad). Anyway, ignore those for now, and just know that, instead, a lot of your editing work will be spent finding a good balance between the two Edge Glow sliders. The Radius slider controls the size of the edge glow, and the Strength slider controls the contrast of that glow. Move these two sliders in small increments and you'll stay out of trouble. In my Scott5 preset, I set the Radius at 176 and the Strength at 0.47 (as shown here).

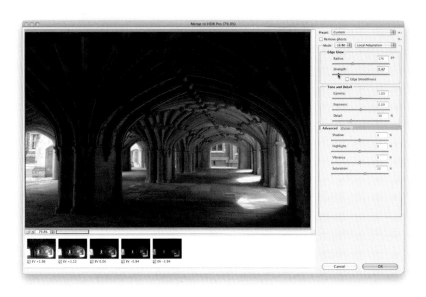

Step Four:

A new feature in Photoshop CS6 is Edge Smoothness (at the bottom of the Edge Glow section) and it's well named—when you turn it on, it kind of smooths out the edges a bit, but at the same time, it also enhances the detail. If you turn it on at this stage of the game (when you've only tweaked the Radius and Strength sliders), it's not going to look like it's doing much of anything (and right now, it's not), but once we juice this baby up and turn it on, then I think you'll really like it (but as with any slider, it doesn't look good on every image, so you'll just have to try it and see). For now, let's keep it turned off, and once we crank things up, we'll come back and turn it on, and you'll get a better look at what it really does.

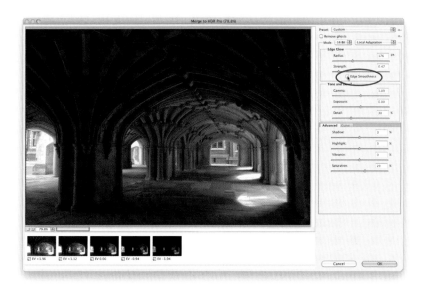

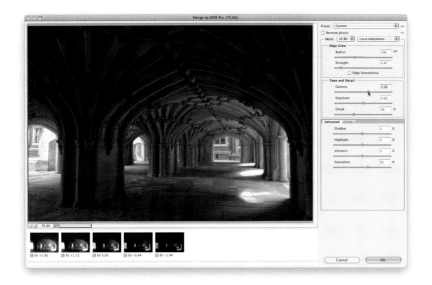

Step Five:

The next section down is Tone and Detail, and we'll start with the Gamma slider. If your overall exposure looks pretty decent, you probably won't have to mess with the Gamma slider much (especially if you're trying to create a photorealistic HDR image, rather than the hyper-contrast fantasy look). The Gamma slider controls the midtones, and if you drag the slider in either direction, you'll see how it affects the image. For this image, which is going more in the hyperreal direction, set the Gamma to the right at 0.76 (as shown here).

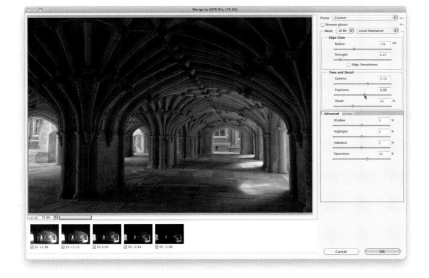

Step Six:

The Exposure slider controls the overall exposure, much in the same way the Exposure slider does in Camera Raw (dragging to the left darkens the overall image; dragging to the right brightens it). In this case, go ahead and drag the Exposure to 0.30 to lighten things just a little bit. If you look back at Step Three, you can see this doesn't look a whole lot different yet, but that's about to change.

(Continued)

Step Seven:

The next slider down is the Detail slider, which kind of acts like the Clarity slider in Camera Raw (it adds something similar to midtone contrast). Think of this as the "Make it look like HDR" slider, and cranking this one way up helps to create the hyperreal artistic look. In this case, set the Detail amount at 300% (as shown here). It's starting to now get that "HDR look."

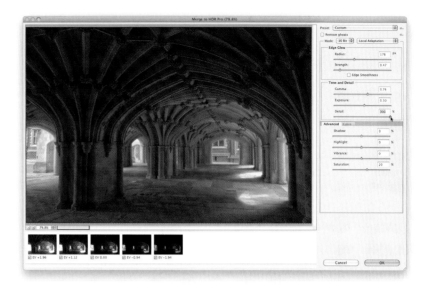

Step Eight:

Now, on to the Advanced tab (I have no idea why these are called "Advanced," since these sliders live in the Basic panel in Camera Raw and do very similar things). The top two sliders—Shadow and Highlight—don't usually have a big effect. Dragging the Shadow slider to the right makes the shadow detail lighter—kind of like Camera Raw's Shadows (but without as much power). The Highlight slider acts like Camera Raw's Highlights slider and dragging it to the left pulls back the very brightest highlight areas, but again, it doesn't have nearly as much effect as Camera Raw's Highlights slider. Here, go ahead and set the Shadow amount at 100%, which brightens up the shadow areas inside the arches, and lower the Highlight amount to –30%, which reduces some of the really bright lights in the stone floor. Now, keep in mind that these are two sliders that will change some from image to image. Most of the time, I wind up lowering the Highlight amount either a little or a lot (depending on the image), and raising the Shadow amount to keep the shadows from getting too dark. But, again, it just depends on the image.

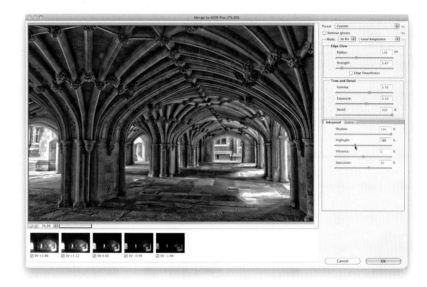

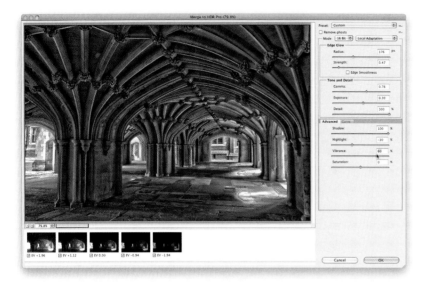

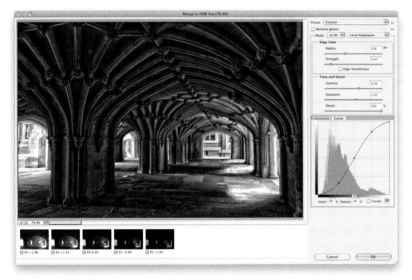

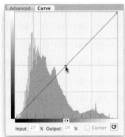
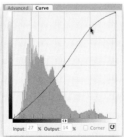
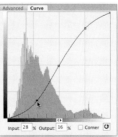

Click to add a point to the center

Add a point halfway from the center to the top, then click-and-drag upward

Add a point halfway from the center to the bottom, then click-and-drag downward

Step Nine:

The next two sliders down, Vibrance and Saturation, are also in Camera Raw, but again, the versions here in HDR Pro don't have nearly as much power. Basically, these make the colors more punchy, so if your image needs more color, try dragging the Vibrance slider to the right. If you want to take your image to "Harry Potter land," then boost the Saturation amount, as well. Here, we'll set the Vibrance at 60% and set the Saturation at 0%. Be careful about adding too much Vibrance or Saturation at this point, because in the next step, when we add contrast, that usually makes the colors automatically more vibrant.

Step 10:

Lastly, there is no Contrast slider here in HDR Pro, so click on the Curve tab to reveal a point curve like the one in Camera Raw. You see that diagonal line going across the curve grid? Well, we bend that line into a subtle S-curve and that adds contrast. The steeper we make this S-curve, the more contrast it adds. So, start by clicking once in the center of the line and it adds an adjustment point there (see bottom left). Now, add another point halfway between that center point and the top right, then click-and-drag it upward a bit (as seen in the bottom center). Now, add another point halfway between the center and the bottom-left corner, click-and-drag it downward a bit (as seen in the bottom right), and there's your contrast. Remember, if you need more contrast, click-and-drag the top point up higher and the bottom point down lower, which makes the curve steeper.

(Continued)

Step 11:

Okay, now we can go back and turn on the Edge Smoothness checkbox. You'll see the image soften a bit, but at the same time, you'll see more detail come out (which is great for this type of look). Remember back in Step Four when we turned it on, we really didn't see much of anything? Well, toggle it on/off a few times and you'll see that it now really adds a lot. By the way, in the previous step, when we increased the contrast, it made the highlights a little too bright, so I went back to the Highlight slider and pulled them back to –80, since the stone floor was starting to blow out in some areas. *Note:* At this point, you could save this as an HDR Pro preset (click on the icon to the right of the Preset pop-up menu and choose **Save Preset** to add it to the list).

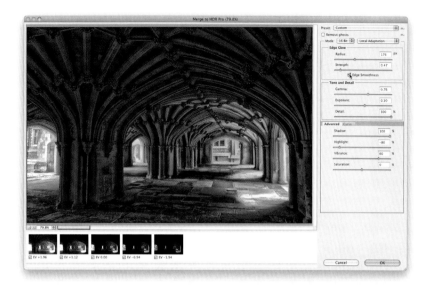

Step 12:

Now, click the OK button at the bottom right to have Photoshop process the image. When it's done, the HDR image appears in Photoshop (as seen here). There's something many people don't re-alize about the post-production process of HDR images: there's always a second round of processing in Camera Raw. How do you get your image back into Camera Raw? First, you have to save it as a TIFF, PSD, or JPEG (if you want to keep it in 16-bit mode, save it as a TIFF or PSD), so choose **Save As** from the File menu (as shown here), give your image a name, click Save, and then close the image. Next, under the File menu, choose **Open (PC: Open As)**. When the dialog appears, click on the image you just saved, and from the Format (PC: Open As) pop-up menu at the bottom, choose **Camera Raw** (as shown here) to have the image open in Camera Raw for processing, and then click Open.

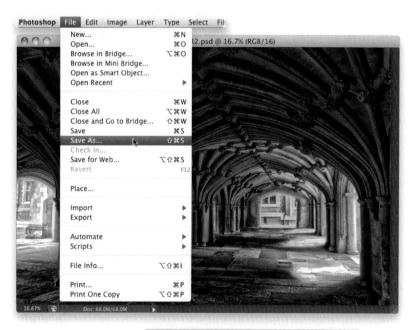

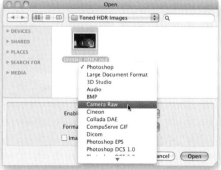

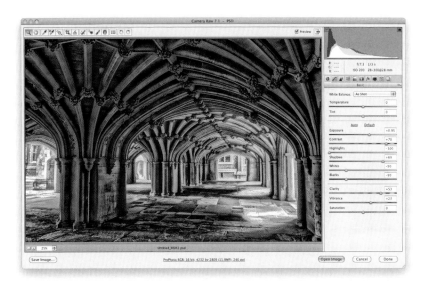

Step 13:

The image looks a little bit dark over-all, so increase the Exposure to +0.95. Okay, the image looks brighter, but it also looks kinda flat, so this is where you want to bump up the Contrast. Here, I bumped it up to +70. The light outside looks like it's blowing out and we need to recover as much of that as we can, so drag the Highlights slider all the way to the left to –100. To open up the shadow areas in the ceiling, we're going to bump up the Shadows to +60. That brings in a lot more detail, too. We still have a prob-lem with the bright light, so we're going to have to lower the Whites. There's such a broad contrast between the dark ceil-ings and the bright light streaming in that we need to lower them to –50. And, to keep the image from looking washed out, we need to lower the Blacks. Anytime I see an image looking washed out, the first thing I think of is I need to lower the Blacks, so drag that slider to the left to –50. Of course, since an image like this has so much texture, it's perfect for Clarity, which enhances the texture, so increase the Clarity to +53. And to bring out the color, we're going to increase just the Vibrance to +23, which gives us the nice, vibrant look that we see here.

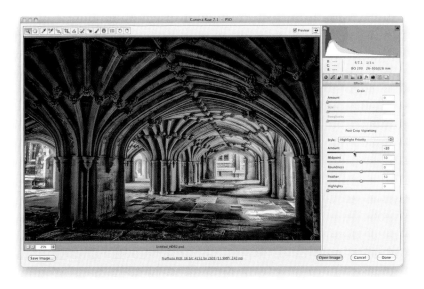

Step 14:

The last finishing move for this would be to darken the edges all the way around, so the focus isn't on the outside of the photo, but kind of leads your eye to the center. To do this, click on the Effects icon (the fourth one from the right) at the top of the Panel area, and go under Post Crop Vignetting. Make sure your Style is set to **Highlight Priority**, which is the default, because it's the best look-ing one, and then lower the Amount to –20. That's really all we're going to have to do—just lower the Amount to –20 and we're looking pretty good.

(Continued)

Step 15:

Click the Open Image button to re-open the image in Photoshop. At this point, I generally add two finishing moves (the same two I did in the Down & Dirty HDR project before this one): (1) I add High Pass sharpening (you can look back at the Down & Dirty project, or just check out page 189 to see how to add this), and (2) I add a soft overall glow by duplicating the Background layer, then adding a 50-pixel Gaussian Blur (that's based on a 12-megapixel camera file. If you're shooting a higher megapixel camera, you might have to use 60 or 70 pixels of blur), then lower the Opacity of this layer to 60%, and lastly change the blend mode of this blurry layer to **Soft Light** (as shown here) to create the glow effect (you can find more on exactly how to do this in the Down & Dirty project). A before and after is shown below.

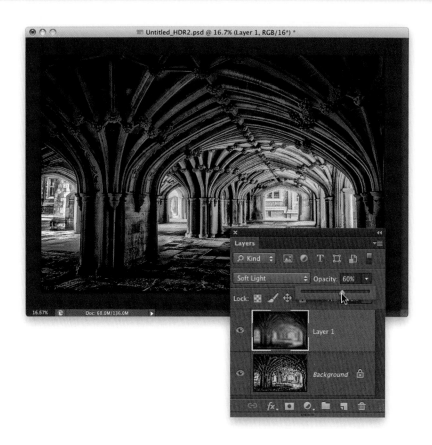

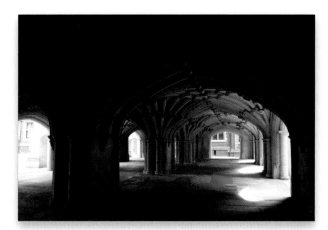

The original normal-exposure image

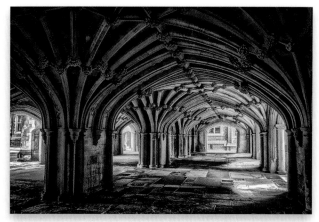

The HDR image after being processed with HDR Pro, along with edge vignetting, sharpening, and the glow finishing move

In the previous projects, we looked at the very popular, hyperreal tone-mapped look, which is definitely a creative, artistic use of HDR, but if you're looking to simply expand the dynamic range of what your digital camera can capture, without adding an "HDR look" to it, you'll be happy to know that getting that look is even easier (though I recommend going through the previous projects first, so you know what all the sliders do, because here I'm just going to give you a recipe for photorealistic HDR images).

Creating Photorealistic HDR Images

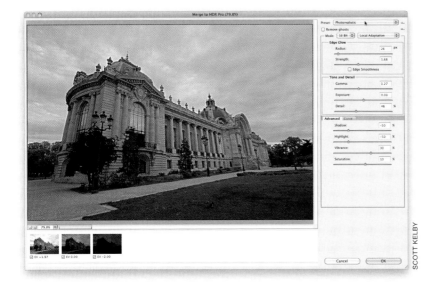

SCOTT KELBY

Step One:

Start by selecting your HDR-bracketed images in Mini Bridge, then Right-click on any one of those thumbnails and, under Photoshop, choose **Merge to HDR Pro**. After a few moments, you'll see the Merge to HDR Pro dialog appear (seen here). Go ahead and choose **Photorealistic** from the Preset pop-up menu at the top right, and you'll find out (like I did) that the Photorealistic preset doesn't look so photorealistic sometimes. It actually looks like it has an effect applied. In fact, if you look at the side of this building, you can see an edge glow around it. Nothing screams HDR like an edge glow.

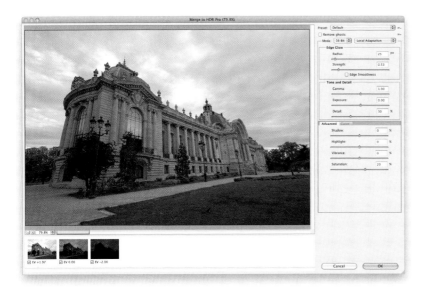

Step Two:

Surprisingly, the one that looks the most photorealistic to me is the preset called Default. So, choose **Default** from the Preset pop-up menu, and take a look at the image. The edge glow is gone, and look at, for example, the grass, trees, and left side of the building. You can now easily see there is a bird on the lawn, and you can see detail in the two trees on the left and in the left side of the building—things that were completely lost in the original exposure, as you'll see on the next page.

(Continued)

Step Three:

If you hand-held the shots, you may want to turn on the Remove Ghosts checkbox just to see if that makes a difference (it doesn't make a big difference in this one). You also might want to add a little bit of contrast using an S-curve, as shown here (see page 183 in this chapter for more on this). Below is a before and after, comparing the normal-exposure image and the HDR image. Again, notice how the HDR image reveals so much more in the details, and in the texture of the building, without it getting clogged up and turning to black in areas. You have detail in areas you wouldn't normally have it.

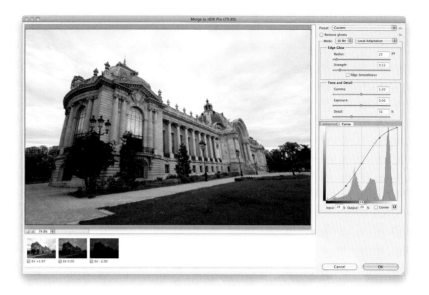

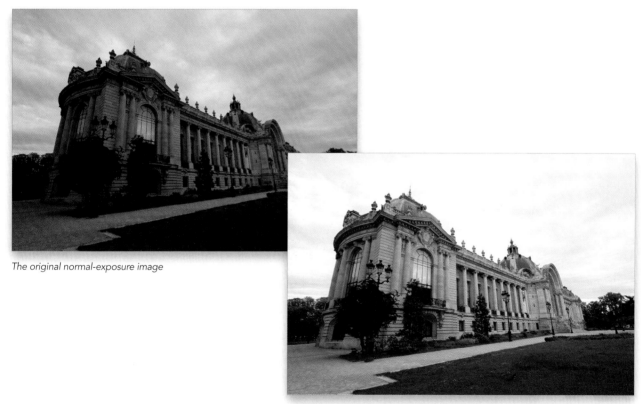

The original normal-exposure image

The HDR image using the Default preset settings and then adding an S-curve

Although I cover High Pass sharpening in the sharpening chapter, and in a few of the other projects in this chapter, I thought it was important to include it here as its own project, because High Pass sharpening has kind of become synonymous with HDR editing. High Pass sharpening is sometimes called "extreme sharpening" and that's a really good description of what it is. Here, I'm going to show you how to apply it, how to control it afterward, and an optional method that I use myself quite a bit.

High Pass Sharpening for HDR Images

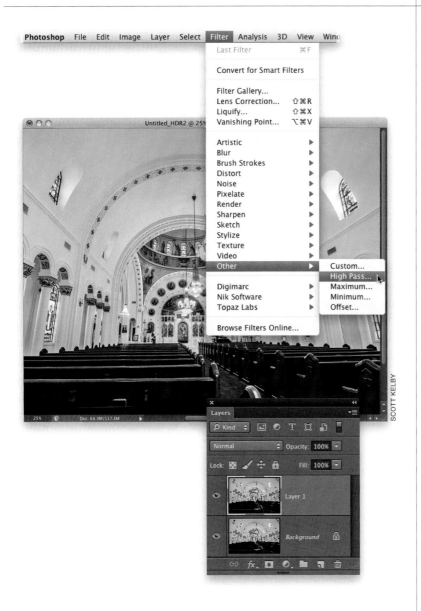

Step One:
Once you've finished creating your HDR image using Merge to HDR Pro, and it's open in Photoshop, start by pressing **Command-J (PC: Ctrl-J)** to duplicate the Background layer. Now go under the Filter menu, under Other, and choose **High Pass** (as shown here).

(Continued)

Step Two:

When the High Pass filter dialog appears, drag the Radius slider all the way to the left, so that everything turns solid gray. Now, drag the slider to the right until you can just start to see the color peek through the solid gray (as shown here)—the farther you drag, the more intense the effect will be (here, as an example, I dragged to 7 pixels, and you can see lots of edge detail starting to appear). When you're done, click OK.

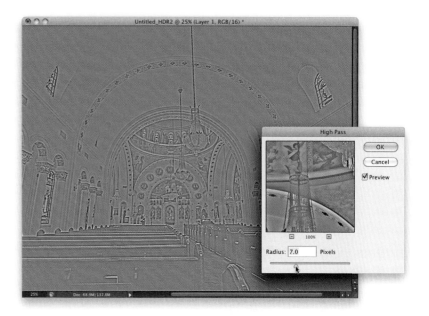

Step Three:

To bring the sharpening into the image, go to the top of the Layers panel and change the duplicate layer's blend mode from Normal to one of these three modes: (1) for medium sharpening, choose Soft Light; (2) for heavy sharpening, choose Overlay; or (3) for just insane sharpening, choose Hard Light (as shown here). If the sharpening seems like it's too much, you can lower the opacity of this duplicate layer. Think of this as the control for the amount of sharpening, so try lowering the Opacity amount (at the top of the Layers panel) to 75% (for 75% of the sharpening), or 50% if that's still too much. So, that's High Pass sharpening, but there's another option, and in the next step, we'll look at limiting where the sharpening is applied (and keeping some of the glow around the edges in check).

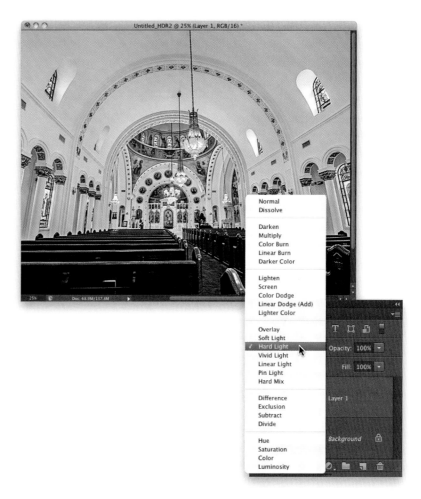

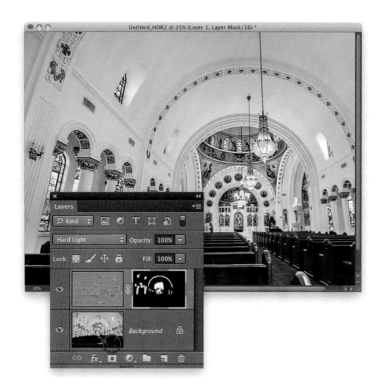

Step Four:

If you just need this level of intense sharpening over particular areas of your photo (like in this case, maybe over the gold tops of the columns and over the artwork), just press-and-hold the Option (PC: Alt) key and click on the Add Layer Mask icon at the bottom of the Layers panel (shown circled here) to hide your sharpened layer behind a black mask. Get the Brush tool **(B)**, and make sure your Foreground color is set to white. Then from the Brush Picker in the Options Bar, choose a medium-sized, soft-edged brush and paint over just the parts of the image you want to be super-sharp (here, I've painted over the gold tops of the columns, the chandeliers, the paintings, and tiles). Once you've painted over those areas, also try the Overlay and Soft Light blend modes to see which of the three you like best.

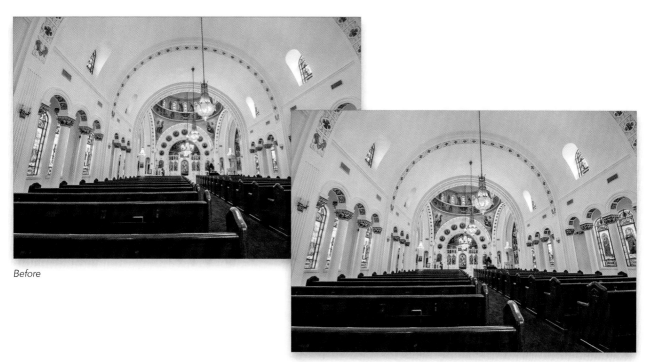

Before

After

Getting the HDR Look on a Single Image

You could actually get kinda close to an HDR look with a single image back in Photoshop CS5, but now in Photoshop CS6, with its new Camera Raw controls, and especially the enhancements and expanded power of Clarity, you can really get incredibly close to an HDR look using just one photo (instead of combining a number of bracketed photos). Here's the recipe to make it happen:

Step One:

Here's the original single-image exposure, and it's the perfect kind of image to apply an HDR look to. There's a wide tonal gap between the bright light coming in from the windows and the dark shadows in the rest of the image; plus, things with lots of texture and detail tend to look great as HDR images, and if they look great as HDR, they'll look great with an HDR effect applied, even though we're applying it to one single image, rather than a set of bracketed exposures in HDR Pro. Start by opening the image in Camera Raw. Here's the basic recipe we follow: crank up the Shadows, crush down the Highlights, add lots of Blacks, max out the Clarity, add a dark edge vignette, and then add some sharpening. Okay, let's try it.

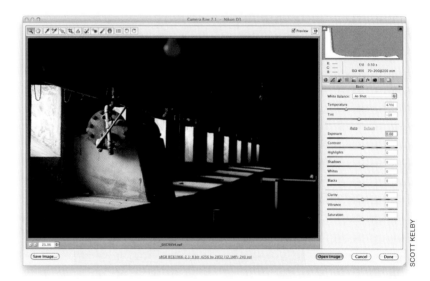

Step Two:

Drag the Highlights slider all the way to the left. Then, drag the Shadows slider all the way to the right, which tends to make the image look washed out. So, then drag the Blacks slider way to the left, until the photo doesn't look washed out anymore. Now, increase the Clarity to +100, and if the photo needs a little boost in color (I sure think this one does), crank up the Vibrance slider a bit (here I dragged it to +25). This particular image looks pretty dark overall, so I increased the Exposure to +1.40 (as shown here), but you won't always have to do that.

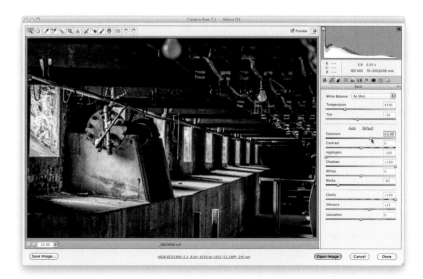

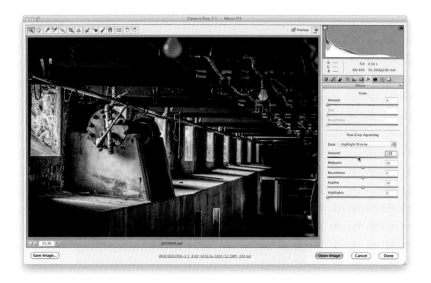

Step Three:

Next, let's darken the edges of the image (very popular with real HDR images) by clicking on the Effects icon (the fourth icon from the right) at the top of the Panel area and, in the Post Crop Vignetting section, dragging the Amount slider to the left until the edges look nice and dark (here, I dragged over to –13).

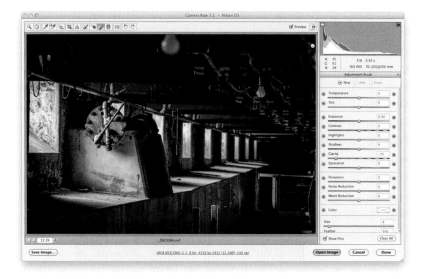

Step Four:

Now, we're going to apply a soft glow to the image (again, another typical effect you'd apply to a real HDR image), and we can do it right here in Camera Raw. Click on the Adjustment Brush **(K)** in the toolbar up top, and then click three times on the little – (minus sign) button to the left of Clarity. This resets all the other sliders to 0, and then sets the Clarity to a negative amount (–75), which creates a softening effect. Turn off the Auto Mask checkbox near the bottom of the panel (to speed up your painting) and paint over the entire image using this negative Clarity setting, giving you a similar effect to a soft glow you'd apply in Photoshop as a finishing move.

(Continued)

Step Five:

The final step here is to jump over to the Detail panel (it's the third icon from the left) and crank up the Sharpening Amount quite a bit (here, I cranked it up to 70), which completes the HDR look (a before/after is shown on the next page, along with some other images where I used Camera Raw to create the HDR look). Besides using Camera Raw, there is an HDR Toning feature in Photoshop that you can apply to a single image, and it uses the same presets and underlying techniques as HDR Pro. It doesn't do a bad job, but honestly I think you can get a better HDR look for single images using the new Camera Raw, so I just go with that. However, you at least should know where HDR Toning is and give it a try to see what you think.

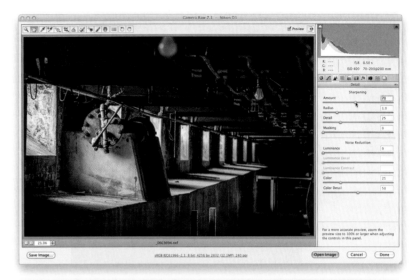

Step Six:

Go under the Image menu, under Adjustments, and choose **HDR Toning** (of course, before you do that, open your original image in Photoshop). Here are some settings that get you a decent faux-HDR look: Set your Edge Glow Radius to 100, the Strength to 0.84, and turn on Smooth Edges to hide the harsh edge lines. In the Tone and Detail section, set your Gamma to 0.82 and your Exposure to –0.57 to darken the image a bit. Set your Detail to +214% to add lots of crispness, then set your Shadow slider to –100% to darken and hide some of the speckled dots that are starting to appear in the shadow areas. Crank up the Vibrance and Saturation a bit to add in some color. Lastly, add an S-Curve (see page 183 earlier in this chapter for more on this) to add more contrast to your image. You'll notice there are some funky edge problems along the windows and in some other areas, which is another reason I prefer Camera Raw.

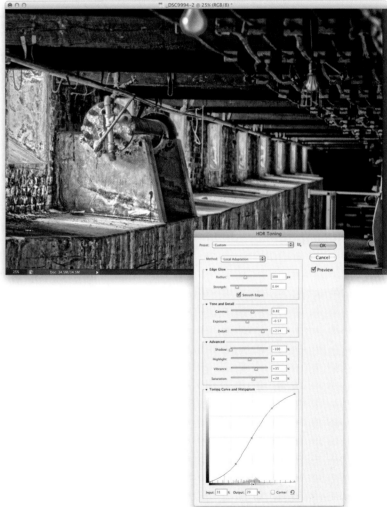

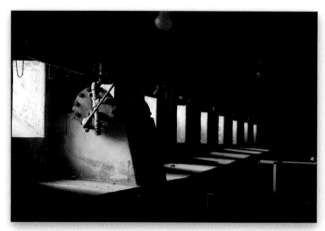

The original normal-exposure image

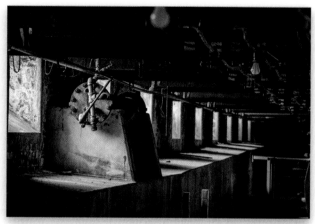

Using just Camera Raw to create the HDR look

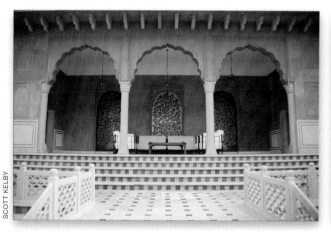

The original normal-exposure image

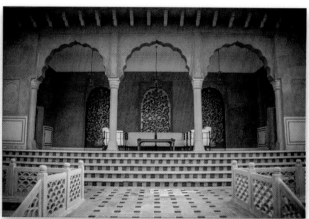

Using just Camera Raw to create the HDR look

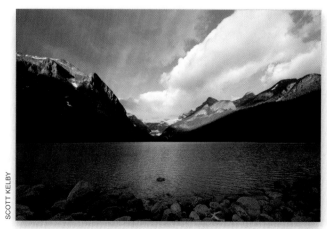

The original normal-exposure image

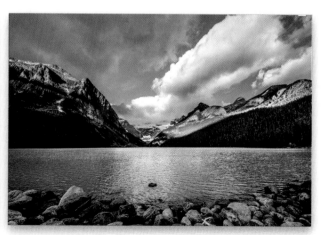

Using just Camera Raw to create the HDR look

Dealing with Ghosting in Merge to HDR Pro

If anything was moving slightly in the scene you were photographing (like water in a lake, or tree branches in the wind, or people walking by, etc.), you'll have a ghosting problem, where that object is either blurry (at best), or you'll actually see a transparent ghost of that part of the image (hence the name). In this hand-held photo of the Forbidden City, there are people moving in the scene, but in most cases, fixing that is just one click away.

Step One:

Open the HDR bracketed images in Merge to HDR Pro (see Step One on page 175 for more on how to do this). Here are some settings you can use for this image: Radius: 175, Strength: 0.25, Gamma: 0.75, Exposure 0.25, Detail: 300%, Shadow: –100%, Highlight: –50%, Vibrance: 25%, Saturation 25%, then click on the Curve tab and create an S-curve (see page 183 for more on this). Lastly, turn on the Edge Smoothness checkbox to enhance the detail and smooth out the edges. Now, if you look just right of front center, you see the problem: you can't keep tourists from moving (well, not without duct tape). You can see what looks like a semi-transparent version of the tourist in the foreground (which is why it's called ghosting).

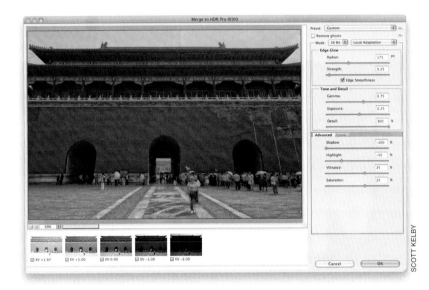

Step Two:

Luckily, fixing this is pretty darn easy: turn on the Remove Ghosts checkbox at the top right of the dialog (it's shown circled here in red). Merge to HDR Pro tries to deal with the ghosting by look-ing for things that are in common in all your exposures to lock onto and it does a pretty amazing job of it. Of course, sometimes it makes the wrong guess (more likely, if you're creating HDR from JPEG images rather than from RAW images), and if this happens, you can choose which of your bracketed photos you think it should lock onto, by clicking on its thumbnail in the filmstrip at the bottom of the dialog.

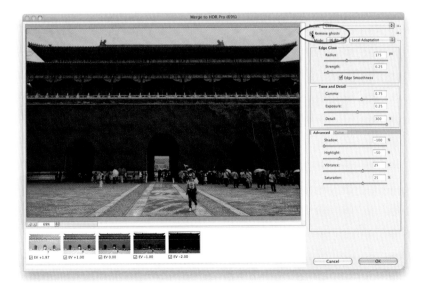

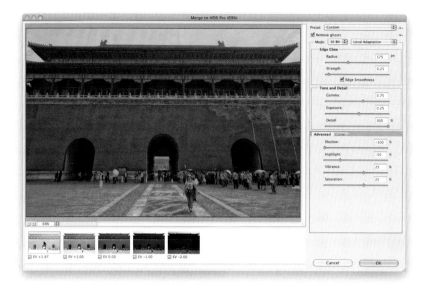

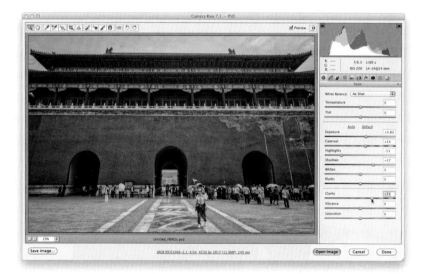

Step Three:

The thumbnail with the green highlight around it is the one it chose to lock onto for de-ghosting purposes (you'll only see this green highlight when the Remove Ghosts checkbox is on), and if you look back in Step Two, you'll see that it originally chose the thumbnail on the far right. If you want to try one of the other images, and see if using it does a better job than the one Photoshop chose, just click on it down in the filmstrip. Here, I clicked on the first image, but it actually looks worse. (Note: If you shot a multi-photo exposure of something, like waves rushing to the shore, you can actually choose which individual wave you want visible using this same technique, so it's not just for ghosting.) So, at this point, I'd click back on the far-right thumbnail.

Step Four:

Now, what would you do if the Remove Ghosts checkbox didn't work at all? Then, you'd use the trick you'll learn in the next project ("Creating a Blended HDR"), and you'd paint in the original person from the single still image (it works really well actually). In this case, it worked (yay), so now you would just finish this HDR image off just like you learned earlier in this chapter—by saving it as a TIFF, PSD, or JPEG, then reopening it in Camera Raw for the finishing moves. In this case, I added an edge vignette in the Lens Corrections panel (what's an HDR without a huge vignette, eh?), and then I used the settings you see here in the Basic panel: it's kind of underexposed, so increase the Exposure to +0.80, add some Contrast by increasing it to +14, pull back the bright highlights by dragging the Highlights slider to the left to –53, and open up those shadows in the three archways by dragging the Shadows slider to +37. Lastly, as always, I pumped up the Clarity (in this case, to +33, as shown here).

Creating a Blended HDR

We've all seen HDR images where parts of the image look funky, with big glows around the edges of things and dark or black skies that look obviously "HDR'd," plants and trees that look plastic, and lots of weird-looking areas that instantly tip you off that you're looking at a heavily "HDR'd" image (and not in a good way). The technique we're going to learn here takes the image with the regular exposure and blends it with the HDR image to get the advantages of a tone-mapped HDR image, without all that bad stuff that can come with it. That way, people say, "Hey, is that an HDR image?" instead of, "Oh, that's been HDR'd!"

Step One:
Go to Mini Bridge, select your bracketed photos, then Right-click on any one of those thumbnails and, from the pop-up menu that appears, under Photoshop, choose **Merge to HDR Pro** (as shown here).

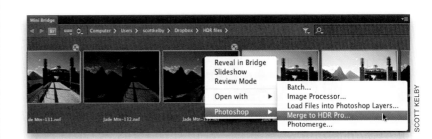

Step Two:
When the Merge to HDR Pro dialog appears, go ahead and choose the **Scott5** preset from the Preset pop-up menu at the top right of the dialog. Then, turn on the Edge Smoothness checkbox (as shown here) to reduce some of the harsh edges around the Piton mountains off in the distance and on the edges of the railing's shadow in the foreground. When you do this, you can see some of the funky stuff I was talking about up in the intro—a fakey-looking sky, glows around the mountains and the two colorful glass creations on top of the two columns in the foreground. The sidewalk is so textured now it almost looks like they need to clean it, and the trees on the left side look a bit "HDR'd" (not to mention, I apparently have a lot of sensor dust on my camera, because there are little spots and specks visible all over the sky, which we'll deal with later, so don't worry—we will deal with them). For now, just click OK to open the over-HDR'd image in Photoshop.

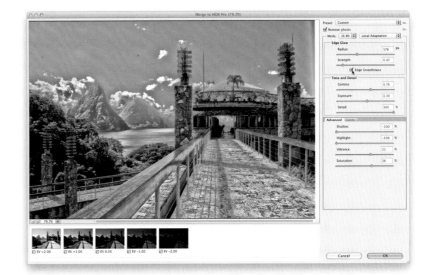

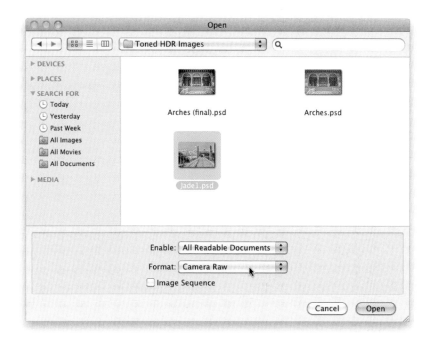

Step Three:

Once the image opens in Photoshop, go ahead and save it as a PSD, and close the image window, because we need to open this image in Camera Raw and do some tweaking there. Once you've saved it, go under the File menu and choose **Open (PC: Open As)** to bring up the Open dialog and find that image you just saved as a PSD. Click on it and, from the Format (PC: Open As) pop-up menu, choose **Camera Raw** (as shown here), and now when you click Open, your image will open in Camera Raw.

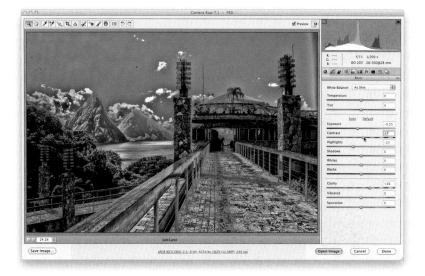

Step Four:

Here's our HDR image opened in Camera Raw. We're going to make it more contrasty by dragging the Contrast slider to the right (here I dragged it over to +7), then let's pull back the Highlights a bit to –23, and then let's enhance the detail even more by increasing the Clarity amount to +26. Also, the photo looks a little bright (to me, anyway), so lower the Exposure to –0.55. That's all we need to do in Camera Raw, so go ahead and click the Open Image button to open your HDR image in Photoshop.

(Continued)

Step Five:

Now, go back to Mini Bridge and find your bracketed shots. Double-click directly on the shot that is the normal, regular exposure (the one that's not over- or underexposed intentionally), so it opens in Camera Raw (as seen here). This regular-exposure image has its problems, too: The building is pretty much in the shade, so you don't see any detail at all back there, or in the two columns in front. At the same time, the sky and Piton mountains in the background look great, the trees look okay, and the sidewalk doesn't look filthy, so there's good stuff here, too. We're going to mix the best parts of this regular-exposure image with the best parts of the HDR image. But, so this photo doesn't look too flat when we do this, I generally add contrast, open up the shadows a bit, increase the Clarity (to enhance texture and detail), and increase the Vibrance (so the sky looks nice and blue).

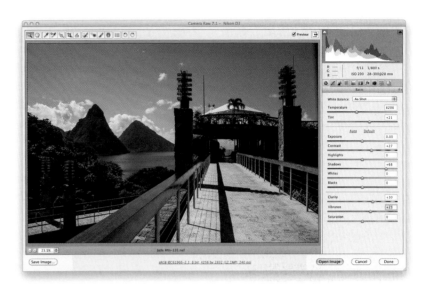

Step Six:

Click the Open Image button to open your regular-exposure image in Photoshop, and now you should have two images open: (1) the HDR image (with its problems), and (2) the normal-exposure image (with its problems). Now, it's time to take the best of each of these to help make an image that has the benefits of HDR, but without all the bad stuff.

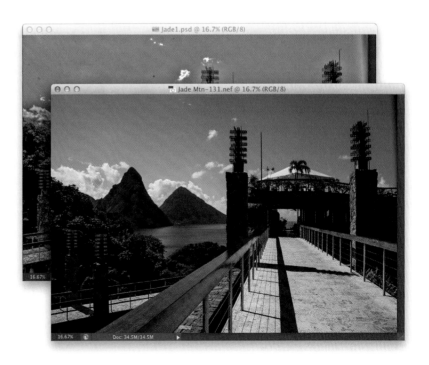

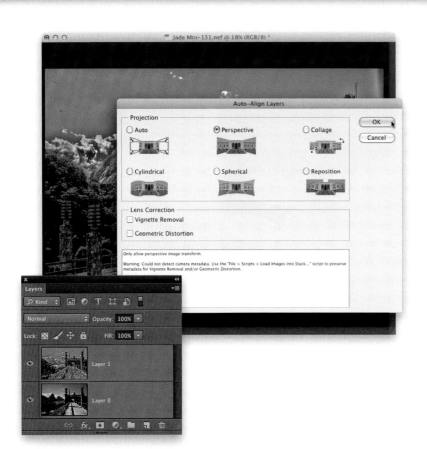

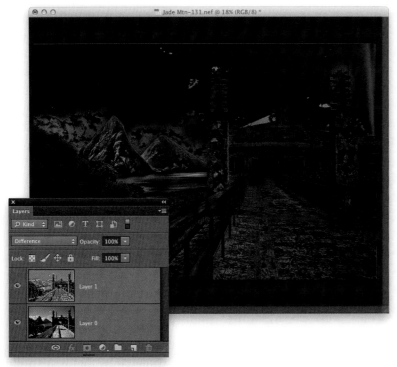

Step Seven:

Get the Move tool **(V)**, press-and-hold the Shift key, and drag-and-drop the HDR image on top of your regular-exposure image (holding the Shift key makes sure the two line up). *Note:* If you hand-held your HDR bracketed shots, and Photoshop had to do some layer alignment as it applied the HDR effect, holding the Shift key may not be enough to line these two perfectly up. If that's the case (and it usually is), then in the Layers panel, Command-click (PC: Ctrl-click) on both layers to select them both, go under the Edit menu, choose **Auto-Align Layers**, and click OK to have Photoshop align them (as shown here).

Step Eight:

To make sure the images are actually perfectly in alignment, go to the Layers panel and toggle on/off the little Eye icon that appears to the left of the top layer's thumbnail. This shows/hides that layer, and you'll be able to immediately see whether they're perfectly lined up (if the image seems to shift a pixel or two, either left/right or up/down, you'll see it right away). Now, you may not need to do this, but just in case you do see that it's off by a few pixels, I want to show you how I fix this. At the top of the Layers panel, change your layer blend mode from Normal to **Difference**. This highlights any alignment differences between the two layers. Your image should look almost solid black (like this does), but if you see a strong color edge, it's probably off by a pixel or two. It's been my experience that if it's off, more often than not it just needs to be nudged one pixel to the right and one pixel down. You do this, with the Move tool still active, by hitting the **Right Arrow key** on your keyboard once and the **Down Arrow key** once. Now, toggle on/off the Eye icon, again, and see how that looks.

(Continued)

Step Nine:

Now, if things look aligned correctly, switch your blend mode back to Normal (if not, keep nudging this top image a pixel or two until they're right on the money). Next, click on your top layer, so that only it is active, press-and-hold the Option (PC: Alt) key, and click on the Add Layer Mask icon at the bottom of the Layers panel to hide the HDR image layer behind a black mask. Get the Brush tool **(B)**, choose a soft-edged brush from the Brush Picker in the Options Bar and, since your mask is black, you need to paint in the opposite color, so make sure your Foreground color is set to white. Now, begin painting over the parts of the image that you want to have a more HDR look. For example, here I'm painting over the railing on the left side, and it reveals the railing on the HDR image layer, which has more detail and dimension than the original image has.

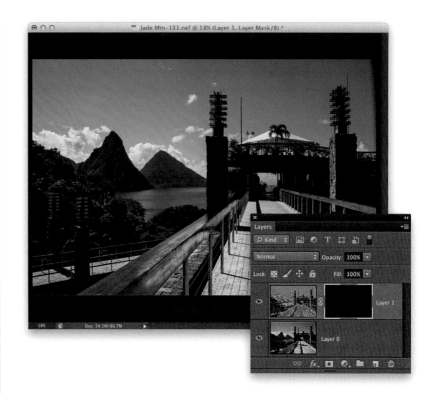

Step 10:

So, that's the plan: paint in white over things where you want more detail and dimension from the HDR image layer. For example, I'd paint over the building (but, I'd avoid the tent on the top, which looks okay), then I'd paint over the stone columns in front (as seen here), and you can see the effect it's having. All that detail is coming out now, but look at our sky and the mountains—they look realistic. We're kind of blending fantasy and reality in the same image.

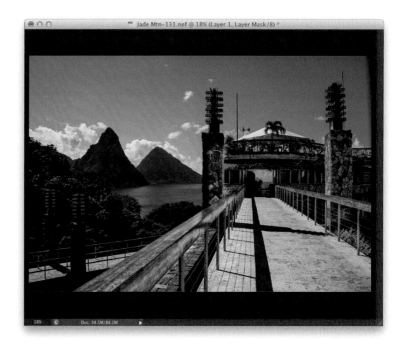

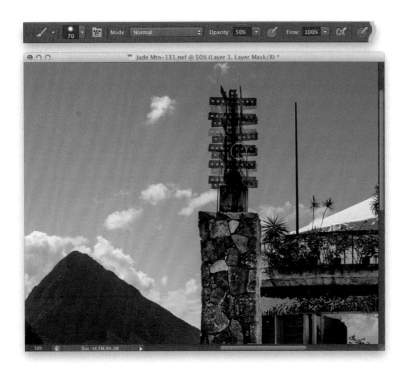

Step 11:

Here's a tip that really makes all of this work together pretty seamlessly: There will be areas in your image, like the glass ornaments on top of the columns, where it would be really tedious and tricky to paint over them without really affecting the sky. In those cases (and I do this in almost every image), you want to blend "some" of the HDR image here, but not the full strength. So, go up to the Options Bar and lower the Opacity of the Brush tool to 50%. Now when you paint in white, it only paints in the HDR image at half-strength, so bringing out these glass ornaments is much easier, because you don't have to mask it perfectly.

Step 12:

Now that you're at 50%, you can bring out other parts of the image without them looking "over-the-top." For example, here I painted at 50% over the trees on the left side to bring out some of that detail. I painted over the sidewalk, as well, to bring out half the HDR in it. But, I avoided that shadow of the railing, because once I painted over it, it got a funky-looking edge, so I just pressed **Command-Z (PC: Ctrl-Z)** to undo my painting, and then re-painted the sidewalk while avoiding that shadow. I painted over the other walkway on the left, too, but when I painted over the red glass ornaments, it looked weird, so I used Undo, and painted those col-umns again, but not the red glass. When you're done, choose **Flatten Image** from the Layers panel's flyout menu. Then, finally, get the Spot Healing Brush **(J)** and click once on each of those sensor dust spots in the sky to remove them, giving you the image seen here.

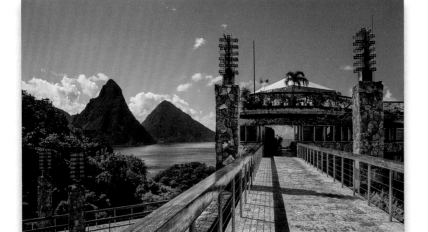

(Continued)

Single Image Regular Exposure

Here's the original exposure—one of the five bracketed photos taken for an HDR image.

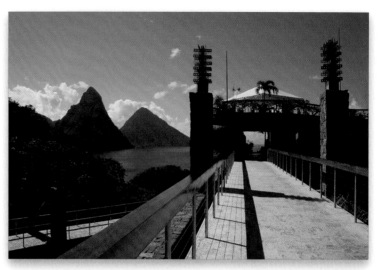

Five Images Combined into HDR

Here's the image after having those five bracketed exposures merged into one image using HDR Pro and the Scott5 preset (which looks kind of funky for this shot, but it was the best choice from the presets).

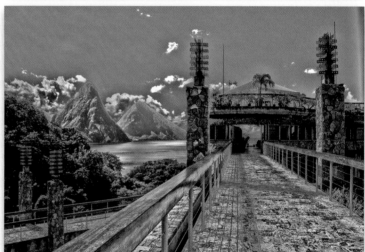

A Blend of the Two

Here's where we blended the two images, using the sky and Pitons from the original single image, mixed with varying amounts of the HDR image. For example, compare the three sidewalks: the top one looks like a regular exposure, the middle "totally HDR'd," and this one has only 50% of the HDR look. Also, look at the glass ornaments on top of the columns—too dark in the top shot, then they have those awful glows in the middle one, but this one has the right mix.

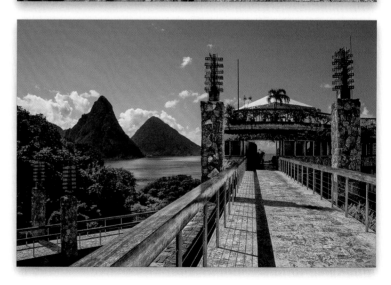

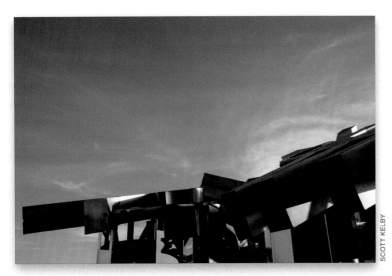

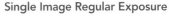

Single Image Regular Exposure

Here's another example using the same technique and similar settings. Shown here is the regular exposure—one of the five bracketed photos taken for an HDR image.

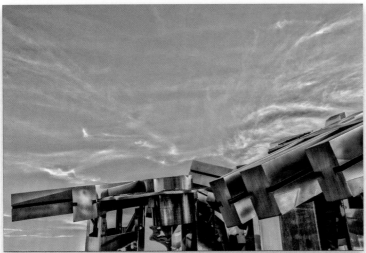

Five Images Combined into HDR

Here's the image after having those five bracketed exposures merged into one image using HDR Pro and the Scott5 preset (it looks great on the metal sculpture, but the sky looks totally "HDR'd").

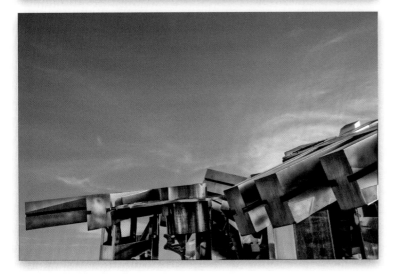

A Blend of the Two

Here's where I blended the two images, using the nice clean blue sky from the normal-exposure single image, mixed with the HDR image. In this instance, I didn't have to paint with the brush at 50% at all—I was able to just paint in the entire sculpture at 100% opacity, to give the blended image you see here.

HDR Finishing Techniques (Vignetting & Soft Glow)

Both of these are totally optional (but very popular) finishing moves for HDR images. I actually briefly covered these two effects earlier in this chapter when I applied them to our projects as finishing moves. But, I wanted to put them here separately, so if you wanted to just add one of these finishing techniques, you wouldn't have to go fishing through all those steps to find them. Plus, I'm going to show an alternate way to apply vignettes that keeps you from having to go back to Camera Raw.

Step One:

Once you've processed your bracketed photos in HDR Pro, you'll usually be re-opening your HDR image in Camera Raw for a second round of tweaking (see page 184 in this chapter for how to open it in Camera Raw). We'll start with our first finishing move: adding a dark edge vignette. There are actually two different places to apply vignettes in Camera Raw, and they both produce different looks, but the one I think looks the best (and gives you the most control) is Post Crop Vignetting (designed to be used after you've cropped the image, but you can apply it to an uncropped image, no problem). To get to this feature, in Camera Raw, click on the Effects icon (the fourth icon from the right) at the top of the Panel area.

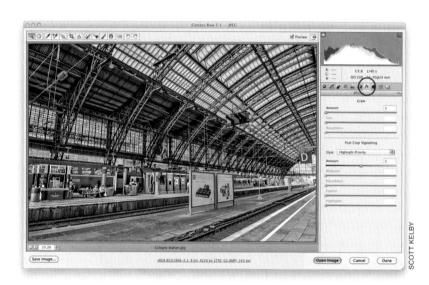

Step Two:

In the Post Crop Vignetting section, first make sure **Highlight Priority** is the selected Style (it's the only one that actually looks good), then drag the Amount slider to the left to darken the edges all the way around your image (as seen here). The Midpoint slider determines how far that darkening extends in toward the center of your photo (so I dragged it just a little to the left to make the dark edge bigger). If you want the edges extending inward to be softer, you can increase the Feather amount (although I normally don't).

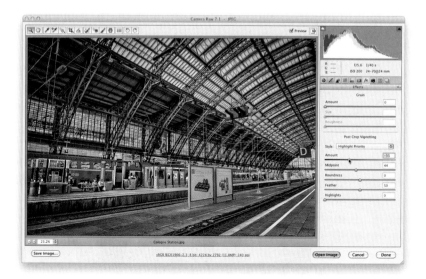

SCOTT KELBY

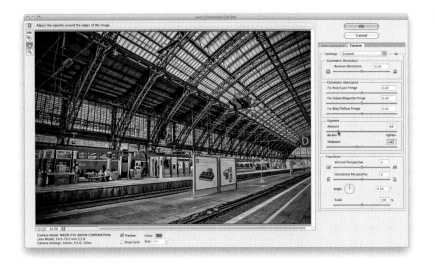

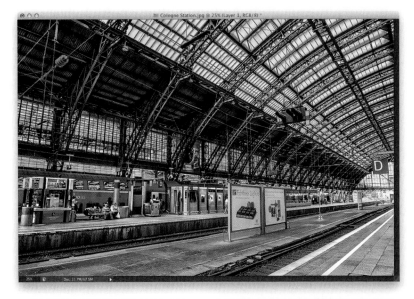

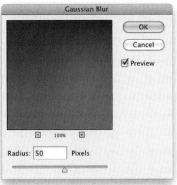

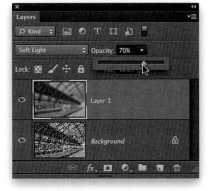

Step Three:

Now, if you're already done with your second round of tweaking in Camera Raw, and you decide you want to add an edge vignette, you don't have to go back to Camera Raw again, because the Lens Correction filter in Photoshop also lets you do vignetting (although I don't like the quality nearly as much as the Post Crop Vignetting in Camera Raw). To get to this, go under the Filter menu in Photoshop and choose **Lens Correction**. When the dialog appears (shown here), click on the Custom tab near the top right. In the Vignette section, drag the Amount slider to the left to darken the edges, and then drag the Midtone slider to the left a bit, too. These same controls are also found in Camera Raw and do the same thing (if you go to the Lens Corrections panel and click on the Manual tab).

Step Four:

To get the Soft Glow finishing move that's so popular for HDR images, try this: Press **Command-J (PC: Ctrl-J)** to duplicate your Background layer, then go under the Filter menu, under Blur, and choose **Gaussian Blur**. Enter 50 pixels for your Blur amount, and click OK, then at the top of the Layers panel, lower the Opacity of this blurry layer to 70%. It still looks really blurry, but what gives this the right look is when you change the blend mode of this blurry layer from Normal to **Soft Light**. Now, you get that soft glow across the image that takes the edge off the harsh HDR look. Again, both of these finishing moves are optional, so don't think you have to apply them, but now at least if you do want to apply them, you know how to do it.

Photoshop Killer Tips

Zooming In Really Tight? There's a Pixel Grid to Help You Out

You won't see this neat little feature unless you zoom in to 600% magnification or more—it's a little pixel grid that appears that makes it visually easier to tell pixels apart when you're zoomed in crazy tight. It's on by default (give it a try—zoom in crazy tight and see), but if you want to turn it off, just go under the View menu, under Show, and choose **Pixel Grid**.

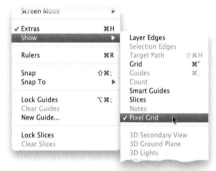

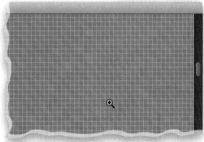

Duplicate Multiple Layers at Once

Pressing **Command-J (PC: Ctrl-J)** is not only the fastest way to duplicate a layer, it is also now the fastest way to duplicate multiple layers. Just go to the Layers panel, Command-click (PC: Ctrl-click) on the layers you want duplicated to select them, then use that same shortcut to duplicate all the selected layers (this is new in CS6).

Keeping Your Third-Party Plug-Ins from Loading into Photoshop

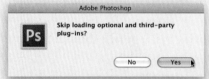

Before you launch Photoshop, press-and-hold the Shift key. A dialog will appear and, if you click the Yes button, it disables any third-party plug-ins. This can come in handy if you think you're having a problem in Photoshop caused by one. If you restart with them disabled and the problem goes away, you've probably found your culprit.

Create a New Document Just Like the Last One

There's a super-handy, yet little known shortcut, that lets you create a brand new document using the exact same specs (size, resolution, color mode, etc.) as the last one you made. Instead of choosing **Command-N (PC: Ctrl-N)** to bring up the New dialog, just press **Command-Option-N (PC: Ctrl-Alt-N)**, and when the New dialog appears, all the specs for your last document will be entered for you.

Saving Time in HDR Pro

The more images you use to create your HDR images, the longer it takes HDR Pro to compile your final image, so this is a case where less is more. I usually use five images (as I explained at the beginning of this chapter), but an interesting tidbit I learned from one of the Photoshop product managers is that, for the best results, you need more darker photos than lighter ones. So, if you don't mind the extra wait, you're better off having just one image with a really bright exposure and four darker ones, than you are with an equal balance.

Editing the Lens Correction Grid

When you use the Lens Correction filter in CS6, the first thing you'll notice is that "annoying grid" isn't turned on by default (by the way, the only reason it was annoying was because it used to be turned on by default). Now, not only is it off by default, but you can edit the size and color of the grid itself. When you turn on the Show Grid checkbox at the bottom of the Lens

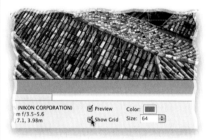

Correction dialog, a Size field and a color swatch become available to the right of the checkbox. Also, although there is a grid in the Lens Corrections panel of Camera Raw (press **V** to toggle it on/off), you can't change the size or color of that grid.

Hide All Your Panels Fast

If you want to focus on your photo, and temporarily hide your Toolbox, Options Bar, and all your panels, just press the **Tab key**. Press it again to bring them all back.

Renaming Multiple Layers Fast

Want to rename a bunch of layers? Just double-click directly on the first layer's name to highlight it, type in a new name, and then press the **Tab key** to jump to the next layer and its name field will be highlighted, ready to be renamed. The Tab key takes you to the next layer down; to jump back to a previous layer, press **Shift-Tab**.

Photoshop Killer Tips

Need Help Finding the Right Colors?

Back in CS4, Adobe introduced this very cool little utility called "Kuler" which was designed to help you find, mix, match, and try out different color schemes, and it was so popular that it spawned its own online community, with users sharing and rating different sets of colors based on themes. You can find Kuler built right into Photoshop in its own panel. Just go under the Window menu, under Extensions, and choose **Kuler**, and browse some of the most popular color combos right within Photoshop. If you see a set of colors you like, double-click on it to see them as larger swatches in a panel. To make any of those color swatches your Foreground color, just double-click on it.

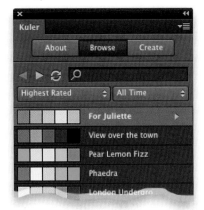

Putting Your Drop Shadow Right Where You Want It

If you're adding a drop shadow behind your photo using a Drop Shadow layer style (choose **Drop Shadow** from the Add a Layer Style icon's pop-up menu),

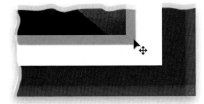

you don't have to mess with the Angle or Distance fields whatsoever. Instead, move your cursor outside the Layer Style dialog—over into your image area—and just click-and-drag the shadow itself right where you want it.

Getting Rid of Your Empty Layers Fast

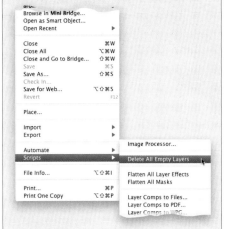

In CS5, Adobe included a built-in script that will go through your Layers panel and remove any empty layers (layers with nothing on them) automatically (once you get a large multi-layered project going, you wind up with more of these than you'd think). To have Photoshop tidy things up for you, go under the File menu, under Scripts, and choose **Delete All Empty Layers**.

Removing Noise from Cell Phone Photos

Since Photoshop is a pro tool, most of us probably wouldn't even think of using Camera Raw's built-in Noise Reduction feature to remove the noise from our cell phone camera's photos, but…why not? Cell phone photos are notorious for color noise, which Camera Raw cleans up really well. Try it one time, and I'll bet you'll use it more than you ever dreamed (to open

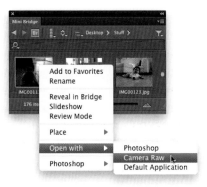

a cell phone photo in Camera Raw, just find it on your computer in Mini Bridge, then Right-click on it and, from under Open With, choose **Camera Raw**).

Using the HUD Pop-Up Color Picker

If you've ever thought, "There's got to be an easier way to pick colors than clicking on the Foreground color swatch every time," you're gonna love this: It's a pop-up color picker (Adobe calls it the HUD [Heads-Up Display], because you keep your eyes on the image, instead of looking over and down at the Foreground/Background color swatches). First, choose a Brush tool, then press **Command-Option-Ctrl (PC: Alt-Shift)** and **click (PC: Right-click)** on your image. It brings up a simplified color picker where you can choose your color (I find it easier to choose the hue first, from the bar on the right, then choose the tint and saturation of the color from the box on the left).

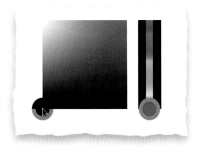

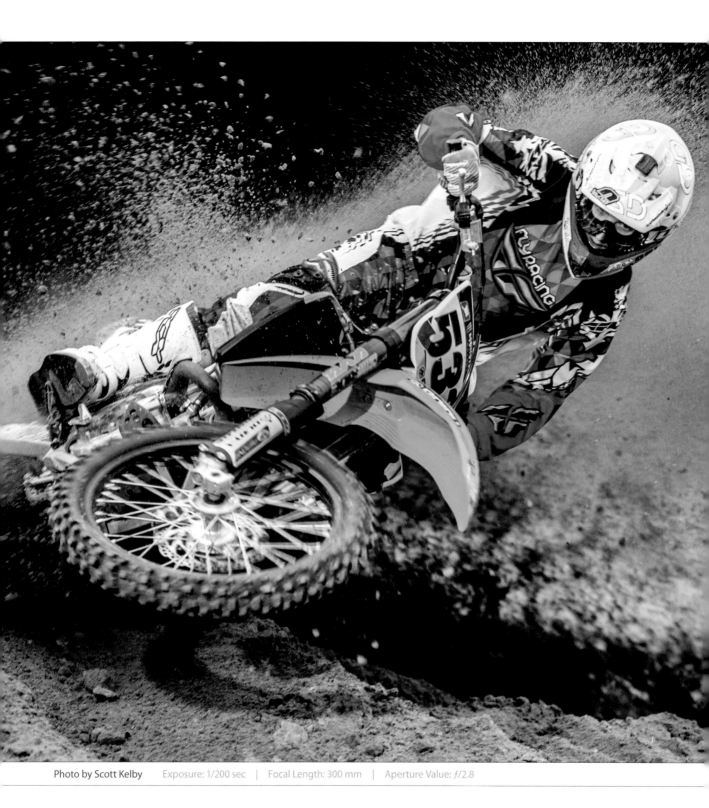

Photo by Scott Kelby   Exposure: 1/200 sec | Focal Length: 300 mm | Aperture Value: *f*/2.8

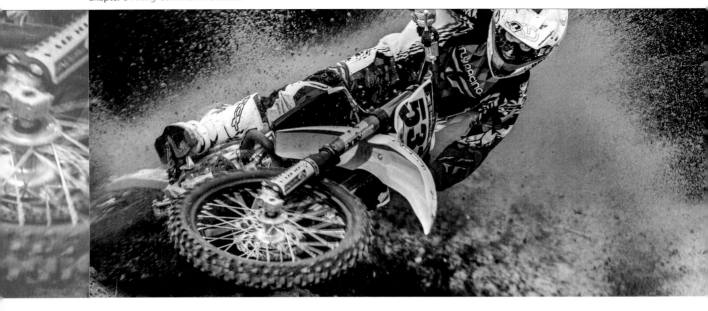

Little Problems
fixing common problems

The title for this chapter comes from the 2009 movie *Little Problems* (written and directed by Matt Pearson), but I could have just as easily gone with the 2008 short *Little Problems* (written and directed by Michael Lewen), but there was one big thing that made the choice easy. The first movie was about zombies. You just can't make a bad movie about zombies. It's a lock. Throw a couple of hapless teens (or in this case "an unlikely couple") into some desolate location with a couple hundred flesh-starved undead, and you've got gold, baby, gold! Now, has anyone ever wondered, even for a second, why every zombie in the rich and colorful history of zombies has an insatiable hunger for human flesh and only human flesh? Why can't there be zombies that have an insatiable hunger for broccoli? Then, in their bombed-out shell of a desolate vacant city, on every corner there would be other zombies selling broccoli the size of azalea bushes.

Anyway, it's just a little too coincidental that every zombie wants to eat you, but they don't want to eat something that might actually keep them alive, and is in ample and easily reproducible supply, like broccoli, or spring rolls, or chowder. Nope, it has to be human flesh, even though you know and I know (say it with me) it tastes like chicken (well, that's what I've been told, anyway). Another thing that drew me to the first *Little Problems* was the director's last name, seeing as all my books are published by subsidiaries of Pearson Education, a company who somehow chose to hire Ted Waitt as my editor, despite the fact that they were forewarned by the DCBGC (the Desolate City Broccoli Growers' Consortium) that Ted might not actually be the strict vegetarian he claimed to be in his resume. I probably shouldn't say anything bad about Ted, though. I don't want to bite the hand that feeds me.

When Your Subject Is in the Shadows

We all wind up shooting subjects that are backlit (where the light is behind your subject). That's because our eyes automatically adjust to the situation and we see the subject just fine in our viewfinder. The problem is our cameras aren't nearly as sophisticated as our eyes are, so you're almost guaranteed to get some shots where the subject is way too dark. Although I feel you get better results using Camera Raw's Exposure and Highlights sliders, the Shadows/Highlights adjustment does a fairly decent job, and there's a trick you can use to make the adjustment re-editable.

Step One:

Open a photo where your subject is in the shadows (it can be a person, or a building, or anything backlit). In this example, the light is behind our subject, so he's pretty much fully in the shadows. Ideally, we'd like to brighten him up, and the area around him, as well, to balance out the light in the photo. To do this, first go under the Filter menu and choose **Convert for Smart Filters**. This lets you apply the adjustment as if it was an adjustment layer (meaning you can re-edit it later if you need to, or even delete the adjustment altogether). Even though the adjustment we're going to apply isn't found under the Filter menu, for some reason Adobe lets it act like it is a smart filter, so why not take advantage of it, eh? Now go under the Image menu, under Adjustments, and choose **Shadows/Highlights**.

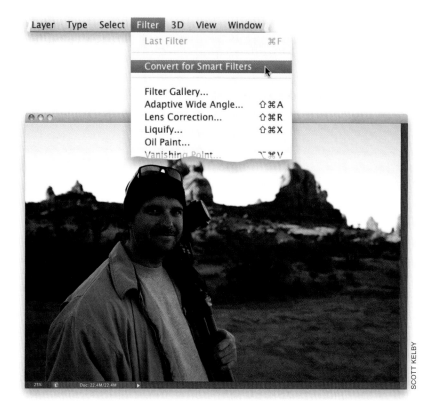

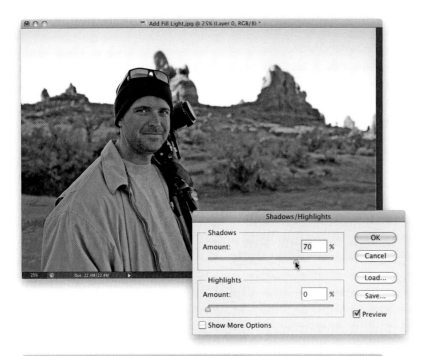

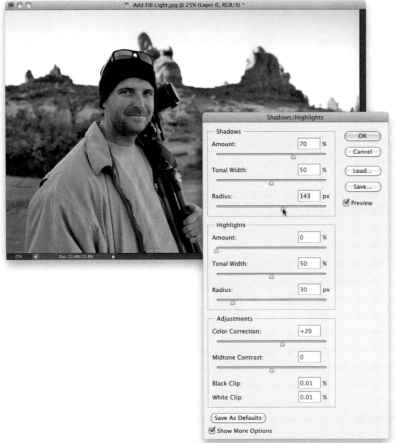

Step Two:

If you're choosing Shadows/Highlights, you probably have a problem in the shadow areas, which is why, by default, it's set to open up (lighten) the shadow areas in your photo by 35%. However, in this case, our subject is so buried in the shadows that we'll have to open the shadows quite a bit. The problem with opening the shadows 50% or higher is your photos tend to look kinda "weird and milky" (as you can see here, where I've increased it to 70%, and now he almost looks like he has a sunburn).

Step Three:

To get around that, turn on the Show More Options checkbox at the bottom of the dialog. This brings up an expanded version of the dialog (as shown here). The key to fixing this "weird and milky" look is to drag the Radius slider over to the right until it smooths out the effect and looks normal (here, I dragged it over to 143 pixels because that's where it looked most natural to me, but it really just depends on the photo. I would say that most of the time I set the Radius to around 125 to 175). By the way, the Radius amount determines how many pixels each adjustment affects, so to affect a wider range of pixels, you'd increase the amount, which is what we did here.

TIP: Save a New Default

If you come up with some settings you like, click the Save As Defaults button in the bottom-left corner of the dialog, and now it will open with your settings.

(Continued)

Step Four:

Now that the shadows are opened up (and look reasonably realistic), if you want, you can darken the highlights behind him. In most cases, you'll only have to fix one or the other—the shadows or the highlights—but not both. For example, to darken the sky behind him a bit, go to the Highlights section and drag the Amount slider to the right (as shown here; I also increased the Radius slider quite a bit, as well). If you drag too far, you might start to see some banding in the sky (where you start to see lines where the colors change, instead of a smooth transition between colors), so just keep an eye on the sky as you drag. If later you need to tweak these settings, because you applied this as a smart filter, you can go to the Layers panel, double-click directly on the words "Shadows/Highlights" (as shown here), and the Shadows/Highlights dialog re-opens, with the settings you used previously. Just make any changes you want, then click OK.

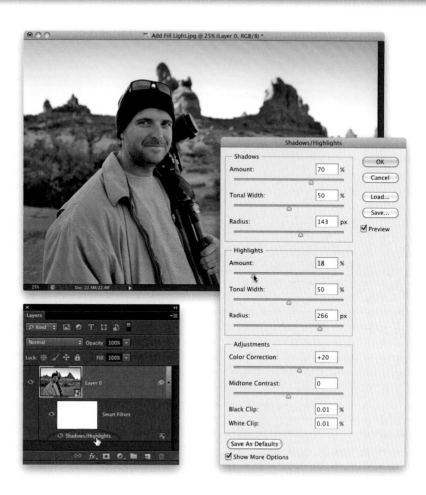

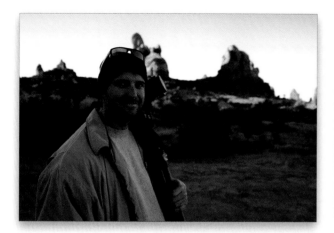

Before

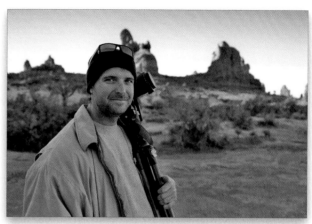

After (opening up the shadows and pulling back the highlights)

Nothing ruins an outdoor shot like a dull gray sky, but luckily, in many cases, you can save the shot by darkening the midtones a bit, and adding a blue tint or gradient to the sky. Here's how to do both:

Fixing Shots with a Dull Gray Sky

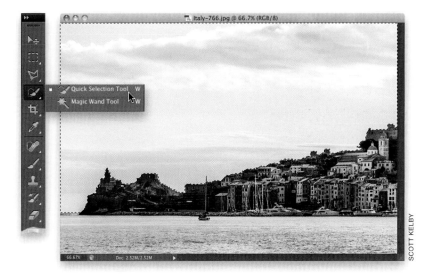

SCOTT KELBY

Step One:

Here's a shot where the sky is really blah. Not totally 100%, but close enough. Also, the clouds are a little dark, so even if you went into Camera Raw and lowered the exposure, those darkish clouds would look like rain clouds, and you'd have a whole different problem to deal with (an underexposed photo with the buildings in the shadows). So, this technique will work pretty well for this image. You'll start by making a selection of the sky and your first thought might be to use the Magic Wand tool. Now, if the sky was just a flat sky with no clouds, that would probably work out okay, but in this case (a sky with clouds), you're much better off using the Quick Selection tool (it'll select that sky in all of 5 seconds). So, get the Quick Selection tool **(W)** from the Toolbox, click it on the far-left side of the sky, then drag it over to the right side, and—BAM!—it's selected (as shown here).

(Continued)

Step Two:

When I make a selection like this, to make sure it didn't miss any little areas, I usually expand (grow) the selection outward by a pixel or two (that way, it kind of "digs-in" to the city a little and eliminates any little gaps that would be a giveaway you tweaked the sky). To do this, go under the Select menu, under Modify, and choose **Expand**. When the dialog appears, if it's a really high-resolution image, use 2 pixels. If it's a 6- or 8-megapixel image (or smaller), just use 1 pixel, then click OK (you probably won't see anything onscreen when you do this—you just have to trust that it actually expanded outward by a pixel or two).

Step Three:

To get a realistic color for the sky, we're going to open another photo that already has a nice sky color (you can download this same photo, and most of the key photos used in this book, at the web address listed in the introduction at the front of the book). Once you open the image, switch to the Eyedropper tool (**I**), and click once on the brightest blue area in the image (as shown here) to make that your Foreground color. Now, press the letter **X** to swap your Foreground and Background colors, then click the Eyedropper on the darkest blue in the photo (higher in the sky), so that now your Foreground is a darker blue, and your Background is a lighter blue.

TIP: The Color Selector Ring

That ring that appears when you use the Eyedropper tool is there to help you see which color you're selecting. The outside ring is a neutral gray, which just helps to make sure you're seeing the right color without being influenced by other colors around it. The bottom half of the inside ring shows the old color, and the top half shows what your Foreground color would change to if you clicked right now.

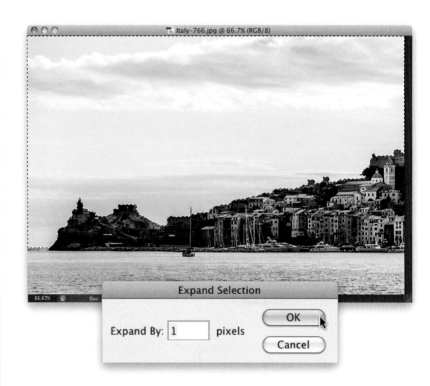

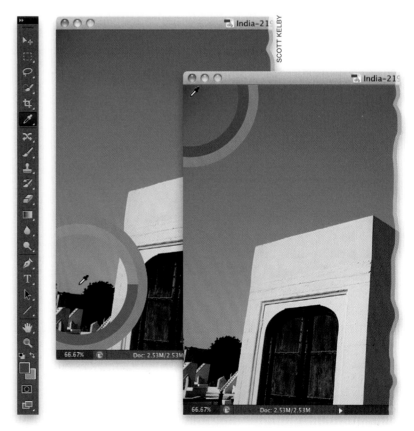

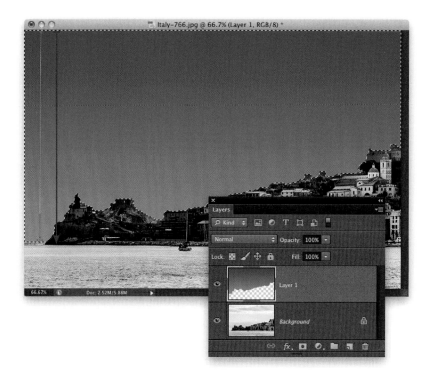

Step Four:
Go back to the original image, then go to the Layers panel and add a new, blank layer by clicking on the Create a New Layer icon at the bottom of the panel, then switch to the Gradient tool **(G)**, and click-and-drag your gradient from the top of the photo down to the bottom of the sky (the light blue color should be at the bottom of the gradient). This fills the new layer with a gradient made up of your Foreground and Background colors (as seen here). For some images, you can leave this gradient as is (or maybe just lower the layer opacity a little to let it blend in), but I think it usually looks a little too fakey, which is why there are two more steps.

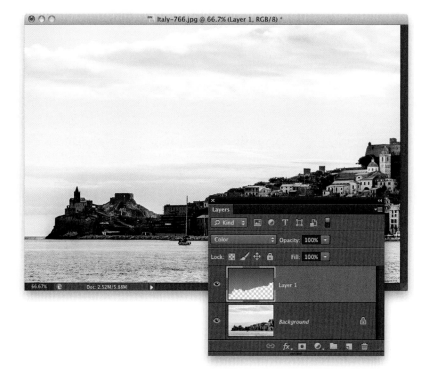

Step Five:
First, press **Command-D (PC: Ctrl-D)** to Deselect, then go to the Layers panel and change the layer's blend mode from Normal to **Color** (shown here), just to see how the color itself looks. In this case, it looks a bit too cyan and fakey, so we'll have to take it another step further (don't worry—it's easy), but at least we can see that we're in the ballpark (so to speak).

(Continued)

Step Six:

There are two layer blend modes that add contrast to our layer: Soft Light and Overlay. Let's try both of those. When you try Soft Light, you can see its effect is more subtle, and Overlay (shown here) is more contrasty (and in this case, that's what I'd go with, because it looks darker, but not at all over-the-top. If you want a really dramatic sky, try Color Burn, and then lower the layer's Opacity to around 50%). If you're not sure which one you want, just press **Shift-+** (plus sign) to toggle through all the different blend modes until you find one you like. A before and after are shown below (it's subtle, but it's supposed to be).

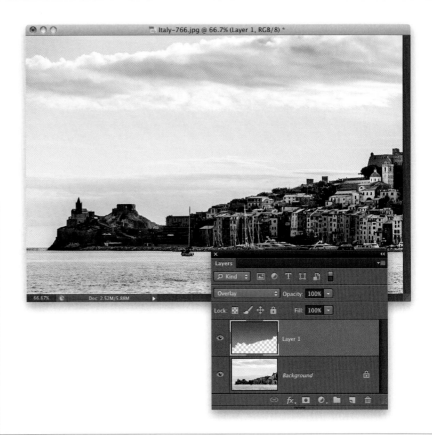

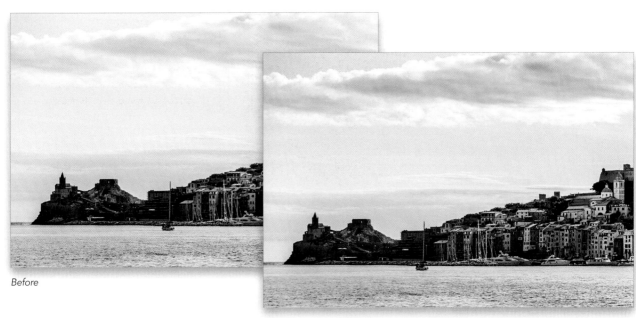

Before

After

In CS4 and earlier versions of Photoshop, when we wanted to dodge and burn, we had to jump through a bunch of hoops (creating special layers, and using blend modes and such), because the Dodge and Burn tools were…well…let's just say they weren't the best (and that's being kind). Luckily, back in Photoshop CS5, Adobe updated these tools, which totally fixed the problem, and now it's safe to use the Dodge and Burn tools for lightening and darkening different parts of your image.

Using the Dodge and Burn Tools

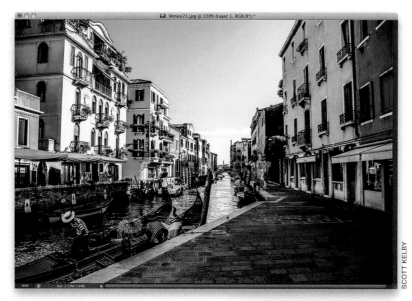

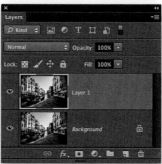

Step One:
Before we dig into this, I just want to you let you know up front that I would normally do my dodging and burning inside Camera Raw using the Adjustment Brush (and do the lightening and darkening using only the Exposure slider). However, if you're already in Photoshop and don't want to go back to Camera Raw, then here's how you'd do it: In the photo shown here, our light is kind of out of balance. The thing I want people drawn to is the gondola on the left in the foreground, but the brightest thing in the photo (the thing that draws your eye) is the building in the top-left corner, which is where I don't want the viewer looking. In fact, almost the entire foreground is in shadow, so first, we're going to dodge (lighten) the gondola, and then we'll brighten up the buildings and sidewalk on the right side of the image. Then, we're going to burn (darken) the buildings on the left and the sky. Basically, we're just going to rearrange how the light is falling on our photo. Now, I don't use the Dodge and Burn tools directly on the original photo. Instead, press **Command-J (PC: Ctrl-J)** to duplicate the Background layer. That way, if we don't like what we've done, we can lessen the effect (by lowering the layer's opacity) or undo it altogether by throwing the layer away.

(Continued)

Step Two:

Get the Dodge tool **(O)** from the Tool-box (as shown here), and begin painting over the area you want to lighten (in our case, we'll start by painting over the gon-dola on the left—you can see the brush cursor near the front of it here). Keep holding the mouse button down as you paint, because the Dodge and Burn tools have a build-up effect—each time you release the mouse button and start paint-ing again, the amount of Dodge (or Burn) builds up.

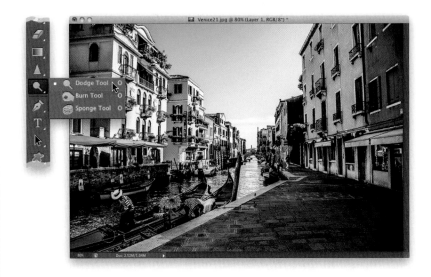

Step Three:

Release the mouse button, and paint over that same gondola area again, and you'll see how it gets another level brighter. Remember: While the mouse button is held down, you're painting one level of brightness. Release the mouse button, then click-and-paint over that area again, and you're painting over the original brightness with more brightness, and so on (it's kind of like polishing a silver platter—the more times you polish it, the brighter it gets). Now look at how much brighter the gondola is here, compared with the original image in Step One. Next, let's work on the buildings on the right and the walkway.

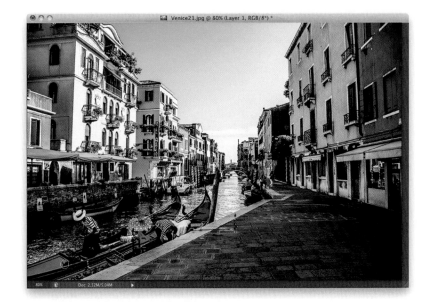

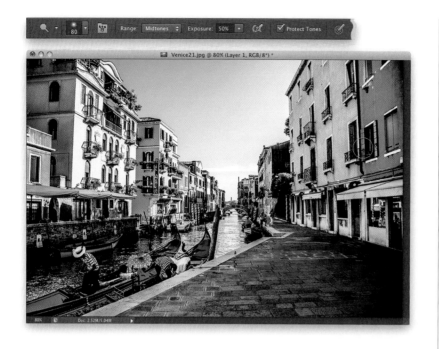

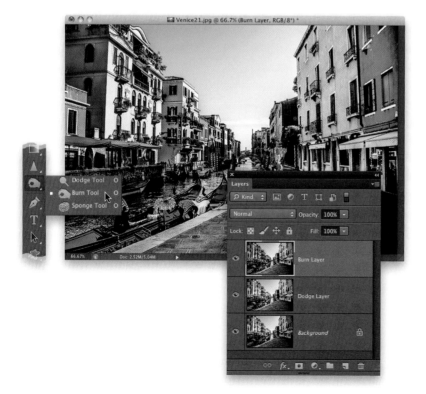

Step Four:

Start painting over both buildings and the walkway to dodge (brighten) them, but keep the mouse button held down the whole time to paint just one level of brightness over them. Now, release the mouse button and paint over just the orange building on the far right again (it's pretty dark, so we need to brighten it more than the rest, like you see here). Now, before we switch to burning on the buildings on the left, take a look up in the Options Bar for this tool, and you can see that we've been dodging just the Midtones (and that's generally where I do my dodging and burning), but if you wanted the tool to just affect the Highlight or Shadow areas, you can choose that from that Range pop-up menu. Also, the 50% Exposure amount is fine for something like this, but if I were doing this on a portrait, I'd usually want something much more subtle, and I'd lower the amount to around 10%–15%.

Step Five:

Now let's switch to burning: first start by pressing **Command-J (PC: Ctrl-J)** to duplicate your top layer. So, at this point, you've got the original untouched image as your Background layer, the brightened Dodge Layer in the middle (I renamed it "Dodge Layer" just to make it easier to see), and a copy of the brightened layer on top, which is the one we're going to burn on (I named it "Burn Layer"). By keeping everything on separate layers, if you don't like the burning effect, you can reduce it by lowering the opacity, or delete it altogether and you won't lose the dodging you did on the layer below it. Now get the Burn tool (as shown here), and paint over the buildings on the left. By darkening those areas, it takes the focus off of them, which helps lead the eye to the gondola. (Whether you realize it or not, you're painting with light. Cool!)

(Continued)

Step Six:

Lastly, we can darken the sky a bit by burning over it, as well. Just remember— while you're painting, keep your mouse button held down the whole time, or part of your sky will be one shade darker, and then another part might be two shades darker (where the two areas overlap). One more thing: up in the Options Bar you'll see a checkbox for Protect Tones. That's the checkbox that helps to keep the color of what you're dodging and burning intact, so things just get brighter or darker, and not sunburned and color saturated. I leave this on all the time, even when I'm not dodging and burning portraits (which is when it's most useful). Below is a before/after, and while I'm usually fairly subtle with my dodging and burning, here I took things a little farther than I normally would, just to show a clear example of the power of dodging and burning.

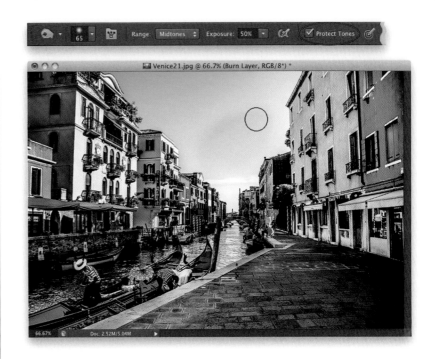

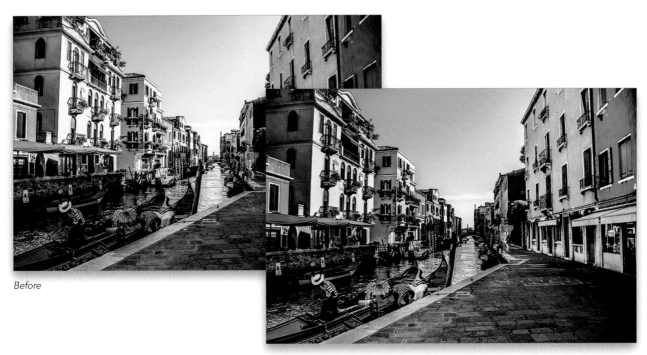

Before

After

I get more requests for how to fix this problem than probably all the rest combined. The reason is it's so darn hard to fix. If you're lucky, you get to spend an hour or more desperately cloning. In many cases, you're just stuck with it. However, if you're smart, you'll invest an extra 30 seconds while shooting to take one shot with the glasses off (or ideally, one "glasses off" shot for each new pose). Do that, and Photoshop will make this fix absolutely simple. If this sounds like a pain, then you've never spent an hour desperately cloning away a reflection.

Fixing Reflections in Glasses

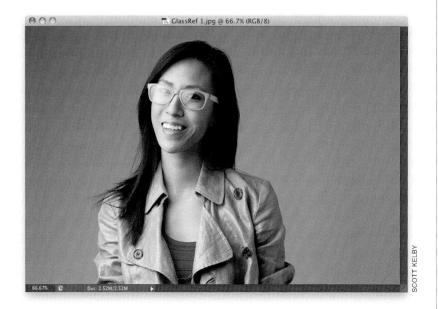

Step One:
Before we get into this, make sure you read the short intro up top here first, or you're going to wonder what's going on in Step Two. Okay, here's a photo of our subject with her glasses on, and you can see the reflection in them (pretty bad on the left side, not quite as bad on the right, but it definitely needs fixing). The ideal situation is to tell your subject that after you take the first shot, they need to freeze for just a moment while you (or a friend, assistant, etc.) walk over and remove their glasses (that way they don't change their pose, which they absolutely will if they take their own glasses off), then take a second shot. That's the ideal situation.

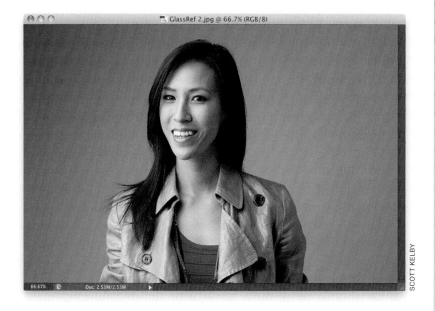

Step Two:
Unfortunately, that's not what happened for my second shot—our subject decided (maybe 10 minutes later) to remove her glasses. But, luckily, I had shots in the same shoot both with and without her glasses on (of course, that was luck—you should definitely plan to shoot some with them on, then some off, during the shoot). So, I had to look for one where her head position was somewhat similar. This shot isn't right on the money, so we'll have to tweak it a bit to make it work, but at least we have a shot to work with, so I'm not complaining.

(Continued)

Step Three:

With both images open in Photoshop, get the Move tool **(V)**, press-and-hold the Shift key, and then click-and-drag the "no glasses" photo on top of the "glasses" photo (as I did here). Now, if you planned ahead and took shots with and without the glasses (one right after the other), then you can take a shortcut and use Auto-Align Layers to perfectly match up the two shots. In the Layers panel, Command-click (PC: Ctrl-click) on each layer to select both (as shown here), then go under the Edit menu and choose **Auto-Align Layers**. Leave the Auto option selected and click OK, and in just a few seconds, they will be aligned right on the money. Now, if you did all of this "the right way" in the studio, then you can jump to the second part of Step Six. However, since the shots we're using here were taken hand-held, about 10 minutes apart, we can't use Auto-Align Layers (I tried it and it distorted things really badly), so we'll have to do it manually (another reason why setting this up the right way in the studio really pays off).

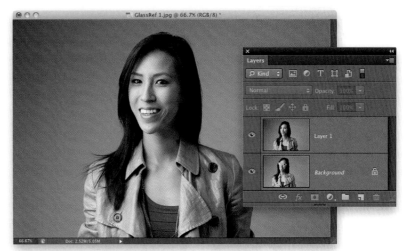

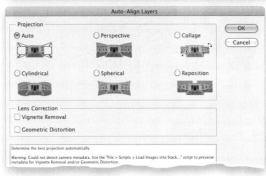

Step Four:

You need to be able to "see through" the top layer, so you can see her eyes on the bottom layer (that way, you can line them up). So, start by going to the Layers panel and lowering the Opacity of the top layer to around 50% or 60% (as shown here). Now, with the Move tool, position the eyes on the top layer as close as you can get to those on the bottom layer (it won't match exactly, of course, because her head is tilted differently. So, at this point, just get as close as you can, even though you'll still be quite a bit off, as seen here at bottom. We're a little closer, but still not there).

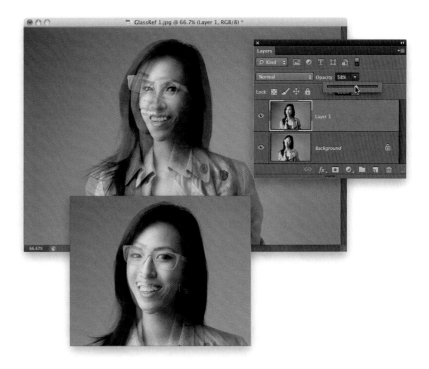

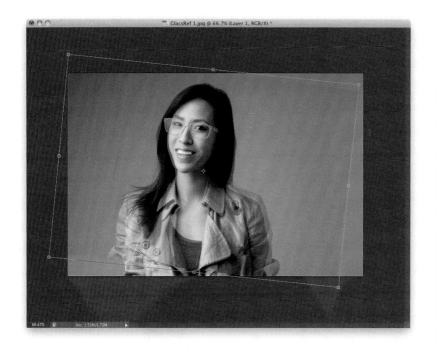

Step Five:

If you look at her shoulders back in Step Four, you can see that not only is her head tilted, but I either zoomed in or zoomed out just a little because she is a different size in the each of the photos. So, press **Command-T (PC: Ctrl-T)** to bring up Free Transform, press-and-hold the Shift key (to keep everything proportional), then click on a corner point and drag inward until her shoulders look about the same size in each of the photos. Now, we can rotate the top photo, so her eyes better match up. To rotate this top layer, go ahead and zoom out (to shrink the size of your image window), then pull out the corners of the image window, so you see some of the dark gray canvas area around your image (as seen here). Now, when you move your cursor outside the Free Transform bounding box, it will change into a two-headed rounded arrow, so you can click-and-drag in a circular motion to rotate the top layer. (*Note:* You may need to move your cursor inside the bounding box to reposition the top layer, as well.)

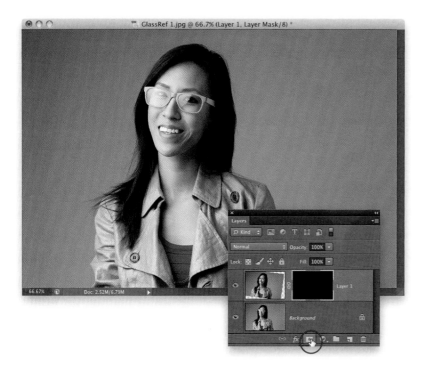

Step Six:

Once it looks pretty well lined up, press the **Return (PC: Enter) key** on your keyboard to lock in your resizing and rotation, then raise the Opacity of this top layer back to 100%. Now, all we really need from the image on the top layer is the area that appears inside her frames. So, press-and-hold the Option (PC: Alt) key and click on the Add Layer Mask icon at the bottom of the Layers panel to hide this rotated layer behind a black layer mask (as shown here).

(Continued)

Step Seven:

Now, with your Foreground color set to white, get the Brush tool **(B)**, choose a small, soft-edged brush from the Brush Picker up in the Options Bar, then simply start painting over the lens on the right, and it reveals the version of her eye without the glasses on (as seen here). What you're doing is revealing the top layer, but just where you want it.

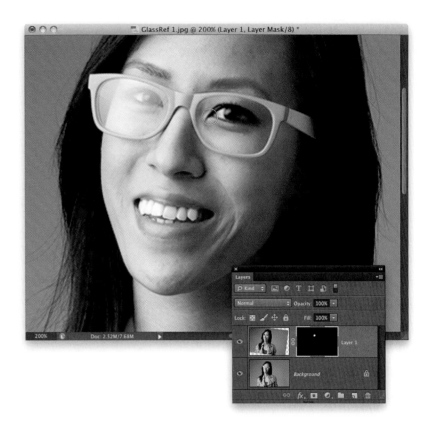

Step Eight:

Once the eye on the right is done, do the same thing for the eye on the left. Make sure you use a small brush and be careful not to accidentally paint over any of the frames. If you do make a mistake, no biggie, just press **X** to switch your Foreground color to black and paint the frames back in. Now, remember, this whole process would be made a whole lot easier (you could skip Steps Four and Five altogether) if you remember, once you get a look you like in the studio, to have your subject freeze, remove their glasses, and take another shot. Then, Auto-Align Layers can do its thing and save you a lot of time and trouble. A before and after are shown on the next page.

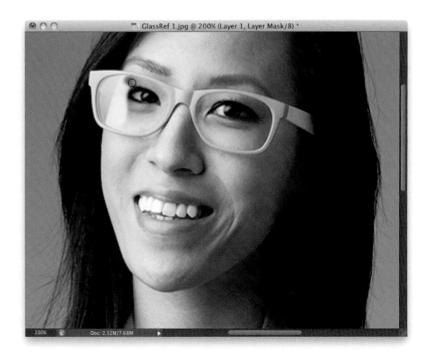

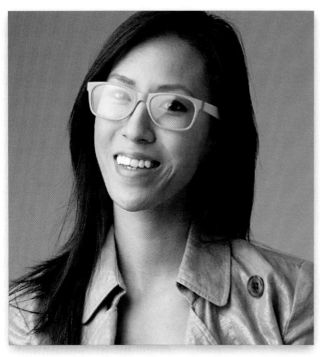

Before (with the softboxes reflecting in her glasses)

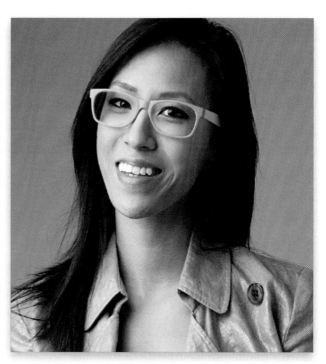

After (the reflections are gone)

Fixing Group Shots the Easy Way

Group shots are always a challenge because, without a doubt, somebody in the group will be totally hammered (at least, that's been the experience with my family. You know I'm kidding, right?). Okay, the real problem is that in group photos there's always one or more people who blinked at just the wrong time, or forgot to smile, or weren't looking at the camera, etc. Of course, you could just take their expression from another frame and combine it with this one, but that takes a lot of work. Well, at least it did before the Auto-Align Layers feature. This thing rocks!

Step One:

Here's a group shot where one of the subjects (the guy on the right) is kind of squinting and looking away.

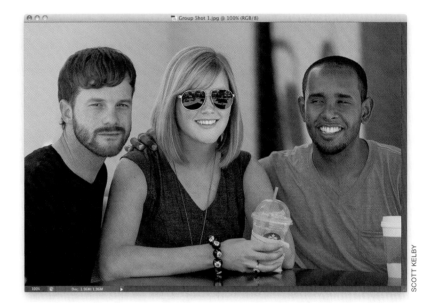

Step Two:

Of course, with group shots, you take as many shots as the group will endure, and, luckily, a few frames later, we have one where the guy on the right looks great. But, we can't use this shot, because now the guy on the left is looking away (and he's a bit out of focus, as well). So, the idea here is to take the guy on the right from this shot and combine him with the first photo to make one single group photo where they're all smiling and looking at the camera.

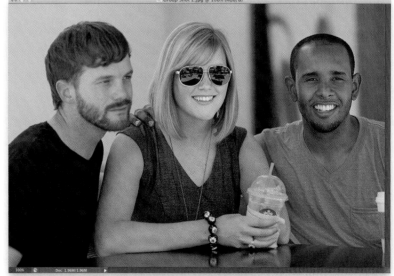

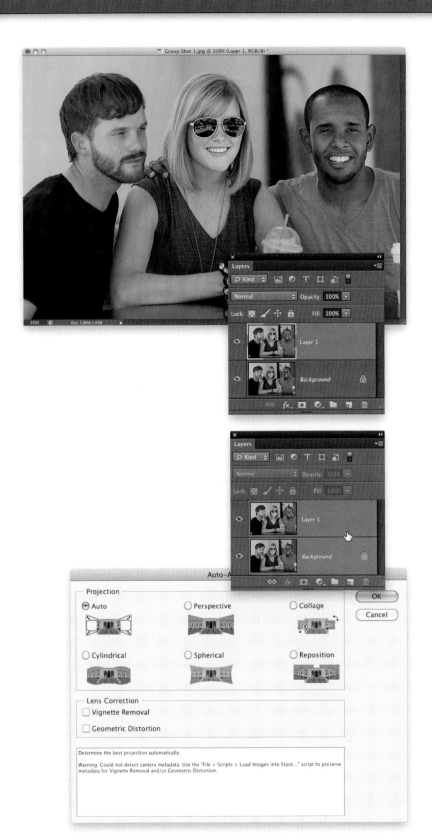

Step Three:
Start by opening both photos in Photoshop and dragging them into the same document: get the Move tool **(V)**, press-and-hold the Shift key, and click-and-drag the photo where the guy on the right looks good over on top of the other photo, where he's squinting and looking away (it will appear as its own layer in the other document, as you can see in the Layers panel shown here).

Step Four:
Usually, just pressing-and-holding the Shift key will help the photos line up pretty well (especially if the shots were taken with your camera on a tripod), but if you hand-held the shots, or if your subjects moved a bit, you'll need Photoshop to line them up precisely for you. You do this by going to the Layers panel, Command-clicking (PC: Ctrl-clicking) on both layers to select them (as shown here), then going under the Edit menu and choosing **Auto-Align Layers**. When the Auto-Align Layers dialog appears, leave Auto selected at the top, and then click OK to have Photoshop align the two layers for you (and it usually does a pretty darn amazing job, too!).

(Continued)

Step Five:

Now that they're aligned, click on the top layer in the Layers panel to make it the active layer. Press-and-hold the Option (PC: Alt) key and click on the Add Layer Mask icon at the bottom of the Layers panel to hide the top layer (with the guy on the right looking at the camera) behind a black layer mask. Now, get the Brush tool **(B)**, choose a medium-sized, soft-edged brush from the Brush Picker in the Options Bar, and with your Foreground color set to white, paint over the guy on the right's head. As you do, it reveals the good version of him where he's looking at the camera (as shown here). Keep painting until his head, shirt, and basically as much as you need, look natural in the photo (in this case, his body position shifted a bit, so I had to paint over his neck, chest, and shoulders, as well). When you're done, get the Crop tool **(C)** and crop the image down to size. The final is shown below.

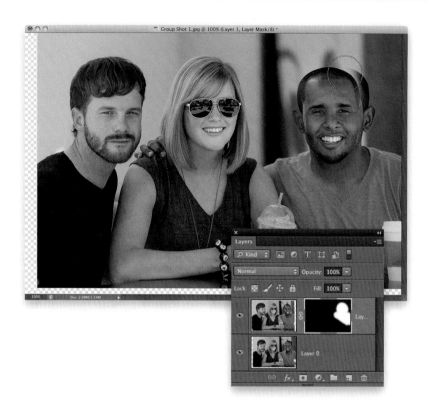

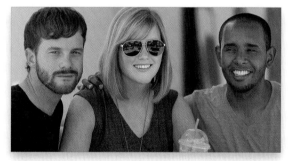

Before: The guy on the right is squinting and looking away

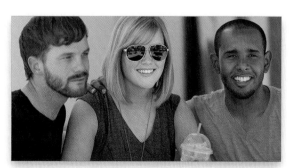

Before: The guy on the left is looking away and is out of focus

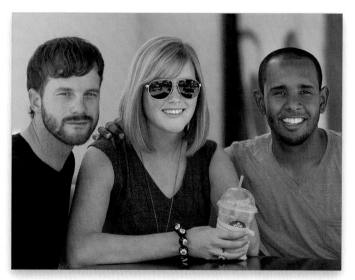

After: Parts of the two photos are combined to make one perfect group shot

Most of the selecting jobs you'll ever have to do in Photoshop are pretty easy, and you can usually get away with using the Magic Wand, Lasso, or Pen tools for most jobs, but the one that has always kicked our butts is when we have to select hair. Over the years we've come up with all sorts of tricks, including the intricate Channels techniques I covered in my Photoshop Channels Book, but all these techniques kind of went right out the window when Adobe supercharged the Quick Selection tool in Photoshop CS5 with the new Refine Edge feature. This is, hands down, one of the most useful, and most powerful, tools in all of Photoshop.

Making Really Tricky Selections, Like Hair (and Some Cool Compositing Tricks, Too!)

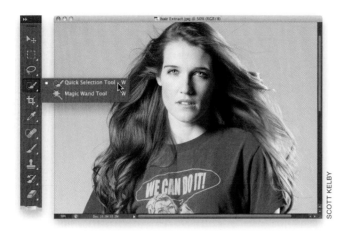

SCOTT KELBY

Step One:
Start by opening an image that has a challenging area to select (like our subject's hair here, which is being blown by a fan). Then, get the Quick Selection tool **(W)** from the Toolbox (as shown here).

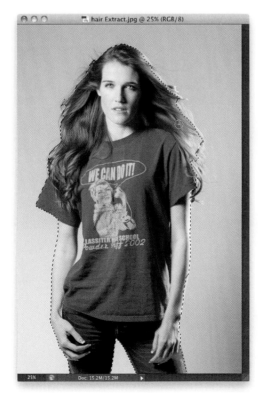

Step Two:
Here's how it works: you just take the tool and paint loosely over the areas you want to select, and it expands to select the area (kind of like a much smarter version of the Magic Wand tool, but using different technology). One thing I've learned about this tool is it actually seems to work best when you use it quickly—really zoom over your subject with the tool and it does a pretty decent job. Here, I selected the subject, and while you can see some problems with the selection (the area of gray between her arm on the left and her shirt), it's not that bad overall. If it selects too much, press-and-hold the **Option (PC: Alt) key** and paint over that accidentally selected area to remove it from your selection. Don't worry—it's not going to look perfect at this point.

(Continued)

Step Three:

Now, here's something else I've learned about the Quick Selection tool: while it's pretty good at selecting, it's not nearly as good at deselecting areas that you don't want selected (like that gray area between her arm and her shirt). I've found that when it misses areas like that, you're honestly better off switching to the Magic Wand tool **(Shift-W)**, pressing-and-holding the **Option (PC: Alt) key**, and just clicking once in that area to instantly deselect it. So, let's go ahead and do that under her arm, and you'll see that in just that one click with the Magic Wand tool, that area is deselected (as shown here).

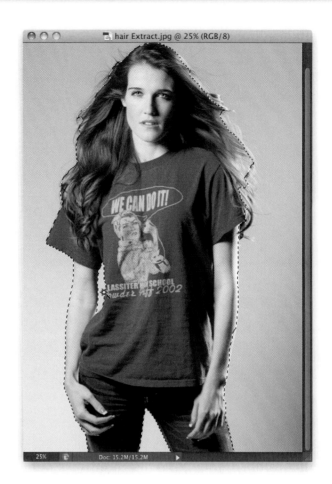

Step Four:

Okay, here comes a very important part of this stage of the process, and that is making sure that when you select her hair, you don't select any background area with it. In other words, don't let there be any hair selected with gray background showing through. In fact, I basically follow the rule that I don't get too close to the outside edges of my subject's hair unless an area is pretty flat (in other words, no flyaway, tough-to-select hair in that area). You can see what I mean in the close-up here, where I avoided the thinner edges of her hair (we'll let Photoshop select those hard parts—we'll just get close to the edge then stop). Also, you can see where I stopped before some areas where the hair is finer. Again, we'll let Photoshop grab those parts later, but for now we're most concerned with avoiding selecting areas where you can see gray background through her hair. If you accidentally select an area with gaps, then it's okay to switch back to the Quick Selection tool, press-and-hold the Option (PC: Alt) key, and paint over those gap areas to deselect them.

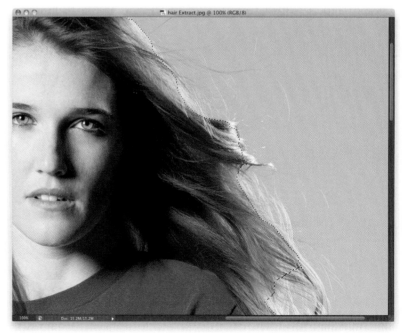

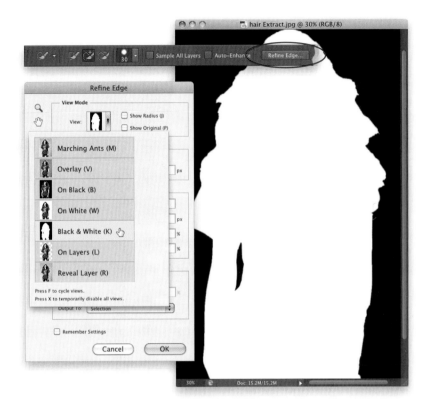

Step Five:

Once your selection looks pretty decent, it's time to unlock the real selection power (the Quick Selection tool is just the warm-up act). Go up to the Options Bar and click on the Refine Edge button (shown circled here). This is where the magic happens. In the Refine Edge dialog, you have a number of choices for how you can view your selected image (including just the standard old marching ants), but just for now, as part of our learning process, go ahead and choose **Black & White**, from the View pop-up menu. This shows your selection as a standard layer mask. As you can see, the Quick Selection tool, by itself, isn't gettin' the job done (the edges are jaggy and harsh, and there's no wispy hair selected at all). That's okay, though, because we're just gettin' started.

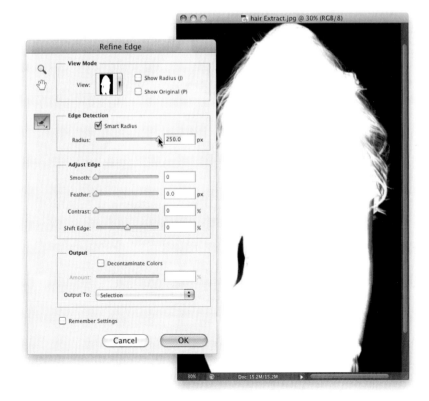

Step Six:

Next, turn on the Smart Radius checkbox (you won't see anything happen yet, but turn it on anyway). Smart Radius is the edge technology that knows the difference between a soft edge and a hard edge, so it can make a mask that includes both. This checkbox is so important that I leave it on all the time (if you want it always on, as well, just turn it on and then turn on the Remember Settings checkbox at the bottom of the dialog). Now, again, just for learning purposes, drag the Radius slider all the way over the right (to 250), and all of her hair gets selected instantly (pretty amazing isn't it?). While it did a great job on her hair, there are parts of her (like her right arm) that are being "over-selected." Those areas will wind up being transparent, and you don't want that, so we always have to back it way down. But, I just wanted you to see the incredible math at work.

(Continued)

Step Seven:

Okay, let's drag that Radius slider back down until her arm on the right looks more solid white. Here's how this works: We want our subject to be solid white and we want the background to be solid black. Anything that appears in gray will be semi-transparent. That's okay if this happens in her hair in wispy areas, but it's not good on her arms or clothes or anything that's supposed to have a well-defined hard edge. Otherwise, we'd leave the Radius up at 250 and be done with it. But, there's more to most portraits than just hair, so we have to keep those other areas pretty much intact, too. Here, I rolled back the Radius to around 47, but you might be able to bring it up a bit more, maybe to somewhere in the mid-50s. By the way, for simple selections, leave the Radius amount down low. When you have a tricky selection, like fine hair blowing in the wind, you'll have to increase it. So, just remember: trickier selections mean higher Radius amounts.

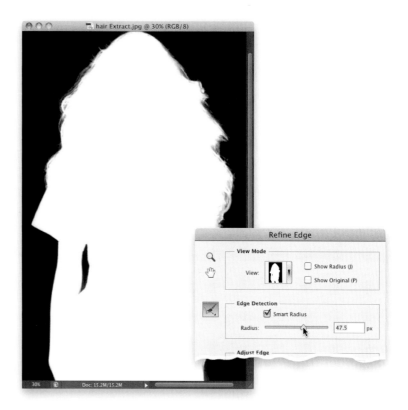

Step Eight:

Now, let's change the View to **Overlay** to see if there are any areas we missed. The parts that are selected appear in full-color, and the parts that aren't appear in red. If you see the background color showing through (in our case, gray), you've got a problem (and we do here, on the left side). You need to tell Photoshop exactly where the problem areas are, so it can better define those areas. You do that with the Refine Radius tool (**E**; shown circled here). It's active by default, so just take your cursor and simply paint over the areas where you see the background peeking through (as shown here), and it redefines those areas. This is what picks up that fine hair detail.

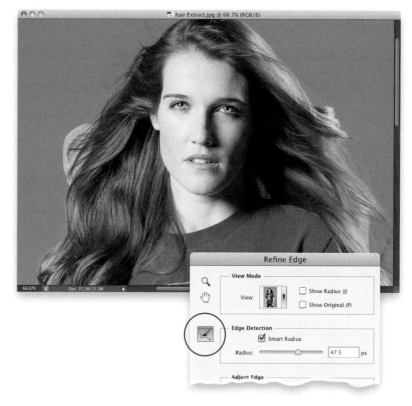

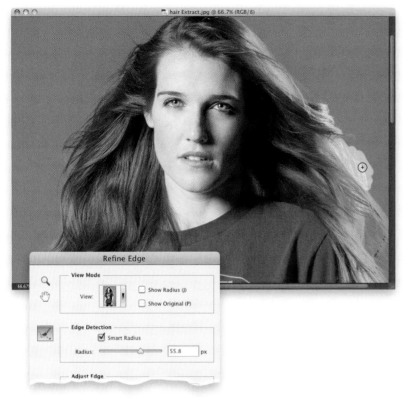

Step Nine:

As you look around her hair, if you see parts of it that are tinted red, those parts aren't selected. So, just paint a stroke or two over those areas (like I'm doing here), and they become full-color (letting you know they're added to your selection) as Photoshop refines those edge areas where you're painting. It'll look like it's painting in white sometimes, but when you're done, it just redefines the area and tells Photoshop that this area needs some work, and it "redoes" its thing. Here, I've gone over some areas that were tinted red on the left side of her hair, and on the right side, too, and you can see those areas are now appearing in color. I also increased the Radius amount a bit.

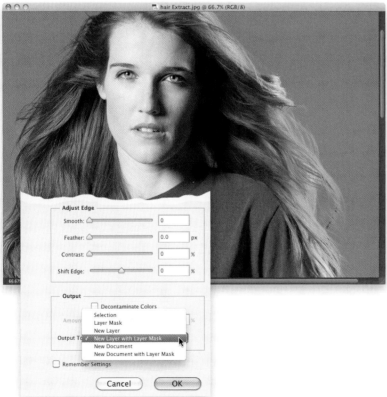

Step 10:

I recommend avoiding the Adjust Edge section sliders in the center of the dialog altogether, because you'll spend too much time fussing with them, trying to make them work. (I figure you want me to tell you when to avoid stuff, too.) Down at the bottom of the dialog, there's a Decontaminate Colors checkbox, which basically desaturates the edge pixels a bit. So, when you place this image on a different background, the edge color doesn't give you away. Just below that, you get to choose what the result of all this will be: will your selected subject be sent over to a new blank document, or just a new layer in this document, or a new layer with a layer mask already attached, etc.? I always choose to make a new layer with a layer mask in the same document. That way, I can just grab the Brush tool and fix any areas that might have dropped out, which we're probably going to have to do next, so choose **New Layer with Layer Mask** and click OK.

(Continued)

Step 11:

When you click OK, your image will now appear on a transparent layer (as seen here) and if you look in the Layers panel, you'll see a new layer with a layer mask attached (just what you asked for). You can also see it does a pretty amazing job. It won't get every little thin, wispy hair strand, but it gets most of the important ones. Also, I've got a trick or two coming up that will help a bit more, but first, let's do a quick check of that mask and fine-tune it just a bit before we put her over a different background (that's right, baby, we're doing some compositing!). Press-and-hold the Option (PC: Alt) key and click directly on that layer mask thumbnail in the Layers panel to see just the mask (you can see it in the next step).

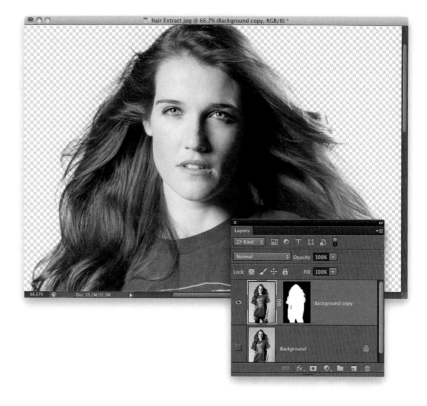

Step 12:

Now, zoom in tight near the bottom of her arm on the right, and you can see some areas that aren't solid white (which means these areas will be semi-trans-parent and that's not what you want for her arm). So, get the Brush tool **(B)** and, with your Foreground color set to white, choose a small, hard-edged brush from the Brush Picker in the Options Bar, and then paint along that edge, right over the grayish area, to make it solid white. You can see some areas on the inside of her legs here that need a cleanup, as well. Next, press **X** to switch your Foreground color to black to clean up that mess on the right side of her leg where the white has spilled over onto the black. That should be solid black in the background areas. For a little help cleaning up tricky areas, switch your Brush's blend Mode to **Overlay**. That way, when you're painting with white, it automatically avoids paint-ing over the color black (and vice versa).

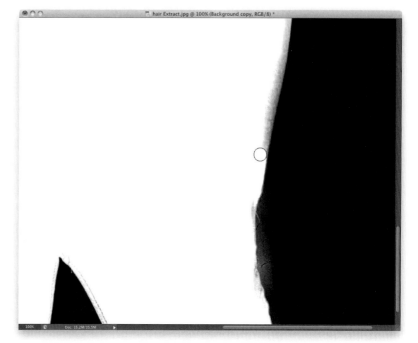

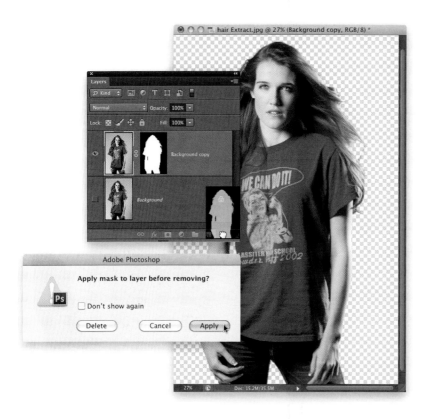

Step 13:

At this point, we're done with our mask, so you can apply it permanently to your image by clicking directly on the layer mask thumbnail (in the Layers panel) and dragging it onto the Trash icon at the bottom of the panel (as shown here) to delete it. When you do this, a warning dialog pops up asking if you want to "Apply mask to layer before removing?" You want to click Apply, and the masking you did is now applied to the layer (and the layer mask thumbnail is deleted). This just makes things a little easier from here on out.

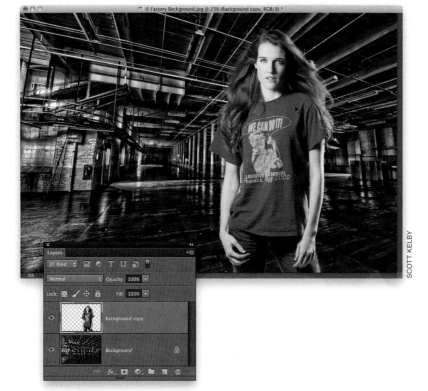

Step 14:

Next, open the background image you want to use in your composite. Get the Move tool (**V**), then drag-and-drop your subject right onto this background image (as shown here). (*Note:* This is easier if you have the Application Frame turned off and can see at least part of both images on your screen. If you have it turned on, so you can't see both images at once, just click-and-drag the subject image up to the tab of the background image and hover there for a moment or two until it lets you drop the image on the background. If all else fails, copy-and-paste it onto this background; it will appear on its own layer.) Now, you see our next challenge here? Her color tone makes it look like she wasn't photographed in these surroundings (plus, she has a tiny white fringe around her outside edge, which is a dead giveaway that this is a composite).

(Continued)

Step 15:

First, let's get rid of that thin white fringe around her, then we'll deal with our color issue. To remove the fringe, go under the Layer menu, under Matting (it's at the very bottom of the menu), and choose **Defringe**. When the Defringe dialog appears (shown here), enter 1 (use 2 pixels for a higher-megapixel image), click OK, and that fringe is gone! (Photoshop basically replaces the outside edge pixels with a new set of pixels that is a combination of the background its sitting on and your subject's edge, so the fringe goes away.)

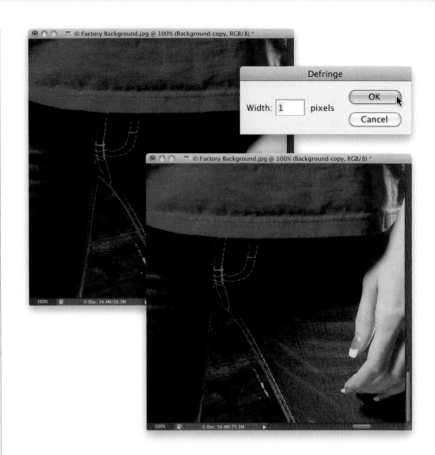

Step 16:

Here's a trick I stumbled upon years ago when making composites (back when we used channels for stuff like this). This trick gives you more detail and brings back some of those lost wisps of hair by building up some pixels. It's going to sound really simple and it is. Just press **Command-J (PC: Ctrl-J)** to duplicate your layer (the one with your subject). That's it. Just duplicate your subject layer, and it has a "building up" effect around the edges of her. Suddenly, it looks more defined, and it fills in some of the weaker wispy areas. If for any reason it looks like too much, at the top of the Layers panel, just lower the Opacity of this duplicate layer until it looks right (here, I lowered it to 50% and it looks about right). Next, merge this duplicate layer with your original subject layer by pressing **Command-E (PC: Ctrl-E)**. Okay, now to tackle the fact that the color of our subject doesn't match the surroundings she was supposedly shot in.

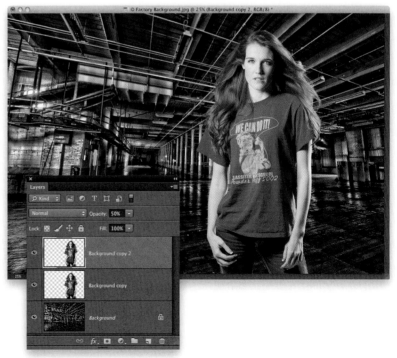

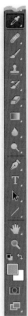

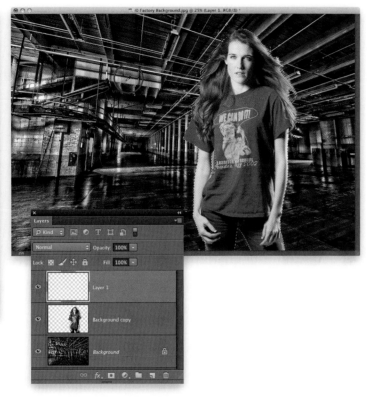

Step 17:
We need a selection around our subject layer again, so Command-click (PC: Ctrl-click) on your subject layer's thumbnail to load it as a selection. Once the selection is in place (as seen here), add a new blank layer by clicking on the Create a New Layer icon at the bottom of the Layers panel. Now, look at your image and ask yourself, "Which color really stands out to me in this background?" Here, I see purple, brown (on the floor), and gray (in some parts of the ceiling), but the color that's really jumping out to me is green. So, get the Eyedropper tool **(I)** from the Toolbox and click it once on an area of green in the photo to make that exact green your Foreground color (as shown here, where I'm clicking near the ceiling).

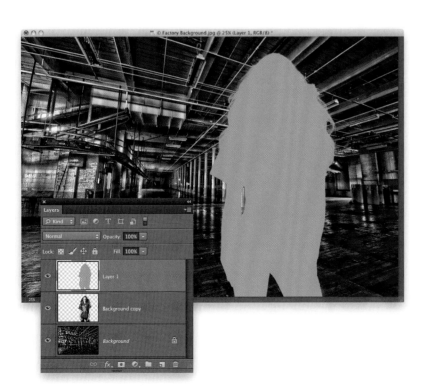

Step 18:
Now, fill the selection (on your empty layer) with this green color by pressing **Option-Delete (PC: Alt-Backspace)**. Then, deselect by pressing **Command-D (PC: Ctrl-D)**.

(Continued)

Step 19:

To make this green area blend in:
(1) change the layer's blend mode from Normal to **Color** (so just the color shows through, instead of being solid). Then, (2) lower the Opacity to the point where you see the color image start to emerge, but it has enough of the green tint to it that it really looks like she was photographed there on location (at least color-wise, anyway). For this image, I lowered the Opacity of the green layer to 35%, which ties the color of the two together (as seen here, where her overall color is more muted, like the background colors, but with a hint of that green). Now, press Command-E (PC: Ctrl-E) once more to merge this green layer with the subject's layer below it. The last step is to unify her tonally with the background.

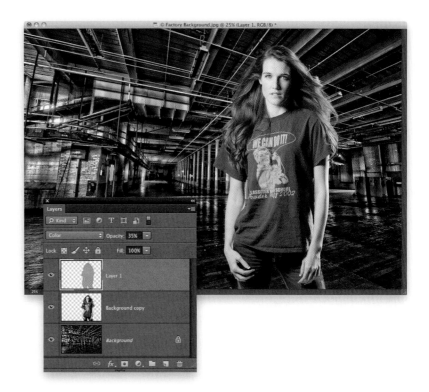

Step 20:

In this case, our background is a multi-exposure HDR, so we need to add a high-contrast effect to her to match the background (if the background wasn't an HDR, I'd apply the effect to the background first, then to her). This is a multi-step process, so jump to page 272 in the special effects chapter to see how this is done, or if you already learned it, you can follow this shorthand version: Duplicate the subject layer, change the blend mode to **Vivid Light**, and then Invert by pressing **Command-I (PC: Ctrl-I)**. Now, apply the Surface Blur filter set at a Radius of 40 and a Threshold of 40. Hide the Background layer (click on its Eye icon), then press **Command-Option-Shift-E (PC: Ctrl-Alt-Shift-E)** to create a merged layer on top of your layer stack. Press **Command-Shift-U (PC: Ctrl-Shift-U)** to desaturate it. Delete the middle layer (Background copy 2), then change the blend mode of the top layer to **Overlay** (as seen here). Lastly, make the Background layer visible again, flatten the image, then go to the Lens Correction filter and add a dark edge vignette.

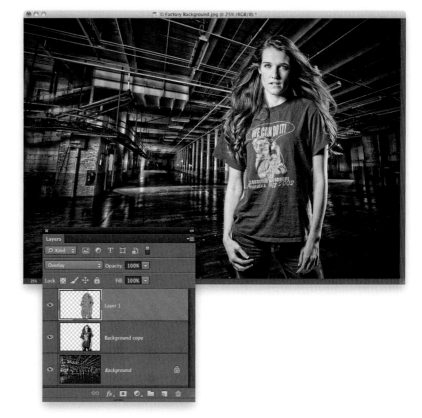

How's that one for a title? Well, that's the best explanation of what happens sometimes when you shoot really wide, and in Photoshop CS6, there's a tool called Adaptive Wide Angle that was invented for these situations. However, there are three things you need to know about this filter: (1) you're not going to use it very often, (2) you're either going to have to crop pretty massively after using it or use Content-Aware Fill to fill in the gaps, and (3) it actually does a pretty darn good job when you do need it.

Fixing Really Messed Up Wide-Angle Shots

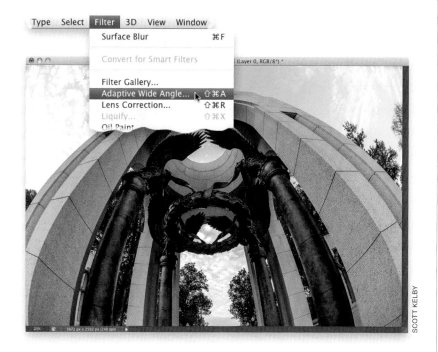

SCOTT KELBY

Step One:

Open the photo that has a serious lens issue you want to fix. I personally don't use smart filters a bunch, because once I apply a filter, I'm usually pretty much done with it. But, in this case, it's not a bad idea to first go under the Filter menu and choose **Convert for Smart Filters**, and then choose **Adaptive Wide Angle** from that same menu. The reason why this might come in handy is that, depending on the image, you may need to come back and tweak your existing filter settings (well, it's been the case for me anyway), and by making it a smart filter, you can apply the filter, and then re-open it with all the Constraint lines still in place, so you can tweak them (this will all make more sense in just a minute).

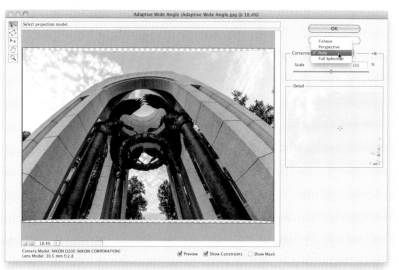

Step Two:

When the Adaptive Wide Angle dialog opens (shown here), it reads the lens data embedded into the photo by your camera (see the bottom-left corner of the dialog), and it tries to apply an Auto correction. Sometimes it does a pretty good job, but in this case, you can see the monument is still really bent, so we'll have to help the filter out. If you know the image is a fisheye, or if you just want to try to fix perspective, choose either from the Correction pop-up menu in the top right to give you a better starting point.

(Continued)

Step Three:

We help the filter do its thing by letting it know which parts of the image need to be fixed, and we do that using the Constraint tool (it's the default tool and the first one in the toolbar in the top left). Basically, you click at the base of the object you want straightened (like the column on the right side here), and then as you move your cursor up toward the top of the object, the green line you're dragging literally bends (it does this automatically, because it knows the lens you used and what kind of problems you're dealing with). You get a zoomed-in close-up of where your cursor is currently located in the Detail preview on the right side of the dialog (as seen here), which is really handy for situations like this where you want the end of your line to be right along an edge (see how it's off a bit in the Detail preview?). *Note:* If you mess up, you can delete a Constraint line by just press-and-holding the Option (PC: Alt) key, clicking once on it, and it's gone.

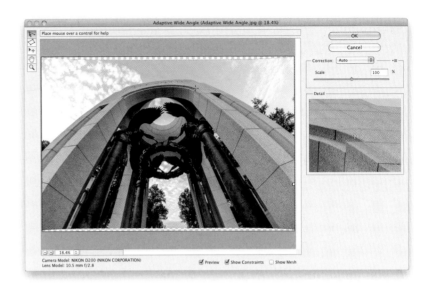

Step Four:

Once you click your mouse near the top of the column (like I did here), it straightens that column. It also gives you a preview of the cropping work that you'll need to do pretty shortly (either that, or Content-Aware Fill, but you can see how it's having to the warp the image around to pull this straightening trick off). Also, if part of the top or bottom of the column still looks bent after adding the Constraint line, you can grab the end of the line near where the problem is and literally just drag it out longer. That will usually get rid of the problem, even if you have to drag it off the image area. If you do, you can move your image over in the preview window, so you can reach that end handle if you need to tweak it again, by switching to the Adaptive Wide Angle's own Move tool (it's the third tool down in the toolbar).

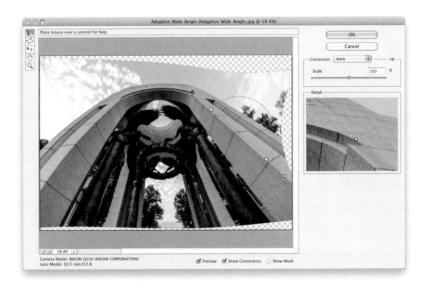

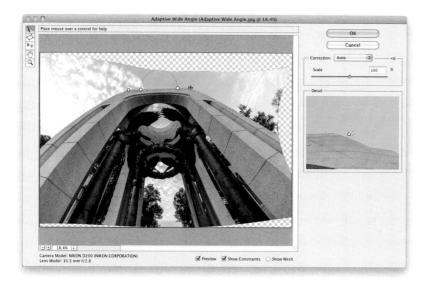

Step Five:

So, that's the basic plan: you take the Constraint tool and drag it over parts of your image that need to be straightened and it does its thing. Now, see how the top of the monument is arched (well, look back at it in Step Four)? Just drag a new Constraint line across the top of the monument from left to right to straighten it (as seen here). Just know that you'll usually have to do this more than once (in this case, you'll have to do just about every column individually to get things looking decent). Also, while we're here, when you lay down one of these Constraint lines, you'll see a round circle with two round handles appear with it. That lets you fine-tune the angle of that line after you've laid it down. So, if it's off a little (or a lot), you can grab one of those round handles and literally rotate the circle in a clockwise (or counter-clockwise) motion to change the angle of the fix. As you do this, a little pop-up appears giving you a readout with the amount of rotation (in degrees, as seen here on the bottom left). Once you let go, it readjusts the fix based on how much you rotated (as seen here on the bottom right).

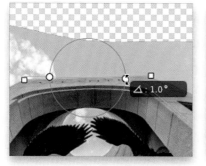

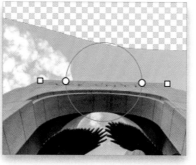

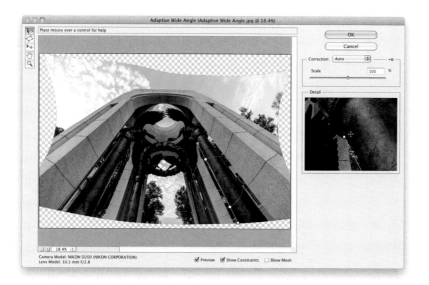

Step Six:

After tracing the inner and outer edges of the column on the left and the black column on the right (as seen here), for a total of five Constraint lines (four on the columns and one across the top), the image looks pretty good. So, go ahead and click OK to apply your changes.

(Continued)

Step Seven:

Now, remember, if you click OK and something doesn't look quite right, *and* you converted this image for smart filters before you opened the filter itself (see Step One), then you can go to the Layers panel and double-click directly on the words "Adaptive Wide Angle" (as shown here). This will reopen the Adaptive Wide Angle dialog with all your Constraint lines still in place, so you can tweak them, rather than starting over from scratch.

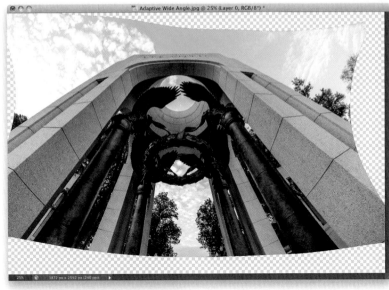

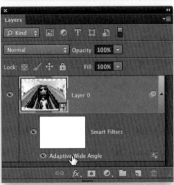

Step Eight:

Once you click OK, you'll see all the gaps that will need to be cropped away, so get the Crop tool **(C)** and click-and-drag in the corner and side handles until most of the gaps are cropped away (all that grayed out area outside the cropping border here will be cropped away, and you can see it's a pretty good amount). Press **Return (PC: Enter)** to crop your image, then go ahead and choose **Flatten Image** from the Layers panel's flyout menu to flatten it.

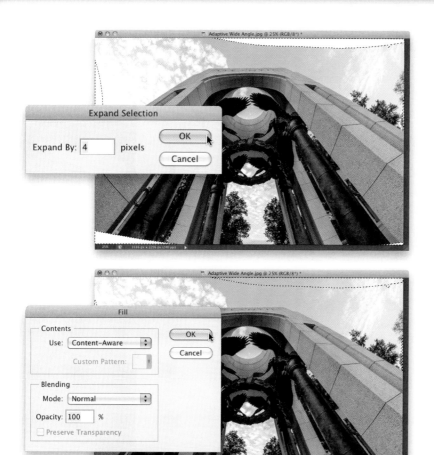

Step Nine:

Now, you're still going to have some gaps, so get the Magic Wand tool (press **Shift-W** until you have it). Click it in one of those gaps (like the one at the top right), and once that area is selected, press-and-hold the Shift key and click in the other gap areas. Then, go under the Select menu, under Modify, and choose **Expand**. Enter 4 pixels and click OK (as shown here) to grow your selection out a bit (this helps Content-Aware Fill do a better job).

Step 10:

Next, go under the Edit menu, and choose **Fill**. From the Use pop-up menu, choose **Content-Aware**, then click OK to have it fill in those areas. Press **Command-D (PC: Ctrl-D)** to deselect. Below is a before and after (I'm showing this now, because we need to open a different image to show the rest of the Adaptive Wide Angle tools).

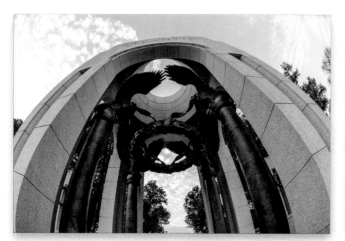

Before

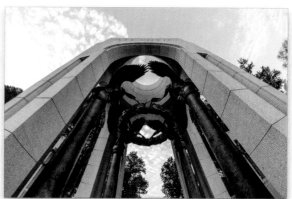

After

(Continued)

Step 11:

If you have an image where you know that a part of it is supposed to be absolutely level and flat (like a horizon line or, in this case, the floor of the basketball court), then before you drag out your Constraint line, press-and-hold the Shift key. Your line will turn yellow, and you'll drag it out like usual along the curved edge of the court (as shown here).

TIP: If Your Constraint Lines Don't Bend

If Photoshop recognized your lens and has a profile for it, then the lines will bend automatically. But, if it doesn't recognize your lens, then there's no lens profile for it to work from (if you choose Auto correction, a warning dialog will appear telling you that no matching lens profile was found), and it's then up to you to make the bend manually. Just click the Constraint tool on one end of what you want to fix, then click it again on the other end to complete your straight line. Then, click on the center point within the circle and bend the line so it fits.

Step 12:

Here's the result of our Shift-clicking: the floor is straight and flat. Well, most of it is. Take a look at the far-right side of it. See how it bends up? To fix that, just click-and-drag the point on the right end of the line out to the right. You'll see the line automatically bend up along the floor and then when you release your mouse button, it will immediately straighten it out, as seen here at the bottom (that's pretty amazing when you think about it).

TIP: Straightening Rectangles

If you need to quickly fix something like a doorway or window (a rectangle), then use the Polygon Constraint tool (the second tool down in the toolbar), which works like the Polygonal Lasso tool—just trace around your rectangle and it straightens it.

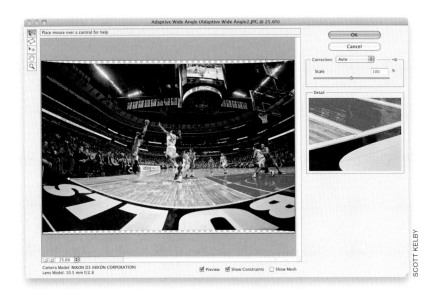

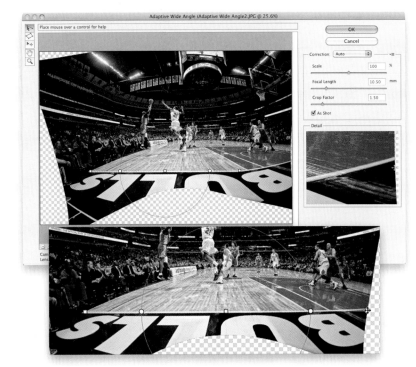

SCOTT KELBY

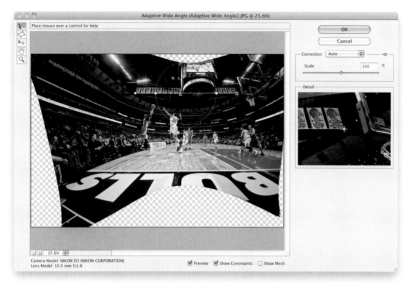

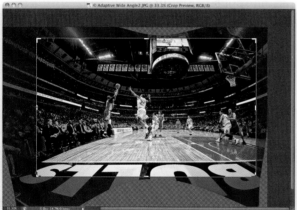

Step 13:

Now, let's fix that row of championship banners across the top of the image by Shift-clicking a Constraint line across the bottom of them. This immediately straightens those out, as well. Again, we do the Shift-click thing when we know something should be either perfectly horizontal or perfectly vertical.

TIP: Making a Curved Line Straight

Once you have a curved line in place, if you decide you want it to be a perfectly straight line (a flat horizontal or vertical line), just Right-click on the line and a pop-up menu will appear where you can choose the type of line you want to convert it to.

Step 14:

Now, just click OK and flatten your image (because it's a Smart Filter layer). Then, get the Crop tool and crop the image down, so you don't see those gaps along the edges (as shown here, where I cropped tight enough that I didn't have to deal with the edges at all). A before/after is shown below.

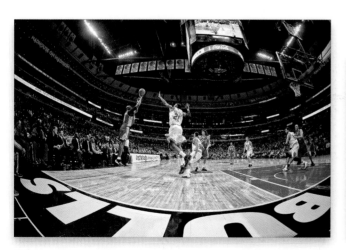

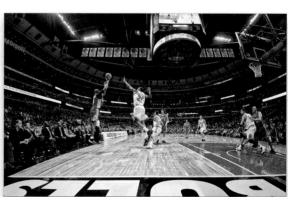

Before

After

Fixing Problems Caused by Your Camera's Lens

Photoshop definitely has some overlap with the included Camera Raw 7 that comes with CS6 (and is part of Photoshop), in that you can do a lot of the same things in Photoshop that you can do in Camera Raw. If you shoot in RAW mode on your camera, you're better off doing things like lens corrections right within Camera Raw (see Chapter 3), because it's faster and does less harm to your pixels. However, if for whatever reason, you don't want to use Camera Raw's Lens Corrections panel (it works for JPEGs and TIFFs, too. Hint, hint), then you can use the Lens Correction filter in CS6.

Step One:

Here's a problem image. Look at the columns on either side, which are bowing outward. Luckily, we've got a filter for that. Go under the Filter menu and, right near the top, choose **Lens Correction**.

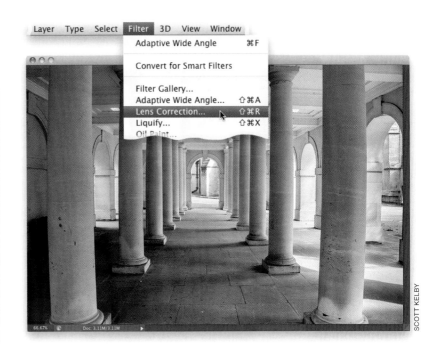

SCOTT KELBY

Step Two:

When the Lens Correction dialog opens, you'll see two tabs in the top right: Auto Correction and Custom (Custom means "do-it-yourself"). I always try Auto Correction first, because if it can find a profile for your lens in its database of lenses, it will pretty much fix the problem for you instantly (it looks at the embedded lens data in your image, then searches its internal database for a built-in profile based on your camera make and model, and lens type). In the Auto Correction tab, turn on the Geometric Distortion checkbox and, as you can see here, it found a lens profile for my lens and did a pretty darn good job of removing that bowing from the columns. If you're seeing any lens vignetting (darkening of the corners in your image), then also turn on the Vignette checkbox and it will fix that at the same time automatically.

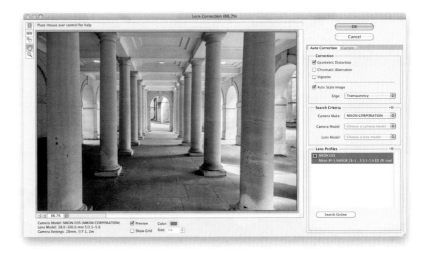

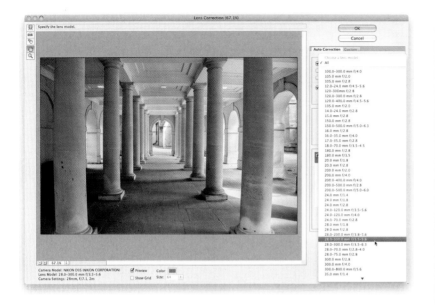

Step Three:

Now, what if it doesn't instantly come up with a profile (or the camera data is missing from the file) when you turn on Geometric Distortion? In that case, you can sometimes help it along by choosing your camera's make, model, and even lens from the pop-up menus in the Search Criteria section. In this case, they didn't actually have my camera model listed in the Camera Model pop-up menu, and even when I chose the lens I did use, here, the Auto Correction doesn't look right. This is why this works best if it can match it to a profile in its database automatically, rather than having you choose it here. However, sometimes this works great. If you don't see the exact lens model, I usually try the next closet profile, and that will often do the trick.

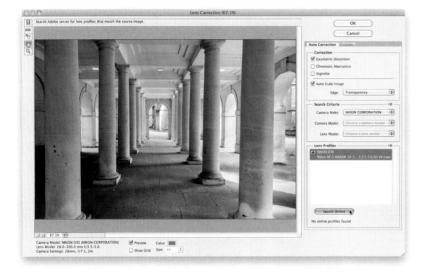

Step Four:

If, after choosing your camera make and model, no profiles show up in the Lens Profiles listing box, try clicking the Search Online button (as shown here). It will go to Adobe's own servers, and check to see if any additional profiles for your camera make and model have been added by end users (as long as you're connected to the Internet, of course). If it does find some, they'll be listed there, and all you have to do is click on one to apply it. In this case, it didn't find any additional profiles for my lens, so it reverted back to the original profile it first provided (which actually looks pretty good). Although it did a pretty good job of fixing the barrel distortion (the bowing out of the columns), there's still kind of a perspective problem (look at how the columns are leaning out to the left and right—smaller at the bottom and leaning outward as you get to the top).

(Continued)

Step Five:

This bending outward has to be fixed manually, so click on the Custom tab. Anything you do in this Custom tab is added to any corrections you already applied in the Auto Correction tab, so you don't lose what it already did for you. At the top, you'll see a slider for fixing problems like the bowing columns, but since the Auto Correction already fixed that, we'll go down near the bottom of the dialog to the Transform section. The little icons on the left and right of the sliders give you a good idea of what they do. We need to fix the perspective (they're wider apart at the top than the bottom), so drag the Vertical Perspective slider to the right until they look pretty much even at the top and bottom (for this image, I dragged over to +7 and it looked about right). A before and after appears below. Okay, ready for a more challenging fix (meaning, no Auto Correction at all)?

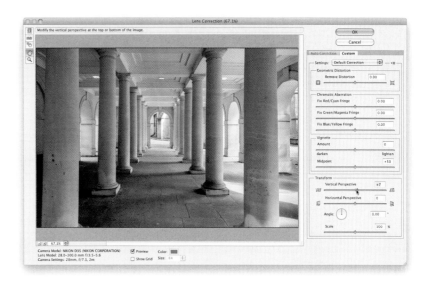

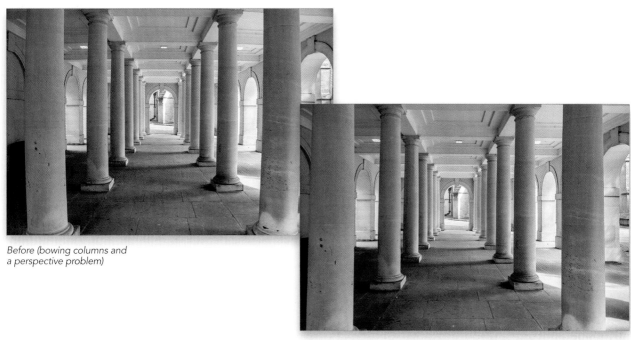

Before (bowing columns and a perspective problem)

After

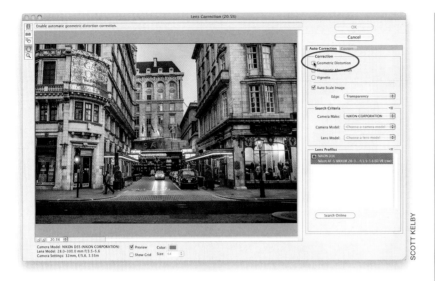

SCOTT KELBY

Step Six:

This image has all sorts of lens night-mares going on. First, the buildings look like they're leaning in toward each other. Secondly, there's a geometric distortion problem here (the buildings are bowing outward), as well, and lastly, the image is a little crooked. We can fix all of these in the Custom tab. Let's start by turning off Auto Correction (turn off the Geo-metric Distortion checkbox in the Auto Correction tab, as shown here).

TIP: It's Auto-Cropping Behind the Scenes

When you make geometric distortion corrections like this, you'll see that it seems to crop in a little bit tighter on your photo. That's because it does. What it's doing is automatically correcting for the fact that when it unbowed your image, it had to bow the outside edges a bit (leav-ing big gaps on the edges), so it automati-cally scales up the image a little to crop off those messed-up edges. If you want to see what's really going on, drag the Scale slider (at the bottom of the dialog) to anything less than 100%, and you'll see the edges.

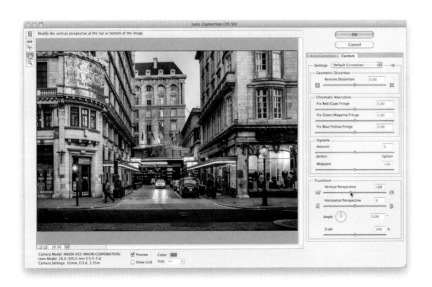

Step Seven:

Now, let's get the buildings straight, so they don't fall over into the road. Go down to the Transform section, but this time you'll need to drag the Vertical Per-spective slider to the left (the perspective problem is the opposite of what it was with the columns—these buildings are leaning inward). So, drag it over until the buildings look straighter (as shown here). I dragged over to –14, which gets the fronts of the buildings looking good, but the right side of the building on the left still looks a little off. If I drag any farther, though, the rest of the image starts to lean, so we should stop about there.

(Continued)

Step Eight:

There's only some minor bowing (barrel distortion), but it doesn't appear that obvious. So, drag the Remove Distortion slider to the right to +3.00 (as seen here), and now that it's gone, it'll be more obvious (drag it back and forth a couple of times and you'll see it). The last tweak is to go back down to the Transform section, to the Angle control. While you can drag the little line around the circle, it's very sensitive. So much so, that I wouldn't use it (go ahead and try it, then press **Command-Z [PC: Ctrl-Z]** to Undo). Instead, click your cursor in the Angle field. You can use the **Up/Down Arrow keys** on your keyboard to change it, however, it's very precise (moving in tenths of a degree), so to speed things up, press-and-hold the Shift key while you use the Arrow keys and it'll move in larger increments. Slowly rotate it until you feel like it's straight (I felt like it was around +0.70°, as shown here).

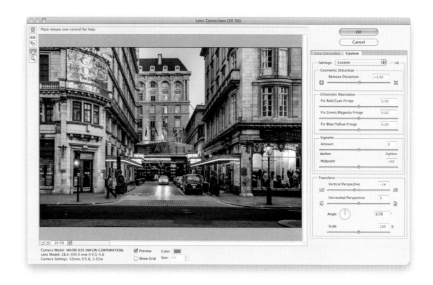

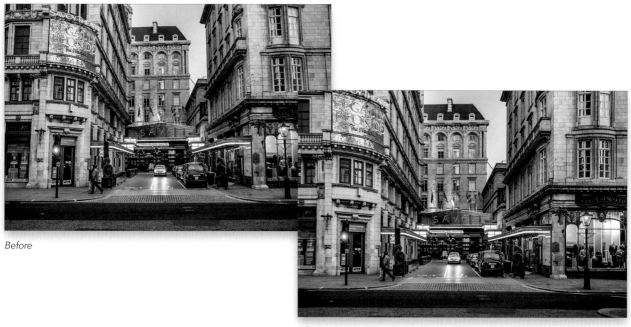

Before

After

The first of the Content-Aware features we'll cover comes in handy when you need to resize just part of your image without totally trashing the main subject of it. This is great when you have to make your image fit into a document size that doesn't match the aspect ratio of a digital camera image (for example, like when you add a still image to a video slide show). That's when Content-Aware Scale rocks, because it's "aware" of the important part of the image, and so it only stretches the non-important parts (and if it's not quite sure, you can help it out). It's like an "intelligent" resizer.

Stretching Stuff to Fit Using Content-Aware Scale

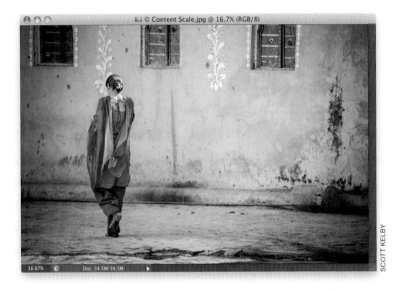

SCOTT KELBY

Step One:
Here are the two documents we're going to work with. The first is our digital camera photo, and the second is a blank document that's more like the widescreen aspect ratio of video.

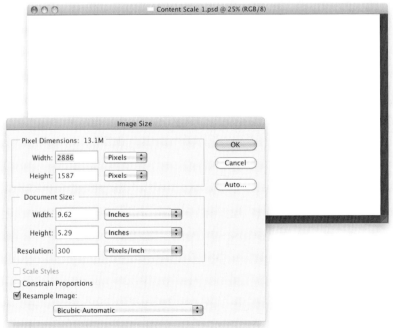

(Continued)

Step Two:

Get the Move tool **(V)** and click-and-drag your photo into the widescreen document. To shrink your image down so it fits fully inside the document, press **Command-T (PC: Ctrl-T)** to bring up Free Transform (if you can't reach the Free Transform handles, press **Command-0** [zero; **PC: Ctrl-0**], and the image window will expand enough so you can reach all the handles). Press-and-hold the Shift key, click on a corner handle, and drag to resize your image. When you get it so it fits fully inside the document (as seen here), press the **Return (PC: Enter) key** to lock in your resizing. You can see the problem, here: to get it to fit, without cropping, leaves white gaps to the left and right of your image.

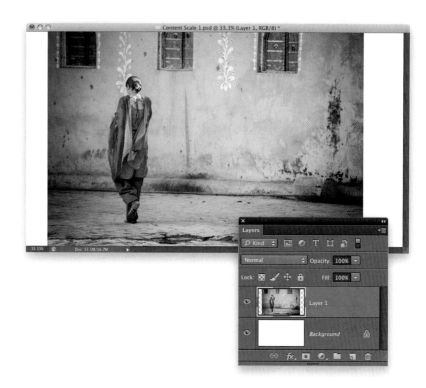

Step Three:

Now, you could just bring up Free Transform again, drag the left side handle over so it covers the gap on the left side, and then do the same thing to stretch the image over to the right side (as shown here), but that stretches our subject out and her body is now thicker and distorted (take a look back at the image in Step Two and you'll see how much wider she looks here). This will not win you any fans (or repeat business), so don't hit the Return key to lock in your transformation. Instead, hit the **Esc key** to cancel your transformation. Then, go under the Edit menu and choose **Content-Aware Scale**.

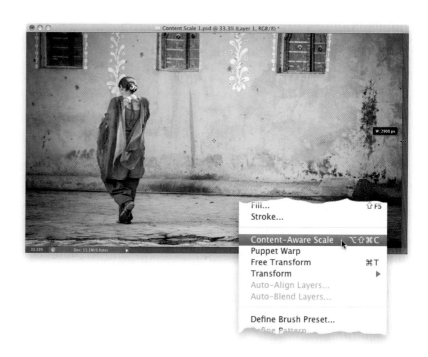

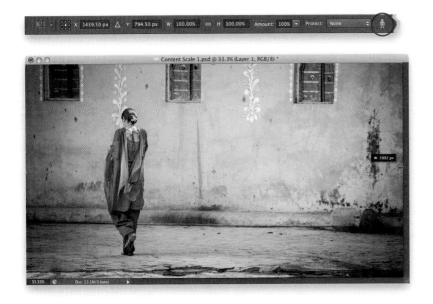

Step Four:

Choosing this brings up what looks just like the Free Transform handles (but these have "special powers"). Now, do the same thing you just did in Step Three—drag the left side handle over to cover the gap on the left, and then do the same thing on the right side (as shown here). It knows where your subject is (and that it's the most important part), so it only stretches the background (parts that can be scaled), and not her (which should not be scaled). It also expands the area it stretches in a very smart way, so the image doesn't look like it has been stretched. If you're using this on a different image, and it doesn't recognize that there's a person in your photo, click the Protect Skin Tones button up in the Options Bar (shown circled here), and that will alert Photoshop that there's a person in the image that it should avoid stretching. Of course, it can still get confused and miss that there's a person (or object) that you don't want stretched, which is why you'll want to know this next trick.

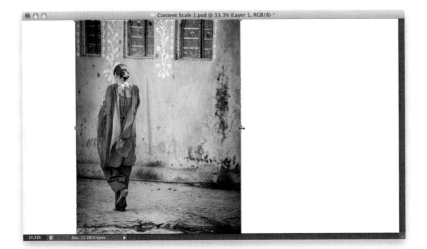

Step Five:

Before we go on to that, you'll want to know that you can also use this to shrink the width of the photo without distorting your subject (it'll slide her over, but it won't distort her, which is pretty amazing—maybe more amazing than the stretching). You do it the same way: just go into Content-Aware Scale and click-and-drag the side handles inward, and the scene just kind of collapses in around her, but she stays intact (as seen here). Notice how the windows are now closer together, but even they don't look squished? Pretty amazing, eh? Okay, now on to how to protect your subject when Photoshop doesn't recognize which part of the photo is the important part.

(Continued)

Step Six:

Let's open up a different image (shown here) and drag it over into our main document (you can click-and-drag the layer for the previous image onto the Trash icon at the bottom of the Layers panel to get rid of it). Press Command-T (PC: Ctrl-T) to go into Free Transform again and resize the image to fit in the document. Then, let's go ahead and use Content-Aware Scale again to shrink her down, so you can see what happens when Photoshop, for whatever reason, doesn't recognize our subject. Grab the side handles and drag way in toward our subject, and you can see it totally squishes her (as seen here at the bottom). Luckily, we can fix this easier than you'd think.

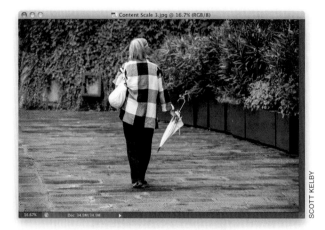

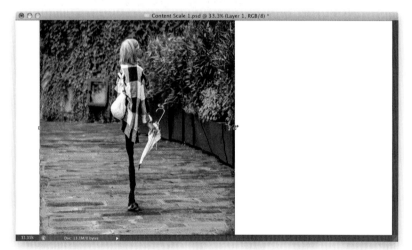

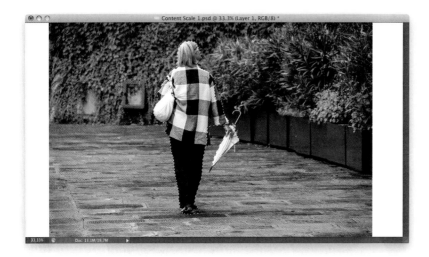

Step Seven:

The trick is simple: make a selection of the subject you want to protect (in our case, the woman), save that selection, then tell Photoshop you've saved it, and it then avoids that selected area like the plague. So, start by getting whichever selection tool you're most comfortable with from the Toolbox, and put a selection around your subject (here I used the Quick Selection tool, which if anything, is quick. It's not the most accurate, but that's okay for what we need to do here). Once your selection is in place, go under the Select menu and choose **Save Selection**. When the Save Selection dialog appears, just click OK, and now you can deselect by pressing **Command-D (PC: Ctrl-D)**.

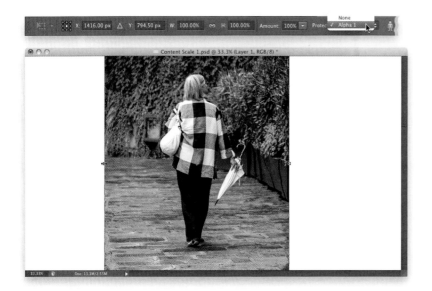

Step Eight:

Next, go under the Edit menu and choose Content-Aware Scale. All you have to do now is tell Photoshop that you have a saved selection (called an Alpha channel). To the left of the Protect Skin Tones button up in the Options Bar, you'll see a Protect pop-up menu. From that menu, choose **Alpha 1** (your saved selection), and now Content-Aware Scale knows exactly what not to stretch. So, grab the side handles, drag way in, and you'll notice that it keeps our subject intact and squishes the background in around her instead.

Removing Stuff Using Content-Aware Fill

When people talk about "Photoshop magic," Content-Aware Fill is one of those things they're talking about. Even after using this feature for a couple of years now to get rid of distracting things in my images, it still amazes me more often than not with the incredible job it does. The fact that it's incredibly easy to use at the same time really makes it a powerful, and indispensable, tool for photographers.

Step One:

Here, we have a tourist crossing into the background scene from the far-left side of the image, and it distracts from our subject (the woman sweeping), so ideally we'd like him out of the shot.

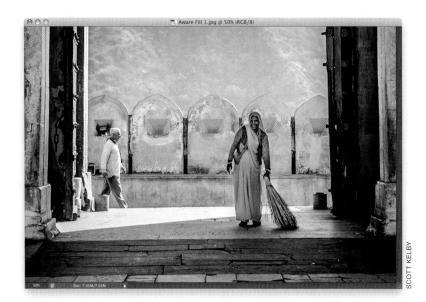

Step Two:

To have Content-Aware Fill remove him, just get the Lasso tool **(L)**, or whichever selection tool you're most comfortable with (like the Quick Selection tool, Pen tool—whatever), and draw a selection around him. Once your selection is in place, you can help Content-Aware Fill do its thing by expanding that selection outward by 4 or so pixels. So, go under the Select menu, under Modify, and choose **Expand**. When the Expand Selection dialog appears (shown here), enter 4 pixels, click OK, and your selection grows outward by that much.

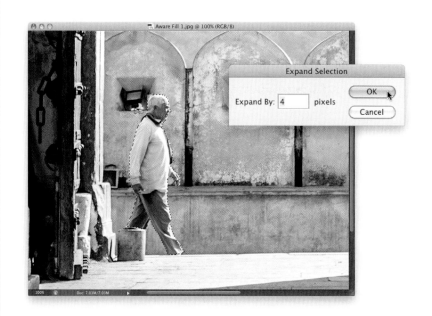

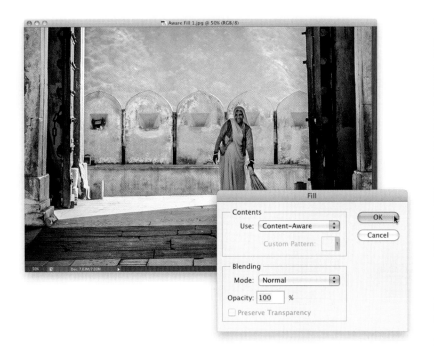

Step Three:

Next, go under the Edit menu and choose **Fill**. When the Fill dialog appears, choose **Content-Aware** from the Use pop-up menu (as seen here). Now, just click OK, sit back, and prepare to be amazed (I know—it's freaky). Not only is the guy gone, but it also patched the wall pretty darn perfectly behind him (that's why it's called "Content-Aware" Fill. It's aware of what is around the object you're removing, and it does an intelligent filling in of what would normally just be a big white hole in your image). Go ahead and deselect by pressing **Command-D (PC: Ctrl-D)**. The more I use it, the more it amazes me, but part of using this effectively is learning its weaknesses, and how to get around them when possible.

Step Four:

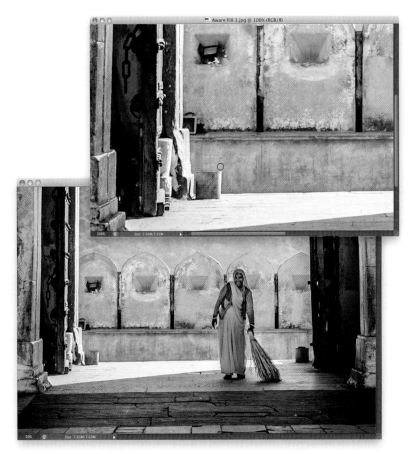

One area it didn't fill perfectly is the top of the stone cylinder his leg was behind, so we'll have to fix that manually using the Clone Stamp tool. Get the Clone Stamp tool **(S)** from the Toolbox, Option-click (PC: Alt-click) above the top edge of the cylinder and paint over the top right of it to fix that spillover (as seen here at the top). Now, you will fall deeply in love with Content-Aware Fill if you can come to peace with the fact that it won't work perfectly every time. But, if it does 70% or 80% of the work for me (in removing something I don't want), that means I only have to do the other 20% (or maybe 3%, like in this case), and that makes it worth its weight in gold. If it does the entire job for me, and sometimes it surely does, then it's even better, right? Right. Also, it helps to know that the more random the background is behind the object you want to remove, the better job Content-Aware Fill generally does for you.

(Continued)

Step Five:

Content-Aware Fill is pretty amazing when it works, but like any other tool in Photoshop, it doesn't work 100% of the time on every single type of photo and every situation. When I use Content-Aware Fill, I usually wind up using the Spot Healing Brush along with it, because it has Content-Aware healing built in. In Photoshop CS6, the Patch tool (the Healing Brush's cousin that works better for removing large objects) also has Content-Aware capabilities now. Let's open another image (this motocross shot) and use all of these tools together to remove the rider in the background, along with all the power lines, light poles, and the signs in the lower-left side of the image.

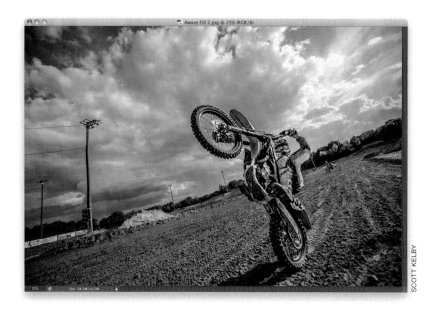

Step Six:

A lot of times you don't have to do as accurate a selection as we just did when removing the tourist in the previous project. For the rider in the background, just take the regular ol' Lasso tool (L), draw a loose selection around him and his bike (as shown here), then go under the Edit menu and choose Fill. When the Fill dialog comes up, make sure Content-Aware is selected in the Use pop-up menu, then click OK, and press Command-D (PC: Ctrl-D) to deselect (you'll see in the next step that the rider and his bike are gone, and it did a great job of filling in the trees and dirt hill behind him).

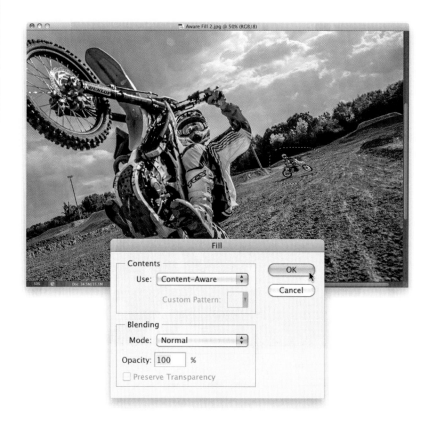

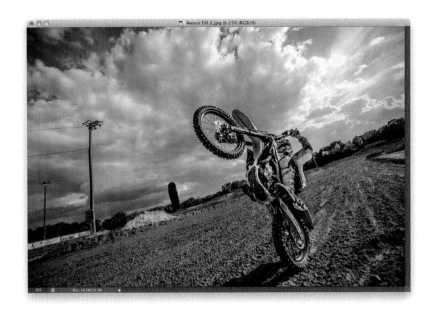

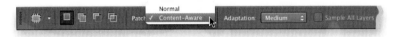

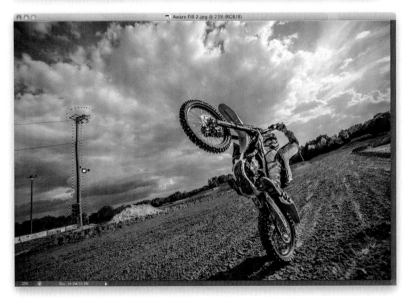

Step Seven:

Take a look at where the second rider used to be. He's outtathere! Let's switch to the Spot Healing Brush tool **(J)** for the light poles on the left. You literally just make your brush size a little bigger than a pole, paint over it, and Photoshop uses the Content-Aware technology to remove it. I removed the one under his wheel first by painting right over it, and here you can see I'm painting over the one in the middle (when I release the mouse button, a second later that one will be gone, too!). *Note:* The regular Healing Brush tool (the one where you have to choose the area to sample from by Option-clicking (PC: Alt-clicking) does *not* have the Content-Aware technology. Only the Spot Healing Brush tool and the Patch tool have it (but you have to turn it on for the Patch tool—it's on by default with the Spot Healing Brush).

Step Eight:

Let's use the Patch tool (press **Shift-J** until you have it), just so you can see how it works. You use it initially just like the Lasso tool: click-and-drag a loose selection around the object you want to remove (the large light pole, here), then click your cursor inside that selected area and drag it to a nearby clean area (you'll see a preview inside the selected area of what your patch will look like). Then, when you release the mouse button, it snaps back and the pole is removed. I use the Patch tool for removing larger objects like this. Also, if you want it to use the Content-Aware technology, in the Options Bar, choose **Content-Aware** from the Patch pop-up menu (as shown here). By the way, using this Content-Aware option won't always be better than the regular Patch tool healing—it just depends on the image. So, if you don't like the results of one, try the other. We're not done here yet, though.

(Continued)

Step Nine:

Here's the result of dragging the selection over to the right (look where my cursor is—over to the right of the original selection), and when it snapped back, it didn't look all that great (I could kind of see a little faint line where the pole had been. In cases like this, we just need to try another method, so press **Command-Z (PC: Ctrl-Z)** to Undo your patch, then Command-D (PC: Ctrl-D) to deselect, and let's go a different route.

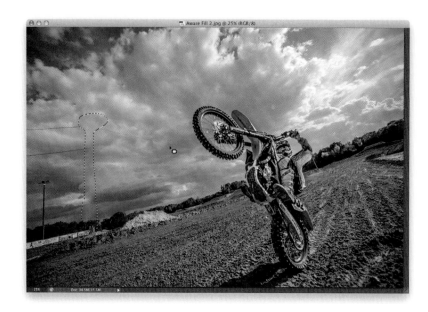

Step 10:

Switch back to the Spot Healing Brush (press **Shift-J** until you have it), then just paint over the pole (as shown here), and let's see how that does. You can see it already did a great job removing the pole on the left and the power lines.

TIP: Fixing Bad Repairs

We were lucky in this photo that the things we wanted to repair were far away from our rider, but in a lot of cases where the objects are in closer proximity, when you try to patch something, it doesn't patch your hole with background, it patches your hole with something in the foreground (imagine if, when we used Content-Aware, it filled the light pole with the motorbike? It happens more often than you'd think). To get around that, put a selection around what you want to tell Photoshop is "off limits" for using as a patch (in this case, you'd put a selection around the motorbike), then save that as a selection (under the Select menu, choose **Save Selection**, then click OK). Now, it will avoid that area when choosing areas to pull fill from.

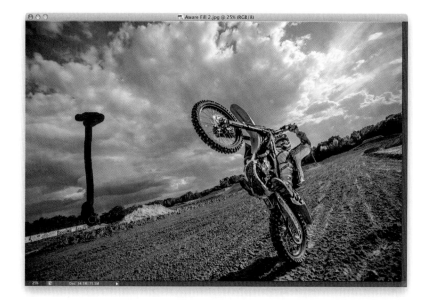

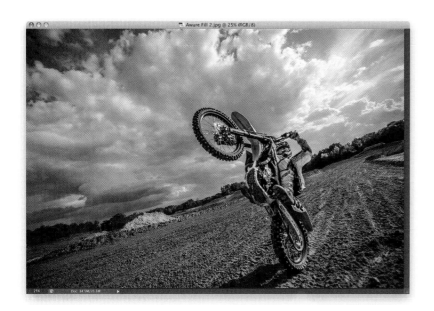

Step 11:

You can see here, in this case, the Spot Healing Brush did a good job. I tried all our different techniques on that pole—everything from the Patch tool with and without Content-Aware, to the regular old Content-Aware Fill from the Fill dialog—but for this particular image, the Spot Healing Brush just seemed to work the best. In fact, it worked so well that as soon as the pole was gone, I took it and painted right over those signs on the lower-left side of the image, and in two seconds they were gone—it filled in the dirt almost perfectly, as if they were never there. Before and After images are shown below.

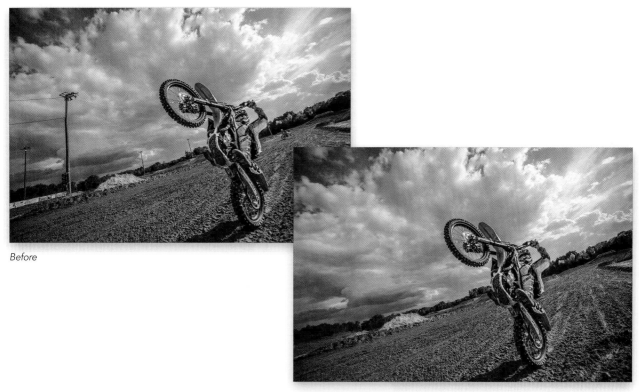

Before

After

Moving Stuff Without Leaving a Hole by Using Content-Aware Move

This is another one of those tools that makes you just scratch your head at the math that must be going on to perform the mini-miracle of letting you select something, then move it someplace else in your image, and Photoshop automatically repairs the area where it used to be. This doesn't work for every image, every time, and it's one of those tools you won't be reaching for every day, but when you need it, and it does its thing perfectly, your jaw hits the floor. It can be finicky sometimes, but I'll show you a few things to help it help you.

Step One:
Here's the image we're going to work on, and in this one, we want our subjects to be on the right side of the image, instead of being on the left.

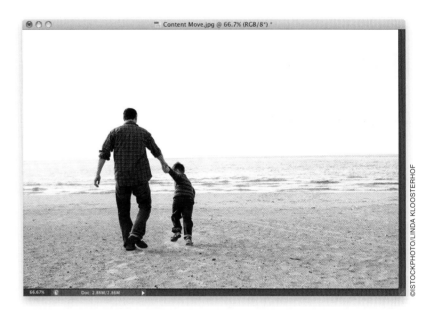

Step Two:
From the Toolbox, grab a selection tool that you're comfortable with and draw a selection around the object(s) you want to move (in this case, the father and son). It doesn't have to be a perfect selection, but get fairly close. (Here, I selected the area between them and their shadow on the sand, as well.) Once your selection is in place, you can usually get better results from Content-Aware Move by expanding your selection outward by 4 or so pixels. So, go under the Select menu, under Modify, and choose **Expand**. When the Expand Selection dialog appears (shown here), enter 4 pixels, click OK, and your selection grows outward by that much.

TIP: Draw Selection with Content-Aware Move
You can use the Content-Aware Move tool to draw your selections, just like you would with the Lasso tool.

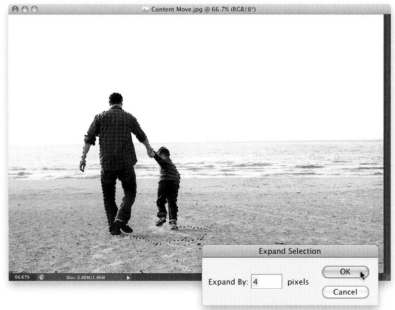

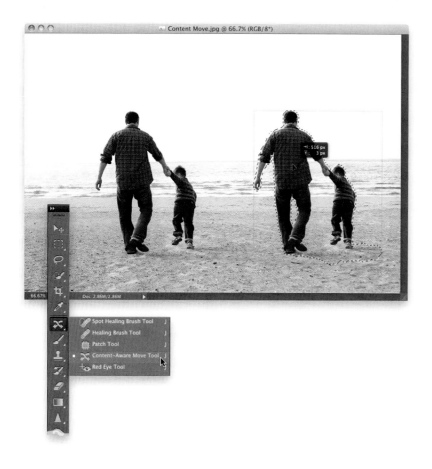

Step Three:

Next, go to the Toolbox, and get the new Content-Aware Move tool (as shown here—it's nested in the same menu as the Healing Brush tool and Patch tool; or just press **Shift-J** until you have it). Now, click on your selected subjects and drag them over to the right side of the image (as shown here). The original of them will still be in the same position for a few seconds while Photoshop is freaking out (kidding. While Photoshop is doing its math).

Step Four:

When you release your mouse button, it's going to take a few moments for the magic to happen (depending on how large your file size is), but then you'll see that not only are your subjects moved, but the hole that would normally have been left behind is instead totally patched and filled (as shown here). However, don't deselect quite yet. Leave your selection in place—especially if it didn't work well—because while it's still selected, you can change how Photoshop creates the background texture that blends with your move. You do this from the Adaptation pop-up menu up in the Options Bar. What's nice is, since your selection is still in place, you can choose a different option from that menu and it will re-render your move. So, all you have to do is try each one and choose the one that looks the best (again, I do this only if there's a problem). Also, the stricter the method you choose, the more Photoshop uses of the actual real background. This looks more realistic in some cases, but it can make the move look weird in others, so it's best to try them all if it just doesn't look right. (*Note:* If needed, you can also switch to the Spot Healing Brush and clean up any stray areas it left behind.)

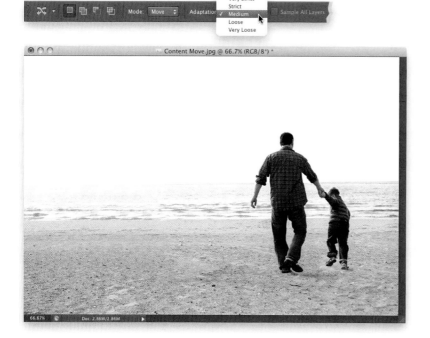

Photoshop Killer Tips

How to Make Shadows/Highlights an Adjustment Layer

Well, it won't technically be an adjustment layer, but it will act and perform exactly like one. Here's what you do: First, go under the Filter menu and choose **Convert for Smart Filters** (which converts the layer into a smart object). Then go under the Image menu, under Adjustments, and choose **Shadows/Highlights**. Now, choose any settings you like, then click OK. If you look in the Layers panel, you'll see that attached below your layer is a layer mask (just like an adjustment layer), and if you

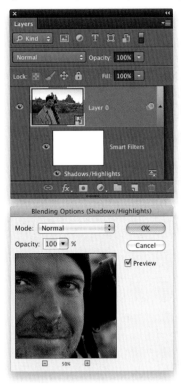

double-click on the words "Shadows/Highlights" below the mask, it brings up the dialog again, with the last settings you applied (just like an adjustment layer).

Also, just like an adjustment layer: if you double-click on the little adjustment sliders icon to the right of the name, it brings up a dialog where you can change the blend mode and opacity; you can click the Eye icon to turn the adjustment on/off; and finally, you can delete it anytime during your project.

Changing the Position of Your Lens Flare

When you use the Lens Flare filter (found under the Filter menu, under Render) it puts the flare in the center of your image,

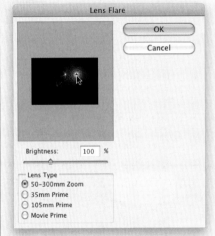

but you can actually choose the position for your flare center (which changes the look of your flare quite a bit) by just clicking-and-dragging the flare center within the filter's Preview window. By the way, a great way to apply this filter is to add a new layer, fill it with black, then run the filter, change its layer blend mode to **Screen**, and it will blend in with your image, so you can drag it wherever you'd like (if an edge shows, add a layer mask and paint over the edges in black with a huge, soft-edged brush).

Not Sure Which Blend Mode Is the Right One?

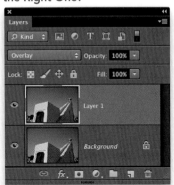

Then just press **Shift-+** to toggle through all the layer blend modes one-by-one, so you can quickly find out which one looks best to you.

How to Change the Order of the Brushes in the Brush Picker

Go under the Edit menu, under Presets, and choose **Preset Manager**. When the dialog opens, by default it's set to display

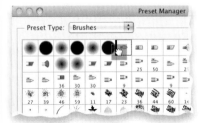

all your brushes, so now all you have to do is click-and-drag them into the order you want them. When you've got everything in the order you want, click the Done button.

Changing the Color of Your Guides

Want to change the color of those guides you drag out from the rulers? Just pull out a guide, then double-click directly on it, and it brings up the Preferences dialog

Photoshop Killer Tips

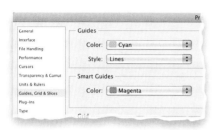

for Guides, Grid & Slices, where you can choose any color you'd like. You can also press **Command-K (PC: Ctrl-K)** and click on Guides, Grid & Slices on the left.

What That Fill Field Does

In the Layers panel, right below the Opacity field is a Fill field, which has had Photoshop users scratching their heads since it debuted several versions ago. It only kicks in when you have a

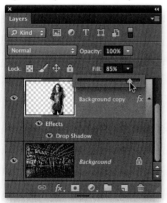

layer style applied to a layer, like a drop shadow or bevel. If you have something on a layer and you apply a drop shadow to it, then lower the Opacity amount, the object and its shadow both fade away, right? But if you lower the Fill amount only, the object starts to fade away, but the drop shadow stays at 100% opacity.

The Hidden Shortcut for Flattening Your Layers

There technically isn't a keyboard shortcut for the Flatten command, but I use a standard shortcut for flattening my image all the time. It's **Command-Shift-E (PC: Ctrl-Shift-E)**. That's actually the shortcut for Merge Visible, so it only works if you don't have any hidden layers, but I usually don't, so it usually works.

Customizing the HUD Pop-Up Color Picker

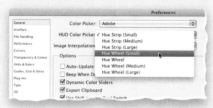

You can have a heads-up display color picker appear onscreen when you're using the Brush tool by pressing **Command-Option-Ctrl (PC: Alt-Shift)** and **clicking (PC: Right-clicking)**. And, did you know you also get to choose which type and size of HUD you want? Press **Command-K (PC: Ctrl-K)** to bring up Photoshop's preferences, click on General on the left, then up near the top of the General preferences is a HUD Color Picker pop-up menu for choosing your style and size.

Changing Brush Blend Modes on the Fly

If you want to change the blend mode for your current brush without traveling up to the Options Bar, just press **Shift-Ctrl (PC: Shift)** and **click (PC: Right-click)** anywhere in your image, and a pop-up menu of Brush tool blend modes appears.

Creating Cast Shadows

To create a cast shadow (rather than a drop shadow), first apply a Drop Shadow layer style to your object (choose Drop Shadow from the Add a Layer Style icon's pop-up menu at the bottom of the Layers panel, change your settings, and click OK), then go under the Layer menu, under Layer Style, and choose **Create Layer**. This puts the drop shadow on its own separate layer. Click on that new drop shadow layer, then press **Command-T (PC: Ctrl-T)** to bring up Free Transform. Now, press-and-hold the Command (PC: Ctrl) key, grab the top center point, and drag down at a 45° angle to create a cast shadow (like your shadow is casting onto the floor).

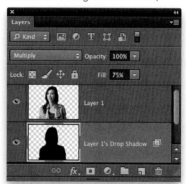

Copying Layer Masks from One Layer to Another

If you've created a layer mask, and you want that same mask to appear on a different layer, press-and-hold the Option (PC: Alt) key and just drag-and-drop that mask onto the layer where you want it. It makes a copy, leaving the original intact. If you want to remove the mask from one layer and apply it to another, then don't hold the Option key and, instead, just click-and-drag the mask to the layer where you want it.

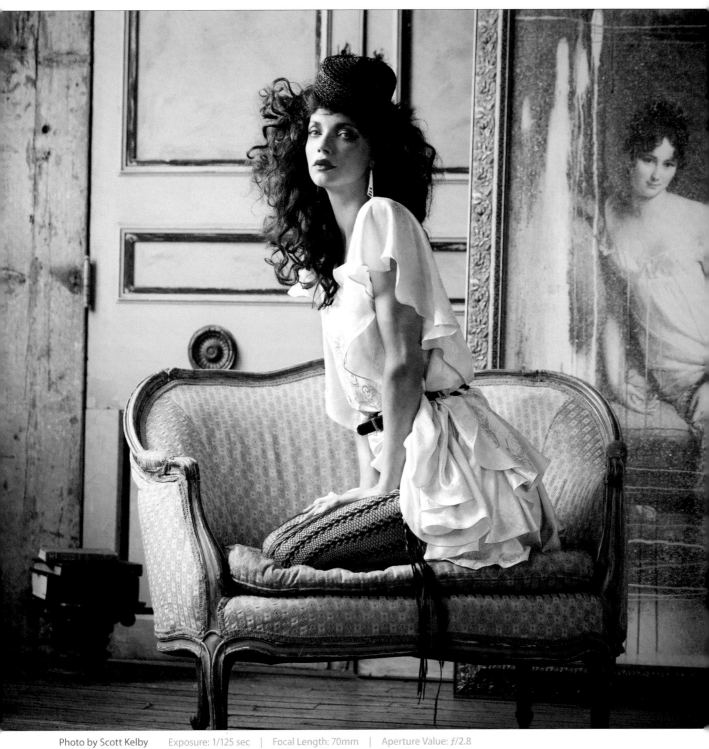

Photo by Scott Kelby   Exposure: 1/125 sec | Focal Length: 70mm | Aperture Value: ƒ/2.8

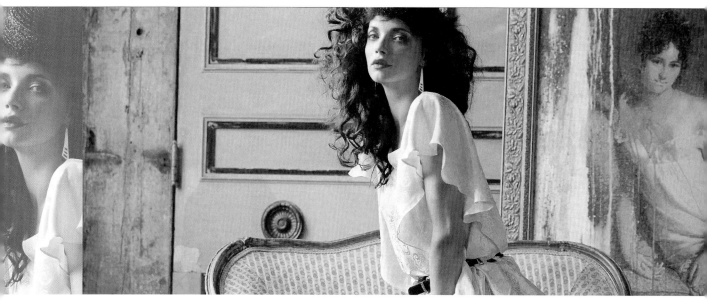

Side Effects
special effects for photographers

The name of this chapter comes from the 2009 movie short *Side Effects* (it's less than 20 minutes long, which is probably why you can buy it for only $1.99 in the iTunes Store. It's either that, or it's so cheap because of its lack of zombies). Anyway, here's how they describe *Side Effects* (say this in your best movie voice-over guy voice): "An ordinary guy becomes a human guinea pig in an experimental drug test and meets the girl of his dreams…" Sounds like a pretty typical everyday story. At least the human guinea pig in an experimental drug test part. Anyway, I looked at the movie poster, and the guys in the poster all have this creepy-looking bluish/green color cast that makes them look kind of sickly, but then the female lead's photo looks fine, with regular-looking flesh tones, and that's when I realized why this guy thinks he's found the woman of his dreams. She doesn't have a creepy bluish/green color cast. I mean, think

about it. If all the girls around you had a serious white balance problem, and then all of sudden you meet a girl carrying around her own 18% gray card, and so she looks correctly color balanced in any lighting situation, wouldn't you fall in love with her, too? Exactly. I'll bet in the last 10 minutes of the movie, you find out that this guy actually starts an online business for people using dating sites like eHarmony, or Match.com, or HandsomeStalker.com, where he offers to remove bluish/green color casts from your profile photo for a price. Things are going pretty well for him for a while, but then in about the eighteenth minute, the experimental drug wears off, and he finds himself trapped in a dank, dimly-lit room, forced to write non-sensical chapter intros late into the night, until his wife comes in and says "Honey, come to bed," but right then, he notices she has a bluish/green color cast, and….

Trendy Desaturated Skin Look

This is just about the hottest Photoshop portrait technique out there right now, and you see it popping up everywhere, from covers of magazines to CD covers, from print ads to Hollywood movie posters, and from editorial images to billboards. It seems right now everybody wants this effect (and you're about to be able to deliver it in roughly 60 seconds flat using the simplified method shown here!).

Step One:
Open the photo you want to apply this trendy desaturated portrait effect to. Duplicate the Background layer by pressing **Command-J (PC: Ctrl-J)**. Then duplicate this layer using the same shortcut (so you have three layers in all, which all look the same, as shown here).

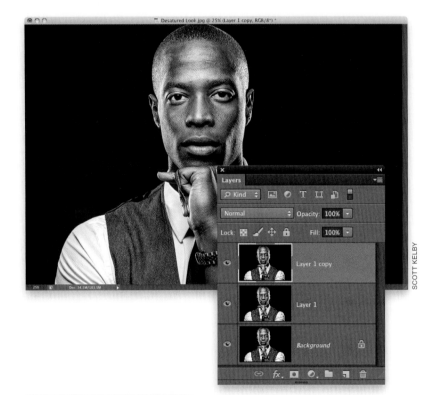

Step Two:
In the Layers panel, click on the middle layer (Layer 1) to make it the active layer, then press **Command-Shift-U (PC: Ctrl-Shift-U)** to Desaturate and remove all the color from that layer. Now, lower the Opacity of this layer to 80%, so just a little color shows through. Of course, there's still a color photo on the top of the layer stack, so you won't see anything change onscreen (you'll still see your color photo), but if you look in the Layers panel, you'll see the thumbnail for the center layer is in black and white (as seen here).

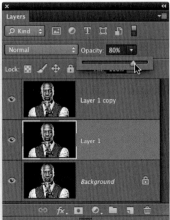

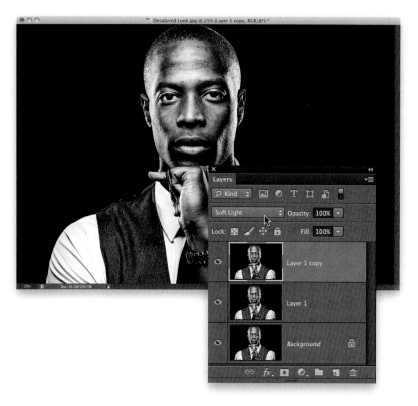

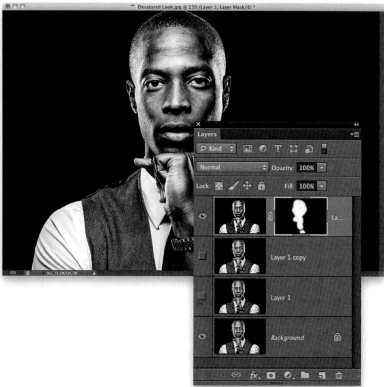

Step Three:

In the Layers panel, click on the top layer in the stack (Layer 1 copy), then switch its layer blend mode from Normal to **Soft Light** (as shown here), which brings the effect into play. Now, Soft Light brings a very nice, subtle version of the effect, but if you want something a bit edgier with even more contrast, try using Overlay mode instead. If the Overlay version is a bit too intense, try lowering the Opacity of the layer a bit until it looks good to you, but honestly, I usually just go with Soft Light myself.

Step Four:

Our last step is to limit the effect to just our subject's skin (of course, you can leave it over the entire image if it looks good, but normally I just use this as a skin effect. So, if it looks good to you as-is, you can skip this step). To limit it to just the skin, press **Command-Option-Shift-E (PC: Ctrl-Alt-Shift-E)** to create a merged layer on top of the layer stack (a merged layer is a new layer that looks like you flattened the image). You don't need the two layers below it any longer, so you can hide them from view by clicking on the Eye icon to the left of each layer's thumbnail (like I did here), or you can just delete them altogether. Now, press-and-hold the Option (PC: Alt) key and click on the Add Layer Mask icon at the bottom of the Layers panel to hide our desaturated layer behind a black mask. Press **D** to set your Foreground color to white, get the Brush tool **(B)**, choose a medium-sized, soft-edged brush from the Brush Picker in the Options Bar, and just paint over his face and hands (or any visible skin) to complete the effect. If you think the effect is too intense, just lower the Opacity of this layer until it looks right to you. That's it!

High-Contrast Portrait Look

The super-high-contrast, desaturated look is incredibly popular right now, and while there are a number of plug-ins that can give you this look, along with a Camera Raw technique I'll show you next, I also wanted to include this version, which I learned from German retoucher Calvin Hollywood, who shared this technique during a stint as my special guest blogger at my daily blog (www.scottkelby.com). The great thing about his version is: (1) you can write an action for it and apply it with one click, and (2) you don't need to buy a third-party plug-in to get this look. My thanks to Calvin for sharing this technique with me, and now you.

Step One:

Open the image you want to apply a high-contrast look to. Let's start, right off the bat, by creating an action to record our steps, so when you're done, you can reapply this same look to other photos with just one click. Go to the Actions panel, and click on the Create New Action icon at the bottom of the panel. When the New Action dialog appears, name this "High-Contrast Look" and click the Record button. Now it's recording every move you make… every step you take, it'll be watching you (sorry, I just couldn't resist).

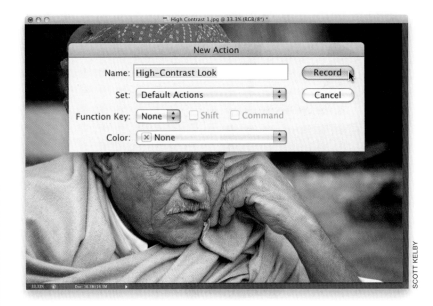

Step Two:

Make a copy of your Background layer by pressing **Command-J (PC: Ctrl-J)**. Now, change the blend mode of this duplicate layer to **Vivid Light** (I know it doesn't look pretty now, but it'll get better in a few more moves).

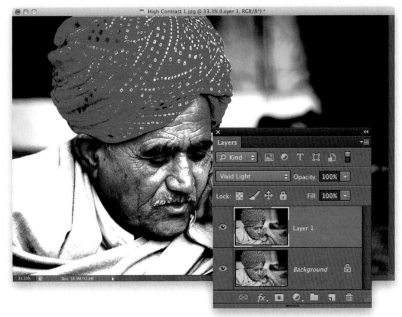

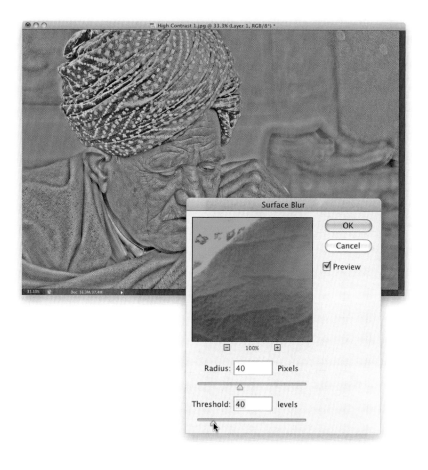

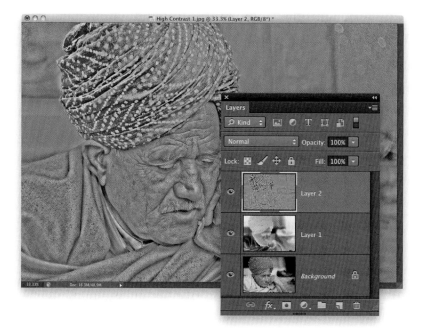

Step Three:

Now press **Command-I (PC: Ctrl-I)** to Invert the layer (it should look pretty gray at this point). Next, go under the Filter menu, under Blur, and choose **Surface Blur**. When the dialog appears, enter 40 for the Radius and 40 for the Threshold, and click OK (it takes a while for this particular filter to do its thing, so be patient. If you're running this on a 16-bit version of your photo, this wouldn't be a bad time to grab a cup of coffee. Maybe a sandwich, too).

Step Four:

We need to change the layer's blend mode again, but we can't change this one from Vivid Light or it will mess up the effect, so instead we're going to create a new layer, on top of the stack, that looks like a flattened version of the image. That way, we can change its blend mode to get a different look. This is called "creating a merged layer," and you get this layer by pressing **Command-Option-Shift-E (PC: Ctrl-Alt-Shift-E)**.

(Continued)

Step Five:

Now that you have this new merged layer, you need to delete the middle layer (the one you ran the Surface Blur upon), so drag it onto the Trash icon at the bottom of the Layers panel. Next, we have to deal with all the funky neon colors on this layer, and we do that by simply removing all the color. Go under the Image menu, under Adjustments, and choose **Desaturate**, so the layer only looks gray. Then, change the blend mode of your merged layer (Layer 2) to **Overlay**, and now you can start to see the effect taking shape. You can stop right there (I usually do), but if you think you need an even stronger high-contrast effect (hey, it's possible. It just depends on the image, and how much texture and contrast you want it to have), you can continue on and crank your amp up to 11 (sorry for the lame *This Is Spinal Tap* movie reference).

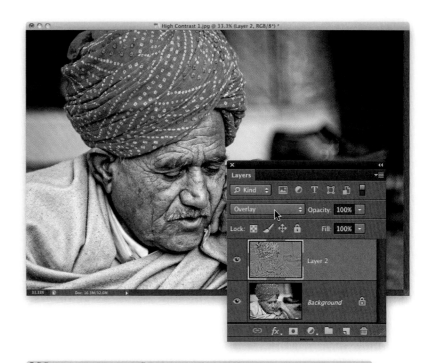

Step Six:

Go under the Image menu, under Adjustments, and choose **Shadows/Highlights**. In the dialog, drag the Shadows Amount down to 0. Turn on the Show More Options checkbox to reveal more editing options. Then, you're going to add what amounts to Camera Raw's Clarity by increasing the amount of Midtone Contrast on this Overlay layer. Go down near the bottom of the dialog and drag the Midtone Contrast slider to the right, and watch how your image starts to get that crispy look (crispy, in a good way). Of course, the farther to the right you drag, the crispier it gets, so don't go too far, because you're still going to sharpen this image. Click OK. The next step is optional, so if you don't need it, go to the Layers panel's flyout menu and choose **Flatten Image**. Don't forget to stop your action here.

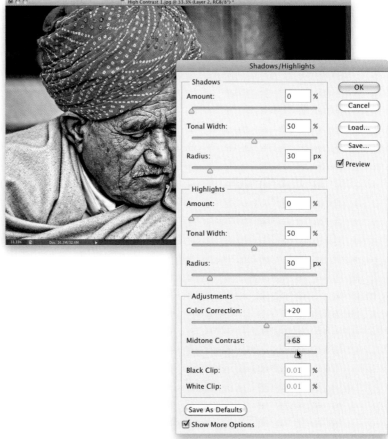

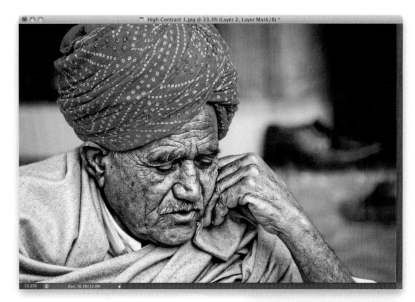

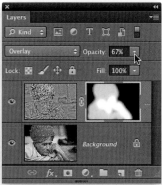

Step Seven:

Okay, this high-contrast look looks great on a lot of stuff, but one area where it doesn't look that good (and makes your image look obviously post-processed) is when you apply this to blurry, out-of-focus backgrounds, like the one you see here. So, I would only apply it to our subject and not the background. Here's how: Option-click (PC: Alt-click) on the Add Layer Mask icon at the bottom of the Layers panel to hide the contrast layer behind a black mask (so the effect is hidden from view). With your Foreground color set to white, get the Brush tool **(B)**, choose a medium-sized, soft-edged brush, and paint over his face to add the high-contract effect there. Now, in the Options Bar, lower the brush's Opacity to 70% (so the effect isn't as intense), then paint over his turban and clothes. This way, you avoid adding the contrast to the blurry background alto-gether. Lastly, go to the Layers panel and lower the Opacity of this layer until it looks more natural, as shown here at 67%. Now, you can flatten the layers and sharpen it using Unsharp Mask (see Chapter 10. Here, I used Amount: 120, Radius: 1, Threshold: 3) to finish off the effect.

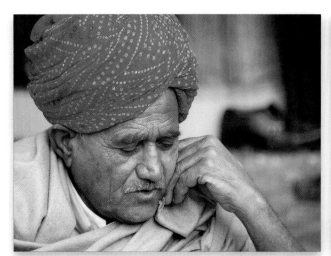

Before

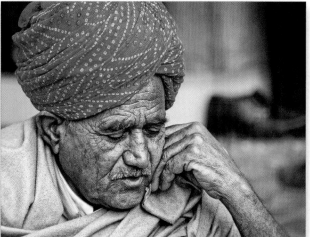

After

Getting the Grungy, High-Contrast Look Within Camera Raw

If you want that extreme-contrast, grungy look, you can create it right within Camera Raw itself by just dragging a few sliders in the Basic panel. If you're going to leave Camera Raw and go to Photoshop at some point anyway, you should try poppin' some High Pass sharpening on this puppy, too. Shots with lots of texture and metal just love a little High Pass tossed on them, too, so give it a try. But let's not get ahead of ourselves—here's the grungy look made easy:

Step One:

Open a photo in Camera Raw. This is one of those effects that needs the right kind of image for it to look right. Photos with lots of detail, texture, along with anything metallic, and lots of contrast seem to work best (it also works great for sports portraits like this one, cars, and even some landscapes. In other words: I wouldn't apply this effect to a shot of a cute little fuzzy bunny). Here's the original RAW image open in Camera Raw. (*Note:* This effect actually seems to come out better when you run it on RAW images, rather than JPEG or TIFF, but it does work on all three.)

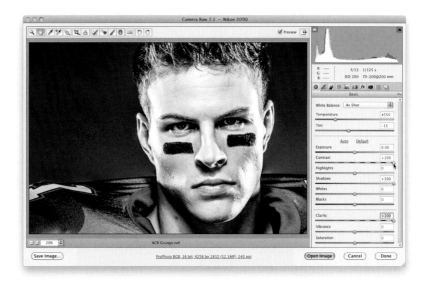

Step Two:

Set these three sliders all at 100: Contrast, Shadows, and Clarity (as shown here). Depending on the photo, this can make it look a little too bright or a little too washed out (his face looks a lot brighter and a bit washed out). So, you might have to tweak the Exposure slider a bit (most likely dragging it to the left to make the overall photo a little darker). I didn't do that here, but I wanted you to be aware just in case it happens to you.

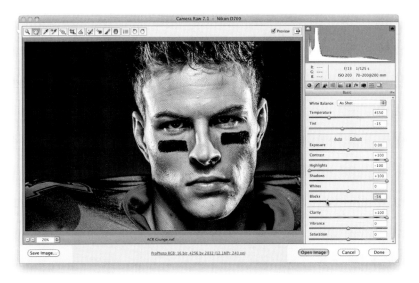

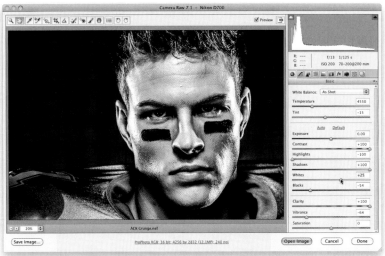

Step Three:

To keep the photo from looking too washed out in the deepest shadow areas, drag the Blacks slider to the left until the photo looks more balanced (like it does here, where I dragged it over to –54). Also, to "crush" back the highlights (it's part of the look of this high-contrast effect), you're going to drag the Highlights slider all the way to the left to –100. Okay, we're getting close.

Step Four:

Dragging that Blacks slider over like you did in the previous step generally makes your colors really vivid and saturated, but part of this effect is to intentionally desaturate the image. So, lower the Vibrance amount until it looks desaturated quite a bit (remember, that's part of the look). Here, I lowered it to –64. Lastly, if the image looks a little too dark, you can bring out the brightest highlights by dragging the Whites slider over to the right (as I did here—just a bit—over to +25). You won't do this to every image, but when it needs that little kicker in the highlights, dragging the Whites slider to the right a bit will often do the trick. A before/after is shown below. One more thing: is this image just screamin' for some High Pass sharpening, or what? (See page 347 for how to add it.)

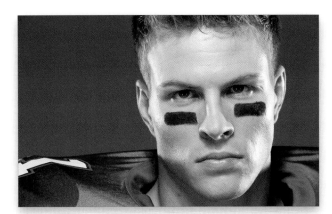

Before

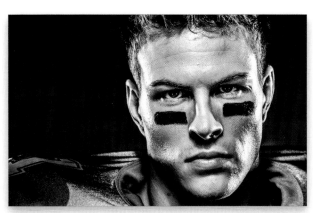

After

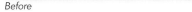

Dreamy Focus Effect for People and Landscapes

This is an effect I get asked about a lot, because I use it a lot. The particular thing I get asked is, "How do you get that look where your image looks sharp, but soft at the same time?" Well, it's actually really simple, but don't tell anybody it's this simple, because I'd prefer that people thought I had to pull off some serious Photoshop magic to make this happen. LOL!

Step One:

The sharpness of this effect comes from sharpening the image right up front, so I usually save this effect for when I'm about to save the file (in other words, I usually save the sharpening for the end, but in this case, there's another move that happens after the sharpening, so let's start with the sharpening first). Go under the Filter menu, under Sharpen, and choose **Unsharp Mask**. When the dialog appears, enter 120% for the Amount, set the Radius to 1.0, and set the Threshold to 3 for some nice punchy sharpening. Click OK.

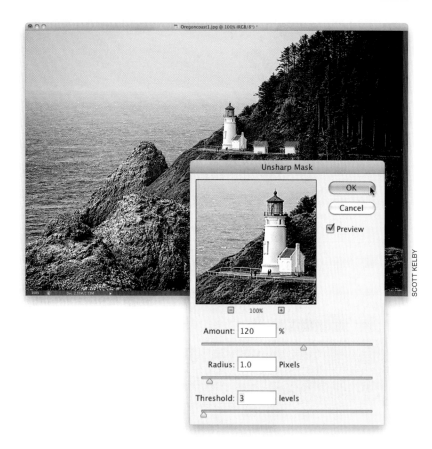

Step Two:

Duplicate this sharpened layer by pressing **Command-J (PC: Ctrl-J)**.

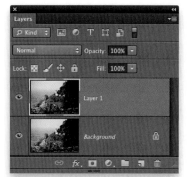

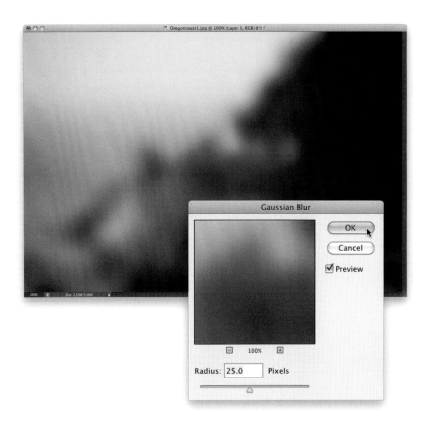

Step Three:

Now, go to the Filter menu, under Blur, and choose **Gaussian Blur**. When the filter dialog appears, enter 25 pixels for the Radius (you may have to go to 35 pixels or higher if you have a 24-mega-pixel, or higher, camera. Don't worry so much about the number, just make sure your image looks at least as blurry as this one does), and click OK.

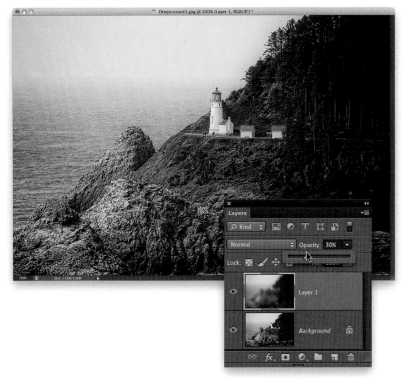

Step Four:

Finally, go to the Layers panel and change the Opacity amount of this blurred layer to 30% (as shown here), and that completes the effect. Now, I know what you're thinking, "Scott. Seriously. Is that all there is to it?" Yes, and that's why it's best we keep this just between us. ;-)

Getting the Instagram Look

Here's a quick and easy, all-in-Camera-Raw way to get the wildly popular Instagram app look. Of course, there isn't just one "look," because Instagram has like 15 different ones, but this will at least take you in the right direction. One more thing: I know you're thinking, "Do people really want to learn how to do phone app looks in Photoshop?" Yup. It's one of the most-requested effects people ask to learn (don't get me started). Luckily, it's easy, and the looks are actually based on classic darkroom effects, so that can't be a bad thing.

Step One:

Start by opening your image in Camera Raw. One of the trademark looks of the Instagram app is its square cropping ratio, so let's start there. Click-and-hold on the Crop tool in the toolbar at the top, and a list of cropping ratios appears (seen here). Choose the **1 to 1** ratio (as shown), which gives you a square crop.

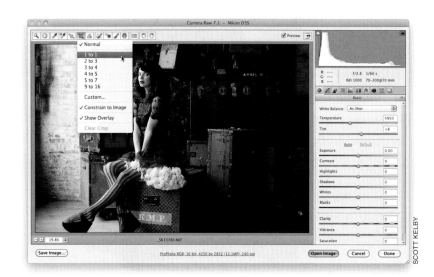

Step Two:

Drag your cropping border out over the part of the image you want to have your effect (in this case, it's pretty obvious which part of the image we should keep). Once the crop is where you want it, just press the **Return (PC: Enter) key** to lock in your square crop. From here on out, it's pretty darn easy—I'll give you some sliders to set, and a couple of minor little moves, and you're there. Let's do it.

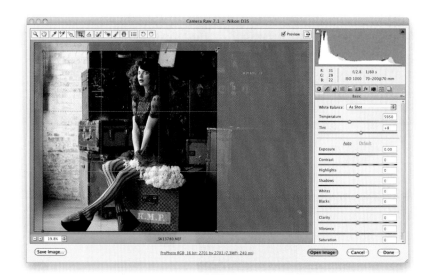

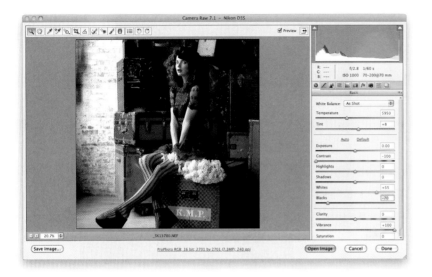

Step Three:

Another trademark part of the Instagram look is that the images have very flat contrast (after all, these are imitating some vintage camera looks), so start by dragging your Contrast slider all the way to the left to –100. Then, go ahead and crank up the Vibrance a bunch to +100. Now, we'll add a little contrast back in by dragging the Whites to the right to increase the very brightest highlights (here, I dragged over to +55), and bring some color back to the darkest shadow areas by dragging the Blacks slider to the left (here, I dragged it over to –70). At this point, the photo looks kind of yellowish. Not for long, though.

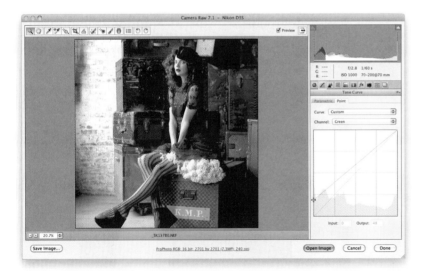

Step Four:

Click on the Tone Curve icon (the second icon from the left) at the top of the Panel area, and when that panel appears, click on the Point tab. Then, from the Channel pop-up menu, choose **Green**. Don't worry—even if you've never used the Tone Curve before, you'll absolutely be able to do this. You see that diagonal line running from the bottom-left corner up to the top-right corner? Well, grab the point at the bottom of the line and drag it up a bit (as shown here) to bump up the greens. See, that was easy, eh?

(Continued)

Step Five:

Now that you've got the hang of adjusting the curve, choose **Blue** from the Channel pop-up menu. Grab the same point (the bottom-left corner point) and drag upward, but this time you're going to keep dragging until you pass the center line and stop about halfway up the next grid square (as seen here). Next, grab the top-right corner point and drag downward to just a hair or two past the center of the first grid square (as seen here). This gives the image more of a teal-and-yellowish feel.

TIP: Add Grain for a Film-Like Look

If you want more of a film look, click on the Effects icon in Camera Raw (the fourth from the right), and at the top is a Grain Amount slider (designed to emulate film grain). Drag it to the right to add more of a grainy look to your Instagram-effect images.

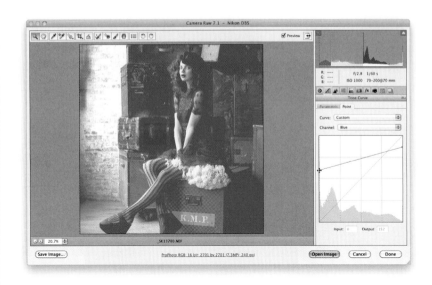

Step Six:

Next, click on the fifth icon from the left, at the top of the Panel area, to bring up the Split Toning panel. Here, you can add one color tint to the highlights in your photo, and a different one to the shadow areas, and then you can control the balance between the two. We'll start with the highlights, so drag the Highlights Saturation slider to 37 (we drag the Saturation slider first, so we can actually see the hue. At its default, you can drag that Hue slider all day and never see any difference). Then, drag the Hue slider to 47, which gives you a yellow tint in the highlights. Jump down to the Shadows and increase the Saturation to 100 and set the Hue at 273 for a blue tint in the shadows. Lastly, we're going to drag the Balance slider to the right—over to +65—so there are more blue shadows than yellow highlights in our split tone (as seen here).

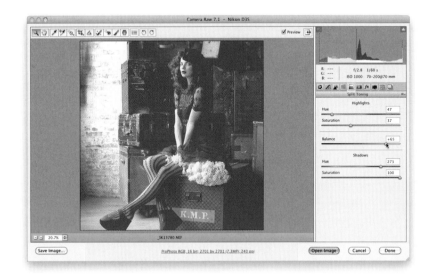

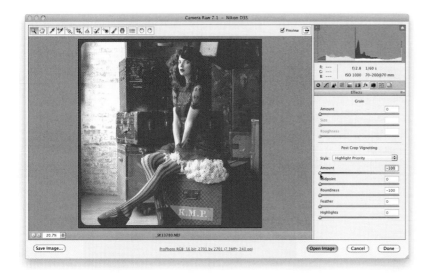

Step Seven:

Now, we're going to add a fake border right in Camera Raw. This is kinda similar to one of the built-in Instagram borders. Click on the Effects icon (the fourth from the right), and then go down to the Post Crop Vignetting section and drag the Amount slider all the way to the left, to –100 (as shown here), to make your border solid black. Then, drag the other three sliders all the way to the left, as well, and that gives you the hard-edged, rounded-corner border you see here.

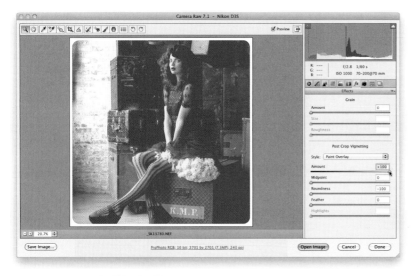

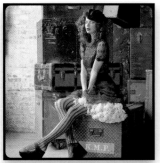

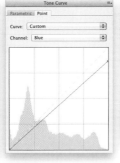

Step Eight:

Instagram also gives you the option of a white border, and you can do that in Camera Raw, too: just change the Style of your Post Crop Vignette to **Paint Overlay**, then drag your Amount slider all the way to the far right (to +100) to get a solid white border like the one you see here. By the way, for a quick color variation of the image, go back to the Tone Curve panel, to the Blue channel, and drag the point on the left side back down to the left corner (as shown below center). Do the same in the Green channel, then take away some of the contrast by lowering the Whites to –100, and lastly bump up the Exposure a little to give you the alternate reddish look you see here, below left. Lastly, once you've adjusted all these sliders, it would be the perfect time to save these settings as a one-click preset (so, next time, this entire look is just one click away). Click on the Presets icon (the second from the right), then click on the Create New Preset icon at the bottom-right of the panel (it looks like the Create a New Layer icon) and save your settings. For more on saving presets, see page 167. Okay, there ya go bunky.

Panoramas
Made Crazy Easy

I used to have an entire segment in my live Photoshop seminars where I'd show you the seven things you needed to do with your camera to shoot a pano that Photoshop would merge seamlessly together. Then, Adobe improved the Photomerge feature so vastly that you now only need to do one simple thing: as you shoot, overlap each frame by around 20% (so if you're shooting in the desert, from left to right, the same rock would appear on the right edge of the first shot and the left edge of the next frame). That way, Photoshop sees how they get stitched together. Outside of that, you can now even hand-hold your shots and it will perfectly align your frames, too.

Step One:

This first thing isn't technically a Photoshop thing, but if you do it, it sure will make working with panos easier. When you're out shooting, and you're about to shoot a pano, before you shoot your first pano frame, hold your index finger up in front of your lens and take a photo. Then go ahead and take your pano, and right after you shoot your last frame, hold up two fingers in front of your lens and take another photo. Here's where this pays off: When you open all your photos from that day's shoot in Mini Bridge, you could easily have hundreds of photos (especially if these are vacation photos). As you scroll through, as soon as you see an index finger, you know these are your pano photos (by the way, if you have that whole self-loathing thing going on, or if you're a teen, you don't have to use your index finger). Plus, it not only tells you that you shot a pano, it tells you exactly where it starts and where it ends (as seen here). It sounds silly, but if you don't do this, you'll actually miss panos you took, and you'll just kind of wonder, "What was I thinking when I took those?" and you'll scroll right by them. It's happened to me, and so many of my friends, that we now all use this technique, and we never miss a pano. Okay, now press-and-hold the Command (PC: Ctrl) key and click on each photo thumbnail between your two finger shots (as shown here).

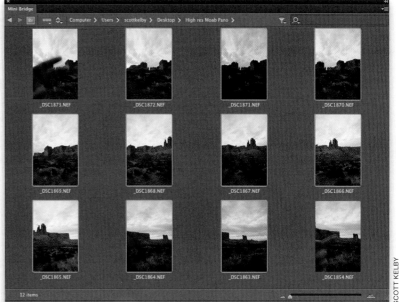

SCOTT KELBY

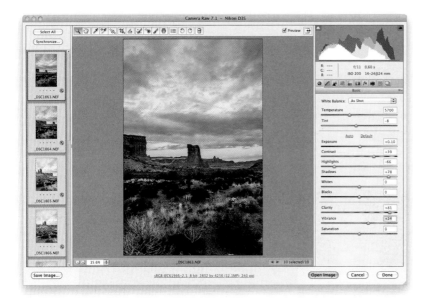

Step Two:

Before you create your pano, here's something to consider: if you just jump over to Photoshop and create your pano, when you see it next, it will be a regular 8-bit Photoshop image (in other words, it won't be a RAW image any longer). That's why I like to do some up-front image tweaking, while those images are still in RAW format, before we "bake it" and turn it into a regular Photoshop file. So, since those pano images are already selected, just double-click on any one of them to open them all in Camera Raw (as shown here). Press **Command-A (PC: Ctrl-A)** to select all the images you just opened (that way, any changes you make to one image are automatically applied to the rest of the pano frames). Now, let's increase the Exposure (here, I went to +0.10) and Contrast (to +39), pull back the Highlights to –66 to bring back some detail and dimension in the sky, bump the Shadows up to +78, so we can see more detail in the shadow areas, and lastly, let's crank the Clarity to +81 and the Vibrance to +24. Now, don't click Open Images, just click Done.

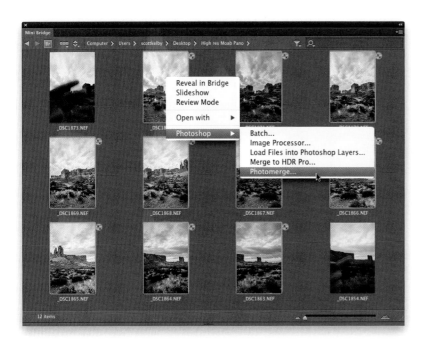

Step Three:

Back in Mini Bridge, the thumbnails of those images will now have a little circular adjustment badge icon, letting you know they've been adjusted in Camera Raw. Make sure those images are still selected (everything between the two finger shots), then Right-click on any one of those thumbnails and from the pop-up menu that appears, under Photoshop, choose **Photomerge** (as shown here). *Note:* If you opened your photos in Photoshop, then you can go under the File menu, under Automate, and choose Photomerge. Either way, they both will get you to the same place, but I prefer going directly from the RAW images, if possible.

(Continued)

Step Four:

When you choose Photomerge, it brings up the dialog you see here, with the images you selected listed in the center column. (*Note: If* you opened your pano photos from within Photoshop, the center column will be empty, so you'll click the Add Open Files button.) We'll look at the Layout part in the next step, and jump down below that center column. Leave the Blend Images Together checkbox turned on. Now, there are two other options you may need, depending on how you shot your pano: (1) If you have lens vignetting (the edges of your images appear darkened), then turn on Vignette Removal (as I did here), and although it will take a little longer to render your pano, it will try to remove the vignetting during the process (it does a pretty decent job). If you're using a Nikon, Sigma, or Canon fisheye lens to shoot your panos, then turn on the Geometric Distortion Correction checkbox at the bottom to correct the fisheye distortion.

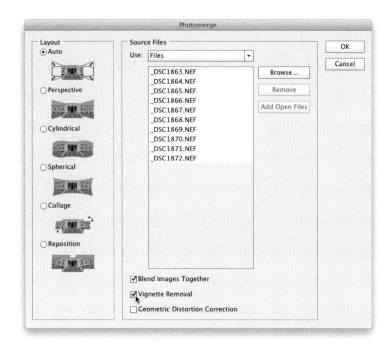

Step Five:

In the Layout section on the left, the default setting is Auto (as seen in Step Four), and I recommend leaving that set to Auto to get the standard wide pano we're looking for. The five Layout choices below Auto (Perspective, Cylindrical, Spherical, Collage, and Reposition) all give you…well…funky looking panos (that's the best description I can give you), but suffice it to say—they don't give you that nice wide pano most of us are looking for. So, let's just stick with Auto. Click OK, and within a few minutes (depending on how many photos you shot for it), your pano is seamlessly stitched together (as seen here). In the Layers panel, you can see all the masks it created to do its thing.

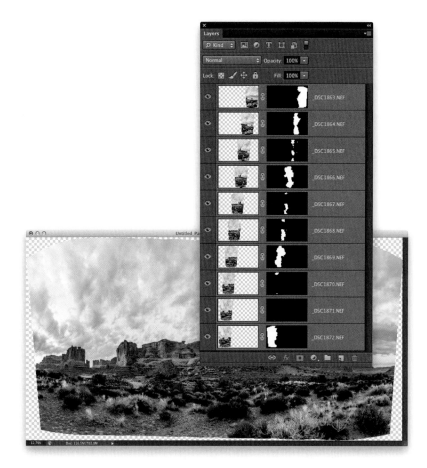

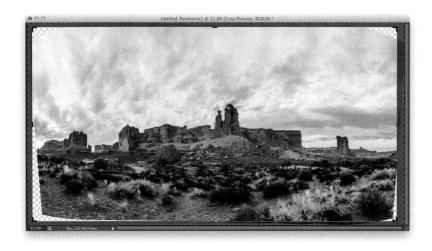

Step Six:

To make your pano fit perfectly together, Photomerge has to move and rearrange things in a way that will cause you to have to crop the photo down to get the final result you want (we get the easy job—cropping only takes about 10 seconds). So, get the Crop tool **(C)**, which brings up a cropping border around your image (like you see here). Don't worry if there are a few gaps along the edges, because we'll fix that in a moment.

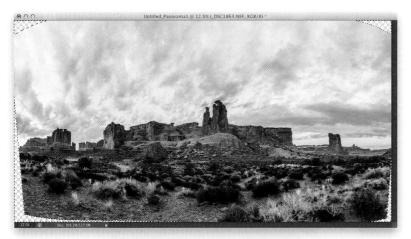

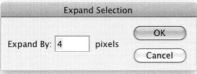

Step Seven:

Press **Return (PC: Enter)**, and your pano is cropped down to size (as seen here), but you can see that we have gaps in all four corners (and a couple of tiny white gaps on the top-right side, which we can fix later with the Clone Stamp tool—that's easy—but we need to deal with these corner problems now). First, from the Layers panel's flyout menu, choose **Merge Visible** to merge all your layers and leave the background transparent. Next, get the Magic Wand tool (press **Shift-W** until you have it), click in the top-left gap once, then press-and-hold the Shift key and click in the other corners (holding the Shift key lets you add the other areas to your current left-corner selection). We're going to use Content-Aware Fill to fill in those gaps, but it works best if you give it some breathing room by expanding your selected areas by 4 pixels. To do that, go under the Select menu, under Modify, and choose **Expand**. Enter 4 pixels (as shown here) to grow your selection outward a bit, and click OK. Now our file is ready to let Content-Aware work its magic.

(Continued)

Step Eight:

Go under the Edit menu and choose **Fill**. When the dialog appears (shown here), from the Use pop-up menu at the top, choose **Content-Aware**, then click OK, sit back, and prepare to be amazed. Well, most of the time it's pretty darn amazing. Every once in a while, it's just way, way off and you have to undo it and go a different route. But, when it's fixing things like gaps in the sky, or in a desert floor, or anything that's kind of random by nature, it works wonders, and in an image like this, it does a really great job (as shown here). Press **Command-D (PC: Ctrl-D)** to deselect.

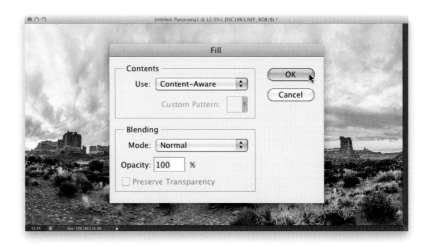

Step Nine:

Now for some finishing moves. I would generally create a neutral density gradient filter effect here to darken the sky (like we did in Camera Raw in Chapter 4), which is simple to do in Photoshop. Click on the Create New Adjustment Layer icon at the bottom of the Layers panel and choose **Gradient** from the pop-up menu. When the dialog appears, turn on the Reverse checkbox (otherwise, it does the opposite of what you want—it darkens the foreground instead of the sky). Now, click on the Gradient itself to bring up the Gradient Editor. Click on the last gradient in the default Presets list—that's the Neutral Density gradient. To control how far down this gradient extends into your image, click-and-drag the white Opacity stop (shown circled here in the red) to the left. The farther you drag, the shorter the gradient extends down into your image. I usually like it in the top ¼ to ⅓ of the sky. When you're done, click OK twice, then, in the Layers panel, change the blend mode of this layer to **Overlay**.

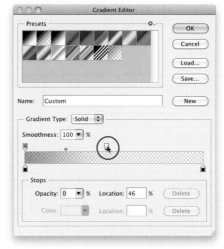

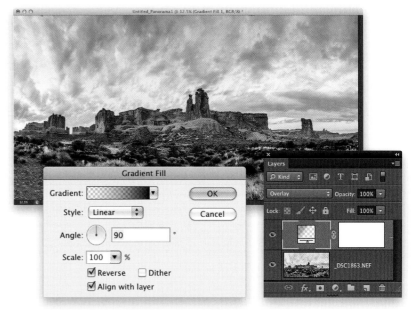

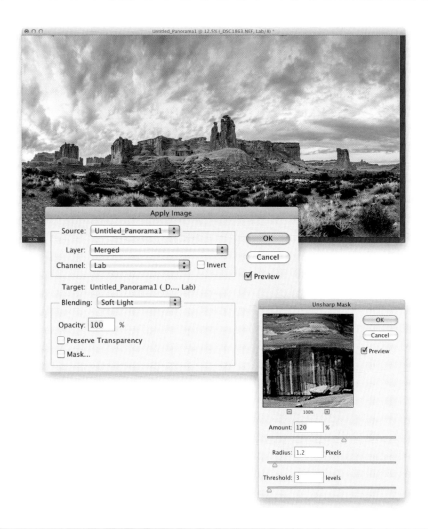

Step 10:

At this point, to make the color more vibrant, you could save the file as a JPEG, TIFF, or PSD, then reopen the image in Camera Raw and increase the Vibrance amount. If that sounds like a lot of work, try this instead: Press **Command-E (PC: Ctrl-E)** to merge your two layers, then go under the Image menu, under Mode, and choose **Lab Color** (don't worry, this is a non-destructive move). Go under the Image menu, again, and choose **Apply Image**. In the dialog (shown here), first change the Blending mode to **Soft Light**, which builds up the contrast. Then, from the Channel pop-up menu, try all three channels, Lab, "a," and "b" (ignore the Lightness channel—you'll never use it), and see which one looks best to you. In this case, I chose "a," which added a lot of warmth to the foreground and rock formations in back. When it looks good to you, click OK, then go back under the Image menu, under Mode, and choose **RGB Color**. Now you can sharpen it by going under the Filter menu, under Sharpen, and choosing **Unsharp Mask**. Pick some nice strong settings (here, I chose Amount: 120, Radius: 1.2, Threshold: 3), and click OK to finish the image (seen below).

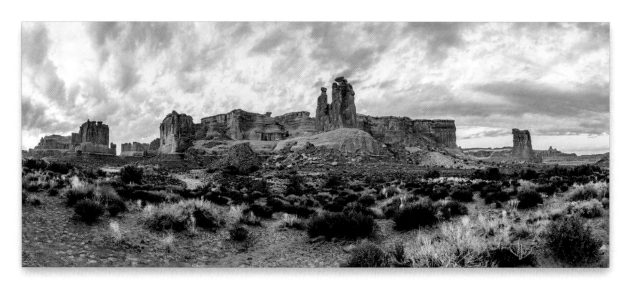

Turning a Photo into an Oil Painting in One Click

Being able to easily turn a photo into a realistic-looking painting has been on the photographer's wish list for quite some time (this look is very popular with wedding and portrait photographers), and after years of being a painstakingly tedious and complex technique to get even close, now in Photoshop CS6, it literally is a one-click process (because as soon as you open the Oil Paint filter—boom— it's an oil painting before you even touch a single slider). Now, of course, there are sliders, and that's why this isn't just a one-page project, but you are going to love how simple this really is.

Step One:

Open an image you want to turn into an oil painting. Here's a shot of Byron Hamburgers in London (mmmmm… burger) taken on vacation late at night (think "midnight burger run"). I did a little HDR on this image (as if there was such a thing as "a little" HDR), but we're going to turn it into an oil painting in one click. For reasons I can't even begin to understand, there is no Preview checkbox in the Oil Paint filter, so I usually start by pressing **Command-J (PC: Ctrl-J)** to duplicate the Background layer (as shown here), so at least that way you can easily see a before/after.

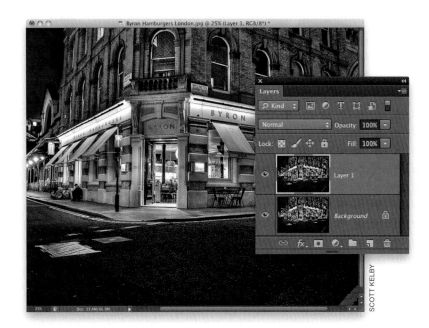

Step Two:

Now, go under the Filter menu, choose **Oil Paint** (it's near the top of the menu), and that's it—you've got an oil painting. But to really see the effect, zoom in to 100% (like you see here), and you can see it does a pretty amazing job of keeping detail, while looking very painterly at the same time. Of course, you can just click OK and be done with it, but you actually have quite a bit of control over how your oil painting looks (and messing around with the sliders in this filter is actually fun, so it's worth giving it a go).

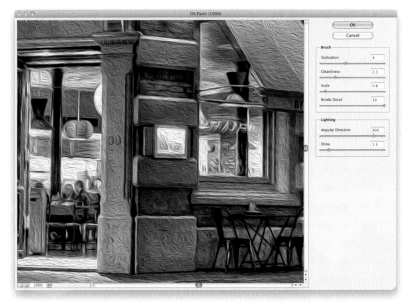

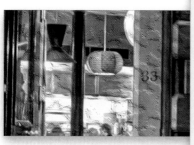

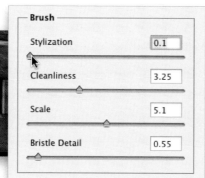

Brush Stylization set to 0.1

Step Three:

I'll take you through the sliders here, so you can see how each one affects part of the image, and I'll show before/after images, as well, so it makes more sense. At the top, you've got the Brush controls, and the first is the Stylization slider. This lets you choose the style of the brush that paints the image. Set to 0.1 (all the way to the left), it paints with small, hard brush strokes, which gives you the look you see here at the top (it almost looks like stucco on the walls, right?). If you drag that slider over all the way to the right, the strokes get longer, and the effect looks more smooth and graceful (if not a little Van Gogh-esque). I usually prefer something more toward the middle or higher numbers, and of course it always depends on the image you're working on, but I've yet to find one where I want to leave it set at 0.1.

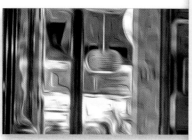

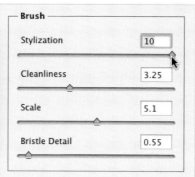

Brush Stylization set to 10

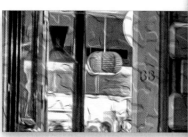

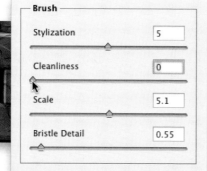

Brush Cleanliness set to 0.1

Step Four:

A good name for the second Brush slider would have been Detail, but then we would have known exactly what it does, so instead, it's named Cleanliness. If you want the brush to paint your image with a cleaner, more detailed look (more realistic), drag the slider to the left, and for more of a softer, more painterly look (at bottom), drag the slider to the right. Also note that I've set the Stylization slider to 5 (the midway point). I'll do that for each previous slider as we move on through the rest of the sliders.

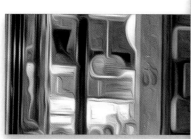

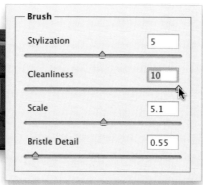

Brush Cleanliness set to 10

(Continued)

Step Five:

The Scale slider controls the size of your brush, so dragging it way over to the left would paint your image with a very thin brush, and dragging it all the way over to the right would paint it with a very thick strokes. Take at look at the top example here and you can see how tiny and detailed those brush stroke are compared with the strokes below when you set the size (thickness) much larger. Totally different look.

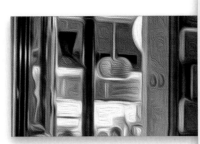
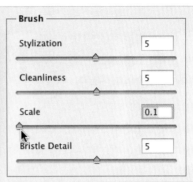

Brush Scale (thickness) set to 0.1

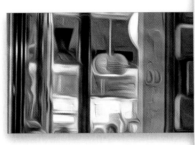
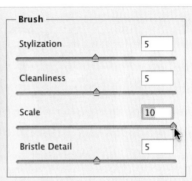

Brush Scale (thickness) set to 10

Step Six:

Okay, the last Brush slider should be called the Sharpness slider, as it makes the overall image look sharper or softer in how it affects the brush. Dragging it to the left takes away the detail of the brush bristles, so it's very soft, smooth, and undefined (like you see here at the top). Dragging to the right gives it a harder, more detailed look that makes the image look sharper, as you really see the bristles in the stroke now. Just for the record, I'm glad there are only four sliders here. :) Now, on to the two lighting controls.

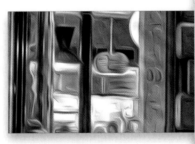
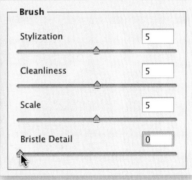

Brush Bristle Detail set to 0

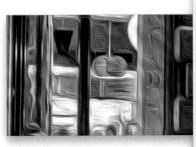
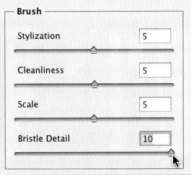

Brush Bristle Detail set to 10

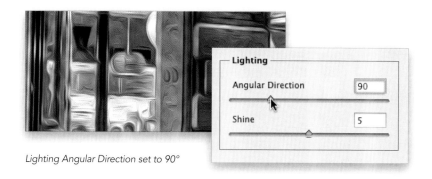

Lighting Angular Direction set to 90°

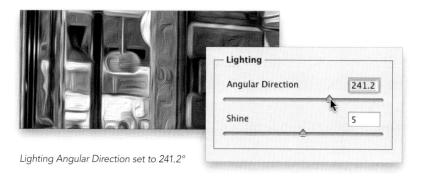

Lighting Angular Direction set to 241.2°

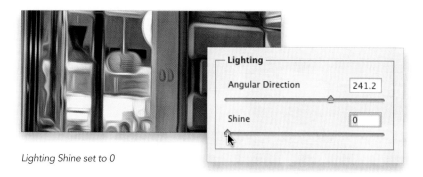

Lighting Shine set to 0

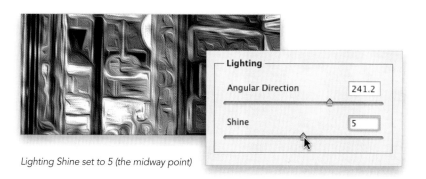

Lighting Shine set to 5 (the midway point)

Step Seven:

There are two sliders in the Lighting section: The Angular Direction slider controls the angle of the light hitting your painting. When it's a direction of light, Adobe usually gives us a round dial-like controller (like the one in the Bevel & Emboss section of the Layer Style dialog), but here, they just went with a regular ol' slider. The best way to totally "get" this slider is to just drag it back and forth a few times and you'll totally get what it does, because the light changes as you drag from 0 to 360 degrees.

Step Eight:

The last slider in this section is the Shine amount, and it controls how the light reflects. Dragging it to the left makes your image very flat-looking (as seen here, at top), and dragging over to the right adds contrast to the highlights and shadows, and kind of makes the paint look thicker, almost like it's embossed. I only dragged halfway here, to a setting of 5, because it looked *so* bad at a setting of 10 that I was afraid you'd look at it and think, "Okay, I'm never going to touch that slider." It actually has a nice effect, and of course, the setting amount (as always) depends on the image you're applying it to.

(Continued)

Step Nine:

Now that I've messed with all the sliders, I'm going to go back and put them where I think they look good for this particular image (if I do an oil painting effect, I really want it to look painted—I don't go for the subtle look with this). However, once you click OK and the filter is applied to your image, if you think it's a little too heavy (or you just want a little more realism back in your painting), you don't have to go back and mess with the sliders again. Instead, immediately go under the Edit menu and choose **Fade Oil Paint**. This brings up the Fade dialog (shown here below), and the best way I can describe it is it's kind of like "Undo on a slider." So, if you drag the Opacity slider to the left, it lowers the intensity of the effect. If you drag it to 0%, it removes it altogether. Try dragging it to 70% (as shown here), and 30% of the original image comes back, bringing in a hint of the original look and detail. A before/after is shown below.

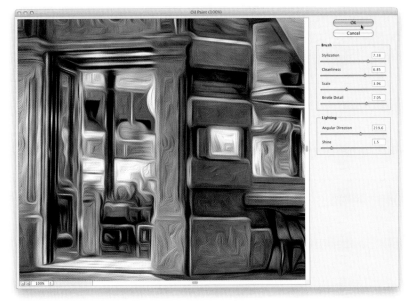

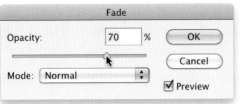

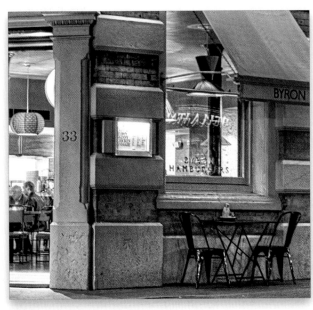

Before

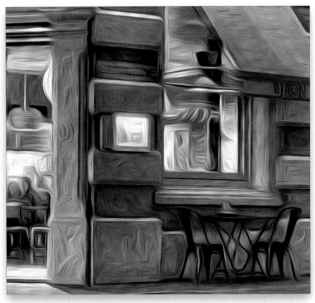

After

This new Blur filter in CS6 gives you a really easy way to create the minia-turization effect you see all over the web, where a photo is transformed to look like a tinytoy model (well, think of it more like an architectural model). Using this filter is easy *if* (this is a big if) you have the right type of photo. Ideally, you'd use one where you photographed from a high point of view, looking downward, and the higher you are, and the steeper the angle, the better it helps sell the idea that you're looking down on a scale model.

Tilt Shift Effect (Using the New Blur Gallery)

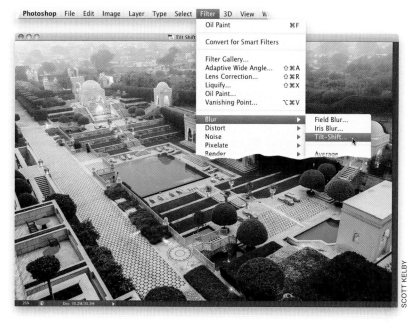

Step One:
Open the image you want to apply the effect to (be sure to read the intro above to make sure you use the right type of image, or this effect will look pretty lame. Of course, as always, you can download the image I'm using here from the book's downloads page men-tioned in the introduction). Now, go under the Filter menu, under Blur, and choose **Tilt-Shift** (as shown here).

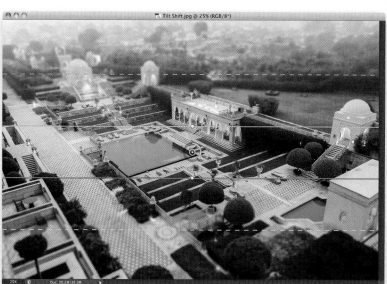

Step Two:
When you use any of the three filters in this section of the Blur submenu, you're using what Adobe calls the Blur Gallery, which is an entirely new, interactive, on-screen way to work with your images. You'll notice it places a round pin in the center of your image, and above and below that are two solid lines, and then two dotted lines. The solid lines show you the area that will remain in focus (the focus area), and the area between each solid line and dotted line is transi-tion, where it fades from sharp to blurry. The wider the distance between the solid and dotted lines, the longer it takes to go from sharp (inside the solid line) to totally blurry (outside the dotted line). *Note:* To remove a pin, just click on it and hit the Delete (PC: Backspace) key on your keyboard.

(Continued)

Step Three:

You control the amount of blur by clicking on the gray part of the ring around the pin, and dragging around the ring. As you drag, the ring turns white to show you how far you've gone, and the actual amount of blur appears in a little pop-up display at the top of the ring (as seen here). I totally dig adjusting the blur this way, but if it gets on your nerves (hey, it could happen), there is a Blur Tools panel that appears over on the right side of your workspace with a Tilt-Shift section. You'll see a Blur slider there, so if you want to go "old school," you can drag that slider and use it to choose how much blur you want. In our example, I clicked-and-dragged the ring (the Blur amount) to 39. While we're here, look inside the two horizontal solid lines. See how that area is sharp and in focus? Okay, now look at the area outside those lines until you reach the dotted lines. See how it transitions to blurry? Got it? Got it!

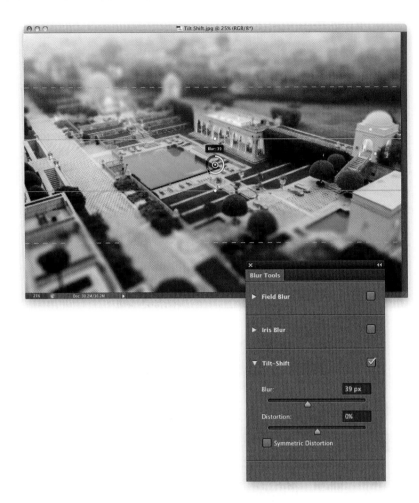

Step Four:

For this particular miniaturization effect, I think it looks better if you compress both of these areas—making the in-focus area smaller and the transition area smaller. Here's how: Click directly on the top solid line and drag inward toward the round pin thingy in the middle (and yes, thingy is the official name given by the International Board of Unsure Naming, or the IBUN). Get it nice and close (as seen here). Now, do the same thing with the bottom solid line, moving it up toward the round pin thingy. Next, drag the center of the top dotted line in closer to the top solid line (as shown here), and then do the same to the bottom dotted line.

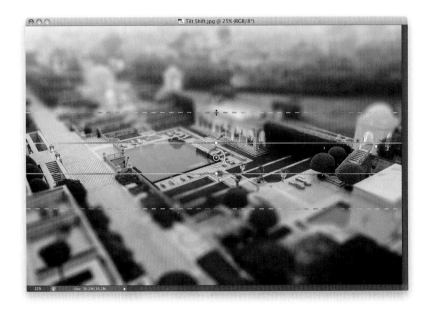

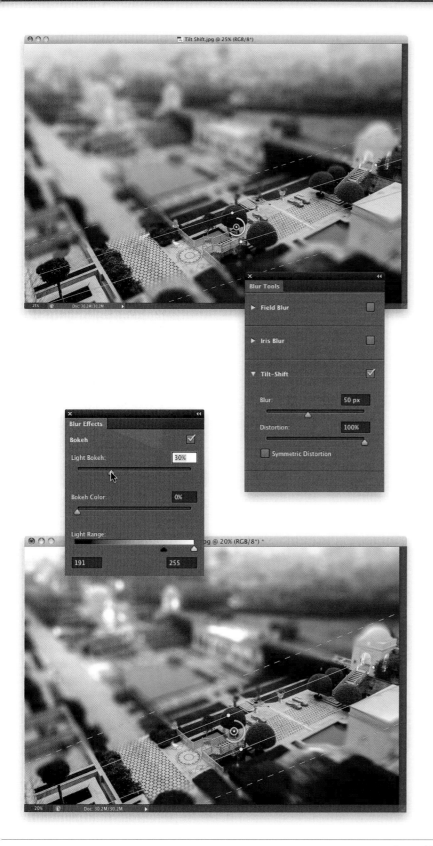

Step Five:

Now, we're going to rotate our in-focus area (and blur, and the whole shebang), so we're just focused on the area we want (which, in my case, is the stairs and bridge near the bottom-center of the photo, as shown here). First, click directly on the center of the round pin thingy and drag it over to that area (put it right near those stairs). Now, to rotate your Tilt-Shift blur, move your cursor over the white center dot on the solid line above the pin, and you'll see it turn into a two-headed rotate arrow. Just click-and-hold on that white dot and rotate by dragging your cursor left/right. So now, it's pretty close to being where and how we want it, but there are some more options you'll want to know about: The first is over in the Blur Tools panel, under Tilt-Shift, and it's the Distortion slider. It lets you change the shape of the blur (I thought it looked best over at 100%, as shown here). Once you add Distortion, if you turn on the Symmetric Distortion checkbox, it makes your blur look really bad and distorted. I personally haven't come up with a reason why I would ever turn this on, unless I was angry at my photo. I also increased my Blur to 50 px.

Step Six:

There is another set of controls in the Blur Effects panel (shown here; it appears below the Blur Tools panel): The top one is kind of useful—it lets you increase the highlights in the blur area, which can be nice for some outdoor portraits, so I dragged it up a bit here (notice the brighter highlights in the top left?). However, this is a *very* sensitive slider, and if you drag too far, it looks like someone dropped a highlights grenade into your image, so use this sparingly. There's a Bokeh Color slider that adds color to your blur and depending on the image, it's either very subtle or a little visible, but like the Symmetric Distortion checkbox, I don't use it.

(Continued)

Step Seven:

When you're done tweaking your blur, press the **Return (PC: Enter) key** to apply it. There are a few more controls in the Options Bar: One is the Focus amount, and it's set at 100% (sharp focus) by default. If you lower that amount, it makes the in-focus area start to blur. The more you lower that amount, the blurrier the in-focus area gets (I haven't found a use for this one yet). Next is the Save Mask to Channels checkbox, which lets you save the area you've masked (using this tool) to a channel (in the Channels panel) in case you want to edit it later (like adding noise to it, or removing all the color, etc.). You can reload that channel and the masked area becomes selected. Lastly, there's a High Quality checkbox, which gives you a better quality blur, but it just takes longer to apply. By the way, if you want to actually see the mask this filter is building, press-and-hold the letter **M** on your keyboard (you can see what the mask looks like here at the bottom). Some other handy shortcuts: Press **P** to hide the blur (press it again to bring it back), and press-and-hold **H** to hide your round pin thingy and all the lines from view.

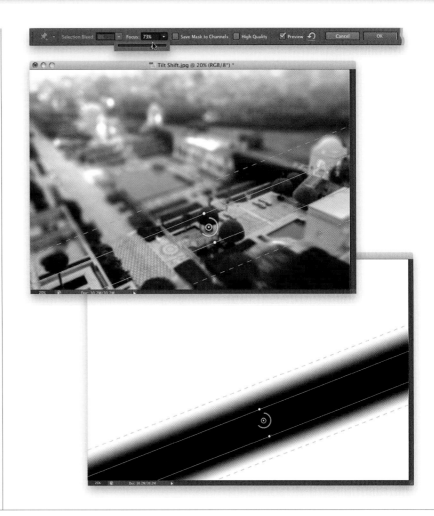

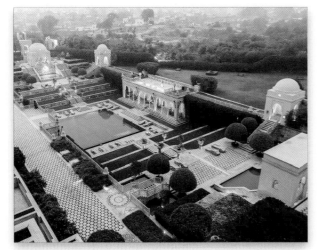

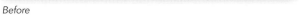

Before

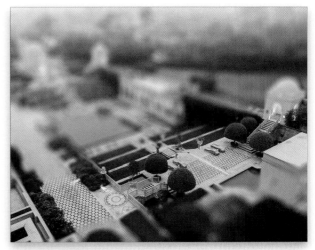

After

This is a really cool feature, because it lets you add a super-shallow depth-of-field effect to your image after the fact, and it lets you place the focus point, and the blur, right where you want it (but doesn't give you the miniature effect like the Tilt-Shift Blur does).

Iris & Field Blur (or How to Fake the 85mm f/1.4 Look)

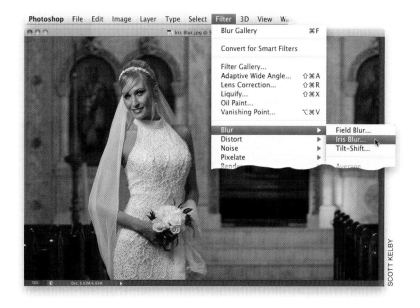

Step One:
Start by opening the photo you want to add a background blur to (like you shot it at a wide-open aperture, like f/1.8 or f/1.4). Now, go under the Filter menu, under Blur, and choose **Iris Blur** (as shown here). The background behind the bride in this image is a tiny bit blurry, but we want to make it a lot blurrier, so she stands out from the background much more.

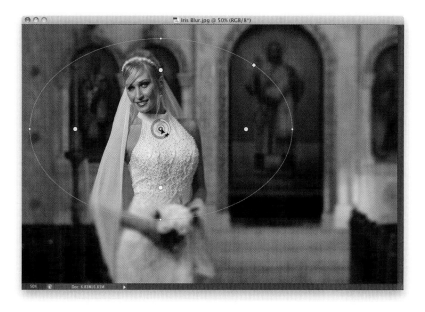

Step Two:
When you choose Iris Blur, it adds a pin to the center of your photo, and that pin represents the center of the area that's going to be in focus. Our bride here is to the left of center, so click directly on that center pin and drag it so it's over the bride (after all, she's what we want in focus). You'll notice it places four round white dots around the center pin, and a solid oval-shaped line outside of those dots. The four round white dots show you the area that will remain in focus (the focus area), and the area between those dots and the solid oval-shaped line is the transition area, where it fades from sharp to blurry. The wider the distance between those white dots and the solid oval, the longer it takes to go from sharp to blurry (the totally blurry area is anything outside that solid oval).

(Continued)

Step Three:

We want our focus squarely on the bride, so we're going to make our oval thinner (so it's closer to her body), and we're going to rotate it to the left so it matches her pose. To shrink in the sides of the oval, click on the small dot on the right side of it and drag inward toward the bride. Now, take that same point and drag upward a bit, and it rotates the oval (as shown here). Our goal is to get the bride's face and her bouquet in focus, so click along the bottom of the oval and drag it straight downward to stretch it out, until one white focus dot is on her forehead and one is on the bouquet (as seen here). You can reshape this oval any time, and rotate it, to fit whatever shape you need (within the constraints of an oval, of course).

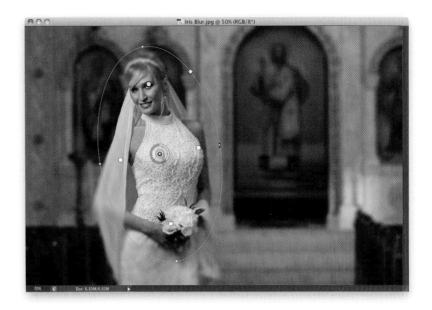

Step Four:

If you look at the image in Step Three, you'll notice that the top of her head is still a bit blurry, and the area below her bouquet is blurry, too. If you like that look—you're done. However, if you want those areas to be in focus, as well, you can add more blur pins to those areas. Click once on her forehead and it adds another blur controller. Shrink the oval way down until it just covers her head. Now, click one more time under her bouquet to add another blur controller, scale it down so it fits, and drag it right where you want it (as shown here). You could even add another one or two on her veil (and position them as tall, thin ovals).

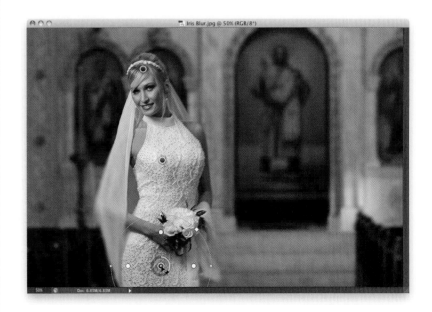

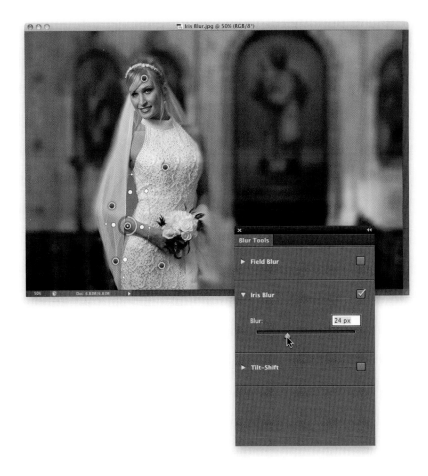

Step Five:

Here, I clicked a few more times to get all of our bride in focus (but I like how her right side goes out of focus, more like a real f/1.4 lens effect would, so I'm leaving that side—the farthest away from the camera—to go blurry). Now that all the pins are in place, let's increase the amount of Blur from 15 to 24 in the Blur Tools panel (as shown here). Look how much blurrier the background looks now and how much separation it gives the bride from the background. So, how long did all those blur pins take to create? Just seconds. Each one takes one click to create and one or two clicks to position, so don't let all those dots on the bride throw you—this is easy stuff. One last thing: once you hit the **Return (PC: Enter) key** to apply your blur effect, you can control the amount of blur after the fact by immediately going under the Edit menu and choosing **Fade Iris Blur**. Lower the Opacity to around 70% and see how that looks (pretty sweet, right?). Below is a before/after, but we're going to move on to another blur filter now.

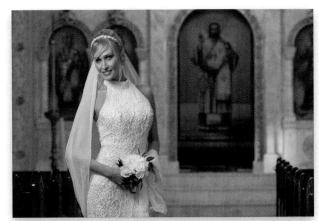

Before

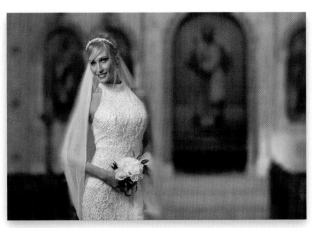

After

(Continued)

Step Six:

By the way, in case you missed the Tilt-Shift project earlier in the chapter, here are some shortcuts that you'll find handy: press-and-hold the letter **M** on your keyboard to see the mask of your blur (you can see a capture of what the mask looks like back in the Tilt-Shift project), press **P** to hide the blur (press it again to bring it back), and press-and-hold **H** to hide your round pin thingy and any lines or dots from view. Also, check Step Seven from that same project for more Blur Gallery tips. Okay, on to Field Blur. Open a new image and choose **Field Blur** from the Filter menu, under Blur. It places a pin in the center of your photo that totally blurs it entirely. Well, it's a start. For this image, drag the pin over onto the roses.

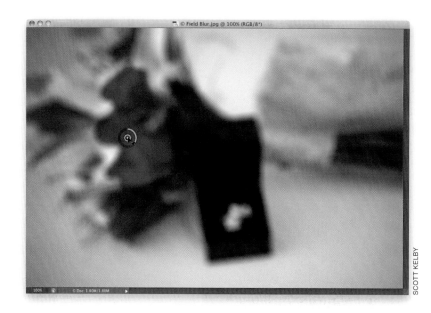

Step Seven:

Next, click on the rings. Still blurry? Yup. Luckily, you can control these two pins separately, so either click-and-drag on that gray-and-white ring around the pin on the rings, or go to the Blur Tools panel and drag the Blur slider all the way to the left to 0 (zero; as shown here), and now the rings are in sharp focus, but the roses are still blurry. That's the way Field Blur works—you place points and decide if the area where you placed them will be sharp or blurry, and if you choose blurry, you get to choose just how blurry.

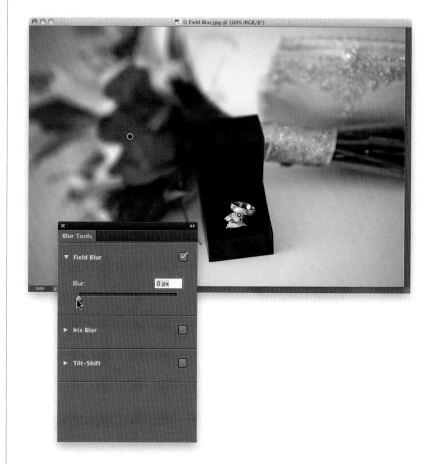

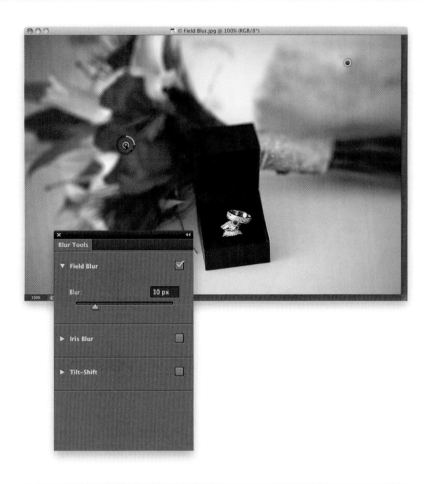

Step Eight:

The default amount of blur is 15 pixels, and that might work for the bride's purse in the background on the right, because it's farther back, but the roses are closer to the ring box. So, click on the pin on the roses, then go to the Blur Tools panel and lower the Blur slider to just 10 px (as seen here), and now the roses aren't quite as blurry. Now, click directly on the purse in the back right (ya know, now that we've brought it up) to add a new pin, and it gets a 15-px blur by default. So, we have three different controls in this image: (1) on the purse on the right in the back, a very blurry pin; (2) the rings have no blur, as their pin's Blur slider is set to 0; and (3) the roses are 33% less blurry than the purse.

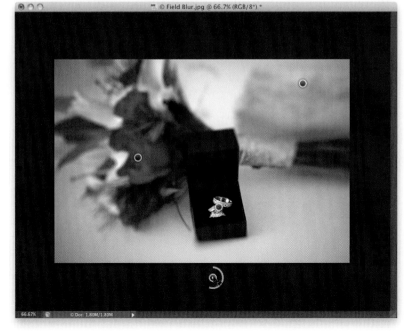

Step Nine:

Okay, so how would you blur the small area in front of the ring box? Well, there's a trick for that: First, you'll need to change your Zoom tool settings (in the Options Bar) so the Resize Windows to Fit checkbox is off, then you can press **Command--** (minus sign; **PC: Ctrl--**) to reduce the image size, but not the window size, so you can see the canvas area around your image. Believe it or not, you can click the Field Blur tool out in this canvas area to add a blurry point. Here, I added one just outside the image, and the edges of the blur spill onto the image (just below the ring box) to give us the final image.

(Continued)

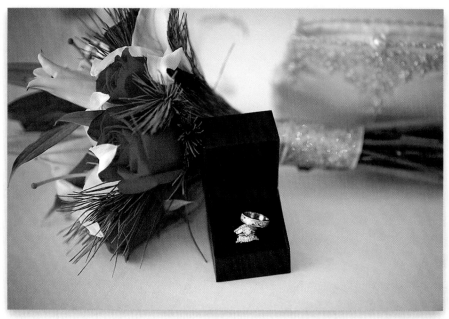

Before

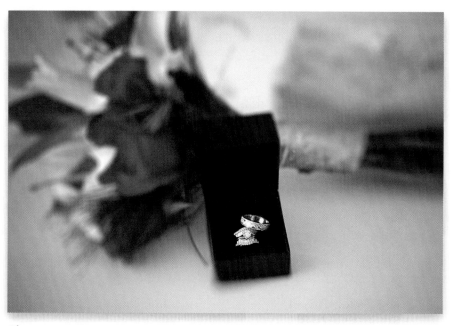

After

The Lighting Effects filter has been in Photoshop for as long as I can remember, but it has needed a major update since about 15 minutes after that, and in Photoshop CS6, it got a complete makeover. It's basically a filter that creates lighting right where you want it, with different styles of lighting, and to be able to do that, it has to darken the rest of your photo first, and then it lights the one (or more) areas you choose. The interface also uses some of the new interactivity that Adobe has introduced in CS6, so besides being better, now it's just plain fun to use, too!

Creating Dramatic Lighting

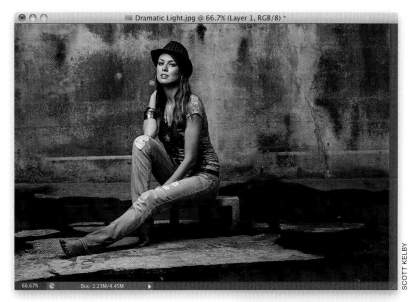

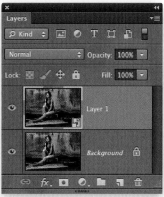

Step One:
Open the image you want to add dramatic lighting to (in the image shown here, the lighting on our subject is pretty decent, but there's so much ambient [existing] light in the room that it's not very dramatic. Of course, I should have done this in-camera by raising my shutter speed to 1/200 or 1/250 of a second to make the background darker, but sadly I didn't, so now I have to do this trick). I always start by duplicating the Background layer (you'll see why in just a few steps), so press **Command-J (PC: Ctrl-J)**. To make it so we can go back and edit this filter later, go under the Filter menu and choose **Convert for Smart Filters**. This makes your top layer a smart object (you can see the little page icon in the bottom-right corner of the layer's thumbnail), and adds your filter below it in the Layers panel, where you can double-click on it to re-open and tweak it later.

(Continued)

Step Two:

Go under the Filter menu, under Render, and choose **Lighting Effects**. The Toolbox gets hidden (you don't need it), a new Lights panel appears on the right, the Properties panel shows the Lighting Effects controls, and we have new options in the Options Bar. Also, you can see that it has greatly darkened your entire image and put a spotlight in place. If all this looks kind of intimidating, I've got good news: you can choose to ignore almost all of it and just use the built-in presets at the left end of the Options Bar. When you click on the Presets pop-up menu, a list of predesigned lights (including multiple-light scenarios) appears (you're just seeing the default spotlight effect here).

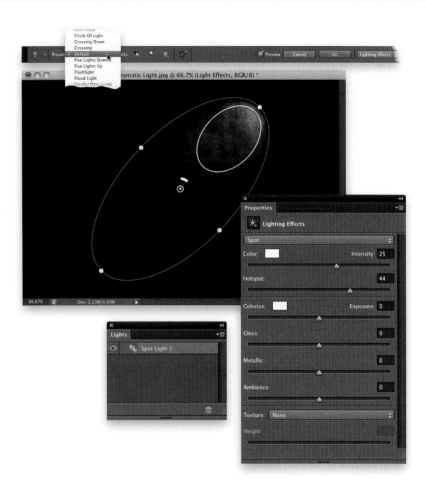

Step Three:

For the dramatic lighting look, my favorite preset is Flashlight (it uses the Point style of light, which is a perfect circle of light, rather than the large, oval shape of the Spot Light style). When you chose **Flashlight** from the Presets menu, you get this soft, round spotlight, and to position it where you want it, just click right in the center of it (you'll see a little HUD [Heads Up Display] appear with the word "Move"), and drag it where you want it. Here I dragged it over onto our subject.

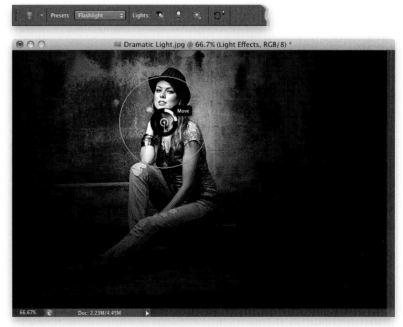

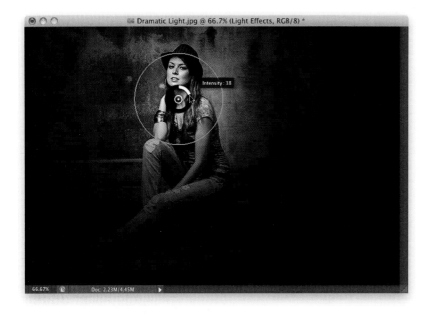

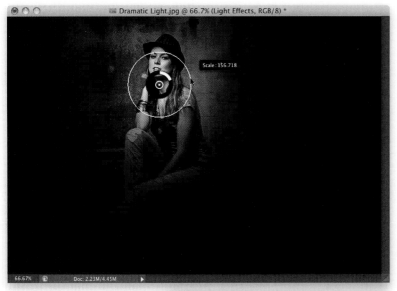

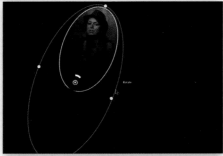

Step Four:

Her face should be the brightest part of the portrait, but the light on her face is a little too bright. Luckily, you can control the intensity of the light without having to mess with any sliders—you do it right on the image itself. The little black/white circular ring that appears just outside the center of your light controls the intensity of the light. Click on it and the HUD will display "Intensity" and the current amount of Intensity ranging from 0 to 100. To lower the amount a bit, click right on that circle and drag in a counter-clockwise motion, and it lowers the brightness (Intensity) of the light (as seen here, where it appears that the light starts on her face and falls off to darkness quickly.

Step Five:

Of course, the light will spill outside your subject's face onto the background quite a bit, but you can control the size (Adobe calls it the "Scale") of the round beam of light, using the outermost ring (the really big green one). Move your cursor right over it and it turns yellow and the HUD displays "Scale" and the amount, from 0 to 100 (as seen here), and then just drag inward/outward to resize the beam. I have to tell you, this green ring is kind of finicky and it might take you moving your cursor over it a few times really slowly to finally get the yellow Scale ring to appear, so don't let it get you frustrated if it doesn't work the first time—just give it another try or two. These three onscreen controls work pretty much the same for the rest of the lights, except for Spotlight—there, the outer-ring controls rotation (as shown here at the bottom), but you can click on the white dots to move it.

(Continued)

Step Six:

To add more lights, click on one of the three light styles up in the Options Bar. Add a Point Light (shown circled here in red) and drag it over near the concrete block she's sitting on. Drag the Scale circle inward, until the size of the beam is very small (as seen here), and lower the Intensity quite a bit. Create another Point Light and do the same, but drag it down by her ankle (as seen here).

TIP: Deleting Lights

To delete a light, click on it, then go over to the Lights panel on the right side of your workspace and click on the Trash icon in the bottom-right corner. It won't let you delete all the lights—it makes you leave one there (or your image would just be black).

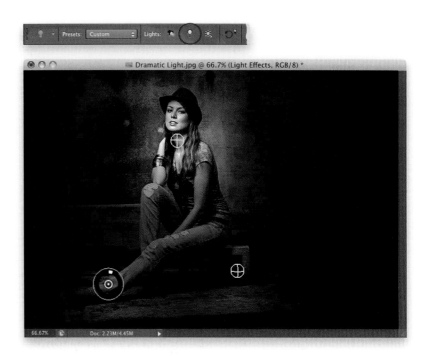

Step Seven:

In the Lights panel, you'll see all your lights listed, kind of like layers. You can toggle them on/off here by clicking on the Eye icon to the left of each light. Also, if you want to change the style of light, click on it, then choose a new style from the pop-up menu in the Properties panel, which should be above the Lights panel. We haven't really talked about the Infinite Light (the third light style), so go ahead and create an Infinite light (click on the third Lights icon in the Options Bar), and then hide the other three from view in the Lights panel by clicking on their Eye icons. This light stays in the center of your image—it doesn't move, so like the sun, all you can do is change its direction (click-and-drag directly on the dot in the center, and you'll see the light icon near the edge of your image move; it's fun to see how it shows the light in a 3D space).

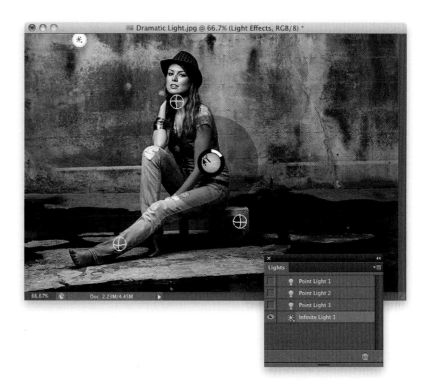

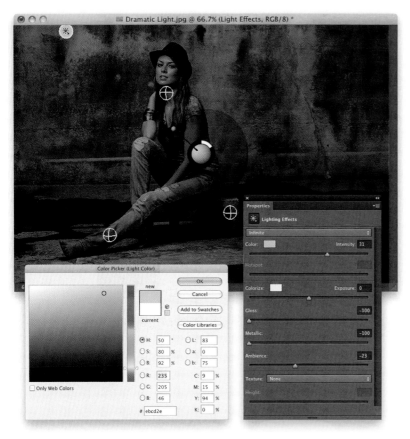

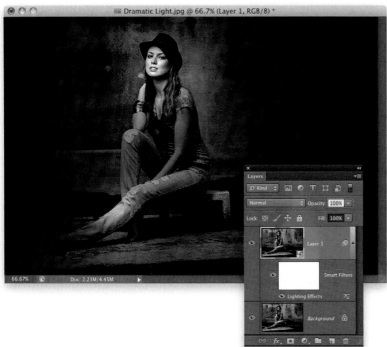

Step Eight:

There are a few other controls you'll want to know about in the Properties panel: (1) To change the color of your light, click on the Color swatch and choose a new color from the Color Picker (as seen here, on the Infinite Light). (2) The Intensity slider is the same as the one you use right on the image itself. (3) The Hotspot slider controls the hot spot (most intense center of the light) if you use the Spot Light style of light. (4) The Colorize swatch actually controls the color cast of the darkened part of your photo (by default, it's flat). (5) The Exposure slider reminds me of the Highlights slider in Camera Raw, so if I use it at all, it's usually dragging it to the left to pull back highlights. (6) The Ambience slider controls the amount of darkening it applies to the rest of the image (more on the next page).

Step Nine:

(7) Right below the Ambience slider is the Texture pop-up menu, which lets you accentuate the texture in your image with kind of an embossed look, on a per color basis (Red, Green, or Blue channel), and you control the amount using the Height slider right below it. Try it and you'll see what I mean. I skipped over the two controls I use the least: the Gloss slider (which theoretically controls the amount of shine to the photo, but it seems to me like more of a contrast control—dragging to the left makes the lit part of your image flatter and less contrasty, and to the right makes it a bit more contrasty and harsh. The Metallic slider only seems to do anything when you have something metallic or reflective in your image, so if you do, dragging it to the right makes it more intense. When you're done, click the OK button in the Options Bar, and it applies the effect to your layer as a smart filter (as seen here). If you want to remove some of the effect, you can paint on the mask that comes with it, or double-click on Lighting Effects to re-open the filter and tweak the settings.

(Continued)

Step 10:

If you look at the image seen here, you'll notice that the light on her face is pretty bright and direct, which is fine, but you can make this blend in a little better and look less harsh with just one click (that's why, at the very beginning, I suggested you duplicate the Background layer—so we can apply this final finishing move). To soften that light, in the Layers panel, change the blend mode of this layer from Normal to **Darken** (as shown here), and it takes the "edge" off that main light and makes it softer-looking with a smoother blend, which completes the effect. One last thing: another benefit of having applied this effect on a layer is that you can control the overall amount of the effect after the fact. For example, if you think the background is too dark and too dramatic now, you can simply lower the Opacity of this layer and it lowers the intensity of the effect.

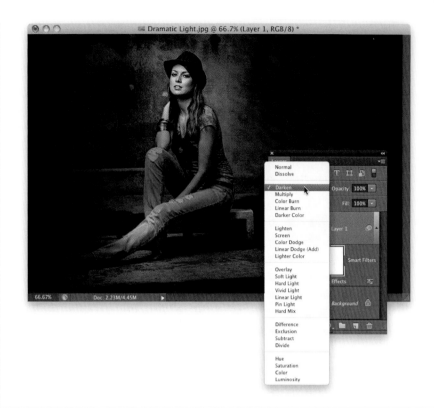

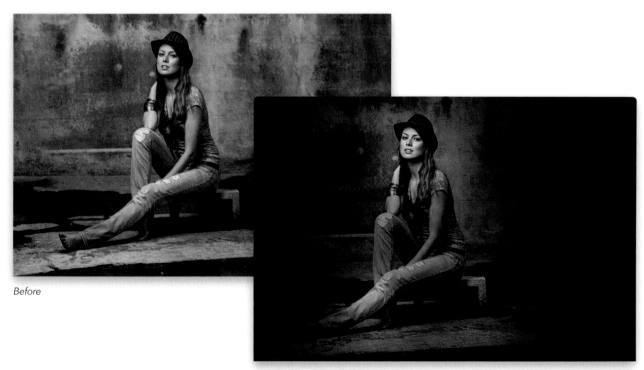

Before

After

One of the most under-used adjustment layers has got to be the Gradient Map. For years, I've only used it for one thing—it makes a pretty mean black-and-white conversion in just one click (well, provided that your Foreground color is black and your Background color is white, so it might technically take one letter and one click). Anyway, in Photoshop CS6, Adobe worked with photographer Steve Weinrebe to add 38 photo-toning and split-toning presets to the Gradient Map feature, making it an even better tool that nobody uses. I hope that changes today.

Photo Toning Effects

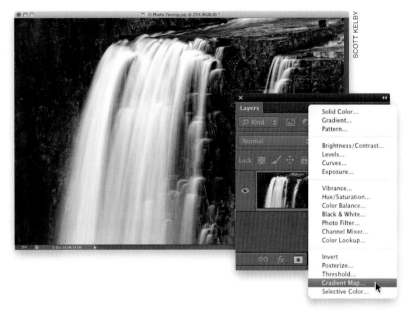

Step One:
Open the photo you want to apply a photo toning effect to. Then, go to the Layers panel and click on the Create New Adjustment Layer icon at the bottom of the panel, and choose **Gradient Map** from the pop-up menu (as shown here), or you can click on the last icon, on the bottom row, of the Adjustments panel.

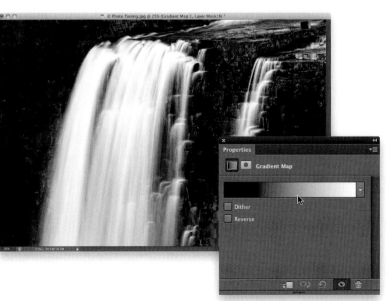

Step Two:
As soon as you choose Gradient Map, it applies the default gradient, which as I said above, makes a pretty darn sweet one-click B&W image (as long as your Foreground and Background colors are set to black/white, respectively, before you choose Gradient Map). Okay, to be able to load the Photo Toning presets, you need to go to the Properties panel and click directly on the gradient itself (as shown here).

(Continued)

Step Three:

This brings up the Gradient Editor (seen here), and if you click on the little "gear" icon at the top-right corner of the Presets section, a pop-up menu appears. Choose **Photographic Toning** from this menu (as shown here). A dialog will appear asking if you want to replace the current default set of gradients with the ones you are loading. I chose yes, because (1) it's easier to work with them if they're not added to the existing set, and (2) I'm going to show you a one-click way to get the default gradients back any time you want, in just a moment. So, for now, click OK to hide the default gradients and load the new set.

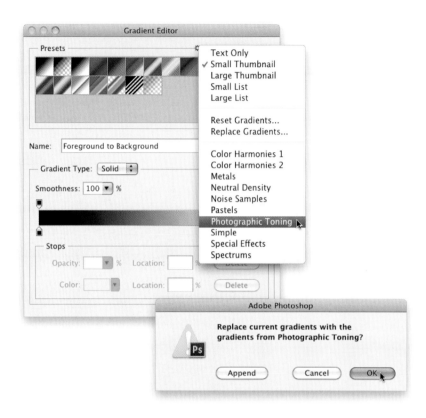

Step Four:

Once they're loaded, now the fun begins, because all you have to do is click on any one of these photographic toning gradients, and it updates your image live, so you can just start clicking until you find one you like. Here's one called Sepia-Selenium 3—you can see the colors that make up the look in the gradient ramp that appears in the middle of the Gradient Editor dialog (seen here).

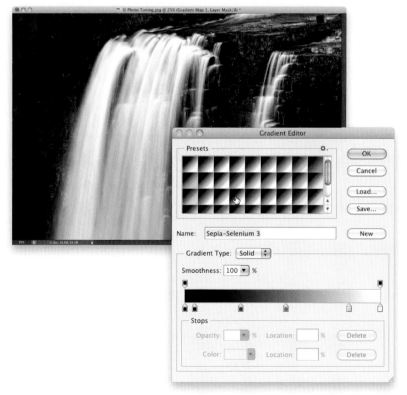

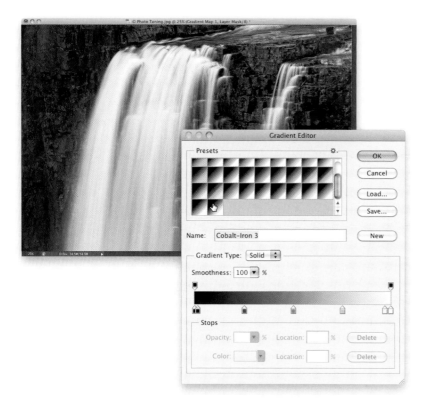

Step Five:

So, now you're pretty much window shopping for the look you like—click a gradient, and if it's not the look you're looking for, click the next one. For example, here's the last gradient in the set, Cobalt-Iron 3 (perhaps not my first choice, but I did want to show you the variety of what's here, and this one has more of a split-tone look, with one color in the shadows [a cyan tone] and one in the highlights [more of a magenta]). Make sure you try out some of the ones in the top row—there are some really useful duotone/sepiatone looks up there, and like most Adobe presets, the best, most-useful ones are near the beginning, and the farther they are down on the list, the less useful they are.

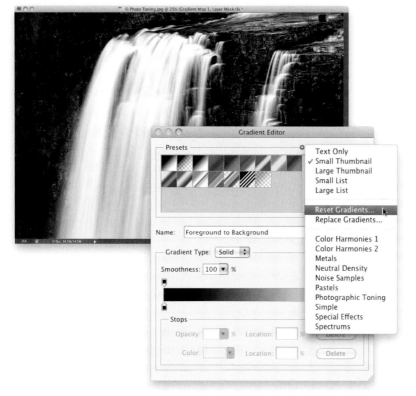

Step Six:

Okay, here's why you never have to worry about replacing the default gradients—you're just one click away from them at any time. Just go to the Gradient Editor, click on the gear icon, and from the pop-up menu, choose **Reset Gradients**, and it reloads just the default gradient set. Now that you know the defaults are always just one click away, I hope that encourages you to load some of the other sets and check them out, as well.

Color Lookup Effects

Another special effect added in Photoshop CS6 is called "Color Lookup." It uses built-in Color Lookup tables to instantly remap the colors in your image to create some pretty cool color effects (inspired by the lookup tables used in movie making and video). There aren't a lot of controls to play around with—most of these are pretty much "one-trick ponies," where you choose a look and you either like the effect or not—but what's nice is it's available as an adjustment layer, so you can control where the effect is applied pretty easily by just painting it on or off. Here's how it works:

Step One:

Open the photo you want to apply a Color Lookup effect to. Then, go to the Layers panel, click on the Create New Adjustment Layer icon at the bottom of the panel, and choose **Color Lookup** from the pop-up menu (as shown here), or you can click on the last icon in the second row of the Adjustments panel. This opens the Color Lookup options in the Properties panel (shown here). There are three different sets of effects, and you choose the one you want from any of the three pop-up menus (you can only choose one at a time).

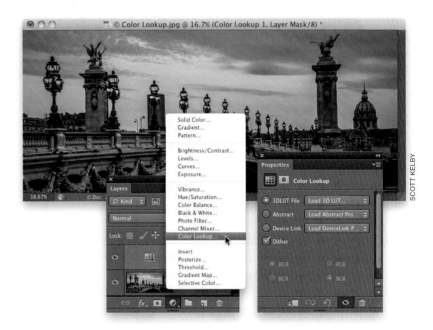

Step Two:

I chose EdgyAmber.3DL from the 3DLUT File pop-up menu, and it applied the color effect you see here. At this point, there are three things you can do: (1) if the effect seems too intense, since this is an adjustment layer, you can lower the layer's Opacity and it lowers the intensity of the effect; (2) you can change the layer's blend mode to control how this effect blends with the image on the layer below it; or (3) you can press **Command-I (PC: Ctrl-I)** to Invert the layer mask, which hides the effect behind a black layer mask, then take the Brush tool **(B)** and, with your Foreground color set to white, just paint the effect right where you want it to appear.

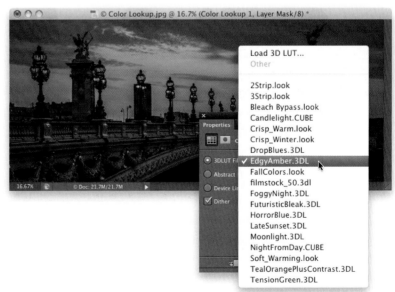

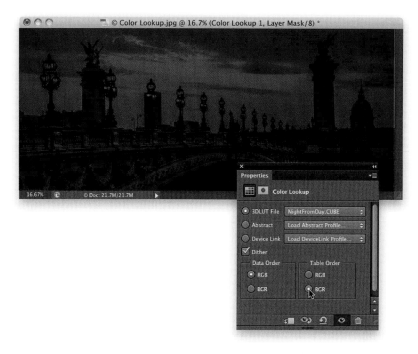

Step Three:

There are a few effects that have extra options. For example, from the same pop-up menu, choose **NightFromDay .CUBE** and some new options appear at the bottom of the Properties panel (shown here). Since they're radio buttons, all you can do is choose one button on the left and one on the right, and as you click on them (as shown here), they create variations of the look you chose. Also, there are a few handy buttons across the bottom of the Properties panel: The one I use the most is the Eye icon, which toggles the Color Lookup adjustment layer on/off (and saves you a trip up to the Layers panel). If you click on the first icon from the left, it makes the effect only affect the layer directly below it (and not all the layers below it, like normal). The next icon over (the eye with an arrow) is a before/after, which is pretty similar to turning the layer on/off with the Eye icon. The next icon (the curved arrow) just resets the entire panel to its defaults.

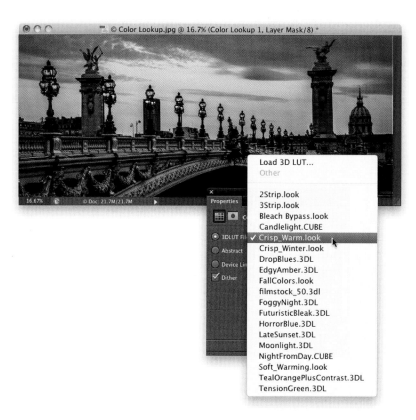

Step Four:

After trying out a few different ones, I think for this particular image the one that looks best to me is Crisp_Warm.look (as shown here). One last thing: If you choose the top choice in any of these pop-up menus, it lets you load in a profile (in case you downloaded some from the web and wanted to apply one of them to your image). It brings up the standard Open dialog, so you can find the profile you want to load. Of course, if you don't have a profile you want to load, there's no reason to choose the top choice in the menus (which makes you wonder why it's not the last choice in each menu, right? Don't get me started).

Sculpting Using the Updated Liquify Filter

This is another filter Adobe updated in Photoshop CS6, and although it's probably most often used in portrait retouching (I used it quite a lot in my portrait retouching techniques book), I did want you to know that: (a) it is much, much faster and more responsive in CS6, because they handed the heavy lifting off to the Graphics Processing Unit (geek speak); and (b) they tweaked lots of little things to make it better and easier to use; plus (c) they added an incredibly helpful new feature that lets you go back and pick up where you left off (very clever). So, here's a quick retoucharoo:

Step One:

Open the image you want to retouch (here, we have a nice headshot), then go under the Filter menu and choose **Liquify** (or press **Command-Shift-X [PC: Ctrl-Shift-X]**), which brings up the dialog you see here. In Photoshop CS6, there are two versions of this dialog: an Advanced Mode version, and the simplified version you see here, with just a few tools on the left, and just the Brush Size and Pressure settings on the right side. For most of what we wind up doing, the simplified version is pretty much all we need (we do most of our work using the Forward Warp tool—the top tool in the Toolbox), so turn off the Advanced Mode checkbox.

TIP: Visual Brush Resizing in Liquify

If you want to quickly jump up to a much larger or down to a smaller brush size, on a Mac, press-and-hold **Option-Ctrl**, and **click-and-drag** your cursor to resize it on-screen. On a PC, press-and-hold the **Alt key**, and then **Right-click-and-drag**.

Step Two:

The Forward Warp tool moves your subject around like they were a thick liquid (like molasses), but the secrets to using it effectively are: (1) make your brush size the size of what you want to move, and (2) make subtle movements with it (just kind of nudge things around, and you'll get great results). So, take the tool, place the center crosshair just to the left of her cheek on the left, and nudge it over to the right to tuck it in a bit (as shown here).

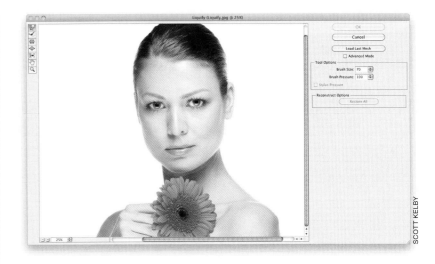

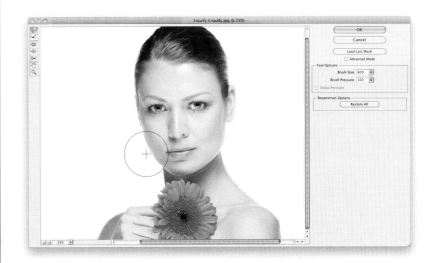

SCOTT KELBY

Step Three:

Then, do the same thing to the cheek on the right (keeping in mind our tip about making the brush size the size of what you want to move). Now, let's tuck her ear on the right side in a bit, as well. You can change the size of your brush using the Brush Size slider over on the right, but honestly, it's easier to use the keyboard shortcuts. The **Left Bracket key** makes the brush smaller; the **Right Bracket key** makes it larger (they're to the right of the letter "P" on your keyboard). By the way, our subject here really doesn't need her cheeks moved in, or her ear moved over, but if we didn't do something, this would be a really short project.

TIP: If You Mess Up, Try This

If you want to start over from scratch, click the Restore All button. If you want to just undo a step or two, you can use the same multiple undo shortcut you normally use in Photoshop: every time you press **Command-Option-Z (PC: Ctrl-Alt-Z)**, it undoes another step.

Step Four:

Long, extended necks are very popular for "beauty style" headshots like this, so let's make our brush really big (don't forget the brush size shortcuts—either the visual one you learned after Step One, or the Bracket keys), and then gently tuck her neck on the right side over a bit (as shown here). Now, before we go to the next page, there is something I actually would do to this image in Liquify, and that is to round out her hair a bit. Take a look, especially on the left side, at the indents along the edges—that is something I would definitely fix, so let's do that in the next step.

(Continued)

Step Five:

Zoom in tight on that area of her hair (Liquify uses the same keyboard shortcuts for zooming in/out that you normally use in Photoshop—**Command-+** [plus sign; **PC: Ctrl-+**] will zoom you in, and **Command--** [minus sign; **PC: Ctrl--**] will zoom you back out). Shrink your brush way down until it's the size of the little dent you want to push out to match the rest of her hair, and then do just that (try not to make it too perfect). Also, sometimes you'll have to push out, and sometimes you may have to push in to make it all fairly even.

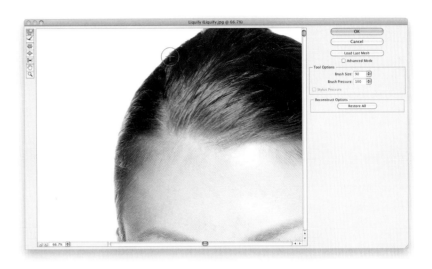

TIP: You Can Have Insane
Brush Sizes

In Photoshop CS6, Adobe increased the maximum brush size to 15,000 pixels, so if you're working with images from huge megapixel cameras, you're covered.

Step Six:

Now let's look at some of the hidden advanced features, so turn the Advanced Mode checkbox back on, and those options appear on the right side of the dialog, and three extra tools are added to the Toolbox. The main feature of this Advanced Mode is the ability to freeze part of the image you don't want to move while you're moving areas right around it. For example, if you needed to make some really big adjustments to her cheeks or head structure, you could freeze her face, but leave the edges of her head unfrozen (as shown here, where I painted with the Freeze Mask tool [**F**; it's the seventh one down in the Toolbox]). So, go ahead and do that now. If you don't see the red mask area, in the View Options section, turn on the Show Mask checkbox, as seen here. To erase any area you accidentally painted over, switch to the Thaw Mask tool (**D**; it's the next tool down).

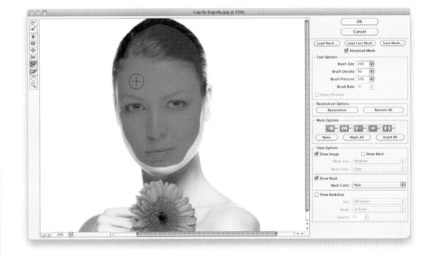

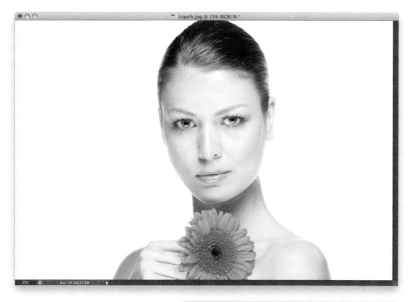

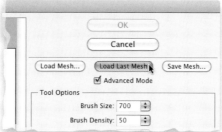

Step Seven:

When you're done, click OK, and your changes are applied (as shown here). Now, these changes are a bit over-the-top, but I didn't want to make them so subtle that you really couldn't see what we were actually doing with this filter. Ready for that cool new CS6 feature I told you about earlier? Okay, here it is: Once you click OK and apply your changes, if you decide you don't like the way they look, of course you can just press Command-Z (PC: Ctrl-Z) to undo them, and then go back and try again in Liquify, right? Right. But, here's the cool thing: Liquify now remembers the last set of adjustments you made (called a "mesh"), and if you reopen the image, and then click the Load Last Mesh button (shown here at the bottom), it reloads the last set of changes you made, so now you can pick up right where you left off. Also, if you shot on a tripod and your subject didn't move (or better yet, your subject was a product), you could save the mesh on the first one, then open the next shot, load the mesh from the previous shot, and be done with it in two clicks.

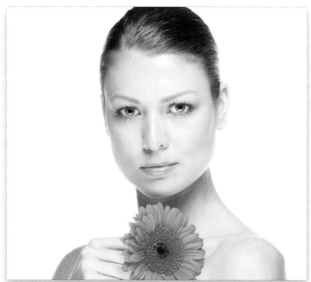

Before

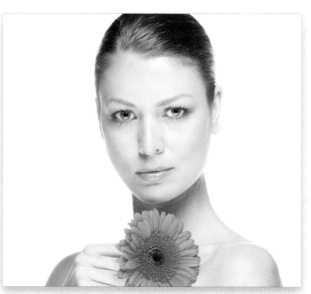

After

Night Lights Background Effect

I learned this technique from my buddy, French photographer and Photoshop trainer Serge Ramelli (http://photoserge.com), and it uses the Iris Blur filter in Photoshop CS6 in a different way to take a nighttime photo and turn it into a great background for compositing. Many thanks to Serge for teaching me the technique, and for letting me share it with you.

Step One:

Start by opening an image of the subject you want to put on our night lights background. Now, make a selection of your subject using the technique for removing people from their background (found on page 231), which is the technique I used here to select our subject playing bass guitar.

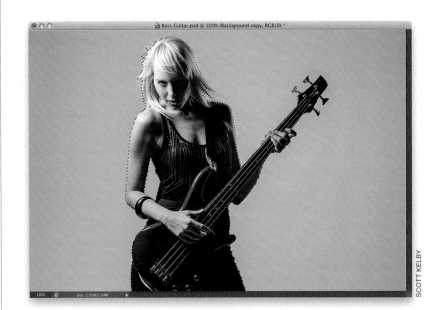

Step Two:

Next, we're going to open a photo taken at night where you can see lights (like the one shown here). With this technique, you don't actually want bright lights (they'll turn into white blobs), but in the shot I chose here, of course, there were some bright lights, but there's a quick fix for that. Open the image in Camera Raw (see the beginning of Chapter 2 if you need a refresher on that), and drag the Highlights slider way over to the left until the lights don't look so bright, as seen here, where I dragged the slider to –30 (you can control the actual brightness of the lights later, but for now they need to be kind of "pulled back" in brightness). Then, click the Open Image button to open it into Photoshop.

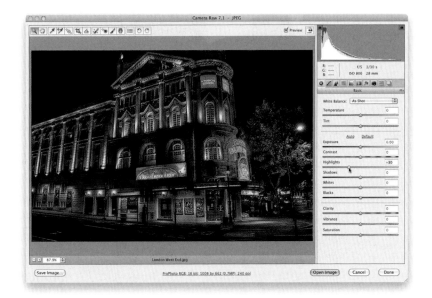

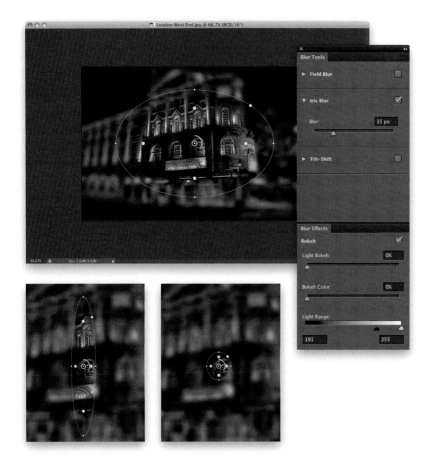

Step Three:
Press **Command--** (minus sign; **PC: Ctrl--**) to zoom out a level. Now, grab the bottom-right corner of your image window and drag outward until you can see the gray canvas area surrounding your image. Then, go under the Filter menu, under Blur, and choose **Iris Blur**. This brings up the Iris Blur interface (seen here) and it puts a large oval in the center of your image—the area inside that oval is where it's clear, and the Iris blur appears outside it. But what we want to do here is blur as much of the background as possible, so what we're going to have to do next is shrink the oval way down and drag it off the image, so it doesn't leave any part of the image clear. Grab one of the side points of the oval and drag it inward to make it a tall, thin oval (as seen here on the bottom left). Then, grab either the top or bottom point on the oval and drag inward to shrink the oval down to a small circle (like what you see here on the bottom right).

Step Four:
Then, click in the center of the circle and drag it right off the image into the upper-left corner of the window (as shown here). By moving it outside your image like this, none of the image will be clear (it all gets blurred). Next, go to the Blur Effects panel on the right, under the Bokeh section, and drag the Light Bokeh slider over to the right to 50%. This slider controls how bright the blurry lights are, so depending on the photo, you might have to make this darker (or even brighter), but just make sure the lights don't get crazy bright.

(Continued)

Step Five:

To make the lights in the background larger, in the Blur Tools panel, you can drag the Blur slider to the right, like I did here, where I dragged it over to 56 pixels. So, you can think of the Blur slider as controlling the size of the night lights.

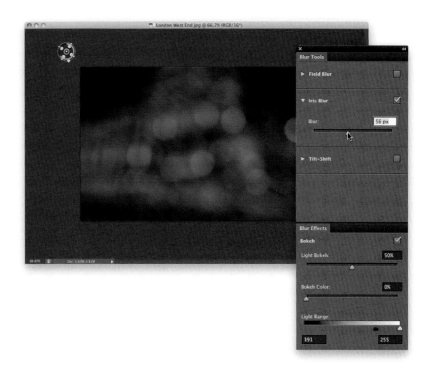

Step Six:

Once I made the lights much larger, they also seemed a lot dimmer, but as I mentioned in Step Four, the Light Bokeh slider controls the brightness of the lights, so let's crank that up to around 65% (as seen here), which makes the lights quite a bit brighter. However, take a look at the lights on the left center, and how they've gotten so bright they've kind of "bloomed" and run together. Once we paste our subject into this spot, we'll either move her away from that side of the image, or we'll have to position her in front of that area, so you don't see that. Now that your blur looks good, go up to the Options Bar and click the blue OK button to apply your blur to the image.

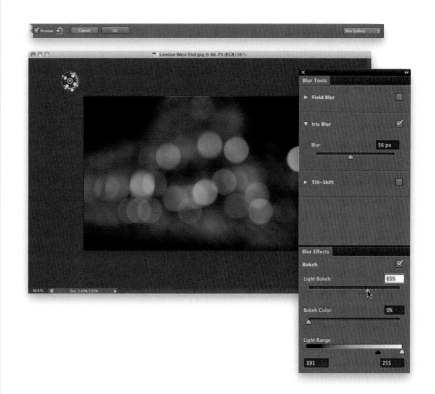

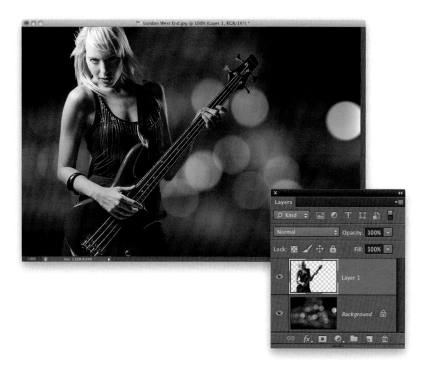

Step Seven:

Go back to the document where you have your subject selected and press **Command-C (PC: Ctrl-C)** to copy your subject into memory, then switch to your background document and press **Command-V (PC: Ctrl-V)** to paste your subject into the background (or you can just get the Move tool **[V]** and drag-and-drop the layer your subject is on over onto your background document). I positioned our subject away from the blooming bright white light also found on the far right, and I made her a little bit larger by using Free Transform (press **Command-T [PC: Ctrl-T]**, then Shift-click on one of the top corner points and drag it upward to scale her up just a small amount. If you drag too far, she will start to look pixelated, so be careful not to scale her up too much).

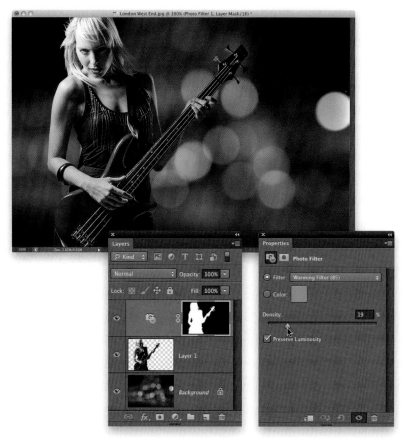

Step Eight:

Lastly, to make your subject look more like she was shot on this warm-colored background, we're going to warm that photo of her up a little bit, too. Start by going to the Layers panel and Command-clicking (PC: Ctrl-clicking) directly on the thumbnail for your subject's layer to put a selection around them. Now, go to the Adjustments panel and click on the Photo Filter icon. When the Properties panel opens with the Photo Filter controls, by default it warms the photo at an amount of 25%, but if you think it needs to be a little more or less warm, drag the Density slider to the right to make it warmer, or left to make it not quite as warm (I dragged it to 19% here).

Photoshop Killer Tips

How to Open Multiple JPEGs or TIFFs in Camera Raw from Mini Bridge

Opening multiple RAW photos from Mini Bridge is easy—just select as many as you want, and then double-click on any one or Right-click and choose Default Application under Open With. The problem is that doesn't work for JPEG or TIFF images. That is, unless you do these two things first: (1) Go under the Photoshop (PC: Edit) menu, under Preferences, and choose **Camera Raw**. Then, at the bottom of the dialog, in the JPEG and TIFF Handling section, change both pop-up menus to **Automatically Open All Supported JPEGs/TIFFs** (luckily, you only have to do this part once). Now, restart Photoshop, then go select multiple JPEG or TIFF images in Mini Bridge, Right-click on any one and, under Open With, choose **Default Application**, and they'll all open in Camera Raw.

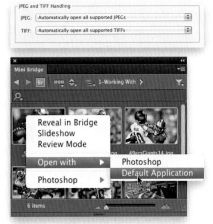

CS6 Tip for Wacom Tablet Users

If you use a Wacom tablet for retouching, there are two buttons that keep you from having to jump to the Brushes panel when you need to control pressure-sensitive opacity or size. These two buttons appear in the Options Bar when you have a brush tool selected (they look like circles with a pen on them), and clicking them overrides the current settings in the Brushes panel, so it saves you a trip to the Opacity or Size controls to turn those two on first.

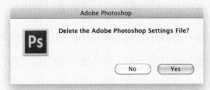

If Photoshop Starts Acting Weird...

....or something doesn't work the way it always did, chances are that your preferences have become corrupt, which hap-

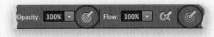

pens to just about everyone at one time or another, and replacing them with a new factory-fresh set of preferences will cure about 99% of the problems that you'll run into with Photoshop (and it's the very first thing Adobe's own tech support will tell you to fix), so it's totally worth doing. To rebuild your preferences, go ahead and quit Photoshop, then press-and-hold Command-Option-Shift (PC: Ctrl-Alt-Shift) and launch Photoshop (keep holding them down). A dialog will pop up asking if you want to Delete the Adobe Photoshop Settings File. Click Yes, and chances are, your problems will be gone.

Creating a New Document with the Same Specs as Another Open Document

If you have an image already open, and you want to create a new blank document with the exact same size, resolution, and color space, just press **Command-N (PC:**

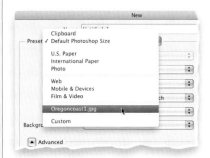

Ctrl-N) to bring up the New dialog, then from the Preset pop-up menu up top, choose the name of your already open document, and it takes all the specs from that document and fills in all the fields for you. All you have to do is click OK.

Retouching Tip for Liquify

If you're using the Liquify filter to do some retouching on a portrait, you can make sure you don't accidentally move an area you don't want to affect by freezing it, and there are freeze tools in Liquify, but it's easier to just put a selection around the area you want to adjust first, then bring up the Liquify filter, and any area outside your selected area is automatically frozen. (You'll see a rectangle with your selection in it in the Preview area, and the areas outside your selection will be masked in red.)

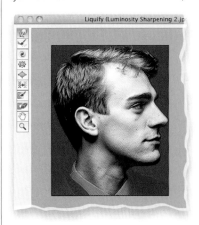

Photoshop Killer Tips

Super-Fast Temporary Tool Switching

This is one Adobe introduced back in CS4, but few people knew it was there. They're called Spring Loaded Tools, and what they let you do is temporarily access any other tool while you're using your current tool. When you're done, Photoshop automatically switches back. Here's how it works: Let's say you have the Brush tool, but you need to put a Lasso selection around an area, so you don't paint outside of it. Just press-and-hold the L key (for the Lasso

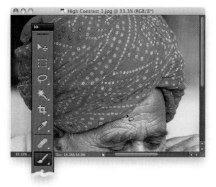

tool), and your Brush tool temporarily switches to the Lasso tool. Make your selection, then just let go of the L key and you're back to the Brush tool. This is a huge time and trouble saver.

Designing for a Cell Phone or Tablet?

Then you'll be happy to know that there are a bunch of new built-in presets for the most common sizes of mobile device screens. From the File menu, choose New, then choose **Mobile & Devices** from the Preset pop-up menu, and then choose the size you need from the Size pop-up menu.

Assigning More RAM to Photoshop

You can control how much of your computer's installed RAM actually gets set aside just for Photoshop's use. You do this within Photoshop itself, by pressing **Command-K (PC: Ctrl-K)** to bring up Photoshop's Preferences, then click Performance in the list on the left side of the dialog. Now you'll see a bar graph with a slider that represents how much of your installed RAM is set aside for Photoshop. Drag the slider to the right

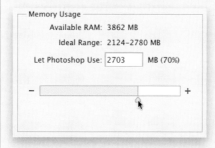

to allocate more RAM for Photoshop (the changes don't take effect until you restart Photoshop).

Save Time When Saving

When you click on the Save Image button in the bottom left of the Camera Raw window, it brings up the Save Options dialog, but if you don't need to make any changes to your settings, you can skip this dialog altogether by pressing-and-holding the Option (PC: Alt) key before clicking the Save Image button. Hey, every click you save, counts.

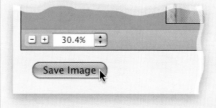

Shortcuts for Changing the Order of Layers

I use these a lot, because it saves a trip over to the Layers panel dozens of times a day. To move your current layer up one layer (in the stack of layers), press **Command-]** (Right Bracket key; **PC: Ctrl-]**) and of course to move down, you'd use the same shortcut with the Left Bracket key **([)**. To move the current layer all the way to the top, add the **Shift key**. Of course, you can't move anything below the locked Background layer.

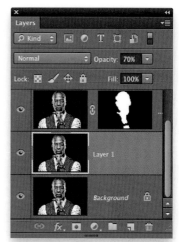

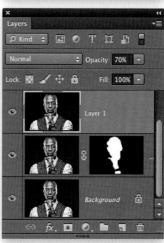

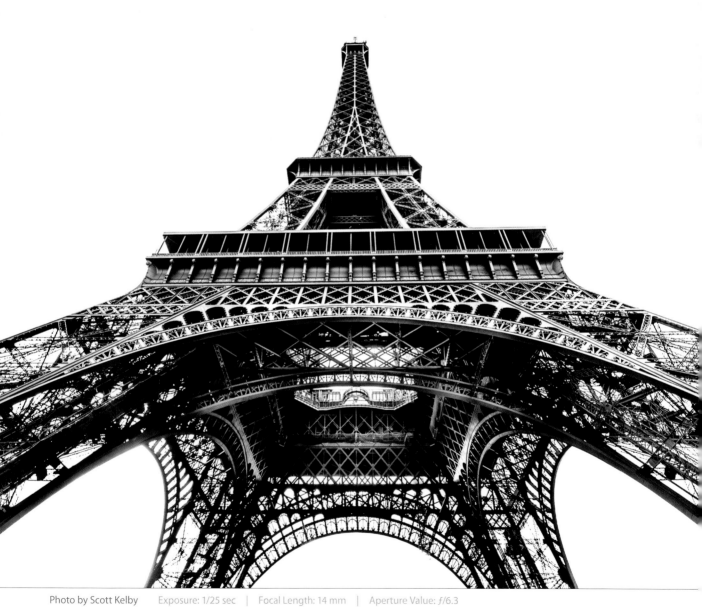

Photo by Scott Kelby   Exposure: 1/25 sec | Focal Length: 14 mm | Aperture Value: f/6.3

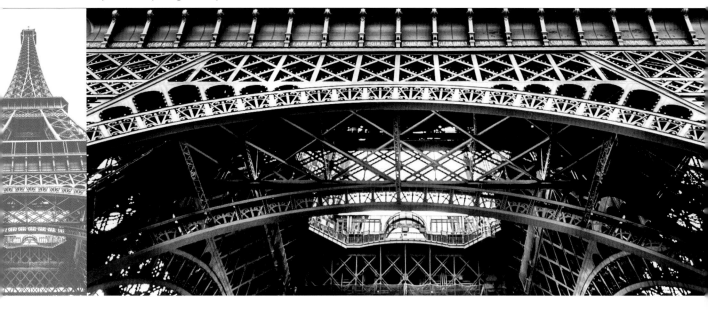

Sharpen Your Teeth
sharpening techniques

I had two really good song titles to choose from for this chapter: "Sharpen Your Teeth" by Ugly Casanova or "Sharpen Your Sticks" by The Bags. Is it just me, or at this point in time, have they totally run out of cool band names? Back when I was a kid (just a few years ago, mind you), band names made sense. There were The Beatles, and The Turtles, and The Animals, and The Monkees, and The Flesh Eating Mutant Zombies, and The Carnivorous Flesh Eating Vegetarians, and The Bulimic Fresh Salad Bar Restockers, and names that really made sense. But, "The Bags?" Unless this is a group whose members are made up of elderly women from Yonkers, I think it's totally misnamed. You see, when I was a kid, when a band was named The Turtles, its members looked and acted like turtles. That's what made it great (remember their hit single "Peeking Out of My Shell," or who could forget "Slowly Crossing a Busy Highway" or my favorite "I Got Hit Crossing a Busy Highway"?). But today, you don't have to look ugly to be in a band named Ugly Casanova, and I think that's just wrong. It's a classic bait-and-switch. If I were in a band (and I am), I would name it something that reflects the real makeup of the group, and how we act. An ideal name for our band would be The Devastatingly Handsome Super Hunky Guys With Six-Pack Abs (though our fans would probably just call us TDHSHGWSPA for short). I could picture us playing at large 24-hour health clubs and Gold's Gyms, and other places where beautiful people (like ourselves) gather to high-five one another on being beautiful. Then, as we grew in popularity, we'd have to hire a manager. Before long he would sit us down and tell us that we're living a lie, and that TDHSHGWSPA is not really the right name for our band, and he'd propose something along the lines of Muscle Bound Studs Who Are Loose With Money or more likely, The Bags.

Sharpening Essentials

After you've tweaked your photo the way you want it, and right before you save it, you'll definitely want to sharpen it. I sharpen every photo, either to help bring back some of the original crispness that gets lost during the correction process, or to help fix a photo that's slightly out of focus. Either way, I haven't met a digital camera (or scanned) photo that I didn't think needed a little sharpening. Here's a basic technique for sharpening the entire photo:

Step One:

Open the photo you want to sharpen. Because Photoshop displays your photo differently at different magnifications, choosing the right magnification (also called the zoom amount) for sharpening is critical. Because today's digital cameras produce such large-sized files, it's now pretty much generally accepted that the proper magnification to view your photos during sharpening is 50%. If you look up in your image window's title bar, it displays the current percentage of zoom (shown circled here in red). The quickest way to get to a 50% magnification is to press **Command-+** (plus sign; **PC: Ctrl-+**) or **Command--** (minus sign; **PC: Ctrl--**) to zoom the magnification in or out.

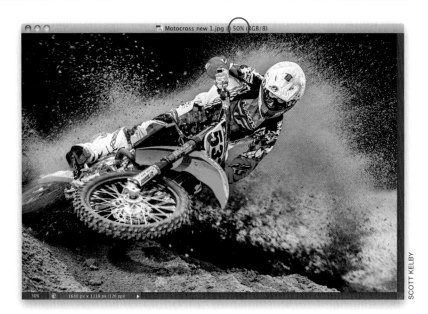

Step Two:

Once you're viewing your photo at 50% size, go under the Filter menu, under Sharpen, and choose **Unsharp Mask**. (If you're familiar with traditional darkroom techniques, you probably recognize the term "unsharp mask" from when you would make a blurred copy of the original photo and an "unsharp" version to use as a mask to create a new photo whose edges appeared sharper.)

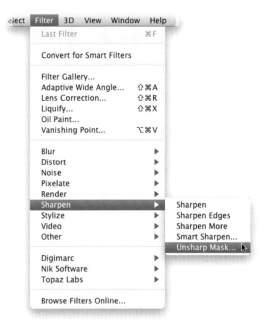

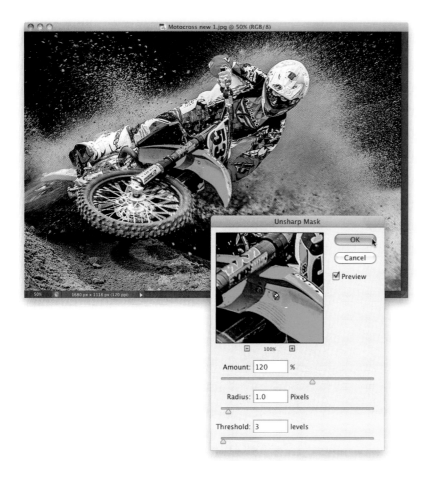

Step Three:
When the Unsharp Mask dialog appears, you'll see three sliders. The Amount slider determines the amount of sharpening applied to the photo; the Radius slider determines how many pixels out from the edge the sharpening will affect; and Threshold determines how different a pixel must be from the surrounding area before it's considered an edge pixel and sharpened by the filter (by the way, the Threshold slider works the opposite of what you might think—the lower the number, the more intense the sharpening effect). So what numbers do you enter? I'll give you some great starting points on the following pages, but for now, we'll just use these settings—Amount: 120%, Radius: 1, and Threshold: 3. Click OK and the sharpening is applied to the entire photo (see the After photo below).

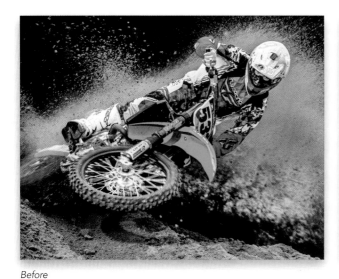

Before

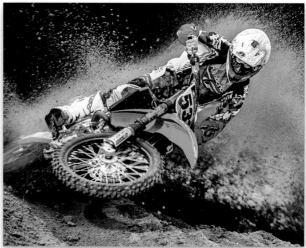

After

(Continued)

Soft subject sharpening:

Here are Unsharp Mask settings—Amount: 120%, Radius: 1, Threshold: 10—that work well for images where the subject is of a softer nature (e.g., flowers, puppies, people, rainbows, etc.). It's a subtle application of sharpening that is very well suited to these types of subjects.

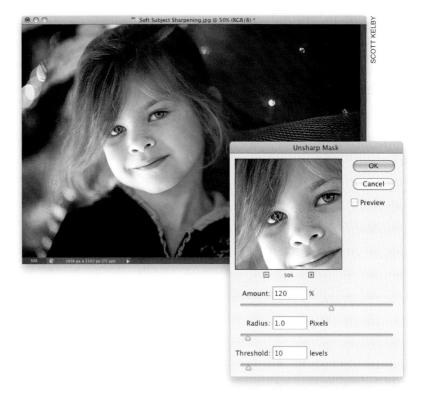

Portrait sharpening:

If you're sharpening close-up portraits, try these settings—Amount: 75%, Radius: 2, Threshold: 3—which apply another form of subtle sharpening, but with enough punch to make eyes sparkle a little bit, and bring out highlights in your subject's hair.

TIP: Sharpening Women

If you need to apply a higher level of sharpening to a portrait of a woman, first go to the Channels panel and click on the Red channel (shown here) to make it the active channel (your image will appear in black and white). Now, apply your sharpening here, using a higher Amount, like 120%, Radius: 1, Threshold: 3, right to this Red channel. By doing this, it avoids sharpening most of the skin texture and instead just sharpens her eyes, eyebrows, lips, hair, and so on. Once it's applied, click on the RGB channel at the top of the Channels panel to return to the full-color image.

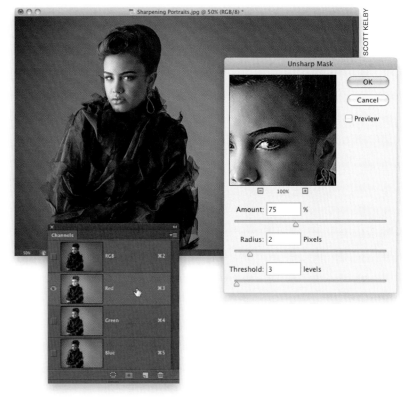

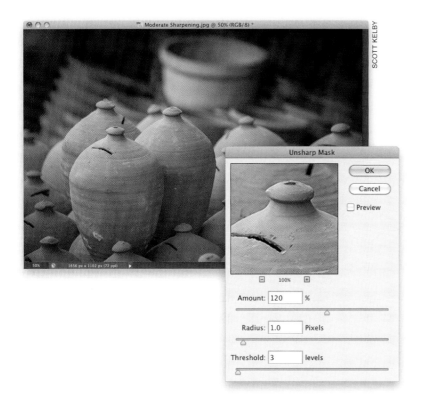

Moderate sharpening:

This is a moderate amount of sharpening that works nicely on everything from product shots, to photos of home interiors and exteriors, to landscapes (and in this case, some clay pots). These are my favorite settings when you need some nice snappy sharpening. Try applying these settings—Amount: 120%, Radius: 1, Threshold: 3—and see how you like it (my guess is you will). Take a look at how it added snap and detail to the rings around the pots and the slits in the tops.

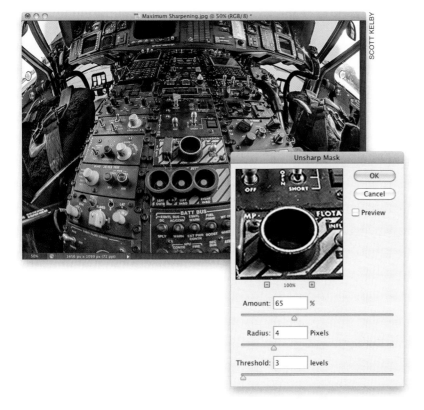

Maximum sharpening:

I use these settings—Amount: 65%, Radius: 4, Threshold: 3—in only two situations: (1) The photo is visibly out of focus and it needs a heavy application of sharpening to try to bring it back into focus. (2) The photo contains lots of well-defined edges (e.g., rocks, buildings, coins, cars, machinery, etc.). In this photo, the heavy amount of sharpening really brings out the detail in this cockpit control panel.

(Continued)

All-purpose sharpening:

These are probably my all-around favorite sharpening settings—Amount: 85%, Radius: 1, Threshold: 4—and I use these most of the time. It's not a "knock-you-over-the-head" type of sharpening—maybe that's why I like it. It's subtle enough that you can apply it twice if your photo doesn't seem sharp enough the first time you run it, but once will usually do the trick.

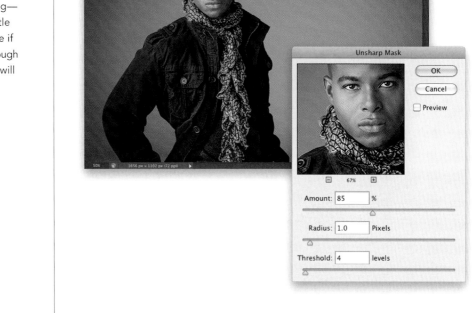

Web sharpening:

I use these settings—Amount: 200%, Radius: 0.3, Threshold: 0—for web graphics that look blurry. (When you drop the resolution from a high-res, 300-ppi photo down to 72 ppi for the web, the photo often gets a bit blurry and soft.) If the sharpening doesn't seem sharp enough, try increasing the Amount to 400%. I also use this same setting (Amount: 400%) on out-of-focus photos. It adds some noise, but I've seen it rescue photos that I would otherwise have thrown away.

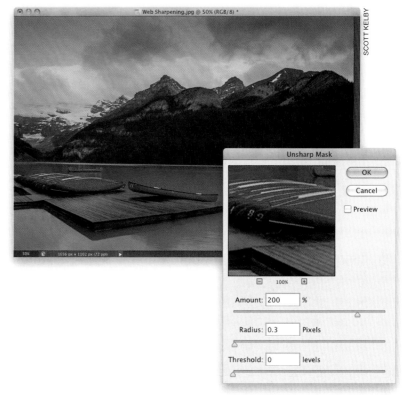

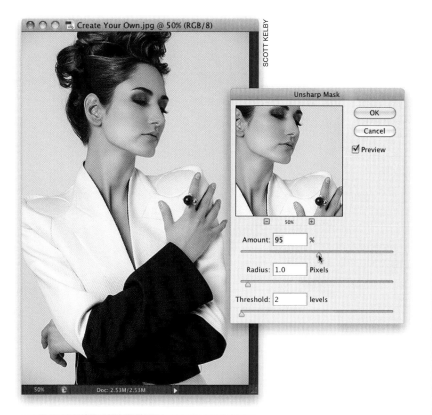

SCOTT KELBY

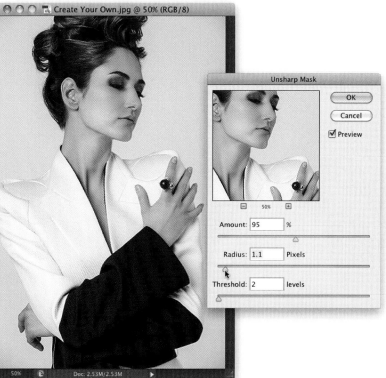

Coming up with your own settings:

If you want to experiment and come up with your own custom blend of sharpening, I'll give you some typical ranges for each adjustment so you can find your own sharpening "sweet spot."

Amount

Typical ranges run anywhere from 50% to 150%. This isn't a hard-and-fast rule—just a typical range for adjusting the Amount, where going below 50% won't have enough effect, and going above 150% might get you into sharpening trouble (depending on how you set the Radius and Threshold). You're fairly safe staying under 150%. (In the example here, I reset my Radius and Threshold to 1 and 2, respectively.)

Radius

Most of the time, you'll use just 1 pixel, but you can go as high as (get ready) 2 pixels. You saw one setting I gave you earlier for extreme situations, where you can take the Radius as high as 4 pixels. I once heard a tale of a man in Cincinnati who used 5, but I'm not sure I believe it. (Incidentally, Adobe allows you to raise the Radius amount to [get this] 250! If you ask me, anyone caught using 250 as their Radius setting should be incarcerated for a period not to exceed one year and a penalty not to exceed $2,500.)

(Continued)

Threshold

A pretty safe range for the Threshold setting is anywhere from 3 to around 20 (3 being the most intense, 20 being much more subtle. I know, shouldn't 3 be more subtle and 20 be more intense? Don't get me started). If you really need to increase the intensity of your sharpening, you can lower the Threshold to 0, but keep a good eye on what you're doing (watch for noise appearing in your photo).

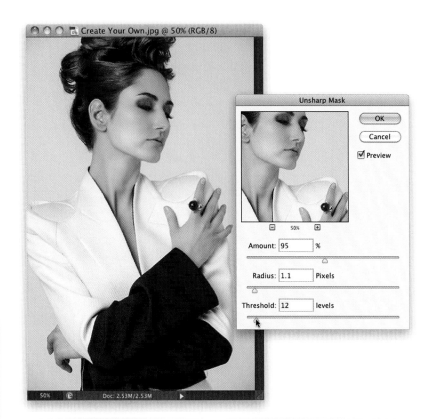

The Final Image

For the final sharpened image you see here, I used the Moderate sharpening settings I gave earlier (Amount: 120%, Radius: 1, Threshold: 3), and I used that tip I gave you after the Portrait sharpening settings for sharpening women, where I only applied this sharpening to the Red channel, so it avoided sharpening her skin texture too much (yet sharpened her hair, eyebrows, lips, clothing, etc.). If you're uncomfortable with creating your own custom Unsharp Mask settings, then start with this: pick a starting point (one of the set of settings I gave on the previous pages), and then just move the Amount slider and nothing else (so, don't touch the Radius and Threshold sliders). Try that for a while, and it won't be long before you'll find a situation where you ask yourself, "I wonder if lowering the Threshold would help?" and by then, you'll be perfectly comfortable with it.

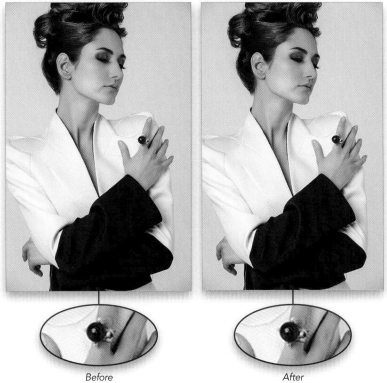

Before   *After*

This sharpening technique is my most often-used technique, and it has replaced the Lab Sharpening technique I've used in the past, because it's quicker and easier, and pretty much accomplishes the same thing, which is helping to avoid the color halos and color artifacts (spots and noise) that appear when you add a lot of sharpening to a photo. Because it helps avoid those halos and other color problems, it allows you to apply more sharpening than you normally could get away with.

Luminosity Sharpening

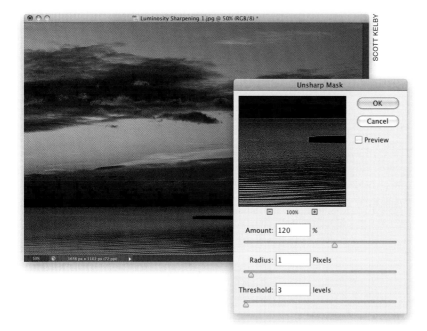

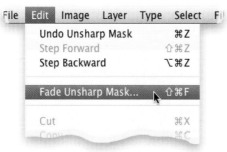

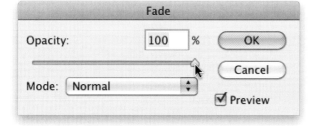

Step One:
Open the RGB photo you want to sharpen, and apply an Unsharp Mask just like you normally would (for this particular photo, let's apply these settings—Amount: 120, Radius: 1, Threshold: 3, which is my recipe for nice, punchy sharpening).

Step Two:
Immediately after you've applied the sharpening, go under the Edit menu and choose **Fade Unsharp Mask** (as shown below).

TIP: Undo on a Slider
I think of Fade's Opacity slider (seen here) as "Undo on a slider," because if you drag it down to 0, it undoes your sharpening. If you leave it at 100%, it's the full sharpening. If you lower the Opacity to 50%, you get half the sharpening applied, and so on. So, if I apply sharpening and I think it's too much, rather than changing all the settings and trying again, I'll just use the Fade Opacity slider to lower the amount a bit. I'll also use Fade when I've applied some sharpening and it's not enough. I just apply the Unsharp Mask filter again, then lower the Opacity to 50%. That way, I get 1½ sharpenings.

(Continued)

Step Three:

So, at this point, you can ignore the Opacity slider altogether, because the only thing you're going to do here is change the Fade dialog's Mode pop-up menu from Normal to **Luminosity** (as shown here). Now your sharpening is applied to just the luminosity (detail) areas of your photo, and not the color areas, and by doing this it helps avoid color halos and other pitfalls of sharpening a color image.

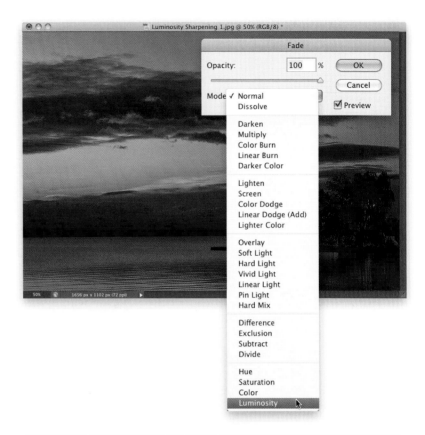

Step Four:

Click the OK button, and now your sharpening is applied to just the luminosity of the image (which is very much like the old Lab mode sharpening we used to do, where you convert your image to Lab Color mode, then just sharpen the Light-ness channel, and then convert back to RGB Color mode). So, should you apply this brand of sharpening to every digital camera photo you take? I would. In fact, I do, and since I perform this function quite often, I automated the process (as you'll see in the next step).

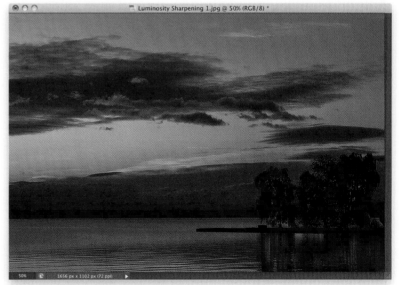

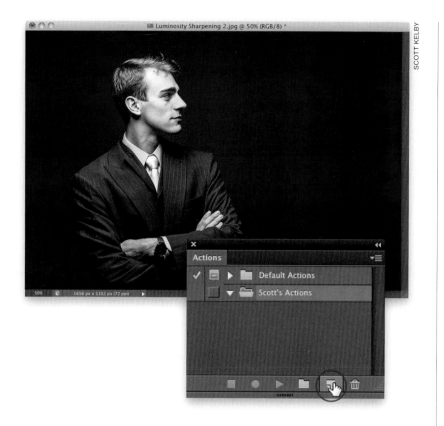

SCOTT KELBY

Step Five:

Open a different RGB photo, and let's do the whole Luminosity sharpening thing again, but this time, before you start the process, go under the Window menu and choose **Actions** to bring up the Actions panel (seen here). The Actions panel is a "steps recorder" that records any set of repetitive steps and lets you instantly play them back (apply them to another photo) by simply pressing one button (you'll totally dig this). In the Actions panel, click on the Create New Action icon at the bottom of the panel (it looks just like the Create a New Layer icon from the Layers panel, and it's shown circled in red here).

Step Six:

Clicking that icon brings up the New Action dialog (shown here). The Name field is automatically highlighted, so go ahead and give this new action a name. (I named mine "Luminosity Sharpen." I know—how original!) Then, from the Function Key pop-up menu, choose the number of the Function key (F-key) on your keyboard that you want to assign to the action (this is the key you'll hit to make the action do its thing). I've assigned mine F11, but you can choose any open F-key that suits you (but everybody knows F11 is, in fact, the coolest of all F-keys—just ask anyone. On a Mac, you may need to turn off the OS keyboard shortcut for F11 first). You'll notice that the New Actions dialog has no OK button. Instead, there's a Record button, because once you exit this dialog, Photoshop starts recording your steps. So go ahead and click Record.

(Continued)

Step Seven:

With Photoshop recording every move you make, do the Luminosity sharpening technique you learned on the previous pages (apply your favorite Unsharp Mask setting, then go under the Edit menu, choose Fade Unsharp Mask, and when the dialog appears, change the blend mode to Luminosity and click OK. Also, if you generally like a second helping of sharpening, you can run the filter again, but don't forget to Fade to Luminosity right after you're done). Now, in the Actions panel, click on the Stop icon at the bottom of the panel (it's the square icon on the left, shown circled here in red).

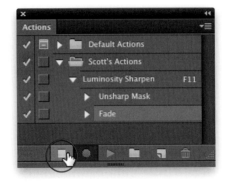

Step Eight:

This stops the recording process. If you look in the Actions panel, you'll see all your steps recorded in the order you did them. Also, if you expand the right-facing triangle beside each step (as shown here), you'll see more detail, including individual settings, for the steps it recorded. You can see here that I used the Amount: 120%, Radius: 1, and Threshold: 3 Unsharp Mask settings.

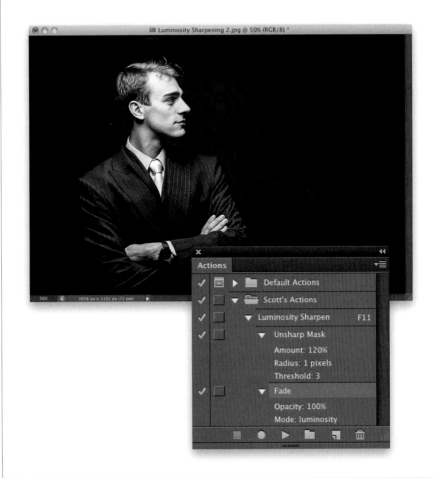

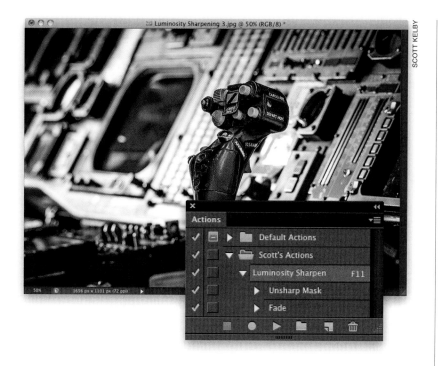

SCOTT KELBY

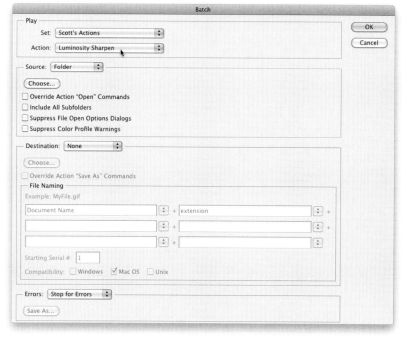

Step Nine:

Now, open a different RGB photo and let's test your action to see that it works (it's important to test it now before moving on to the next step). Press the F-key you assigned to your action (you chose F11, right? I knew it!) or click on the Play Selection icon at the bottom of the Actions panel. Photoshop immediately applies the sharpening to the Luminosity for you, and does it all faster than you could ever do it manually, because it takes place behind the scenes with no dialogs popping up.

Step 10:

Now that you've tested your action, we're going to put that baby to work. Of course, you could open more photos and then press F11 to have your action Luminosity sharpen them one at a time, but there's a better way. Once you've written an action, you can apply that action to an entire folder full of photos and Photoshop will totally automate the whole process for you (it will literally open every photo in the folder and apply your Luminosity sharpening, and then save and close every photo—all automatically. How cool is that?). This is called batch processing, and here's how it works: Go under the File menu, under Automate, and choose **Batch** to bring up the Batch dialog (or you can select all the images within a folder in Mini Bridge, then Right-click on any one of those thumbnails, and then under Photoshop, choose Batch). At the top of the dialog, within the Play section, choose your Luminosity Sharpen action from the Action pop-up menu (if it's not already selected, as shown here).

(Continued)

Step 11:

In the Source section of the Batch dialog, you tell Photoshop which folder of photos you want to Luminosity sharpen. So, choose **Folder** from the Source pop-up menu (you can also choose Bridge to run this batch action on selected photos from Mini Bridge or Big Bridge, or you can import photos from another source, or choose to run it on images that are already open in Photoshop). Then, click on the Choose button. A standard Open dialog will appear (shown here), so you can navigate to your folder of photos you want to sharpen. Once you find that folder, click on it (as shown), then click the Choose (PC: OK) button.

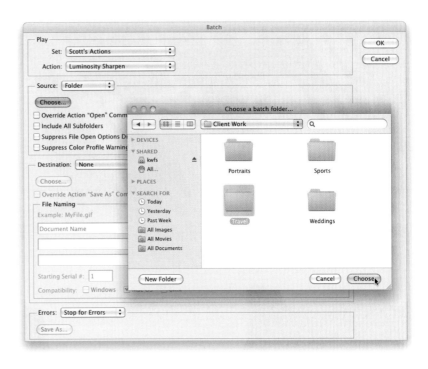

Step 12:

In the Destination section of the Batch dialog, you tell Photoshop where you want to put these photos once the action has done its thing. If you choose Save and Close from the Destination pop-up menu (as shown here), Photoshop will save the images in the same folder they're in. If you select Folder from the Destination pop-up menu, Photoshop will place your Luminosity-sharpened photos into a totally different folder. To do this, click on the Choose button in the Destination section, navigate to your target folder (or create a new one), and click Choose (PC: OK).

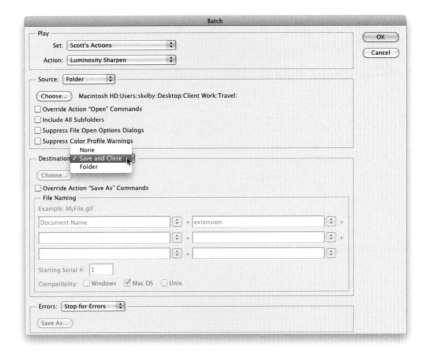

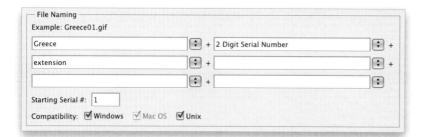

Step 13:

If you do choose to move them to a new folder, you can automatically re-name your photos in the process. In short, here's how the file naming works: In the first field within the File Naming section, you type the basic name you want all the files to have. In the other fields, you can choose (from a pop-up menu) the automatic numbering scheme to use (adding a 1-digit number, 2-digit number, etc., and if you choose this, there's a field near the bottom where you can choose which number to start with). You can also choose to add the appropriate file extension (JPG, TIFF, etc.) in upper- or lowercase to the end of the new name. At the bottom of the dialog, there's a row of checkboxes for choosing compatibility with other operating systems. I generally turn all of these on, because ya never know. When you're finally done in the Batch dialog, click OK and Photoshop will automatically Luminosity sharpen, rename, and save all your photos in a new folder for you. Nice!

The Most Advanced Sharpening in Photoshop

Back in Photoshop CS5, Adobe rewrote the underlying logic of the Sharpen tool—taking it from its previous role as a "noise generator/pixel destroyer" to what Adobe Product Manager Bryan O'Neil Hughes has called "...the most advanced sharpening in any of our products." Here's how it works:

Step One:

Start by applying your regular sharpening to the overall image using Unsharp Mask or Smart Sharpen (more on this coming up next)—your choice. In this case, since this is a portrait of a woman, I'd apply this overall sharpening to just the Red channel (see the tip on page 330 in this chapter). Now, get the Sharpen tool from the Toolbox (it's found nested beneath the Blur tool, as seen here). Once you've got the tool, go up to the Options Bar and make sure the Protect Detail checkbox (shown circled here in red) is turned on (this is the checkbox that makes all the difference, as it turns on the advanced sharpening algorithm for this tool).

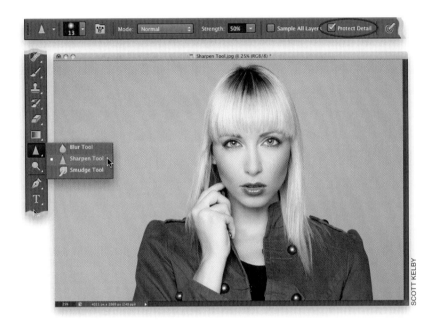

Step Two:

I recommend duplicating the Background layer at this point (by pressing **Command-J [PC: Ctrl-J]**) and applying this extra level of sharpening to this duplicate layer. That way, if you think the sharpening looks too intense, you can just lower the amount of it by lowering the opacity of this layer. I also usually zoom in (by pressing **Command-+** [plus sign; **PC: Ctrl-+**]) on a detail area (like her eyes), so I can really see the effects of the sharpening clearly (another benefit of applying the sharpening to a duplicate layer is that you can quickly see a before/after of all the sharpening by showing/hiding the layer).

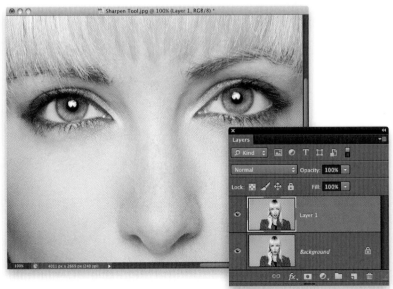

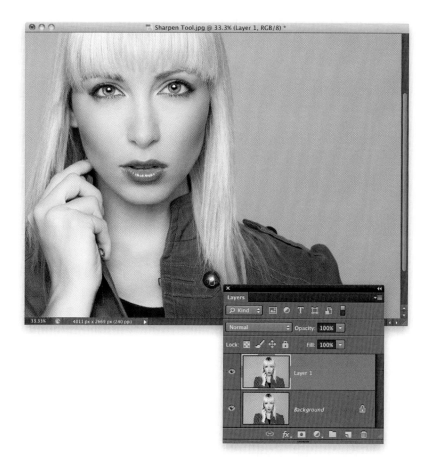

Step Three:

Now, choose a medium-sized, soft-edged brush from the Brush Picker in the Options Bar, and then simply take the Sharpen tool and paint over just the areas you want to appear sharp (this is really handy for portraits like this, because you can avoid areas you want to remain soft, like skin, but then super-sharpen areas you want to be really nice and crisp, like her irises and the buttons on her jacket, like I'm doing here). Below is a before/after, after painting over other areas that you'd normally sharpen, like her eyes, eyebrows, eyelashes, and lips, while avoiding all areas of flesh tone. One more thing: This technique is definitely not just for portraits. The Sharpen tool does a great job on anything metal or chrome, and it's wonderful on jewelry, or anything that needs that extra level of sharpening.

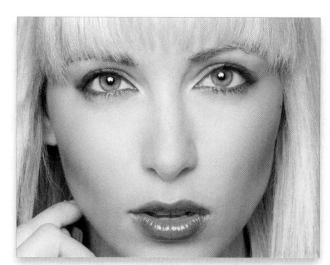

Before

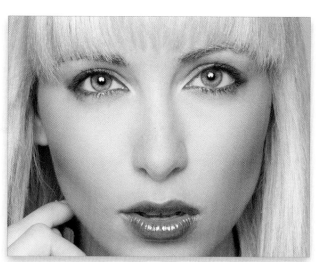

After

When to Use the Smart Sharpen Filter Instead

Although it hasn't caught on like many of us hoped, the Smart Sharpen filter offers some of the most advanced sharpening available in Photoshop CS6 (along with the improved Sharpen tool), because within it is a special sharpening algorithm that's better than the one found in the ever popular Unsharp Mask filter—you just have to know where to turn it on. Because Unsharp Mask is still so popular (old habits are hard to break), I find that I generally switch to Smart Sharpen when I run into a photo that's just a little soft (maybe I moved a bit when taking the shot, so it's not really sharp right out of the camera).

Step One:

Go under the Filter menu, under Sharpen, and choose **Smart Sharpen**. This filter is in Basic mode by default, so there are only two sliders: Amount controls the amount of sharpening (I know, "duh!") and Radius determines how many pixels the sharpening will affect. The default Amount setting of 100% seems too high to me for everyday use, so I usually find myself lowering it to between 60% and 70%. The Radius is set at 1 by default, and I rarely change that, but for this image, I raised it to 2.

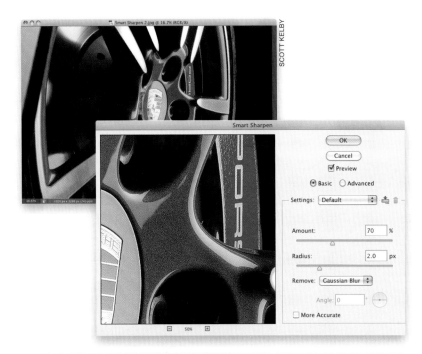

Step Two:

Below the Radius slider is the Remove pop-up menu (shown here), which lists the three types of blurs you can reduce. Gaussian Blur (the default) applies the same sharpening you get using the regular Unsharp Mask filter. Motion Blur is useless, unless you can accurately determine the angle of blur in your image (which I've yet to be able to do even once). The third one is the one I recommend: Lens Blur. This uses a sharpening algorithm created by Adobe's engineers that's better at detecting edges, so it creates fewer color halos than you'd get with the other choices, and overall I think it gives you better sharpening for most images.

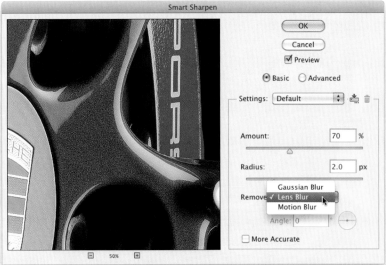

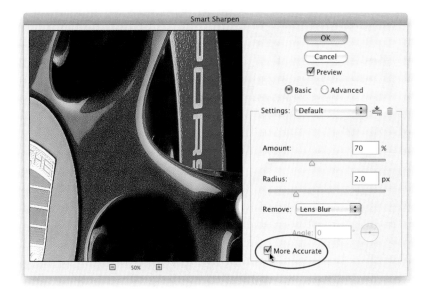

Step Three:

The only downside to choosing Lens Blur is that it makes the filter take a little longer to "do its thing." (That's why it's not the default choice, even though it provides better-quality sharpening.) After you choose Lens Blur, go to the bottom of the dialog and you'll see a checkbox for More Accurate. It gives you (according to Adobe) more accurate sharpening by applying multiple iterations of the sharpening. I leave More Accurate turned on all the time. (After all, who wants "less accurate" sharpening?) *Note:* If you're working on a large file, the More Accurate option can cause the filter to process slower, so it's up to you if it's worth the wait (I think it is). By the way, the use of the More Accurate checkbox is one of those topics that Photoshop users debate back and forth in online forums. For regular everyday sharpening it might be overkill, but again, the reason I use Smart Sharpen is because the photo is visibly blurry, slightly out of focus, or needs major sharpening to save. So I leave this on all the time.

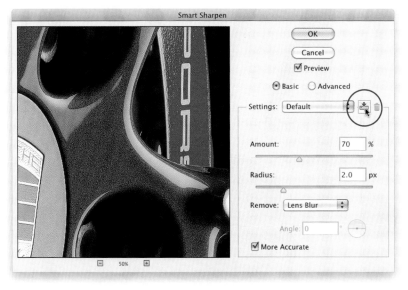

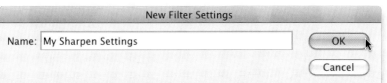

Step Four:

If you find yourself applying a setting such as this over and over again, you can save these settings and add them to the Settings pop-up menu at the top of the dialog by clicking on the icon to the right of the pop-up menu. This brings up a dialog for you to name your saved settings, and then click OK. Now, the next time you're in the Smart Sharpen filter dialog and you want to instantly call up your saved settings, just choose it from the Settings pop-up menu.

(Continued)

Step Five:

If you click the Advanced radio button, it reveals two additional tabs with controls for reducing the sharpening in just the shadow or just the highlight areas that are applied to the settings you chose back in the Basic section. That's why in the Shadow and Highlight tabs, the top slider says "Fade Amount" rather than just "Amount." As you drag the Fade Amount slider to the right, you're reducing the amount of sharpening already applied, which can help reduce any halos in the highlights. (*Note:* Without increasing the amount of fade, you can't tweak the Tonal Width and Radius amounts. They only kick in when you increase the Fade Amount.) Thankfully, I rarely have had to use these Advanced controls, so 99% of my work in Smart Sharpen is done using the Basic controls.

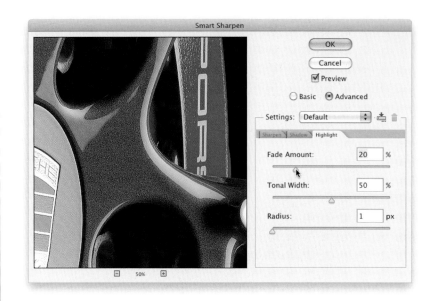

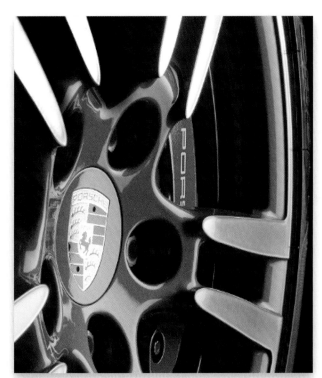

Before

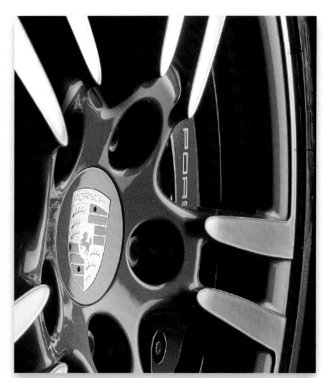

After

High Pass Sharpening

I don't normally include the same technique twice in the same book, but if you read the HDR chapter, I included High Pass sharpening there, too, because it has become kind of synonymous with HDR processing. Of course, what I'm concerned about is that you skipped over the HDR chapter altogether, and came here to the sharpening chapter, and you'd be wondering why the very popular High Pass sharpening technique (which creates extreme sharpening) wasn't included in the book. Well, it's so good, it is covered twice. :)

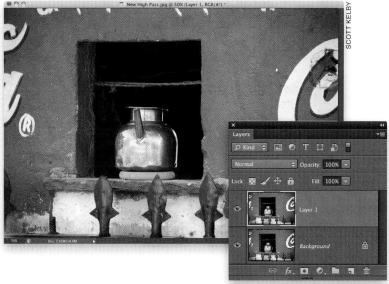

SCOTT KELBY

Step One:
Open a photo that needs some extreme sharpening, like this photo taken in India. Duplicate the Background layer, as shown here, by pressing **Command-J (PC: Ctrl-J)**.

Step Two:
Go under the Filter menu, under Other, and choose **High Pass**. You use this filter to accentuate the edges in the photo, and making those edges stand out can really give the impression of mega-sharpening. I start by dragging the Radius slider all the way to the left (everything turns gray onscreen), then I drag it over to the right. For non-HDR images, I don't drag it all that far—I just drag until I see the edges of objects in the photos appear clearly, and then I stop. The farther you drag, the more intense the sharpening will be, but if you drag too far, you start to get these huge glows and the effect starts to fall apart, so don't get carried away. Now, click OK to apply the sharpening.

(Continued)

Step Three:

In the Layers panel, change the layer blend mode of this layer from Normal to **Hard Light**. This removes the gray color from the layer, but leaves the edges accentuated, making the entire photo appear much sharper (as seen here). If the sharpening seems too intense, you can control the amount of the effect by lowering the layer's Opacity in the Layers panel, or try changing the blend mode to Overlay (which makes the sharpening less intense) or Soft Light (even more so).

Step Four:

If you want even more sharpening, duplicate the High Pass layer to double-up the sharpening. If that's too much, lower the Opacity of the top layer. One problem with High Pass sharpening is that you might get a glow along some edges. The trick to getting rid of that is to: (1) press **Command-E (PC: Ctrl-E)** to merge the two High Pass layers, (2) click the Add Layer Mask button at the bottom of the panel, (3) get the Brush tool **(B)**, and with a small, soft-edged brush and your Foreground color set to black, (4) paint right along the edge, revealing the original, unsharpened edge with no glow.

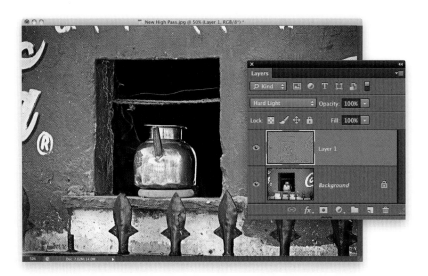

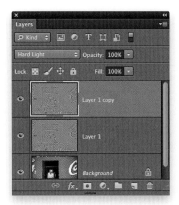

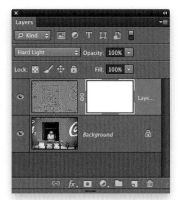

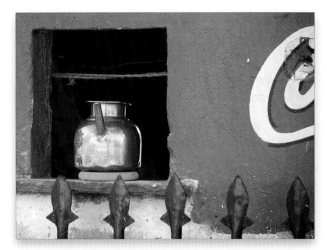

Before

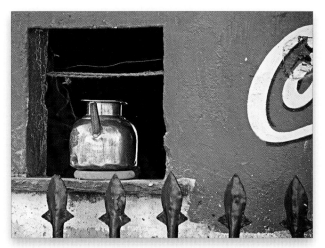

After

If you wind up doing all your edits from right within Camera Raw, and then you save straight to a JPEG or TIFF right from Camera Raw, as well (skipping the jump to Photoshop altogether), you'll still want to sharpen your image for how the image will be viewed (onscreen, in print, etc.). This is called "output sharpening" (the sharpening you do in Camera Raw's Detail panel is called "input sharpening," because it's designed to replace the sharpening that would have been done in your camera if you had shot in JPEG or TIFF mode).

Output Sharpening in Camera Raw

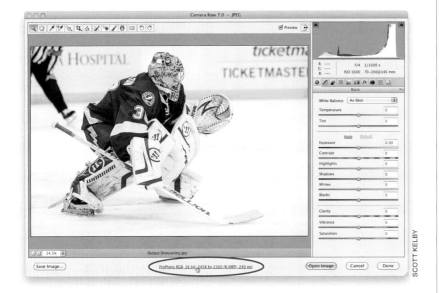

SCOTT KELBY

Step One:
Before we do this output sharpening, it's important to note that this sharpening only kicks in if you're going to save your image from right here within Camera Raw by clicking the Save Image button in the bottom-left corner of the Camera Raw window. If you click the Open Image or Done button, the output sharpening is not applied. Okay, now that you know, you find output sharpening by clicking on the line of text (which looks like a web link) below the Preview area (it's circled here in red).

Step Two:
First, choose how you want this image sharpened from the Sharpen For pop-up menu near the bottom: Screen is for images you're going to post on the web, email to a client, or present in a slide show. If the image is going to be printed, choose whether you'll be printing to Glossy Paper or Matte Paper. Lastly, choose the amount of sharpening you want from the Amount pop-up menu. Camera Raw will do the math based on the image's resolution, your Sharpen For choice, and Amount choice (I never choose Low, by the way) to calculate the exact right amount of output sharpening. *Note:* When you click OK, the sharpening stays on from now on. To turn it off, choose **None** from the Sharpen For pop-up menu.

Photoshop Killer Tips

Content-Aware Fill Tips

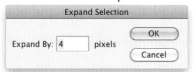

If you made a selection in an image and tried Content-Aware Fill on it, but you're not happy with the results, try one of these two tips: (1) Press **Command-Z (PC: Ctrl-Z)** to Undo the Fill, then try Content-Aware Fill again. It's somewhat random in choosing the area it samples to fill its area from, so simply trying it again might do the trick (this works more often than you might think). (2) Try to expand your selection a little bit. Once you've put a selection around what you want to remove, then go under the Select menu, under Modify, and choose **Expand**, and try expanding your selection by 3 or 4 pixels, and try Content-Aware Fill again. It just might do the trick.

If One of Your Tools Starts Acting Weird...

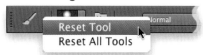

...chances are something has changed in the options for that tool (up in the Options Bar) that may not be obvious by just looking at the Options Bar. In that case, you can reset the tool to its factory defaults by Right-clicking directly on the little down-facing arrow next to the tool's icon at the far-left side of the Options Bar, and a pop-up menu will appear where you can choose to reset your current tool, or all your tools.

Tip for When You're Zoomed In Tight

If you're zoomed in tight on a photo, there is nothing more frustrating than trying to move to a different part of the image using

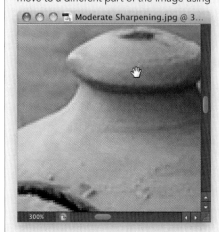

the scroll bars (they always seem to move you way too far, and then eventually you just have to zoom back out and then zoom back in again). Instead, just press-and-hold the **Spacebar**, and it temporarily switches you to the Hand tool, so you can click-and-drag the image right where you want it. When you release the Spacebar, it returns you to the tool you were using.

Merge to HDR Pro Can Make Killer B&W Images

I know that when you say "HDR" most folks picture those surreal, super-vibrant images that you see all over the web, which is why you may not think of Merge to HDR Pro as a choice for creating black-and-white images, but it actually does a pretty amazing job (and although most of the built-in presets that come

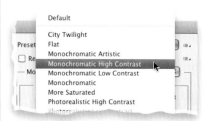

with Merge to HDR Pro kinda stink, the Monochromatic (B&W) presets aren't half bad. Give this a try the next time you shoot a bracketed image.

Giving Your RAW Image to Someone Else (Along with Your Edits)

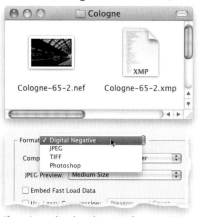

If you've edited a photo in Camera Raw, and you give the RAW file to a client, they won't see the edits you've made to the file, unless: (a) you include the separate XMP file along with your RAW file (it should be found right beside the RAW file in your image folder), or (2) you save the file in DNG format in the Format pop-up menu in Camera Raw's Save Options dialog (DNG is Adobe's open-source format for RAW images, and it embeds your edits in the DNG file).

Photoshop Killer Tips

Lock Multiple Layers at Once

In CS6, if you want to lock more than one layer at a time, it's no sweat. Just Command-click (PC: Ctrl-click) to select

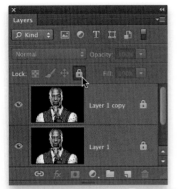

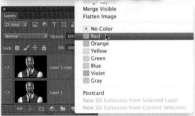

as many layers as you want locked, and then click on the Lock icon at the top of the Layers panel. This works the same when assigning Color labels—just select the layers you want to label, then Right-click on one of the layers, and choose the Color label you want to assign to the selected layers from the pop-up menu.

Making Selections Near the Edge of Your Document

When you're making a selection (with the Polygonal Lasso or regular Lasso tool), and you reach the edge of your document window, you don't have to release

and start over—just press-and-hold the **Spacebar**, and your Lasso tool temporarily switches to the Hand tool, so you can move over enough to complete your

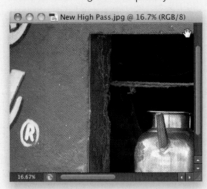

selection, then release the Spacebar and it switches you back to the Lasso tool, and (here's what's so cool) your selection-in-process has been frozen in place, so now you can pick right up where you were.

Keeping Your Camera Settings to Yourself

If you're posting an image on the web, or sending an image to a client, you might not want to have all your camera settings, and camera serial number, included in the image where anyone can view it (after all, does your client really need to know you shot this at f/5.6 at 800 ISO?). So, to keep your camera settings to yourself, just press

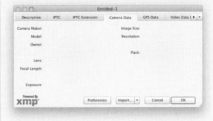

Command-A (PC: Ctrl-A) to select your entire image, then press **Command-C (PC: Ctrl-C)** to copy it into memory. Now, press **Command-N (PC: Ctrl-N)** and Photoshop will automatically create a new document that is the exact size, resolution, and color mode as the image you copied vinto memory. Next, press **Command-V (PC: Ctrl-V)** to paste your image into this new blank document. Then, press **Command-E (PC: Ctrl-E)** to flatten the image, and you can send this file anywhere without having your camera data in the file. However, I would go under the File menu and choose **File Info**, then click on the Description tab, and I'd enter my copyright info in the Copyright section.

Want to See Your Adjustment Layer Controls Larger?

If you add a Levels, or Hue/Saturation, or Curves (and so on) adjustment layer, those controls appear in the new Properties panel at its default size. But, if you want more precision when working with those settings in the panel, just click on the left side of the panel and drag it out to the left. As the panel gets larger, so do the adjustment's controls themselves.

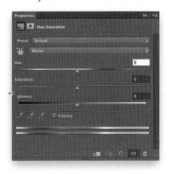

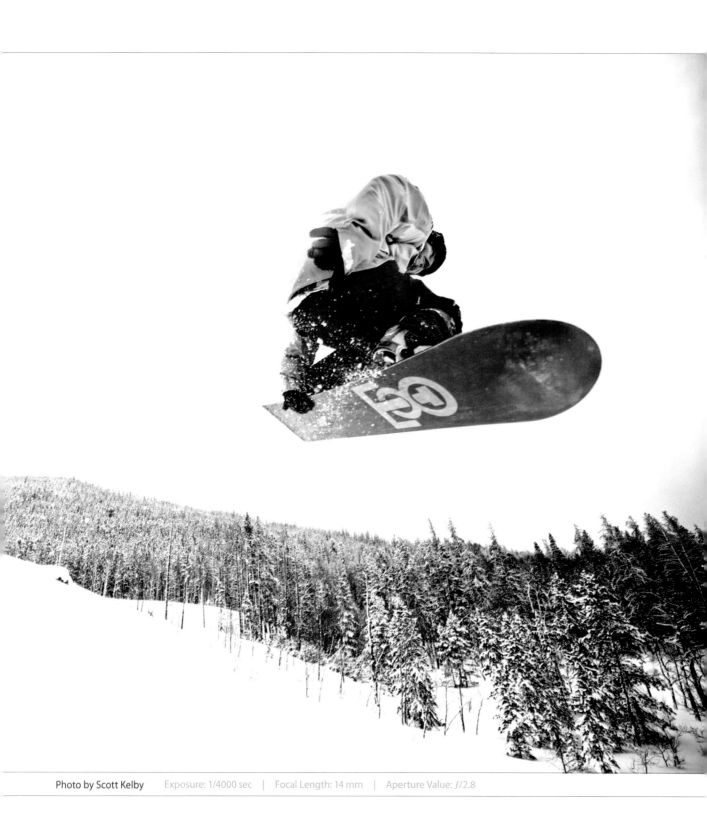

Photo by Scott Kelby   Exposure: 1/4000 sec | Focal Length: 14 mm | Aperture Value: ƒ/2.8

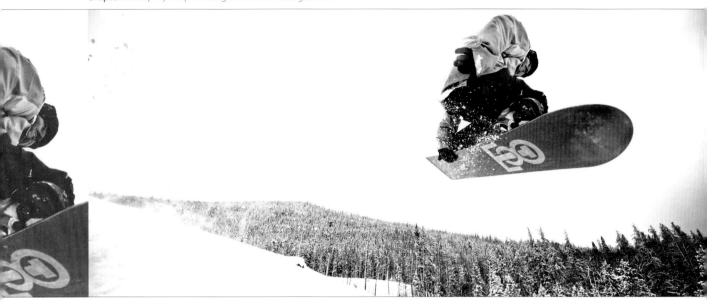

Fine Print
step-by-step printing and color management

There is nothing like a photographic print. It's the moment when your digitally captured image, edited on a computer, moves from a bunch of 1s and 0s (computer code) into something real you can hold in your hand. If you've never made a print (and sadly, in this digital age, I meet people every day who have never made a single print—everything just stays on their computer, or on Facebook, or someplace else where you can "look, but don't touch"), today, all that changes, because you're going to learn step by step how to make your own prints. Now, if you don't already own a printer, this chapter becomes something else. Expensive. Actually, in all fairness, it's not the printer—it's the paper and ink, which is precisely why the printers aren't too expensive. But once you've bought a printer—they've got you. You'll be buying paper and ink for the rest of your natural life, and it seems like you go through ink cartridges faster than a gallon of milk. This is precisely why I've come up with a workflow that literally pays for itself—I use my color inkjet printer to print out counterfeit U.S. bills. Now, I'm not stupid about it— I did some research and found that new ink cartridges for my particular printer run about $13.92 each, so I just make $15 bills (so it also covers the sales tax). Now—again, not stupid here—I don't go around using these $15 bills to buy groceries or lunch at Chili's, I only use them for ink cartridges, and so far, it's worked pretty well. I must admit, I had a couple of close calls, though, mainly because I put Dave Cross's face on all the bills, which seemed like a good idea at the time, until a sales clerk looked closely at the bill and said, "Isn't Dave Canadian?" (By the way, this chapter title comes from the song "Fine Print" by Nadia Ali. According to her website, she was born in the Mediterranean, which is precisely why you don't see her on my newly minted $18.60 bills.)

Setting Up Your Camera's Color Space

Although there are entire books written on the subject of color management, in this chapter we're going to focus on just one thing—getting what comes out of your color inkjet printer to match what you see onscreen. That's what it's all about, and if you follow the steps in this chapter, you'll get prints that match your screen. We're going to start by setting up your camera's color space, so you'll get the best results from screen to print. *Note:* You can skip this if you only shoot in RAW.

Step One:

If you shoot in JPEG or TIFF mode (or JPEG + Raw), you'll want to set your camera's color space to match what you're going to use in Photoshop for your color space (to get consistent color from your camera to Photoshop to your printer, you'll want everybody speaking the same language, right?). I recommend you change your camera's color space from its default sRGB to Adobe RGB (1998), which is a better color space for photographers whose final image will come from a color inkjet printer.

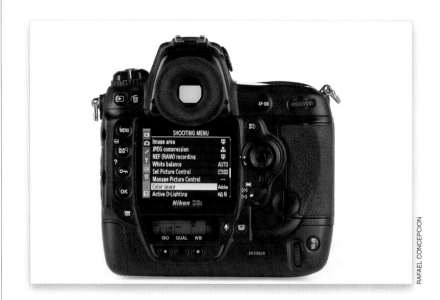

RAFAEL CONCEPCION

Step Two:

On a Nikon DSLR, you'll usually find the Color Space control under the Shooting Menu (as shown here at left). On most Canon DSLRs, you'll find the Color Space control under the Shooting 2 menu (as shown here on the right). Change the space to Adobe RGB. If you're not shooting Nikon or Canon, it's time to dig up your owner's manual (or, ideally, download it in PDF format from the manufacturer's website) to find out how to make the switch to Adobe RGB (1998). Again, if you're shooting in RAW, you can skip this altogether.

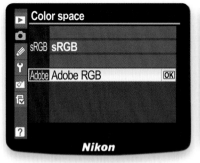

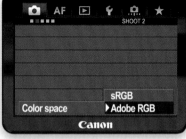

Resolution for Printing

This is one of those topics that tend to make people crazy, and since there is no Official Board of Resolution Standards, this is the type of thing that gets argued endlessly in online discussion forums. That being said, I take the word of my friend and fellow photographer Dan Steinhardt from Epson (the man behind the popular Epson Print Academy), who lives this stuff day in and day out (Dan and I did an online training class on printing and this was just about the first topic we covered, because for so many, this is a real stumbling block). Here's what we do:

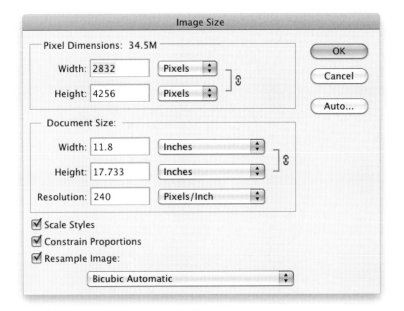

Step One:

To see what your current photo's resolution is, go under the Image menu and choose **Image Size** (or press **Command-Option-I [PC: Ctrl-Alt-I]**). Ideally, for printing to a color inkjet printer, I like to be at 240 ppi (pixels per inch), but I often print at 200 ppi, and will go as low as 180 ppi (but 180 ppi is absolutely the lowest I'll go. Anything below that and, depending on the image, you'll start to visibly lose print quality). So, I guess the good news here is: you don't need as much resolution as you might think (even for a printing press). Here's an image taken with a 12-megpixel camera and you can see that at 240 ppi, I can print an image that is nearly 12x18".

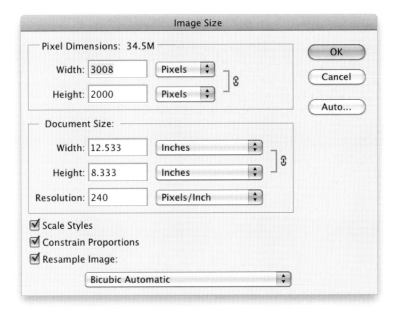

Step Two:

Here's the resolution from a 6-megapixel camera. At 240 ppi I can only print an 8x12.5" image. So, to make it larger, I turn off the Resample Image checkbox, type in 200 as my new resolution, and then I'd have an image size of 10x15" (with no loss of quality). If I lower it to 180 ppi (as low as I would ever go), then I get the print up to a finished size of 11x16.75" (nearly that of a 12-megapixel camera), and I did it all without losing quality (because I turned off the Resample Image checkbox, but before you do this, you need to read about resizing in Chapter 5).

Setting Up Photoshop's Color Space

Photoshop's default color space is sRGB (some pros refer to it as "stupid RGB"), which is fine for photos going on the web, but your printer can print a wider range of colors than sRGB (particularly in the blues and greens). So, if you work in sRGB, you're essentially leaving out those rich, vivid colors you could be seeing. That's why we either change our color space to Adobe RGB (1998) if you're shooting in JPEG or TIFF, which is better for printing those images, or ProPhoto RGB if you shoot in RAW or work with Photohsop Lightroom. Here's how to set up both:

Step One:

Before we do this, I just want to reiterate that you only want to make this change if your final print will be output to your own color inkjet. If you're sending your images out to an outside lab for prints, you should probably stay in sRGB—both in the camera and in Photoshop—as most labs are set up to handle sRGB files. Your best bet: ask your lab which color space they prefer. Okay, now on to Photoshop: go under the Edit menu and choose **Color Settings** (as shown here).

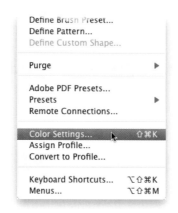

Step Two:

This brings up the Color Settings dialog. By default, it uses a group of settings called "North America General Purpose 2." Now, does anything about the phrase "General Purpose" sound like it would be a good space for pro photographers? Didn't think so. The tip-off is that under Working Spaces, the RGB space is set to sRGB IEC61966–2.1 (which is the long-hand technical name for what we simply call sRGB). In short, you don't want to use this group of settings. They're for goobers—not for you (unless of course, you are a goober, which I doubt because you bought this book, and they don't sell this book to goobers. It's in each book-store's contract).

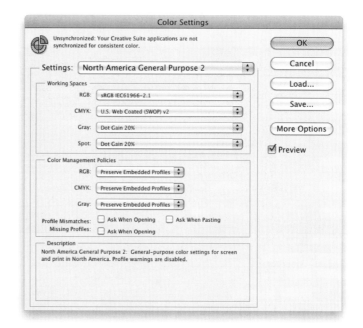

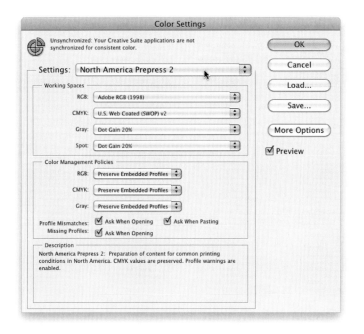

Step Three:

To get a preset group of settings that's better for photographers, from the Settings pop-up menu, choose **North America Prepress 2**. Don't let it throw you that we're using prepress settings here—they work great for color inkjet printing because it uses the Adobe RGB (1998) color space. It also sets up the appropriate warning dialogs to help you keep your color management plan in action when opening photos from outside sources or other cameras (more on this on the next page).

Step Four:

If you're shooting in RAW exclusively, or using Lightroom (Adobe's awesome application for photographers), then you'll want to change your color space in Photoshop to **ProPhoto RGB** to get the best prints from your RAW images (plus, if you use Lightroom, you'll wind up moving images back and forth between Lightroom and Photoshop from time to time, and since Lightroom's native color space is ProPhoto RGB, you'll want to keep everything consistent. While you might use Lightroom for your JPEG or TIFF images, there's really no advantage to choosing ProPhoto RGB for them). You change Photoshop's Color Space to PhotoPro RGB in the Color Settings dialog (just choose it from the RGB menu, as shown here). That way, when you open a RAW photo in Photoshop (or import a file from Lightroom), everything stays in the same consistent color space and if you wind up bringing an image from Lightroom over to Photoshop, and end up printing it in Photoshop (instead of jumping back to Lightroom for printing), you'll get better results.

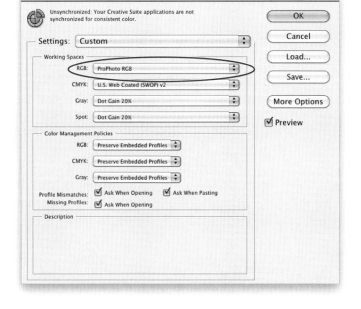

(Continued)

Step Five:

About those warnings that help you keep your color management on track: Let's say you open a JPEG photo, and your camera was set to shoot in Adobe RGB (1998), and your Photoshop is set the same way. The two color spaces match, so no warnings appear. But, if you open a JPEG photo you took six months ago, it will probably still be in sRGB, which doesn't match your Photoshop working space. That's a mismatch, so you'd get the warning dialog shown here, telling you this. Luckily it gives you the choice of how to handle it. I recommend converting that document's colors to your current working space (as shown here).

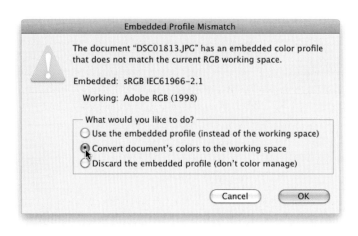

Step Six:

You can have Photoshop do this conversion automatically anytime it finds a mismatch. Just reopen the Color Settings dialog, and under Color Management Policies, in the RGB pop-up menu, change your default setting to **Convert to Working RGB** (as shown here). For Profile Mismatches, turn off the Ask When Opening checkbox. Now when you open sRGB photos, they will automatically update to match your current working space. Nice!

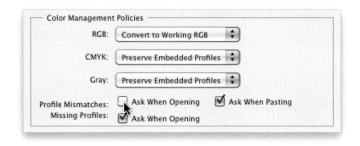

Step Seven:

Okay, so what if a friend emails you a photo, you open it in Photoshop, and the photo doesn't have any color profile at all? Well, once that photo is open in Photoshop, you can convert that "untagged" image to Adobe RGB (1998) by going under the Edit menu and choosing **Assign Profile**. When the Assign Profile dialog appears, click on the Profile radio button, ensure Adobe RGB (1998) is selected in the pop-up menu, then click OK.

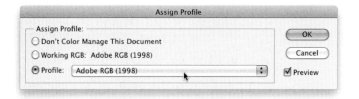

When we apply sharpening, we apply it so it looks good on our computer screen, right? But when you actually make a print, a lot of that sharpening that looks fine on a 72- or 96- dpi computer screen gets lost on a high-resolution print at 240 ppi. Because the sharpening gets reduced when we make a print, we have to sharpen so our photo looks a bit too sharp onscreen, but then looks perfect when it prints. Here's how I apply sharpening for images I'm going to print:

Sharpening for Printing

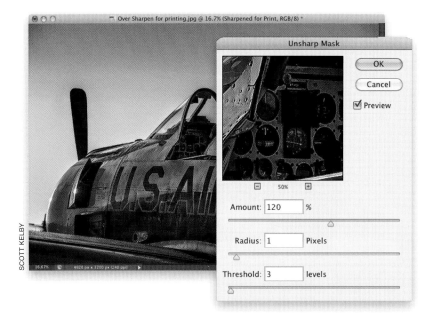

Step One:
Start by doing a trick my buddy Shelly Katz shared with me: duplicate the Background layer (by pressing **Command-J [PC: Ctrl-J]**) and do your print sharpening on this duplicate layer (that way, you don't mess with the already sharpened original image on the Background layer). Name this new layer "Sharpened for Print," then go under the Filter menu, under Sharpen, and choose **Unsharp Mask**. For most 240 ppi images, I apply these settings: Amount 120; Radius 1; Threshold 3. Click OK.

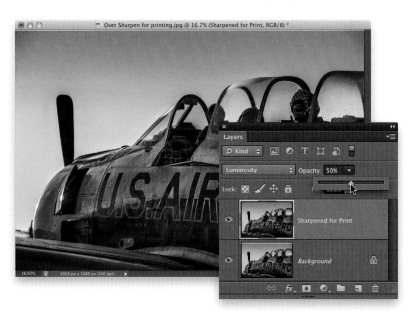

Step Two:
Next, reapply the Unsharp Mask filter with the same settings by pressing **Command-F (PC: Ctrl-F)**. Then, at the top of the Layers panel, change the layer blend mode to **Luminosity** (so the sharpening is only applied to the detail of the photo, and not the color), then use the Opacity slider to control how much sharpening is applied. Start at 50% and see if it looks a little bit oversharpened. If it looks like a little bit too much, stop—you want it to look a little oversharpened. If you think it's way too much, lower the opacity to around 35% and re-evaluate. When it looks right (a little too sharp), make a test print. My guess is that you'll want to raise the opacity up a little higher, because it won't be as sharp as you thought.

Sending Your Images to Be Printed at a Photo Lab

Besides printing images on my own color inkjet printer, I also send a decent amount of my print work out to a photo lab (I use Mpix as my lab) for a number of reasons— like if I want metallic prints, or I want the image mounted, matted, and/or framed with glass, or I want a print that's larger than I can print in-house. Here's how to prep your images for uploading to be printed at a photo lab:

Step One:
First, contact the photo lab where you're sending your image, and ask what color profile they want you to use. Chances are they are going to want you to convert your image to sRGB color mode. I know this flies in the face of what we do when we print our own images, but I know a number of big, high-quality photo labs (Mpix included) that all request that you convert your images to sRGB first, and for their workflow, it works. If they don't request you convert to sRGB, they may have you download a color profile they've created for you, and you'll use it the same way as you'll assign sRGB in the next step.

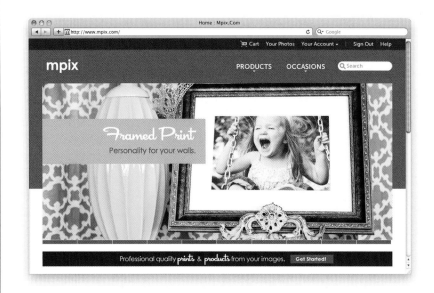

Step Two:
With your image open in Photoshop, go under the Edit menu, choose **Convert to Profile**, and you'll see the image's current color profile at the top of the dialog (here, my image is a RAW image, and so it's set to ProPhoto RGB). Under Destination Space, from the Profile pop-up menu, choose **sRGB IEC61966-2.1**. If you down- loaded a profile from your lab, you'll choose that instead (more on where to save downloads on page 367). Click OK, and don't be surprised if the image looks pretty much the same. In fact, be happy if it does, but at least now it's set up to get the best results from your photo lab.

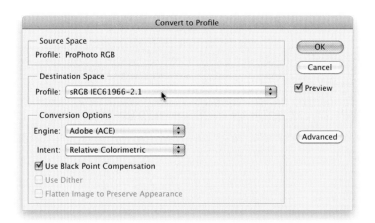

If you really want what comes out of your printer to match what you see onscreen, then I don't want to have to be the one to tell you this, but…you absolutely, positively have to calibrate your monitor using a hardware calibrator. The good news is that today it's an absolutely simple, totally automated process. The bad news is that you have to buy a hardware calibrator. With hardware calibration, it's measuring your actual monitor and building an accurate profile for the exact monitor you're using, and yes—it makes that big a difference.

You Have to Calibrate Your Monitor Before You Go Any Further

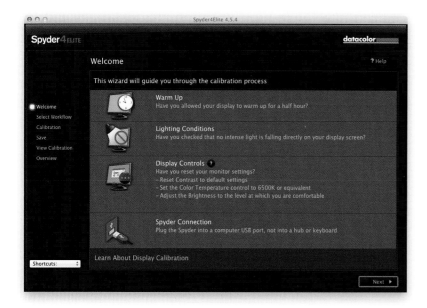

Step One:
I use Datacolor's Spyder4ELITE hardware color calibrator (around $249 street price), because it's simple, affordable, and a lot of the pros I know have moved over to it. So, I'm going to use it as an example here, but it's not necessary to get this same one, because they all work fairly similarly. You start by installing the software that comes with the Spyder4ELITE. Then, plug the Spyder4ELITE sensor into your computer's USB port and launch the software, which brings up the main window (seen here). You follow the "wizard," which asks you a couple of simple questions (stuff like, "Is this the first time you've calibrated your monitor using Spyder4ELITE?" Or, maybe, "What's the capital of Nebraska?"), and then it does the rest.

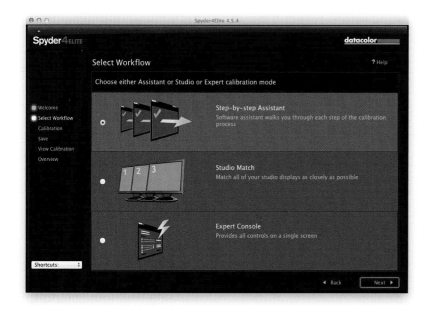

Step Two:
Start by clicking the Next button in the bottom right, and the window you see here will appear. If you're new to calibrating your monitor, I recommend using the Step-by-Step Assistant (which is already selected by default), so at this point just click the Next button again.

(Continued)

Step Three:

The next screen asks you which type of calibration you want to do. Are you going to just update an older calibration you did previously with the Spyder4ELITE (then you would choose the ReCAL radio button), or do you just want to check to see how accurate your current calibration is (CheckCAL), or are you doing this for the first time (which you are, so you'd click the FullCAL radio button, as shown here)? Then, just click the Next button, because you're going to leave all the pop-up menus here at their default recommended settings.

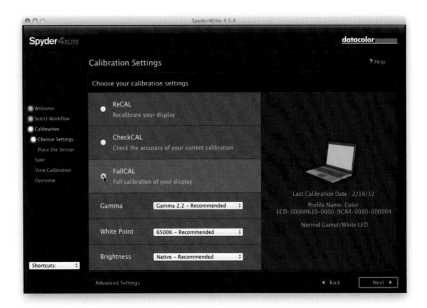

Step Four:

The next screen asks you to put the Spyder unit on your monitor, which means you drape the sensor over your monitor so it sits flat against it and the cord hangs over the back. It shows you exactly where to place it (the two blue arrows you see beside its outline actually flash on/off, so you can't possibly miss where it goes). The sensor comes with a counterweight you can attach to the cord, so you can position the sensor approximately in the center of your screen without it slipping down. Once the sensor is in position over your screen, click the Next button, sit back, and relax. You'll see the software conduct a series of onscreen tests, using gray, white, and various color swatches, as shown here.

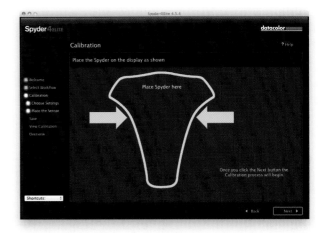

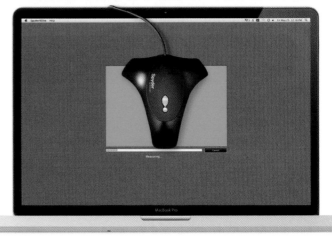

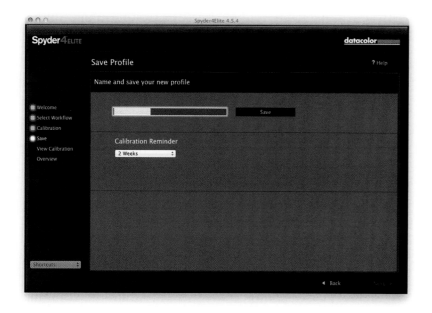

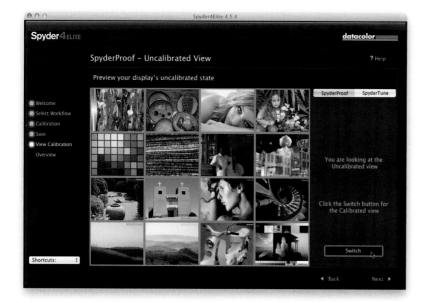

Step Five:
This testing only goes on for a few minutes (at least, that's all it took for my laptop), and then it's done. It asks you to name your profile (it puts a default name in place for you), so enter a name, and then click the Save button. Below that is a pop-up menu where you can choose when you want an automatic reminder to "Recalibrate your monitor" to pop up on your screen. The default choice is 2 Weeks (so please don't tell anyone that I actually set mine to 1 Month). Make your choice and then click the Next button.

Step Six:
Now you get to see the usually shocking before/after. Click on the Switch button at the bottom right and you can switch back and forth between your now fully calibrated monitor and your uncalibrated monitor. It's at that moment you say, "Ohhhhhh…that's why my prints never match my screen." Well, it's certainly one part of the puzzle, but without this one critical piece in place, you don't have a chance with the rest, so you did the right thing. Click Next one last time, and then click the Quit button in the Profile Overview screen.

The Other Secret to Getting Pro-Quality Prints That Match Your Screen

When you buy a color inkjet printer and install the printer driver that comes with it, it basically lets Photoshop know what kind of printer is being used, and that's about it. But to get pro-quality results, you need a color profile for your printer based on the exact type of paper you'll be printing on. Most inkjet paper manufacturers now create custom profiles for their papers, and you can usually download them free from their websites. Does this really make that big a difference? Ask any pro. Here's how to find and install these profiles:

Step One:

Your first step is to go to the website of the company that makes the paper you're going to be printing on and search for their downloadable color profiles for your printer. I use the term "search" because they're usually not in a really obvious place. I use two Epson printers—a Stylus Photo R2880 and a Stylus Pro 3880—and I generally print on Epson paper. When I installed the 3880's printer driver, I was tickled to find that it also installed custom color profiles for all Epson papers (this is rare), but my R2880 (like most printers) doesn't. So, the first stop would be Epson's website, where you'd click on the Printers & All-in-One Printers link under Get Drivers & Support (as shown here). *Note:* Even if you're not an Epson user, still follow along (you'll see why).

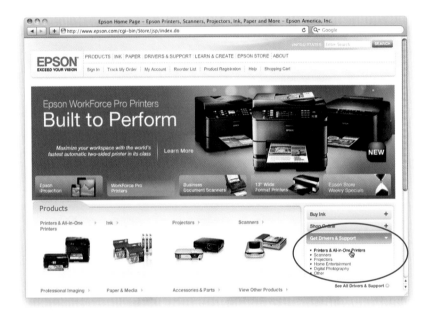

Step Two:

Once you get to Drivers & Support, find your particular printer in the list. Click on that link, and on the next page, click on Drivers & Downloads (choose Windows or Macintosh). On that page is a link to the printer's Premium ICC Profiles page.

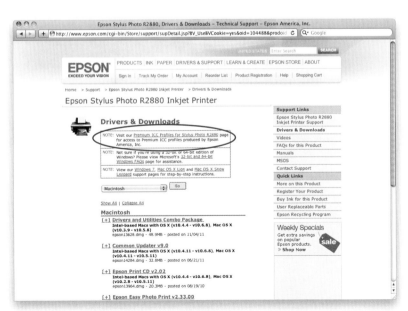

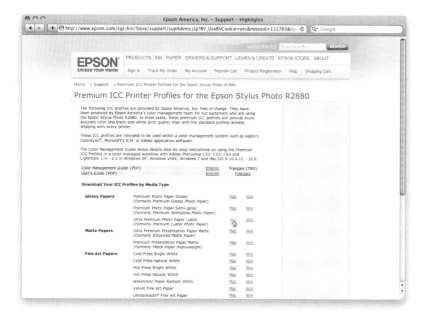

Step Three:

When you click that link, a page appears with a list of Mac and Windows ICC profiles for Epson's papers and printers. I primarily print on two papers: (1) Epson's Ultra Premium Photo Paper Luster, and (2) Epson's Velvet Fine Art paper. So, I'd download the ICC profiles for them under Glossy Papers (as shown here) and Fine Art Papers (at the bottom of the window). They download onto your computer, and you just double-click the installer for each one, and they're added to your list of profiles in Photoshop (I'll show how to choose them in the Print dialog a little later). That's it—you download them, double-click to install, and they'll be waiting for you in Photoshop's print dialog. Easy enough. But what if you're not using Epson paper? Or if you have a different printer, like a Canon or an HP?

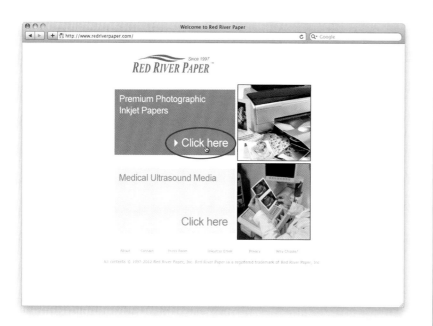

Step Four:

We'll tackle the different paper issue first (because they're tied together). I mentioned earlier that I usually print on Epson papers. I say usually because sometimes I want a final print that fits in a 16x20" standard pre-made frame, without having to cut or trim the photo. In those cases, I use Red River Paper's 16x20" Ultra Pro Satin instead (which is very much like Epson's Ultra Premium Luster, but it's already pre-cut to 16x20"). So, even though you're printing on an Epson printer, now you'd go to Red River Paper's site (www.redriverpaper.com) to find their color profiles for my other printer—the Epson 3880. (Remember, profiles come from the company that makes the paper.) On the Red River Paper homepage is a link for Premium Photographic Inkjet Papers, so click on that.

(Continued)

Step Five:

Once you click that link, things get easier, because on the left side of the next page (under Helpful Info) is a clear, direct link right to their free downloadable color profiles (as seen here). Making profiles easy to find like this is extremely rare (it's almost too easy—it must be a trap, right?). So, click on that Color Profiles link and it takes you right to the profiles for Epson printers, as seen in Step Six (how sweet is that?).

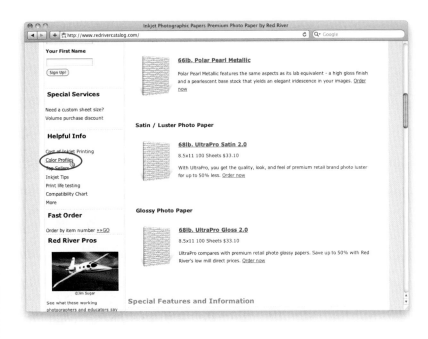

Step Six:

Under the section named Epson Wide Format, there's a direct link to the Epson Pro 3880 (as shown here), but did you also notice that there are ICC Color profiles for the Canon printers, as well? See, the process is the same for other printers, but be aware: although HP and Canon both make pro-quality photo printers, Epson had the pro market to itself for quite a while, so while Epson profiles are created by most major paper manufacturers, you may not always find paper profiles for HP and Canon printers. As you can see at Red River, they widely support Epson, and some Canon profiles are there, too, but there are only a few for HP. That doesn't mean this won't change, but as of the writing of this book, that's the reality. Speaking of change—the look and navigation of websites change pretty regularly, so if these sites look different when you visit them, don't freak out. Okay, you can freak out, but just a little.

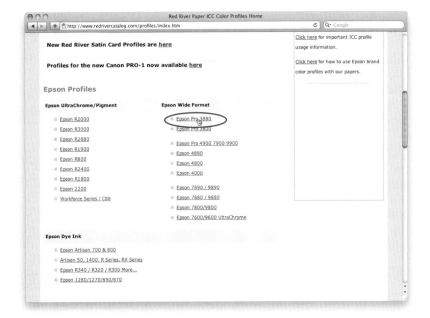

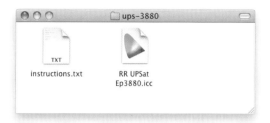

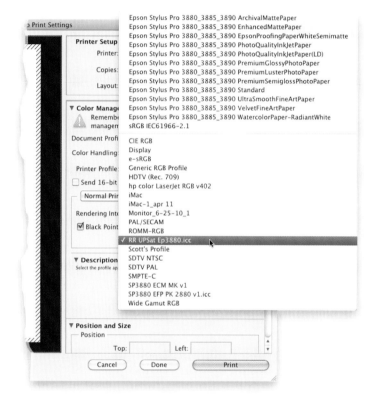

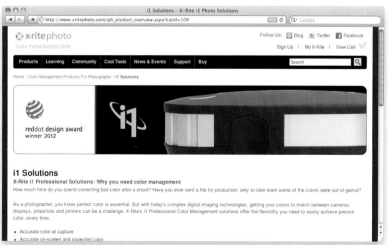

Step Seven:

Although profiles from Epson's website come with an installer, in Red River's case (and in the case of many other paper manufacturers), you just get the profile (shown here) and instructions, so you install it yourself (don't worry—it's easy). On a PC, just Right-click on the profile and choose **Install Profile**. Easy enough. On a Mac, go to your hard disk, open your Library folder, and open your ColorSync folder, where you'll see a Profiles folder. Just drag the file in there and you're set (in Photoshop CS6, you don't even have to restart Photoshop—it automatically updates).

Step Eight:

Now, you'll access your profile by choosing **Print** from Photoshop's File menu. In the Print dialog, change the Color Handling pop-up menu to **Photoshop Manages Color**. Then, click on the Printer Profile pop-up menu, and your new color profile(s) will appear (as shown here). In our example, I'm printing to an Epson 3880 using Red River's Ultra Pro Satin paper, so that's what I'm choosing here as my printer profile (it's named RR UPSat Ep3880.icc). More on using these color profiles later in this chapter.

TIP: Creating Your Own Profiles

You can also pay an outside service to create a custom profile for your printer. You print a test sheet (which they provide), overnight it to them, and they'll use an expensive colorimeter to measure your test print and create a custom profile. The catch: it's only good for that printer, on that paper, with that ink. If anything changes, your custom profile is just about worthless. Of course, you could do your own personal printer profiling (using something like one of X-Rite's i1 Solutions), so you can re-profile each time you change paper or inks. It's really determined by your fussiness/time/money factor (if you know what I mean).

Making the Print (Finally, It All Comes Together)

Okay, so at this point, you've set Photoshop to the proper color space for the type of photo you're going to be printing (RAW, JPEG, TIFF, etc., see page 356), you've hardware calibrated your monitor (see page 361), and you've even downloaded a printer profile for the exact printer model and style of paper you're printing on. In short—you're there. Luckily, you only have to do all that stuff once—now we can just sit back and print. Well, pretty much. Also, in CS6, Adobe added some nice new tweaks to the Photoshop Print Settings dialog, which we'll cover here.

Step One:
Go under Photoshop's File menu and choose **Print** (as shown here) or just press **Command-P (PC: Ctrl-P)**.

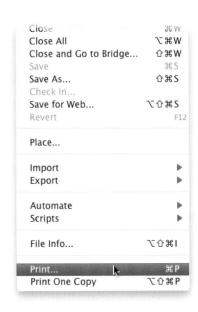

Step Two:
When the Photoshop Print Settings dialog appears, let's choose your printer first. At the top right, choose the printer you want to print to from the Printer pop-up menu (here, I'm going to be printing to my Epson Stylus Pro 3880). You can choose your page orientation by clicking on the portrait and landscape Layout icons at the bottom of the Printer Setup section (as shown here). By the way, if you've used this dialog before in previous versions of Photoshop, you'll be happy to know that now, in Photoshop CS6, you can actually resize the dialog to any size you'd like by clicking on the bottom-right corner and dragging it out. Here I dragged it out to the right, so I could see my preview much larger, and it was at that moment that I realized that I wasn't seeing the full image (it's not cropped that tight to the top of her head).

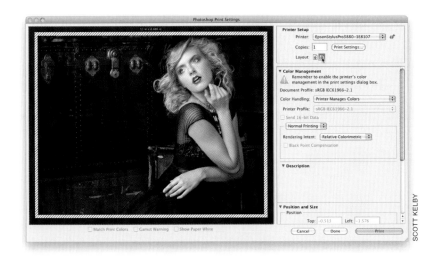

SCOTT KELBY

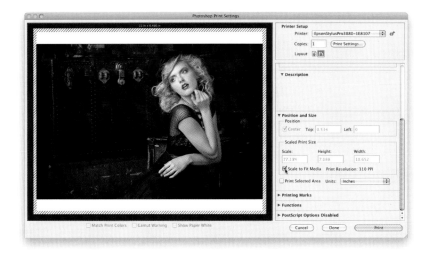

Step Three:

If you want your image to fit fully on the page, scroll down to the Position and Size section and turn on the Scale to Fit Media checkbox (as shown here) and it scales the image down in size, so the entire image fits on the page without being cropped (now you can see the rest of her hat, and the image is much wider than what we saw back in Step Two). Just so you know: I have no problem turning this Scale to Fit Media checkbox on if my image is going to shrink in size to fit the paper, but if turning that on would wind up increasing the size, I'll hit the Cancel button and go to the Image Size dialog (under the Image menu) and resize it there, so I have control over the upsizing process (see page 139).

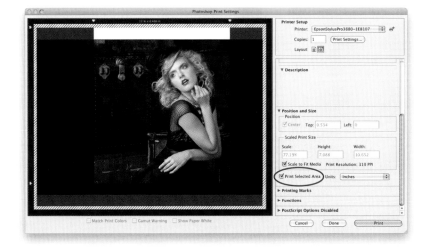

Step Four:

While we're talking about size; there's another new Print feature added in Photoshop CS6 called Print Selected Area, and it gives you the ability to just print part of your image (so, it's kind of like cropping the print without actually cropping the image itself). You do this in the Position and Size section of the dialog by turning on the Print Selected Area checkbox. When you turn this on, you'll see little arrows appear around the corners of your image. Just click-and-drag these in toward your image, and as you do, it darkens the areas to be cropped away (as seen here, where I've dragged those arrows on the top left, top right, and lower left). Now, only the area that's not darkened will actually wind up being printed on the page.

(Continued)

Step Five:

Another new resizing feature added in Photoshop CS6 is the ability to just click-and-drag on your photo to reposition and/or resize it (I know what you're thinking: "Couldn't we always do that?" Believe it or not, no). To use this new feature, first make sure the Scale to Fit Media check-box is turned off, and then click-and-drag the image around so you can reach a corner handle surrounding your image. Then, just click-and-drag a corner handle inward, and it resizes your image (kind of like Free Transform does, but you don't have to hold the Shift key to keep the resizing proportional—it does that automatically). Here, I scaled the image down in size and positioned it where I wanted by just clicking-and-dragging it in the preview area. Now, before we go on to the next step, you're probably wondering what that lined area around the outside edge of your paper is all about. That's showing you where the margins are (the non-printable areas of your paper).

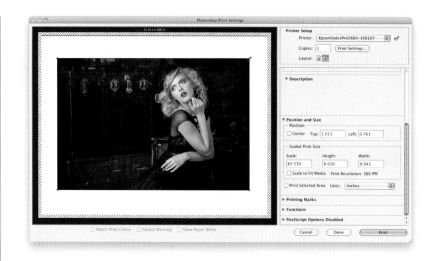

Step Six:

If you want to be able to print all the way to the border (and have those margin lines and non-printable areas go away), all you have to do is to set your margins to 0 inches. You do this by clicking on the Print Settings button in the top right of the dialog (it's shown circled here in red) to bring up your OS Print (PC: Printer Properties) dialog (shown here at the bottom). (Note: I use Epson printers, but if you have a Canon or HP, the dialog will have the same basic function, just in a different layout.) When you choose a paper size that is borderless (as shown here), you can now print to the edges of the paper (well, as long as your printer supports edge-to-edge printing, of course). Now, take a look at the preview—the margin area lines are gone.

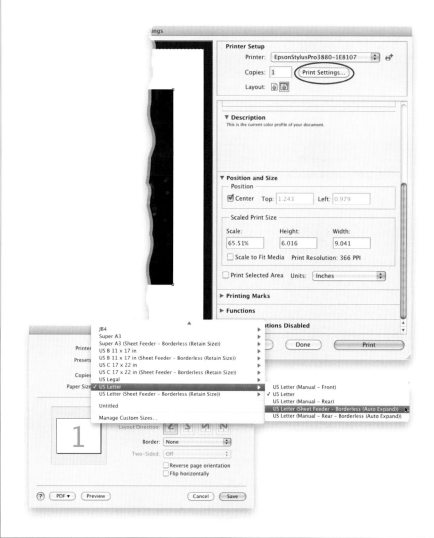

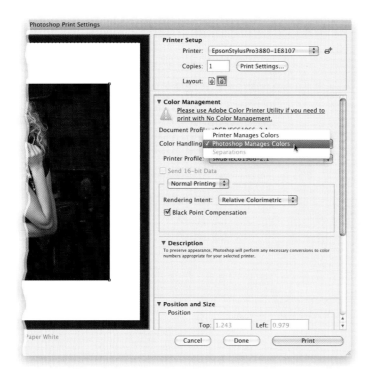

Step Seven:

Okay, now let's turn on our Color Management, so our prints will match what we see onscreen. In the Color Management section, you'll see that, by default, the Color Handling is set up to have your printer manage colors (instead of Photoshop). You really only want to choose this if you weren't able to download any printer/paper profiles for your printer. Having your printer manage colors like this is your backup plan, not your first choice. But, today's printers have gotten to the point that if you have to go with this, it still does a decent job (that wasn't the case just a few years ago). Instead, I recommend that you choose **Photoshop Manages Colors** (as shown here). That way, it uses the color profile we downloaded earlier for our printer and paper combination, which will give us the best possible match.

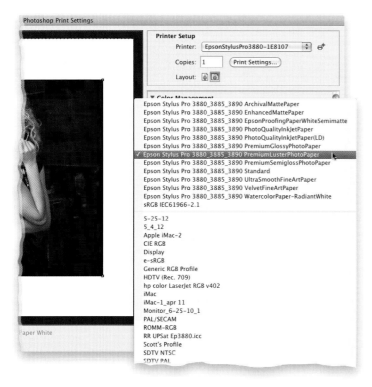

Step Eight:

Next, you'll need to choose that printer/paper profile you downloaded and installed earlier. So, from the Printer Profile pop-up menu, choose the printer/paper profile that matches your printer and paper (here, I'll choose the profile for Ultra Premium Photo Paper Luster). Now, Photoshop and the printer know exactly which paper I'll be printing on, and it's optimized to give us the best possible color print on that printer using that paper (this is very important, because this sends a whole series of instructions to the printer, including everything from the amount of ink it should lay down, to the drying time of the paper, to the proper platen gap for the printer, and so on).

(Continued)

Step Nine:

Next, you'll need to choose the Rendering Intent. There are four choices here, but only two I recommend: either Relative Colorimetric (which is the default setting) or Perceptual. Here's the thing: I've had printers where I got the best looking prints with my Rendering Intent set to Perceptual, but currently, on my Epson Stylus Pro 3880, I get better results when it's set to Relative Colorimetric. So, which one gives the best results for your printer? I recommend printing a photo once using Perceptual, then printing the same photo using Relative Colorimetric, and when you compare the two, you'll know.

TIP: The Gamut Warning Isn't for Us

The Gamut Warning checkbox (beneath the preview area) is not designed for use when printing to a color inkjet (like we are here) or any other RGB printer. It warns you if colors are outside the printable range for a CMYK printing press, so unless you are outputting to a printing press, you can leave this turned off.

Step 10:

Lastly, just make sure the Black Point Compensation checkbox is turned on (it should be by default) to help maintain more detail and color in the shadow areas. Now, click the Print Settings button in the top-right corner (we're not quite done yet).

WARNING: If you're printing to a color inkjet printer, don't ever convert your photo to CMYK format (even though you may be tempted to because your printer uses cyan, magenta, yellow, and black inks). The conversion from RGB to CMYK inks happens within the printer itself, and if you do it first in Photoshop, your printer will attempt to convert it again in the printer, and your printed colors will be way off.

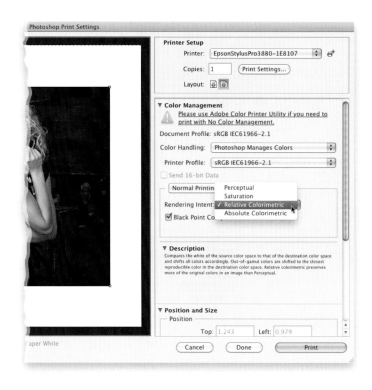

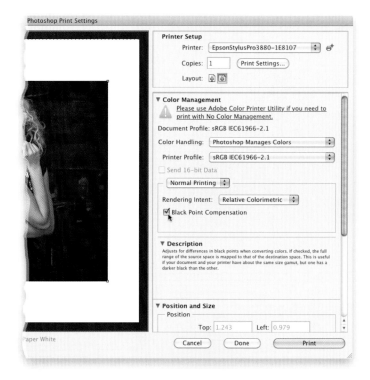

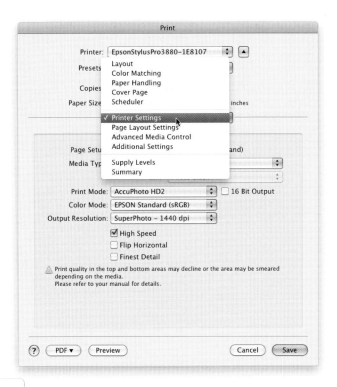

Step 11:

In your OS Print (PC: Printer Properties) dialog (again, I use Epson printers, so your dialog may look different), your printer will already be chosen in the Printer pop-up menu. On a PC, you'll skip the Print dialog and just see your printer's options. From the Layout pop-up menu, choose **Print Settings** (as shown here), so we can configure the printer to give us the best-quality prints.

WARNING: From this point on, what appears in the Layout pop-up menu is contingent on your particular printer's options. You may or may not be able to access these same settings, so you may need to view each option to find the settings you need to adjust. If you're using a Windows PC, you may have to click on the Advanced tab or an Advanced button to be able to choose from similar settings.

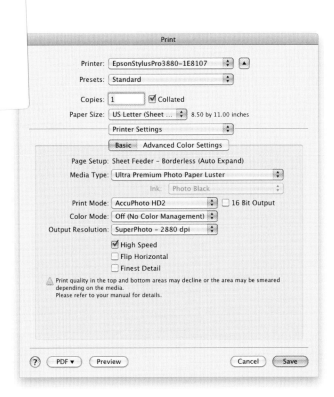

Step 12:

First, from the Media Type pop-up menu, choose your paper type. Then, choose your Output Resolution from that pop-up menu (on a PC, choose Quality Options from the Print Quality pop-up menu, then use the slider to set the quality level). I use SuperPhoto - 2880 dpi, because I want to get the highest possible quality (little known fact: at 2880 dpi, it doesn't use more ink—it just takes longer). Next, choose **Off (No Color Management)** from the Color Mode pop-up menu (on a PC, click on the Custom radio button and choose Off [No Color Adjustment] from the Mode pop-up menu). You want no color adjustment from your printer— you're letting Photoshop manage your color instead. Now you're ready to print, so click the Save (PC: OK) button to go back to Photoshop's Print dialog, and hit the Print button to get prints that match your screen, as you've now color man-aged your photo from beginning to end.

Soft Proofing in Photoshop

This is only the second edition of this book to include how to do soft proofing, because I don't use—or recommend—soft proofing myself, and I don't want to include techniques I don't really use. But, I have had so many people ask me about it, I felt I had to include it. Just know that my advice about this is simple: nothing beats a real proof. If you're serious about making great prints, make a test print—soft proofing just gives you a hint of what it might look like. A test print is what it actually looks like. Okay, I'm off my soap box. Here's how it's done:

Step One:

Start by downloading the free color profile from the company that makes the paper you're going to be printing on (see page 364 for where to get these and how to install them). Open the image you want to soft proof, then under the View menu, under Proof Setup, choose **Custom** (as shown here).

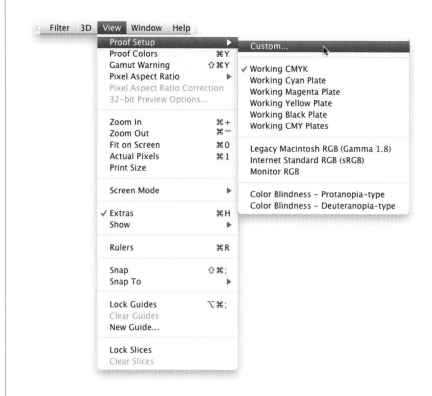

Step Two:

When the Customize Proof Condition dialog appears, from the Device to Simulate pop-up menu, choose the color profile for the printer/paper combo you'll be using (here, I've chosen an Epson Stylus Pro 3880 printing to Velvet Fine Art Paper). Next, choose the Rendering Intent (see page 372 for more on this), and make sure you leave Black Point Compensation turned on. Down in the Display Options (On-Screen) section, leave Simulate Paper Color and Simulate Black Ink both turned off. You can toggle the Preview checkbox on/off to see a before/after of the simulation of what your print might look like with that profile on that paper (though, of course, it can't simulate how your sharpening might look on different papers, just the color. Kinda). Give it a try and then compare it with a real test print, and you'll be able to determine if soft proofing is for you.

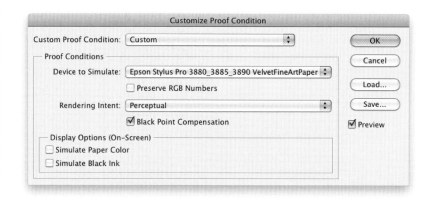

Okay, what do you do if you followed all these steps—you've hardware calibrated your monitor, you've got the right paper profiles, and color profiles, and profiles of profiles, and so on, and you've carefully turned on every checkbox, chosen all the right color profiles, and you've done everything right—but the print still doesn't match what you see onscreen? You know what we do? We fix it in Photoshop. That's right—we make some simple tweaks that get the image looking right fast.

What to Do If the Print Still Doesn't Match Your Screen

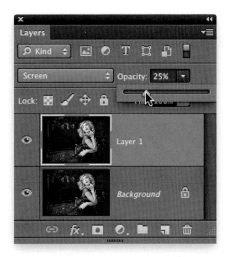

Your Print Is Too Dark

This is one of the most common problems, and it's mostly because today's monitors are so much more incredibly brighter (either that, or you're literally viewing your images in a room that's too dark). Luckily, this is an easy fix and here's what I do: Press **Command-J (PC: Ctrl-J)** to duplicate the Background layer, then at the top of the Layers panel, change the layer blend mode to **Screen** to make everything much brighter. Now, lower the Opacity of this layer to 25% and (this is key here) make a test print. Next, look at the print, and see if it's a perfect match, or if it's still too dark. If it's still too dark, set the Opacity to 35% and make another test print. It'll probably take a few test prints to nail it, but once you do, your problem is solved (by the way, this is a great thing to make into an action).

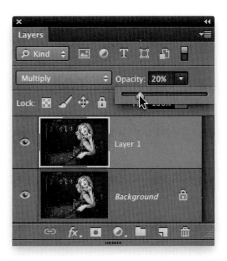

Your Print Is Too Light

This is less likely, but just as easy to fix. Duplicate the Background layer, then change the layer blend mode to **Multiply** to make everything darker. Now, lower the Opacity of this layer to 20% and make a test print. Again, you may have to make a few test prints to get the right amount, but once you've got it, you've got it. Now, make that into an action (name it something like "Prep for Print") and any time you print, just run that action first.

(Continued)

Your Print Is Too Red (Blue, etc.)

This is one you might run into if your print has some sort of color cast. First, before you mess with the image, press the letter **F** on your keyboard to put a solid gray background behind your photo, and then just look to see if the image onscreen actually has too much red. If it does, then press **Command-U (PC: Ctrl-U)** to bring up Hue/Saturation. From the second pop-up menu, choose **Reds**, then lower the Saturation amount to –20%, and then (you knew this was coming, right?) make a test print. You'll then know if 20% was too much, too little, or just right. Once you make a few test prints and nail it, save those steps as an action and run it before you print each time.

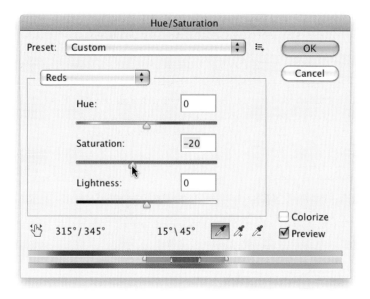

Your Print Has Visible Banding

The more you've tweaked an image, the more likely you'll run into this (where the colors have visible bands, rather than just smoothly graduating from color to color. It's most often seen in blue skies). There are two ways to deal with this: If you shot in RAW, make sure you keep the image in 16-bit mode (don't have it down sample to 8-bit when it leaves Camera Raw). Click the Workflow Options link beneath the Preview area in Camera Raw, and choose **16 Bits/Channel** from the Depth pop-up menu. Stay in 16-bit through the entire printing process. If your original was a JPEG, then there's no going back to a 16-bit original (and just converting to 16-bit mode does nothing), so instead try this: Go under the Filter menu, under Noise, and choose **Add Noise**. In the dialog, set the Amount to 4%, click on the Gaussian radio button, and turn on the Monochromatic checkbox. You'll see the noise onscreen, but it disappears when you print the image (and usually, the banding disappears right along with it).

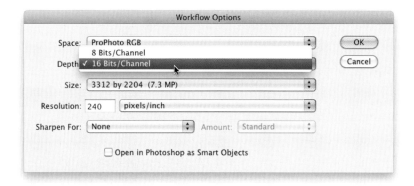

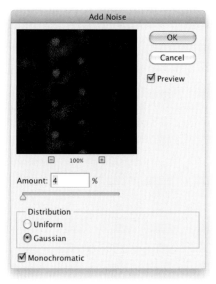

For reasons known only to a secret society of Adobe engineers (who meet in underground catacombs buried deep below Adobe's headquarters and lit solely by torches), they chose to remove the Contact Sheet feature from the previous version of Photoshop (CS5). I guess they assumed we'd use the PDF Contact Sheet in Bridge, which can only mean they never actually tried it themselves. Thankfully, after the public stormed Adobe's headquarters with axes and pitchforks, they brought Contact Sheet II back in CS6, and the balance of power has been restored to the kingdom. Here's how to unleash its wrath:

Making Contact Sheets (Yup, It's Back!)

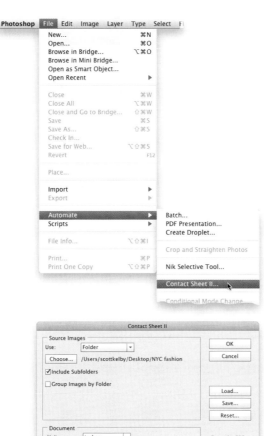

Step One:

To launch Contact Sheet II (the II part comes from the fact that this is the second version of this automated script, a big improvement over the first one. But, honestly when I heard Adobe was bringing this back, I was hoping for Contact Sheet III. Sigh), go under the File menu, under Automate, and choose **Contact Sheet II** (as shown here).

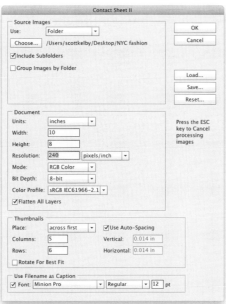

Step Two:

This brings up the Contact Sheet II dialog, where you get to choose how your contact sheet will look. You start at the top by clicking on the Choose button and selecting which folder of images you want to create a contact sheet of. In the next section down, Document, you get to choose the size and resolution of your contact sheet. In our example, we're going to make a wide 10x8" sheet at a resolution of 240 ppi (pretty standard resolution for a color inkjet printer). I always leave the Flatten All Layers checkbox turned on, so when it's done I'm not looking in my Layers panel and seeing 36 different layers, and that's pretty much what you'll get if you choose not to flatten all layers.

(Continued)

Step Three:

The next section down, Thumbnails, is where you choose how many columns and rows you want. In our example, we're going to do six across, with three rows deep. I generally leave the Use Auto-Spacing checkbox turned on, because it has Photoshop do the math to figure out how to make the thumbnails in your contact sheet as large as possible. However, if you turn that checkbox off, you can type in what you'd like for your vertical and horizontal spacing (the only time I would do this is if I wanted more space along the top and sides. As you'll see in the next step, this one has them spread out, so they're really close to the side edges of the paper and pretty darn close to the top and bottom).

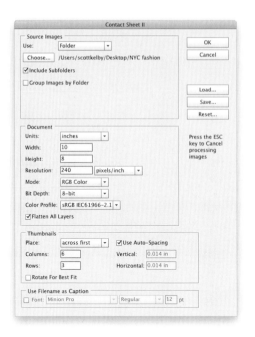

Step Four:

The last section, at the bottom of the dialog, is pretty important (even though I don't have it turned on here), and that is the option for the filename of each photo to appear below the thumbnail. If you're using this as a proof sheet for a client, that's pretty important. My only recommendation for this would be to use a smaller font size than the default 12 point, which always seems too large to me (especially if you have a long file-name). Try 9 or 10 point, and I also would try a sans serif font, like Myriad Pro (rather than the default Minion Pro), simply because it looks better. Now, click the OK button up top, and in about 20 or 30 seconds, the contact sheet you see here appears. This particular one uses 18 photos (6 columns by 3 rows), but if your folder contains more than 18 photos, it just keeps making more contact sheets until every photo is accounted for.

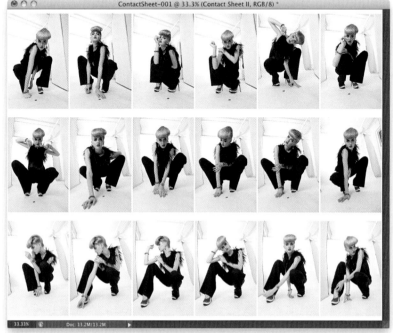

Photoshop Killer Tips

Using CS6 on a MacBook Pro?

Then you've probably experienced a weird thing where all of a sudden your screen rotates, or your image suddenly zooms in (or out). It's because the track pad on a MacBook Pro supports Gestures, which are great for most things, but tend to drive you insane when using Photoshop. You can turn off Gestures by pressing **Command-K (PC: Ctrl-K)** to bring up Photoshop's Preferences, then click on Interface (in the list on the left) and, in the Options section, turn off the Enable Gestures checkbox.

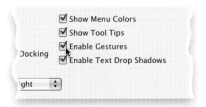

Canceling an Adjustment Layer Edit

If you're working with an adjustment layer, and you want to cancel your edit and return to the adjustment defaults, click the curved arrow at the bottom of the Properties panel. If you don't want the adjustment layer at all, you can quickly delete it by clicking on the Trash icon, also at the bottom of the panel.

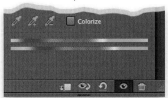

What's That ✳ Up in Your Document's Title Bar Mean?

That's just letting you know that the image you're working on has an embedded color profile that's different from the one you chose in Photoshop (for example, you'd see this if you brought an image over from Lightroom, whose default color space is

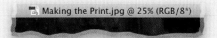

ProPhoto RGB, but Photoshop's default color space is sRGB, so since the two don't match, it just puts that asterisk up top in case you care).

Tip for Finding Out Which Fonts Look Best with Your Layout

This is a handy tip, especially if you're doing poster layouts, and you want to find just the right font to complement your photo. Go ahead and create some type, then double-click on the Type layer's thumbnail in the Layers panel to select

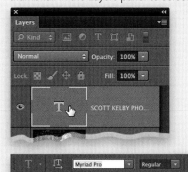

all your type. Now, click your cursor once in the Font field up in the Options Bar, and you can use the **Up/Down Arrow keys** on your keyboard to scroll through all the installed fonts on your system, and your highlighted type changes live onscreen as you do.

Refining Your Masks Using Color Range

If you've created a layer mask, and want to tweak it a bit, you can add the Color Range feature as part of your tweaking arsenal. I use this to quickly select images that are on a white background. Try this: Click on the Add Layer Mask icon at the bottom of the Layers panel (you'll have to be on

a duplicate or unlocked layer), then go under the Select menu, and choose **Color Range**. With the first Eyedropper tool on the left (below the Save button), click on the background once (not in the image itself, in the mask preview right there in the Color Range dialog), and then raise the Fuzziness amount until it selects the background. That usually does most of the masking for me. Click OK, and now you can quickly paint in any missing parts using the Brush tool set to paint in black. This gives you a mask of the background selection. To make your mask a selection of your subject, make sure the mask is selected, and press **Command-I (PC: Ctrl-I)** to Invert it.

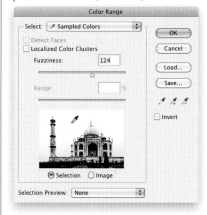

Change Your Background Canvas Color

By default, the area around your document is a dark gray color, but you can choose any color you'd like by just Right-clicking anywhere on that gray canvas area and choosing **Select Custom Color** from the pop-up menu.

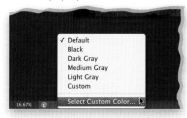

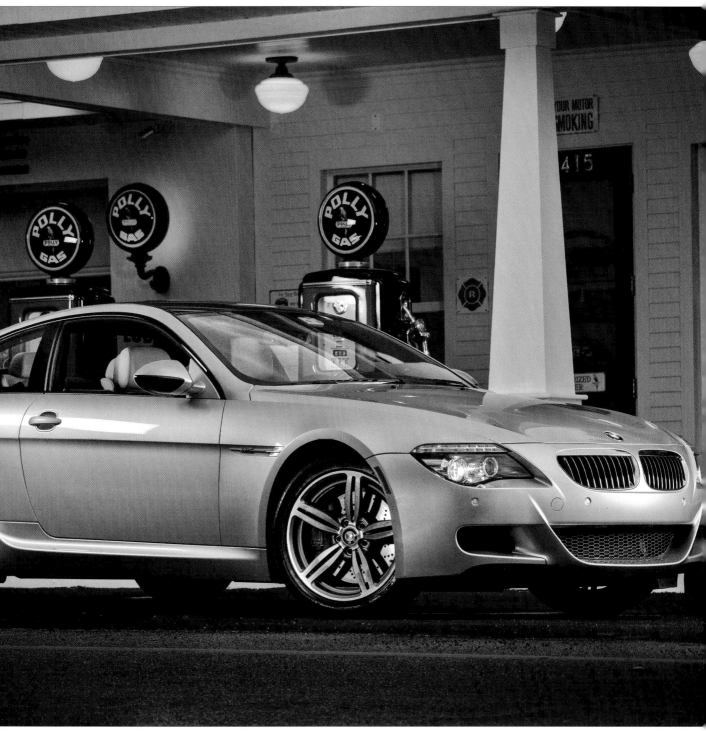

Photo by Scott Kelby   Exposure: 1/125 sec | Focal Length: 116 mm | Aperture Value: ƒ/8

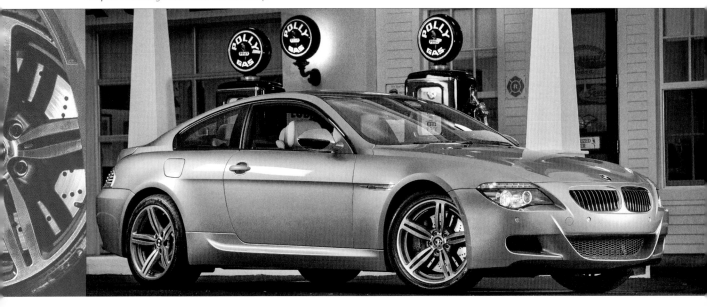

Videodrome
editing DSLR video in photoshop

The name of this chapter comes from the 1983 movie of the same name starring Debbie Harry, lead singer of the '80s band Blondie, in what I can only imagine was her film debut and simultaneous film career exit, since I never heard of Debbie Harry starring in any other movies. Now, in all honesty, I might be jumping the gun on this one, so in all fairness to Ms. Harry, I'm pausing this chapter intro right now to go and check the official online source for anything to do with movies, and that is, of course, www.homedepot.com (okay, not really, but I gotta tell ya, they had a pretty sweet deal on a DeWalt 18-Volt ½ in. Cordless Impact Wrench). Anyway, instead, I went and checked IMDb (the Internet Movie Database), and I have to tell you, I was pretty shocked to find out that Debbie Harry was actually listed as an actress in 53 movies and TV shows. 53! Digging a little deeper (not really), I learned that none of those were put together using Photoshop's built-in video capabilities, because prior to CS6, Photoshop barely had any serious video editing capabilities. I mean, you could do a few things, but nothing like the complexity you see in Debbie Harry's 2011 (pre-CS6) movie short *Pipe Dreams*, where she played Iris, a young undocumented worker from Ecuador. (Oh, I can see where this is going. They never have their documentation, now, do they?) According to IMBb, the movie pretty much takes place in an aging smoking-pipe manufacturing plant. Geesh—not that tired old scenario again. I can probably tell you the ending already. Let me guess: she gets hooked on tobacco products and winds up hitch-hiking to North Carolina, where she meets an aging nicotine salesman from Raleigh who convinces her to become a documented worker, and then the two open a small pet bakery/mobile spray-tanning business in Jacksonville, against the wishes of her controlling Canadian rebel–fighting parents and Kreshnik, her half-blind Albanian ex-fiancé and father of their illegitimate teacup schnauzer, Mr. Buttersticks. Tell me you didn't see that one coming, right?

Four Things You'll Want to Know Now About Creating Video in Photoshop CS6

I truly believe this video feature in Photoshop is a game changer. You can hardly find a digital camera today (DSLR or point-and-shoot) that doesn't shoot HD-quality video, yet most of the photographers I talk to that have shot video with their DSLR just have a bunch of individual movie clips in a folder on their computer, and never create a movie with them. I asked why and they basically said, "Photoshop is hard enough. I don't have time to learn a video-editing program." That's why I think this is so important. Now, we can edit video in a program we already know, and finally, we'll start turning those clips into movies.

① It Helps to Have Lots of RAM

When it comes to video, more is more. Ideally, you'd have a minimum of 8 GB of RAM, but the more the merrier, because unlike still images, video has to "render" (which it does in RAM), and the more RAM you have, the faster you'll be able to preview clips without them being jumpy or jittery.

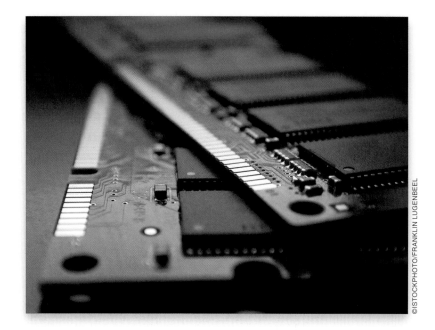

©ISTOCKPHOTO/FRANKLIN LUGENBEEL

② It's Ideal for Making Short Movies

Although you could make a 20- or 30-minute movie in Photoshop, it's really best suited for short movies—the kind of videos wedding photographers might create, or promo videos for a photographer's website, or short demos, or commercials. If you need to make something longer and more complex, then you should make a number of short movies in Photoshop, and then combine all these shorter clips into one longer final version at the end. If you're thinking of making an epic motion picture, you should probably choose something made for that type of stuff, like Premiere Pro.

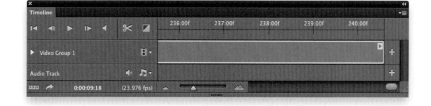

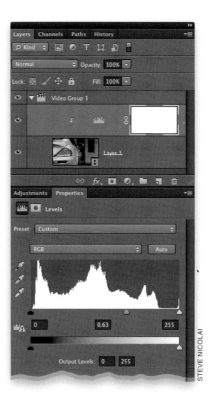

STEVE NICOLAI

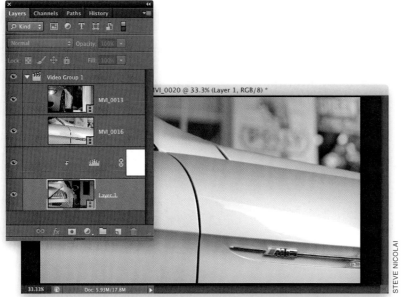

STEVE NICOLAI

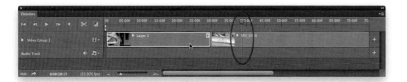

❸ You Can Apply Photoshop Adjustments and Filters to Your Movies

I think one of the best things about editing video in Photoshop is that you get to use the same tools you're already familiar with from working on digital photos. We're talking everything from Levels and Curves adjustments, to filters like Gaussian Blur and Unsharp Mask, and you resize things using Free Transform. Once you learn the timeline (which you'll do in this chapter), then the rest seems very familiar.

❹ What You See Onscreen Is Different When You Do Video

You can't just click on things (like a video clip or a Type layer) and have them display onscreen. If you want to see something, you have to move the playhead in the timeline to the spot in the movie where that thing appears. That's because wherever the playhead is right now is what you're seeing onscreen. This takes a bit of getting used to. For example, here I clicked on the first clip to select it, and in regular Photoshop thinking, that would mean, "Hey, I want to see this clip," but if you look at the playhead (the blue knob with the red vertical line, circled in red here), it's on the second clip, and what's under the playhead is what you see onscreen. That's exactly what you're seeing here—that part of the second clip. You'll get used to it, but it'll catch you a few times where you're just sitting there wondering, "Why isn't it showing my clip?" Now when that happens, you'll go look to see where the playhead is.

Opening Your Video Clips into Photoshop

You can open a video clip to start building your movie like it was any other file, so getting a clip to open in Photoshop is easy (especially since Photoshop supports all the most common movie file formats found in DSLRs), but this isn't about just opening a video clip in Photoshop to start your movie project. This is really about what to do after you've started your video project, because knowing what to do next (how to add more clips to your movie) can save you a lot of time and frustration. Later, you'll get to mix video and still (and have audio, as well), so learning this first is worth the quick read.

Step One:
Once your movie clips have been imported from your DSLR onto your computer, you can open these clips in Photoshop just like you would any other file—by going under the File menu and choosing **Open**, or double-clicking on a video clip in Mini Bridge, which is what I did here (go ahead and open a video clip. If you don't have one, you can download the ones I'm using here). When it opens, Photoshop knows it's a video file and it automatically opens the Timeline panel across the bottom (seen here), which is where we put our movie together. The length of the blue bar corresponds to how long the video is (in minutes and seconds). The longer the bar, the longer the video clip.

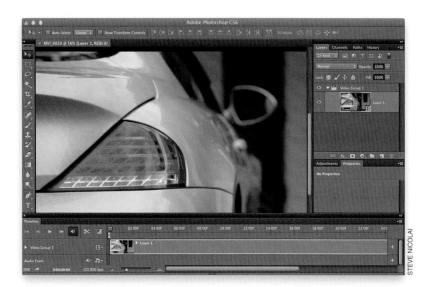

Step Two:
If you want to add another video clip to play right after this clip, then you'd click on that little filmstrip icon to the right of Video Group 1 on the left side of the Timeline panel (it's shown circled here in red), and choose **Add Media**. In the Add Clips dialog, navigate to the next video clip, select it, and click Open. This adds that video clip right after your first clip (the clips play in order, from left to right in the Timeline panel).

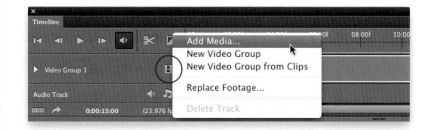

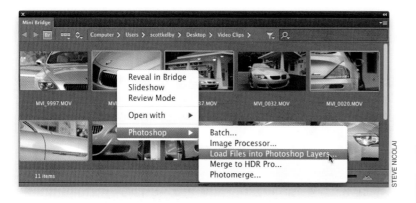

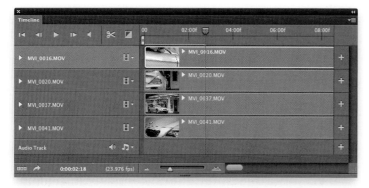

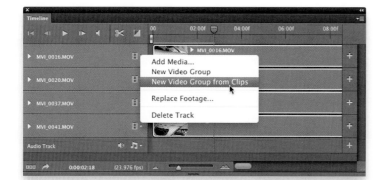

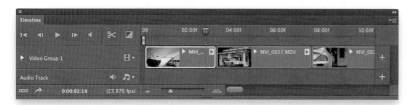

Step Three:

If you want to load multiple clips at once, just Command-click (PC: Ctrl-click) on each one to select them in Mini Bridge, then Right-click on any one of them and, from the pop-up menu that appears, go under Photoshop, and choose **Load Files into Photoshop Layers**. That opens the files in Photoshop with each on its own layer. But if you look in the Timeline panel, you'll see that they're not appearing one after another (meaning one clip plays, then the next clips plays, and so on). Instead, they're stacked one on top of another (all the clips play at once, which is bad, since all you'll see is the top clip—it covers the rest).

Step Four:

Luckily, we can have Photoshop move them into a Video Group, which puts them one after another for us. Just select all the clips in the Timeline panel (click on one, then Command-click [PC: Ctrl-click] on the rest). Then, click on the little filmstrip icon next to any track and, from the pop-up menu, choose **New Video Group from Clips**. That's it—Photoshop rearranges them so they're now one after another in the timeline, and the clips will play one after the other now, as well. If you look in the Layers panel, you'll see them inside what looks like a layer group. What's cool is that you can actually change the order your clips play in by changing the order of your layers in the Layers panel. The layer on the bottom plays first, then the layer above that plays right after it, and so on.

Your Basic Controls for Working with Video

The panel where almost everything video-related happens is called the Timeline panel. Most video editors are based on this same idea, because it's a very visual way to put together a movie. You build your movie from left to right, just like you would a slide show, where the first thumbnail is the first slide, then the one to the right of that is the second, and so on. Same thing with video, except, of course, that the thumbnails are videos. Take two minutes now to learn the Timeline panel and its basic controls, and it'll make your video editing life a lot easier.

Step One:
You play, rewind, and fast-forward your video in Photoshop just like you would in any other video player (using the standard Rewind [Go to Previous Frame], Play, and Fast-Forward [Go to Next Frame] icons). However, there is a "rewind to the beginning" icon (it's actually the Go to First Frame icon) that you'll wind up using quite a bit (it's the first icon, just to the left of Rewind).

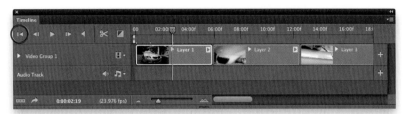

The Go to First Frame icon takes you back to the very beginning

Step Two:
Now, click on the down-facing arrow in the top right of the Timeline panel, and from the flyout menu, choose **Enable Timeline Shortcut Keys** to turn on your shortcuts for the panel. There's a great shortcut you can use to play your video: just hit the **Spacebar** on your keyboard. It starts (and then stops) your video. To jump to the beginning of the individual clip that is curently selected, press the **Up Arrow key** on your keyboard. To jump to the end of that clip, press the **Down Arrow key**.

TIP: Put Your Playhead at Any Spot
To move your playhead to any spot you want it in the timeline, just click once up at the top of the timeline, right on where the seconds are listed, and your playhead immediately jumps to that spot.

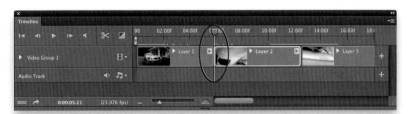

Pressing the Up Arrow key jumps the playhead back to the beginning of the selected clip. The Down Arrow key jumps you to the end

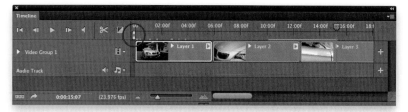

By default, the start of the work area is the start of your movie

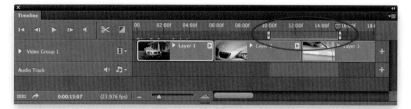

Drag the Start and End Work Area bars to change where your playhead starts and stops (so when you click Play, it will start 10 seconds into your movie, at the left bar, and stop 15 seconds in, at the right one)

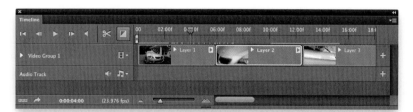

To jump back 1 second in the timeline, press Shift–Up Arrow. To jump forward 1 second, press Shift–Down Arrow

Step Three:

If you know you want your movie to be a specific length, like maybe 30 or 60 seconds for a commercial, or 90 seconds for a promo movie, you can keep from having to scroll back and forth down your timeline by setting up your work area to display just that amount of time from the very beginning. You do that by dragging the little Set Start of Work Area bar at the beginning of the timeline or the Set End of Work Area bar at the end of the timeline to the length you want your movie. That way, when your playhead hits the end of your work area (after playing for 30 seconds), it stops (it doesn't just keep playing nothing). Also, if you want to work on just one part of a longer video, then you can drag the Set Start of Work Area bar to the beginning of that part, and then drag the Set End of Work Area bar to the end of that area. Now, when you click Play, it starts where you set the start of you work area and stops where you set the end.

Step Four:

There are some other shortcuts you might want to use once you really dig into this, but for now, I'd just concentrate on those ones I've given you here, because they're the ones you'll use every time you make a movie. Just in case you need them, though, here are a few more: To jump back one frame, press the **Left Arrow key**. Add the **Shift key** to jump back 10 frames. Use the **Right Arrow key** to jump forward one frame; add the Shift key to jump 10 forward. To jump to the end of your timeline, press the **End key** on your keyboard. To jump back 1 second in time, press **Shift–Up Arrow key**. To jump forward 1 second, press **Shift–Down Arrow key**. Again, you may not ever use these, but at least you know they're there.

(Continued)

Step Five:

There are some other important things you'll want to know about the Timeline panel: One is that you can change the size of the thumbnails in the Timeline panel by dragging the size slider at the bottom of the panel (it's shown circled here in red). Dragging to the left makes the thumbnails smaller; dragging to the right makes them larger. The advantage of choosing a smaller thumbnail size is that you'll see more of your movie in the timeline without scrolling (of course, it helps if you have the eyes of a 14-year-old, because if you're any older, you're probably going to need bifocals).

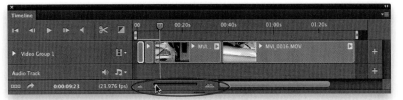

If you zoom out, you can fit the whole 01:40 movie in the timeline without having to scroll over to the right at all

TIP: Rearranging the Order of Clips

There are two ways to change the order of how your clips play: (1) you can drag-and-drop the clips into the order you want right there in the timeline, or (2) you can change the order over in the Layers panel. They stack from bottom (being the first clip to play) to top, so just drag-and-drop the layers into the order you want the clips to play.

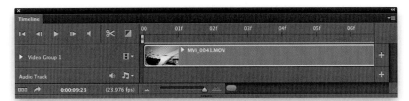

If you zoom way in, now you're just seeing the first 7 seconds of your movie. This is handy when you've got a lot going on (like a bunch of very short clips close together with transitions)

Step Six:

If you want to see a quick preview of any part of your video, you can just grab the playhead and, as you drag it right or left across your video, it plays a preview of the video that's below it (you don't hear any audio, you just see the video). This is called "scrubbing" in "Video Land" (they have a secret code name for everything). This is a huge time saver and you'll find yourself scrubbing over clips quite often.

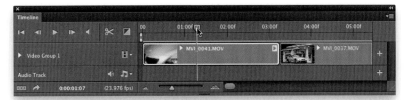

Here, I'm "scrubbing" across the first clip to see a preview of it, without clicking Play

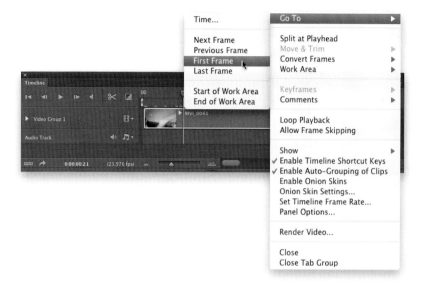

Step Seven:

You know that flyout menu at the top-right corner of the Timeline panel? If you ever can't remember the shortcut to do something, you can most likely do it there. Also, by default, Photoshop uses its regular keyboard shortcuts for everything. For example, if you have the Move tool active, and you press the Up or Down Arrow key on your keyboard, it will move your clip up or down onscreen. However, if you turn on Enable Timeline Shortcut Keys, as we did in Step Two, then it uses the shortcuts I mentioned in that step. So, now the Up Arrow key jumps you to the beginning of the currently selected clip, and the Down Arrow key jumps you to the end of that clip.

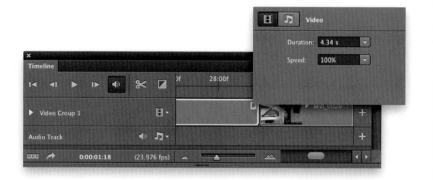

Step Eight:

There's a little right-facing triangle at the end of each video clip and clicking on it brings up a settings dialog with more options for that clip. For example, you can set the Duration in the Video settings here. So, if the clip needed to be 4 minutes exactly, you could set it to 4 minutes exactly by dragging the slider or simply entering 4 minutes in the Duration field. There's also a speed control here. If you click the music notes icon at the top, you'll get the Audio options for just this clip, including the overall volume for the clip's audio (or you can mute the audio), and you can set the audio Fade In and Fade Out points numerically.

Editing (Trimming) Your Clips

When we shoot digital photos, we wind up taking a lot of shots that nobody ever sees in our quest to find a "keeper." Same thing in video. We shoot a lot of footage where some parts at the beginning or end of our video (like us saying "Cut!" at the end of a clip) just need to be deleted. This cropping off of the beginning and/or end of our videos is called "trimming" (you trim off the parts that you don't want anyone to see), but we cover a bit more here than just this, so make sure you don't skip over it if you already know how to trim.

Step One:

Open clip 0020.mov to start a new movie, then click on the little filmstrip icon (to the right of Video Group 1), and choose **Add Media** from the pop-up menu, then choose clip 0008.mov, and it adds that clip right after the first one. Now, click the Play icon and you'll see that the first clip does the same "slide" (moving slowly from left to right) four times in this video clip. We only need one slide move from this angle for our movie, so we need to trim away the other parts of the video we don't need (we need to trim off a lot from the front and a little from the back, as the third time through the slide looked like the best one). All you have to do is click-and-hold directly on the beginning of the clip in the timeline and a little trimming preview window will pop up (as seen here).

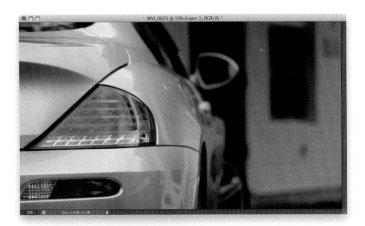

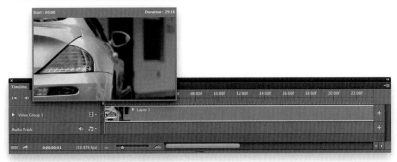

Step Two:

As you drag to the right (this is called "scrubbing" in video world), the preview shows the slide, and then it being reset, and then sliding again. The good one starts right around the 15-second mark in the video, so keep dragging to the right until you get to that point, but stop dragging right before it starts to slide to the left. Now, just let go of your mouse button and it trims off everything before that third slide. It shows the new start time of that clip as 15 seconds and 5 frames.

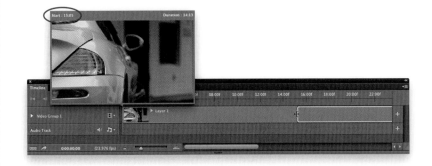

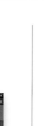

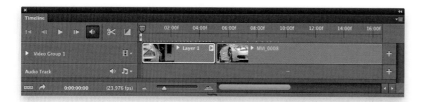

Step Three:

Next, let's do the same thing to the end of the clip and trim away the fourth slide (so all you'll see in this clip is that third slide—the one we want to keep). Scroll sideways down the timeline until you see the end of our first clip. Click-and-hold directly on the end of the clip (that preview window pops up again), and drag to the left while you keep an eye on that preview window. Keep dragging to about the 5:03 end mark (look up in the top-left corner of the preview window and it shows you the time in seconds and frames, so stop around 5 seconds and 3 frames, as shown here). You've now trimmed off everything past the third slide, and your original 28-second video is down to about a 5-second clip overall.

Step Four:

Now, what about that second clip we added that appears immediately after the clip we just trimmed? Won't there be a big gap of nothing between the two clips? Nope. Photoshop automatically moves that clip over for you, so there are no gaps in your movie. Pretty sweet, eh? Here, you can see your two clips, which, even after trimming, are still back-to-back. If you look up at the top of the timeline, you'll see that the first clip is now only around 5 seconds of your movie, and the second clip starts immediately after it. Also, don't worry, even though you trimmed that video away, you can always bring it right back the same way you trimmed it—just click on either end and drag it out (so it's really more like it's hidden, than trimmed, but again, in the world of video, its referred to as "trimming"). Okay, that's all there is to it.

Working with Audio and Background Music

There are three types of audio you'll wind up dealing with in your movies: (1) there's audio in the video you captured with your camera, and you get to decide whether your audience will hear that or not, (2) you can add a background music track behind your video, and (3) you can add additional audio tracks for things like narration or sound effects. Luckily, managing these is fairly easy.

Step One:

We'll pick up with the two clips we used in the previous trimming project. If you look in the Timeline panel, directly below your movie clips, you'll see an empty track right below it (and it says Audio Track to the left of it, below Video Group 1). That's where your audio (background music or narration tracks) goes. To add an audio track, click directly on the little music notes icon and, from the pop-up menu that appears, choose **Add Audio** (as shown here).

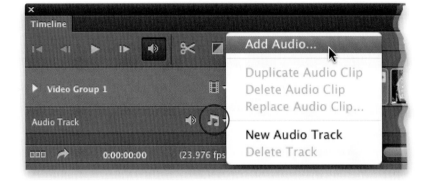

Step Two:

Find the audio track you want to use as your background music (Photoshop supports most common audio file formats, from AAC to MP3). You can go to the book's download page and download the track I used, which is a royalty-free background music track from iStockphoto (they have lots of great background music tracks you can buy and use in your projects. They were gracious enough to let me use this one and share it with you to practice along with. This track was actually featured as their "Free Track of the Day" the day I needed a background track, and it worked perfectly for this project. Total luck). Anyway, once you select your audio file and click Open, it adds your background music to the timeline, where it appears in green so you know instantly it's audio (video clips appear in blue).

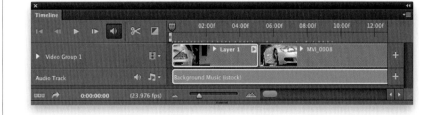

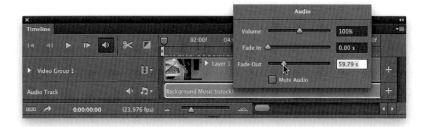

Step Three:

Click the Play icon (or just press the **Spacebar**) to play our short video, and now the background music plays, as well. Makes a huge difference, doesn't it? At the end of this chapter, we're going to build a 60-second-or-so demo video, so just like the video clip, trim the music down to around 60 seconds. But, our music clip is 236 seconds long (almost 4 minutes), so it's going to cut off really abruptly at the end of our video, unless we gently fade the music out. So, Right-click directly on your green audio track and an Audio settings dialog appears, where you can choose when you want the music to fade in (since we're starting at the beginning of the song, we don't need to fade in, but if we started later in the song, we would want it to) and fade out. Drag the Fade Out slider over to around the 60-second mark (as shown here) and click anywhere outside the dia-log to close it. Now, play your movie again and, at the 60-second mark, your music will gently fade away.

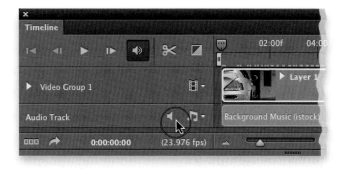

TIP: Muting Your Background Music

If you want to temporarily turn off your background music track, just click the little speaker icon (shown circled here) to the left of the music notes icon, and it mutes your background track.

Step Four:

When you played the video clip in Step Three, did you hear people talking in the background? That's me and my team talk-ing and directing during the shoot. Of course, you don't want to hear that in this case—you just want to hear the back-ground music—so you need to mute the audio on the video clip. Right-click on your first video clip and a settings dialog appears (shown here). Click on the music notes icon to see the Audio settings, then turn on the Mute Audio checkbox (as shown here), so you don't hear us talking while we were taping.

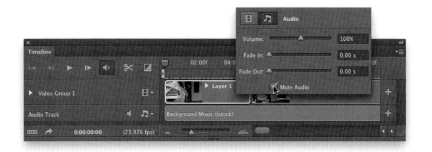

(Continued)

Step Five:

Besides your background music track, you can add a narration track (or a voice-over track), or even sound effects (maybe a car revving its engine?). To add another audio track, click on the music notes icon again (to the left of your existing music track), and choose **New Audio Track** (as shown here at top). This adds a blank audio track below your background music track, and it will be empty until you go back under that same pop-up menu and choose **Add Audio**, then find a narration or voice-over track to add. Here, I chose a voice-over track, and you'll see it appear in the new audio track right below the background track (seen here in the center). If you were to click the Play icon right now, our background music would start, but our voice-over would start immediately, as well. If you want your voice-over to start a little later (maybe after a few seconds of background music), just click-and-drag the voice-over clip to the right (don't try to trim it, you want to move the whole clip), until you get to the point in time you want it to start (at the bottom here, you can see I dragged it over so it will start around the 7-second mark).

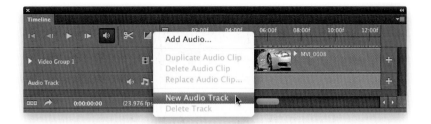

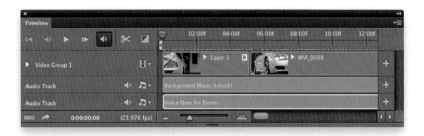

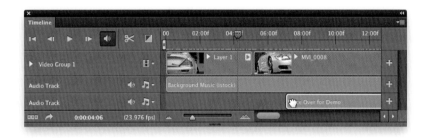

Step Six:

If you are going to have a voice-over track, you'll probably want the volume of the music to lower once the talking starts (this is called "ducking" in the video world). To do that, click on the background music track, then click-and-drag your playhead over to a second or so before the point where your voice-over starts. Now, click on the Split at Playhead icon (it looks like a pair of scissors and is circled in red here) to split your background music into two sections. Then, Right-click on this second section and, in the Audio settings dialog, you can lower the volume from 100% (full volume) to maybe 50% or 60% (as shown here).

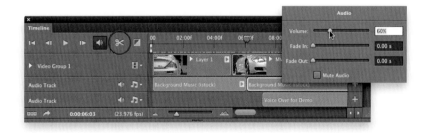

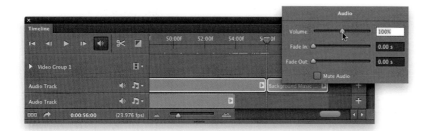

Step Seven:
Of course, at some point your voice-over will end, and you'll probably want the background music to return to full volume. You pretty much do the same thing. Just scroll down the timeline to the point where you can see your voice-over ends and move your playhead to a second or two after that point. Click on the track you want to split (your background music track), then click the Split at Playhead icon again to create a third section of your background music track. Right-click on this third section and set your volume back to 100% (as shown here).

Adding Transitions Between Clips and Fade Ins/Fade Outs

When you make a movie, you get to decide how your movie starts and ends. For example, at the end of the movie, does it just abruptly stop, or does it smoothly fade away to black? Same thing for the opening. Does it just start immediately when you click Play, or fade in from white or black? You also get to decide how your clips transition from clip to clip—a quick cut, or does it smoothly dissolve from one clip to the next? Of course, it depends on the type of movie you're creating, but adding these transitions can help give your movie a more polished look.

Step One:

Here are same two video clips again, and if you click the Play icon (or press the **Spacebar**), the first clip plays and then when it's done, the second clip plays immediately—it just cuts from one clip to the other. To add a nice fade between the two, click on the Transition icon (it looks like a square with a diagonal line), and the Drag to Apply dialog, with your transition choices, appears (seen here). The top one, Fade, doesn't work very well between two clips like this (it fades out at the end of the first clip, then fades in the second clip).

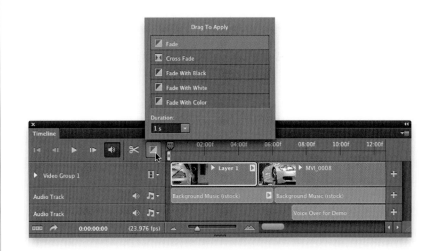

Step Two:

Instead, you'd probably choose a Cross Fade, which fades directly from one clip into the next (kind of like a dissolve in a slide show). To add a cross fade between your clips, first click on Cross Fade in the dialog, and then you get to choose how long you want this cross fade to take. The default choice is 1 second, but you can choose longer if you'd like by clicking on the Duration slider (I chose 1.15 seconds here). Now, just click-and-drag that cross fade down onto your timeline and position it between your two clips (as shown here), and then let go of your mouse button. It adds a little blue rectangle with two triangles (as seen in the next step) letting you know there's a transition added there. To remove a transition, click on that little rectangle and hit the **Delete (PC: Backspace) key** on your keyboard.

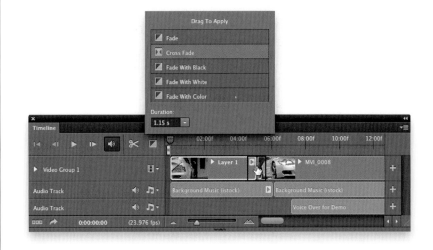

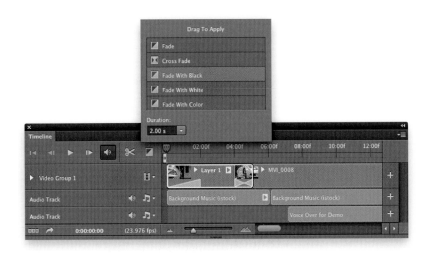

Step Three:

Of the other choices here, I usually use Fade with Black, which is a great way to start your movie, because it starts with a black screen and then fades into your first video clip. However, the default 1-second duration always seems too short and abrupt to me (for the start of a video anyway), so I generally increase the duration to 2 seconds. To add this Fade with Black transition to the beginning of your movie, just click-and-drag it down to the beginning of your video clip and let go of the mouse button. It adds a little blue rectangle with a diagonal line letting you know there's a transition added there.

Tip: Editing Transitions

If you want to make any changes to a transition, just Right-click on it and you can make those changes in the Transition settings that pops up.

Step Four:

So, if you know what Fade with Black does, you can probably imagine what Fade with White does. If you choose Fade with Color, a little color swatch will appear in the bottom-right corner of the dialog (shown here at bottom right). Click on the color swatch and Photoshop's standard Color Picker appears for you to choose a solid color to fade to. At the end of your video, you're probably going to want to Fade with Black (dramatic ending, right?) and you do this the same way as adding any transition. Scroll down the timeline to the very end of your movie and then click the Transition icon to bring up the Drag to Apply dialog. Now, drag the Fade with Black transition and drop it on the end of your video clip. It adds a little "fade out" rectangle to let you know it's there. That's it.

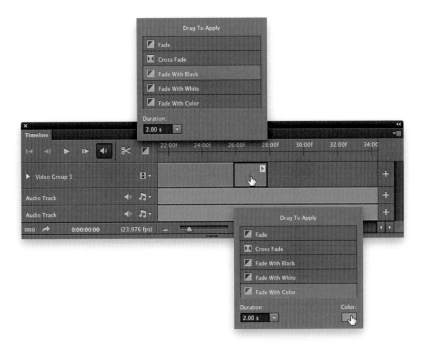

Creating Lower Thirds (or Adding Logos)

If you're doing an interview as your movie, it's pretty common to have the person's name appear in the bottom third of the frame, usually within a rectangle or graphic bar of some kind (called a "lower third" in video world). The trick is to have the background behind your graphic bar appear transparent, so it doesn't cover your video with a solid white background. They're easy to create in Photoshop and then take directly over to your timeline. Plus, the same technique we use for lower thirds, you can use for bringing logos or other graphics into your timeline.

Step One:

Start by creating a regular ol' new document in Photoshop (go under the File menu and choose **New**). You want to make this pretty close to the dimensions of the movie you're creating, so from the Preset pop-up menu, choose **Film & Video**, and then choose a Size that is closest to the size of what you're editing (in this case, we're editing 1080p HD video, so I choose the HDV 1080p/29.97 preset, as shown here), then click OK to create a new blank Photoshop document.

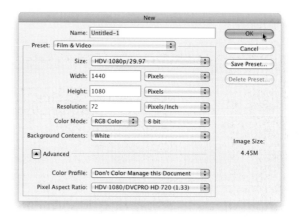

Step Two:

Go to the Layers panel, click on the Create a New Layer icon to create a new blank layer, and then get the Rectangular Marquee tool **(M)** and drag out a long, thin horizontal selection like the one you see here (this will be our simple lower third shape). Press **D** to set your Foreground color to black, and then fill your selected area with black by pressing **Option-Delete (PC: Alt-Backspace)**. Now, while your selection is still in place, click on the Create New Adjustment Layer icon at the bottom of the Layers panel, and choose **Gradient** from the pop-up menu (as shown here). When the Gradient Fill dialog appears, click on the little downward-facing triangle to the right of the Gradient thumbnail, and in the Gradient Picker, click on the little gear icon, and choose **Pastels**. Click Append in the dialog that appears.

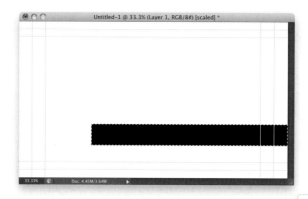

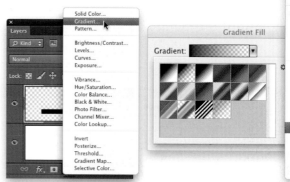

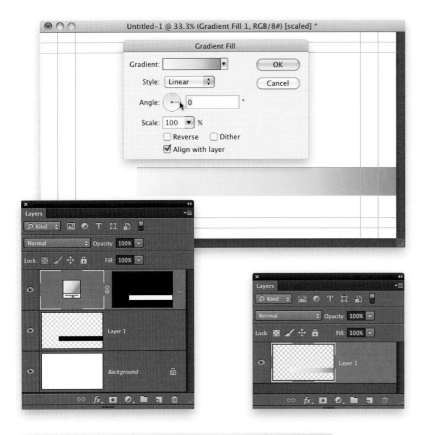

Step Three:

Once they're loaded, choose the Yellow, Green, Blue gradient (seen here), and then change the Angle to 0°, so the gradient is applied sideways (rather than top to bottom). Once it looks like the one you see here, press **Command-E (PC: Ctrl-E)** to merge the Gradient adjustment layer with the black bar layer to make it just one gradient bar layer. Now, we can't just save the file at this point, because we have a solid white Background layer, and that's exactly how this file would appear on our timeline—as a big white box with a gradient bar on it. So, what you need to do is simply drag your Background layer onto the Trash icon at the bottom of the panel. Now, you just have that gradient bar all by itself with a transparent background (as seen in the Layers panel at bottom right), which is exactly what we want in our video (so just the bar sits over our video).

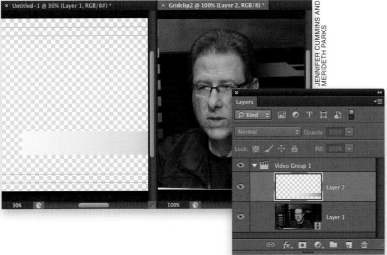

JENNIFER CUMMINS AND MERIDETH PARKS

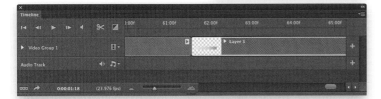

Step Four:

Arrange the two windows (your gradient bar and video clip windows) so you can see them both onscreen at the same time (try going under the Window menu, under Arrange, and choosing **Tile All Vertically**), get the Move tool **(V)**, click on the gradient bar layer, and then just drag-and-drop it right onto your video. Now, you'll see the gradient bar with a transparent background in your Layers panel (which is exactly what we want), but it's not in the place where we want it. By default, it adds it at the end of the video clip, like it was another clip or still (it appears in purple though, because it's a still). We need it to appear "over" the video clip.

(Continued)

Step Five:

What we need to do is get that gradient bar outside our Video Group 1, so it can appear over our video clip (not after it). To do this, click-and-drag the gradient bar layer straight up to the very top of the layer stack in the Layers panel—right outside Video Group 1). The trick to making this work is to move it up top until you see a thin white horizontal line appear. That's your cue to let go of the mouse button, and then it appears outside the group (as seen in the Layers panel here). Here's the "Gotcha!" You still can't see your gradient bar. That's because, although it's now on its own graphics track in the Timeline panel (above your video), it starts after the end of your clip. So, click on the gradient bar in the timeline, and drag it to the left so it appears over the video (as shown here at the bottom). Now (finally), you can see your gradient bar. Switch to the Move tool to reposition your bar wherever you'd like it.

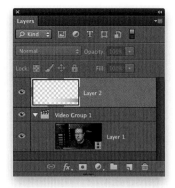

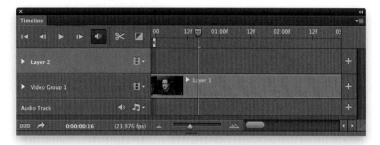

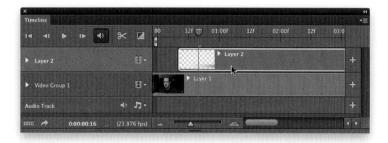

Step Six:

If you want your lower third to fade in, click on the Transition icon (shown circled here in red), and in the Drag to Apply dialog, click on Fade, choose a nice long Duration (like around 1½ seconds), and then click-and-drag the Fade transition and drop it on the beginning of your gradient bar in the timeline (as shown here). Now when the playhead reaches your gradient, it will fade it in over 1½ seconds. We're almost done.

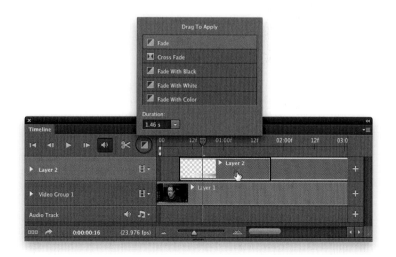

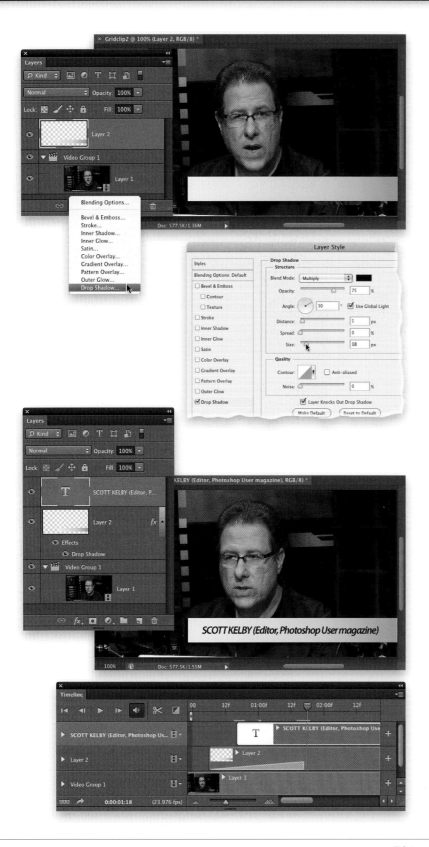

Step Seven:

You can add layer styles to your project, as well. In this case, let's add a Drop Shadow layer style to our gradient bar (so it casts a shadow back onto our video, which helps add depth and adds to the impression that our bar is "floating above" our video). To do this, make sure your playhead is over the gradient bar in the timeline, so you can see it onscreen, then click on the Add a Layer Style icon at the bottom of the Layers panel, and choose **Drop Shadow** (as shown here). When the dialog comes up, you can change the softness of the shadow by dragging the Size slider to the right (as shown here). Also, you can change the position of the shadow by moving your cursor outside the dialog—right onto your image itself—and just dragging it where you want it. When you're done, click OK, and now you've created extra depth.

Step Eight:

Now let's finish off our Lower Third project. Get the Type tool **(T)**, click right on your lower third in your image window, and simply enter your text (as shown here, where I added some text in the font Myriad Pro Semibold Italic). You can switch to the Move tool and reposition this text just like you would with a text layer on a photo. Once again, take a look at the stacking order over in the Layers panel: the Type layer is on top, which means the type appears over the gradient bar, then you see the gradient bar next (it's over the video), and then the video clip itself. By the way, we didn't have to drag the Type layer up to the top, since we were already working outside Video Group 1. Finally, like I mentioned in the intro, you can use this same technique to add logos or other graphics to your video.

Applying Photoshop Filters and Adjustments

This is one of my favorite features: the ability to apply Photoshop adjustments (everything from Curves to Levels and a whole lot more) and regular Photoshop filters. There are just a few little things you need to know so it works the way you want it to.

Step One:

Let's start a new movie (just so we don't get totally sick of seeing one video clip again and again). Go to Mini Bridge and double-click on the file named "0037 .mov," which is the full car in front of the 1950s gas station, to open it. Of course, it needs some trimming, so you can do that now if you'd like, but when you're done, go to the Layers panel, click on the Create New Adjustment Layer icon, and from the pop-up menu, you can choose any of the regular adjustment layers we'd use for digital photos (in this case, just choose **Black & White**, as shown here).

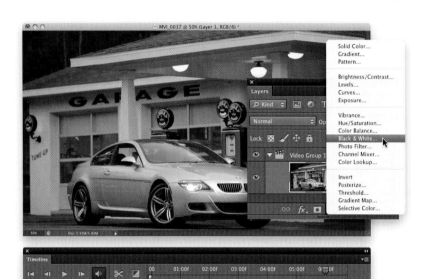

Step Two:

When you choose this, your clip instantly becomes black and white (as seen here), and if you look in the Properties panel, you'll see all the regular Black & White sliders (I'm not a big fan of this adjustment layer for doing black-and-white conversions for photos, but just for this example, I don't think it'll hurt anybody). ;-) One thing to note: look in the Layers panel—it automatically groups this adjustment layer with just this one video clip. That's really helpful, because we just want to affect only this clip (not all our clips).

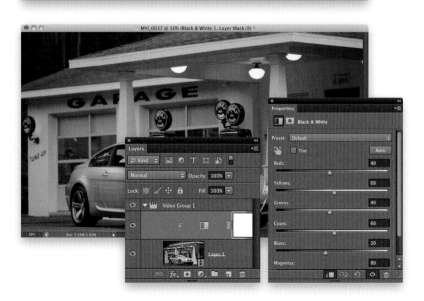

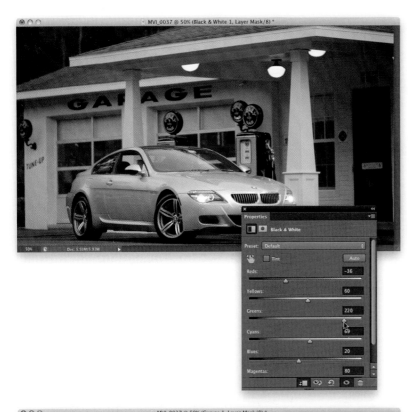

Step Three:

Here's something to keep in mind: these adjustment layers aren't just "one-click video effects"; you added a regular Photoshop adjustment layer. So, now think like you would if you were adjusting a digital camera photo, and do the same type of things (like, here, I lowered the amount of red to darken the windows of the garage, and then increased the greens to make the gas pumps brighter, just like I would on a still, but it's applied to the entire video. This is what is so darn powerful about having video in Photoshop like this. We can take the stuff we already know in Photoshop and apply it to video without having to learn a whole new program. That, I love!

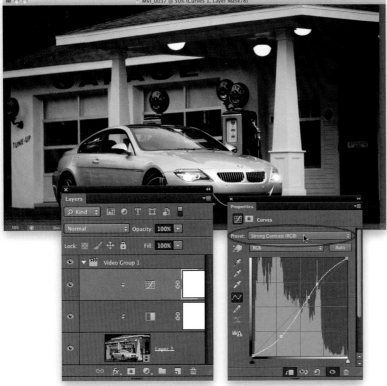

Step Four:

To further illustrate this, let's add another adjustment layer. Click on the Create New Adjustment Layer icon again, but this time choose **Curves**. Now you can adjust the curve any way you'd like (or in this case, we want to add lots of contrast, so just choose **Strong Contrast** from the Preset pop-up menu—it's shown circled in red here). Notice that it's automatically grouped with your video clip, as well. Seriously, this is pretty darn amazing that we can treat moving video just like it was a still photo (can you tell I am just so digging this?). Okay, now let's take it up a notch and leverage this for video.

(Continued)

Step Five:

Go to the Layers panel and delete those two adjustment layers, because now we're going to look at how to apply Photoshop filters to your video. First, go up under the Filter menu, under Sharpen, and choose **Unsharp Mask**. When the dialog appears, we're going to add some really heavy sharpening—try Amount: 135, Radius: 1.5, and Threshold: 3, and click OK. Now, click the Play icon to see how your video clip looks all sharpened. You're probably wondering why you could see the sharpening onscreen for a moment, but then as soon as it started playing, the sharpening was gone. That's because you can't just apply a filter directly to a clip—it will only apply it to the first frame (which is why you saw it for a split-second, and then it was gone). You have to do one extra step, so the filter is applied to the entire clip.

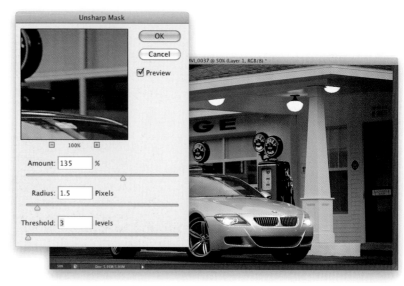

Step Six:

Press **Command-Option-Z (PC: Ctrl-Alt-Z)** a couple of times until the sharpening is removed from that first frame. Now, to apply a filter to the entire clip at once, you'll need to first convert this clip into a smart object layer. Go under the Filter menu and choose **Convert for Smart Filters** (as shown here), and a little tiny page icon will appear in the bottom-right corner of your clip's thumbnail in the Layers panel, letting you know it's now a smart object. Then, go back to the Unsharp Mask filter, apply those same settings, and click OK. (*Note:* Applying a smart filter turns your video clip's bar purple in the timeline, as if it were a still image.) Now when you click the Play icon, the sharpening appears throughout the entire clip. But, there's a decent chance on that playback you ran into a problem.

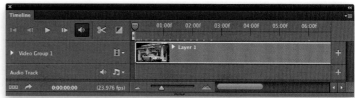

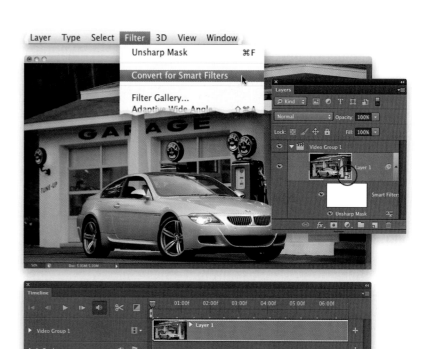

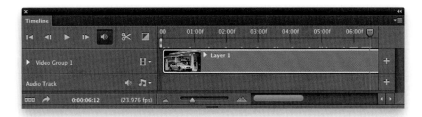

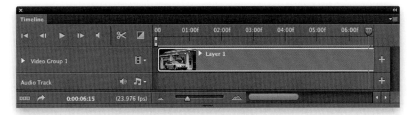

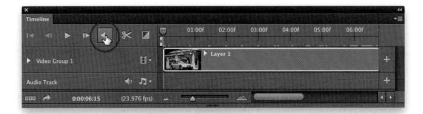

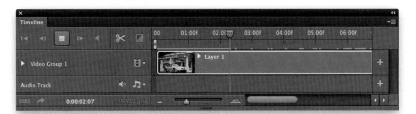

Step Seven:

So, chances are somewhat likely that when you played that clip it either was a bit jittery, or it played for a few seconds and then the playhead literally stopped. That's because the clip hadn't fully rendered a preview yet (this is a phenomenon video people deal with all the time, but as photographers we're like, "Huh?" because we're used to everything happening in real time). When you apply an effect like a filter, it takes some time (and a lot of your computer's RAM) to apply that sharpening to 24 frames every second. So, how do you know if your video has rendered and will play without being choppy? You'll see a thin, solid green bar directly above your video clip in the Timeline panel (as shown here at the bottom). If, instead, you see a broken green line, or just some green dots (as shown here at the top), that means it hasn't fully rendered, so your preview will be choppy at best. Now, on to the fix.

Step Eight:

I learned this fix from my buddy Richard Harrington (author of the book, *Photoshop for Video*, by Peachpit Press), and it works great. First, turn off the master audio (click that little icon that looks like a speaker, shown circled here in red) and then play the clip one time through. For whatever reason, that forces the preview to build, and with the audio turned off, you'll actually see the thin green solid bar appear as your playhead moves through the clip. *Note:* I noticed that if I applied a filter that does some serious math, like the new Oil Paint filter, I had to let it run through more than once with the audio off before the preview would fully render. Just a heads up on that.

Titles and Working with Text

There are two ways to work with text in your video project: one is to create your text in a separate Photoshop document (as if you were creating a slide for a slide show), and then bring that into your project, or you can just add your text directly into your video project, and here you'll learn both (and a couple of tips along the way).

Step One:

The nice thing about adding text to your videos in Photoshop is that you get to use all the regular type controls. But, before we start adding type to our video, if you're primarily going to do title slides (an opening slide or a closing slide), you might want to consider just building those separately in Photoshop and then dragging them into your video timeline. To do that, go under the File menu, choose **New**, and then from the Preset pop-up menu, choose **Film & Video**. That gives you a bunch of preset video sizes in the Size pop-up menu. Choose the one that matches the video you're going to be working with (in my case, it was HDV 1080p/29.97). This creates a new document, which you can treat just like a photo (add backgrounds, text, and so on).

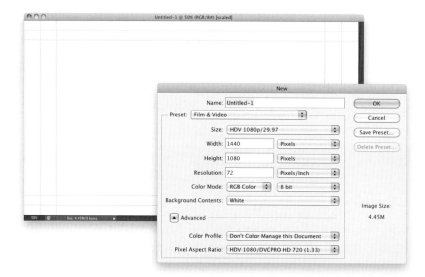

Step Two:

If you want to use a photo as your background, just open the photo and, using the Move tool **(V)**, click-and-drag it onto your HD-sized document. Then, press **Command-T (PC: Ctrl-T)** to bring up Free Transform. Press-and-hold the Shift key to keep things proportional, and click-and-drag a corner point to resize your photo so it fits (as best it can) within this wide-screen document. Now, get the Type tool **(T)**, click on your image, and type in your text (it's best to keep your text inside those guides. The area inside those guides is safe for putting text without it clipping off if you were to broadcast this video on television. Hey, it could happen).

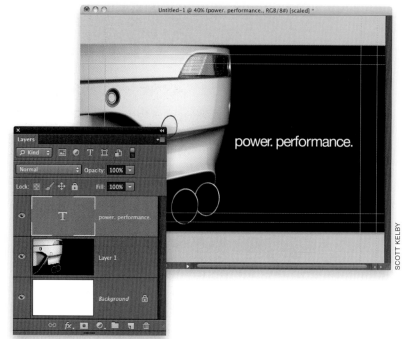

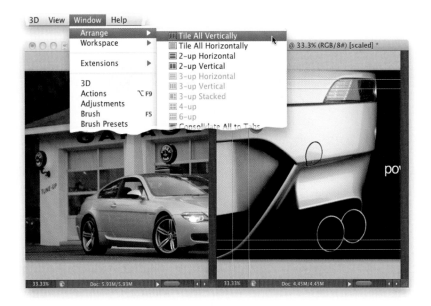

Step Three:

Once you've created your title slide the way you want it, go ahead and flatten the file (click on the down-facing arrow in the top right of the Layers panel, and choose **Flatten Image**), and then it's decision time. You can either: (a) save the file, and then, in the Timeline panel, click on the filmstrip icon and choose **Add Media** to add this slide to your timeline, or (b) drag-and-drop it right onto your timeline. To drag-and-drop it, you'll need to be able to see both your slide document and your video document, so go under the Window menu, under Arrange, and choose **Tile All Vertically** to put both windows side-by-side (as seen here).

Step Four:

Then, get the Move tool again, press-and-hold the Shift key (so everything lines up perfectly), click on your flattened title slide (it's the window on the right in the previous step), and drag that image over onto your video clip (you should see a faint outline of your document as you drag. If you don't see it, hold the cursor down a little longer on the slide before you drag). Because you held the Shift key, the title slide fits perfectly onscreen (otherwise, you'd have to reposition it to fit onscreen afterward). This adds your title slide to your timeline, after the video clip (as seen here at top). To make it appear as the opening slide instead, just go to the Layers panel, click on that layer (the top layer), and drag it below your video clip layer (as seen at bottom here). Now, your title slide is the first thing in your timeline and will appear first when you play your movie.

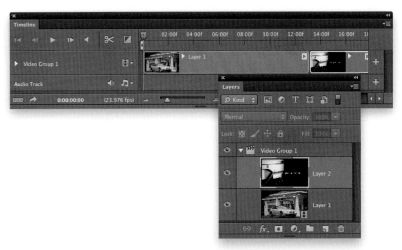

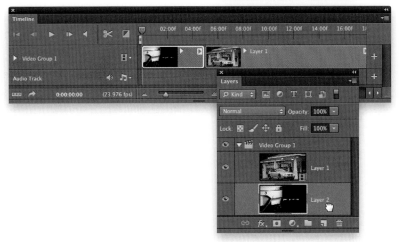

(Continued)

Step Five:

Besides creating your title slides separately in Photoshop, you can add text over any still or video clip in your movie. However, if you just get the Type tool, and with your video layer active in the Layers panel, click on your video and start typing, it assumes you want to add this text to the end of your movie (here, I typed the word "passion," and it added a Type frame to the end of my movie, as seen in the timeline). What we actually want is for this text to appear on top of (over) our video clip, rather than after it. We're going to fix that in just a moment, but before we do, take a look at the Layers panel and notice that our title slide is at the bottom (which makes it play first), then our movie clip is right above that (meaning it plays second), and then our Type layer is above that, meaning it plays after the movie clip. Okay, now we can go fix it.

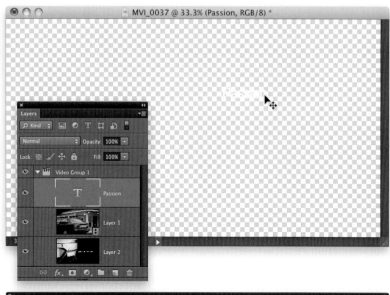

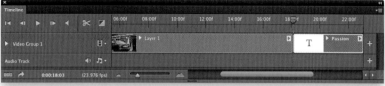

Step Six:

If your layers are all in the same Video Group (like a layer group when you're working on still images), each layer plays one after another. However, if you want something to appear over part of your video track, you have to move it outside that Video Group, so it's on its own separate track. So, go to the Layers panel, click-and-drag that Type layer up toward the top of the layer stack (above Video Group 1), and you'll see a white horizontal line appear. When you see that, let go of the mouse button, and your layer moves outside the group, and above it (as seen here), and your type now appears in its own track above your main video track in the Timeline panel. Now, click on that Type clip in the timeline, and drag it to the left, so it appears over the video clip, and now you can see the type appear over your video (as seen here).

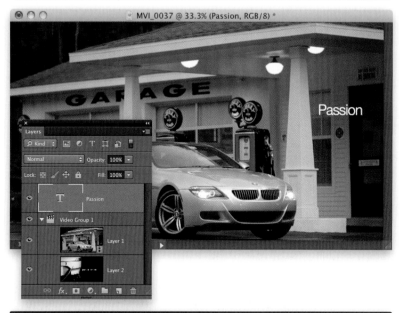

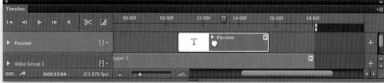

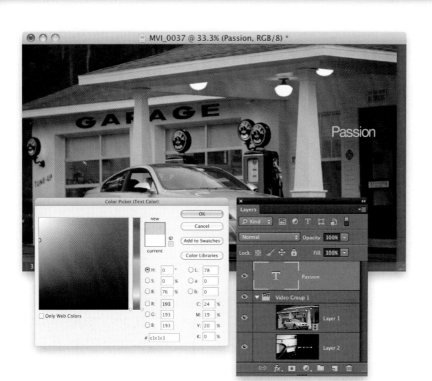

Step Seven:

Before we move on, one thing to keep in mind is if you're not seeing your text (but you can see that it's at the top of the Layers panel, outside your group), that's probably because you need to move your playhead over the part of your movie where the text appears. Okay, now that your text is in place, you can move it anywhere you want over the video by simply dragging it with the Move tool. If you want to change the color of your text, you'd do it the same way you do any other time: double-click directly on the little "T" thumbnail in the Layers panel (that's a shortcut to select all the text on the layer), then go to the Options Bar and click on the color swatch, which brings up the Color Picker, where you choose a new color and click OK. Besides the controls in the Options Bar, other Type controls are found in the Character panel (go under the Window menu and choose **Character**).

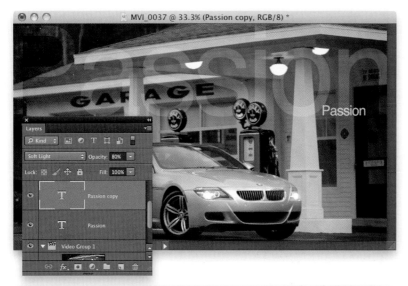

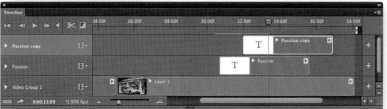

Step Eight:

While we're here, let's try a few more type techniques. Press **Command-J (PC: Ctrl-J)** to duplicate your Type layer. Press **Command-T (PC: Ctrl-T)** to bring up Free Transform, press-and-hold the Shift key, grab a corner point, and drag the text on this duplicate layer out so it fills the entire image area from side to side (as seen here), then position it near the top of the video. Because you can pretty much do the same stuff to a video that you can do to a still image, you can do things like changing the blend mode of the Type layer (go ahead and change it to **Soft Light**, so it blends in with the video), and lowering the layer's Opacity (lower it to 80%, as seen here). Lastly, drag this Type clip a little further to the right in the timeline, so the smaller word "Passion" appears first, then the larger one.

(Continued)

Step Nine:

If you want the larger type to fade in (rather than just appearing abruptly), Click on the Transition icon, and in the Drag to Apply dialog (seen here), click on Fade, and then drag-and-drop it right at the beginning of your duplicate Type clip (as shown here), and now it will smoothly fade in. Okay, you ready to take it up a notch? Let's do some type animation.

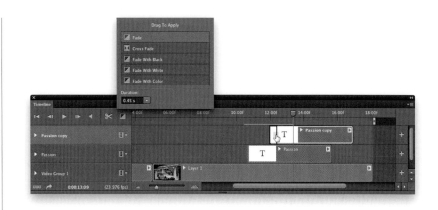

Step 10:

In the Layers panel, click on the smaller Type layer, then go to the Timeline panel and click on the little right-facing arrow to the left of the word "Passion" on the far left to reveal the animation controls (shown here). Move your playhead just past the beginning of where your type appears, then click on the Enable Keyframe Animation control to the left of Text Warp (as shown here) and it adds a diamond icon to your timeline (shown circled here in red), which marks the spot at which your text warp animation will start. Now, drag your playhead over to where you want it to stop and just leave it there for now. Double-click on your Type layer's thumbnail in the Layers panel to select your text, then go up to the Options Bar, and click on the Create Warped Text icon (also shown circled here). When the Warp Text dialog appears, choose any Style you like (I chose Arch), change the Bend amount (I chose +26), and click OK. Go back to the Timeline panel, to the Text Warp animation control, click the diamond icon (to the left of Text Warp) to mark the end of your animation (as shown here at the bottom), and you're done. Now when you click the Play icon, your text will be regular text when it first appears, and then it will animate a bending move into arched text.

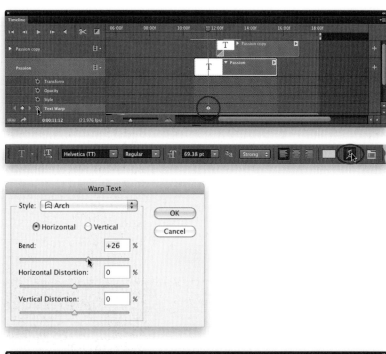

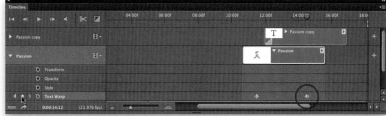

Using Blend Modes to Create "Looks"

Besides adding the standard stuff in the Adjustments panel, we can also add overlays and different texture effects using layer blend modes, just like we would to a still image in Photoshop, but as always, there are a few little things to know about how these are handled when adding them over video.

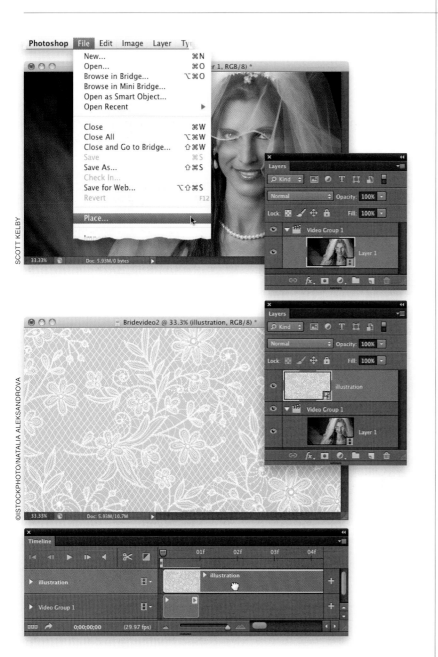

SCOTT KELBY

©ISTOCKPHOTO/NATALIA ALEKSANDROVA

Step One:

Open the video you want to apply a blend mode look to. I downloaded a lace texture for this from iStockphoto (they've got loads of these—just search for "wedding," then choose the Illustrations filter at the right end of the Search field, so it doesn't show photos, just illustrations. The pattern we're using here, which you can see in the next step, in high resolution, costs $8). Now, go under the File menu and choose **Place** (this will let us open the pattern and scale it to the size we want it).

Step Two:

Navigate to the pattern file, click on it, and then click Place. When your illustration appears, it will appear as a box with a big X in it. Press-and-hold the Shift key, grab one of the corner points, and resize it so it fills the entire image area, then press the **Return (PC: Enter) key** to lock in your resizing. You're probably wondering why you're seeing the pattern appear in the Layers panel, but you don't see it in your image window, right? That's because, by default, it adds the new file to the end of your video. To change that, go to the Layers panel, click on the pattern layer, and drag it out of Video Group 1, up to the very top of the layer stack, and then release the mouse button. This puts the pattern on its own track in the Timeline panel, but now you'll need to click on it there and slide it over to the left, until it's directly above your video clip, and now you'll be able to see it.

(Continued)

Step Three:

Now, change the blend mode of this layer to **Overlay**, and you can see how, by just changing the blend mode, the pattern is now blending with our bride video. Unfortunately, it's covering her face, and that's generally not what we're going for. So, we'll do three quick things to fix this: (1) Add a layer mask to this pattern layer by clicking on the Add Layer Mask icon at the bottom of the Layers panel (it's the third icon from the left). (2) Get the Rectangular Marquee tool **(M)**, and drag out a selection over your bride's face. Make it very loose, so if your bride moves a bit in the video, you won't see the texture appear over her face. And, (3) you're going to need to really soften the edges of this selection, so there's a smooth blend between the texture and the bride. You do this by going under the Select menu, under Modify, and choosing **Feather**. Enter 200 pixels and click OK.

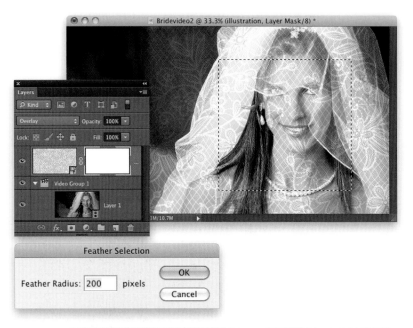

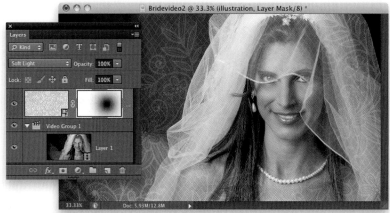

Step Four:

Press **D**, then **X**, to set your Foreground color to black, then press **Option-Delete (PC: Alt-Backspace)** to fill your selection with black. Since you're on the layer mask on this layer, it masks away that area over the bride's face, and leaves the pattern everywhere but her face (as seen here). Now, you can try out different blend modes by pressing **Shift-+** (plus sign) and just stop at the one that looks best to you. In this case, I liked Soft Light, but also try Hard Light, and lower the Opacity to 50% to get the look you see below.

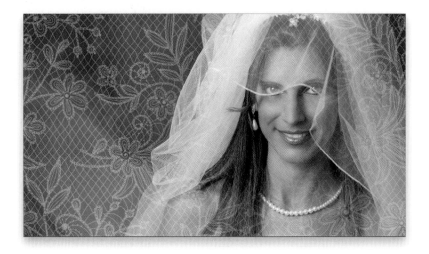

Before you jump into this start-to-finish project, you really need to have already read the rest of this chapter, because I'm not going to explain in-depth the stuff already covered in this chapter—I'm just going to tell you what to do. This is a great way to take what you've learned in this chapter and put it to use (plus, this is where everything you've learned so far comes together). So, if you've read the rest of this chapter, you've probably already gone to the downloads page and downloaded these same video clips and photos, so let's get to work.

Our Start-to-Finish Project

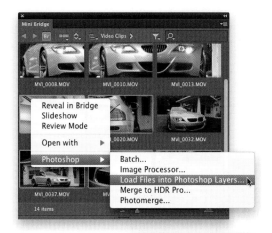

Step One:
Go to Mini Bridge and select the video clips you want to use in your movie (you can see the ones I used here in the Layers panel in the next step). Then Right-click on any of those selected clips, and from the pop-up menu that appears, go under Photoshop, and choose **Load Files into Photoshop Layers**. In just a minute or so, you'll see your clips, each appearing on its own layer in the Layers panel (they'll have a little filmstrip icon in the lower-right corner of the thumbnail).

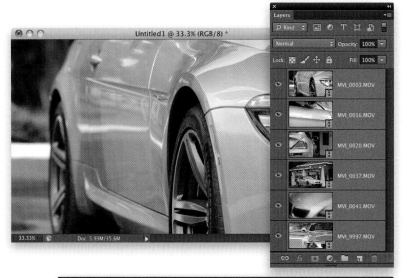

Step Two:
Of course, these videos are stacked one on top of another, and we need them to appear in our timeline one right after another instead. So, select all your clips (either in the Layers panel, or in the Timeline panel, whichever you prefer) by Command-clicking (PC: Ctrl-clicking) on them, then click on the filmstrip icon to the left of any of your selected clips in the Timeline panel and, from the pop-up menu, choose **New Video Group from Clips**. Photoshop then rearranges the selected clips so they appear one after another. By the way, our movie is going to be 60 seconds long, so if you want, you can move your Set End of Work Area bar to the 60-second mark, just to save you some time (see page 370 for more on your Work Area).

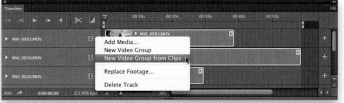

(Continued)

Step Three:

Let's go ahead and make the clip of the back of the car our opening clip, so go to the Layers panel and drag this clip down in the layer stack, so it's the bottommost layer (as shown here). Now, let's trim the clip (the first couple of slide moves aren't that good, so we'll go with the third one): trim the front (as seen here) and the back to get it so it's just that one slide move from left to right. Trim it so the clip stops just a second after the slide move ends (see page 390 for more on trimming). *Note:* If you have trouble trimming the end of the clip so there's no movement back toward the left (I sure did), this is where zooming in on your timeline (using the slider at the bottom left of the timeline) really pays off (I zoomed in tight, then it was a breeze getting to just the right spot, because the blue clip got a lot longer, which makes it easier to trim).

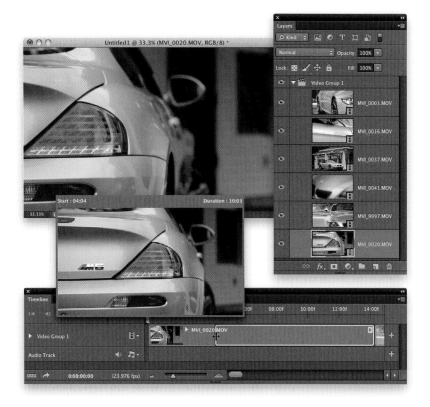

Step Four:

Let's make the car hood unfocused-to-focused shot the second clip, so in the Layers panel, drag that clip down in the stack so it's the second layer. We'll need to trim this one a bit to get just the second unfocused-to-focused move, and make sure the end cuts off right after it's in focus for just a second. Go ahead and play the first two clips and see how it looks. Looks like it needs a transition between those two clips, right? Click on the Transition icon at the top left of the Timeline panel, and choose **Cross Fade**. Choose a short Duration (like 0.75 seconds), and then click on Cross Fade and drag-and-drop it right over the spot where the first and second clips meet in the timeline (as shown here) to make it dissolve between the two (see page 396 for more on transitions).

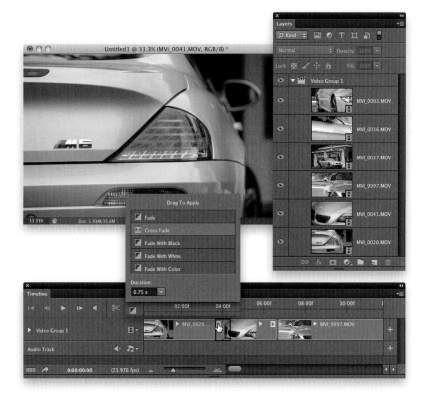

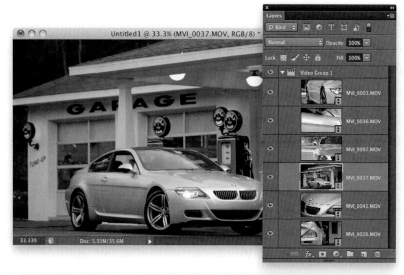

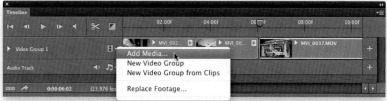

Step Five:

Technically, things go faster in the editing process if you wait until the end to add things like transitions and Photoshop adjustments and effects, so usually you'd put all your clips in order first, and then go back and add all these little enhancements, but since this movie is so short, I thought we could bend the rules a bit here. Okay, let's choose our third clip, and move it to the third position from the bottom in our Layers panel (let's use the wide shot). Go ahead and trim the front and back of that clip, so you just see the slide move, and cut it a second or so after the move. Now, let's add a digital photo to our movie, so click on the filmstrip icon to the right of Video Group 1 in the Timeline panel, and choose **Add Media** (as shown here), navigate to the image, and click Open.

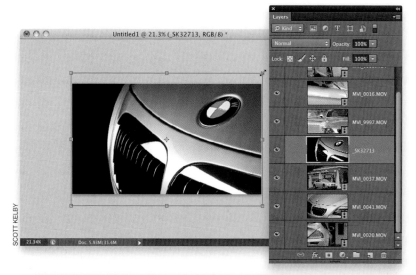

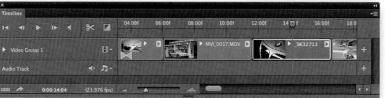

Step Six:

Your photo appears at the end of your video, but we want it after our third video clip, so in the Layers panel, click-and-drag it downward in the stack so it's the fourth layer (as seen here). You can see it now in the timeline after the third clip (photos appear in purple on the timeline). The photo is fairly large in size (dimension-wise), so we'll have to scale it down to fit onscreen, and we can do that using the same thing we use to scale down any image on a layer in Photoshop: Free Transform. Press **Command-T (PC: Ctrl-T)**, but when the Free Transform handles appear, the image is so large you won't be able to reach them. So, press **Command-0** (zero; **PC: Ctrl-0**) and the document window will resize so you can reach all the handles. Press-and-hold the Shift key, grab a corner point, and drag inward until the photo fits the image how you want it (as seen here), then press **Return (PC: Enter)** to lock in your transformation.

(Continued)

Step Seven:

Let's go ahead and bring in three more photos using the same Add Media command we just used in the previous step. Also, like the previous step, we need to change their order in the Layers panel so they're right above the first photo in the layer stack, and of course, you'll have to resize them all to fit using Free Transform, as well.

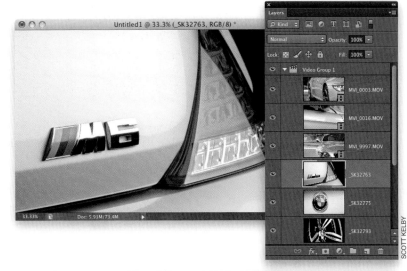

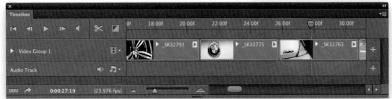

Step Eight:

At this point (at the end of these photos), we're about at the 30-second point in our video, so let's go back to including some video clips. We've already added them, so it's just a matter of moving them into the order we want and trimming the in/out points. Keep in mind, when you're trimming, start just before the movement starts and end right after it stops, so we have tight, short clips. After we add in the other clips, we're right at about 56 seconds.

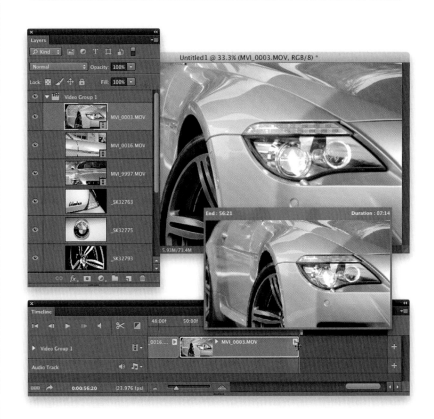

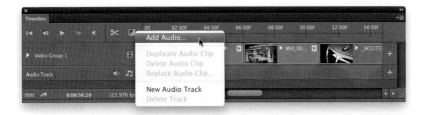

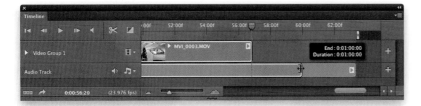

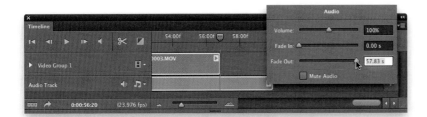

Step Nine:

Okay, now that our clips in are order, let's add some music (and make sure we like how the order flows once we drop a background music track in). Go to the Timeline panel, click-and-hold on the little musical notes icon to the right of Audio Track, and from the pop-up menu that appears, choose **Add Audio**. Select your background music track (we'll use the same one we used back on page 392), click Open, and it's added to your movie (audio tracks appear in green). This music track is actually around 4 minutes long, so go ahead and trim this back to around 1 minute (audio tracks trim the same way video tracks do, but since there is no video, instead of a pop-up video preview, you get a pop-up with the length of time at the current end position, so just watch that number until you get down to around an End at 1:00, as shown at the bottom here).

Step 10:

You'll probably want the music to fade out at the end (rather than just cutting off abruptly), and you do that by clicking on that little triangle at the end of the audio track. That brings up the Audio settings dialog with controls for when the music fades in and out. Choose a second or two before the end of your movie for the Fade Out, then click anywhere outside the dialog to close it and accept your Fade Out.

(Continued)

Step 11:

While we're at the end of the timeline like this, let's go ahead and set a fade to black for the end of our movie. Click on the Transition icon, click on Fade with Black, set the Duration, and then drag-and-drop Fade with Black right onto the end of your last video clip (as shown here). Also, press the **Home key** on your keyboard (or the Go to First Frame icon at the top left of the Timeline panel) to get back to the beginning of your movie, then add a Fade with Black transition to the beginning of your first video clip, so when your movie starts, it fades in from a solid black screen.

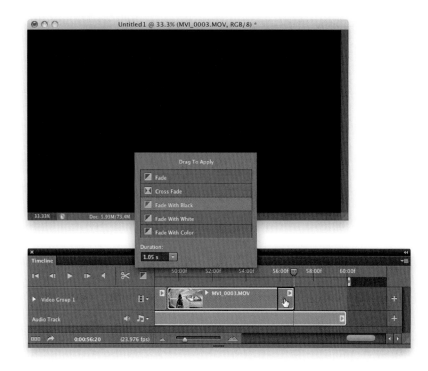

Step 12:

If you go ahead and hit Play at this point, you'll see your video fade in from black, you'll hear your background music, but you'll also hear something else: any audio your camera picked up when you recorded your video clips. In some cases, you might want to hear this, but in our case, we only want to hear the background music (and not us calling out cues to each other during the shoot). So, let's turn off the audio that's in our clips. We can't just click on that speaker icon to the right of Audio Track (that's the main on/off for audio), so what you'll do is click on the little triangle at the end of the video clip you want to affect and a settings dialog pops up with video and audio controls. Click on the music notes icon to bring up the Audio settings, then turn on the Mute Audio checkbox. Okay, now do that for all your video clips.

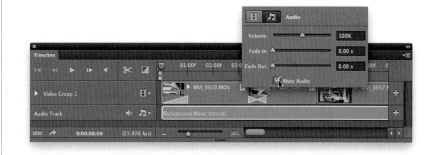

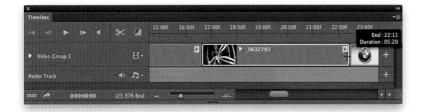

Step 13:

Once you're at the end of the timeline, if you're wondering how we're going to stretch this video out to fill a full 60 seconds, we can either: (a) add another photo or a video clip, or (b) extend the length of time one of the photos is onscreen (that's the great thing about using a still—you can make it any length you'd like). So, just click on a photo clip, and click-and-drag out the end of that purple bar (as shown here) to any length you'd like (kind of the opposite of trimming). Rather than doing it all to just one photo (so that one stays onscreen really long), you should probably add a little to one, and a little to another, until you reach 60 seconds right on the money.

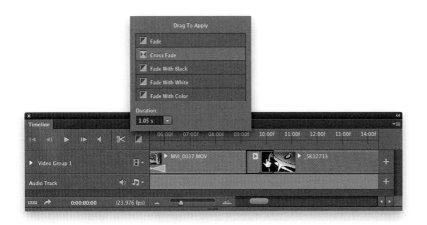

Step 14:

Now it's time for some finishing touches. Let's add some Cross Fade transitions between our video clips and our photos by clicking on the Transition icon, clicking on Cross Fade, setting the Duration amount (I use around 1 second, generally), and dragging-and-dropping Cross Fade right between the various clips and photos on your timeline. Go ahead and do that now for all our clips, so there are no hard cuts between images. *Note:* There will be times, depending on the subject and the theme of your video, where hard cuts will be what you want to use, but for this particular project, we're going with Cross Fades.

(Continued)

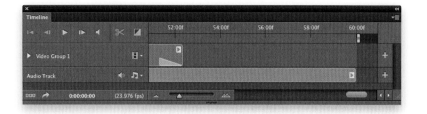

Step 15:

Okay, it's time to experience another "Weird Photoshop Video Quirk." Now that you've put in all your transitions, scroll to the end of your timeline, where you'll probably be shocked to see that your video, which was 60 seconds long a few steps ago, is now around 52 seconds. Why in the world is that? It's because of a weird way that Photoshop handles transitions—it actually shortens each clip a little to create that cross-fade effect (I know, I know, don't get me started). Anyway, it is what it is, and so all we can do is adjust the length of either our video clips or photos to fill in that missing time. You know how to do it (since you did it earlier in this project), so let's go ahead and stretch things out until the movie is 60 seconds long. By the way, if you don't actually need the video to be a certain time length, you can skip this part altogether.

Step 16:

We have two last things to do to finish our movie off. The first is adding some text (which you learned about back on page 406). Easy enough, just scroll to the first frame of our video, get the Type tool, choose Helvetica as your font, and type in "performance." (as shown here). As you know from before, something funky is going to happen here: it doesn't add the text above your video track, by default it adds it right to your track, immediately after your selected clip (it treats it like you added another video or photo).

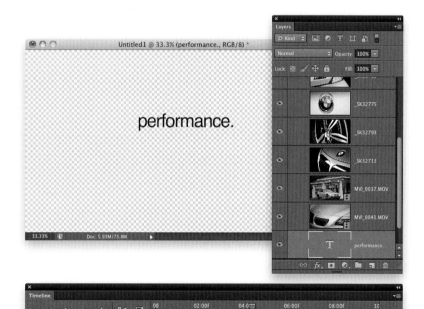

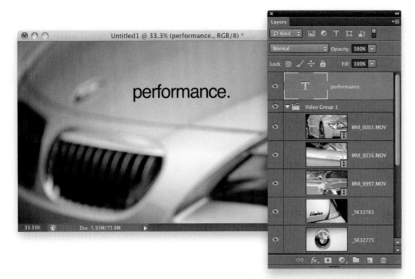

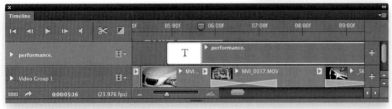

Step 17:

To get this text layer to appear on top of your video, you have to go to the Layers panel and drag it to the top of the layer stack and out of Video Group 1, so it creates a new track above your video track. Sadly, you still won't see your text at this point, because while it does take your text and adds it to a new track, it also moves it so it starts wherever your playhead is. So, find your type clip, click on it, and drag it back to the beginning of your movie. Actually, the text doesn't look that good over the first clip, so drag it above the second clip, and indent it a little, so the second clip plays for a moment before the text appears. Also, add a Fade transition to your text, so it fades in (you can see the transition in the next step).

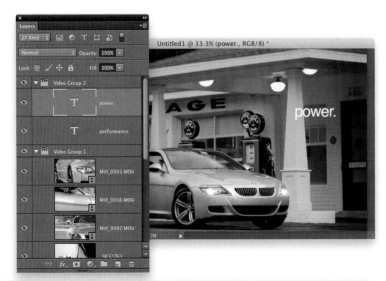

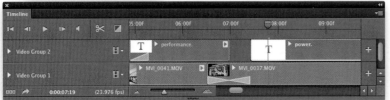

Step 18:

To add more text above other video clips is actually easier: first, drag your playhead over to the video clip where you want the next text clip to appear (I went to the third clip here). Now, just click on your Type layer, and press **Command-J (PC: Ctrl-J)** to duplicate your text layer. This automatically creates a new track above your existing text track in the timeline. You really don't need more tracks to keep track of (no pun intended), so once it appears, just click-and-drag it back down to your original text track in the timeline (as shown here, where they're both on the same track). Double-click on the "T" thumbnail over in the Layers panel to highlight your text, go up to the Options Bar and change the text color to white, and then type in "power." Next, use the Move tool **(V)** to reposition it.

(Continued)

Step 19:

Go ahead and duplicate that text layer a few more times so you can add "prestige." and "passion." and "pricey." Just kidding on that last one—how about "perfection." (ahhh, much better)? Add these over whichever clips you like best, and position them where you want them, as well (totally your call). Okay, one last tweak before we save our movie—let's add some motion to our photos. That's right baby, we can make 'em move. Go to the first photo, click on the little triangle at the end of the purple bar, and the Motion dialog appears. Choose **Pan & Zoom** from the pop-up menu (as shown here) and now this still photo moves slowly from side-to-side as it also slowly zooms in tighter (it's a pretty cool effect). Add any one of these motion effects to as few, or as many, of the photos as you like. Of course, go ahead and play your entire video and make sure it's just like you want it.

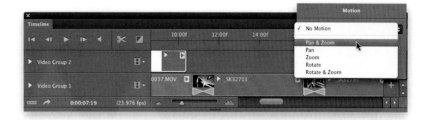

Step 20:

Now it's time to save out our project as a movie (so we can share it, email it, put in on YouTube, or our phones, etc.). Click on the Render Video icon at the bottom-left corner of the Timeline panel (shown circled in red above), to bring up the Render Video (export) dialog shown here. Give your file a name, and then from the Preset pop-up menu, choose the format you want for your video (in our case, we'll be sending our video to YouTube). Lastly, this preset is choosing 29 fps, but we're not certain that's what your camera shot, so to keep from having jittery or jumpy video playback, from the Frame Rate pop-up menu, choose **Document Frame Rate**, then click the Render button. In about five (errrr…10?) minutes your video is exported and ready for upload (of course, play it once to make sure everything came out the way you wanted).

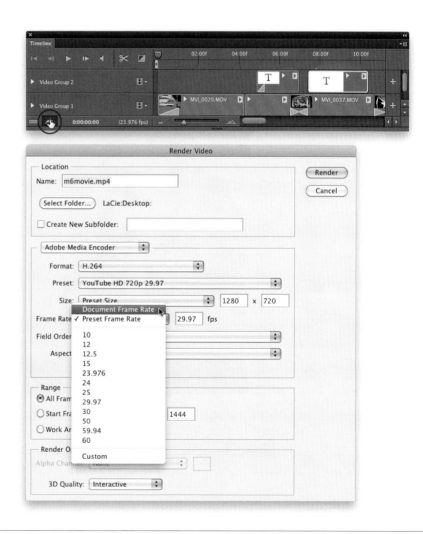

Photoshop Killer Tips

How to Have Mini Bridge Tuck Itself Away After You Open an Image

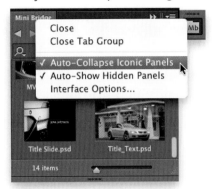

If you have Mini Bridge docked to the right side of your screen (rather than its default location along the bottom), you can Right-click directly on Mini Bridge's tab and from the pop-up menu that appears choose **Auto-Collapse Iconic Panels**. That way, when you double-click on an image to open it, as soon as it opens and you click anywhere outside Mini Bridge, it will tuck itself out of sight automatically (saving you from having to close it yourself each time).

Contact Sheet II Brought Two More Friends Along

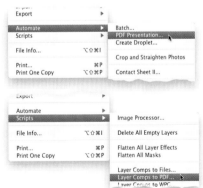

In Photoshop CS6, Adobe brought back the Contact Sheet II automation

(see Chapter 11), but they also brought back two more built-in automations that users have missed since they were removed back in CS4. We have PDF Presentation and Layer Comps to PDF back in Photoshop CS6 (they're found under the File menu, under Automate and Scripts).

Opening a Second Image from Mini Bridge Using Drag-and-Drop

In the Mini Bridge chapter, I mentioned that you can drag-and-drop a thumbnail out into Photoshop's image area and it opens (Mac users must have the Application Frame [found under the Window menu] turned on). Anyway, what happens if you drag one image out to the image

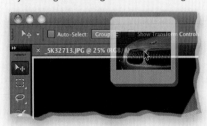

area and it opens, but then you want to drag another image out there? If you drag over the open image, it thinks you want to add the second image as a layer on top of the first image (and hey, maybe you do, in which case this is a tip on how to do that). If you want to open a second image in its own separate document, then make sure your documents open as tabs, and click-and-drag its thumbnail up until it's just to the right of the first image's document tab. Release your mouse and it adds your second image as a separate document.

Changing Your Brush's Size, Hardness, and Even Opacity on the Fly

If you press-and-hold **Option-Ctrl (PC: Alt)** and **click (PC: Right-click)** your brush anywhere within your image, it brings up

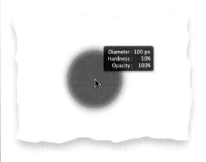

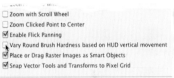

a preview of your currently selected brush tip (as shown here), with a little heads-up display showing you the current size, hardness amount, and brush opacity. Now you can drag straight upward to make it softer or down to make it harder. Drag left to make the brush size smaller; right to make it larger. That's cool, but now here's the trick: You can change one setting so that, instead of softness/hardness, dragging up/down changes the brush opacity. To do that, press **Command-K (PC: Ctrl-K)** to bring up Photoshop's Preferences, and then in the General preferences, turn off the checkbox for Vary Round Brush Hardness Based on HUD Vertical Movement. Now when you drag up/down, it changes the brush opacity instead.

Applying a Layer Style to More Than One Layer at a Time

Put your layers in a group by Command-clicking (PC: Ctrl-clicking) on each one in the Layers panel to select them, and choosing **New Group from Layers** from

Photoshop Killer Tips

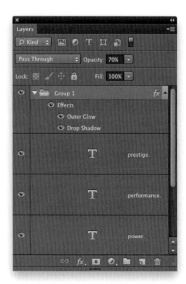

the panel's flyout menu. Now you can apply your group style (say, a drop shadow, for example) directly to that group, and it automatically applies that layer style to every layer in that group (and it doesn't matter how many layers you put inside that group—it adds it to all of them instantly). You can also add more than one layer style, if you like: just click on the group, then double-click on the fx icon to the right of the group name to re-open the dialog, and choose a layer style in the list on the left (let's say Outer Glow, for example) and it adds that style, along with the Drop Shadow you added earlier.

If You Work with a Lot of Layers, You're Going to Want to Learn This!

If you've created a big multi-layer file, you're going to have a long scrolling list of layers, and sometimes finding the layer you're looking for gets really time-consuming. Luckily, in CS6, there's now a filter bar

at the top of the Layers panel. On the left side of this bar is a search pop-up menu, which changes your choices to the right of it. It's set to Kind by default, which gives you icons, and if you click on those icons, it filters to just show you particular kinds of layers. For example, if you click on the "T" icon, it hides all the other layers but your Type layers. I don't mean it hides them from view on your image, I mean now you only see Type layers in the Layers panel (every other kind of layer is hidden). There are filters to just show pixel layers (regular old image layers), just adjustment layers, just shape layers, or just smart object layers, and all it takes is one click on any of these to quickly see just those types of layers. You can also search for layers by Name (a text field appears, so you can type in a name to search for), or by Effect (a pop-up menu of layer styles appears), or which blend mode you used, or a specific attribute, or assigned color. It's really pretty slick, and blindingly fast. When you're done (and you want to turn the filtering off), click on the little toggle switch on the far right of the filter bar.

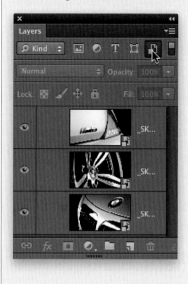

Want to Get Rid of All Your Hidden Layers Before You Save Your File?

Go to the Layers panel, and from the search pop-up menu at the top left of the filter bar at the top of the panel, choose **Attribute**, and then, from the pop-up menu that appears to the right, choose **Not Visible**. Now it displays any

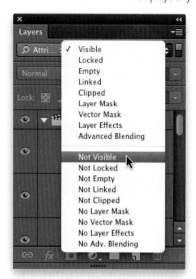

layers you're not using (since they're hidden). Select them all and hit the **Delete (PC: Backspace) key**, and they're gone. Not only does this make your Layers panel shorter (less layers to scroll through), but it also makes your file size smaller by getting rid of layers you're not using.

A Faster Way to Resize

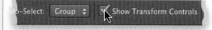

If you find yourself doing a lot of resizing of objects or selections, you'll be pressing **Command-T (PC: Ctrl-T)** a lot to bring up Free Transform, but there's a faster way: Click on the Move tool **(V)**, and then up in the Options Bar, turn on the checkbox

Photoshop Killer Tips

for Show Transform Controls. This leaves the Free Transform handles visible all the time, around any selection or object on a layer, so all you have to do is grab a corner point and drag (of course, press-and-hold the Shift key to keep things resizing proportionally).

New Maximum Brush Size

Back in CS5, the maximum size you could make any brush was 2,500 pixels, which seems like a lot until you have all these new DSLRs that are over 30 megapixels, and all of sudden, your biggest brush isn't big enough. That's why you'll be happy to know, not only can you make your brush sizes more than 2,500 pixels, you can go all the way 5,000 pixels. Yeah, baby!

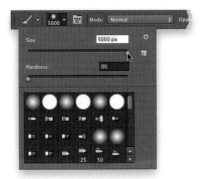

New Power for the Eyedropper

If you've added an adjustment layer above an image, and you use the Eyedropper tool to sample a color from that image, of course the color it picks is going to be based on how the adjustment layer is affecting that image, right? Right. However, in CS6, you can now make the Eyedropper tool ignore the effect of any adjustment layer and, instead, sample from your image layers. You do this by choosing **All Layers No Adjustments** from the Sample pop-up menu in the Options Bar.

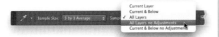

Not Sure Which Method to Choose for Resizing Your Image? Let Photoshop Choose

If having to choose which interpolation method to use when resizing made your head hurt (and it did for a lot of folks), then you'll be happy to see the new default is Bicubic Automatic, which means Photoshop will automatically choose the best one for what you want to do.

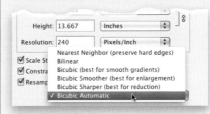

New Trick for Selecting Skin Tones

If you have skin tones that needs adjusting (maybe your subject's skin tone looks too red, but the rest of the photo looks good, which is more common than you might think), then you'll want to know this new little tweak in Photoshop CS6: if you go to under the Select menu and choose **Color Range**, and then

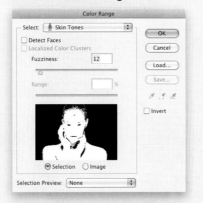

from the Select pop-up menu at the top of the dialog, choose **Skin Tones**, it looks for flesh tones and selects them. If you're just trying to select skin tones in your subject's face, then turn on the

Detect Faces checkbox to refine it even further. Then, drag the Fuzziness slider (kind of like the Tolerance amount in the Magic Wand tool) down to 1 and see what that looks like. If you need to raise the amount to select more skin, drag it to the right.

Saving Your Work Automatically

Photoshop is an amazingly stable program (it hardly ever crashes for me, well... unless I'm in front of an audience, then it senses fear), but if for some reason it does crash (hey, it happens), you're not out of luck if you haven't saved the document you're working on in a while. Well, at least not in CS6, because there's a new Auto Save feature that saves your document automatically at whatever amount of time you choose. You do this by going under the Photoshop (PC: Edit) menu, under Preferences, and choosing **File Handling**. At the bottom of the File Saving Options section, you'll

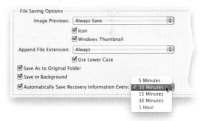

see the Automatically Save Recovery Information Every checkbox and a pop-up menu set to 10 Minutes by default (so, the most you can lose at any time is 10 minutes worth of work). But, if you can't bear to lose even that, you can choose 5 Minutes, or go the other way and increase the amount of time before it saves (for the brave at heart).

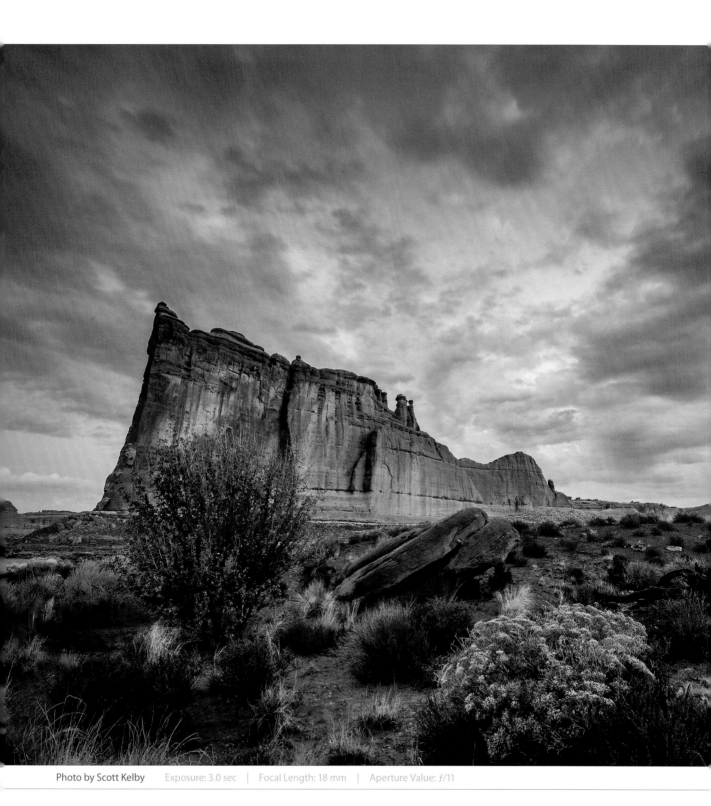

Photo by Scott Kelby | Exposure: 3.0 sec | Focal Length: 18 mm | Aperture Value: *f*/11

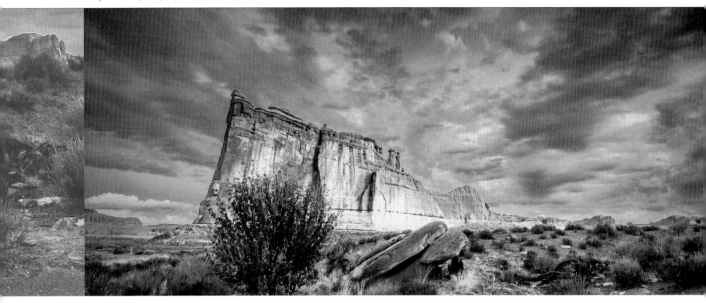

Workflow
my step-by-step workflow

I'm about to let you behind the curtain and into the world of my own personal workflow. Not my Photoshop workflow, mind you, but the workflow I use to find the names for titles of chapter intros (it would be more useful to write a chapter on my Photoshop CS6 workflow, though. Maybe I'll do that after this page). Anyway, this has been a highly guarded, super-secretive process, shrouded in mystery and ensconced in velvet, but today, for you, I'm revealing it for the first time ever. So, here's what I do: First, I choose which word I want to search for (so, for a chapter on color correction, I can search for either color or correction), then I type my first choice into Apple's iTunes Store, because it shows movies, TV shows, and music. For the word "color," you get about a bazillion matches (especially songs), but depending on the word you choose, it might not return any results at all, in which case, I go to IMDb (Internet Movie Database;

www.imdb.com) and type in the word there. So, for this chapter, I figured I'd type in the word "work" and I'd get lots of results (like "Workin' for a Livin'" by Huey Lewis & The News, for example), but on a lark, I typed in "workflow" and son-of-a-gun if one result didn't come up: the two-song album "Workflow" by Ricky Ambilotti. In the world of psychotic chapter intro writers, this is as good as it gets. Now, you're probably thinking, "Wow, that's a surprisingly easy process," and to some extent it is, but there is something I didn't tell you that makes this process much, much harder. I never learned to read. I know that sounds kind of weird coming from someone who writes books for a living, but sadly, it's true. When I was in grade school, I skipped the reading class, because back then I was much more interested in hacking into the WOPR using my 300-baud dial-up modem and playing chess with Dr. Falken.

My Photoshop CS6 Digital Photography Workflow

I've been asked many times, "What is your Photoshop digital photography workflow?" (What should I do first? What comes next? Etc.) So, I thought I would add this chapter here in the back of the book to bring it all together. This chapter isn't about learning new techniques (you've already learned all the things you'll need for your workflow), it's about seeing the whole process, from start to finish, in order. Every photographer has a different workflow that works for them, and I hope that sharing mine helps you build a workflow that works for you and your style of work.

Step One:

Like most photographers today, most of my workflow takes place in Camera Raw. I honestly believe it is the fastest and easiest way to get your images looking the way you want them (even if you didn't shoot in RAW format). So, I start in Mini Bridge by navigating to the folder of images I imported from my camera's memory card, then Right-clicking on the image I want to edit and, under Open With, choosing **Camera Raw** (as shown here). I'm going to edit one of the photos that I shot during a workshop I was teaching out in Moab, Utah. It's not a great shot on any level, but it has enough problems to deal with that I thought it would give you a good insight into how I deal with them (of course, you can download this same image and follow right along with me—the web address for the book's companion website is in the book's introduction up front).

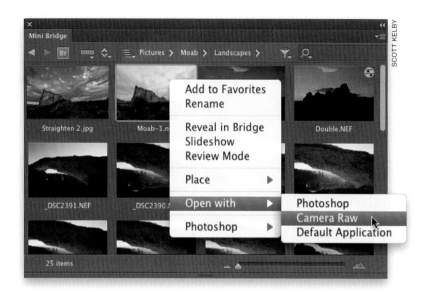

Step Two:

Here's the original RAW image open in Camera Raw. The first thing I do at this point is figure out what's wrong with the photo, and the question I ask myself is simple: "What do I wish were different?" Here, I wish the sky was darker and there was more definition in the clouds. I wish the whole photo had a lot more contrast and detail and was more vibrant overall. Of course, I wish everything was sharper, but since I always sharpen every photo, that's a given.

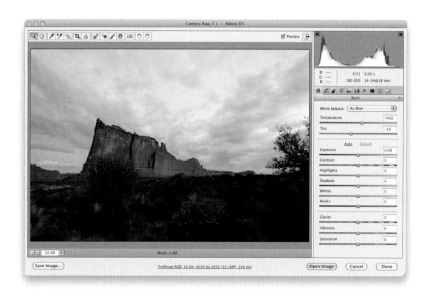

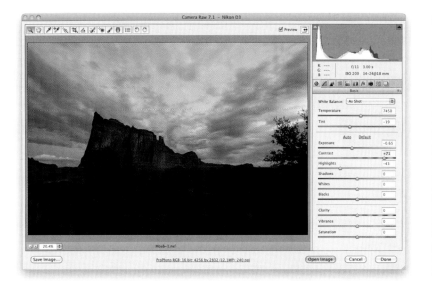

Step Three:

Normally, I start by adjusting the white balance (see page 26), but in this case, I'm okay with the overall color temperature (don't get me wrong, I'm going to pump up the color in just a moment, but as far as it being too warm or too cool, or just totally wrong, I'm okay with that part for this particular photo. That's pretty common for shots taken outdoors, where white balance usually isn't a big issue). We're going to start with the thing that bugs me the most (which is what I usually do), and in this case, it's the sky. It's just too stark and bland (take a look at the image in Step Two for a reference). Here's the recipe for darkening the sky: (1) Lower the Highlights slider a lot (here, I dragged it down to –43). Then, (2) lower the Exposure a bit (I lowered it to –0.65), which affects the sky big time (since it controls the midtones). Then, (3) increase the Contrast a lot (to +71 here) to give it some "oomph," and you can see that helped a lot (again, compare it to Step Two). If you need a refresher on the Basic panel sliders, go back to Chapter 2.

Step Four:

Now, we stop and see what it needs next. Back in Step Three, the mountains look way too dark, so we'll have to open up those dark shadow areas by dragging the Shadows slider way over to the right (here I went to +91). When you increase the Shadows a lot, like we did here, it can make the blacks look washed out, so I generally drag the Blacks slider to the left to balance it out (here, I dragged to –38). To bring out some highlights, I increased the Whites to +17 (I couldn't increase the Highlights—they were busy keeping the sky dark). The sky started getting a little bright from all that, so I lowered the Highlights even more (down to –89).

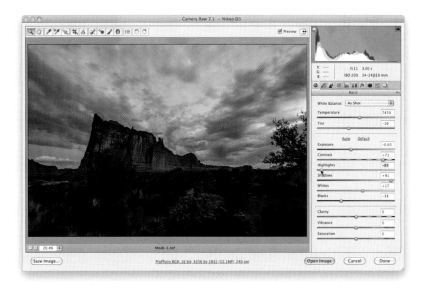

(Continued)

Step Five:

A landscape photo like this, with lots of well-defined edges and texture, is just screaming out for Clarity! (You can hear it, can't you?) So, I cranked it up here quite a bit, to +53. This tends to give the image a little tiny bit of an HDR feel, so if you're an anti-HDRite (and you know who you are), then don't drag it as far as I did (you might want to stop at +20 or +25). I also increased the Vibrance to +17 to punch up the colors a little more. As I go through this process, at certain times the overall image may look a little too dark or two bright, and if either is the case, I just drag the Exposure slider a little to the right if I need it brighter, or left if it's too bright. It was looking a little dark, so I increased the Exposure from −0.65 up to −0.50.

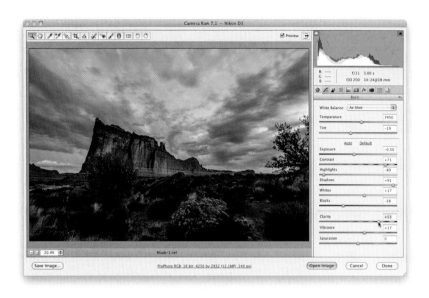

Step Six:

Okay, to me that sky is starting to look too light again, and I can't lower the Exposure any more, or the whole photo will be underexposed, so we're going to add a neutral density gradient filter effect (out in the field, I'd do this by putting a filter in front of my lens that graduates from a dark gray down to transparent. That way, it darkens the sky, but leaves the foreground alone, which helps balance landscape photos where your foreground exposure looks right, so your sky isn't way too bright). However, if you didn't have that filter with you, you can replicate it here in Camera Raw. Click on the Graduated Filter tool in the toolbar up top. When the panel appears, lower the Exposure and the Highlights amounts, then increase the Saturation. Now, click-and-drag from the top of the image to around the horizon line, and it darkens the top of the sky, then trails off (but it also intensifies the blue color in the sky, because you increased the color saturation, too). For more on how to use the Graduated Filter, see page 109.

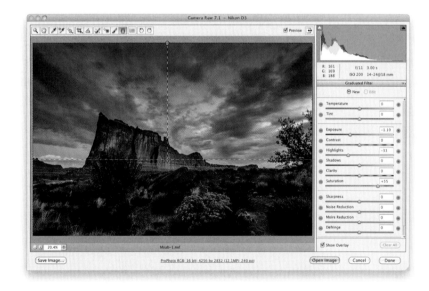

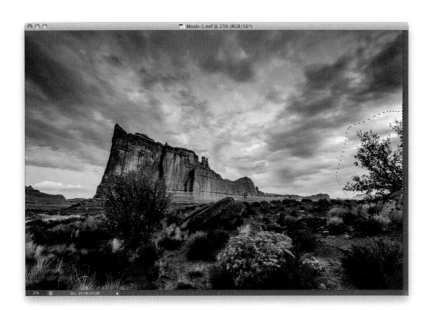

Step Seven:

Click the Open Image button to open this photo into Photoshop. Now that the sky has been fixed, the next most annoying thing has got to be that ugly tree creeping into the frame from the right side. A "creeping edge tree" has killed more landscape photos than I can count, but it's not going to kill this one, because we have Content-Aware Fill. Get the Lasso tool **(L)**, and draw a selection around the offending tree (as shown here).

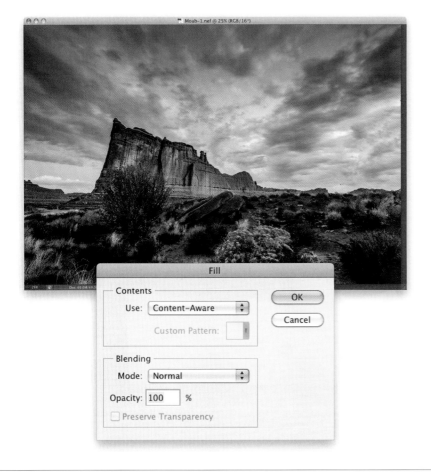

Step Eight:

Press the **Delete (PC: Backspace) key** to bring up the Fill dialog (shown here). By the way, this only works if your image is the Background layer. If this image is on a regular layer (you have a multi-layered file), then pressing Delete just deletes your selection, which probably is a bad thing, so in that case go under the Edit menu and choose Fill. When the dialog appears, just click OK, and in a few seconds, that nasty-looking tree is gone. You'll probably need to grab the Healing Brush (press **Shift-J** until you have it) and clean up any little spots or areas it missed (just Option-click [PC: Alt-click] in a clean area, then move your cursor over the area you need to fix and click), but at this point, it should only take a few seconds with either that or the Clone Stamp tool. For more on Content-Aware Fill, see page 258.

(Continued)

Step Nine:

Okay, it's decision time once again. What does it need next? I think the whole image could be a little more vibrant, so I can: (a) Reopen this image in Camera Raw and drag the Vibrance slider to the right until it looks good to me. You'll have to save the file as a JPEG, PSD, or TIFF first. (See page 19 if you don't remember how to do this.) Or, (b) do this right in Photoshop. Go under the Image menu, under Mode, and choose **Lab Color**, then do the Apply Image move we learned back on page 289. I chose the "a" channel here. Whichever you choose, it will add color and contrast. Don't forget to switch back to **RGB Color** mode when you're done.

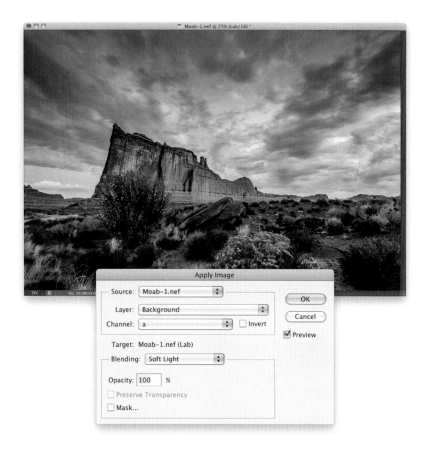

Step 10:

I try to keep the viewer's attention off the outside edges of my image and focused on the subject instead. One trick to do that (well, my favorite anyway) is to darken the edges all the way around with an edge vignette. I used the Lens Correction dialog here, which we learned two ways to do, starting on page 206.

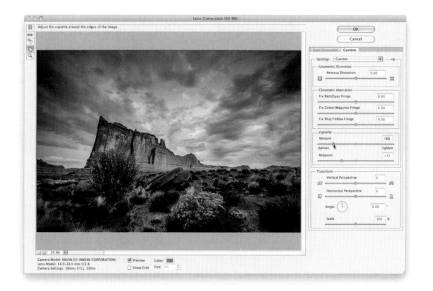

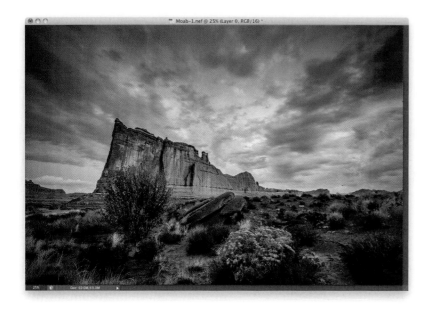

Step 11:

Here's the image after you've added the edge darkening, and you can see how it focuses your attention through the use of light (your eye is automatically drawn to the brightest thing in the photo), to the mountains.

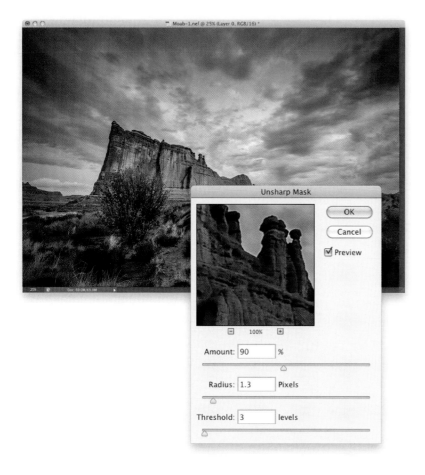

Step 12:

At this point, it's time to sharpen (I usually save this until last), so go under the Filter menu, under Sharpen, and choose **Unsharp Mask**. Enter 90% for Amount, set the Radius to 1.3, and set the Threshold to 3 (more on sharpening, starting back on page 328). This is some really punchy sharpening (note the Radius being increased past 1), but an image like this (and most landscape images), can really take a lot of sharpening and they look great. Go ahead and click OK.

(Continued)

Step 13:

After I run the Unsharp Mask filter, I try to limit any halos or other color nasties that might appear by immediately going under the Edit menu and choosing **Fade**. Then, I change the blend Mode to **Luminosity** (as seen here), which applies my sharpening to just the detail areas of the image, and not the color areas, which helps me avoid lots of sharpening hazards. I also lowered the Opacity to 90%. A before/after is shown on the next page. Since we did wind up opening the shadows quite a bit, and adding lots of clarity, it has a little bit of an HDR look to it. If you want less, use less clarity (back in Step Five), but if you want even more of an HDR effect, then go under the Image menu, under Adjustments, and choose **Shadows/Highlights**. Lower the Shadows Amount to 0 (zero), but increase the Midtone Contrast slider (if you don't see it, turn on the Show More Options checkbox) to around +25. I didn't add that here, but I thought you should know it's there. That's pretty typical of what I do for my workflow. Remember, it all starts with asking "What do I wish were different?" Once you know that, go back and find the techniques in this book that will get you there.

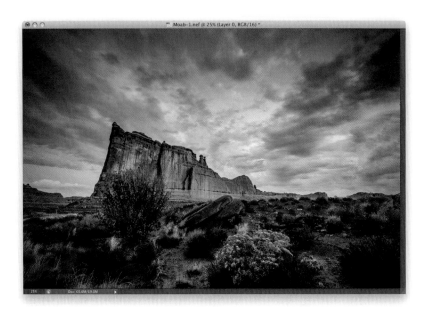

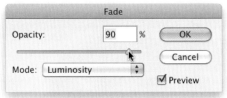

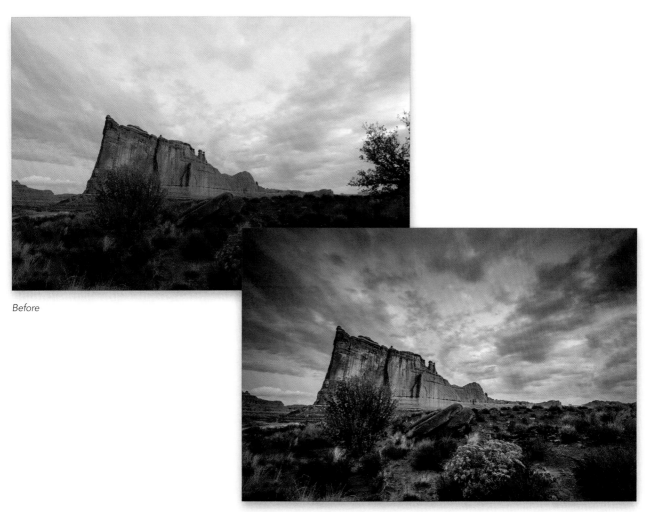

Before

After

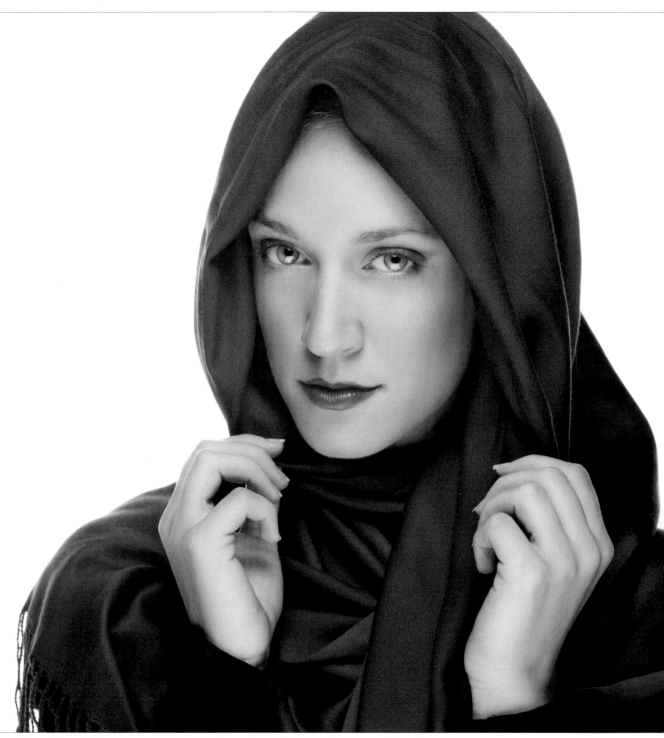

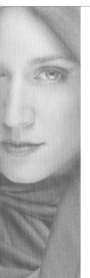
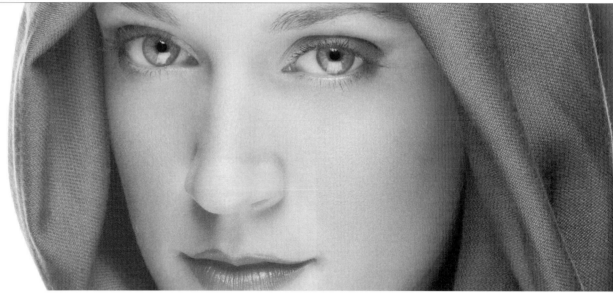

Beyond the Clouds
extra photoshop features for creative cloud users

Okay, I don't normally use French movie titles for chapter names, but *Beyond the Clouds* (the 1995 movie from directors Michelangelo Antonioni and Wim Wenders) had such a vaguely risqué movie poster I had to use it. By "vaguely," I mean it kinda looks like there's some nudie nakedness going on (in the movie poster I saw on IMDb's website), but it's so blurry I'm not quite certain whether (a) it's a person lying seductively on a bed entirely unclothed, or (b) it's a fully grown Antarctic leopard seal lying on a huge block of ice in a northern coastal breeding region, where these marine mammals come to mate each season. Either way, it's kinda naughty, so I'm going with it. But, honestly, the title *Beyond the Clouds* is perfect for this chapter because it's all about the extra features Adobe provides for Creative Cloud users (if you have a Creative Cloud subscription, Adobe releases new features as soon as they're ready, so you don't have to wait for the next release of Photoshop). Now, if you're using Photoshop CS6 and don't have an Adobe Creative Cloud subscription, you can just skip this chapter altogether because the features included in this chapter aren't in the regular version of Photoshop CS6 (hey, don't shoot the messenger, or the guy writing this book, who may be telling you something you didn't already know and, thus, should be seen as a happy courier and not a guy bringing bad news). The French have a name for this phenomenon, which is *ce chapitre n'est pas pour vous*, which roughly translates to either (a) this chapter is not for you, or (b) I have a bunion the size of a grapefruit. I'm not sure which. Anyway, we skipped over a very important part of this chapter introduction, which is there's a director out there whose parents were cool enough to name him "Michelangelo," which has to make women instantly fall in love with him and want to take off their clothes and lie on a block of northern coastal ice until a photographer comes along to take such a blurry photo of them that it attracts leopard seals looking for a mate. I'm just sayin'.

Using Camera Raw Like It's a Filter

Okay, I'm starting off with this particular new feature because the ability to reopen any currently open image in Camera Raw has been at the top of my Photoshop wish list for years now. Before this was possible, if you had an image open in Photoshop and you wanted to re-edit it in Camera Raw, you had to save the image and close it. Then, you'd have to go to the Open (PC: Open As) dialog, find the image on your computer, change the Format to Camera Raw and then open it. Now, it's finally just a one-click process (like applying any other filter).

Step One:
When you have an image already open in Photoshop and want to edit it in Camera Raw, just go under the Filter menu and choose **Camera Raw Filter** (as shown here).

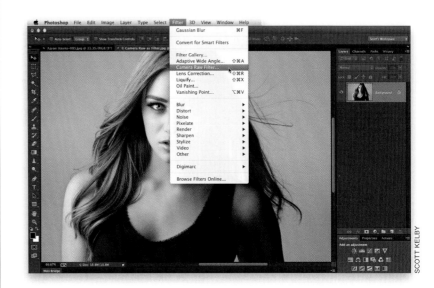

Step Two:
The Camera Raw window opens, and now you can make any changes you'd like. When you're done, just click OK, and you're back in Photoshop with your Camera Raw changes applied. Just a heads up: if your image is already open in Photoshop, even if it was shot in RAW format on your camera, it's no longer a RAW photo at this point, so it doesn't go back and reopen the RAW version—it takes the 8- or 16-bit photo you have already open in Photoshop and it opens that in Camera Raw. This isn't a bad thing, and works as expected, but I just thought I'd address it in case you were wondering.

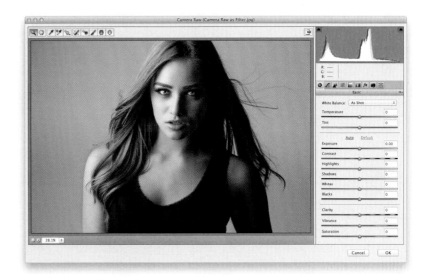

If you're planning on creating a photorealistic HDR (skipping the HDR-style toning), you can expand the range of your HDR image by creating a 32-bit HDR image. You can do this part in the regular Photoshop CS6 version, but now Creative Cloud subscribers can take that 32-bit HDR image straight into Camera Raw and edit it right on the spot before heading to Photoshop.

Opening 32-Bit HDR Images Directly in Camera Raw

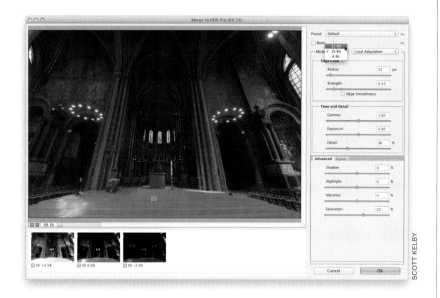

Step One:

Select your HDR-bracketed images in Mini Bridge, and then Right-click on any one of the images and, from the pop-up menu that appears, go under the Photoshop menu and choose **Merge to HDR Pro**. This brings up the Merge to HDR Pro dialog (seen here) and to open this as a photorealistic 32-bit HDR, choose **32 Bit** from the Mode pop-up menu (as shown here).

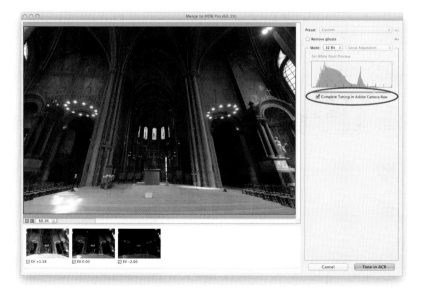

Step Two:

When you choose 32 Bit, in the Creative Cloud version of HDR Pro, a Complete Toning in Adobe Camera Raw checkbox appears on the right side of the dialog. With this checkbox turned on, you can click the Tone in ACR button at the bottom, and it takes your completed 32-bit image directly to Camera Raw for editing. When you click the OK button in Camera Raw, you get a smart object filter layer, with a layer mask in place all ready to go (pretty sweet, eh?).

Liquify Is Now Re-Editable (and It Has a Handy New Tool!)

I do a lot of portrait retouching (heck, I even wrote a bestselling book on the topic, but if you think I'm going to plug my *Professional Portrait Retouching Techniques for Photographers Using Photoshop* book here in this book, man are you right). Anyway, one feature on every retoucher's wish list was the ability to apply Liquify as a smart object, so we could edit or undo our Liquify retouches anytime. This is now available in the Creative Cloud version of Photoshop. What wasn't on our radar was the handy new Smooth tool, which helps hide our Liquify retouches.

Step One:

To use Liquify as a smart object, start by converting your image layer into a smart object layer (either go under the Filter menu and choose **Convert for Smart Filters**, or go to the Layers panel, Right-click on the Background layer, and choose **Convert to Smart Object**, as shown here).

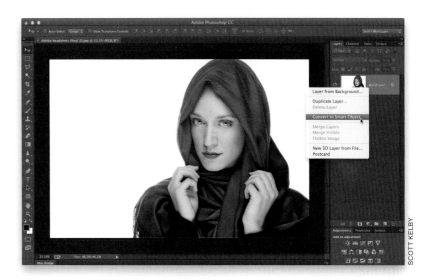

Step Two:

Now, choose **Liquify** from the Filter menu and make any changes you want (here, we'll use the Forward Warp tool **[W]**—the first tool at the top of the Toolbox—to flatten the part of our subject's scarf that's sticking out on the right side, just above her hand). Use a large-sized brush to nudge that area inward until it looks nice and flat (like you see here). Let's also nudge in the scarf on the left side, as well, and maybe tuck in her shoulder a little on the left side, too (so, we adjusted three areas in all). When you're done, click OK and that layer now appears as an editable smart filter layer with a layer mask attached (so, if you wanted to, you could hide any part of the Liquify edit you just made by painting over that area in black).

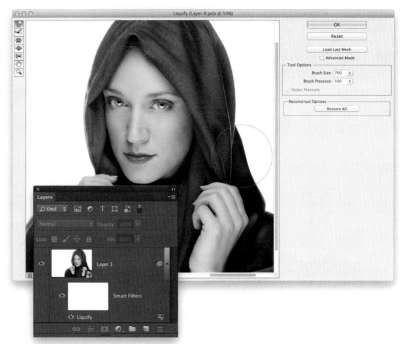

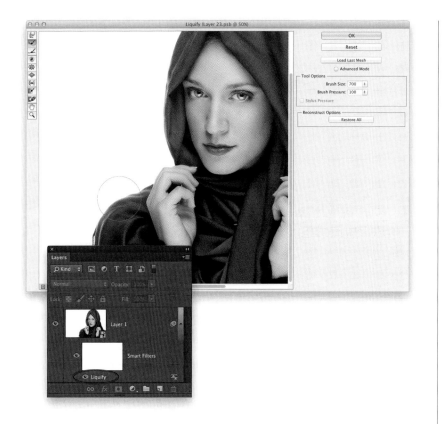

Step Three:

If you decide maybe you went a bit too far in Liquify, normally you'd have to start over from scratch. But, since you made this a smart object first, you can reopen the image with your retouches still "live," so you can edit them. To do this, just double-click directly on the word "Liquify" (shown circled in red here) directly below the smart filter layer in the Layers panel, and it reopens the layer in Liquify. Now all your edits are not only in place, they're editable. For example, if you want to undo just part of your last edit (let's say you wanted to undo the changes you made on the left side to her shoulder), you can just get the Reconstruct tool (**R**; the second tool from the top in the Toolbox) and paint over that area to return it to the original look while leaving the rest of your edits as-is. Now, click OK.

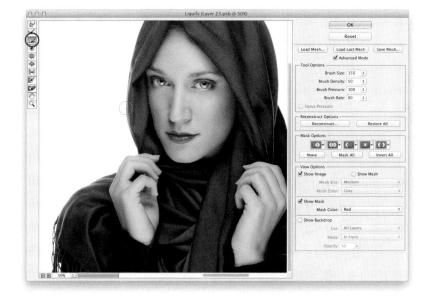

Step Four:

Okay, so that's the smart object part (easy enough, right?). Now let's look at the new Smooth tool. To get to this new tool, you have to turn on the Advanced Mode checkbox (near the top right of the dialog), which reveals more tools and controls. The Smooth tool **(E)** now appears in the Toolbox and is the third tool down. You'd generally use this tool if you see that an edit you made with one of the other tools looks rippled or obviously retouched. The Smooth tool actually works kind of like the Reconstruct tool, but instead of bringing the full original image back where you paint, it only brings back part of it. The first pass with the tool undoes "part" of your retouch; another pass undoes a little more. So, you can use it with a small brush for a more realistic retouch.

Auto Straightening and Perspective Fixes in Camera Raw

This is a fairly amazing one- (or sometimes two-, but occasionally three-) button quick fix for images that have the typical perspective or lens problems (like a building tipping back, or crooked horizon lines). The fixes for 'em are now pretty much automated. This new feature for Creative Cloud subscribers is called "Upright," and it straightens and fixes both horizontal and vertical perspective automatically.

Step One:

Here's the original image, taken with a wide-angle lens, and you can immediately see the problems: the buildings are leaning back (they're larger at the bottom and narrower at the top), and it's a little bit crooked, and, well, it's all kind of a mess. Now, while I'm going to take you through the different automatic fixes, in this case, I'm going to take things farther than I normally would, but the final result of the Upright feature is pretty amazing. Start by going to the Lens Corrections panel in Camera Raw (the fifth icon from the right at the top of the Panel area), click on the Profile tab, and turn on the Enable Lens Profile Corrections checkbox (the Upright feature works better with this turned on first). The auto profile correction is very subtle in this case.

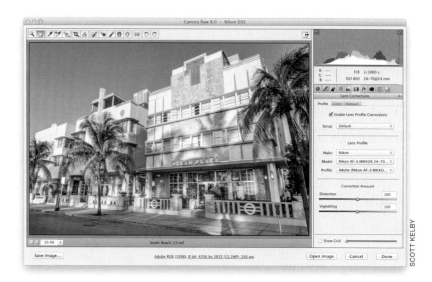

Step Two:

Let's apply the auto Upright correction by clicking on the Manual tab, then clicking on the Auto button (it's the second button from the left under Upright and shown circled here in red), and it straightens the perspective of the buildings (as seen here; take a look at the right edge of the building on the right, and the face of the building). This takes the three different auto Upright options (you'll learn about each in a moment), and it applies a balanced version of each. In this case, it's certainly a step in the right direction, but it's not quite there.

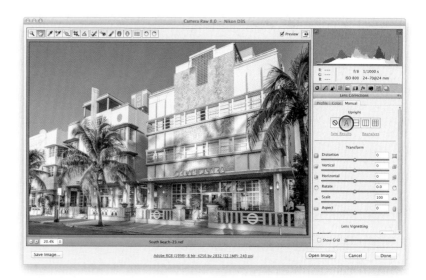

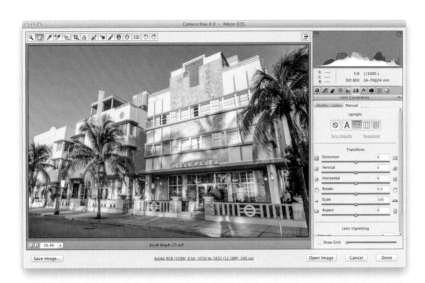

Step Three:

Now, let's try each of the three individual Upright options and see how they affect the image. The first is just a Level adjustment (the third button from the left) and this is what I'd click if it were a regular image where the only problem was a crooked horizon line. It looks for a straight line somewhere in your photo and tries to straighten it out. In this case, it did very little, but depending on the photo, it can definitely save time and trouble.

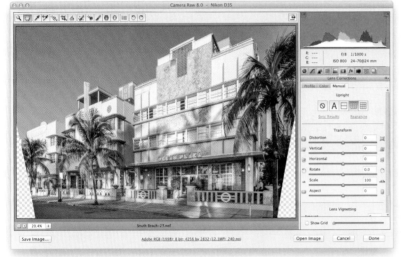

Step Four:

Next, let's try the Vertical option (the second button from the right) and it changes the perspective of the image (as shown here). Of course, you'd have to crop the image down a bit (pretty standard for perspective corrections of any kind).

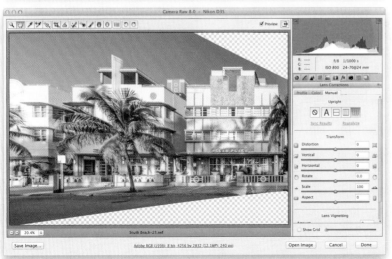

Step Five:

For this particular image, the last option, Full (the button on the right), I think is the most intriguing because it literally flattens out the image (as seen here), which is pretty darn amazing. Now, there are certainly some problems—the image needs to be cropped down, and the left side looks like it's been stretched (which is has)—but both of these can easily be fixed.

(Continued)

Step Six:

To crop the image, while you're still in Camera Raw, drag out the Crop tool **(C)** and, by default, it snaps to the point where you can crop the image without having any missing areas (like at the right-side corners). If you want to extend it further (I did), click on the Crop tool in the toolbar and, from the pop-up menu that appears, choose **Constrain to Image** to deselect it. You can now click-and-drag the right-middle cropping point out to the far right like you see here (I also moved the top-middle and bottom-middle points up just a little). Press the **Return (PC: Enter) key** to lock in your crop. Now, to fix the transparent corners and stretched-image problem, click the Open Image button to open it in Photoshop.

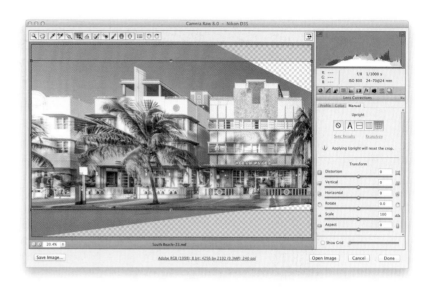

Step Seven:

The fix I use for stretched images is actually incredibly easy and effective. Get the Rectangular Marquee tool **(M)** from the Toolbox and select a good part of the left side of the image. Now, press **Command-T (PC: Ctrl-T)** to bring up the Free Transform handles and simply click-and-drag the left-middle point to the right to squeeze this part of the image. Keep dragging until it looks normal (not stretched), press the **Return (PC: Enter) key** to lock in your transformation, and then press **Command-D (PC: Ctrl-D)** to Deselect. Believe it or not, you won't see a line or anything whatsoever to indicate that part of the image has been squeezed—it's a seamless transformation. Once you've squeezed it in, you'll need to get the Crop tool **(C)** and re-crop the image to get rid of that transparent area on the far left created by the squeeze.

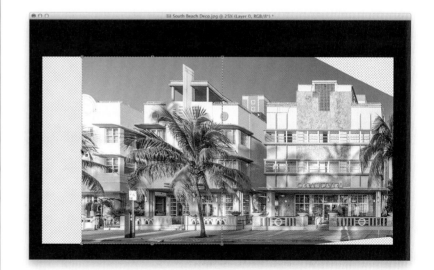

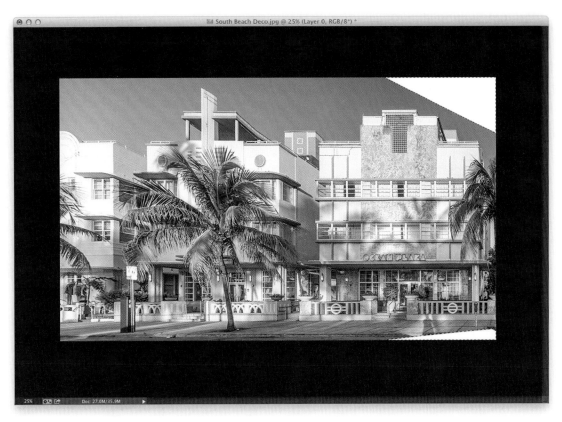

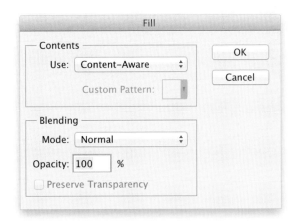

Step Eight:

Now, let's use Content-Aware Fill to take care of those empty corners on the right (for more on Content-Aware Fill, see page 258). One trick we use to make Content-Aware Fill work better is how we select the areas we want to fill. So, choose **Flatten Image** from the Layers panel's flyout menu to flatten the image, and then select the corners using the Magic Wand tool (press **Shift-W** until you have it)—click to select the top corner, press-and-hold the **Shift key** to add to that selection, and then click in the triangle at the bottom right. The trick now is to expand that selection by 4 pixels. So, go under the Select menu, under Modify, choose **Expand**, enter 4 pixels, and click OK. Now, go under the Edit menu, and choose **Fill**. Then, choose **Content-Aware** from the Fill dialog's Use pop-up menu, click OK, and then deselect.

(Continued)

Step Nine:

Content-Aware Fill did a pretty good job, here, but I did have to do some cleanup with the Clone Stamp tool **(S)**. If it doesn't work well for you the first time, press **Command-Z (PC: Ctrl-Z)** before you deselect and try it again. A before and after are shown here.

TIP: Shortcut for Changing UI Color

Back in Photoshop CS6, Adobe introduced the new "dark" color scheme (replacing the old light gray look that had been Photoshop's look since Photoshop 1.0). But, if you want a lighter or darker version of Photoshop's user interface, you can press **Shift-F1** to make the interface one shade darker or **Shift-F2** to make it one shade brighter (you can press more than once, depending on how light/dark your current interface is set). Also, if you're using a laptop, depending on how you have your laptop's preferences set, to make this shortcut work you might have to add the Fn key (so, Fn-Shift-F1 or Fn-Shift-F2).

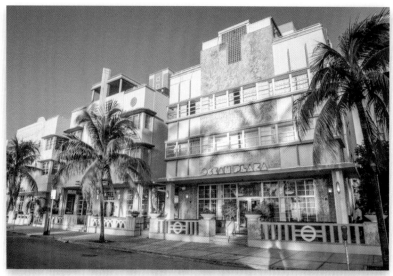

Before

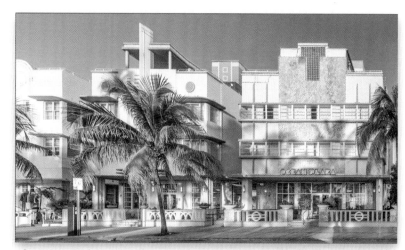

After: Here's the final image after the Upright correction, cropping, and Content-Aware Fill

Another thing I love that Adobe's engineers do in each new version of Photoshop is that they go back and make existing features even better. In this Creative Cloud update, they came up with a new option for upsizing images (making them larger using the Image Size dialog) with a new mathematical algorithm for upsizing your image while maintaining more detail and sharpness than ever before (and this includes better results from upsizing a low-res 72 ppi image).

Smarter Image Upsizing (Even for Low-Res Images)

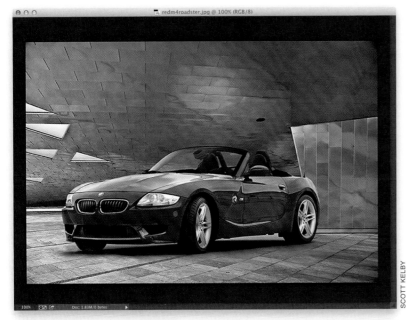

SCOTT KELBY

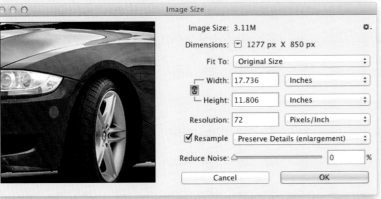

Step One:

Here's a low-resolution 72-ppi image we want to resize to a high-enough resolution to make a print of it. Go under the Image menu and choose **Image Size** to bring up the new Image Size dialog (by the way, this new Image Size dialog is resizable). You can see our image has a resolution of just 72 pixels per inch (or ppi, for short). Make sure the Resample checkbox is turned on and then choose **Preserve Details (Enlargement)** from the Resample pop-up menu. When you do this, a Reduce Noise slider appears beneath the menu that might come in handy if you notice that the noise gets increased along with the size of your photo (but using it adds a little blurring, so use it gingerly). By the way, you can compare different sizing methods by pressing **Option-1–Option-7 (PC: Alt-1–Alt-7)** to toggle through the different Resample options.

(Continued)

Step Two:

Now, in the Resolution field, enter the new resolution you want. Here, we'll enter 300 ppi (if you don't want to change the resolution, you can just type in new physical dimensions instead, a resize percentage, or both). The preview window shows you how the image is going to look at its new size or resolution. That's it! In the before and after shown below, you can see how much more detail and sharpness is now maintained after the upsize. One last thing: if you resize to some particular sizes a lot, you can save your own custom size presets. Just go under the Fit To pop-up menu and choose **Save Preset**.

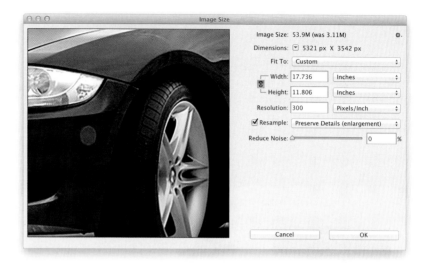

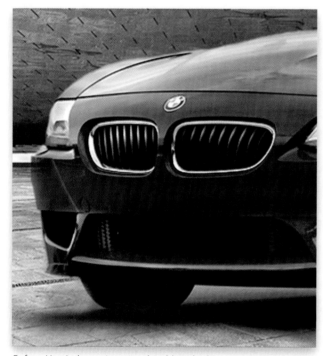

Before: Here's the upsize using the old method

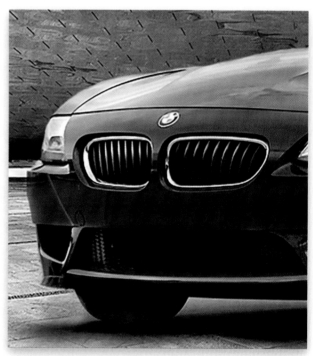

After: Here's the new method. Much better!

You've been able to add edge vignettes (where the outside edge around your image is darkened) for a while now, but the problem had always been your subject had to be right in the center, since it darkened evenly around the outside edges. With the new Radial Filter you can control placement of your vignette, so it's right where you want it, and you can have multiple sources of light, so you can also use it as a spotlight effect or to re-light your image after the fact.

Camera Raw's Radial Filter (Custom Vignettes & Spotlights)

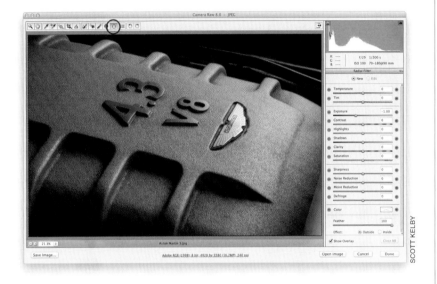

SCOTT KELBY

Step One:
Here, we want to focus the viewer's attention on the car's logo badge and engine specs (using dramatic lighting) rather than the outside edges of the image. So, click on the Radial Filter tool **(J)** up in the toolbar (it's shown circled here in red). Since we want to darken the outside edges, click the – (minus sign) button to the left of the Exposure slider a couple times, so when we use the tool it will be easy to see the effect (we can always change the amount later).

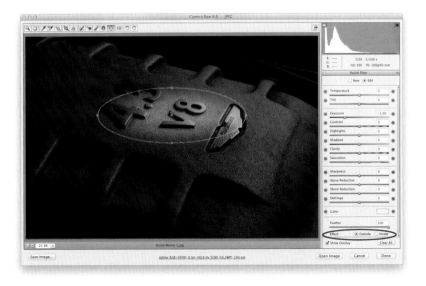

Step Two:
At the bottom of the this panel, you'll see an Effect option, which lets you choose whether it's the area inside the circle that gets affected or the area outside. In this case, we want what's inside to remain un-changed and everything outside it to be darker, so click the Outside radio button. Now, click-and-drag out the tool in the basic direction you want your oval (or circular) pool of light to appear. Here, I dragged it out over the center of the area I want to affect.

TIP: Repositioning as You Drag
As you're dragging out your oval, you can reposition it as you're dragging by pressing-and-holding the **Spacebar**. Try it. It's really handy.

(Continued)

Step Three:

Once your oval is in place, you can rotate it by moving your cursor outside the green overlay and clicking-and-dragging in the direction you want to go. To resize the oval, just click on any one of the little handles on the edges, and drag out or in. To move the oval, just click anywhere inside the overlay and drag it where you want it. While we're here, let's make the area outside of the "lit" area darker. Drag the Exposure slider to the left until it reads –2.00 (as seen here).

TIP: Two Handy Keyboard Shortcuts

Pressing the letter **V** hides the green overlay oval from view (press V again to get it back; you'll see I turned it off in the next step), and pressing the letter **X** swaps the Effect from Outside to Inside (so, instead of the outside being dark in this case, it makes the center dark and everything outside the oval unchanged).

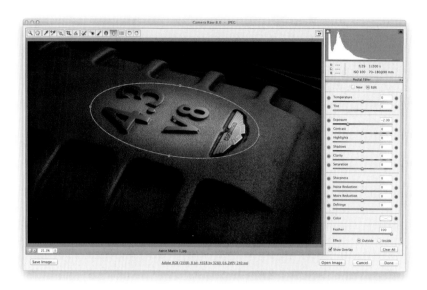

Step Four:

The nice thing about this filter is that you can do more than just adjust Exposure. For example, drag the Contrast slider over to the right (as I did here to +34) and this makes that outside area more contrasty. If it wasn't already so gray (it is an engine after all), you could lower the Saturation and then everything outside the oval would not only be darker, but black and white (or vice versa if you increased the Saturation). Now, I mentioned in the intro on the previous page that you could add multiple filters on the same image and that you could use it to effectively re-light an image. So, let's do that next.

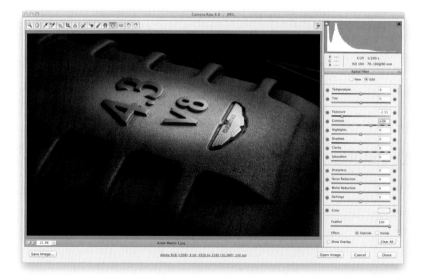

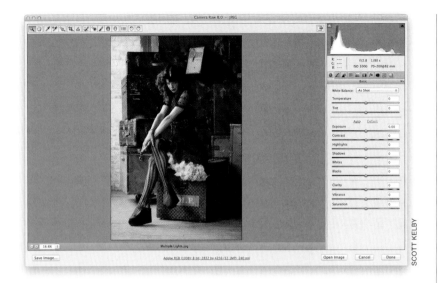

SCOTT KELBY

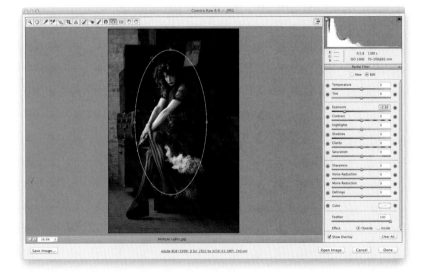

Step Five:

Here we're going to re-light this image using the Radial Filter. The viewer's eye is drawn to the brightest part of the image first, but unfortunately, in this shot, I let the light on the left side of our subject become so bright that your eye is drawn there first (instead of to her face), and the floor is brightly lit, too (this wasn't, ahem, my best day for controlling light apparently). Anyway, the light on our subject is at least directional, nice, and soft—it's just not quite bright enough, and I lost some detail in her dark dress against the dark luggage props. In short, lots of stuff to fix here.

Step Six:

We'll start the same way we did the last one—by selecting the Radial Filter tool and dragging out an oval in the direction we want it. In this case, I want her to remain the same, but I want the area around her much darker. So, make sure the Outside Effect radio button is selected and drag the Exposure slider way over to the left to darken the area outside the oval (here I dragged it to –2.30).

TIP: Removing Ovals

If you want to remove an oval you've created, either just click on it and hit the **Delete (PC: Backspace) key**, or move your cursor over the center point of the oval, press-and-hold the **Option (PC: Alt) key**, and your cursor will turn into a pair of scissors. Now, just click on the center point of the oval to delete it. Also, just as a general rule, when you have this scissor tool, don't run. Sorry, I couldn't help myself.

(Continued)

Step Seven:

To add another oval, click the New radio button at the top of the Panel area (so Camera Raw knows you want to create a new pool of light), then at the bottom of the panel, switch the Effect to Inside (or use the shortcut I mentioned earlier: X). Now, we're going to use this oval to light the part of her dress that's getting a bit lost. So, drag out a small oval over the frilly pink part of her dress (I'm certain there's a better name for it, but there's no way I should actually know what it would be, right? I'll bet my daughter knows, but I'm too embarrassed to ask), but this time, you'll brighten this area by dragging the Exposure slider to the right a bit (as I did here, where I dragged to +0.80).

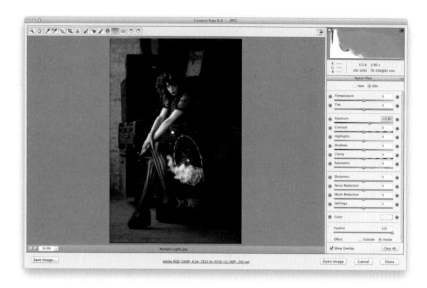

Step Eight:

We need another of the exact same oval to light her face a bit better. Rather than starting from scratch, we'll duplicate the second oval. Press-and-hold **Command-Option (PC: Ctrl-Alt)** and when your cursor changes into two small arrows, click-and-drag on the center of your second oval, release your mouse button and those keys, and a third oval (a duplicate of your second one) appears. Place it right on her hat (as shown here) and rotate and resize it as necessary. Decrease the Exposure a little (here, I set it to +0.65), and you could try increasing the Shadows to open up detail there (as I did here, where I increased it to +82). Remember, you can use any of the sliders in the panel.

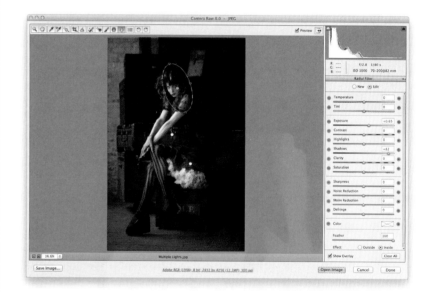

TIP: Controlling the Edge Blending

The softness of the transition between the center of your oval and the area being affected by the sliders is controlled by the Feather amount and, at a setting of 100, you get the softest, smoothest blending between the two. If you lower the Feather amount, the transition area becomes smaller and, of course, if you drag it to zero, it becomes a downright hard edge. Never had a use for that. Ever.

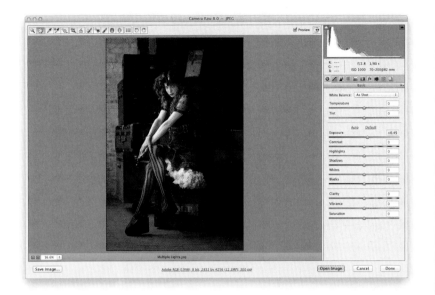

Step Nine:

One more thing to think about: What we've mostly done here is darken the area around our subject (well, except for those two small areas we brightened). But, if we want to make her brighter overall, we'll need to go back to the Basic panel and drag the Exposure slider to the right (as I did here, where I increased it to +0.45). This makes her brighter, but also makes the entire photo brighter at the same time. So, if the edges of the image now look too bright, you can go back to the Radial Filter tool, click on the first oval you made, and decrease (darken) the Exposure slider some more (that will only affect the area around her). I'm showing the before image here, as well, so you can see how dramatically we've re-lit the image using the Radial Filter.

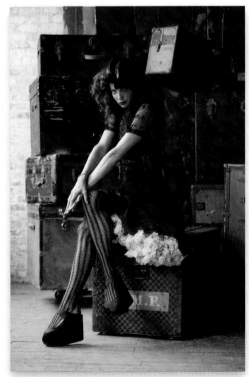

Before

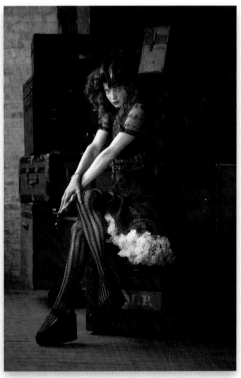

After

Finding Spots and Specks the Easy Way

There is nothing worse than printing a nice big image, and then seeing all sorts of sensor dust, spots, and specks in your image. If you shoot landscapes or travel shots, it is so hard to see these spots in a blue or grayish sky, and if you shoot in a studio on seamless paper, it's just as bad (maybe worse). I guess I should say: it used to be bad. Now, it's absolutely a breeze, thanks to a new feature in Camera Raw that makes every little spot and speck really stand out so you can remove them fast!

Step One:

Here's an image taken out in Moab, Utah, and you see some spots and specks in the sky. I can see five or six pretty clearly, but it's the spots that you can't see clearly at this size that "Getcha!"

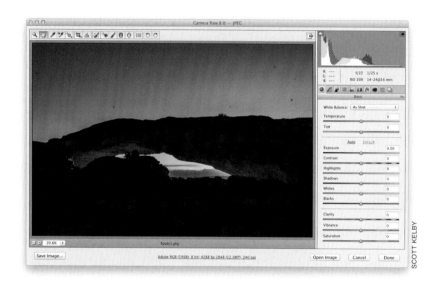

SCOTT KELBY

Step Two:

Click on the Spot Removal tool up in the toolbar (**B**; it's shown here circled in red), and at the bottom of its panel, there's a new checkbox for Visualize Spots. Turn that checkbox on and it gives you an inverted view of your image. Now, slowly drag the Visualize Spots slider to the right and, as you do, the spots will start to clearly appear. Next, just take the Spot Removal tool and, right on the image (with the Visualize Spots option still on), click once right over each spot to remove them until they're all gone.

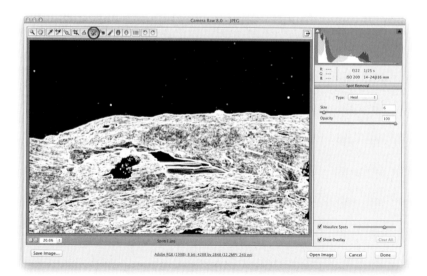

One thing we always had to go to Photoshop for was to use the Healing Brush. Sure, if you wanted to remove a spot or a blemish, you could use Camera Raw's Spot Removal tool, but since it did "circular" healing, even though you had "healing power," you couldn't paint a stroke to remove a wrinkle, or a power line, or, well, much of anything other than a spot. All you could do was draw more circles. Well, finally (finally!), we have a tool that lets us paint a stroke and heal those problems away (but, of course, it's for more than just wrinkles. It's for all the stuff you used to have to jump over to Photoshop to remove).

Oh Hallelujah, It's a Regular Healing Brush! (Finally!)

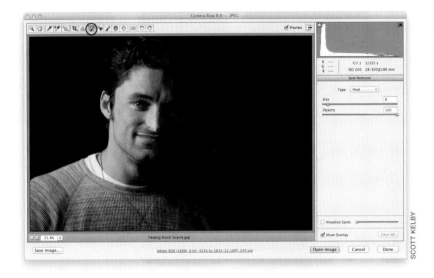

Step One:

Here's the image we want to retouch. Our subject has some small wrinkles on the left, under his eye, that we want to remove (something we definitely would not have been able to do easily in previous versions of Camera Raw). Get the Spot Removal tool **(B)** from the toolbar up top (shown circled here in red). By the way, I think they totally should rename this tool now that it works more like the Healing Brush, and it does more than just remove spots.

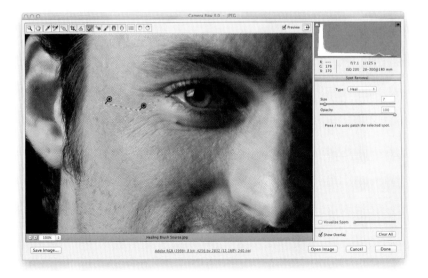

Step Two:

Double-click on the Zoom tool in the toolbar to jump to a 100% view, so we can see an up-close view of the area where we want to remove the wrinkles. Now, take the Spot Removal tool and just paint a stroke over the wrinkle you want to remove and, as you do, you'll see an outline showing the area you're healing as you paint.

TIP: More Realistic Retouching

If you remove a guy's wrinkles completely, it will probably look a bit unrealistic, but you can adjust the Opacity slider (in the panel on the right) to bring back a tiny bit of the original wrinkle. So, you're actually reducing the wrinkles, rather than totally removing them.

(Continued)

Step Three:

When you finish your stroke, you'll see two outlined areas: (1) the area inside the red-dotted line is the area you're healing, and (2) the area inside the green-dotted line is the area that the Spot Removal tool chose to sample the texture it's going to use to make your retouch. Usually this sample area is pretty close to the area you're trying to fix, but sometimes it does what it did here—it chooses an area far enough away that it doesn't actually create a perfect match (in this case, the direction and type of skin found on the sides of his nose are a lot different than the skin texture and direction under the far corner of his eye). That's okay, we can easily make the Spot Removal tool choose a different area to sample from.

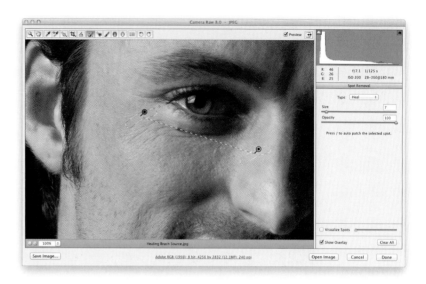

Step Four:

Take your cursor, click inside the green sample area, and just drag it somewhere else on your subject's face that's a better match (here, I dragged it over to the left of the area we painted over). Once you drag it over a new area, let go of the mouse button for just a moment and it draws a preview of how this sample area looks (that way, you can see if moving it actually helped or not). If it doesn't look good, just drag the green sample area somewhere else and let go of the mouse button again for a quick preview of how it looks now. That's pretty much all there is to it.

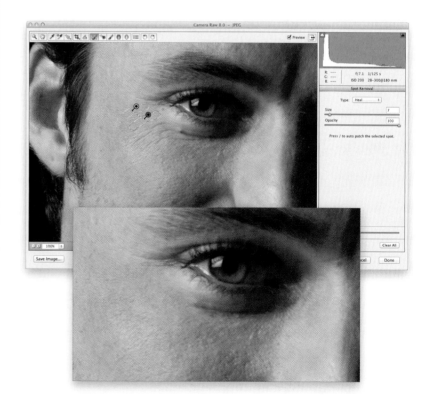

Imagine being able to sit down at a friend's or co-worker's computer to do some Photoshop work and, within seconds, you have all your own brushes, swatches, actions, patterns, and more, so it's just like working on your version of Photoshop, your way. Or, wouldn't it be nice to have your laptop's and your desktop's settings exactly alike? You can do just that by syncing your important settings with the Creative Cloud, so they're always just one click away (plus, now you have a copy of your important settings backed up to the cloud, so if your hard drive dies or your computer gets lost or stolen, you can quickly get back up and running).

Sync Settings

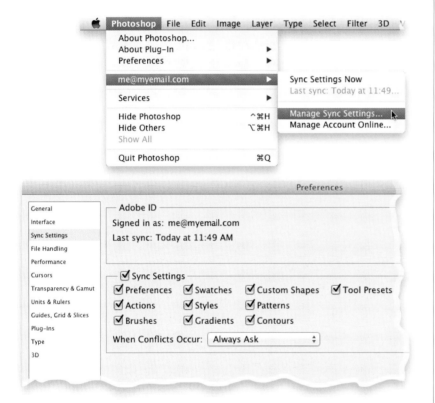

Step One:
Start by going under the Photoshop (PC: Edit) menu, under your Adobe ID and, from the submenu, choose **Manage Sync Settings** (as shown here) to go directly to the preference settings for syncing (also shown here). By default, it assumes you want all your stuff synced, but if you'd prefer to not have one or more of the options synced, just turn off those checkboxes.

Step Two:
If the date of your Last Sync was quite a while ago (time flies when you're not syncing), you can go under the Photoshop (PC: Edit) menu, under your Adobe ID, and choose **Sync Settings Now** and it will update your Creative Cloud settings with your current ones (it only updates any settings you've changed since your last sync). Okay, so how do you use all of this on a different computer? Well, you start in the same place (in your Adobe ID submenu), but instead choose **Manage Account Online**, sign in to your Creative Cloud account, and then choose Sync Settings Now.

TIP: Sync Shortcut
You can one-click sync by clicking the Sync icon at the bottom-left corner of your currently open document.

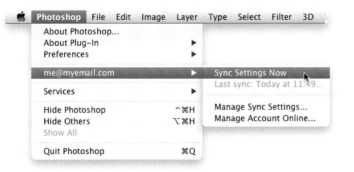

Conditional Actions
(At Last!)

Actions are basically tape recordings that live inside of Photoshop and you can use them to automate boring, repetitive tasks. Actions have been in Photoshop for many years now and ever since they were added, users have been asking for the ability to have conditional actions (meaning, a step in the recording where you can insert a condition, like "if this particular thing exists, then do this instead"). For example, if you wanted to have one action that properly resizes both your wide and your tall images for your online portfolio, you'd want your action to be "conditional" (if it's wide, run this action; if it's tall, run this one instead).

Step One:
Start by opening a wide image, and then go under the Window menu and choose **Actions** to bring up the Actions panel. Click on the Create New Action icon at the bottom of the panel (it looks like the Create a New Layer icon in the Layers panel and is circled in red here) and, when the New Action dialog appears, name your new action "Wide Portfolio," then click the Record button.

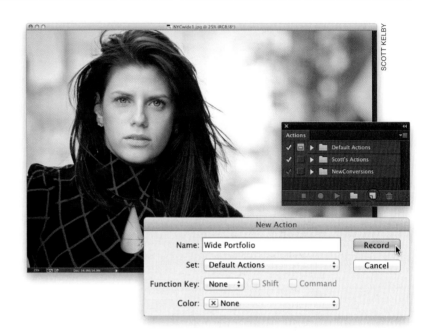

Step Two:
Now it's recording what you're doing, so go under the Image menu, choose **Image Size**, and resize your image, so it's about 1200 pixels wide by 800 pixels tall, and then click OK. Next, press the square Stop Recording icon at the bottom of the Actions panel to stop recording (as shown here). Okay, that's one action done.

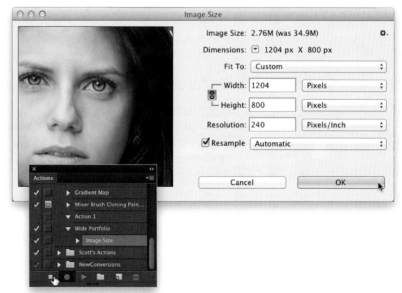

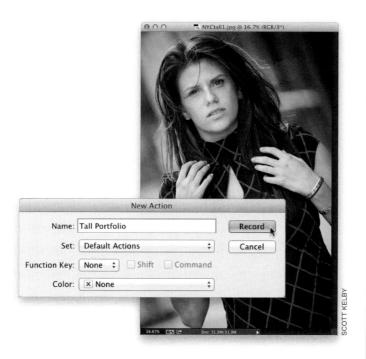

SCOTT KELBY

Step Three:

Next, open a tall image and do the same thing, but name this action "Tall Portfolio" and, in the Image Size dialog, make this one 532 pixels wide by 800 pixels tall. Click OK, then click the Stop Recording icon. Now we have our two actions, so we can use those to make our conditional action in the next step.

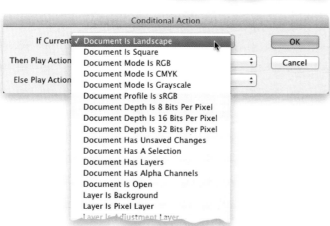

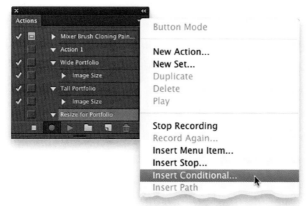

Step Four:

Click on the Create New Action icon, once again, name this one "Resize for Portfolio," and click the Record button. Now, go right to the Actions panel's flyout menu and choose **Insert Conditional** (as shown here). This is where we tell Photoshop which action to run if it opens a wide image and which one to run if it opens a tall image. So, no matter what their orientation, they'll wind up being 800 pixels tall, so they look uniform side-by-side in our portfolio. You'll see that you have a bunch of different conditions to choose from in the Conditional Action dialog (also shown here).

(Continued)

Step Five:

For our project, here, from the If Current (meaning, the currently open document) pop-up menu, we're going to chose **Document Is Landscape**, and if that's the case, from the Then Play Action pop-up menu, choose the **Wide Portfolio** action you made earlier. Finally, from the Else Play Action pop-up menu, choose **Tall Portfolio**. Click OK, and then click the Stop Recording icon at the bottom of the Actions panel.

Step Six:

Now, to apply this conditional action to a folder full of images, go under the File menu, under Automate, and choose **Batch** (we use Batch to process an entire folder of images at one time automatically). When the dialog appears, in the Play section at the top, choose the **Resize for Portfolio** conditional action you just created in the previous step from the Action pop-up menu. Then, choose the folder you want to run this action on (click the Choose button in the Source section), choose **Save and Close** from the Destination pop-up menu (or if you want them to be resized and saved in a different folder, choose Folder and then pick the folder you want them to be moved into after you've resized them), and then click the OK button at the top right.

Step Seven:

Once the batch runs, even though the folder had both wide and tall images, you'll see that the height of all the images is exactly the same. Again, this is just one use for conditional actions, but now you know how to create them (they're pretty easy, right?), and now that you know, you can start creating smarter actions.

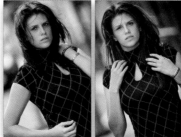
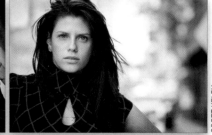

SCOTT KELBY

Smart Sharpen has been in Photoshop for a while now, but Adobe went back and updated both the math and the interface to make it the most powerful sharpening tool ever! Interface-wise, the window is now resizable (just drag a corner in/out) and they've streamlined the look, as well. But, it's what's "under the hood" that really makes it special, because now you can apply a higher level of sharpening without getting halos. There's also a new slider that allows you to sharpen without sharpening any noise that's already in the image.

New Smarter Smart Sharpen

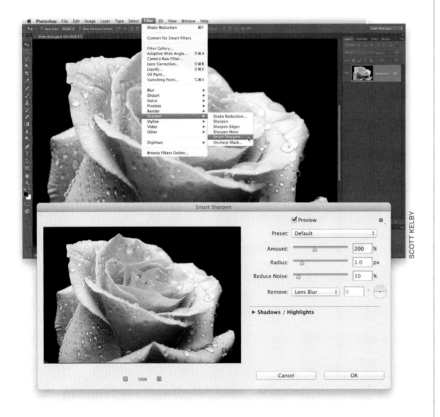

SCOTT KELBY

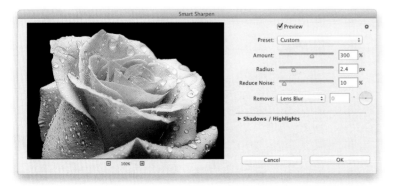

Step One:
Smart sharpening is in the same place it's always been: go under the Filter menu, under Sharpen, and choose **Smart Sharpen** (as shown here). This brings up the improved Smart Sharpen filter dialog, (which, as I mentioned above, is totally resizable). The controls are all in the same place as in the previous Smart Sharpen dialog (see page 344), except for the addition of the Reduce Noise slider. The goal with this slider is not to decrease noise, it's to let you add a lot of sharpening without increasing the noise. So, after you apply your sharpening, you'll drag this slider to the right until the noise in the photo looks just about like it did before you sharpened the image.

Step Two:
One of the downsides of sharpening has always been that if you apply a lot of sharpening, the edges start to get "halos" around them, but Smart Sharpen's new algorithm lets you apply a higher amount of sharpening before halos start to appear. So, how do you know how far you can push the sharpening? Adobe recommends that you start by increasing the Amount slider to at least 300%, and then start dragging the Radius slider to the right until you start to see halos appear around the edges. When they appear, back the slider off by a little bit (until the halos go away).

(Continued)

Step Three:

Now you've got your Radius set correctly, so go back to the Amount slider and start dragging it to the right (above 300%) until the sharpening looks good to you (or haloing appears, but you'd have to crank it quite a bit before that happens). I think this new sharpening algorithm is dramatically better than in the previous Smart Sharpen, but if you'd like to use the old method (or just use it to compare), just press the letter **L** on your keyboard and it applies the legacy Smart Sharpen (the old version, before the new math). Press it again to turn it off and return to the new Smart Sharpening. You can also choose **Use Legacy** from the settings pop-up menu at the top-right corner of the filter dialog.

Step Four:

In the previous version of Smart Sharpen, there was an Advanced radio button, and if you clicked on it, two other tabs would show up: one for reducing the amount of sharpening in the highlight areas (I never used that one), and one for reducing sharpening in the shadow areas (I only occasionally used this one, but just on really noisy images—it allowed you to reduce or turn off sharpening in the shadow areas where noise is usually most visible—but now with the Reduce Noise slider, I'm not sure if I'll ever use it again). You can still access both of these features by clicking on the little right-facing triangle to the left of Shadows/Highlights—just click on the triangle and the two sets of sliders appear (shown here).

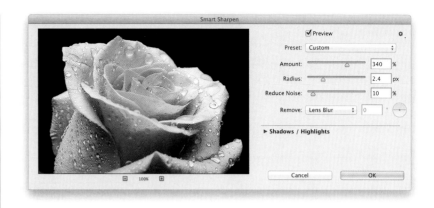

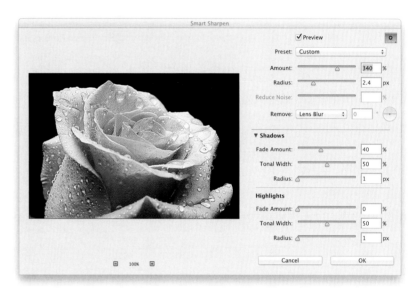

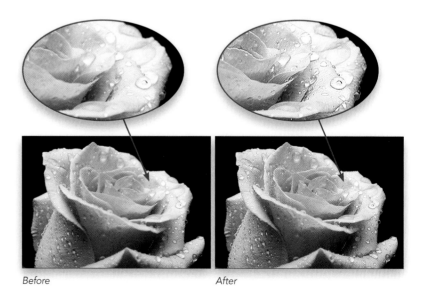

Before   After

Saving Blurry Pictures Using the Shake Reduction Filter

If you have a shot you took handheld in low light (so the blurriness was caused by shooting with a slow shutter speed), or if your blurry shot came from a long lens, you may be in luck using a new filter called Shake Reduction. It can greatly reduce the blur caused by shots where your camera moved a bit (it's not for shots where your subject is moving). This filter works best on images that don't have a lot of noise, have a pretty decent overall exposure, and where you didn't use flash. It doesn't work on every image, but when it does, it's pretty jaw-dropping.

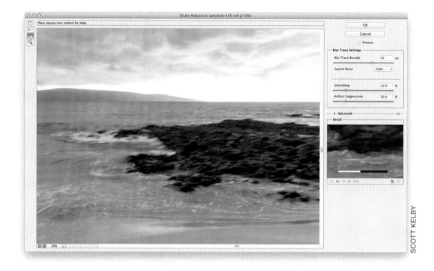

SCOTT KELBY

Step One:

Here's a shot I took handheld in low light; it's a blurry mess, and this is exactly when you'd reach for the Shake Reduction filter (it's found under the Filter menu, under Sharpen). When the filter opens, it immediately starts analyzing the image, starting in the middle (where most blurring occurs) and searching outward from there. You'll see a little progress bar appear (as it's thinking) near the bottom of the small preview on the right side of the dialog (that preview is called the Detail Loupe; more on this in a moment). If you want to cancel the analyzing process, just click the little circular "No!" symbol at the end of the progress bar.

Step Two:

Once it's done doing the math, it shows you its automated blur correction (seen here), where I have to say, on this image, it did a pretty darn good job. It's not perfectly sharp, but the original was completely unusable. At least now if I wanted to put it on Facebook or Twitter at web resolution, it would be totally passable, which I think is saying a lot. For most users, this is all you'll need to do: open the filter, let it do its thing, and you're done. However, if you're a "tweaker," then read on.

(Continued)

Step Three:

The filter automatically calculates what it thinks is the amount of camera shake based on how many pixels it thinks have moved, but if the auto method doesn't look good, it may be that it either needs to affect more or fewer pixels. That's what the Blur Trace Bounds slider is for. This slider controls how many pixels the filter affects (kind of like how the Tolerance slider for the Magic Wand tool determines how far out the tool selects). Dragging the slider to the left affects fewer pixels (so, if there's just a little blurring, it may need to affect fewer pixels) and dragging to the right affects more pixels. Its own estimation is pretty darn good but, again, you can override it (in this case, there's a lot of blur and the image looks better with a higher amount, but that's not the only way to get better results).

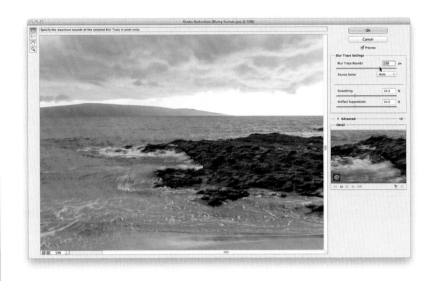

Step Four:

On the right side of the filter dialog is that small preview called the Detail Loupe, which shows you a zoomed-in view of your image (you can change its level of magnification by clicking the zoom amount buttons right below it). If you press the letter **Q** on your keyboard, the Detail Loupe now floats, so you can reposition it anywhere you'd like (press Q again to re-dock it). If you click-and-hold inside the Detail Loupe, it gives you a quick "before" view of your image (before you removed the camera shake). When you release the button, it brings you back to the edited "after" image.

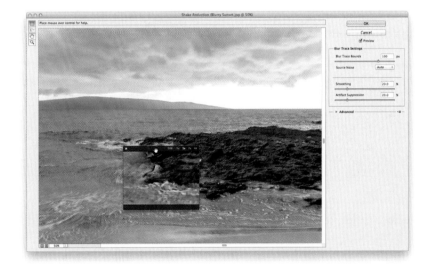

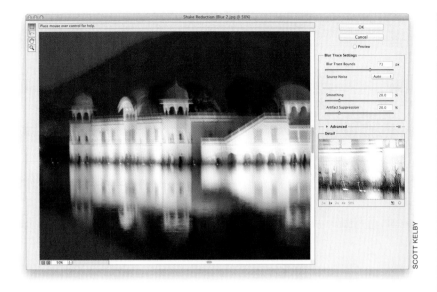

SCOTT KELBY

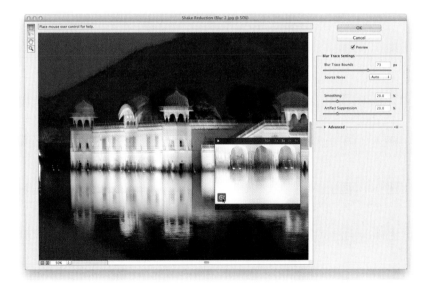

Step Five:

Luckily, there's more to the Detail Loupe than just that. Its power comes when you position it over an area you want analyzed. Let's open a different image and put this Detail Loupe to work (this is a shot taken in Jaipur, India, and as you can see, it's another blurry mess—a shot you'd de-lete for sure). This is the "before" image (I turned off the Preview checkbox, so you can see what it looks like before the filter is applied). Now, let's use the Detail Loupe to help us correct the blurriness.

Step Six:

Double-click on the spot within your image where you want that Detail Loupe to appear (it'll leave its home on the right side and jump to that spot in your image). Now, click the circular button in the bot-tom-left corner of the Loupe (as seen here) and it analyzes the area right under the Loupe. (*Note:* If you already had the Loupe floating, you don't need to double-click, a single click will do.) Look at how much better the image looks with the camera shake reduced. So, in this case, we double-clicked on the area right in front, but what if there's more than one place where you want the emphasis on camera shake reduction placed? Well, luckily, you can have multiple Regions of Interest (that's what Adobe calls the areas being analyzed).

TIP: Manually Choosing Blur Direction

If you think the filter got the direction of the blur wrong, you can choose it manually using the Blur Direction tool (the second tool down in the Toolbox in the top left—it becomes active after you expand the Advanced section on the right). Just click-and-drag it in the direction of the blur, for the approximate length of the blur. Use the **Bracket keys** to nudge the length; add the **Command (PC: Ctrl) key** to nudge the Angle.

(Continued)

Step Seven:

To see how much area is inside the Blur Estimation Region, expand the Advanced section (on the right side of the dialog) by clicking on its right-facing triangle, and you'll now see a bounding box around the area that's being analyzed (press Q to re-dock the Detail Loupe). You can click directly in the center of that box to drag it to a new location to have it analyze that area instead. You can also click-and-drag the corners in/out to resize it.

TIP: Reducing Junk Sharpening Creates

Sharpening generally brings out noise (which is why Adobe says this filter works best on images that were not shot at a high ISO), but there are two sliders that can help: (1) the Smoothing slider tries to reduce grain in the image, and (2) the Artifact Suppression slider helps to get rid of spots and other junk that appear when you apply extreme sharpening like this. These are both applied before the standard noise reduction (see tip below).

Step Eight:

If you need to analyze more than one area, you can use the Blur Estimation tool (it's the first tool in the Toolbox) to drag out another Blur Estimation Region (as seen here). Now it will focus on those two areas when analyzing the image to reduce blur.

TIP: Auto Noise Reduction

By default, the Shake Reduction filter applies an Auto noise reduction to the source image, but if you don't think it did a great job, you can use the Source Noise pop-up menu to try one of the three different noise reduction amounts (Low, Medium, and High).

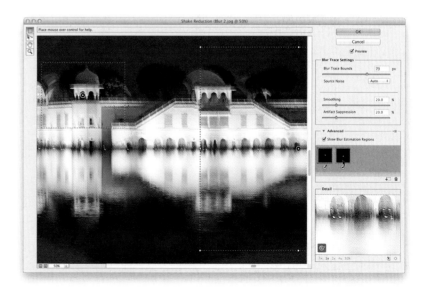

Crop Tool Refinements

Adobe majorly tweaked (and improved) the Crop tool functions back in Photoshop CS6, and now in the Creative Cloud version, they've further refined and enhanced what they introduced back in CS6. Most of these are the direct result of feedback from Photoshop users, so there are lots of little things that just make using the tool easier (plus, they brought something back that made some users a little crazy that it wasn't there in CS6).

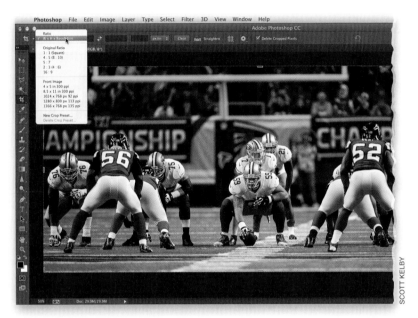

SCOTT KELBY

Step One:

Okay, this really isn't a step, it's more of a run-down of the new stuff, but we'll start with the fact that Adobe brought back the Resolution field (yay!), so you can choose **W x H x Resolution** from the preset pop-up menu in the Options Bar. When you choose that preset (shown here), the Resolution field now appears. There's also a Clear button that clears all the settings, so you can do an uncon-strained crop. There are new presets in this list, as well, including the return of the option to crop to the size of the front image. The double-arrow icon that lets you swap the settings in the width and height fields is back now, too.

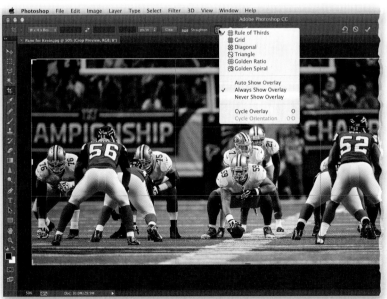

Step Two:

Yeah, this isn't a step either (just more Crop tool changes). The View pop-up menu has been replaced with a grid icon pop-up menu that has icons show-ing what each of the different cropping overlays looks like (you're seeing Rule of Thirds here). Okay, there ya have it.

Index

D

Darken blend mode, 310
darkening prints, 375
Darks slider, 40
Datacolor Spyder4ELITE, 361
Decontaminate Colors checkbox, 235
Default button, 35, 48
Default HDR preset, 187
Defringe dialog, 238
Defringe sliders, 75
Delete key, 45, 48
deleting
    adjustments, 101
    cropped pixels, 127
    empty layers, 209
    hidden layers, 424
    layer masks, 237
    lights, 308
    photos, 10, 13, 48
    presets, 133
    star ratings, 11
    See also removing
Density slider, 105
Desaturate command, 240, 270, 274
desaturated portrait effect, 270–271
Deselect command, 217, 239, 245, 257
Detail icon, 61
Detail Loupe, 463, 464–465, 466
Detail slider
    Camera Raw, 64
    Merge to HDR Pro dialog, 182
Detect Faces checkbox, 425
Difference blend mode, 201
digital cameras
    calibrating Camera Raw for, 87
    camera profiles for, 24–25
    color space configuration, 354
    HDR setup for, 172–174
    hiding info from, 351
    lens profiles for, 66–67, 248–249
    reducing shake from, 463–466
    resizing photos from, 134–136
    white balance settings, 26, 27, 115
digital noise reduction, 88–90
digital photography workflow, 428–435
distortion fixes
    Content-Aware Fill option, 70–71
    Free Transform used for, 70, 71–72

    Geometric Distortion checkbox, 248, 251
    Lens Corrections panel, 69
    Remove Distortion slider, 252
Distortion slider
    Blur Tools panel, 297
    Lens Corrections panel, 69
distraction removal, 258–263
DNG (Digital Negative) format
    converting RAW files to, 80–81, 350
    setting preferences for, 81
DNG Profile Editor utility, 25
docking Mini Bridge, 5
Document Frame Rate option, 422
documents
    duplicating specs for, 208, 324
    presets for creating, 132–133
Dodge and Burn tools, 219–222
dodging and burning
    in Camera Raw, 100–105
    in Photoshop CS6, 219–222
double-processing images, 52–57
double-stacking adjustments, 117
download website, xiv, xvi
downsizing photos, 143–144
Drag to Apply dialog, 410
dragging-and-dropping
    photos from Mini Bridge, 14–15, 169, 423
    size/resolution issues with, 145
    title slides into videos, 407
dramatic lighting effect, 305–310
drawing straight lines, 118
dreamy focus effect, 278–279
drop shadows, 209, 267, 401
dull gray skies, 215–218
duotone effects, 164, 166
Duotone Options dialog, 166
duplicating layers, 208, 219, 221, 238, 270
Duration field, 389

E

Edge Glow sliders, 180
Edge Smoothness feature, 180, 184, 196, 198
edge vignetting, 76–79
    adding, 77–79, 432
    HDR image, 185, 193, 197, 206–207
    post-crop, 78–79, 185, 206, 283
    Radial Filter for, 449–453
    removing, 76

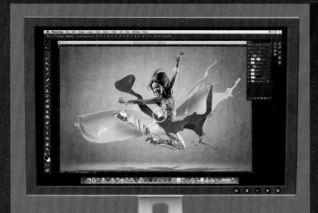
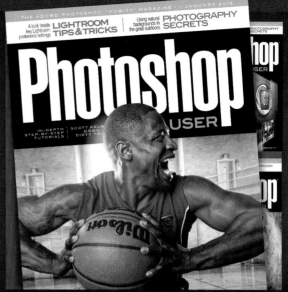
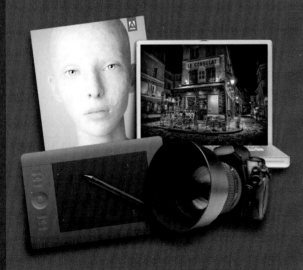
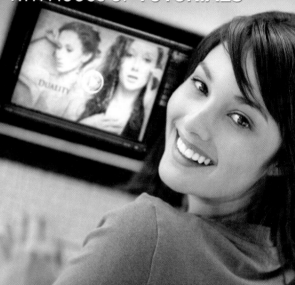

CAMERA RAW WHITE BALANCE CARD

From Scott Kelby's *The Adobe® Photoshop® Book for Digital Photographers (for Versions CS6 and CC)*